TOUCHSTONE

EXISTENCE

A New Dimension in Psychiatry and Psychology

Rollo May
Ernest Angel
Henri F. Ellenberger
Editors

A Touchstone Book

ISBN 0-671-20314-2

Library of Congress Catalog Card Number 58-8348
Manufactured in the United States of America

9   10   11   12   13   14   15   16   17

To
Eugene Minkowski
Pioneer in
Phenomenological Psychiatry

Ludwig Binswanger
Explorer in
Existential Analysis

And to all those in the science of man who have opened new realms in our understanding of what it means to be a human being

Preface

THIS BOOK represents the fruition of four years' labor—most of it, fortunately, a labor of love. The idea of translating these papers, originating with Ernest Angel, was welcomed by Basic Books because of their enthusiasm for bringing out significant new material in the sciences of man. I was glad to accept their invitation to participate as one of the editors since I, too, had long been convinced of the importance of making these works available in English, particularly at this crucial moment in the development of modern psychiatry and psychology.

We asked Dr. Ellenberger to join us as the third editor because of his extensive knowledge of the literature of phenomenological and existential psychiatry and his clinical experience in using these methods in Switzerland. He and Mr. Angel are chiefly responsible for the selection of the particular papers translated. In our introductory chapters, Dr. Ellenberger and I have undertaken the task of making a bridge between these contributions and American psychiatry and psychology, while Mr. Angel has borne the major weight of the translations themselves.

But no sooner had we commenced work than we found ourselves up against grave difficulties. How could one render into English the key terms and concepts of this way of understanding man, beginning with even such a basic word as *Dasein*? We were indeed facing what has often been called the genius and demonic character of the German language. I vividly remember a comment made by Dr. Paul Tillich, who is himself a representative of one wing of the existential movement and who likewise possesses a penetrating understanding of psychoanalysis. Driving together to East Hampton one day during the early stages of this work, Tillich and I stopped at a "diner." Over our coffee I handed him a list of some of the key terms and their proposed equivalents in English.

Suddenly he exclaimed, "Ach, it is impossible!" I hoped he meant the coffee and not the definitions! But it soon became clear he meant the latter. "It is impossible," he continued. "But you must do it anyway."

The present volume is proof that we kept to the task, and we trust that by and large we have achieved success in rendering into clear English the profound and oftentimes exceedingly subtle meanings in these papers. The most severe obstacles arose in "The Case of Ellen West." This remarkable paper by Binswanger was generally considered to be untranslatable into English, chiefly because the key terms in the analysis of the patient are built up—as is so often the case in German philosophical and scientific writing—out of a complex interrelation of concepts. We had reluctantly decided in our original plans to omit it from this volume. Then we heard that Dr. Werner Mendel and Dr. Joseph Lyons in Topeka had had the courage to undertake a translation of Ellen West. We warmly appreciated their willingness to offer us the results of their labors. So great are the difficulties inherent in this paper that their draft was revised by Professor Bayard Morgan and reworked in part by Dr. Ellenberger and, in connection with special problems, by Dr. Straus. Finally, Mr. Angel and I worked through the ultimate version in detail. Despite the travails involved in such combined efforts, we are indeed happy—for reasons the reader of this case will quickly see—that the paper is available in English. Due to pressures of time, Dr. Binswanger was unable to study this translation in detail, and hence it is not termed authorized although it is published with the author's permission. All of the other translations are authorized versions.

On completing such a labor, the moods of editors and translators are of course complex. But, for myself, may I say that time and again in working on these papers during these years I have had the experience of discovery that Keats so beautifully describes:

> "Then felt I like some watcher of the skies
> When a new planet swims into his ken . . ."

This indeed is its own reward. But we are also deeply gratified if we have made it possible for our colleagues and others to have this same experience of discovery.

ROLLO MAY

New York, February 1958

Contents

ix

PART III: EXISTENTIAL ANALYSIS

PART I

Introduction

I

The Origins and Significance of the Existential Movement in Psychology*

by Rollo May

IN RECENT YEARS there has been a growing awareness on the part of some psychiatrists and psychologists that serious gaps exist in our way of understanding of human beings. These gaps may well seem most compelling to psychotherapists, confronted as they are in clinic and consulting room with the sheer reality of persons in crisis whose anxiety will not be quieted by theoretical formulae. But the lacunae likewise present seemingly unsurmountable difficulties in scientific research. Thus many psychiatrists and psychologists in Europe and others in this country have been asking themselves disquieting questions, and others are aware of gnawing doubts which arise from the same half-suppressed and unasked questions.

Can we be sure, one such question goes, that we are seeing the patient as he really is, knowing him in his own reality; or are we seeing merely a projection of our own theories *about* him? Every psychotherapist, to be sure, has his knowledge of patterns and mechanisms of behavior and has at his finger tips the system of concepts developed by his particular school. Such a conceptual system is entirely necessary if we are to observe scientifically. But the crucial question is always the bridge between the system and the patient —how can we be certain that our system, admirable and beautifully wrought as it may be in principle, has anything whatever to do with this specific Mr. Jones, a living, immediate reality sitting opposite us in the consulting room? May not just this particular person require another system, another quite different frame of reference? And does not this patient, or any person for that matter, evade our investigations, slip through our scientific fingers like seafoam, precisely to the extent that we rely on the logical consistency of our own system?

* I wish to thank Drs. Henri Ellenberger, Leslie Farber, Carl Rogers, Erwin Straus, Paul Tillich, and Edith Weigert for reading and making suggestions for these two chapters.

Another such gnawing question is: How can we know whether we are seeing the patient in his real world, the world in which he "lives and moves and has his being," and which is for him unique, concrete, and different from our general theories of culture? In all probability we have never participated in his world and do not know it directly; yet we must know it and to some extent must be able to exist in it if we are to have any chance of knowing him.

Such questions were the motivations of psychiatrists and psychologists in Europe who later comprised the *Daseinsanalyse,* or existential-analytic, movement. The "existential research orientation in psychiatry," writes Ludwig Binswanger, its chief spokesman, "arose from dissatisfaction with the prevailing efforts to gain scientific understanding in psychiatry. . . . Psychology and psychotherapy as sciences are admittedly concerned with 'man,' but not at all primarily with mentally *ill* man, but with *man as such.* The new understanding of man, which we owe to Heidegger's analysis of existence, has its basis in the new conception that man is no longer understood in terms of some theory—be it a mechanistic, a biologic or a psychological one. . . ." [1]

I *What Called Forth This Development?*

Before turning to what this new conception of man is, let us note that this approach sprang up spontaneously in different parts of Europe and among different schools, and has a diverse body of researchers and creative thinkers. There were Eugene Minkowski in Paris, Erwin Straus in Germany and now in this country, V. E. von Gebsattel in Germany, who represent chiefly the first, or phenomenological, stage of this movement. There were Ludwig Binswanger, A. Storch, M. Boss, G. Bally, Roland Kuhn in Switzerland, J. H. Van Den Berg and F. J. Buytendijk in Holland, and so on, representing more specifically the second, or existential, stage. These facts—namely, that the movement emerged spontaneously, without these men in some cases knowing about the remarkably similar work of their colleagues, and that, rather than being the brain-child of one leader, it owes its creation to diverse psychiatrists and psychologists—testify that it must answer a widespread need in our times in the fields of psychiatry and psychology. Von Gebsattel, Boss, and Bally are Freudian analysts; Binswanger, though in Switzerland, became a member of the Vienna Psychoanalytic Society at Freud's recommendation when the Zurich group split off from the International. Some of the existential therapists had also been under Jungian influence.

These thoroughly experienced men became disquieted over the fact that, although they were effecting cures by the techniques they had learned, they could not, so long as they confined themselves to Freudian and Jungian as-

[1] L. Binswanger, "Existential Analysis and Psychotherapy," in *Progress in Psychotherapy,* ed. by Fromm-Reichmann and Moreno (New York: Grune & Stratton, 1956), p. 144.

sumptions, arrive at any clear understanding of why these cures did or did not occur or what actually was happening in the patients' existence. They refused the usual methods among therapists of quieting such inner doubts— namely, of turning one's attention with redoubled efforts to perfecting the intricacies of one's own conceptual system. Another tendency among psycho-therapists, when anxious or assailed by doubts as to what they are doing, is to become preoccupied with technique; perhaps the most handy anxiety-reducing agent is to abstract one's self from the issues by assuming a wholly technical emphasis. These men resisted this temptation. They likewise were unwilling to postulate unverifiable agents, such as "libido," or "censor," as Ludwig Lefebre points out,[2] or the various processes lumped under "trans-ference," to explain what was going on. And they had particularly strong doubts about using the theory of the unconscious as a *carte blanche* on which almost any explanation could be written. They were aware, as Straus puts it, that the "unconscious ideas of the patient are more often than not the con-scious theories of the therapist."

It was not with specific techniques of therapy that these psychiatrists and psychologists took issue. They recognize, for example, that psychoanalysis is valid for certain types of cases, and some of them, bona fide members of the Freudian movement, employ it themselves. But they all had grave doubts about its theory of man. And they believed these difficulties and limitations in the concept of man not only seriously blocked research but would in the long run also seriously limit the effectiveness and development of therapeutic techniques. They sought to understand the particular neuroses or psychoses and, for that matter, any human being's crisis situation, not as deviations from the conceptual yardstick of this or that psychiatrist or psychologist who hap-pened to be observing, but as deviations in the structure of that particular patient's existence, the disruption of his *condition humaine.* "A psychother-apy on existential-analytic bases investigates the life-history of the patient to be treated, . . . but it does not explain this life-history and its pathologic idiosyncrasies according to the teachings of any school of psychotherapy, or by means of its preferred categories. Instead, it *understands* this life-history as modifications of the total structure of the patient's being-in-the-world. . . ."[3] If these phrases seem confusing, we may only remark that it will be the task of these introductory chapters to make as clear as possible what this approach means in the understanding of specific persons. Most of the succeeding chap-ters in the book, written by the pioneers in this movement themselves, will exemplify the method in case studies.

Binswanger's own endeavor to understand how existential analysis throws light on a given case, and how it compares with other methods of under-

---

[2] Personal communication from Dr. Lefebre. an existential psychotherapist who was a student of Jaspers and Boss.

[3] L. Binswanger, *op. cit.,* p. 145.

standing, is graphically shown in his "Ellen West." [4] After he had completed his book on existential analysis, in 1942,[5] Binswanger went back into the archives in the sanatorium of which he is director to select the case history of this young woman who had ultimately committed suicide. The case is rich not only in the respect that the eloquent diaries, personal notes, and poems of Ellen West were available but also in the respects that she had been treated over two periods of time by psychoanalysts before her admission to the sanatorium and, while in the sanatorium, had received consultations by Bleuler and Kraepelin. Binswanger uses this case as a basis for discussing how Ellen West was diagnosed and understood first by the psychoanalysts, then by Bleuler and Kraepelin and the authorities at the sanatorium, and finally how she would now be understood on the basis of existential analysis.

It is relevant here to note the long friendship between Binswanger and Freud, a relationship which both greatly valued. In his recent small book giving his recollections of Freud, which he published at the urging of Anna Freud, Binswanger recounts the many visits he made to Freud's home in Vienna and the visit of several days Freud made to him at his sanatorium on Lake Constance. Their relationship was the more remarkable since it was the sole instance of a lasting friendship of Freud with any colleague who differed radically with him. There is a poignant quality in a message Freud wrote to Binswanger in reply to the latter's New Year's letter: "You, quite different from so many others, have not let it happen that your intellectual development—which has taken you further and further away from my influence—should destroy our personal relations, and you do not know how much good such fineness does to one." [6] Whether the friendship survived because the intellectual conflict between the two was like the proverbial battle between the elephant and the walrus, who never met on the same ground, or because of some diplomatic attitude on Binswanger's part (a tendency for which Freud mildly chided him at one point) or because of the depth of their respect and affection for each other, we cannot of course judge. What was certainly important, however, was the fact that Binswanger and the others in the existential movement in therapy were concerned not with arguing about specific dynamisms as such but with analyzing the underlying assumptions about human nature and arriving at a *structure* on which all specific therapeutic systems could be based.

It would be a mistake, therefore, simply to identify the existential movement in psychotherapy as another in the line of schools which have broken off from Freudianism, from Jung and Adler on down. Those previous deviating schools, although called forth by blind spots in orthodox therapy and

4 Included in this volume, published originally in 1945.

5 *Grundformen und Erkenntnis menschlichen Daseins* (Zurich: Niehans, 1942).

6 L. Binswanger, *Erinnerungen an Sigmund Freud*, just published in this country under the title, *Sigmund Freud: Reminiscences of a Friendship*, trans. by Norbert Guterman (New York: Grune and Stratton, 1957).

typically emerging when orthodoxy had struck an arid plateau, were nevertheless formed under the impetus of the creative work of one seminal leader. Otto Rank's new emphasis on the *present time* in the patient's experience emerged in the early twenties when classical analysis was bogging down in unvital intellectualized discussion of the patient's past; Wilhelm Reich's *character analysis* arose in the late twenties as an answer to the special need to break through the "ego defenses" of the character armor; new *cultural approaches* developed in the 1930's through the work of Horney and, in their distinctive ways, Fromm and Sullivan, when orthodox analysis was missing the real significance of the social and interpersonal aspects of neurotic and psychotic disturbances. Now the emergence of the existential therapy movement does have one feature in common with these other schools, namely, that it was also called forth by blind spots, as we shall make clearer later, in the existing approaches to psychotherapy. But it differs from the other schools in two respects. First, it is not the creation of any one leader, but grew up spontaneously and indigenously in diverse parts of the continent. Secondly, it does not purport to found a new school as over against other schools or to give a new technique of therapy as over against other techniques. It seeks, rather, to analyze the structure of human existence—an enterprise which, if successful, should yield an understanding of the reality underlying all situations of human beings in crises.

Thus this movement purports to do more than cast light upon blind spots. When Binswanger writes, ". . . existential analysis is able to widen and deepen the basic concepts and understandings of psychoanalysis," he is on sound ground, in my judgment, not only with respect to analysis but other forms of therapy as well.

It requires no brilliance, however, to predict that this approach will encounter a good deal of resistance in this country, despite the fact that it has been rapidly growing in importance in Europe and is now reported by some observers to be the dominant movement on the continent. In the early period when they were colleagues, Freud once wrote to Jung that it was always better to identify and call forth openly the resistances of that still-Victorian culture to psychoanalysis. We shall take Freud's advice and name what we believe will be the chief resistances to this present approach.

The *first* source of resistance, of course, to this or any new contribution is the assumption that all major discoveries have been made in these fields and we need only fill in the details. This attitude is an old interloper, an uninvited guest who has been notoriously present in the battles between the schools in psychotherapy. Its name is "blind-spots-structuralized-into-dogma." And though it does not merit an answer, nor is it susceptible to any, it is unfortunately an attitude which may be more widespread in this historical period than one would like to think.

The *second* source of resistance, and one to be answered seriously, is the suspicion that existential analysis is an encroachment of philosophy into psychiatry, and does not have much to do with science. This attitude is partly a hang-over of the culturally inherited scars from the battle of the last of the nineteenth century when psychological science won its freedom from metaphysics. The victory then achieved was exceedingly important but, as in the aftermath of any war, there followed reactions to opposite extremes which are themselves harmful. Concerning this resistance we shall make several comments.

It is well to remember that the existential movement in psychiatry and psychology arose precisely out of a passion to be not *less* but *more* empirical. Binswanger and the others were convinced that the traditional scientific methods not only did not do justice to the data but actually tended to hide rather than reveal what was going on in the patient. The existential analysis movement is a protest against the tendency to see the patient in forms tailored to our own preconceptions or to make him over into the image of our own predilections. In this respect it stands squarely within the scientific tradition in its widest sense. But it broadens its knowledge of man by historical perspective and scholarly depth, by accepting the facts that human beings reveal themselves in art and literature and philosophy, and by profiting from the insights of the particular cultural movements which express the anxiety and conflicts of contemporary man. One has only to read the following chapters to see with what intellectual probity and scholarly discipline these students of man explore their fields. To my mind they represent a uniting of science and humanism.

It is also important here to remind ourselves that every scientific method rests upon philosophical presuppositions. These presuppositions determine not only how much reality the observer with this particular method can see —they are indeed the spectacles through which he perceives—but also whether or not what is observed is pertinent to real problems and therefore whether the scientific work will endure. It is a gross, albeit common, error to assume naïvely that one can observe facts best if he avoids all preoccupation with philosophical assumptions. All he does, then, is mirror uncritically the particular parochial doctrines of his own limited culture. The result in our day is that science gets identified with methods of *isolating* factors and observing them from an allegedly *detached base*—a particular method which arose out of the split between subject and object made in the seventeenth century in Western culture and then developed into its special compartmentalized form in the late nineteenth and twentieth centuries.[7] We in our day, of course, are no less subject to "methodolatry" than are members of any other culture. But it seems especially a misfortune that our understanding in such a crucial area as the psychological study of man, with the understand-

7 See p. 22.

ing of emotional and mental health depending upon it, should be curtailed by uncritical acceptance of limited assumptions. Helen Sargent has sagely and pithily remarked, "Science offers more leeway than graduate students are permitted to realize." [8]

Is not the essence of science the assumption that *reality is lawful* and therefore understandable, and is it not an inseparable aspect of scientific integrity that any method continuously criticize its own presuppositions? The only way to widen one's "blinders" is to analyze one's philosophical assumptions. In my judgment it is very much to the credit of the psychiatrists and psychologists in this existential movement that they seek to clarify their own bases. This enables them, as Dr. Ellenberger points out in a later chapter in this book, to see their human subjects with a fresh clarity and to shed original light on many facets of psychological experience.

The *third* source of resistance, and to my mind the most crucial of all, is the tendency in this country to be preoccupied with technique and to be impatient with endeavors to search below such considerations to find the foundations upon which all techniques must be based. This tendency can be well explained in terms of our American social background, particularly our frontier history, and it can be well justified as our optimistic, activistic concern for helping and changing people. Certainly our genius in the field of psychology has been in the behavioristic, clinical, and applied areas, and our special contributions in psychiatry have been in drug therapy and other technical applications. Gordon Allport has described the fact that American and British psychology (as well as general intellectual climate) has been Lockean, that is, pragmatic, a tradition fitting behaviorism, stimulus and response systems, and animal psychology. The continental tradition, in contrast, has been Leibnitzian.[9] Now it is very sobering to remind one's self that every new theoretical contribution in the field of psychotherapy which has had the originality and germinating power to lead to the developing of a new school has come from continental Europe with only two exceptions—and, of these, one was grandsired by a European-born psychiatrist.[10] In this

---

[8] *Methodological Problems in the Assessment of Intrapsychic Change in Psychotherapy* (to be published).

[9] Gordon Allport, *Becoming, Basic Considerations for a Psychology of Personality* (New Haven: Yale University Press, 1955). The Lockean tradition, Allport points out, consists of an emphasis on the mind as *tabula rasa* on which experience writes all that is later to exist therein, whereas the Leibnitzian tradition views the mind as having a potentially active core of its own.

[10] To see this one has only to name the originators of new theory: Freud, Adler, Jung, Rank, Stekel, Reich, Horney, Fromm, etc. The two exceptions, so far as I can see, are the schools of Harry Stack Sullivan and Carl Rogers, and the former was indirectly related to the work of the Swiss-born Adolph Meyer. Even Rogers may partly illustrate our point, for although his approach has clear and consistent theoretical implications about human nature, his focus has been on the "applied" rather than the "pure" science side, if we may make that distinction, and his theory about human nature owes much to Otto Rank. We

country we tend to be a nation of practitioners; but the disturbing question is, where shall we get *what* we practice? In our preoccupation with technique, laudable enough in itself, we tend to overlook the fact that *technique emphasized by itself in the long run defeats even technique*. One of the reasons that European thought has been so much richer in yielding original and fresh discoveries in these fields is its tradition of broad historical and philosophical perspective in science and thought. This is abundantly clear in the specific area with which we are concerned in this book, the existential psychotherapy movement. Binswanger, Straus, Von Gebsattel and the other founders of this movement, though their thought is related to real problems and patients, have the flavor of "pure" science. They search not for techniques as such but rather for an understanding of the foundations on which all technique must stand.

These resistances we have named, far from undermining the contribution of existential analysis, precisely demonstrate its potential importance to our thinking, in my judgment. Despite its difficulties—due partly to its language, partly to the complexity of its thought—we believe that it is a contribution of significance and originality meriting serious study.

II *What Is Existentialism?*

We must now remove a major stumbling block—namely, the confusion surrounding the term, "existentialism." The word is bandied about to mean

---

are not making a value judgment in the distinction between the "applied" science tendency in America as contrasted to the "pure" science tendencies in Europe; but we do wish to point out that a serious problem confronts us that goes far beyond the borders of psychology and psychiatry. Professor Whitehead of Harvard, in his inaugural address several years ago as Director of the Harvard School of Economics, undertook to list the twenty outstanding contributors to the intellectual scientific development of Western civilization during the last three centuries, such as Einstein, Freud; every one of them came from Europe or the Near East; not one was born in America. One cannot explain this simply on the basis of the longer time Europe has been training scientists, says Whitehead, for in America in the last four decades we have trained more scientists and engineers than in all the rest of Western civilization put together. Since the sources of "pure" science in Europe may be drying up, this predilection for "applications" presents us with a serious problem for the future.

We obviously have no desire at all to set up any "Europe vs. America" issue. We are all part of modern Western culture, and for quite understandable historical reasons certain aspects of the historical destiny of Western man fell more heavily on Europe and others on America. It is precisely in this context that the existential approach may have a particular and significant contribution. For this approach combines the basic scientific quest for understanding the underlying structure of human existence both with a suspicion of abstraction *per se* and with an emphasis on truth produced in action. It seeks theory not in the realm of abstraction but in the realm of the concrete, existing human being. Thus it has a profound, potential (though as yet unrealized) affinity for the American genius for combining thought and action (as shown so beautifully in William James). The chapters which follow, therefore, may yield important help in our finding the "pure" science bases we so sorely need in the sciences of man.

everything—from the posturing defiant dilettantism of some members of the *avant garde* on the left bank in Paris, to a philosophy of despair advocating suicide, to a system of anti-rationalist German thought written in a language so esoteric as to exasperate any empirically minded reader. Existentialism, rather, is an expression of profound dimensions of the modern emotional and spiritual temper and is shown in almost all aspects of our culture. It is found not only in psychology and philosophy but in art, *vide* Van Gogh, Cezanne, and Picasso—and in literature, *vide* Dostoevski, Baudelaire, Kafka, and Rilke. Indeed, in many ways it is the unique and specific portrayal of the psychological predicament of contemporary Western man. This cultural movement, as we shall see later in detail, has its roots in the same historical situation and the same psychological crises which called forth psychoanalysis and other forms of psychotherapy.

Confusions about the term occur even in usually highly literate places. *The New York Times,* in a report commenting on Sartre's denunciation of, and final break with, the Russian Communists for their suppression of freedom in Hungary, identified Sartre as a leader in "existentialism, a broadly materialistic form of thought." The report illustrates two reasons for the confusion—first, the identification of existentialism in the popular mind in this country with the writings of Jean-Paul Sartre. Quite apart from the fact that Sartre is known here for his dramas, movies, and novels rather than for his major, penetrating psychological analyses, it must be emphasized that he represents a nihilistic, subjectivist extreme in existentialism which invites misunderstanding, and his position is by no means the most useful introduction to the movement. But the second more serious confusion in the *Times* report is its definition of existentialism as "broadly materialistic." Nothing could be less accurate—nothing, unless it be the exact opposite, namely, describing it as an idealistic form of thinking. For the very essence of this approach is that it seeks to analyze and portray the human being—whether in art or literature or philosophy or psychology—on a level which undercuts the old dilemma of materialism versus idealism.

Existentialism, in short, is the endeavor to understand man by cutting below the cleavage between subject and object which has bedeviled Western thought and science since shortly after the Renaissance. This cleavage Binswanger calls "the cancer of all psychology up to now . . . the cancer of the doctrine of subject-object cleavage of the world." The existential way of understanding human beings has some illustrious progenitors in Western history, such as Socrates in his dialogues, Augustine in his depth-psychological analyses of the self, Pascal in his struggle to find a place for the "heart's reasons which the reason knows not of." But it arose specifically just over a hundred years ago in Kierkegaard's violent protest against the reigning rationalism of his day, Hegel's "totalitarianism of reason," to use Maritain's phrase. Kierkegaard proclaimed that Hegel's identification of abstract truth with reality was an illusion and amounted to trickery. "Truth exists," wrote Kierkegaard, "only as the individual himself produces it in action." He and the existentialists following him protested firmly against the rationalists and idealists who would see man only as a subject—that is, as having reality only as a thinking being. But just as strongly they fought against the tendency to treat man as an object to be calculated and controlled, exemplified in the almost overwhelming tendencies in the Western world to make human beings into anonymous units to fit like robots into the vast industrial and political collectivisms of our day.

These thinkers sought the exact opposite of intellectualism for its own sake. They would have protested more violently than classical psychoanalysis against the use of thinking as a defense against vitality or as a substitute for immediate experience. One of the early existentialists of the sociological wing, Feuerbach, makes this appealing admonition, "Do not wish to be a philosopher in contrast to being a man . . . do not think as a thinker . . . think as a living, real being. Think in Existence." [11]

The term "existence," coming from the root *ex-sistere,* means literally to *stand out, to emerge.* This accurately indicates what these cultural representatives sought, whether in art or philosophy or psychology—namely, to portray the human being not as a collection of static substances or mechanisms or patterns but rather as emerging and becoming, that is to say, as existing. For no matter how interesting or theoretically true is the fact that I am composed of such and such chemicals or act by such and such mechanisms or patterns, the crucial question always is that I happen to exist at this given moment in time and space, and my problem is how I am to be aware of that fact and what I shall do about it. As we shall see later, the existential psychologists and psychiatrists do not at all rule out the study of dynamisms, drives, and patterns of behavior. But they hold that these cannot be understood in any given person except in the context of the overarching fact that here is a person who happens *to exist, to be,* and if we do not keep this in mind, all else we know about this person will lose its meaning. Thus their approach is always dynamic; existence refers to coming into being, becoming. Their endeavor is to understand this becoming not as a sentimental artifact but as the fundamental structure of human existence. When the term "being" is used in the following chapters, as it often is, the reader should remember that it is not a static word but a verb form, the participle of the verb "to be." Existentialism is basically concerned with *ontology,* that is, the science of being (*ontos,* from Greek "being").

We can see more clearly the significance of the term if we recall that traditionally in Western thought "existence" has been set over against "es-

[11] Quoted by Paul Tillich, "Existential Philosophy," in the *Journal of the History of Ideas,* 5:1, 44–70, 1944.

sence." Essence refers to the greenness of this stick of wood, let us say, and its density, weight, and other characteristics which give it substance. By and large Western thought since the Renaissance has been concerned with essences. Traditional science seeks to discover such essences or substances; it assumes an essentialist metaphysics, as Professor Wild of Harvard puts it.[12] The search for essences may indeed produce higly significant universal laws in science or brilliant abstract conceptualizations in logic or philosophy. But it can do this only by abstraction. The *existence* of the given individual thing has to be left out of the picture. For example, we can demonstrate that three apples added to three make six. But this would be just as true if we substituted unicorns for apples; it makes no difference to the mathematical truth of the proposition whether apples or unicorns actually exist or not. That is to say, a proposition can be *true* without being *real*. Perhaps just because this approach has worked so magnificently in certain areas of science, we tend to forget that it necessarily involves a detached viewpoint and that the living individual must be omitted.[13] There remains the chasm between truth and reality. And the crucial question which confronts us in psychology and other aspects of the science of man is precisely this chasm between what is *abstractly true* and what is *existentially real* for the given living person.

Lest it seem that we are setting up an artificial, straw-man issue, let us point out that this chasm between truth and reality is openly and frankly admitted by sophisticated thinkers in behavioristic and conditioning psychology. Kenneth W. Spence, distinguished leader of one wing of behavior theory, writes, "The question of whether any particular realm of behavior phenomena is more real or closer to real life and hence should be given priority in investigation does not, or at least should not, arise for the psychologist *as scientist*." That is to say, it does not primarily matter whether what is being studied is real or not. What realms, then, should be selected for study? Spence gives priority to phenomena which lend themselves "to the degrees of control and analysis necessary for the formulation of abstract laws." [14] Nowhere has our point been put more unabashedly and clearly—

12 John Wild, *The Challenge of Existentialism* (Bloomington: Indiana University Press, 1955). Modern physics, with Heisenberg, Bohr (see p. 26), and similar trends have changed at this point, paralleling, as we shall see later, one side of the existentialist development. We are talking above of the traditional ideas of Western science.

13 Reality makes a difference to the person who *has* the apples—that is the *existential* side—but it is irrelevant to the truth of the mathematical proposition. For a more serious example, that all men die is a truth; and to say that such and such a percentage die at such and such ages gives a statistical accuracy to the proposition. But neither of these statements says anything about the fact which really matters most to each of us, namely, that you and I must alone face the fact that at some unknown moment in the future we shall die. In contrast to the essentialist propositions, these latter are *existential facts*.

14 Kenneth W. Spence, *Behavior Theory and Conditioning* (New Haven: Yale University Press, 1956).

what can be reduced to *abstract laws* is selected, and whether what you are studying has reality or not is irrelevant to this goal. On the basis of this approach many an impressive system in psychology has been erected, with abstraction piled high upon abstraction—the authors succumbing, as we intellectuals are wont, to their "edifice complex"—until an admirable and imposing structure is built. The only trouble is that the edifice has more often than not been separated from human reality in its very foundations. Now the thinkers in the existential tradition hold the exact opposite to Spence's view, and so do the psychiatrists and psychologists in the existential psychotherapy movement. They insist that it is necessary and possible to have a science of man which studies human beings in their reality.

Kierkegaard, Nietzsche, and those who followed them accurately foresaw this growing split between truth and reality in Western culture, and they endeavored to call Western man back from the delusion that reality can be comprehended in an abstracted, detached way. But though they protested vehemently against arid intellectualism, they were by no means simple activists. Nor were they anti-rational. Anti-intellectualism and other movements in our day which make thinking subordinate to acting must not at all be confused with existentialism. Either alternative—making man subject *or* object—results in losing the living, existing person. Kierkegaard and the existential thinkers appealed to a reality *underlying both subjectivity and objectivity*. We must not only study a person's experience as such, they held, but even more we must study the man to whom the experience is happening, the one who is doing the experiencing. They insist, as Tillich puts it, that "Reality or Being is not the object of cognitive experience, but is rather 'existence,' is Reality as immediately experienced, with the accent on the inner, personal character of man's immediate experience." [15] This comment, as well as several above, will indicate to the reader how close the existentialists are to present-day depth-psychology. It is by no means accidental that the greatest of them in the nineteenth century, Kierkegaard and Nietzsche, happen also to be among the most remarkable psychologists (in the dynamic sense) of all time and that one of the contemporary leaders of this school, Karl Jaspers, was originally a psychiatrist and wrote a notable text on psychopathology. When one reads Kierkegaard's profound analyses of anxiety and despair or Nietzsche's amazingly acute insights into the dynamics of resentment and the guilt and hostility which accompany repressed emotional powers, one must pinch himself to realize that he is reading works written seventy-five and a hundred years ago and not some new contemporary psychological analysis. The existentialists are centrally concerned with rediscovering the living person amid the compartmentalization and dehumanization of modern culture, and in order to do this they engage in depth psychological analysis. Their concern is not with isolated psychological reactions in themselves

[15] Paul Tillich, *op. cit.*

but rather with the psychological being of the living man who is doing the experiencing. That is to say, they use psychological terms with an ontological meaning.[16]

Martin Heidegger is generally taken as the fountainhead of present-day existential thought. His seminal work, *Being and Time,* was of radical importance in giving Binswanger and other existential psychiatrists and psychologists the deep and broad basis they sought for understanding man. Heidegger's thought is rigorous, logically incisive, and "scientific" in the European sense of pursuing with unrelenting vigor and thoroughness whatever implications his inquiries led him to. But his work is almost impossible

[16] For readers who wish more historical background, we append this note. In the winter of 1841, Schelling gave his famous series of lectures at the University of Berlin before a distinguished audience including Kierkegaard, Burckhardt, Engels, Bakunin. Schelling set out to overthrow Hegel, whose vast rationalist system, including, as we have said, the identification of abstract truth with reality and the bringing of all of history into an "absolute whole," held immense and dominant popularity in the Europe of the middle of the nineteenth century. Though many of Schelling's listeners were bitterly disappointed in his answers to Hegel, the existential movement may be said to have begun there. Kierkegaard went back to Denmark and in 1844 published his *Philosophical Fragments,* and two years later he wrote the declaration of independence of existentialism, *Concluding Unscientific Postscript.* Also in 1844 there appeared the second edition of Schopenhauer's *The World as Will and Idea,* a work important in the new movement because of its central emphasis on vitality, "will," along with "idea." Two related works were written by Karl Marx in 1844-45. The early Marx is significant in this movement in his attack upon abstract truth as "ideology," again using Hegel as his whipping boy. Marx' dynamic view of history as the arena in which men and groups bring truth into being and his meaningful fragments pointing out how the money economy of modern industrialism tends to turn people into things and works toward the dehumanization of modern man are likewise significant in the existentialist approach. Both Marx and Kierkegaard took over Hegel's dialectical method but used it for quite different purposes. More existential elements were latently present in Hegel, it may be noted, than his antagonists acknowledged.

In the following decades the movement subsided. Kierkegaard remained completely unknown, Schelling's work was contemptuously buried, and Marx and Feuerbach were interpreted as dogmatic materialists. Then a new impetus came in the 1880's with the work of Dilthey, and particularly with Friedrich Nietzsche, the "philosophy of life" movement, and the work of Bergson.

The third and contemporary phase of existentialism came after the shock to the Western world caused by World War I. Kierkegaard and the early Marx were rediscovered, and the serious challenges to the spiritual and psychological bases of Western society given by Nietzsche could no longer be covered over by Victorian self-satisfied placidity. The specific form of this third phase owes much to the phenomenology of Edmund Husserl, which gave to Heidegger, Jaspers, and the others the tool they needed to undercut the subject-object cleavage which had been such a stumbling-block in science as well as philosophy. There is an obvious similarity between existentialism, in its emphasis on truth as produced in action, with the process philosophies, such as Whitehead's, and American pragmatism, particularly as in William James.

Those who wish to know more about the existential movement as such are referred to Paul Tillich's classical paper, "Existential Philosophy." For most of the above historical material I am indebted to Tillich's paper.

We may add that part of the confusion in this field is due to the misleading titles which books are given. Wahl's *A Short History of Existentialism* is short but by no means a history of existentialism, just as the book by Sartre published under the title of *Existential Psychoanalysis* has very little to do with psychoanalysis or, for that matter, existential therapy.

to translate. Only a few essays are available in English.[17] Jean-Paul Sartre's best contribution to our subject are his phenomenological descriptions of psychological processes. In addition to Jaspers, other prominent existential thinkers are Gabriel Marcel in France, Nicolas Berdyaev, originally Russian but until his recent death a resident of Paris, and Ortega y Gasset and Unamuno in Spain. Paul Tillich shows the existential approach in his work, and in many ways his book *The Courage to Be* is the best and most cogent presentation of existentialism as an approach to actual living available in English.[18]

The novels of Kafka portray the despairing, dehumanized situation in modern culture from which and to which existentialism speaks. *The Stranger* and *The Plague*, by Albert Camus, represent excellent examples in modern literature in which existentialism is partially self-conscious. But perhaps the most vivid of all portrayals of the meaning of existentialism is to be found in modern art, partly because it is articulated symbolically rather than as self-conscious thought and partly because art always reveals with special clarity the underlying spiritual and emotional temper of the culture. We shall frequently refer to the relation of modern art and existentialism in the following pages. Here let us only note that some of the common elements in the work of such outstanding representatives of the modern movement as Van Gogh, Cezanne, and Picasso are, *first,* a revolt against the hypocritical academic tradition of the late nineteenth century, *second,* an endeavor to pierce below surfaces to grasp a new relation to the reality of nature, *third,*

[17] Published, along with an introduction and a summary of "Being and Time," by Werner Brock, in *Existence and Being* (Chicago: Henry Regnery Co., 1949). Heidegger disclaimed the title "existentialist" after it became identified with the work of Sartre. He would call himself, strictly speaking, a philologist or ontologist. But in any case, we must be existential enough not to get twisted up in controversies over titles and to take the meaning and spirit of each man's work rather than the letter. Martin Buber likewise is not happy at being called an existentialist, although his work has clear affinities with this movement. The reader who has difficulty with the terms in this field is indeed in good company!

[18] *The Courage to Be* (New Haven: Yale University Press, 1952) is existential as a living approach to crises in contrast to books *about* existentialism. Tillich, like most of the thinkers mentioned above, is not to be tagged as *merely* an existentialist, for existentialism is a way of approaching problems and does not in itself give answers or norms. Tillich has both rational norms—the structure of reason is always prominent in his analyses—and religious norms. Some readers will not find themselves in agreement with the religious elements in *The Courage to Be*. It is important to note the very significant point, however, that these religious ideas, whether one agrees with them or not, do illustrate an authentic existential approach. This is seen in Tillich's concept of "the God beyond God" and "absolute faith" as faith not *in* some content or somebody but as a state of being, a way of relating to reality characterized by courage, acceptance, full commitment, etc. The theistic arguments for the "existence of God" are not only beside the point but exemplify the most deteriorated aspect of the Western habit of thinking in terms of God as a substance or object, existing in a world of objects and in relation to whom we are subjects. This is "bad theology," Tillich points out, and results in "the God Nietzsche said had to be killed because nobody can tolerate being made into a mere object of absolute knowledge and absolute control" (p. 185).

an endeavor to recover vitality and honest, direct aesthetic experience, and, *fourth*, the desperate attempt to express the immediate underlying meaning of the modern human situation, even though this means portraying despair and emptiness. Tillich, for example, holds that Picasso's painting "Guernica" gives the most gripping and revealing portrayal of the atomistic, fragmentized condition of European society which preceded World War II and "shows what is now in the souls of many Americans as disruptiveness, existential doubt, emptiness and meaninglessness." [19]

The fact that the existential approach arose as an indigenous and spontaneous answer to crises in modern culture is shown not only in the fact that it emerged in art and literature but also in the fact that different philosophers in diverse parts of Europe often developed these ideas without conscious relation to each other. Though Heidegger's main work, *Being and Time*, was published in 1927, Ortega y Gasset already in 1924 had developed and partially published strikingly similar ideas without any direct knowledge of Heidegger's work.[20]

It is true, of course, that existentialism had its birth in a time of cultural crisis, and it is always found in our day on the sharp revolutionary edge of modern art, literature, and thought. To my mind this fact speaks for the validity of its insights rather than the reverse. When a culture is caught in the profound convulsions of a transitional period, the individuals in the society understandably suffer spiritual and emotional upheaval; and finding that the accepted mores and ways of thought no longer yield security, they tend either to sink into dogmatism and conformism, giving up awareness, or are forced to strive for a heightened self-consciousness by which to become aware of their existence with new conviction and on new bases. This is one of the most important affinities of the existential movement with psychotherapy—both are concerned with individuals in crisis. And far from saying that the insights of a crisis period are "simply the product of anxiety and despair," we are more likely to find, as we do time and again in psychoanalysis, that a crisis is exactly what is required to shock people out of unaware dependence upon external dogma and to force them to unravel layers of pretense to reveal naked truth about themselves which, however unpleasant, will at least be solid. Existentialism is an attitude which accepts man as always becoming, which means potentially in crisis. But this does not mean it will be despairing. Socrates, whose dialectical search for truth in the individual is the prototype of existentialism, was optimistic. But this approach is understandably more apt to appear in ages of transition, when one age is dying and the new one not yet born, and the individual is either homeless

---

[19] "Existential Aspects of Modern Art," in *Christianity and the Existentialists*, edited by Carl Michalson (New York: Scribners, 1956), p. 138.

[20] Ortega y Gasset, *The Dehumanization of Art, and Other Writings on Art and Culture* (New York: Doubleday Anchor, 1956), pp. 135–137.

and lost or achieves a new self-consciousness. In the period of transition from Medievalism to the Renaissance, a moment of radical upheaval in Western culture, Pascal describes powerfully the experience the existentialists later were to call *Dasein:* "When I consider the brief span of my life, swallowed up in the eternity before and behind it, the small space that I fill, or even see, engulfed in the infinite immensity of spaces which I know not, and which know not me, I am afraid, and wonder to see myself here rather than there; for there is no reason why I should be here rather than there, now rather than then. . . ." [21] Rarely has the existential problem been put more simply or beautifully. In this passage we see, first, the profound realization of the contingency of human life which existentialists call "thrownness." Second, we see Pascal facing unflinchingly the question of *being there* or more accurately "being where?" Third, we see the realization that one cannot take refuge in some superficial explanation of time and space, which Pascal, scientist that he was, could well know; and lastly, the deep shaking anxiety arising from this stark awareness of existence in such a universe.[22]

It remains, finally, in this orientation section to note the relation between existentialism and oriental thought as shown in the writings of Laotzu and Zen Buddhism. The similarities are striking. One sees this immediately in glancing at some quotations from Laotzu's *The Way of Life:* "Existence is beyond the power of words to define: terms may be used but none of them is absolute." "Existence, by nothing bred, breeds everything, parent of the universe." "Existence is infinite, not to be defined; and though it seem but a bit of wood in your hand, to carve as you please, it is not to be lightly played with and laid down." "The way to do is to be." "Rather abide at the center of your being; for the more you leave it, the less you learn." [23]

One gets the same shock of similarity in Zen Buddhism.[24] The likenesses between these Eastern philosophies and existentialism go much deeper than the chance similarity of words. Both are concerned with ontology, the study of being. Both seek a relation to reality which cuts below the cleavage between subject and object. Both would insist that the Western absorption in

[21] *Pensées of Pascal* (New York: Peter Pauper Press, 1946), p. 36. *Dasein* is defined on page 41.

[22] It is not surprising, thus, that this approach to life would speak particularly to many modern citizens who are aware of the emotional and spiritual dilemmas in which we find ourselves. Norbert Wiener, for example, though the actual implications of his scientific work may be radically different from the emphases of the existentialists, has stated in his autobiography that his scientific activity has led him personally to a "positive" existentialism. "We are not fighting for a definitive victory in the indefinite future," he writes. "It is the greatest possible victory *to be,* and *to have been.* [ITALICS MINE.] No defeat can deprive us of the success of having existed for some moment of time in a universe that seems indifferent to us." *I Am a Mathematician* (New York: Doubleday).

[23] Witter Bynner, *The Way of Life, according to Laotzu, an American version* (New York: John Day Company, 1946).

[24] See William Barrett, ed., *Zen Buddhism, the Selected Writings of D. T. Suzuki* (New York: Doubleday Anchor, 1956), Introduction, p. xi.

conquering and gaining power over nature has resulted not only in the estrangement of man from nature but also indirectly in the estrangement of man from himself. The basic reason for these similarities is that Eastern thought never suffered the radical split between subject and object that has characterized Western thought, and this dichotomy is exactly what existentialism seeks to overcome.

The two approaches are not at all to be identified, of course; they are on different levels. Existentialism is not a comprehensive philosophy or way of life, but an endeavor to grasp reality. The chief specific difference between the two, for our purposes, is that existentialism is immersed in and arises directly out of Western man's anxiety, estrangement, and conflicts and is indigenous to our culture. Like psychoanalysis, existentialism seeks not to bring in answers from other cultures but to utilize these very conflicts in contemporary personality as avenues to the more profound self-understanding of Western man and to find the solutions to our problems in direct relation to the historical and cultural crises which gave the problems birth. In this respect, the particular value of Eastern thought is not that it can be transferred, ready-born like Athena, to the Western mind, but rather that it serves as a corrective to our biases and highlights the erroneous assumptions that have led Western development to its present problems. The present widespread interest in oriental thought in the Western world is, to my mind, a reflection of the same cultural crises, the same sense of estrangement, the same hunger to get beyond the vicious circle of dichotomies which called forth the existentialist movement.

III *How Existentialism and Psychoanalysis Arose Out of the Same Cultural Situation*

We shall now look at the remarkable parallel between the problems of modern man to which the existentialists on one hand and psychoanalysts on the other devote themselves. From different perspectives and on different levels, both analyze anxiety, despair, alienation of man from himself and his society.

Freud describes the neurotic personality of the late nineteenth century as one suffering from fragmentation, that is, from repression of instinctual drives, blocking off of awareness, loss of autonomy, weakness and passivity of the ego, together with the various neurotic symptoms which result from this fragmentation. Kierkegaard—who wrote the only known book before Freud specifically devoted to the problem of anxiety—analyzes not only anxiety but particularly the depression and despair which result from the individual's self-estrangement, an estrangement he proceeds to classify in its different forms and degrees of severity.[25] Nietzsche proclaims, ten years before Freud's

25 Sören Kierkegaard, *The Sickness Unto Death,* trans. by Walter Lowrie (New York: Doubleday & Co., 1954).

first book, that the disease of contemporary man is that "his soul had gone
stale," he is "fed up," and that all about there is "a bad smell . . . the smell
of failure. . . . The leveling and diminution of European man is our greatest danger." He then proceeds to describe, in terms which remarkably predict
the later psychoanalytic concepts, how blocked instinctual powers turn
within the individual into resentment, self-hatred, hostility, and aggression.
Freud did not know Kierkegaard's work, but he regarded Nietzsche as one
of the authentically great men of all time.

What is the relation between these three giants of the nineteenth century,
none of whom directly influenced either of the others? And what is the relation between the two approaches to human nature they originated—exten-
tialism and psychoanalysis—probably the two most important to have shaken,
and indeed toppled, the traditional concepts of man? To answer these questions we must inquire into the cultural situation of the middle and late
nineteenth century out of which both approaches to man arose and to which
both sought to give answers. The real meaning of a way of understanding
human beings, such as existentialism or psychoanalysis, can never be seen
in abstracto, detached from its world, but only in the context of the historical
situation which gave it birth. Thus the historical discussions to follow in
this chapter are not at all detours from our central aim. Indeed, it is precisely this historical approach which may throw light on our chief question,
namely, how the specific scientific techniques that Freud developed for the
investigation of the fragmentation of the individual in the Victorian period
are related to the understanding of man and his crises to which Kierkegaard
and Nietzsche contributed so much and which later provided a broad and
deep base for existential psychotherapy.

Compartmentalization and Inner Breakdown in the Nineteenth Century

The chief characteristic of the last half of the nineteenth century was the
breaking up of personality into fragments. These fragmentations, as we shall
see, were symptoms of the emotional, psychological, and spiritual disintegration occurring in the culture and in the individual. One can see this splitting up of the individual personality not only in the psychology and the
science of the period but in almost every aspect of late nineteenth-century
culture. One can observe the fragmentation in family life, vividly portrayed
and attacked in Ibsen's *A Doll's House.* The respectable citizen who keeps
his wife and family in one compartment and his business and other worlds
in others is making his home a doll's house and preparing its collapse. One
can likewise see the compartmentalization in the separation of art from the
realities of life, the use of art in its prettified, romantic, academic forms as
a hypocritical escape from existence and nature, the art as *art*ificiality against

which Cezanne, Van Gogh, the impressionists, and other modern art movements so vigorously protested. One can furthermore see the fragmentation in the separating of religion from weekday existence, making it an affair of Sundays and special observances, and the divorce of ethics from business. The segmentation was occurring also in philosophy and psychology—when Kierkegaard fought so passionately against the enthronement of an arid, abstract reason and pleaded for a return to reality, he was by no means tilting at windmills. The Victorian man saw himself as segmented into reason, will, and emotions and found the picture good. His reason was supposed to tell him *what* to do, then voluntaristic will was supposed to give him the means to do it, and emotions—well, emotions could best be channeled into compulsive business drive and rigidly structuralized in Victorian mores; and the emotions which would really have upset the formal segmentation, such as sex and hostility, were to be stanchly repressed or let out only in orgies of patriotism or on well-contained week-end "binges" in Bohemia in order that one might, like a steam engine which has let off surplus pressure, work more effectively on returning to his desk Monday morning. Naturally, this kind of man had to put great stress on "rationality." Indeed, the very term "irrational" means a thing not to be spoken of or thought of; and Victorian man's repressing, or compartmentalizing, what was not to be thought of was a precondition for the apparent stability of the culture. Schachtel has pointed out how the citizen of the Victorian period so needed to persuade himself of his own rationality that he denied the fact that he had ever been a child or had a child's irrationality and lack of control; hence the radical split between the adult and the child, which was portentous for Freud's investigations.[26]

This compartmentalization went hand in hand with the developing industrialism, as both cause and effect. A man who can keep the different segments of his life entirely separated, who can punch the clock every day at exactly the same moment, whose actions are always predictable, who is never troubled by irrational urges or poetic visions, who indeed can manipulate himself the same way he would the machine whose levers he pulls, is of course the most profitable worker not only on the assembly line but even on many of the higher levels of production. As Marx and Nietzsche pointed out, the corollary is likewise true: the very success of the industrial system, with its accumulation of money as a validation of personal worth entirely separate from the actual product of a man's hands, had a reciprocal depersonalizing and dehumanizing effect upon man in his relation to others and himself. It was against these dehumanizing tendencies to make man into a machine, to make him over in the image of the industrial system for which he labored, that the early existentialists fought so strongly. And they were aware that the most serious threat of all was that reason would join mechanics in sapping

26 Ernest Schachtel, *On Affect, Anxiety and the Pleasure Principle*, paper to be published.

the individual's vitality and decisiveness. *Reason,* they predicted, *was becoming reduced to a new kind of technique.*

Scientists in our day are often not aware that this compartmentalization, finally, was also characteristic of the sciences of the century of which we are heirs. This nineteenth century was the era of the "autonomous sciences," as Ernest Cassirer phrases it. Each science developed in its own direction; there was no unifying principle, particularly with relation to man. The views of man in the period were supported by empirical evidence amassed by the advancing sciences, but "each theory became a Procrustean bed on which the empirical facts were stretched to fit a preconceived pattern. . . . Owing to this development our modern theory of man lost its intellectual center. We acquired instead a complete anarchy of thought. . . . Theologians, scientists, politicians, sociologists, biologists, psychologists, ethnologists, economists all approached the problem from their own viewpoints . . . every author seems in the last count to be led by his own conception and evaluation of human life." [27] It is no wonder that Max Scheler declared, "In no other period of human knowledge has man ever become more problematic to himself than in our own days. We have a scientific, a philosophical, and a theological anthropology that know nothing of each other. Therefore we no longer possess any clear and consistent idea of man. The ever-growing multiplicity of the particular sciences that are engaged in the study of men has much more confused and obscured than elucidated our concept of man." [28]

On the surface, of course, the Victorian period appeared placid, contented, ordered; but this placidity was purchased at the price of widespread, profound, and increasingly brittle repression. As in the case of an individual neurotic, the compartmentalization became more and more rigid as it approached the point—August 1, 1914—when it was to collapse altogether.

Now it is to be noted that the compartmentalization of the culture had its *psychological parallel in radical repression within the individual personality.* Freud's genius was in developing scientific techniques for understanding, and mayhap curing, this fragmentized individual personality; but he did not see—or until much later, when he reacted to the fact with pessimism and some detached despair [29]—that the neurotic illness in the individual was only one side of disintegrating forces which affected the whole of society. Kierkegaard, for his part, foresaw the results of this disintegration upon the inner emotional and spiritual life of the individual: endemic anxiety, loneliness, estrangement of one man from another, and finally the condition that would lead to ultimate despair, man's alienation from himself. But it remained for Nietzsche to paint most graphically the approaching

---

[27] Ernest Cassirer, *An Essay on Man* (New Haven: Yale University Press, 1944), p. 21.
[28] Max Scheler, *Die Stellung des Menschen im Kosmos* (Darmstadt: Reichl, 1928), pp. 13f.
[29] Cf. *Civilization and Its Discontents.*

situation: "We live in a period of atoms, of atomic chaos," and out of this chaos he foresaw, in a vivid prediction of collectivism in the twentieth century, "the terrible apparition . . . the Nation State . . . and the hunt for happiness will never be greater than when it must be caught between today and tomorrow; because the day after tomorrow all hunting time may have come to an end altogether. . . ." [30] Freud saw this fragmentation of personality in the light of natural science and was concerned with formulating its technical aspects. Kierkegaard and Nietzsche did not underestimate the importance of the specific psychological analysis; but they were much more concerned with understanding *man as the being who represses,* the being who surrenders self-awareness as a protection against reality and then suffers the neurotic consequences. The strange question is: What does it mean that man, the being-in-the-world who can be conscious that he exists and can know his existence, should choose or be forced to choose to block off this consciousness and should suffer anxiety, compulsions for self-destruction, and despair? Kierkegaard and Nietzsche were keenly aware that the "sickness of soul" of Western man was a deeper and more extensive morbidity than could be explained by the specific individual or social problems. Something was radically wrong in man's relation to himself; man had become fundamentally problematic to himself. "This is Europe's true predicament," declared Nietzsche; "together with the fear of man we have lost the love of man, confidence in man, indeed, *the will to man.*"

Kierkegaard, Nietzsche, and Freud

We turn now to a more detailed comparison of the approach to understanding Western man given by Kierkegaard and Nietzsche, with the hope of seeing more clearly their interrelationship with the insights and methods of Freud.

Kierkegaard's penetrating analysis of anxiety—which we have summarized in another volume [31]—would alone assure him of a position among the psychological geniuses of all time. His insights into the significance of self-consciousness, his analysis of inner conflicts, loss of the self, and even psychosomatic problems are the more surprising since they antedate Nietzsche by four decades and Freud by half a century. This indicates in Kierkegaard a re-

---

[30] Walter A. Kaufmann, *Nietzsche. Philosopher, Psychologist, AntiChrist* (Princeton: Princeton University Press, 1950), p. 140.

[31] *The Meaning of Anxiety* (New York: Ronald Press, 1950), pp. 31–45. Those pages may be recommended as a short survey of the importance of Kierkegaard's ideas for the psychologically minded reader. His two most important psychological books are *The Concept of Anxiety* (translated into English as the *Concept of Dread,* a term which may in literary terms be closer to the meaning but is not psychologically), and *The Sickness Unto Death.* For further acquaintance with Kierkegaard, *A Kierkegaard Anthology,* ed. by Bretall, is recommended.

markable sensitivity to what was going on under the surface of Western man's consciousness in his day, to erupt only half a century later. He died just over a hundred years ago at the early age of forty-four, after an intense, passionate, and lonely period of creativity in which he wrote almost two dozen books in the space of fifteen years. Secure in the knowledge that he would become important in decades to come, he had no illusions about his discoveries and insights being welcomed in his day. "The present writer," he says in one satirical passage about himself, "is nothing of a philosopher; he is . . . an amateur writer who neither writes the System nor promises the System nor ascribes anything to it. . . . He can easily foresee his fate in an age when passion has been obliterated in favor of learning, in an age when an author who wants to have readers must take care to write in such a way that the book can easily be perused during the afternoon nap. . . . He foresees his fate, that he will be entirely ignored." True to his prediction, he was almost unknown in his day—except for satirical lampooning in *Corsair,* the humor magazine of Copenhagen. For half a century he remained forgotten and was then rediscovered in the second decade of this century, not only to have a profound effect on philosophy and religion but also to yield specific and important contributions to depth-psychology. Binswanger, for example, states in his paper on Ellen West that she "suffered from that sickness of the mind which Kierkegaard, with the keen insight of genius, described and illuminated from all possible aspects under the name of 'Sickness Unto Death.' I know of no document which could more greatly advance the existential-analytic interpretation of schizophrenia than that. One might say that in this document Kierkegaard had recognized with intuitive genius the coming of schizophrenia. . . ." Binswanger goes on to remark that the psychiatrist or psychologist who does not concur in Kierkegaard's religious interpretations nevertheless remains "deeply indebted to this work of Kierkegaard." [32]

Kierkegaard, like Nietzsche, did not set out to write philosophy or psychology. He sought only to understand, to uncover, to disclose human existence. With Freud and Nietzsche he shared a significant fact: all three of them based their knowledge chiefly on the analysis of one case, namely, themselves. Freud's germinal books, such as *Interpretation of Dreams,* were based almost entirely on his own experience and his own dreams; he wrote in so many words to Fliess that the case he struggled with and analyzed continually was himself. Every system of thought, remarked Nietzsche, "says only: this is a picture of all life, and from it learn the meaning of your life. And conversely; read only your life and understand from it the hieroglyphics of universal life." [33]

The central psychological endeavor of Kierkegaard may be summed up under the heading of the question he pursued relentlessly—how can you

[32] Chap. IX.
[33] Kaufmann, *op. cit.,* p. 135.

become an individual? The individual was being swallowed up on the rational side by Hegel's vast logical "absolute Whole," on the economic side by the increasing objectification of the person, and on the moral and spiritual side by the soft and vapid religion of his day. Europe was ill, and was to become more so, not because knowledge or techniques were lacking but because of the want of *passion, commitment*.[34] "Away from Speculation, away from the System," he called, "and back to reality!" He was convinced not only that the goal of "pure objectivity" is impossible but that even if it were possible it would be undesirable. And from another angle it is immoral: we are so involved in each other and the world that we cannot be content to view truth disinterestedly. Like all the existentialists, he took the term "interest" (inter-est) seriously.[35] Every question is the "question for the Single One," that is, for the alive and self-aware individual; and if we don't start with the human being there, we shall have spawned, with all our technical prowess, a collectivism of robots who will end up not just in emptiness but in self-destructive despair.

One of the most radical contributions of Kierkegaard to later dynamic psychology is his formulation of truth-as-relationship. In the book which was later to become the manifesto for existentialism, he writes:

When the question of truth is raised in an objective manner, reflection is directed objectively to the truth, as an object to which the knower is related. Reflection is not focused upon the relationship, however, but upon the question of whether it is the truth to which the knower is related. If only the object to which he is related is the truth, the subject is accounted to be in the truth. *When the question of the truth is raised subjectively, reflection is directed subjectively to the nature of the individual's relationship; if only the mode of this relationship is in the truth, the individual is in the truth, even if he should happen to be thus related to what is not true.*[36]

---

34 Thus the very increase of truth may leave human beings less secure, if they let the objective increase of truth act as a substitute for their own commitment, their own relating to the truth in their own experience. He "who has observed the contemporary generation," wrote Kierkegaard, "will surely not deny that the incongruity in it and the reason for its anxiety and restlessness is this, that in one direction truth increases in extent, in mass, partly also in abstract clarity, whereas certitude steadily decreases."

35 See Walter Lowrie, *A Short Life of Kierkegaard* (Princeton: Princeton University Press, 1942).

36 Quoted from the "Concluding Unscientific Postscript," in *A Kierkegaard Anthology*, Robert Bretall, ed. (Princeton: Princeton University Press, 1951), pp. 210–211. (Kierkegaard has the whole passage in italics; we have limited them, for purposes of contrast, to the new element, namely, the subjective relation to truth.) It is highly interesting that the example Kierkegaard goes on to cite, after the above sentences, is the knowledge of God, and points out—a consideration that would have saved endless confusions and futile bickerings—that the endeavor to prove God as an "object" is entirely fruitless, and that truth rather lies in the nature of the relationship ("even if he should happen to be thus related to what is not true"!). It should certainly be self-evident that Kierkegaard is not in the slightest implying that whether or not something is objectively true doesn't matter. That would be absurd. He is referring, as he phrases it in a footnote, to "the truth which is essentially related to existence."

It would be hard to exaggerate how revolutionary these sentences were and still are for modern culture as a whole and for psychology in particular. Here is the radical, original statement of *relational truth*. Here is the fountainhead of the emphasis in existential thought on truth as *inwardness* or, as Heidegger puts it, truth as freedom.[37] Here, too, is the prediction of what was later to appear in twentieth-century physics, namely, the reversal of the principle of Copernicus that one discovered truth most fully by detaching man, the observer. Kierkegaard foretells the viewpoint of Bohr, Heisenberg, and other contemporary physicists that the Copernican view that nature can be separated from man is no longer tenable. The "ideal of a science which is completely independent of man [*i.e.*, completely objective] is an illusion," in Heisenberg's words.[38] Here is, in Kierkegaard's paragraph, the forerunner of relativity and the other viewpoints which affirm that the human being who is engaged in studying the natural phenomena is in a particular and significant relationship to the objects studied and he must make himself part of his equation. That is to say, the *subject,* man, can never be separated from the *object* which he observes. It is clear that the cancer of Western thought, the subject-object split, received a decisive attack in this analysis of Kierkegaard's.

But the implications of this landmark are even more specific and more incisive in psychology. It releases us from bondage to the dogma that truth can be understood only in terms of external *objects*. It opens up the vast provinces of inner, subjective reality and indicates that such reality may be true even though it contradicts objective fact. This was the discovery Freud was later to make when, somewhat to his chagrin, he learned that the "childhood rape" memories so many of his patients confessed were generally lies from a factual point of view, the rape never having in fact occurred. But it turned out that the experience of rape was as potent even if it *existed only in phantasy*, and that in any case the crucial question was how the patient *reacted to* the rape rather than whether it was true or false in fact. We have, thus, the opening of a continent of new knowledge about inner dynamics when we take the approach that the *relation to* a fact or person or situation is what is significant for the patient or person we are studying and the question of whether or not something objectively occurred is on a quite different level. Let us, to avoid misunderstanding, emphasize even at the price of repetition that this truth-as-relationship principle does not in the slightest imply a sloughing off of the importance of whether or not something is objectively true. This is not the point. Kierkegaard is not to be confused with the subjectivists or idealists; he opens up the subjective world without losing

[37] See the essay "On the Essence of Truth" in *Existence and Being,* by Martin Heidegger, edited by Werner Brock, *op. cit.*

[38] From mimeographed address by Werner Heisenberg, Washington University, St. Louis, Oct. 1954.

objectivity. Certainly one has to deal with the real objective world; Kierkegaard, Nietzsche, and their ilk took nature more seriously than many who call themselves naturalists. The point rather is that the meaning for the person of the objective fact (or phantasied one) depends on how he relates to it; there is no existential truth which can omit the relationship. An objective discussion of sex, for example, may be interesting and instructive; but once one is concerned with a given person, the objective truth depends for its meaning upon the relationship between that person and the sexual partner and to omit this factor not only constitutes an evasion but cuts us off from seeing reality.

The approach stated in Kierkegaard's sentences is, furthermore, the forerunner of concepts of "participant observation" of Sullivan and the other emphases upon the significance of the therapist in the relationship with the patient. The fact that the therapist participates in a real way in the relationship and is an inseparable part of the "field" does not, thus, impair the soundness of his scientific observations. Indeed, can we not assert that unless the therapist is a real participant in the relationship and consciously recognizes this fact, he will *not* be able to discern with clarity what is in fact going on? The implication of this "manifesto" of Kierkegaard is that we are freed from the traditional doctrine, so limiting, self-contradictory, and indeed often so destructive in psychology, *that the less we are involved in a given situation, the more clearly we can observe the truth.* The implication of that doctrine was, obviously enough, that there is an inverse relation between involvement and our capacity to observe without bias. And the doctrine became so well-enshrined that we overlooked another one of its clear implications, namely, that he will most successfully discover truth who is not the slightest bit interested in it! No one, of course, would argue against the obvious fact that *disruptive* emotions interfere with one's perception. In this sense it is self-evident that anyone in a therapeutic relationship, or any person observing others, for that matter, must clarify very well what his particular emotions and involvement are in the situation. But the problem cannot be solved by detachment and abstraction. That way we end up with a handful of sea foam; and the reality of the person has evaporated before our eyes. The clarification of the pole in the relationship represented by the therapist can only be accomplished by a fuller awareness of the existential situation, that is, the real, living relationship.[39] When we are dealing with human beings, no truth has reality by itself; it is always dependent upon the reality of the immediate relationship.

[39] It should be possible to demonstrate—possibly it has already been done—in perception experiments that the interest and involvement of the observer increase the accuracy of his perception. There are indications already in Rorschach responses that in the cards where the subject becomes emotionally involved, his perception of form becomes more, not less. sharp and accurate. (I am of course speaking not of neurotic emotion; that introduces quite different factors.)

A second important contribution of Kierkegaard to dynamic psychology lies in his emphasis upon the necessity of commitment. This follows from the points already made above. Truth becomes reality only as the individual produces it in action, which includes producing it in his own consciousness. Kierkegaard's point has the radical implication that we cannot even *see* a particular truth unless we already have some commitment to it. It is well known to every therapist that patients can talk theoretically and academically from now till doomsday about their problems and not really be affected; indeed, particularly in cases of intellectual and professional patients, this very talking, though it may masquerade under the cloak of unbiased and unprejudiced inquiry into what is going on, is often the defense against seeing the truth and against committing one's self, a defense indeed against one's own vitality. The patient's talking will not help him to get to the reality until he can experience something or some issue in which he has an immediate and absolute stake. This is often expressed under the rubric of "the necessity of arousing anxiety in the patient." I believe, however, that this puts the matter too simply and partially. Is not the more fundamental principle that the patient must find or discover some point in his existence where he can commit himself before he can permit himself even to see the truth of what he is doing? This is what Kierkegaard means by "passion" and "commitment" as over against objective disinterested observation. One corollary of this need for commitment is the commonly accepted phenomenon that we cannot get to the underlying levels of a person's problems by laboratory experimentation; only when the person himself has some hope of getting relief from his suffering and despair and of receiving some help in his problems will he undertake the painful process of investigating his illusions and uncovering his defenses and rationalizations.

We turn now to Friedrich Nietzsche (1844–1900). He was very different from Kierkegaard in temperament, and, living four decades later, he reflected nineteenth-century culture at a different stage. He never read Kierkegaard; his friend Brandes called his attention to the Dane two years before Nietzsche's death, too late for Nietzsche to know the works of his predecessor, who was superficially so different but in many essentials so alike. Both represent in fundamental ways the emergence of the existential approach to human life. Both are often cited together as the thinkers who discerned most profoundly and predicted most accurately the psychological and spiritual state of Western man in the twentieth century. Like Kierkegaard, Nietzsche was not anti-rational, nor is he to be confused with the "philosophers of feeling" or the "back to nature" evangelists. He attacked not reason but *mere* reason, and he attacked it in the arid, fragmentized rationalistic form it assumed in his day. He sought to push reflection—again like Kierkegaard—to its uttermost limits to find the reality which underlies *both* reason and unreason. For reflection is, after all, a turning in on itself, a mirroring, and the issue for the living existential person is *what* he is reflecting; otherwise reflecting empties the person of vitality.[40] Like the depth psychologists to follow him, Nietzsche sought to bring into the scope of existence the unconscious, irrational sources of man's power and greatness as well as his morbidity and self-destructiveness.

Another significant relationship between these two figures and depth psychology is that they both developed a great intensity of self-consciousness. They were well aware that the most devastating loss in their objectivating culture was the individual's consciousness of himself—a loss to be expressed later in Freud's symbol of the ego as weak and passive, "lived by the Id," having lost its own self-directive powers.[41] Kierkegaard had written, "the more consciousness, the more self," a statement which Sullivan was to make in a different context a century later and which is implied in Freud's description of the aim of his technique as the increasing of the sphere of consciousness: "Where Id was, there ego shall be." But Kierkegaard and Nietzsche could not escape, in their special historical situations, the tragic consequences of their own intensity of self-consciousness. Both were lonely, anti-conformist in the extreme, and knew the deepest agonies of anxiety, despair, isolation. Hence they could speak from an immediate personal knowledge of these ultimate psychological crises.[42]

Nietzsche held that one should experiment on all truth not simply in the laboratory but in one's own experience; every truth should be faced with the question, "Can one live it?" "All truths," he put it, "are bloody truths for me." Hence his famous phrase, "error is cowardice." In taking religious leaders to task for their being alien to intellectual integrity, he charges that

40 Both Kierkegaard and Nietzsche knew that "man cannot sink back into unreflective immediacy without losing himself; but he can go this way to the end, not destroying reflection, but rather coming to the basis in himself in which reflection is rooted." Thus speaks Karl Jaspers in his enlightening discussion of the similarities of Nietzsche and Kierkegaard, whom he regards as the two greatest figures of the nineteenth century. See his book, *Reason and Existence,* Chapter I, "Origin of the Contemporary Philosophic Situation (the Historical Meaning of Kierkegaard and Nietzsche)" (The Noonday Press, 1955, trans. from the German edition of 1935 by William Earle). This chapter is reprinted in the paperbound Meridian book, *Existentialism from Dostoevsky to Sartre,* Walter Kaufmann, ed., 1956.

41 The existential thinkers as a whole take this loss of consciousness as the centrally tragic problem of our day, not at all to be limited to the psychological context of neurosis. Jaspers indeed believes that the forces which destroy personal consciousness in our time, the juggernaut processes of conformity and collectivism, may well lead to a more radical loss of individual consciousness on the part of modern man.

42 Both Kierkegaard and Nietzsche also share the dubious honor of being dismissed in some allegedly scientific circles as pathological! I assume this fruitless issue needs no longer to be discussed; Binswanger quotes Marcel in a following paper concerning those who dismiss Nietzsche because of his ultimate psychosis, "One is free to learn nothing if one wishes." A more fruitful line of inquiry, if we wish to consider the psychological crises of Kierkegaard and Nietzsche, is to ask whether any human being can support an intensity of self-consciousness beyond a certain point, and whether the creativity (which is one manifestation of this self-consciousness) is not paid for by psychological upheaval?

they never make "their experiences a matter of conscience for knowledge. 'What have I really experienced? What happened then in me and around me? Was my reason bright enough? Was my will turned against all deceptions . . . ?' thus none of them questioned. . . . We, however, we others who thirst for reason want to look our experiences in the eye as severely as at a scientific experiment . . . ! We ourselves want to be our experiments and guinea-pigs!" [43] Neither Kierkegaard nor Nietzsche had the slightest interest in starting a movement—or a new System, a thought which would indeed have offended them. Both proclaimed, in Nietzsche's phrase, "Follow not me, but you!"

Both were aware that the psychological and emotional disintegration which they described as endemic, if still underground, in their periods was related to man's loss of faith in his essential dignity and humanity. Here they expressed a "diagnosis" to which very little attention was paid among the schools of psychotherapy until the past decade, when man's loss of faith in his own dignity began to be seen as a real and serious aspect of modern problems. This loss, in turn, was related to the breakdown of the convincing and compelling power of the two central traditions which had given a basis for values in Western society, namely the Hebrew-Christian and the humanistic. Such is the presupposition of Nietzsche's powerful parable, "God Is Dead." Kierkegaard had passionately denounced, with almost nobody listening, the softened, vapid, and anemic trends in Christianity; by Nietzsche's time the deteriorated forms of theism and emotionally dishonest religious practices had become part of the illness and had to die. [44] Roughly speaking, Kierkegaard speaks out of a time when God is dying, Nietzsche when God is dead. Both were radically devoted to the nobility of man and both sought some basis on which this dignity and humanity could be re-established. This is the meaning of Nietzsche's "man of power" and Kierkegaard's "true individual."

One of the reasons Nietzsche's influence upon psychology and psychiatry has so far been unsystematic, limited to a chance quotation of an aphorism here and there, is precisely that his mind is so unbelievably fertile, leaping incredibly from insight to flashing insight. The reader must take care not to be carried away in uncritical admiration or, on the other hand, to overlook Nietzsche's real importance because the richness of his thought beggars all our tidy categories. Hence we shall here endeavor briefly to clarify more systematically some of his central points.

His concept of "will to power" implies the self-realization of the individual in the fullest sense. It requires the courageous living out of the individual's potentialities in his own particular existence. Like all existential-

43 Kaufmann, op. cit., p. 93.
44 See Paul Tillich's reference to Nietzsche's "God Is Dead," footnote, p. 16.

ists, Nietzsche is not using psychological terms to describe psychological attributes or faculties or a simple pattern of behavior, such as aggression or power over someone. Will to power rather is an ontological category, that is to say, an inseparable aspect of being. It does not mean aggression or competitive striving or any such mechanism; it is the individual affirming his existence and his potentialities as a being in his own right; it is "the courage to be as an individual," as Tillich remarks in his discussion of Nietzsche. The word "power" is used by Nietzsche in the classical sense of *potentia, dynamis.* Kaufmann succinctly summarizes Nietzsche's belief at this point:

Man's task is simple: he should cease letting his "existence" be "a thoughtless accident." Not only the use of the word *Existenz,* but the thought which is at stake, suggests that [this essay] is particularly close to what is today called *Existenz-philosophie.* Man's fundamental problem is to achieve true "existence" instead of letting his life be no more than just another accident. In *The Gay Science* Nietzsche hits on a formulation which brings out the essential paradox of any distinction between self and true self: "What does your conscience say?—*You shall become who you are.*" Nietzsche maintains this conception until the end, and the full title of his last work is *Ecce Homo, Wie man wird, was man ist*—how one becomes what one is.[45]

In an infinite variety of ways, Nietzsche holds that this power, this expansion, growing, bringing one's inner potentialities into birth in action is the central dynamic and need of life. His work here relates directly to the problem in psychology of what the fundamental drive of organisms is, the blocking of which leads to neurosis: it is not urge for pleasure or reduction of libidinal tension or equilibrium or adaptation. The fundamental drive rather is to live out one's *potentia.* "*Not* for pleasure does man strive," holds Nietzsche, "but for power." [46] Indeed, happiness is not absence of pain but "the most alive feeling of power," [47] and joy is a "*plus-feeling* of power." [48] Health, also, he sees as a by-product of the use of power, power here specifically described as the ability to overcome disease and suffering.[49]

Nietzsche was a naturalist in the sense that he sought at all times to relate every expression of life to the broad context of all of nature, but it is precisely at this point that he makes clear that human psychology is always more than biology. One of his most crucial existential emphases is his insistence that the values of *human* life never come about automatically. The human being *can lose his own being by his own choices,* as a tree or stone cannot. Affirming one's own being creates the values of life. "Individuality, worth and dignity are not *gegeben,* i.e., given us as data by nature, but

45 Kaufmann, *op. cit.,* pp. 133–134.
46 *Ibid.,* p. 229.
47 *Ibid.,* p. 168.
48 *Ibid.,* p. 239.
49 Kaufmann, *op. cit.,* p. 169.

aufgegeben—i.e., given or assigned to us as a task which we ourselves must solve." [50] This is an emphasis which likewise comes out in Tillich's belief that courage opens the way to being: if you do not have "courage to be," you lose your own being. And it similarly appears in extreme form in Sartre's contention, you *are* your choices.

At almost any point at which one opens Nietzsche, one finds psychological insights which are not only penetrating and astute in themselves but amazingly parallel to the psychoanalytic mechanisms Freud was to formulate a decade and more later. For example, turning to the *Genealogy of Morals,* written in 1887, we find, "All instincts that are not allowed free play turn inward. This is what I call man's *interiorization.*" [51] One looks twice, noting the curiously close prediction of the later Freudian concept of repression. Nietzsche's eternal theme was the unmasking of self-deception. Throughout the whole essay mentioned above he develops the thesis that altruism and morality are the results of repressed hostility and resentment, that when the individual's *potentia* are turned inward, bad conscience is the result. He gives a vivid description of the "impotent" people "who are full of bottled-up aggressions: their happiness is purely passive and takes the form of drugged tranquillity, stretching and yawning, peace, 'sabbath,' emotional slackness." [52] This in-turned aggression breaks out in sadistic demands on others—the process which later was to be designated in psychoanalysis as symptom-formation. And the demands clothe themselves as morality—the process which Freud later called reaction-formation. "In its earliest phase," Nietzsche writes, "bad conscience is nothing other than the instinct of freedom forced to become latent, driven underground, and forced to vent its energy upon itself." At other points we find staring us in the face striking formulations of sublimation, a concept which Nietzsche specifically developed. Speaking of the connection between a person's artistic energy and sexuality, he says that it "may well be that the emergence of the aesthetic condition does not suspend sensuality, as Schopenhauer believed, but merely *transmutes it in such a way that it is no longer experienced as a sexual incentive.*" [53]

What, then, are we to conclude from this remarkable parallel between Nietzsche's ideas and Freud's? The similarity was known to the circle around Freud. One evening in 1908 the Vienna Psychoanalytic Society had as its program a discussion of Nietzsche's *Genealogy of Morals.* Freud mentioned that he had tried to read Nietzsche, but found his thought so rich he renounced the attempt. He then stated that "Nietzsche had a more penetrating knowledge of himself than any other man who ever lived or was

50 *Ibid.,* p. 136.
51 *Genealogy of Morals,* p. 217.
52 *Ibid.,* p. 102.
53 *Ibid.,* p. 247.

ever likely to live." [54] This judgment, repeated on several occasions, was, as Jones remarks, no small compliment from the inventor of psychoanalysis. Freud always had a strong but ambivalent interest in philosophy; he distrusted and even feared it.[55] Jones points out that this distrust was on personal as well as intellectual grounds. One of the reasons was his suspicion of arid intellectual speculation—a point on which Kierkegaard, Nietzsche, and the other existentialists would have enthusiastically agreed with him. In any case, Freud felt that his own potential proclivity for philosophy "needed to be sternly checked, and for that purpose he chose the most effective agency—scientific discipline." [56] At another point Jones remarks, "The ultimate questions of philosophy were very near to him in spite of his endeavor to keep them at a distance and of distrusting his capacity to solve them." [57]

Nietzsche's works may not have had a direct, but most certainly had an indirect, influence on Freud. It is clear that the ideas which were later to be formulated in psychoanalysis were "in the air" in the Europe of the end of the nineteenth century. The fact that Kierkegaard, Nietzsche, and Freud all dealt with the same problems of anxiety, despair, fragmentalized personality, and the symptoms of these bears out our earlier thesis that psychoanalysis and the existential approach to human crises were called forth by, and were answers to, the same problems. It does not detract, of course, from the genius of Freud to point out that probably almost all of the specific ideas which later appeared in psychoanalysis could be found in Nietzsche in greater breadth and in Kierkegaard in greater depth.

But the particular genius of Freud lies in his translating these depth-psychological insights into the natural scientific framework of his day. For this task he was admirably fitted—in temperament highly objective and rationally controlled, indefatigable, and capable of taking the infinite pains necessary for his systematic work. He did accomplish something new under the sun, namely, the transmuting into the scientific stream of Western culture the new psychological concepts, where they could be studied with some objectivity, built upon, and within certain limits rendered teachable.

[54] *The Life and Work of Sigmund Freud*, by Ernest Jones, Basic Books, Inc., Vol. II, p. 344. Dr. Ellenberger, commenting on the affinities of Nietzsche with psychoanalysis, adds, "In fact, the analogies are so striking that I can hardly believe that Freud never read him, as he contended. Either he must have forgotten that he read him, or perhaps he must have read him in indirect form. Nietzsche was so much discussed everywhere at that time, quoted thousands of times in books, magazines, newspapers, and in conversations in everyday life, that it is almost impossible that Freud could not have absorbed his thought in one way or another." Whatever one may assume at this point, Freud did read Edward von Hartmann (Kris points out), who wrote a book, *The Philosophy of the Unconscious*. Both Von Hartmann and Nietzsche got their ideas of the unconscious from Schopenhauer, most of whose work also falls in the existential line.

[55] *Ibid.*, Vol. II, p. 344.

[56] *Ibid.*, Vol. I, p. 295.

[57] *Ibid.*, Vol. II, p. 432.

But is not the very genius of Freud and of psychoanalysis likewise also its greatest danger and most serious shortcoming? For the translation of depth-psychological insights into objectivated science had results which could have been foreseen. One such result has been the limiting of the sphere of investigation in man to what fits this sphere of science. In one of the succeeding chapters in this book, Binswanger points out that Freud deals only with the *homo natura* and that, whereas his methods admirably fitted him for exploring the *Umwelt,* the world of man in his biological environment, they by the same token prevented him from comprehending fully the *Mitwelt,* man in personal relations with fellowmen, and the *Eigenwelt,* the sphere of man in relation to himself.[58] Another more serious practical result has been, as we shall indicate later in our discussion of the concepts of determinism and passivity of the ego, a new tendency to objectivate personality and to contribute to the very developments in modern culture which caused the difficulties in the first place.

We now come to a very important problem, and in order to understand it we need to make one more preliminary distinction. That is between "reason" as the term was used in the seventeenth century and the enlightenment and "technical reason" today. Freud held a concept of reason which came directly from the enlightenment, namely, "ecstatic reason." And he equated this with science. This use of reason involves, as seen in Spinoza and the other thinkers of the seventeenth and eighteenth centuries, a confidence that reason can by itself comprehend all problems. But those thinkers were using reason as including the capacity to transcend the immediate situation, to grasp the whole, and such functions as intuition, insight, poetic perception were not rigidly excluded. The concept also embraced ethics: reason in the enlightenment meant justice. Much, in other words, that is "irrational" was included in their idea of reason. This accounts for the tremendous and enthusiastic faith they could lodge in it. But by the end of the nineteenth century, as Tillich demonstrates most cogently, this ecstatic character had been lost. Reason had become "technical reason": reason married to techniques, reason as functioning best when devoted to isolated problems, reason as an adjunct and subordinate to technical industrial progress, reason as separated off from emotion and will, reason indeed as opposed to existence—the reason finally which Kierkegaard and Nietzsche so strongly attacked.

Now, part of the time Freud uses the concept of reason in the ecstatic form, as when he speaks of reason as "our salvation," reason as our "only recourse," and so on. Here one gets the anachronistic feeling that his sentences are directly out of Spinoza or some writer of the enlightenment. Thus

---

[58] The point that Freud deals with *homo natura* was centrally made by Binswanger in the address he was invited to give in Vienna on the occasion of the eightieth birthday of Freud.

he tried on one hand to preserve the ecstatic concept, tried to save the view of man and reason which transcends techniques. But, on the other hand, in equating reason with science, Freud makes it technical reason. His great contribution was his effort to overcome the fragmentation of man by bringing man's irrational tendencies into the light, bringing unconscious, split off, and repressed aspects of personality into consciousness and acceptance. But the other side of his emphasis, namely, the identification of psychoanalysis with technical reason, is an expression of the precise fragmentation which he sought to cure. It is not unfair to say that the prevailing trend in the development of psychoanalysis in late decades, particularly after the death of Freud, has been to reject his efforts to save reason in its ecstatic form and to accept exclusively the latter—namely, reason in its technical form. This trend is generally unnoticed, since it fits in so well with dominant trends in our whole culture. But we have already noted that seeing man and his functions in their technical form is one of the central factors in the compartmentalization of contemporary man. Thus a critical and serious dilemma faces us. On the theoretical side, psychoanalysis (and other forms of psychology to the extent that they are wedded to technical reason) themselves add to the chaos in our theory of man, both scientific and philosophical, of which Cassirer and Scheler spoke above.[59] On the practical side, there is considerable danger that psychoanalysis, as well as other forms of psychotherapy and adjustment psychology, will become new representations of the fragmentation of man, that they will exemplify the loss of the individual's vitality and significance, rather than the reverse, that the new techniques will assist in standardizing and giving cultural sanction to man's alienation from himself rather than solving it, that they will become expressions of the new mechanization of man, now calculated and controlled with greater psychological precision and on the vaster scale of unconscious and depth dimensions—that psychoanalysis and psychotherapy in general will become part of the neurosis of our day rather than part of the cure. This would indeed be a supreme irony of history. It is not alarmism nor showing unseemly fervor to point out these tendencies, some of which are already upon us; it is simply to look directly at our historical situation and to draw unflinchingly the implications.

We are now in a position to see the crucial significance of the existential psychotherapy movement. It is precisely the movement that protests against the tendency to identify psychotherapy with technical reason. It stands for basing psychotherapy on an understanding of what makes man the *human* being; it stands for defining neurosis in terms of what destroys man's capacity to fulfill his own being. We have seen that Kierkegaard and Nietzsche, as well as the representatives of the existential cultural movement following them, not only contributed far-reaching and penetrating

[59] See p. 22.

psychological insights, which in themselves form a significant contribution to anyone seeking scientifically to understand modern psychological problems, but also did something else—they placed these insights on an ontological basis, namely, the study of *man as the being who has* these particular problems. They believed that it was absolutely necessary that this be done, and they feared that the subordination of reason to technical problems would ultimately mean the making of man over in the image of the machine. Science, Nietzsche had warned, is becoming a factory, and the result will be ethical nihilism.

Existential psychotherapy is the movement which, although standing on one side on the scientific analysis owed chiefly to the genius of Freud, also brings back into the picture the understanding of man on the deeper and broader level—man as the being who is human. It is based on the assumption that it is possible to have a science of man which does not fragmentize man and destroy his humanity at the same moment as it studies him. It unites science and ontology. It is not too much to say, thus, that we are here not merely discussing a new method as over against other methods, to be taken or left or to be absorbed into some vague catch-all eclecticism. The issues raised in the chapters in this volume strike much deeper into our contemporary historical situation.

II

Contributions of
Existential Psychotherapy

by Rollo May

THE FUNDAMENTAL CONTRIBUTION of existential therapy is its understanding of man as *being*. It does not deny the validity of dynamisms and the study of specific behavior patterns in their rightful places. But it holds that drives or dynamisms, by whatever name one calls them, can be understood only in the context of the structure of the existence of the person we are dealing with. The distinctive character of existential analysis is, thus, that it is concerned with *ontology*, the science of being, and with *Dasein*, the existence of this particular being sitting opposite the psychotherapist.

Before struggling with definitions of *being* and related terms, let us begin existentially by reminding ourselves that what we are talking about is an experience every sensitive therapist must have countless times a day. It is the experience of the instantaneous encounter with another person who comes alive to us on a very different level from what we know *about* him. "Instantaneous" refers, of course, not to the actual time involved but to the quality of the experience. We may know a great deal about a patient from his case record, let us say, and may have a fairly good idea of how other interviewers have described him. But when the patient himself steps in, we often have a sudden, sometimes powerful, experience of here-is-a-new-person, an experience that normally carries with it an element of surprise, not in the sense of perplexity or bewilderment, but in its etymological sense of being "taken from above." This is of course in no sense a criticism of one's colleagues' reports; for we have this experience of encounter even with persons we have known or worked with for a long time.[1] The data we learned

1 We may have it with friends and loved ones. It is not a once-and-for-all experience; indeed, in any developing, growing relationship it may—probably should, if the relationship is vital—occur continually.

about the patient may have been accurate and well worth learning. But the point rather is that *the grasping of the being of the other person occurs on a quite different level from our knowledge of specific things about him.* Obviously a knowledge of the drives and mechanisms which are in operation in the other person's behavior is useful; a familiarity with his patterns of interpersonal relationships is highly relevant; information about his social conditioning, the meaning of particular gestures and symbolic actions is of course to the point, and so on *ad infinitum.* But all these fall on to a quite different level when we confront the overarching, most real fact of all—namely, the immediate, living person himself. When we find that all our voluminous knowledge about the person suddenly forms itself into a new pattern in this confrontation, the implication is not that the knowledge was wrong; it is rather that it takes its meaning, form, and significance from the reality of the person of whom these specific things are expressions. Nothing we are saying here in the slightest deprecates the importance of gathering and studying seriously all the specific data one can get about the given person. This is only common sense. But neither can one close his eyes to the experiential fact that this data forms itself into a configuration given in the encounter with the person himself. This also is illustrated by the common experience we all have had in interviewing persons; we may say we do not get a "feeling" of the other person and need to prolong the inter- view until the data "breaks" into its own form in our minds. We particularly do not get this "feeling" when we ourselves are hostile or resenting the relationship—that is, keeping the other person out—no matter how intellec- tually bright we may be at the time. This is the classical distinction between *knowing* and *knowing about.* When we seek to know a person, the knowl- edge *about* him must be subordinated to the overarching fact of his actual existence.

In the ancient Greek and Hebrew languages the verb "to know" is the same word as that which means "to have sexual intercourse." This is il- lustrated time and again in the King James translation of the Bible— "Abraham knew his wife and she conceived . . ." and so on. Thus the ety- mological relation between knowing and loving is exceedingly close. Though we cannot go into this complex topic, we can at least say that knowing another human being, like loving him, involves a kind of union, a dialecti- cal participation with the other. This Binswanger calls the "dual mode." One must have at least a readiness to love the other person, broadly speak- ing, if one is to be able to understand him.

The encounter with the being of another person has the power to shake one profoundly and may potentially be very anxiety-arousing. It may also be joy-creating. In either case, it has the power to grasp and move one deeply. The therapist understandably may be tempted for his own comfort to abstract himself from the encounter by thinking of the other as just a "patient" or by focusing only on certain mechanisms of behavior. But if the technical view is used dominantly in the relating to the other person, obviously one has defended himself from anxiety at the price not only of the isolation of himself from the other but also of radical distortion of reality. For one does not then really *see* the other person. It does not disparage the importance of technique to point out that technique, like data, must be subordinated to the fact of the reality of two persons in the room.

This point has been admirably made in a slightly different way by Sartre. If we "consider man," he writes, "as capable of being analyzed and reduced to original data, to determined drives (or 'desires'), supported by the subject as properties of an object," we may indeed end up with an imposing system of substances which we may then call mechanisms or dynamisms or patterns. But we find ourselves up against a dilemma. Our human being has become "a sort of indeterminate clay which would have to receive [the desires] passively—or he would be reduced to a simple bundle of these irreducible drives or tendencies. In either case the *man* disappears; we can no longer find 'the one' to whom this or that experience has happened." [2]

I *To Be and Not To Be*

It is difficult enough to give definitions of "being" and *Dasein,* but our task is made doubly difficult by the fact that these terms and their connotations encounter much resistance. Some readers may feel that these words are only a new form of "mysticism" (used in its disparaging and quite inaccurate sense of "misty") and have nothing to do with science. But this attitude obviously dodges the whole issue by disparaging it. It is interesting that the term "mystic" is used in this derogatory sense to mean anything we cannot segmentize and count. The odd belief prevails in our culture that a thing or experience is not real if we cannot make it mathematical, and somehow it must be real if we can reduce it to numbers. But this means making an abstraction out of it—mathematics is the abstraction par excellence, which is indeed its glory and the reason for its great usefulness. Modern Western man thus finds himself in the strange situation, after reducing something to

2 Jean-Paul Sartre, *Being and Nothingness,* trans. by Hazel Barnes (1956), p. 561. Sartre goes on, ". . . either in looking for the *person* we encounter a useless, contradictory metaphysical substance—or else the being whom we seek vanishes in a dust of phenomena bound together by external connections. But what each of us requires in this very effort to comprehend another is that he should never resort to this idea of substance, which is inhuman because it is well this side of the human" (p. 52). Also, "If we admit that the person is a totality, we can not hope to reconstruct him by an addition or by an organization of the diverse tendencies which we have empirically discovered in him. . . ." Every attitude of the person contains some reflection of this totality, holds Sartre. "A jealousy of a particular date in which a subject posits himself in history in relation to a certain woman, signifies for the one who knows how to interpret it, the total relation to the world by which the subject constitutes himself as a self. In other words this *empirical attitude* is by itself the expression of the 'choice of an intelligible character.' There is no mystery about this" (p. 58).

an abstraction, of having then to persuade himself it is real. This has much to do with the sense of isolation and loneliness which is endemic in the modern Western world; for the only experience we let ourselves believe in as real is that which precisely is not. Thus we deny the reality of our own experience. The term "mystic," in this disparaging sense, is generally used in the service of obscurantism; certainly avoiding an issue by derogation is only to obscure it. Is not the scientific attitude rather, to try to see clearly what it is we are talking about and then to find whatever terms or symbols can best, with least distortion, describe this reality? It should not so greatly surprise us to find that "being" belongs to that class of realities, like "love" and "consciousness" (for two other examples), which we cannot segmentize or abstract without losing precisely what we set out to study. This does not, however, relieve us from the task of trying to understand and describe them.

A more serious source of resistance is one that runs through the whole of modern Western society—namely, the psychological need to avoid and, in some ways, repress, the whole concern with "being." In contrast to other cultures which may be very concerned with being—particularly Indian and Oriental—and other historical periods which have been so concerned, the characteristic of our period in the West, as Marcel rightly phrases it, is precisely that the awareness of "the sense of the ontological—the sense of being —is lacking. Generally speaking, modern man is in this condition; if ontological demands worry him at all, it is only dully, as an obscure impulse." [3] Marcel points out what many students have emphasized, that this loss of the sense of being is related on one hand to our tendency to subordinate existence to function: a man knows himself not as a man or self but as a ticket-seller in the subway, a grocer, a professor, a vice president of A. T. & T., or by whatever his economic function may be. And on the other hand, this loss of the sense of being is related to the mass collectivist trends and widespread conformist tendencies in our culture. Marcel then makes this trenchant challenge: *"Indeed I wonder if a psychoanalytic method, deeper and more discerning than any that has been evolved until now, would not reveal the morbid effects of the repression of this sense and of the ignoring of this need."* [4]

"As for defining the word 'being,'" Marcel goes on, "let us admit that it is extremely difficult; I would merely suggest this method of approach: being is what withstands—or what would withstand—an exhaustive analysis bearing on the data of experience and aiming to reduce them step by step to elements increasingly devoid of intrinsic or significant value. (An analysis of this kind is attempted in the theoretical works of Freud.)" [5] This last

3 Gabriel Marcel, *The Philosophy of Existence* (1949), p. 1.
4 *Ibid*. Italics mine. For data concerning the "morbid effects of the repression" of the sense of being, cf. Fromm, *Escape from Freedom*, and David Riesman, *The Lonely Crowd*.
5 *Ibid.*, p. 5.

sentence I take to mean that when Freud's analysis is pushed to the ultimate extreme, and we know, let us say, everything about drives, instincts, and mechanisms, we have everything *except* being. Being is that which remains. It is that which constitutes this infinitely complex set of deterministic factors into a person *to whom* the experiences happen and who possesses some element, no matter how minute, of freedom to become aware that these forces are acting upon him. This is the sphere where he has the potential capacity to pause before reacting and thus to cast some weight on whether his reaction will go this way or that. And this, therefore, is the sphere where he, the human being, is never merely a collection of drives and determined forms of behavior.

The term the existential therapists use for the distinctive character of human existence is *Dasein*. Binswanger, Kuhn, and others designate their school as *Daseinsanalyse*. Composed of *sein* (being) plus *da* (there), *Dasein* indicates that man is the being who *is there* and implies also that he *has* a "there" in the sense that he can know he is there and can take a stand with reference to that fact. The "there" is moreover not just any place, but the particular "there" that is mine, the particular point *in time* as well as space of my existence at this given moment. Man is the being who can be conscious of, and therefore responsible for, his existence. It is this capacity to become aware of his own being which distinguishes the human being from other beings. The existential therapists think of man not only as "being-in-itself," as all beings are, but also as "being-for-itself." Binswanger and other authors in the chapters that follow speak of "*Dasein* choosing" this or that, meaning "the person-who-is-responsible-for-his-existence choosing. . . ."

The full meaning of the term "human being" will be clearer if the reader will keep in mind that "being" is a participle, a verb form implying that someone is in the process of *being something*. It is unfortunate that, when used as a general noun in English, the term "being" connotes a static substance, and when used as a particular noun such as *a* being, it is usually assumed to refer to an entity, say, such as a soldier to be counted as a unit. Rather, "being" should be understood, when used as a general noun, to mean *potentia*, the source of potentiality; "being" is the potentiality by which the acorn becomes the oak or each of us becomes what he truly is. And when used in a particular sense, such as *a* human being, it always has the dynamic connotation of someone in process, the person being something. Perhaps, therefore, *becoming* connotes more accurately the meaning of the term in this country. We can understand another human being only as we see what he is moving toward, what he is becoming; and we can know ourselves only as we "project our *potentia* in action." The significant tense for human beings is thus the *future*—that is to say, the critical question is what I am pointing toward, becoming, what I will be in the immediate future.

Thus, being in the human sense is not given once and for all. It does not unfold automatically as the oak tree does from the acorn. For an intrinsic and inseparable element in being human is self-consciousness. Man (or *Dasein*) is the particular being who has to be aware of himself, be responsible for himself, if he is to become himself. He also is that particular being who knows that at some future moment he will not be; he is the being who is always in a dialectical relation with non-being, death. And he not only knows he will sometime not be, but he can, in his own choices, slough off and forfeit his being. "To be and not to be"—the "and" in our subtitle to this section is not a typographical error—is not a choice one makes once and for all at the point of considering suicide; it reflects to some degree a choice made at every instant. The profound dialectic in the human being's awareness of his own being is pictured with incomparable beauty by Pascal:

Man is only a reed, the feeblest reed in nature, but he is a thinking reed. There is no need for the entire universe to arm itself in order to annihilate him: a vapour, a drop of water, suffices to kill him. But were the universe to crush him, man would yet be more noble than that which slays him, because he knows that he dies, and the advantage that the universe has over him; of this the universe knows nothing.[6]

In the hope of making clearer what it means for a person to experience his own being, we shall present an illustration from a case history. This patient, an intelligent woman of twenty-eight, was especially gifted in expressing what was occurring within her. She had come for psychotherapy because of serious anxiety spells in closed places, severe self-doubts, and eruptions of rage which were sometimes uncontrollable.[7] An illegitimate child, she had been brought up by relatives in a small village in the southwestern part of the country. Her mother, in periods of anger, often reminded her as a child of her origin, recounted how she had tried to abort her, and in times of trouble had shouted at the little girl, "If you hadn't been born, we wouldn't have to go through this!" Other relatives had cried at the child, in family quarrels, "Why didn't you kill yourself?" and "You should have been choked the day you were born!" Later, as a young woman, the patient had become well-educated on her own initiative.

In the fourth month of therapy she had the following dream: "I was in a crowd of people. They had no faces; they were like shadows. It seemed like a wilderness of people. Then I saw there was someone in the crowd who had compassion for me." The next session she reported that she had

6 Pascal's *Pensées*, Gertrude B. Burford Rawlings, trans. and ed. (Peter Pauper Press), p. 35. Pascal goes on, "Thus all our dignity lies in thought. By thought we must raise ourselves, not by space and time, which we cannot fill. Let us strive, then, to think well,— therein is the principle of morality." It is perhaps well to remark that of course by "thought" he means not intellectualism nor technical reason but self-consciousness, the reason which also knows the reasons of the heart.

7 Since our purpose is merely to illustrate one phenomenon, namely, the experience of the sense of being, we shall not report the diagnostic or other details of the case.

had, in the intervening day, an exceedingly important experience. It is reported here as she wrote it down from memory and notes two years later.

I remember walking that day under the elevated tracks in a slum area, feeling the thought, "I am an illegitimate child." I recall the sweat pouring forth in my anguish in trying to accept that fact. Then I understood what it must feel like to accept, "I am a Negro in the midst of privileged whites," or "I am blind in the midst of people who see." Later on that night I woke up and it came to me this way, "I accept the fact that I am an illegitimate child." *But* "I am not a child anymore." So it is, "I am illegitimate." That is not so either: "I was born illegitimate." Then what is left? What is left is this, *"I Am."* This *act* of contact and acceptance with "I am," once gotten hold of, gave me (what I think was for me the first time) the experience "Since I Am, I have the right to be."

What is this experience like? It is a primary feeling—it feels like receiving the deed to my house. It is the experience of my own aliveness not caring whether it turns out to be an ion or just a wave. It is like when a very young child I once reached the core of a peach and cracked the pit, not knowing what I would find and then feeling the wonder of finding the inner seed, good to eat in its bitter sweetness. . . . It is like a sailboat in the harbor being given an anchor so that, being made out of earthly things, it can by means of its anchor get in touch again with the earth, the ground from which its wood grew; it can lift its anchor to sail but always at times it can cast its anchor to weather the storm or rest a little. . . . It is my saying to Descartes, *"I Am, therefore* I think, I feel, I do."

It is like an axiom in geometry—never experiencing it would be like going through a geometry course not knowing the first axiom. It is like going into my very own Garden of Eden where I am beyond good and evil and all other human concepts. It is like the experience of the poets of the intuitive world, the mystics, except that instead of the pure feeling of and union with God it is the finding of and the union with my own being. It is like owning Cinderella's shoe and looking all over the world for the foot it will fit and realizing all of a sudden that one's own foot is the only one it will fit. It is a "Matter of Fact" in the etymological sense of the expression. It is like a globe before the mountains and oceans and continents have been drawn on it. It is like a child in grammar finding the *subject* of the verb in a sentence—in this case the subject being one's own life span. It is ceasing to feel like a theory toward one's self. . . .

We shall call this the "I-am" experience.[8] This one phase of a complex case, powerfully and beautifully described above, illustrates the emergence

8 Some readers will be reminded of the passage in Exodus 3:14 in which Moses, after Yahweh had appeared to him in the burning bush and charged him to free the Israelites from Egypt, demands that the God tell his name. Yahweh gives the famous answer, "I am that I am." This classical, existential sentence (the patient, incidentally, did not consciously know this sentence) carries great symbolic power because, coming from an archaic period, it has God state that *the quintessence of divinity is the power to be.* We are unable to go into the many rich meanings of this answer, nor the equally intricate translation problems, beyond pointing out that the Hebrew of the sentence can be translated as well, "I shall be what I shall be." This bears out our statement above that being is in the future tense and inseparable from becoming; God is creative *potentia,* the essence of the power to become.

and strengthening of the sense of being in one person. The experience is etched the more sharply in this person because of the more patent threat to her being that she had suffered as an illegitimate child and her poetic articulateness as she looked back on her experience from the vantage point of two years later. I do not believe either of these facts, however, makes her experience different in fundamental quality from what human beings in general, normal or neurotic, go through.

We shall make four final comments on the experience exemplified in this case. First, the "I-am" experience is not in itself the solution to a person's problems; it is rather the *precondition* for their solution. This patient spent some two years thereafter working through specific psychological problems, which she was able to do on the basis of this emerged experience of her own existence. In the broadest sense, of course, the achieving of the sense of being is a goal of all therapy, but in the more precise sense it is a relation to one's self and one's world, an experience of one's own existence (including one's own identity), which is a prerequisite for the working through of specific problems. It is, as the patient wrote, the "primary fact," a *ur* experience. It is not to be identified with any patient's discovery of his or her specific powers—when he learns, let us say, that he can paint or write or work successfully or have successful sexual intercourse. Viewed from the outside, the discovery of specific powers and the experience of one's own being may seem to go hand in hand, but the latter is the underpinning, the foundation, the psychological precondition of the former. We may well be suspicious that solutions to a person's specific problems in psychotherapy which do not presuppose this "I-am" experience in greater or lesser degree will have a pseudo quality. The new "powers" the patient discovers may well be experienced by him as merely compensatory—that is, as proofs that he is of significance despite the fact that he is certain on a deeper level that he is not, since he still lacks a basic conviction of "*I Am,* therefore I think, I act." And we could well wonder whether such compensatory solutions would not represent rather the patient's simply exchanging one defense system for another, one set of terms for another, without ever experiencing himself as existing. In the second state the patient, instead of blowing up in anger, "sublimates" or "introverts" or "relates," but still without the act being rooted in his own existence.

Our second comment is that this patient's "I-am" experience is not to be explained by the transference relationship. That the positive transference, whether directed to therapist or husband,[9] is obviously present in the above case is shown in the eloquent dream the night before in which there was one

---

[9] We omit for purposes of the above discussion the question whether this rightly should be called "transference" or simply human trust at this particular point in this case. We do not deny the validity of the concept of transference rightly defined (see p. 83), but it never makes sense to speak of something as "just transference," as though it were all carried over simply from the past.

person in the barren, depersonalized wilderness of the crowd who had compassion for her. True, she is showing in the dream that she could have the "I-am" experience only if she could trust some other human being. But this does not account for the experience itself. It may well be true that for any human being the possibility of acceptance by and trust for another human being is a necessary condition for the "I-am" experience. But the awareness of one's own being occurs basically on the level of the grasping of one's self; it is an experience of *Dasein,* realized in the realm of self-awareness. It is not to be explained *essentially* in social categories. The acceptance by another person, such as the therapist, shows the patient that he no longer needs to fight his main battle on the front of whether anyone else, or the world, can accept him; the acceptance *frees* him to experience his own being. This point must be emphasized because of the common error in many circles of assuming that the experience of one's own being will take place automatically if only one is accepted by somebody else. This is the basic error of some forms of "relationship therapy." The attitude of "If-I-love-and-accept-you, this-is-all-you-need," is in life and in therapy an attitude which may well minister to increased passivity. The crucial question is what the individual himself, in his own awareness of and responsibility for his existence, does with the fact that he can be accepted.

The third comment follows directly from the above, that *being* is a category which cannot be reduced to introjection of social and ethical norms. It is, to use Nietzsche's phrase, "beyond good and evil." To the extent that my sense of existence is authentic, it is precisely *not* what others have told me I should be, but is the one Archimedes point I have to stand on from which to judge what parents and other authorities demand. Indeed, *compulsive and rigid moralism arises in given persons precisely as the result of a lack of a sense of being.* Rigid moralism is a compensatory mechanism by which the individual persuades himself to take over the external sanctions because he has no fundamental assurance that his own choices have any sanction of their own. This is not to deny the vast social influences in anyone's morality, but it is to say that the ontological sense cannot be wholly reduced to such influences. The ontological sense *is not a superego* phenomenon. By the same token the sense of being gives the person a basis for a self-esteem which is not merely the reflection of others' views about him. For if your self-esteem must rest in the long run on social validation, you have, not self-esteem, but a more sophisticated form of social conformity. It cannot be said too strongly that the sense of one's own existence, though interwoven with all kinds of social relatedness, is in basis not the product of social forces; it always presupposes *Eigenwelt,* the "own world" (a term which will be discussed below).

Our fourth comment deals with the most important consideration of all, namely that the "I-am" experience must not be identified with what is called in various circles the "functioning of the ego." That is to say, it is an error to define the emergence of awareness of one's own being as one phase of the "development of the ego." We need only reflect on what the concept of "ego" has meant in classical psychoanalytic tradition to see why this is so. The ego was traditionally conceived as a relatively weak, shadowy, passive, and derived agent, largely an epiphenomenon of other more powerful processes. It is "derived from the Id by modifications imposed on it from the external world" and is "representative of the external world." [10] "What we call the ego is essentially passive," says Groddeck, a statement which Freud cites with approval.[11] The developments in the middle period of psychoanalytic theory brought increased emphasis on the ego, to be sure, but chiefly as an aspect of the study of defense mechanisms; the ego enlarged its originally buffeted and frail realm chiefly by its negative, defensive functions. It "owes service to three masters and is consequently menaced by three dangers: the external world, the libido of the Id, the severity of the Super-ego." [12] Freud often remarked that the ego does very well indeed if it can preserve some semblance of harmony in its unruly house.

A moment's thought will show how great is the difference between this ego and the "I-am" experience, the sense of being which we have been discussing. The latter occurs on a more fundamental level and is a precondition for ego development. The ego is a *part* of the personality, and traditionally a relatively weak part, whereas the sense of being refers to one's whole experience, unconscious as well as conscious, and is by no means merely the agent of awareness. The ego is a reflection of the outside world; the sense of being is rooted in one's own experience of existence, and if it is a mirroring of, a reflection of, the outside world alone, it is then precisely not one's own sense of existence. My sense of being is *not* my capacity to see the outside world, to size it up, to assess reality; it is rather my capacity to see myself as a being in the world, *to know myself as the being who can do these things.* It is in this sense a precondition for what is called "ego development." The ego is the *subject* in the subject-object relationship; the sense of being occurs on a level prior to this dichotomy. Being means not "I am the subject," but "I am the being who can, among other things, know himself as the subject of what is occurring." The sense of being is not in origin set against the outside world but it must include this capacity to set one's self against the external world if necessary, just as it must include the capacity to confront non-being, as we shall indicate later. To be sure, both what is

[10] Healy, Bronner and Bowers, *The Meaning and Structure of Psychoanalysis* (1930), p. 38. We give these quotations from a standard summary from the classical middle period of psychoanalysis, not because we are not aware of refinements made to ego theory later, but because we wish to show the essence of the concept of the ego, an essence which has been elaborated but not basically changed.

[11] *Ibid.*, p. 41.

[12] *Ibid.*, p. 38.

called the ego and the sense of being presuppose the emergence of self-awareness in the child somewhere between the first couple of months of infancy
and the age of two years, a developmental process often called the "emergence of the ego." But this does not mean these two should be identified. The
ego is said normally to be especially weak in childhood, weak in proportion
to the child's relatively weak assessment of and relation to reality; whereas
the sense of being may be especially strong, only later to diminish as the
child learns to give himself over to conformist tendencies, to experience his
existence as a reflection of others' evaluation of him, to lose some of his originality and primary sense of being. Actually, the sense of being—that is, the
ontological sense—is presupposed for ego development, just as it is presupposed for the solution of other problems.[13]

We are of course aware that additions and elaborations are occurring in
ego theory of late decades in the orthodox psychoanalytic tradition. But one
cannot strengthen such a weak monarch by decking him with additional
robes, no matter how well-woven or intricately tailored the robes may be.
The real and fundamental trouble with the doctrine of the ego is that it
represents, par excellence, the subject-object dichotomy in modern thought.
Indeed, it is necessary to emphasize that *the very fact that the ego is conceived of as weak, passive, and derived is itself an evidence and a symptom
of the loss of the sense of being in our day, a symptom of the repression of
the ontological concern.* This view of the ego is a symbol of the pervasive
tendency to see the human being primarily as a passive recipient of forces
acting upon him, whether the forces be identified as the Id or the vast industrial juggernaut in Marxian terms or the submersion of the individual
as "one among many" in the sea of conformity, in Heidegger's terms. The
view of the ego as relatively weak and buffeted about by the Id was in Freud
a profound symbol of the fragmentation of man in the Victorian period and
also a strong corrective to the superficial voluntarism of that day. But the
error arises when this ego is elaborated as the basic norm. The sense of
being, the ontological awareness, must be assumed below ego theory if that
theory is to refer with self-consistency to man as man.

We now come to the important problem of *non-being* or, as phrased in
existential literature, *nothingness.* The "and" in the title of this section,
"To Be *and* Not To Be," expresses the fact that non-being is an inseparable
part of being. To grasp what it means to exist, one needs to grasp the fact
that he might not exist, that he treads at every moment on the sharp edge

13 If the objection is entered that the concept of the "ego" at least is more precise and
therefore more satisfactory scientifically than this sense of being, we can only repeat what
we have said above, that precision can be gained easily enough on paper. But the question
always is the bridge between the concept and the reality of the person, and the scientific
challenge is to find a concept, a way of understanding, which does not do violence to
reality, even though it may be less precise.

of possible annihilation and can never escape the fact that death will arrive at some unknown moment in the future. Existence, never automatic, not only can be sloughed off and forfeited but is indeed at every instant threatened by non-being. Without this awareness of non-being—that is, awareness of the threats to one's being in death, anxiety, and the less dramatic but persistent threats of loss of potentialities in conformism—existence is vapid, unreal, and characterized by lack of concrete self-awareness. But with the confronting of non-being, existence takes on vitality and immediacy, and the individual experiences a heightened consciousness of himself, his world, and others around him.

Death is of course the most obvious form of the threat of non-being. Freud grasped this truth on one level in his symbol of the death instinct. Life forces (being) are arrayed at every moment, he held, against the forces of death (non-being), and in every individual life the latter will ultimately triumph. But Freud's concept of the death instinct is an ontological truth and should not be taken as a deteriorated psychological theory. The concept of the death instinct is an excellent example of our earlier point that Freud went beyond technical reason and tried to keep open the tragic dimension of life. His emphasis on the inevitability of hostility, aggression, and self-destructiveness in existence also, from one standpoint, has this meaning. True, he phrased these concepts wrongly, as when he interpreted the "death instinct" in chemical terms. The use of the word "thanatos" in psychoanalytic circles as parallel to libido is an example of this deteriorated phraseology. These are errors which arise from trying to put ontological truths, which death and tragedy are, into the frame of technical reason and reduce them to specific psychological mechanisms. On that basis Horney and others could logically argue that Freud was too "pessimistic" and that he merely rationalized war and aggression. I think that is a sound argument against the usual oversimplified psychoanalytic interpretations, which are in the form of technical reason; but it is not a sound argument against Freud himself, who tried to preserve a real concept of tragedy, ambivalent though his frame of reference was. He had indeed a sense of non-being, despite the fact that he always tried to subordinate it and his concept of being to technical reason.

It is also an error to see the "death instinct" only in biological terms, which would leave us hobbled with a fatalism. The unique and crucial fact, rather, is that the human being is the one who *knows* he is going to die, who anticipates his own death. The critical question thus is how he relates to the fact of death: whether he spends his existence running away from death or making a cult of repressing the recognition of death under the rationalizations of beliefs in automatic progress or providence, as is the habit of our Western society, or obscuring it by saying "one dies" and turning it into a matter of public statistics which serve to cover over the one ultimately important fact, that he himself at some unknown future moment will die.

The existential analysts, on the other hand, hold that the confronting of death gives the most positive reality to life itself. It makes the individual existence real, absolute, and concrete. For "death as an irrelative potentiality singles man out and, as it were, individualizes him to make him understand the potentiality of being in others [as well as in himself], when he realizes the inescapable nature of his own death." [14] Death is, in other words, the one fact of my life which is not relative but absolute, and my awareness of this gives my existence and what I do each hour an absolute quality.

Nor do we need to go as far as the extreme example of death to see the problem of non-being. Perhaps the most ubiquitous and ever-present form of the failure to confront non-being in our day is in *conformism,* the tendency of the individual to let himself be absorbed in the sea of collective responses and attitudes, to become swallowed up in *das Man,* with the corresponding loss of his own awareness, potentialities, and whatever characterizes him as a unique and original being. The individual temporarily escapes the anxiety of non-being by this means, but at the price of forfeiting his own powers and sense of existence.

On the positive side, the capacity to confront non-being is illustrated in the ability to accept anxiety, hostility, and aggression. By "accept" we mean here to tolerate without repression and so far as possible to utilize constructively. Severe anxiety, hostility, and aggression are states and ways of relating to one's self and others which would curtail or destroy being. But to preserve one's existence by running away from situations which would produce anxiety or situations of potential hostility and aggression leaves one with the vapid, weak, unreal sense of being—what Nietzsche meant in his brilliant description we quoted in the previous chapter of the "impotent people" who evade their aggression by repressing it and thereupon experience "drugged tranquillity" and free-floating resentment. Our point does not at all imply the sloughing over of the distinction between the *neurotic* and *normal* forms of anxiety, hostility, and aggression. Obviously the one constructive way to confront neurotic anxiety, hostility, and aggression is to clarify them psychotherapeutically and so far as possible to wipe them out. But that task

14 This is an interpretation of Heidegger, given by Werner Brock in the introduction to *Existence and Being* (Regnery, 1949), p. 77. For those who are interested in the logical aspects of the problem of being vs. non-being, it may be added that the dialectic of "yes vs. no," as Tillich points out in *The Courage to Be,* is present in various forms throughout the history of thought. Hegel held that non-being was an integral part of being, specifically in the "antithesis" stage of his dialectic of "thesis, antithesis, and synthesis." The emphasis on "will" in Schelling, Schopenhauer, Nietzsche, and others as a basic ontological category is a way of showing that being has the power of "negating itself without losing itself." Tillich, giving his own conclusion, holds that the question of how being and non-being are related can be answered only metaphorically: "Being embraces both itself and non-being." In everyday terms, being embraces non-being in the sense that we can be aware of death, can accept it, can even invite it in suicide, in short, can by self-awareness encompass death.

has been made doubly difficult, and the whole problem confused, by our failure to see the normal forms of these states—"normal" in the sense that they inhere in the threat of non-being with which any being always has to cope. Indeed, is it not clear that *neurotic* forms of anxiety, hostility, and aggression develop precisely because the individual has been unable to accept and deal with the *normal* forms of these states and ways of behaving? Paul Tillich has suggested far-reaching implications for the therapeutic process in his powerful sentence, which we shall quote without attempting to elucidate, "The self-affirmation of a being is the stronger the more non-being it can take into itself."

II *Anxiety and Guilt as Ontological*

Our discussion of being and non-being now leads to the point where we can understand the fundamental nature of anxiety. Anxiety is not an affect among other affects such as pleasure or sadness. It is rather an ontological characteristic of man, rooted in his very existence as such. It is not a peripheral threat which I can take or leave, for example, or a reaction which may be classified beside other reactions; it is always a threat to the foundation, the center of my existence. Anxiety is *the experience of the threat of imminent non-being.*[15]

In his classical contributions to the understanding of anxiety, Kurt Goldstein has emphasized that anxiety is not something we "have" but something we "are." His vivid descriptions of anxiety at the onset of psychosis, when the patient is literally experiencing the threat of dissolution of the self, make his point abundantly clear. But, as he himself insists, this threat of dissolution of the self is not merely something confined to psychotics but describes the neurotic and normal nature of anxiety as well. Anxiety is the subjective state of the individual's becoming aware that his existence can become destroyed, that he can lose himself and his world, that he can become "nothing." [16]

This understanding of anxiety as ontological illuminates the difference between anxiety and fear. The distinction is not one of degree nor of the intensity of the experience. The anxiety a person feels when someone he respects passes him on the street without speaking, for example, is not as

[15] The points in this summary of ontological anxiety are given in epigrammatic form, since for reasons of space we are forced to omit the considerable empirical data which could be cited at each point. A fuller development of some aspects of this approach to anxiety will be found in my book, *The Meaning of Anxiety.*

[16] We speak here of anxiety as the "subjective" state, making a distinction between subjective and objective that may not be entirely justified logically but shows the viewpoint from which one observes. The "objective" side of the anxiety experience, which we can observe from the outside, shows itself in severe cases in disordered, catastrophic behavior (Goldstein) or in cases of neurotics in symptom-formation or in cases of "normal" persons in ennui, compulsive activity, meaningless diversions, and truncation of awareness.

intense as the fear he experiences when the dentist seizes the drill to attack a sensitive tooth. But the gnawing threat of the slight on the street may hound him all day long and torment his dreams at night, whereas the feeling of fear, though it was quantitatively greater, is gone forever as soon as he steps out of the dentist's chair. The difference is that the anxiety strikes at the center core of his self-esteem and his sense of value as a self, which is one important aspect of his experience of himself as a being. Fear, in contrast, is a threat to the periphery of his existence; it can be objectivated, and the person can stand outside and look at it. In greater or lesser degree, anxiety overwhelms the person's awareness of existence, blots out the sense of time, dulls the memory of the past, and erases the future [17]—which is perhaps the most compelling proof of the fact that it attacks the center of one's being. While we are subject to anxiety, we are to that extent unable to conceive in imagination how existence would be "outside" the anxiety. This is of course why anxiety is so hard to bear, and why people will choose, if they have the chance, severe physical pain which would appear to the outside observer much worse. Anxiety is ontological, fear is not. Fear can be studied as an affect among other affects, a reaction among other reactions. But anxiety can be understood only as a threat to *Dasein*.

This understanding of anxiety as an ontological characteristic again highlights our difficulty with words. The term which Freud, Binswanger, Goldstein, Kierkegaard (as he is translated into German) use for anxiety is *Angst,* a word for which there is no English equivalent. It is first cousin to anguish (which comes from Latin *angustus,* "narrow," which in turn comes from *angere,* "to pain by pushing together," "to choke"). The English term *anxiety,* such as in "I am anxious to do this or that," is a much weaker word.[18] Hence some students translate *Angst* as "dread," as did Lowrie in his translations of Kierkegaard and as the translators of Ellen West have done in this volume. Some of us have tried to preserve the term "anxiety" for *Angst* [19] but we were caught in a dilemma. It seemed the alternative was either to use "anxiety" as a watered-down affect among other affects, which will work scientifically but at the price of the loss of power of the word; or to use such a term as "dread," which carries literary power but has no role as a scientific category. Hence so often laboratory experiments on anxiety have seemed to fall woefully short of dealing with the power and devastating qualities of anxiety which we observe every day in clinical work, and also even clinical discussions about neurotic symptoms and psychotic con-

17 See discussion of this phenomenon in connection with Minkowski's chapter in this book, pp. 66 and 127.

18 It is an interesting question whether our pragmatic tendencies in English-speaking countries to avoid reacting to anxiety experiences—by being stoical in Britain and by not crying or showing fear in this country, for examples—is part of the reason we have not developed words to do justice to the experience.

19 See *Meaning of Anxiety*, p. 32.

ditions seem often to coast along the surface of the problem. The upshot of the existential understanding of anxiety is to give the term back its original power. It is an experience of threat which carries both anguish and dread, indeed the most painful and basic threat which any being can suffer, for it is the threat of loss of existence itself. In my judgment, our psychological and psychiatric dealings with anxiety phenomena of all sorts will be greatly helped by shifting the concept to its ontological base.

Another significant aspect of anxiety may now also be seen more clearly, namely, the fact that anxiety always involves inner conflict. Is not this conflict precisely between what we have called being and non-being? Anxiety occurs at the point where some emerging potentiality or possibility faces the individual, some possibility of fulfilling his existence; but this very possibility involves the destroying of present security, which thereupon gives rise to the tendency to deny the new potentiality. Here lies the truth of the symbol of the birth trauma as the prototype of all anxiety—an interpretation suggested by the etymological source of the word "anxiety" as "pain in narrows," "choking," as though through the straits of being born. This interpretation of anxiety as birth trauma was, as is well known, held by Rank to cover all anxiety and agreed to by Freud on a less comprehensive basis. There is no doubt that it carries an important symbolic truth even if one does not take it as connected with the literal birth of the infant. If there were not some possibility opening up, some potentiality crying to be "born," we would not experience anxiety. This is why anxiety is so profoundly connected with the problem of freedom. If the individual did not have some freedom, no matter how minute, to fulfill some new potentiality, he would not experience anxiety. Kierkegaard described anxiety as "the dizziness of freedom," and added more explicitly, if not more clearly, "Anxiety is the reality of freedom as a potentiality before this freedom has materialized." Goldstein illustrates this by pointing out how people individually and collectively surrender freedom in the hope of getting rid of unbearable anxiety, citing the individual's retreating behind the rigid stockade of dogma or whole groups collectively turning to fascism in recent decades in Europe.[20] In whatever way one chooses to illustrate it, this discussion points to the positive aspect of *Angst*. For the experience of anxiety itself demonstrates that some potentiality is present, some new possibility of being, threatened by non-being.

We have stated that the condition of the individual when confronted with the issue of fulfilling his potentialities is *anxiety*. We now move on to state that when the person denies these potentialities, fails to fulfill them, his condition is *guilt*. That is to say, guilt is also an ontological characteristic of human existence.

[20] *Human Nature in the Light of Psychopathology* (Cambridge: Harvard University Press, 1940).

This can be no better illustrated than to summarize a case Medard Boss cites of a severe obsessional-compulsive which he treated.[21] This patient, a physician suffering from washing, cleaning compulsions, had gone through both Freudian and Jungian analyses. He had had for some time a recurrent dream involving church steeples which had been interpreted in the Freudian analysis in terms of phallic symbols and in the Jungian in terms of religious archetype symbols. The patient could discuss these interpretations intelligently and at length, but his neurotic compulsive behavior, after temporary abeyance, continued as crippling as ever. During the first months of his analysis with Boss, the patient reported a recurrent dream in which he would approach a lavatory door which would always be locked. Boss confined himself to asking each time only why the door needed to be locked—to "rattling the doorknob," as he put it. Finally the patient had a dream in which he went through the door and found himself inside a church, waist deep in faeces and being tugged by a rope wrapped around his waist leading up to the bell tower. The patient was suspended in such tension that he thought he would be pulled to pieces. He then went through a psychotic episode of four days during which Boss remained by his bedside, after which the analysis continued with an eventual very successful outcome.

Boss points out in his discussion of this case that the patient was guilty because he had locked up some essential potentialities in himself. *Therefore* he had guilt feelings. If, as Boss puts it, we "forget being"—by failing to bring ourselves to our entire being, by failing to be authentic, by slipping into the conformist anonymity of *das Man*—then we have in fact missed our being and to that extent are failures. "If you lock up potentialities, you are guilty against (or *indebted to,* as the German word may be translated) what is given you in your origin, in your 'core.' In this existential condition of being indebted and being guilty are founded all guilt feelings, in whatever thousand and one concrete forms and malformations they may appear in actuality." This is what had happened to the patient. He had locked up both the bodily and the spiritual possibilities of experience (the "drive" aspect and the "god" aspect, as Boss also phrases it). The patient had previously accepted the libido and archetype explanations and knew them all too well; but that is a good way, says Boss, to escape the whole thing. Because the patient did not accept and take into his existence these two aspects, he was guilty, indebted to himself. This was the origin (*Anlass*) of his neurosis and psychosis.

The patient, in a letter to Boss sometime after the treatment, pointed out that the reason he could not really accept his anality in his first analysis was

21 Medard Boss, *Psychoanalyse und Daseinsanalytik* (Bern and Stuttgart: Verlag Hans Huber, 1957). I am grateful to Dr. Erich Heydt, student and colleague of Boss, for translating parts of this work for me as well as discussing at length with me the viewpoint of Boss.

that he "sensed the ground was not fully developed in the analyst himself." The analyst had always attempted to reduce the dream of the church steeple to genital symbols and the "whole weight of the holy appeared to him as a mere sublimation mist." By the same token, the archetypal explanation, also symbolic, never could be integrated with the bodily, and for that matter never did really mesh with the religious experience either.

Let us note well that Boss says the patient *is* guilty, not merely that he *has guilt feelings*. This is a radical statement with far-reaching implications. It is an existential approach which cuts through the dense fog which has obscured much of the psychological discussion of guilt—discussions that have proceeded on the assumption that we can deal only with some vague "guilt feelings," as though it did not matter whether guilt was real or not. Has not this reduction of guilt to mere guilt feelings contributed considerably to the lack of reality and the sense of illusion in much psychotherapy? Has it not also tended to confirm the patient's neurosis in that it implicitly opens the way for him not to take his guilt seriously and to make peace with the fact that he has indeed forfeited his own being? Boss's approach is radically existential in that it takes the real phenomena with respect, here the real phenomenon being guilt. Nor is the guilt exclusively linked up with the religious aspect of this, or any patient's, experience: we can be as guilty by refusing to accept the anal, genital, or any other corporeal aspects of life as the intellectual or spiritual aspects. This understanding of guilt has nothing whatever to do with a judgmental attitude toward the patient. It has only to do with taking the patient's life and experience seriously and with respect.

We have cited only one form of ontological guilt, namely, that arising from forfeiting one's own potentialities. There are other forms as well. Another, for example, is ontological guilt against one's fellows, arising from the fact that since each of us is an individual, he necessarily perceives his fellow man through his own limited and biased eyes. This means that he always to some extent does violence to the true picture of his fellow man and always to some extent fails fully to understand and meet the other's needs. This is not a question of moral failure or slackness—though it can indeed be greatly increased by lack of moral sensitivity. It is an inescapable result of the fact that each of us is a separate individuality and has no choice but to look at the world through his own eyes. This guilt, rooted in our existential structure, is one of the most potent sources of a sound humility and an unsentimental attitude of forgiveness toward one's fellow men.

The first form of ontological guilt mentioned above, namely, forfeiting of potentialities, corresponds roughly to the mode of world which we shall describe and define in the next section called *Eigenwelt,* or own-world. The second form of guilt corresponds roughly to *Mitwelt,* since it is guilt chiefly related to one's fellow men. There is a third form of ontological guilt which involves *Umwelt* as well as the other two modes, namely, "separation guilt" in relation to nature as a whole. This is the most complex and comprehensive aspect of ontological guilt. It may seem confusing, particularly since we are unable in this outline to explicate it in detail; we include it for the sake of completeness and for the interest of those who may wish to do further research in areas of ontological guilt. This guilt with respect to our separation from nature may well be much more influential (though repressed) than we realize in our modern Western scientific age. It was originally expressed beautifully in a classical fragment from one of the early Greek philosophers of being, Anaximander: "The source of things is the boundless. From whence they arise, thence they must also of necessity return. For they do penance and make compensation to one another for their injustice in the order of time."

Ontological guilt has, among others, these characteristics. *First,* everyone participates in it. No one of us fails to some extent to distort the reality of his fellow men, and no one fully fulfills his own potentialities. Each of us is always in a dialectical relation to his potentialities, dramatically illustrated in the dream of Boss's patient being stretched between faeces and bell tower. *Second,* ontological guilt does not come from cultural prohibitions, or from introjection of cultural mores; it is rooted in the fact of self-awareness. Ontological guilt does not consist of I-am-guilty-because-I-violate-parental-prohibitions, but arises from the fact that I can see myself as the one who can choose or fail to choose. Every developed human being would have this ontological guilt, though its *content* would vary from culture to culture and would largely be given by the culture.

Third, ontological guilt is not to be confused with morbid or neurotic guilt. If it is unaccepted and repressed, it may turn into neurotic guilt. Just as neurotic anxiety is the end-product of unfaced normal ontological anxiety, so neurotic guilt is the result of unconfronted ontological guilt. If the person can become aware of it and accept it (as Boss's patient later did), it is not morbid or neurotic. *Fourth,* ontological guilt does not lead to symptom formation, but has constructive effects in the personality. Specifically, it can and should lead to humility, as suggested above, sharpened sensitivity in relationships with fellow men, and increased creativity in the use of one's own potentialities.

III *Being-in-the-World*

Another one of the major and far-reaching contributions of the existential therapists—to my mind second in importance only to their analysis of being —is the understanding of the person-in-his-world. "To understand the compulsive," writes Erwin Straus, "we must first understand his world"—and this is certainly true of all other types of patients as well as any human being, for that matter. For *being together* means *being together in the same world;* and knowing means knowing in the context of the same world. The world of this particular patient must be grasped from the inside, be known and seen so far as possible from the angle of the one who exists in it. "We psychiatrists," writes Binswanger, "have paid far too much attention to the deviations of our patients from life in the world which is common to all, instead of focusing primarily upon the patients' own or private world, as was first systematically done by Freud." [22]

The problem is how we are to understand the other person's world. It cannot be understood as an external collection of objects which we view from the outside (in which case we never really understand it), nor by sentimental identification (in which case our understanding doesn't do any good, for we have failed to preserve the reality of our own existence). A difficult dilemma indeed! What is required is an approach to world which undercuts the "cancer," namely, the traditional subject-object dichotomy.

The reason this endeavor to rediscover man as being-in-the-world is so important is that it strikes directly at one of the most acute problems of modern human beings—namely, that they have *lost their world,* lost their experience of community. Kierkegaard, Nietzsche, and the existentialists who followed them perdurably pointed out that the two chief sources of modern Western man's anxiety and despair were, first, his loss of sense of being and, secondly, his loss of his world. The existential analysts believe there is much evidence that these prophets were correct and that twentieth-century Western man not only experiences an alienation from the human world about him but also suffers an inner, harrowing conviction of being estranged (like, say, a paroled convict) in the natural world as well.

The writings of Frieda Fromm-Reichmann and Sullivan describe the state of the person who has lost his world. These authors, and others like them, illustrate how the problems of loneliness, isolation, and alienation are being increasingly dealt with in psychiatric literature. The assumption would seem likely that there is an increase not only in awareness of these problems among psychiatrists and psychologists but also in the presence of the conditions themselves. Broadly speaking, the symptoms of isolation and alienation reflect the state of a person whose relation to the world has become broken. Some psychotherapists have pointed out that more and more patients exhibit schizoid features and that the "typical" kind of psychic problem in our day is not hysteria, as it was in Freud's time, but the schizoid type —that is to say, problems of persons who are detached, unrelated, lacking in affect, tending toward depersonalization, and covering up their problems by means of intellectualization and technical formulations.

There is also plenty of evidence that the sense of isolation, the alienation of one's self from the world, is suffered not only by people in pathological conditions but by countless "normal" persons as well in our day. Riesman

[22] P. 197.

presents a good deal of sociopsychological data in his study *The Lonely Crowd* to demonstrate that the isolated, lonely, alienated character type is characteristic not only of neurotic patients but of people as a whole in our society and that the trends in that direction have been increasing over the past couple of decades. He makes the significant point that these people have only a *technical* communication with their world; his "outer-directed" persons (the type characteristic of our day) relate to everything from its technical, external side. Their orientation, for example, was not "I liked the play," but "The play was *well done,*" "the article *well written,*" and so forth. Other portrayals of this condition of personal isolation and alienation in our society are given by Fromm in *Escape from Freedom,* particularly with respect to sociopolitical considerations; by Karl Marx, particularly in relation to the dehumanization arising out of the tendency in modern capitalism to value everything in the external, object-centered terms of money; and by Tillich from the spiritual viewpoint. Camus's *The Stranger* and Kafka's *The Castle,* finally, are surprisingly similar illustrations of our point: each gives a vivid and gripping picture of a man who is a stranger in his world, a stranger to other people whom he seeks or pretends to love; he moves about in a state of homelessness, vagueness, and haze as though he had no direct sense connection with his world but were in a foreign country where he does not know the language and has no hope of learning it but is always doomed to wander in quiet despair, incommunicado, homeless, and a stranger.

Nor is the problem of this loss of world simply one of lack of interpersonal relations or lack of communication with one's fellows. Its roots reach below the social levels to an alienation from the natural world as well. It is a particular experience of isolation which has been called "epistemological loneliness." [23] Underlying the economic, sociological, and psychological aspects of alienation can be found a profound common denominator, namely, the alienation which is the ultimate consequence of four centuries of the outworking of the separation of man as subject from the objective world. This alienation has expressed itself for several centuries in Western man's passion to gain power *over* nature, but now shows itself in an estrangement from nature and a vague, unarticulated, and half-suppressed sense of despair of gaining any real relationship with the natural world, including one's own body.

[23] This phrase, "epistemological loneliness," is used by David Bakan to describe Western man's experience of isolation from his world. He sees this isolation as stemming from the skepticism which we inherited from the British empiricists, Locke, Berkeley, and Hume. Their error specifically, he holds, was in conceiving of the "thinker as essentially alone rather than as a member and participant of a thinking community." ("Clinical Psychology and Logic," *The American Psychologist,* December 1956, p. 656). It is interesting that Bakan, in good psychological tradition, interprets the error as a social one, namely, separation from the community. But is this not more symptom than cause? More accurately stated, is not the isolation from the community simply one of the ways in which a more basic and comprehensive isolation shows itself?

These sentences may sound strange in this century of apparent scientific confidence. But let us examine the matter more closely. In his excellent chapter in this volume, Straus points out that Descartes, the father of modern thought, held that ego and consciousness were separated from the world and from other persons.[24] That is to say, consciousness is cut off and stands by itself alone. Sensations do not tell us anything directly about the outside world; they only give us inferential data. Descartes is commonly the whipping boy in these days and made to shoulder the blame for the dichotomy between subject and object; but he was of course only reflecting the spirit of his age and the underground tendencies in modern culture, about which he saw and wrote with beautiful clarity. The Middle Ages, Straus goes on to say, is commonly thought of as other-worldly in contrast to the "present world" concerns of modern man. But actually the medieval Christian's soul was considered, while it did exist in the world, to be really related to the world. Men experienced the world about them as directly real (*vide* Giotto) and the body as immediate and real (*vide* St. Francis). Since Descartes, however, the soul and nature have had nothing to do with each other. Nature belongs exclusively to the realm of *res extensa,* to be understood mathematically. We know the world only indirectly, by inference. This of course sets the problem we have been wrestling with ever since, the full implications of which did not emerge until the last century. Straus points out how the traditional textbooks on neurology and physiology have accepted this doctrine, and have endeavored to demonstrate that what goes on neurologically has only a "sign" relation to the real world. Only "unconscious inferences lead to the assumption of the existence of an outside world." [25]

Thus it is by no means accidental that modern man feels estranged from

24 P. 142.

25 Readers interested in this history of ideas will recall the important and imposing symbol of the same situation in Leibnitz' famous doctrine that all reality consists of *monads*. The monads had no doors or windows opening to each other, each being separated, isolated. "Each single unit is lonely in itself, without any direct communication. The horror of this idea was overcome by the harmonistic presupposition that in every monad the whole world is potentially present and that the development of each individual is in a natural harmony with the development of all the others. This is the most profound metaphysical situation in the early periods of bourgeois civilization. It fitted this situation because there was still a common world, in spite of the increasing social atomization." (Paul Tillich, *The Protestant Era*, p. 246.) This doctrine of "pre-established harmony" is a carry-over of the religious idea of providence. The relation between the person and the world was somehow "pre-ordained." Descartes, in similar vein, held that God—whose existence he believed he had proved—guaranteed the relation between consciousness and the world. The socio-historical situation in the expanding phases of the modern period were such that the "faith" of Leibnitz and Descartes *worked,* that is, it reflected the fact that there was still a common world (Tillich). But now that God is not only "dead," but a requiem has been sung over his grave, the stark isolation and alienation inherent in the relation between man and the world has become apparent. To put the matter less poetically, when the humanistic and Hebrew-Christian values disintegrated along with the cultural phenomena we have discussed above, the inherent implications of the situation emerged.

nature, that each consciousness stands off by itself, alone. This has been "built in" to our education and to some extent even into our language. It means that the overcoming of this situation of isolation is not a simple task and requires something much more fundamental than merely the rearrangement of some of our present ideas. This alienation of man from the natural and human world sets one of the problems which writers in this volume try to meet.

Let us now inquire how the existential analysts undertake to rediscover man as a being interrelated with his world and to rediscover world as meaningful to man. They hold that the person and his world are a unitary, structural whole; the hyphenation of the phrase being-in-the-world expresses precisely that. The two poles, self and world, are always dialectically related. Self implies world and world self; there is neither without the other, and each is understandable only in terms of the other. It makes no sense, for example, to speak of man in his world (though we often do) as primarily a *spatial* relation. The phrase "match *in* a box" does imply a spatial relation, but to speak of a man *in* his home or in his office or in a hotel at the seashore implies something radically different.[26]

A person's world cannot be comprehended by describing the environment, no matter how complex we make our description. As we shall see below, environment is only one mode of world; and the common tendencies to talk of a person *in* an environment or to ask what "influence the environment has upon him" are vast oversimplifications. Even from a biological viewpoint, Von Uexküll holds, one is justified in assuming as many environments (*Umwelten*) as there are animals; "there is not one space and time only," he goes on to say, "but as many spaces and times as there are subjects." [27] How much more would it not be true that the human being has his own world? Granted that this confronts us with no easy problem: for we cannot describe world in purely objective terms, nor is world to be limited to our subjective, imaginative participation in the structure around us, although that too is part of being-in-the-world.

World is the structure of meaningful relationships in which a person exists and in the design of which he participates. Thus world includes the past events which condition my existence and all the vast variety of deterministic influences which operate upon me. But it is these *as I relate to them,* am aware of them, carry them with me, molding, inevitably forming, build-

---

26 Thus Heidegger uses the terms "to sojourn" and "to dwell" rather than "is" when he speaks of a person being some place. His use of the term "world" is in the sense of the Greek *kosmos*, that is, the "uni-verse" with which we act and react. He chides Descartes for being so concerned with *res extensa* that he analyzed all the objects and things *in* the world and forgot about the most significant fact of all, namely, that there is world *itself*, that is, a meaningful relationship of these objects with the person. Modern thought has followed Descartes almost exclusively at this point, greatly to the impairment of our understanding of human beings.

27 See Binswanger, p. 196.

ing them in every minute of relating. For to be aware of one's world means at the same time to be designing it.

World is not to be limited to the past determining events but includes also all the possibilities which open up before any person and are not simply given in the historical situation. World is thus not to be identified with "culture." It includes culture but a good deal more, such as *Eigenwelt* (the own-world which cannot be reduced merely to an introjection of the culture), as well as all the individual's future possibilities.[28] "One would get some idea," Schachtel writes, "of the unimaginable richness and depth of the world and its possible meanings for man, if he knew all languages and cultures, not merely intellectually but with his total personality. This would comprise the historically knowable world of man, but not the infinity of future possibilities." [29] It is the "openness of world" which chiefly distinguishes man's world from the closed worlds of animals and plants. This does not deny the finiteness of life; we are all limited by death and old age and are subject to infirmities of every sort; the point, rather, is that these possibilities are given within the context of the contingency of existence. In a dynamic sense, indeed, these future possibilities are the most significant aspect of any human being's world. For they are the potentialities with which he "builds or designs world"—a phrase the existential therapists are fond of using.

World is never something static, something merely given which the person then "accepts" or "adjusts to" or "fights." It is rather a dynamic pattern which, so long as I possess self-consciousness, I am in the process of forming and designing. Thus Binswanger speaks of world as "that toward which the existence has climbed and according to which it has designed itself," [30] and

[28] The term "culture" is generally in common parlance set over against the individual, *e.g.*, "the influence of the culture on the individual." This usage is probably an unavoidable result of the dichotomy between subject and object in which the concepts of "individual" and "culture" emerged. It of course omits the very significant fact that the individual is at every moment also forming his culture.

[29] "World-openness is the distinctively human characteristic of man's awake life," Schachtel continues. He discusses cogently and clearly the life-space and life-time which characterize the human being's world in contrast to that of plants and animals. "In the animals, drives and affects remain to a very large extent ties to an inherited instinctive organization. The animal is embedded in this organization and in the closed world (J. v. Uexküll's 'Werkwelt' and 'Wirkwelt') corresponding to this organization. Man's relation to his world is an open one, governed only to a very small extent by instinctive organization, and to the largest extent by man's learning and exploration, in which he establishes his complex, changing and developing relations with his fellow men and with the natural and cultural world around him." So closely interrelated are man and his world, Schachtel demonstrates, that "all our affects arise from . . . spatial and temporal gaps which open between us and our world." "On Affect, Anxiety and the Pleasure Principle," paper to be published, pp. 101–104.

[30] "The Existential Analysis School of Thought," p. 191. In this chapter, it is significant to note the parallels Binswanger draws between his conception of "world" and that of Kurt Goldstein.

goes on to emphasize that whereas a tree or an animal is tied to its "blue-print" in relation to the environment, "human existence not only contains numerous possibilities of modes of being, but is precisely rooted in this manifold potentiality of being."

The important and very fruitful use the existential analysts make of ana-lyzing the patient's "world" is shown in Roland Kuhn's chapter in this vol-ume, the case study of Rudolf, the butcher boy who shot a prostitute. Noting that Rudolf was in mourning in this period following the death of his father, Kuhn goes to considerable lengths to understand the "world of the mourner." At the conclusion of this chapter, the reader is left with a clear and convinc-ing picture of the fact that Rudolf's shooting of the prostitute was an act of mourning for his mother, who died when he was four. I do not think this clarity and completeness of understanding could be gained by any method other than this painstaking description of the patient-in-his-world.

IV *The Three Modes of World*

The existential analysts distinguish three modes of world, that is, three simultaneous aspects of world which characterize the existence of each one of us as being-in-the-world. First, there is *Umwelt,* literally meaning "world around"; this is the biological world, generally called the environment. There is, second, the *Mitwelt,* literally the "with-world,"the world of beings of one's own kind, the world of one's fellow men. The third is *Eigenwelt,* the "own-world," the mode of relationship to one's self.

The first, *Umwelt,* is of course what is taken in general parlance as world, namely, the world of objects about us, the natural world. All organisms have an *Umwelt.* For animals and human beings the *Umwelt* includes biological needs, drives, instincts—the world one would still exist in if, let us hypothe-size, one had no self-awareness. It is the world of natural law and natural cycles, of sleep and awakeness, of being born and dying, desire and relief, the world of finiteness and biological determinism, the "thrown world" to which each of us must in some way adjust. The existential analysts do not at all neglect the reality of the natural world; "natural law is as valid as ever," as Kierkegaard put it. They have no truck with the idealists who would reduce the material world to an epiphenomenon or with the intui-tionists who would make it purely subjective or with anyone who would underestimate the importance of the world of biological determinism. In-deed, their insistence on taking the objective world of nature seriously is one of their distinctive characteristics. In reading them I often have the im-pression that they are able to grasp the *Umwelt,* the material world, with greater reality than those who segment it into "drives" and "substances," precisely because they are not limited to *Umwelt* alone, but see it also in the context of human self-awareness.[31] Boss's understanding of the patient with the "faeces and church steeple" dream cited above is an excellent example. They insist strongly that it is an oversimplification and radical error to deal with human beings as though *Umwelt* were the only mode of existence or to carry over the categories which fit *Umwelt* to make a procrustean bed upon which to force all human experience. In this connection, the existential analysts are *more empirical,* that is, more respectful of actual human phenomena, than the mechanists or positivists.

The *Mitwelt* is the world of interrelationships with human beings. But it is not to be confused with "the influence of the group upon the individual," or "the collective mind," or the various forms of "social determinism." The distinctive quality of *Mitwelt* can be seen when we note the difference between a herd of animals and a community of people. Howard Liddell has pointed out that for his sheep the "herd instinct consists of keeping the environment constant." Except in mating and suckling periods, a flock of collie dogs and children will do as well for the sheep providing such an environment is kept constant. In a group of human beings, however, a vastly more complex interaction goes on, with the meaning of the others in the group partly determined by one's own relationship to them. Strictly speaking, we should say animals have an *environment,* human beings have a *world.* For world includes the structure of meaning which is designed by the interrelationship of the persons in it. Thus the meaning of the group for me depends in part upon how I put myself into it. And thus, also, love can never be understood on a purely biological level but depends upon such factors as personal decision and commitment to the other person.[32]

The categories of "adjustment" and "adaptation" are entirely accurate in *Umwelt.* I adapt to the cold weather and I adjust to the periodic needs of my body for sleep; the critical point is that the weather is not changed by my adjusting to it nor is it affected at all. Adjustment occurs between two objects, or a person and an object. But in *Mitwelt,* the categories of adjustment and adaptation are not accurate; the term "relationship" offers the right category. If I insist that another person adjust to me, I am not taking him as a person, as *Dasein,* but as an instrumentality; and even if I adjust to myself, I am using myself as an object. One can never accurately speak of human beings as "sexual objects," as Kinsey for one example does; once

[31] In this respect it is significant to note that Kierkegaard and Nietzsche, in contrast to the great bulk of nineteenth-century thinkers, were able to take the body seriously. The reason was that they saw it not as a collection of abstracted substances or drives, *but as one mode of the reality of the person.* Thus when Nietzsche says "We think with our bodies," he means something radically different from the behaviorists.

[32] Martin Buber has developed implications of *Mitwelt* in his *I and Thou* philosophy. See his lectures at the Washington School of Psychiatry, printed in *Psychiatry,* May 1957, Vol. 20, No. Two, and especially the lecture on "Distance and Relation."

a person is a sexual object, you are not talking about a person any more. *The essence of relationship is that in the encounter both persons are changed.* Providing the human beings involved are not too severely ill and have some degree of consciousness, relationship always involves mutual awareness; and this already is the process of being mutually affected by the encounter.

The *Eigenwelt,* or "own world," is the mode which is least adequately dealt with or understood in modern psychology and depth-psychology; indeed, it is fair to say that it is almost ignored. *Eigenwelt* presupposes self-awareness, self-relatedness, and is uniquely present in human beings. But it is not merely a subjective, inner experience; it is rather the basis on which we see the real world in its true perspective, the basis on which we relate. It is a grasping of what something in the world—this bouquet of flowers, this other person—means to *me*. Suzuki has remarked that in Eastern languages, such as Japanese, adjectives always include the implication of "for-me-ness." That is to say, "this flower is beautiful" means *"for me* this flower is beautiful." Our Western dichotomy between subject and object has led us, in contrast, to assume that we have said most if we state that the flower is beautiful entirely divorced from ourselves, as though a statement were the more true in proportion to how little we ourselves have to do with it! This leaving of *Eigenwelt* out of the picture not only contributes to arid intellectualism and loss of vitality but obviously also has much to do with the fact that modern people tend to lose the sense of reality of their experiences.

It should be clear that these three modes of world are always interrelated and always condition each other. At every moment, for example, I exist in *Umwelt,* the biological world; but how I relate to my need for sleep or the weather or any instinct—how, that is, I see in my own self-awareness this or that aspect of *Umwelt*—is crucial for its meaning for me and conditions how I will react to it. The human being lives in *Umwelt, Mitwelt,* and *Eigenwelt* simultaneously. They are by no means three different worlds but three simultaneous modes of being-in-the-world.

Several implications follow from the above description of the three modes of world. One is that the reality of being-in-the-world is lost if *one of these modes is emphasized to the exclusion of the other two*. In this connection, Binswanger holds that classical psychoanalysis deals only with the *Umwelt*. The genius and the value of Freud's work lies in uncovering man in the *Umwelt,* the mode of instincts, drives, contingency, biological determinism. But traditional psychoanalysis has only a shadowy concept of *Mitwelt,* the mode of the interrelation of persons as subjects. One might argue that such psychoanalysis does have a *Mitwelt* in the sense that individuals need to find each other for the sheer necessity of meeting biological needs, that libidinal drives require social outlets and make social relationships necessary. But this is simply to derive *Mitwelt* from *Umwelt,* to make *Mitwelt* an epiphenomenon of *Umwelt;* and it means that we are not really dealing with *Mitwelt* at all but only another form of *Umwelt.*

It is of course clear that the interpersonal schools do have a theoretical basis for dealing directly with *Mitwelt.* This is shown, to take only one example, in Sullivan's interpersonal theory. Though they should not be identified, *Mitwelt* and interpersonal theory have a great deal in common. The danger at this point, however, is that if *Eigenwelt* in turn is omitted, interpersonal relations tend to become hollow and sterile. It is well known that Sullivan argued against the concept of the individual personality, and went to great efforts to define the self in terms of "reflected appraisal" and social categories, *i.e.,* the roles the person plays in the interpersonal world.[33] Theoretically, this suffers from considerable logical inconsistency and indeed goes directly against other very important contributions of Sullivan. Practically, it tends to make the self a mirror of the group around one, to empty the self of vitality and originality, and to reduce the interpersonal world to mere "social relations." It opens the way to the tendency which is directly opposed to the goals of Sullivan and other interpersonal thinkers, namely, social conformity. *Mitwelt* does not automatically absorb either *Umwelt* or *Eigenwelt.*

But when we turn to the mode of *Eigenwelt* itself, we find ourselves on the unexplored frontier of psychotherapeutic theory. What does it mean to say, "the self in relation to itself"? What goes on in the phenomena of consciousness, of self-awareness? What happens in "insight" when the inner gestalt of a person reforms itself? Indeed, what does the "self knowing itself" mean? Each of these phenomena goes on almost every instant with all of us; they are indeed closer to us than our breathing. Yet, perhaps precisely because they are so near to us, no one knows what is happening in these events. This mode of the self in relation to itself was the aspect of experience which Freud never really saw, and it is doubtful whether any school has as yet achieved a basis for adequately dealing with it. *Eigenwelt* is certainly the hardest mode to grasp in the face of our Western technological preoccupations. It may well be that the mode of *Eigenwelt* will be the area in which most clarification will occur in the next decades.

Another implication of this analysis of the modes of being-in-the-world is that it gives us a basis for the psychological understanding of love. The

---

[33] This concept was originally formulated by William James as "the self is the sum of the different roles the person plays." Though the definition was a gain in its day in overcoming a fictitious "self" existing in a vacuum, we wish to point out that it is an inadequate and faulty definition. If one takes it consistently, one not only has a picture of an *unintegrated,* "neurotic" self but falls into all kinds of difficulty in adding up these roles. We propose, rather, that the self is not the sum of the roles you play but your capacity *to know that you are the one playing these roles.* This is the only point of integration, and rightly makes the roles *manifestations* of the self.

human experience of love obviously cannot be adequately described within the confines of *Umwelt.* The interpersonal schools, at home chiefly in *Mitwelt,* have dealt with love, particularly in Sullivan's concept of the meaning of the "chum" and in Fromm's analysis of the difficulties of love in contemporary estranged society. But there is reason for doubting whether a theoretical foundation for going further is yet present in these or other schools. The same general caution given above is pertinent here—namely, that without an adequate concept of *Umwelt,* love becomes empty of vitality, and without *Eigenwelt,* it lacks power and the capacity to fructify itself.[34]

In any case, *Eigenwelt* cannot be omitted in the understanding of love. Nietzsche and Kierkegaard continually insisted that to love presupposes that one has already become the "true individual," the "Solitary One," the one who "has comprehended the deep secret that also in loving another person one must be sufficient unto oneself." [35] They, like other existentialists, do not attain to love themselves; but they help perform the psycho-surgical operations on nineteenth-century man which may clear blockages away and make love possible. By the same token, Binswanger and other existential therapists speak frequently of love. And though one could raise questions about how love is actually dealt with by them in given therapeutic cases, they nonetheless give us the theoretical groundwork for ultimately dealing with love adequately in psychotherapy.

V *Of Time and History*

The next contribution of the existential analysts we shall consider is their distinctive approach to *time.* They are struck by the fact that the most profound human experiences, such as anxiety, depression, and joy, occur more in the dimension of time than in space. They boldly place time in the center of the psychological picture and proceed to study it not in the traditional way as an analogy to space but in its own existential meaning for the patient. An example of the fresh light this new approach to time throws upon psy-

---

34 One feels in many of the psychological and psychiatric discussions of love a lack of the *tragic* dimension. Indeed, to take tragedy into the picture in any sense requires that the individual be understood in the three modes of world—the world of biological drive, fate, and determinism (*Umwelt*), the world of responsibility to fellow men (*Mitwelt*), and the world in which the individual can be aware (*Eigenwelt*) of the fate he alone at that moment is struggling with. The *Eigenwelt* is essential to any experience of tragedy, for the individual must be conscious of his own identity in the midst of the vast natural and social forces operating upon him. It has been rightly said that we lack a sense of tragedy in the modern world—and hence produce few real tragedies in drama or other forms of art —because we have lost the sense of the individual's own identity and consciousness in the midst of the overwhelming economic, political, social, and natural forces acting upon him. One of the significant things about the existential psychiatric and psychological approach is that tragedy comes back into the human realm and is to be looked at and understood in its own right.

35 Sören Kierkegaard, *Fear and Trembling,* trans. by Walter Lowrie (New York: Doubleday & Co., 1954), p. 55.

chological problems is seen in the engaging case study by Minkowski published in this volume.[36] Coming to Paris after his psychiatric training, Minkowski was struck by the relevance of the time dimension then being developed by Bergson to the understanding of psychiatric patients.[37] In his study of this depressed schizophrenic in this case, Minkowski points out that the patient could not relate to time and that each day was a separate island with no past and no future, the patient remaining unable to feel any hope or sense of continuity with the morrow. It was obvious, of course, that this patient's terrifying delusion that his execution was imminent had much to do with his being unable to deal with the future. Traditionally, the psychiatrist would reason simply that the patient cannot relate to the future, cannot "temporize," *because* he has this delusion. Minkowski proposes the exact opposite. "Could we not," he asks, "on the contrary suppose *the more basic disorder is the distorted attitude toward the future,* while the delusion is only one of its manifestations?" Minkowski goes on to consider this possibility carefully in his case study. How this approach should be applied in different cases would be, of course, debated by clinicians. But it is indisputable that Minkowski's original approach throws a beam of illumination on these dark, unexplored areas of time, and introduces a new freedom from the limits and shackles of clinical thought when bound only to traditional ways of thinking.

This new approach to time begins with observing that the most crucial fact about existence is that it *emerges*—that is, it is always in the process of becoming, always developing in time, and is never to be defined at static points.[38] The existential therapists propose a psychology literally of *being,* rather than "is" or "has been" or fixed inorganic categories. Though their concepts were worked out several decades ago, it is highly significant that recent experimental work in psychology, such as that by Mowrer and Liddell, illustrates and bears out their conclusions. At the end of one of his most important papers, Mowrer holds that time is the distinctive dimension of human personality. "Time-binding"—that is, the capacity to bring the past into the present as part of the total causal nexus in which living organisms act and react, together with the capacity to act in the light of the long-term future—is "the essence of mind and personality alike." [39] Liddell has shown

[36] "Findings in a Case of Schizophrenic Depression," p. 127. Minkowski's book, *Le Temps Vécu* (Paris: J. L. L. d'Artrey, 1933), a presentation of his concepts of "lived time," is unfortunately not translated into English.

[37] This understanding of time is also reflected in "process philosophies," such as Whitehead's, and has obvious parallels in modern physics.

[38] Cf. Tillich, "Existence is distinguished from essence by its temporal character." Also Heidegger, referring to one's awareness of his own existence in time, "Temporality is the genuine meaning of Care." Tillich, "Existential Philosophy," *Journal of the History of Ideas,* 5:1, 61, 62, 1944.

[39] "Time as a Determinant in Integrative Learning," in *Learning Theory and Personality Dynamics,* selected papers by O. Hobart Mowrer (New York: Ronald Press, 1950).

that his sheep can keep time—anticipate punishment—for about fifteen minutes and his dogs for about half an hour; but a human being can bring the past of thousands of years ago into the present as data to guide his present actions. And he can likewise project himself in self-conscious imagination into the future not only for a quarter of an hour but for weeks and years and decades. This capacity to transcend the immediate boundaries of time, to see one's experience self-consciously in the light of the distant past and the future, to act and react in these dimensions, to learn from the past of a thousand years ago and to mold the long-time future, is the unique characteristic of human existence.

The existential therapists agree with Bergson that "time is the heart of existence" and that our error has been to think of ourselves primarily in spatialized terms appropriate to *res extensa,* as though we were objects which could be located like substances at this spot or that. By this distortion we lose our genuine and real existential relation with ourselves, and indeed with other persons around us. As a consequence of this overemphasis on spatialized thinking, says Bergson, "the moments when we grasp ourselves are rare, and consequently we are seldom free." [40] Or, when we have taken time into the picture, it has been in the sense of Aristotle's definition, the dominant one in the tradition of Western thought, "For the time is this: what is counted in the movement in accordance with what is earlier and later." Now the striking thing about this description of "clock time" is that it really is an analogy from space, and one can best understand it by thinking in terms of a line of blocks or regularly spaced points on a clock or calendar. This approach to time is most fitting in the *Umwelt,* where we view the human being as an entity set among the various conditioning and determining forces of the natural world and acted upon by instinctual drives. But in the *Mitwelt,* the mode of personal relations and love, quantitative time has much less to do with the significance of an occurrence; the nature or degree of one's love, for example, can never be measured by the number of years one has known the loved one. It is true of course that clock time has much to do with *Mitwelt:* many people sell their time on an hourly basis and daily life runs on schedules. We refer rather to the inner meaning of the events. "No clock strikes for the happy one," says a German proverb quoted by Straus. Indeed, the most significant events in a person's psychological existence are likely to be precisely the ones which are "immediate," breaking through the usual steady progression of time.

Finally, the *Eigenwelt,* the own world of self-relatedness, self-awareness, and insight into the meaning of an event for one's self, has practically nothing whatever to do with Aristotle's clock time. The essence of self-awareness and insight are that they are "there"—instantaneous, immediate—and the mo-

40 Bergson, *Essai sur les Données Immédiates de la Conscience,* quoted by Tillich, "Existential Philosophy," p. 56.

ment of awareness has its significance for all time. One can see this easily by noting what happens in oneself at the instant of an insight or any experience of grasping oneself; the insight occurs with suddenness, is "born whole," so to speak. And one will discover that, though mediating on the insight for an hour or so may reveal many of its further implications, the insight is not clearer—and disconcertingly enough, often not as clear—at the end of the hour as it was at the beginning.

The existential therapists also observed that the most profound psychological experiences are peculiarly those which shake the individual's relation to time. Severe anxiety and depression blot out time, annihilate the future. Or, as Minkowski proposes, it may be that the disturbance of the patient in relation to time, his inability to "have" a future, gives rise to his anxiety and depression. In either case, the most painful aspect of the sufferer's predicament is that he is unable to imagine a future moment in time when he will be out of the anxiety or depression. We see a similar close interrelationship between the disturbance of the time function and neurotic symptoms. Repression and other processes of the blocking off of awareness are in essence methods of ensuring that the usual relation of past to present will not obtain. Since it would be too painful or in other ways too threatening for the individual to retain certain aspects of his past in his present consciousness, he must carry the past along like a foreign body *in* him but not *of* him, as it were, an encapsulated fifth column which thereupon compulsively drives to its outlets in neurotic symptoms.

However one looks at it, thus, the problem of time has a peculiar importance in understanding human existence. The reader may agree at this point but feel that, if we try to understand time in other than spatial categories, we are confronted with a mystery. He may well share the perplexity of Augustine who wrote, "When no one asks me what time is, I know, but when I would give an explanation of it in answer to a man's question I do not know." [41]

One of the distinctive contributions of the existential analysts to this problem is that, having placed time in the center of the psychological picture, they then propose that the *future,* in contrast to present or past, is the

[41] Heidegger's *Being and Time* is devoted, as its title indicates, to an analysis of this interrelationship. His over-all theme is "the vindication of time for being" (Straus). He calls the three modes of time, namely, past, present, and future, the "three ecstasies of time," using the term ecstasy in its etymological meaning of "to stand outside and beyond." For the essential characteristic of the human being is the capacity to transcend a given mode of time. Heidegger holds that our preoccupation with objective time is really an evasion; people much prefer to see themselves in terms of objective time, the time of statistics, of quantitative measurement, of "the average," etc., because they are afraid to grasp their existence directly. He holds, moreover, that objective time, which has its rightful place in quantitative measurements, can be understood only on the basis of time as immediately experienced rather than vice versa.

dominant mode of time for human beings. Personality can be understood only as we see it on a trajectory toward its future; a man can understand himself only as he projects himself forward. This is a corollary of the fact that the person is always becoming, always emerging into the future. The self is to be seen in its potentiality; "a self, every instant it exists," Kierkegaard wrote, "is in process of becoming, for the self . . . is only that which it is to become." The existentialists do not mean "distant future" or anything connected with using the future as an escape from the past or present; they mean only to indicate that the human being, so long as he possesses self-awareness and is not incapacitated by anxiety or neurotic rigidities, is always in a dynamic self-actualizing process, always exploring, molding himself, and moving into the immediate future.

They do not neglect the past, but they hold it can be understood only in the light of the future. The past is the domain of *Umwelt,* of the contingent, natural historical, deterministic forces operating upon us; but since we do not live exclusively in *Umwelt,* we are never merely the victims of automatic pressures from the past. *The deterministic events of the past take their significance from the present and future.* As Freud put it, we are anxious *lest* something happen in the future. "The word of the past is an oracle uttered," remarked Nietzsche. "Only as builders of the future, as knowing the present, will you understand it." All experience has a historical character, but the error is to treat the past in mechanical terms. The past is not the "now which was," nor any collection of isolated events, nor a static reservoir of memories or past influences or impressions. The past, rather, is the domain of contingency in which we accept events and from which we select events in order to fulfill our potentialities and to gain satisfactions and security in the immediate future. This realm of the past, of natural history and "thrownness," Binswanger points out, is the mode which classical psychoanalysis has, *par excellence,* made its own for exploration and study.

But as soon as we consider the exploration of a patient's past in psychoanalysis, we note two very curious facts. First is the obvious phenomenon observed every day, that the events in the past which the patient carries with him have very little, if any, necessary connection with the quantitative events that actually happened to him as a child. One single thing that occurred to him at a given age is remembered and thousands of things are forgotten, and even the events that occurred most frequently, like getting up in the morning, are most apt obviously to leave no impression. Alfred Adler used to point out that memory was a creative process, that we remember what has significance for our "style of life," and that the whole "form" of memory is therefore a mirror of the individual's style of life. What an individual seeks *to become* determines what he remembers of his *has been.* In this sense the future determines the past.

The second fact is this: *whether or not a patient can even recall the sig-nificant events of the past depends upon his decision with regard to the fu-ture.* Every therapist knows that patients may bring up past memories *ad interminum* without any memory ever moving them, the whole recital being flat, inconsequential, tedious. From an existential point of view, the problem is not at all that these patients happened to have endured impoverished pasts; it is rather that they cannot or do not commit themselves to the present and future. Their past does not become alive because nothing matters enough to them in the future. Some hope and commitment to work toward changing something in the immediate future, be it overcoming anxiety or other painful symptoms or integrating one's self for further creativity, is necessary before any uncovering of the past will have reality.

One practical implication of the above analysis of time is that psycho-therapy cannot rest on the usual automatic doctrines of historical progress. The existential analysts take history very seriously,[42] but they protest against any tendency to evade the immediate, anxiety-creating issues in the present by taking refuge behind the determinism of the past. They are against the doctrines that historical forces carry the individual along automatically, whether these doctrines take the form of the religious beliefs of predestina-tion or providence, the deteriorated Marxist doctrine of historical mate-rialism, the various psychological doctrines of determinism, or that most common form of such historical determinism in our society, faith in auto-matic technical progress. Kierkegaard was very emphatic on this point:

Whatever the one generation may learn from the other, that which is genuinely human no generation learns from the foregoing. . . . Thus no generation has learned from another to love, no generation begins at any other point than at the beginning, no generation has a shorter task assigned to it than had the previous gen-eration. . . . In this respect every generation begins primitively, has no different task from that of every previous generation, nor does it get further, except in so far as the preceding generation shirked its task and deluded itself.[43]

[42] Not only the existential psychologists and psychiatrists but the existential thinkers in general are to be distinguished precisely by the fact that they do take seriously the his-torical cultural situation which conditions the psychological and spiritual problems for any individual. But they emphasize that to know history we must act in it. Cf. **Heidegger:** "Fundamentally history takes its start not from the 'present' nor from what is 'real' only today, but from the future. The 'selection' of what is to be an object of history is made by the actual, 'existential' choice . . . of the historian, in which history arises." Brock, *op. cit.,* p. 110. The parallel in therapy is that what the patient selects from the past is determined by what he faces in the future.

[43] *Fear and Trembling,* p. 130. What we do learn from previous generations are of course facts; one may learn them by repetition, like the multiplication table, or remember facts or experiences on their "shock" basis. Kierkegaard is not denying any of this. He was well aware that there is progress from one generation to the next in *technical areas.* What he is speaking of above is "that which is genuinely human," specifically, love.

This implication is particularly relevant to psychotherapy, since the popular mind so often makes of psychoanalysis and other forms of psychotherapy the new technical authority which will take over for them the burden of learning to love. Obviously all any therapy can do is to help a person remove the blocks which keep him from loving; it cannot love for him, and it is doing him ultimate harm if it dulls his own responsible awareness at this point.

A last contribution of this existential analysis of time lies in its understanding of the process of insight. Kierkegaard uses the engaging term *Augenblick,* literally meaning the "blinking of an eye" and generally translated "the pregnant moment." It is the moment when a person suddenly grasps the meaning of some important event in the past or future in the present. Its pregnancy consists of the fact that it is never an intellectual act alone; the grasping of the new meaning always presents the possibility and necessity of some personal decision, some shift in gestalt, some new orientation of the person toward the world and future. This is experienced by most people as the moment of most heightened awareness; it is referred to in psychological literature as the "aha" experience. On the philosophical level, Paul Tillich describes it as the moment when "eternity touches time," for which moment he has developed the concept of *Kairos,* "time fulfilled."

VI *Transcending the Immediate Situation*

A final characteristic of man's existence (*Dasein*) which we shall discuss is the capacity to transcend the immediate situation. If one tries to study the human being as a composite of substances, one does not of course need to deal with the disturbing fact that existence is always in process of self-transcending. But if we are to understand a given person as existing, dynamic, at every moment becoming, we cannot avoid this dimension. This capacity is already stated in the term "exist," that is, "to stand out from." Existing involves a continual emerging, in the sense of emergent evolution, a transcending of one's past and present in terms of the future. Thus *transcendere*—literally "to climb over or beyond"—describes what every human being is engaged in doing every moment when he is not seriously ill or temporarily blocked by despair or anxiety. One can, of course, see this emergent evolution in all life processes. Nietzsche has his old Zarathustra proclaim, "And this secret spake Life herself to me, 'Behold' said she, 'I am that which must ever surpass itself.'" But it is much more radically true of human existence, where the capacity for self-awareness qualitatively increases the range of consciousness and therefore greatly enlarges the range of possibilities of transcending the immediate situation.

The term "transcending," appearing often in the following papers, is open to much misunderstanding, and indeed often calls forth violent antagonism.[44] In this country the term is relegated to vague and ethereal things which, as Bacon remarked, are better dealt with in "poesy, where transcendences are more allowed," or associated with Kantian *a priori* assumptions or with New England Transcendentalism or religious other-worldliness, or with anything unempirical and unrelated to actual experience. We mean something different from all of these. It has been suggested that the word has lost its usefulness and another should be found. That would be fine if another were available which would adequately describe the exceedingly important empirical, immediate human experience to which this term, when used by Goldstein and the existential writers, refers; for any adequate description of human beings requires that the experience be taken into account. Some suspicion of the term obviously is sound to the extent that the word serves to elevate any given topic out of any immediate field in which it can be discussed. It must be confessed that occasional usages of the term in some of the papers which follow do have this effect, particularly when the "transcendental categories" of Husserl are assumed without explanation of how they apply. Other objections to the term, less justifiable, may arise from the fact that the capacity to transcend the present situation introduces a disturbing fourth dimension, a *time* dimension, and this is a serious threat to the traditional way of describing human beings in terms of static substances. The term is likewise rejected by those who seek to make no distinction between animal and human behavior or to understand human psychology in terms only of mechanical models. This capacity we are about to discuss does in actual fact present difficulties to those approaches since it is uniquely characteristic of human beings.

The neurobiological base for this capacity is classically described by Kurt Goldstein. Goldstein found that his brain-injured patients—chiefly soldiers with portions of the frontal cortex shot away—had specifically lost the ability to abstract, to think in terms of "the possible." They were tied to the immediate concrete situation in which they found themselves. When their closets happened to be in disarray, they were thrown into profound anxiety and disordered behavior. They exhibited compulsive orderliness—which is a way of holding one's self at every moment rigidly to the concrete situation. When asked to write their names on a sheet of paper, they would typically write in the very corner, any venture out from the specific boundaries of the edges of the paper representing too great a threat. It was as though they were

[44] This antagonism was illustrated to me when a recent paper of mine was read by a discussant prior to its presentation. I had included in the paper a paragraph discussing Goldstein's concept of the neurobiological aspects of the organism's capacity to transcend its immediate situation, not at all under the impression that I was saying anything very provocative. My using the word "transcending" in introducing the topic, however, was like waving a red flag in my discussant's face, for he printed a huge "No!!" in red crayon replete with exclamation marks on the margin before even getting to the discussion of what the word meant. The very word, indeed, seems to carry some inciting-to-riot quality.

threatened with dissolution of the self unless they remained related at every moment to the immediate situation, as though they could "be a self" only as the self was bound to the concrete items in space. Goldstein holds that the distinctive capacity of the normal human being is precisely this capacity to abstract, to use symbols, to orient one's self beyond the immediate limits of the given time and space, to think in terms of "the possible." The injured, or "ill," patients were characterized by loss of range of possibility. Their world-space was shrunk, their time curtailed, and they suffered a consequent radical loss of freedom.

The capacity of the normal human being to transcend the present situation is exemplified in all kinds of behavior. One is the capacity to transcend the boundaries of the present moment in time—as we pointed out in our discussion above—and to bring the distant past and the long-term future into one's immediate existence. It is also exemplified in the human being's unique capacity to think and talk in symbols. Reason and the use of symbols are rooted in the capacity to stand outside the particular object or sound at hand, say these boards on which my typewriter sits and the two syllables that make up the word "table," and agreeing with each other that these will stand for a whole class of objects.

The capacity is particularly shown in social relationships, in the normal person's relation to the community. Indeed, the whole fabric of trust and responsibility in human relations presupposes the capacity of the individual to "see himself as others see him," as Robert Burns puts it in contrasting himself with the field mouse, to see himself as the one fulfilling his fellow men's expectations, acting for their welfare or failing to. Just as this capacity for transcending the situation is impaired with respect to the *Umwelt* in the brain-injured, it is impaired with respect to the *Mitwelt* in the psychopathic disorders which are described as the disorders of those in whom the capacity to see themselves as others see them is absent or does not carry sufficient weight, who are then said to lack "conscience." The term "conscience," significantly enough, is in many languages the same word as "consciousness," both meaning *to know with*. Nietzsche remarked, "Man is the animal who can make promises." By this he did not mean promises in the sense of social pressure or simply introjection of social requirement (which are oversimplified ways of describing conscience, errors which arise from conceiving of *Mitwelt* apart from *Eigenwelt*). Rather, he meant that man can be aware of the fact that he has given his word, can see himself as the one who makes the agreement. Thus, to make promises presupposes conscious self-relatedness and is a very different thing from simple conditioned "social behavior," acting in terms of the requirements of the group or herd or hive. In the same light, Sartre writes that dishonesty is a uniquely human form of behavior: "the lie is a behavior of transcendence."

It is significant at this point to note the great number of terms used in describing human actions which contain the prefix "re"—*re*-sponsible, *re*-collect, *re*-late, and so on. In the last analysis, all imply and rest upon this capacity to "come back" to one's self as the one performing the act. This is illustrated with special clarity in the peculiarly human capacity to be *responsible* (a word combining *re* and *spondere,* "promise"), designating the one who can be depended upon, who can promise to give back, to answer. Erwin Straus describes man as "the questioning being," the organism who at the same moment that he exists can question himself and his own existence.[45] Indeed, the whole existential approach is rooted in the always curious phenomenon that we have in man a being who not only *can* but *must,* if he is to realize himself, question his own being. One can see at this point that the discussion of dynamisms of social adjustment, such as "introjection," "identification," and so forth is oversimplified and inadequate when it omits the central fact of all, namely, the person's capacity to be aware at the moment that he is the one responding to the social expectation, the one choosing (or not choosing) to guide himself according to a certain model. This is the distinction between rote social conformity on one hand and the freedom, originality, and creativity of genuine social response on the other. The latter are the unique mark of the human being acting in the light of "the possible."

Self-consciousness implies self-transcendence. The one has no reality without the other. It will have become apparent to many readers that the capacity to transcend the immediate situation uniquely presupposes *Eigenwelt,* that is, the mode of behavior in which a person sees himself as subject and object at once. The capacity to transcend the situation is an inseparable part of self-awareness, for it is obvious that the mere awareness of one's self as a being in the world implies the capacity to stand outside and look at one's self and the situation and to assess and guide one's self by an infinite variety of possibilities. The existential analysts insist that the human being's capacity for transcending the immediate situation is discernible in the very center of human experience and cannot be sidestepped or overlooked without distorting and making unreal and vague one's picture of the man. This is particularly cogent and true with respect to data we encounter in psychotherapy. All of the peculiarly neurotic phenomena, such as the split of unconsciousness from consciousness, repression, blocking of awareness, self-deceit by way of symptoms, *ad interminum,* are misused, "neurotic" forms of the fundamental capacity of the human being to relate to himself and his world as subject and object at the same time. As Lawrence Kubie has written, "The neurotic process is always a symbolic process: and the split into parallel yet interacting streams of conscious and unconscious processes starts approximately as the child begins to develop the rudiments of speech. . . . It may be accurate to say, therefore, that the neurotic process is the price that we pay for our most precious human heritage, namely our ability to represent experience and communicate our thoughts by means of symbols. . . ." [46] The essence of the use of symbols, we have tried to show, is the capacity to transcend the immediate, concrete situation.

We can now see why Medard Boss and the other existential psychiatrists and psychologists make this capacity to transcend the immediate situation the basic and unique characteristic of human existence. "Transcendence and being-in-the-world are names for the identical structure of Dasein, which is the foundation for every kind of attitude and behavior." [47] Boss goes on in this connection to criticize Binswanger for speaking of different kinds of "transcendences"—the "transcendence of love" as well as the "transcendence of care." This unnecessarily complicates the point, says Boss; and it makes no sense to speak of "transcendences" in the plural. We can only say, holds Boss, that man has the capacity for transcending the immediate situation because he has the capacity for *Sorge*—that is, for "care" or, more accurately, for understanding his being and taking responsibility for it. (This term is from Heidegger and is basic to existential thought; it is used often in the form of *Fürsorge,* meaning "care for," "concerned for the welfare of.") *Sorge* is for Boss the encompassing notion and includes love, hate, hope, and even indifference. All attitudes are ways of behaving in *Sorge* or lack of it. In Boss's sense the capacity of man to have *Sorge* and to transcend the immediate situation are two aspects of the same thing.

We need now to emphasize that this capacity to transcend the immediate situation is not a "faculty" to be listed along with other faculties. It is rather given in the ontological nature of being human. To abstract, to objectivate, are evidences of it; but as Heidegger puts it, "transcendence does not consist of objectivation, but objectivation presupposes transcendence." That is to say, the fact that the human being can be self-related gives him, as one manifestation, the capacity to objectify his world, to think and talk in symbols and so forth. This is Kierkegaard's point when he reminds us that to understand the self we must see clearly that "imagination is not one faculty on a par with others, but, if one would so speak, it is the faculty *instar omnium* [for all faculties]. What feeling, knowledge or will a man has depends in the last resort upon what imagination he has, that is to say, upon how these things are reflected. . . . Imagination is the possibility of all reflection, and the intensity of this medium is the possibility of the intensity of the self." [48]

[46] *Practical and Theoretical Aspects of Psychoanalysis* (New York: International University Press, 1950), p. 19.

[47] Medard Boss, *op. cit.*

[48] *The Sickness Unto Death,* p. 163. The quote continues, "Imagination is the reflection of the process of infinitizing, and hence the elder Fichte quite rightly assumed, even in relation to knowledge, that imagination is the origin of the categories. The self is reflection, and imagination is reflection, it is the counterfeit presentment of the self, which is the possibility of the self."

It remains to make more specific what is implicit above, namely, that this capacity for transcending the immediate situation is the basis of human freedom. The unique characteristic of the human being is the vast range of possibilities in any situation, which in turn depend upon his self-awareness, his capacity to run through in imagination the different ways of reacting he can consider in a given situation. Binswanger, in his discussion of Von Uexküll's metaphor of the contrasting environments of the tree in the forest, the jigger in the tree, the woodsman who comes to chop the tree, the romantic girl who comes to walk in the forest, and so on, points out that the distinctive thing about the human being is that he can one day be the romantic lover, another day the woodchopper, another day the painter. In a variety of ways the human being can select among many self-world relationships. The "self" is the capacity to see one's self in these many possibilities. This freedom with respect to world, Binswanger goes on to point out, is the mark of the psychologically healthy person; to be rigidly confined to a specific "world," as was Ellen West, is the mark of psychological disorder. What is essential is "freedom in designing world," or "letting world occur," as Binswanger puts it. "So deeply founded," he observes indeed, "is the essence of freedom as a necessity in existence that it can also dispense with existence itself." [49]

VII *Some Implications for Psychotherapeutic Technique*

Those who read works on existential analysis as handbooks of technique are bound to be disappointed. They will not find specifically developed practical methods. The chapters in this book, for example, have much more the character of "pure" than of applied science. The reader will also sense that many of the existential analysts are not greatly concerned with technical matters. Part of the reason for this is the newness of the approach. Roland Kuhn wrote, in answer to our inquiry about technique in some of his significant cases, that since existential analysis is a relatively new discipline, it has not yet had time to work out its therapeutic applications in detail.

But there is another, more basic reason for the fact that these psychiatrists are not so concerned with formulating technique and make no apologies for this fact. Existential analysis is a way of understanding human existence, and its representatives believe that one of the chief (if not *the* chief) blocks to the understanding of human beings in Western culture is precisely the overemphasis on technique, an overemphasis which goes along with the tendency to see the human being as an object to be calculated, managed, "analyzed." [50]

49 "Ellen West," p. 308.
50 The term "analyzed" itself reflects this problem, and patients may be doing more than using a semantic difficulty as a way of expressing resistance when they aver that the idea of "being analyzed" makes them objects being "worked upon." The term is carried over into the phrase "existential analysis" partly because it has become standard for deep psycho-

Our Western tendency has been to believe that *understanding follows technique;* if we get the right technique, then we can penetrate the riddle of the patient, or, as said popularly with amazing perspicacity, we can "get the other person's number." The existential approach holds the exact opposite; namely, that *technique follows understanding.* The central task and responsibility of the therapist is to seek to understand the patient as a being and as being-in-his-world. All technical problems are subordinate to this understanding. Without this understanding, technical facility is at best irrelevant, at worst a method of "structuralizing" the neurosis. With it, the groundwork is laid for the therapist's being able to help the patient recognize and experience his own existence, and this is the central process of therapy. This does not derogate disciplined technique; it rather puts it into perspective.

When editing this volume, therefore, we had difficulty piecing together information about what an existential therapist would actually *do* in given situations in therapy, but we kept asking the question, for we knew American readers would be particularly concerned with this area. It is clear at the outset that what distinguishes existential therapy is not what the therapist would specifically do, say, in meeting anxiety or confronting resistance or getting the life history and so forth, but rather the *context* of his therapy. How an existential therapist might interpret a given dream, or an outburst of temper on the patient's part, might not differ from what a classical psychoanalyst might say, if each were taken in isolated fashion. But the context of existential therapy would be very distinct; it would always focus on the questions of how this dream throws light on this particular patient's existence in his world, what it says about *where* he is at the moment and what he is moving toward, and so forth. The context is the patient not as a set of psychic dynamisms or mechanisms but as a human being who is choosing, committing, and pointing himself toward something right now; the context is dynamic, immediately real, and present.

I shall try to block out some implications concerning therapeutic technique from my knowledge of the works of the existential therapists and from my own experience of how their emphases have contributed to me, a therapist trained in psychoanalysis in its broad sense.[51] Making a systematic summary would be presumptuous to try and impossible to accomplish, but I hope the following points will at least suggest some of the important

therapy since the advent of psychoanalysis and partly because existential thought itself (following Heidegger) is an "analysis of reality." This term is of course a reflection of the tendency in our whole culture, called "The Age of Analysis" in the title of a recent survey of modern Western thought. Though I am not happy about the term, I have used the identification "existential analyst" for the writers in this book because it is too clumsy to say "phenomenological and existential psychiatrists and psychologists."

[51] I am indebted to Dr. Ludwig Lefebre and Dr. Hans Hoffman, students of existential therapy, for correspondence and discussion of techniques of *Daseinsanalyse.*

therapeutic implications. It should be clear at every point, however, that the really important contributions of this approach are its deepened understanding of human existence, and one gets no place talking about isolated techniques of therapy unless the understanding we have sought to give in the earlier portions of these chapters is presupposed at every point.

The *first* implication is the variability of techniques among the existential therapists. Boss, for example, uses couch and free association in traditional Freudian manner and permits a good deal of acting out of transference. Others would vary as much as the different schools vary anyway. But the critical point is that the existential therapists have a definite reason for using any given technique with a given patient. They sharply question the use of techniques simply because of rote, custom, or tradition Their approach also does not at all settle for the air of vagueness and unreality that surrounds many therapeutic sessions, particularly in the eclectic schools which allegedly have freed themselves from bondage to a traditional technique and select from all schools as though the presuppositions of these approaches did not matter. Existential therapy is distinguished by a sense of reality and concreteness.

I would phrase the above point positively as follows: existential technique should have flexibility and versatility, varying from patient to patient and from one phase to another in treatment with the same patient. The specific technique to be used at a given point should be decided on the basis of these questions: What will best reveal the existence of this particular patient at this moment in his history? What will best illuminate his being-in-the-world? Never merely "eclectic," this flexibility always involves a clear understanding of the underlying assumptions of any method. Let us say a Kinseyite, for example, a traditional Freudian, and an existential analyst are dealing with an instance of sexual repression. The Kinseyite would speak of it in terms of finding a sexual object, in which case he is not talking about sex in human beings. The traditional Freudian would see its psychological implications, but would look primarily for causes in the past and might well ask himself how this instance of sexual repression *qua* repression can be overcome. The existential therapist would view the sexual repression as a holding back of *potentia* of the existence of this person, and though he might or might not, depending on the circumstances, deal immediately with the sex problem as such, it would always be seen not as a mechanism of repression as such but as a limitation of this person's being-in-his-world.

The *second* implication is that psychological dynamisms always take their meaning from the existential situation of the patient's own, immediate life. The writings of a number of existential psychotherapists, including van den Berg, Frankel, Boss, and especially the recent work of Ronald Laing, are pertinent to the point. Some hold that Freud's practice was right but his theories explaining his practice were wrong. Some are Freudian in technique, but put the theories and concepts of orthodox psychoanalysis on a fundamental existential basis. Take *transference,* for example, a discovery which many greatly value. What really happens is not that the neurotic patient "transfers" feelings he had toward mother or father to wife or therapist. Rather, the neurotic is one who in certain areas never developed beyond the limited and restricted forms of experience characteristic of the infant. Hence in later years he perceives wife or therapist through the same restricted, distorted "spectacles" as he perceived father or mother. The problem is to be understood in terms of perception and relatedness to the world. This makes unnecessary the concept of transference in the sense of a displacement of detachable feelings from one object to another. The new basis of this concept frees psychoanalysis from the burden of a number of insoluble problems.

Take, also, the ways of behaving known as *repression* and *resistance.* Freud saw repression as related to bourgeois morality, specifically, as the patient's need to preserve an acceptable picture of himself and therefore to hold back thoughts, desires, and so forth which are unacceptable according to bourgeois moral codes. Existential therapists see the conflict more basically in the area of the patient's acceptance or rejection of his own potentialities. We need to keep in mind the question—What keeps the patient from accepting in freedom his potentialities? This may involve bourgeois morality, but it also involves a lot more: it leads immediately to the existential question of the person's freedom. Before represssion is possible or conceivable, the person must have some possibility of accepting or rejecting—that is, some margin of freedom. Whether the person is aware of this freedom or can articulate it is another question; he does not need to be. To repress is precisely to make one's self unaware of freedom; this is the nature of the dynamism. Thus, to repress or deny this freedom already presupposes it as a possibility. We wish to emphasize that psychic determinism is always a secondary phenomenon and works only in a limited area. The primary question is how the person relates to his freedom to express potentialities in the first place, repression being one way of so relating.

With respect to *resistance,* the question is to be asked: What makes such a phenomenon possible? One answers that it is an outworking of the tendency of the patient to become absorbed in the *Mitwelt,* to slip back into *das Man,* the anonymous mass, and to renounce the particular unique and original potentiality which is his. Thus "social conformity" is a general form of resistance in life; and even the patient's acceptance of the doctrines and interpretations of the therapist may itself be an expression of resistance.

We do not wish here to go into the question of what underlies these phenomena. We want only to demonstrate that at each point in considering these dynamisms of transference, resistance, and repression. These therapists do something important for the existential approach. *They place each dynamism on an ontological basis.* Each way of behaving is seen and understood in the light of the existence of the patient as a human being. This is shown, too, in his conceiving of drives, libido, and so forth always in terms of *potentialities* for existence. Boss thereby seeks "to throw overboard the painful intellectual acrobatic of the old psychoanalytic theory which sought to derive the phenomena from the interplay of some forces or drives behind them." He does not deny forces as such but holds that they cannot be understood as "energy transformation" or on any other such natural science model but only as the person's *potentia* of existence. "This freeing from unnecessary constructions facilitates the understanding between patient and doctor. Also it makes the pseudo-resistances disappear which were a justified defense of the analysands against a violation of their essence." Boss holds that he thus can follow the "basic rule" in analysis—the one condition Freud set for analysis, namely, that the patient give forth in complete honesty whatever was going on in his mind—more effectively than in traditional psychoanalysis, for he listens with respect and takes seriously and without reserve the contents of the patient's communication rather than sieving it through prejudgments or destroying it by special interpretations. To me this sounds oversimplified and thereby dubious, but Boss holds he is simply engaged in bringing out the underlying meaning of Freud's discoveries and placing them on their necessary comprehensive foundation. Believing that Freud's discoveries have to be understood below their faulty formulation, he points out that Freud himself was not merely a passive "mirror" for the patient in analysis, as traditionally urged in psychoanalysis, but was "translucent," a vehicle and medium through which the patient saw himself.

The *third* implication in existential therapy is the emphasis on *presence.* By this we mean that the relationship of the therapist and patient is taken as a real one, the therapist being not merely a shadowy reflector but an alive human being who happens, at that hour, to be concerned not with his own problems but with understanding and experiencing so far as possible the being of the patient. The way was prepared for this emphasis on presence by our discussion above of the fundamental existential idea of truth-in-relationship.[52] It was there pointed out that existentially truth always involves the relation of the person to something or someone and that the therapist is part of the patient's relationship "field." We indicated, too, that this was not only the therapist's best avenue to understanding the patient but that he cannot really *see* the patient unless he participates in the field.

Several quotations will make clearer what this presence means. Karl Jaspers has remarked, "What we are missing! What opportunities of under-

[52] See page 26.

standing we let pass by because at a single decisive moment we were, with all our knowledge, lacking in the simple virtue of a *full human presence!*" [53] In similar vein but greater detail Binswanger writes as follows, in his paper on psychotherapy, concerning the significance of the therapist's role of the relationship:

If such a (psychoanalytic) treatment fails, the analyst inclines to assume that the patient is not capable of overcoming his resistance to the physician, for example, as a "father image." Whether an analysis can have success or not is often, however, not decided by whether a patient is capable *at all* of overcoming such a transferred father but by the opportunity *this particular physician* accords him to do so; it may, in other words, be the rejection of the therapist as a person, the impossibility of entering into a genuine communicative rapport with him, that may form the obstacle against breaking through the "eternal" repetition of the father resistance. Caught in the "mechanism" and thus in what inheres in it, *mechanical repetition,* the psychoanalytic doctrine, as we know, is altogether strangely blind toward the entire category of the *new,* the properly *creative* in the life of the psyche everywhere. Certainly it not always is true to the facts if one attributes the failure of treatment only to the patient; the question always to be asked first by the physician is whether the fault may not be his. What is meant here is not any technical fault but the far more fundamental failure that consists of an impotence to wake or rekindle that divine "spark" in the patient which only true communication from existence to existence can bring forth and which alone possesses, with its light and warmth, also the fundamental power that makes any therapy work—the power to liberate a person from the blind isolation, the *idios kosmos* of Heraclitus, from a mere vegetating in his body, his dreams, his private wishes, his conceit and his presumptions, and to ready him for a life of *koinonia,* of genuine community. [54]

Presence is not to be confused with a sentimental attitude toward the patient but depends firmly and consistently on how the therapist conceives of human beings. It is found in therapists of various schools and differing beliefs—differing, that is, on anything except one central issue—their assumptions about whether the human being is an object to be analyzed or a being to be understood. Any therapist is existential to the extent that, with all his technical training and his knowledge of transference and dynamisms, he is still able to relate to the patient as "one existence communicating with another," to use Binswanger's phrase. In my own experience, Frieda Fromm-Reichmann particularly had this power in a given therapeutic hour; she used to say, "The patient needs an experience, not an explanation." Erich

[53] Ulrich Sonnemann, in *Existence and Therapy* (New York: Grune & Stratton, 1954), p. 343, quoted from Kolle. Sonnemann's book, we may add, was the first in English to deal directly with existential theory and therapy and contains useful and relevant material. It is therefore the more unfortunate that the book is written in a style which does not communicate.

[54] Quoted by Sonnemann, *op. cit.,* p. 255, from L. Binswanger, "Uber Psychotherapie," in *Ausgewählte Vorträge und Aufsätze,* pp. 142–143.

INTRODUCTION   82

Fromm, for another example, not only emphasizes presence in a way similar to Jasper's statement above but makes it a central point in his teaching
of psychoanalysis.

Carl Rogers is an illustration of one who, never having had, so far as I
know, direct contact with the existential therapists as such, has written a
very existential document in his *apologia pro vita sua* as a therapist:

> I launch myself into the therapeutic relationship having a hypothesis, or a faith,
> that my liking, my confidence, and my understanding of the other person's inner
> world, will lead to a significant process of becoming. I enter the relationship not as
> a scientist, not as a physician who can accurately diagnose and cure, but as a person,
> entering into a personal relationship. Insofar as I see him only as an object, the
> client will tend to become only an object.
>
> I risk myself, because if, as the relationship deepens, what develops is a failure, a
> regression, a repudiation of me and the relationship by the client, then I sense that
> I will lose myself, or a part of myself. At times this risk is very real, and is very
> keenly experienced.
>
> I let myself go into the immediacy of the relationship where it is my total organism
> which takes over and is sensitive to the relationship, not simply my consciousness. I
> am not consciously responding in a planful or analytic way, but simply in an unre
> flective way to the other individual, my reaction being based (but not consciously)
> on my total organismic sensitivity to this other person. I live the relationship on
> this basis.[55]

There are real differences between Rogers and the existential therapists,
such as the fact that most of his work is based on relatively shorter-time
therapeutic relationships whereas the work of the existential therapists in
this volume is generally long-time. Rogers' viewpoint is more optimistic,
whereas the existential approach is oriented more to the tragic crises of life,
and so forth. What are significant, however, are Rogers' basic ideas that
therapy is a "process of becoming," that the freedom and inner growth of
the individual are what counts, and the implicit assumption pervading
Rogers' work of the dignity of the human being. These concepts are all
very close to the existentialist approach to the human being.

Before leaving the topic of *presence*, we need to make three caveats. One
is that this emphasis on relationship is in no way an oversimplification or
short cut; it is not a substitute for discipline or thoroughness of training.
It rather puts these thngs in their context—namely, discipline and thoroughness of training directed to understanding human beings as human. The
therapist is assumedly an expert; but, if he is not first of all a human being,
his expertness will be irrelevant and quite possibly harmful. The distinctive
character of the existential approach is that understanding *being human* is
no longer just a "gift," an intuition, or something left to chance; it is the

[55] C. R. Rogers, "Persons or Science? A Philosophical Question," *American Psychologist,*
10:267–278, 1955.

"proper study of man," in Alexander Pope's phrase, and becomes the center of a thorough and scientific concern in the broad sense. The existential analysts do the same thing with the structure of human existence that Freud did with the structure of the unconscious—namely, take it out of the realm of the hit-and-miss gift of special intuitive individuals, accept it as the area of exploration and understanding, and make it to some extent teachable.

Another caveat is that the emphasis on the reality of presence does not obviate the exceedingly significant truths in Freud's concept of transference, rightly understood. It is demonstrable every day in the week that patients, and all of us to some extent, behave toward therapist or wife or husband as though they were father or mother or someone else, and the working through of this is of crucial importance. But in existential therapy "transference" gets placed in the new context of *an event occurring in a real relationship between two people.* Almost everything the patient does vis-à-vis the therapist in a given hour has an element of transference in it. But nothing is ever "just transference," to be explained to the patient as one would an arithmetic problem. The concept of "transference" as such has often been used as a convenient protective screen behind which both therapist and patient hide in order to avoid the more anxiety-creating situation of direct confrontation. For me to tell myself, say when especially fatigued, that the patient-is-so-demanding-because-she-wants-to-prove-she-can-make-her-father-love-her may be a relief and may also be in fact true. But the real point is that she is doing this to me in this given moment, and the reasons it occurs at this instant of intersection of her existence and mine are not exhausted by what she did with her father. Beyond all considerations of unconscious determinism—which are true in their partial context—she is at some point choosing to do this at this specific moment. Furthermore, the only thing that will grasp the patient, and in the long run make it possible for her to change, is to experience fully and deeply that she is doing precisely this to a real person, myself, in this real moment.[56] Part of the *sense of tim-*

---

[56] This is a point the phenomenologists make consistently, namely, that to know fully *what* we are doing, to feel it, to experience it all through our being, is much more important than to know *why.* For, they hold, if we fully know the *what,* the *why* will come along by itself. One sees this demonstrated very frequently in psychotherapy: the patient may have only a vague and intellectual idea of the "cause" of this or that pattern in his behavior, but as he explores and experiences more and more the different aspects and phases of this pattern, the cause may suddenly become real to him not as an abstracted formulation but as one real, integral aspect of the total understanding of what he is doing. This approach also has an important cultural significance: is not the *why* asked so much in our culture precisely as a way of detaching ourselves, a way of avoiding the more disturbing and anxiety-creating alternative of sticking to the end with the *what?* That is to say, the excessive preoccupation with causality and function that characterizes modern Western society may well serve, much more widely than realized, the need to abstract ourselves from the reality of the given experience. Asking *why* is generally in the service of a need to get power *over* the phenomenon, in line with Bacon's dictum, "knowledge is power" and, specifically, knowledge of nature is power over nature. Asking the question of *what,* on the other hand, is a way of *participating* in the phenomenon.

ing in therapy—which, as Ellenberger indicates in the next chapter, has received special development among the existential therapists—consists of letting the patient experience what he or she is doing until the experience really grasps him.[57] Then and only then will an explanation of *why* help. For the patient referred to above to become aware that she is demanding this particular unconditioned love from this real person in this immediate hour may indeed shock her, and thereafter—or possibly only hours later—she should become aware of the early childhood antecedents. She may well explore and re-experience then how she smoldered with anger as a child because she couldn't make her father notice her. But if she is simply told this is a transference phenomenon, she may have learned an interesting intellectual fact which does not existentially grasp her at all.

Another caveat is that *presence* in a session does not at all mean the therapist imposes himself or his ideas or feelings on the patient. It is a highly interesting proof of our point that Rogers, who gives such a vivid picture of presence in the quotation above, is precisely the psychologist who has most unqualifiedly insisted that the therapist not project himself but at every point follow the affect and leads of the patient. Being alive in the relationship does not at all mean the therapist will chatter along with the patient; he will know that patients have an infinite number of ways of trying to become involved with the therapist in order to avoid their own problems. And he, the therapist, may well be silent, aware that to be a projective screen is one aspect of his part of the relationship. The therapist is what Socrates named the "midwife"—completely real in "being there," but being there with the specific purpose of helping the other person to bring to birth something from within himself.

The *fourth* implication for technique in existential analysis follows immediately from our discussion of presence: therapy will attempt to "analyze out" the ways of behaving which destroy presence. The therapist, on his part, will need to be aware of whatever in him blocks full presence. I do not know the context of Freud's remark that he preferred that patients lie on the couch because he could not stand to be stared at for nine hours a day. But it is obviously true that any therapist—whose task is arduous and taxing at best—is tempted at many points to evade the anxiety and potential discomfort of confrontation by various devices. We have earlier described the fact that real confrontation between two people can be profoundly anxiety-creat-

---

[57] This could well be defined as "existential time"—*the time it takes for something to become real*. It may occur instantaneously, or it may require an hour of talk or some time of silence. In any case, the sense of timing the therapist uses in pondering when to interpret will not be based only on the negative criterion—How much can the patient take? It will involve a positive criterion—Has this become real to the patient? As in the example above, has what she is doing in the present to the therapist been sharply and vividly enough experienced so that an exploration of the past will have dynamic reality and thus give the power for change?

ing.[58] Thus it is not surprising that it is much more comfortable to protect ourselves by thinking of the other only as a "patient" or focusing only on certain mechanisms of behavior. The *technical* view of the other person is perhaps the therapist's most handy anxiety-reducing device. This has its legitimate place. The therapist is presumably an expert. But technique must not be used as a way of blocking presence. Whenever the therapist finds himself reacting in a rigid or preformulated way, he had obviously best ask himself whether he is not trying to avoid some anxiety and as a result is losing something existentially real in the relationship. The therapist's situation is like that of the artist who has spent many years of disciplined study learning technique; but he knows that if specific thoughts of technique preoccupy him when he actually is in the process of painting, he has at that moment lost his vision; the creative process, which should absorb him, transcending the subject-object split, has become temporarily broken; he is now dealing with objects and himself as a manipulator of objects.

The *fifth* implication has to do with the goal of the therapeutic process. The aim of therapy is that the patient *experience his existence as real*. The purpose is that he become aware of his existence fully, which includes becoming aware of his potentialities and becoming able to act on the basis of them. The characteristic of the neurotic is that his existence has become "darkened," as the existential analysts put it, blurred, easily threatened and clouded over, and gives no sanction to his acts; the task of therapy is to illuminate the existence. The neurotic is overconcerned about the *Umwelt*, and underconcerned about *Eigenwelt*.[59] As the *Eigenwelt* becomes real to him in therapy, the patient tends to experience the *Eigenwelt* of the therapist as stronger than his own. Binswanger points out that the tendency to take over the therapist's *Eigenwelt* must be guarded against, and therapy must not become a power struggle between the two *Eigenwelten*. The therapist's function is to *be there* (with all of the connotation of *Dasein*), present in the relationship, while the patient finds and learns to live out his own *Eigenwelt*.

An experience of my own may serve to illustrate one way of taking the patient existentially. I often have found myself having the impulse to ask, when the patient comes in and sits down, not "*How* are you?" but "*Where* are you?" The contrast of these questions—neither of which would I probably actually ask aloud—highlights what is sought. I want to know, as I experience him in this hour, not just how he feels, but rather *where he is*, the "where" including his feelings but also a lot more—whether he is detached or fully present, whether his direction is toward me and toward his problems or away from both, whether he is running for anxiety, whether

58 See p. 38.
59 The point in this and the rest of the sentences in this paragraph is Binswanger's, interpreted by Dr. Hoffman.

this special courtesy when he came in or appearance of eagerness to reveal things is really inviting me to overlook some evasion he is about to make, where he is in relation to the girl friend he talked about yesterday, and so on. I became aware of this asking "where" the patient was several years ago, before I specifically knew the work of the existential therapists; it illustrates a spontaneous existential attitude.

It follows that when mechanisms or dynamisms are interpreted, as they will be in existential therapy as in any other, it will always be in the context of this person's becoming aware of his existence. This is the only way the dynamism will have reality for him, will affect him; otherwise he might as well—as indeed most patients do these days—read about the mechanism in a book. This point is of special importance because precisely the problem of many patients is that they think and talk about themselves in terms of mechanisms; it is their way, as well-taught citizens of twentieth-century Western culture, to avoid confronting their own existence, their method of repressing ontological awareness. This is done, to be sure, under the rubric of being "objective" about one's self; but is it not, in therapy as well as in life, often a systematized, culturally acceptable way of rationalizing detachment from one's self? Even the motive for coming for therapy may be just that, to find an acceptable system by which one can continue to think of himself as a mechanism, to run himself as he would his motor car, only now to do it successfully. If we assume, as we have reason for doing, that the fundamental neurotic process in our day is the repression of the ontological sense—the loss of the sense of being, together with the truncation of awareness and the locking up of the potentialities which are the manifestations of this being—then we are playing directly into the patient's neurosis to the extent that we teach him new ways of thinking of himself as a mechanism. This is one illustration of how psychotherapy can reflect the fragmentation of the culture, structuralizing neurosis rather than curing it. Trying to help the patient on a sexual problem by explaining it merely as a mechanism is like teaching a farmer irrigation while damming up his stream.

This raises some penetrating questions about the nature of "cure" in psychotherapy. It implies that it is not the therapist's function to "cure" the patients' neurotic symptoms, though this is the motive for which most people come for therapy. Indeed, the fact that this is their motive reflects their problem. Therapy is concerned with something more fundamental, namely, helping the person experience his existence; and any cure of symptoms which will last must be a by-product of that. The general ideas of "cure"—namely, to live as long as possible and as satisfactorily adjusted as possible—are themselves a denial of *Dasein*, of this particular patient's being. The kind of cure that consists of adjustment, becoming able to fit the culture, can be obtained by technical emphases in therapy, for it is precisely the central theme of the culture that one live in a calculated, controlled, technically

well-managed way. Then the patient accepts a confined world without conflict, for now his world is identical with the culture. And since anxiety comes
only with freedom, the patient naturally gets over his anxiety; he is relieved
from his symptoms because he surrenders the possibilities which caused his
anxiety. This is the way of being "cured" by giving up being, giving up existence, by constricting, hedging in existence. In this respect, psychotherapists
become the agents of the culture whose particular task it is to adjust people
to it; psychotherapy becomes an expression of the fragmentation of the period rather than an enterprise for overcoming it. As we have indicated
above, there are clear historical indications that this is occurring in the different psychotherapeutic schools, and the historical probability is that it
will increase. There is certainly a question how far this gaining of release
from conflict by giving up being can proceed without generating in individuals and groups a submerged despair, a resentment which will later burst
out in self-destructiveness, for history proclaims again and again that sooner
or later man's need to be free will out. But the complicating factor in our
immediate historical situation is that the culture itself is built around this
ideal of technical adjustment and carries so many built-in devices for nar-
cotizing the despair that comes from using one's self as a machine that the
damaging effects may remain submerged for some time.

On the other hand, the term "cure" can be given a deeper and truer meaning,
namely, becoming oriented toward the fulfillment of one's existence. This may
include as a by-product the cure of symptoms—obviously a desideratum, even
if we have stated decisively that it is not the chief goal of therapy. The important thing is that the person discovers his being, his *Dasein*.

The *sixth* implication which distinguishes the process of existential therapy is the importance of *commitment*. The basis for this was prepared at
numerous points in our previous sections, particularly in our discussion of
Kierkegaard's idea that "truth exists only as the individual himself produces
it in action." The significance of commitment is not that it is simply a
vaguely good thing or ethically to be advised. It is a necessary prerequisite,
rather, for seeing truth. This involves a crucial point which has never to my
knowledge been fully taken into account in writings on psychotherapy,
namely, that *decision precedes knowledge*. We have worked normally on the
assumption that, as the patient gets more and more knowledge and insight
about himself, he will make the appropriate decisions. This is a half truth.
The second half of the truth is generally overlooked, namely, that *the patient cannot permit himself to get insight or knowledge until he is ready to
decide, takes a decisive orientation to life, and has made the preliminary
decisions along the way.*

We mean "decision" here not in the sense of a be-all-and-end-all jump, say,
to get married or to join the foreign legion. The possibility or readiness to
take such "leaps" is a necessary condition for the decisive orientation, but

the big leap itself is sound only so far as it is based upon the minute decisions along the way. Otherwise the sudden decision is the product of unconscious processes, proceeding compulsively in unawareness to the point where they erupt, for example, in a "conversion." We use the term decision as meaning a *decisive attitude toward existence,* an attitude of commitment. In this respect, *knowledge and insight follow decision rather than vice versa.* Everyone knows of the incidents in which a patient becomes aware in a dream that a certain boss is exploiting him and the next day decides to quit his job. But just as significant, though not generally taken into account because they go against our usual ideas of causality, are the incidents when the patient cannot have the dream *until* he makes the decision. He makes the jump to quit his job, for example, and then he can permit himself to see in dreams that his boss was exploiting him all along.

One interesting corollary of this point is seen when we note that a patient cannot recall what was vital and significant in his past until he is ready to make a decision with regard to the future. Memory works not on a basis simply of what is there imprinted; it works rather on the basis of one's decisions in the present and future. It has often been said that one's past determines one's present and future. Let it be underlined that one's present and future—how he commits himself to existence at the moment—also determines his past. That is, it determines what he can recall of his past, what portions of his past he selects (consciously but also unconsciously) to influence him now, and therefore the particular gestalt his past will assume.

This commitment is, furthermore, not a purely conscious or voluntaristic phenomenon. It is also present on so-called "unconscious" levels. When a person lacks commitment, for example, his dreams may be staid, flat, impoverished; but when he does assume a decisive orientation toward himself and his life, his dreams often take over the creative process of exploring, molding, forming himself in relation to his future or—what is the same thing from the neurotic viewpoint—the dreams struggle to evade, substitute, cover up. The important point is that either way the issue has been joined.

With respect to helping the patient develop the orientation of commitment, we should first emphasize that the existential therapists do not at all mean activism. This is no "decision as a short cut," no matter of premature jumping because to act may be easier and may quiet anxiety more quickly than the slow, arduous, long-time process of self-exploration. They mean rather the attitude of *Dasein,* the self-aware being taking his own existence seriously. The points of commitment and decision are those where the dichotomy between being subject and object is overcome in the unity of readiness for action. When a patient discusses intellectually *ad interminum* a given topic without its ever shaking him or becoming real to him, the therapist asks what is he doing existentially by means of this talk? The talk itself, obviously, is in the service of covering up reality, rationalized generally under the idea of unprejudiced inquiry into the data. It is customarily said that the patient will break through such talk when some experience of anxiety, some inner suffering or outer threat, shocks him into committing himself really to getting help and gives him the incentive necessary for the painful process of uncovering illusions, of inner change and growth. True; this of course does occur from time to time. And the existential therapist can aid the patient in absorbing the real impact of such experiences by helping him develop the capacity for silence (which is another form of communication) and thus avoid using chatter to break the shocking power of the encounter with the insight.

But in principle I do not think the conclusion that we must wait around until anxiety is aroused is adequate. If we assume that the patient's commitment depends upon being pushed by external or internal pain, we are in several difficult dilemmas. Either the therapy "marks time" until anxiety or pain occurs, or we arouse anxiety ourselves (which is a questionable procedure). And the very reassurance and quieting of anxiety the patient receives in therapy may work against his commitment to further help and may make for postponement and procrastination.

Commitment must be on a more positive basis. The question we need to ask is: What is going on that the patient has not found some point in his own existence to which he can commit himself unconditionally? In the earlier discussion of non-being and death, it was pointed out that everyone constantly faces the threat of non-being if he lets himself recognize the fact. Central here is the symbol of death, but such threat of destruction of being is present in a thousand and one other guises as well. The therapist is doing the patient a disservice if he takes away from him the realization that it is entirely within the realm of possibility that he forfeit or lose his existence and that may well be precisely what he is doing at this very moment. This point is especially important because patients tend to carry a never-quite-articulated belief, no doubt connected with childhood omnipotent beliefs associated with parents, that somehow the therapist will see that nothing harmful happens to them, and therefore they don't need to take their own existence seriously. The tendency prevails in much therapy to water down anxiety, despair, and the tragic aspects of life. Is it not true as a general principle that we need to engender anxiety only to the extent that we already have watered it down? Life itself produces enough, and the only real, crises; and it is very much to the credit of the existential emphasis in therapy that it confronts these tragic realities directly. The patient can indeed destroy himself if he so chooses. The therapist may not say this: it is simply a reflection of fact, and the important point is that it not be sloughed over. The symbol of suicide as a possibility has a far-reaching positive value;

Nietzsche once remarked that the thought of suicide has saved many lives. I am doubtful whether anyone takes his life with full seriousness until he realizes that it is entirely within his power to commit suicide.[60]

Death in any of its aspects is the fact which makes of the present hour something of absolute value. One student put it, "I know only two things—one, that I will be dead someday, two, that I am not dead now. The only question is what shall I do between those two points." We cannot go into this matter in further detail, but we only wish to emphasize that the core of the existential approach is the taking of existence seriously.

We conclude with two final caveats. One is a danger that lies in the existential approach, the danger of *generality*. It would indeed be a pity if the existential concepts were tossed around among therapists without regard for their concrete, real meaning. For it must be admitted that there is temptation to become lost in words in these complex areas with which existential analysis deals. One can certainly become philosophically detached in the same way as one can be technically detached. The temptation to use existential concepts in the service of intellectualizing tendencies is especially to be guarded against, since, because they refer to things that have to do with the center of personal reality, these concepts can the more seductively give the illusion of dealing with reality. It must be confessed that some of the writers in the papers in this volume may not have fully resisted this temptation, and some readers may feel that I myself have not. I could plead the necessity of having to explain a great deal within a short compass; but extenuating circumstances are not the point. The point is that to the extent that the existential movement in psychotherapy becomes influential in this country —a desideratum which we believe would be very beneficial—the adherents will have to be on guard against the use of the concepts in the service of intellectual detachment. It is, of course, precisely for the above reasons that the existential therapists pay much attention to making clear the verbal utterances of the patient, and they also continually make certain that the necessary interrelation of verbalizing and acting is never overlooked. The "logos must be made flesh." The important thing is *to be* existential.

The other caveat has to do with the existential attitude toward the *unconscious*. In principle most existential analysts deny this concept. They point out all the logical as well as psychological difficulties with the doctrine of the unconscious, and they stand against splitting the being into parts. What is called unconscious, they hold, is still part of this given person; *being,* in any living sense, is at its core indivisible. Now it must be admitted that the doctrine of the unconscious has played most notoriously into the contempo-

[60] We are of course not speaking here of the practical question of what to do when patients actually threaten suicide; this introduces many other elements and is a quite different question. The conscious awareness we are speaking of is a different thing from the overwhelming and persistent depression, with the self-destructive impulse unbroken by self-conscious awareness, which seems to obtain in actual suicides.

rary tendencies to rationalize behavior, to avoid the reality of one's own existence, to act as though one were not himself doing the living. (The man in the street who has picked up the lingo says, "My unconscious did it.") The existential analysts are correct, in my judgment, in their criticism of the doctrine of the unconscious as a convenient blank check on which any causal explanation can be written or as a reservoir from which any deterministic theory can be drawn. But this is the "cellar" view of the unconscious, and objections to it should not be permitted to cancel out the great contribution that the historical meaning of the unconscious had in Freud's terms. Freud's great discovery and his perdurable contribution was to enlarge the sphere of the human personality beyond the immediate voluntarism and rationalism of Victorian man, to include in this enlarged sphere the "depths," that is, the irrational, the so-called repressed, hostile, and unacceptable urges, the forgotten aspects of experience, *ad infinitum*. The symbol for this vast enlarging of the domain of the personality was "the unconscious."

I do not wish to enter into the complex discussion of this concept itself; I wish only to suggest a position. It is right that the blank check, deteriorated, cellar form of this concept should be rejected. But the far-reaching enlargement of personality, which is its real meaning, should not be lost. Binswanger remarks that, for the time being, the existential therapists will not be able to dispense with the concept of the unconscious. I would propose, rather, to agree that being is at some point indivisible, that unconsciousness is part of any given being, that the cellar theory of the unconscious is logically wrong and practically unconstructive; but that the meaning of the discovery, namely, the radical enlargement of being, is one of the great contributions of our day and must be retained.

III

A Clinical Introduction to Psychiatric Phenomenology and Existential Analysis*

by Henri F. Ellenberger

WHAT CLINICALLY are phenomenology and existential analysis? It may be appropriate first to clarify what they are *not*. In contradistinction to a common prejudice, they do *not* represent a confusing interference of philosophy into the field of psychiatry. It is true that there is a *philosophical* trend called "phenomenology," founded by Edmund Husserl, and that there is another *philosophical* trend called "existentialism," whose major representatives are Kierkegaard, Jaspers, Heidegger, Sartre. But there is a wide gap between the philosophical phenomenology of Husserl and the psychiatric phenomenology of Minkowski and between existentialist philosophy and the psychiatric method called existential analysis. Analogously, there is a branch of physics concerned with the investigation of X-rays, and there is a branch of medicine, radiology, concerned with the application of X-rays for medical purposes; yet nobody will contend that medical radiology represents a confusing interference of physics into medicine. In a similar way, psychiatric phenomenologists and existential analysts are psychiatrists utilizing certain new philosophical concepts as tools for psychiatric investigation.

And why did these psychiatrists feel the need of using certain concepts borrowed from philosophy? In all scientific progress, new techniques bring forth new findings which in turn produce new problems; the need to solve these new problems stimulates the search for new techniques, which again bring forth new findings and new problems, *ad infinitum.*

* I wish to express here my thanks to Drs. Ludwig Binswanger, Heinz Graumann, Rollo May, Karl Menninger, Eugene Minkowski, Gardner Murphy, Paul Pruyser, Erwin Straus, H. G. van der Waals for their encouragement and suggestions. Special thanks are due to Dr. Ann Wilkins for her invaluable help in the preparation and editing of this article.

I *Meaning and Purpose of These New Approaches*

If we jump back eighteen centuries, to the time of Galen, we find that psychiatry was very rudimentary. Here, for instance, is a case history quoted from one of Galen's works:

A man afflicted with *phrenitis* lived in his own house, in Rome, with a slave who was a wool-worker. He rose from his bed and went to the window, from whence he could look at the passers-by and be seen by them. He showed to them earthenware pots which he possessed, and asked them whether he should throw them down. With laughter and hand-clappings they urged him to do so, and our man threw one pot after the other, at the noise of laughter and applauding. Then, he asked them whether he should throw down the slave, and since they approved, he did so. When the spectators saw the slave falling, they ceased laughing and they rushed, only to find the unfortunate one crushed to pieces.[1]

What strikes us, in the perspective of modern psychiatry, is the unscientific flavor of this short case history. It seems as if, even in the work of a great medical genius, psychiatry was a field restricted to strange, queer, extraordinary stories. Galen's account of his mental patient is such as one might read in a newspaper today; but for about fifteen centuries, psychiatry knew no better case histories.

Noteworthy progress in the investigation of mental illness was not realized before the seventeenth century, when the Italian physician and lawyer Paolo Zacchias,[2] one of the founders of legal medicine, imagined a kind of schema for psychiatric case studies, a simple but practical frame of reference in which the symptoms of a case of mental illness could be viewed in order to make possible an accurate evaluation, from the medical as well as from the legal point of view. In this frame, not only were the conspicuous disorders of acts and behavior taken into account, but the attention of the examiner was also directed toward specific disorders of each major psychological function—emotions, perception, memory.

New developments as well as new problems arose from the progress of psychology in the eighteenth century. The psychological frame of reference which is generally used today dates from this time. Psychological manifestations were divided into three major groups or "faculties"—intellect, affectivity, and will. Within the faculty of intellect, one distinguished such functions as sensation, perception, association, imagination, intellection, judgment. This psychological frame of reference gradually superseded that of the scholastic philosophers of the Middle Ages and was adopted by the psychiatrists of

---

[1] Ch. Daremberg (ed.), *Oeuvres anatomiques, physiologiques et médicales de Galien* (French trans.) (Paris: Baillière, 1854–56), Vol. 2, p. 588.

[2] Ch. Vallon and G. Génil-Perrin, "La Psychiatrie médico-légale dans l'oeuvre de Zacchias," *Revue de Psychiatrie*, Vol. 16, 1912, pp. 46–84, 90–106.

the beginning of the nineteenth century. They soon began systematically to investigate mental conditions with this new instrument, which facilitated the definition of certain elementary mental disturbances. For instance: "Hallucination is a perception without an object." "Illusion is a perception inadequate to its object." "A delusional idea is erroneous judgment which is maintained by the subject in spite of contrary evidence." Even Bleuler's concept of schizophrenia is a late offspring of eighteenth-century psychology: the major symptom of schizophrenia was "the waning of the strength of associations" and from this basic disturbance all other symptoms of the disease could be deduced.

Whereas Galen's psychiatry included only a description of the patient's most conspicuous behavior, Zacchias' psychiatry comprehended two steps: a careful description of the behavior, followed by a summary investigation of the major psychological functions. Nineteenth-century psychiatry comprehended three steps: The first was the study of the "elements," *i.e.*, the basic types of disturbances of elementary psychological functions, such as hallucinations, illusions, delusional ideas, compulsive ideas, and abulia. The second was the study of "forms" or "syndromes," *i.e.*, how symptoms are combined to form "clinical pictures" such as depression, elation, mental confusion, and amentia. The third step was the attempt to define specific mental disease entities, such as progressive paralysis. History of psychiatry in the nineteenth century is mainly the history of coping with the enormous task of defining the innumerable mental "elements" or "symptoms," the various "forms" or "syndromes," the specific mental disease entities, and of classifying the latter in a nosological system. Such men as Esquirol, Morel, Kahlbaum, Kraepelin, Wernicke, Bleuler were the great pioneers of that period of psychiatry.

Now, at the turn of the nineteenth century new problems arose, together with new techniques and new approaches. Among these new trends were psychiatric genetics, constitution psychiatry, endocrinological and chemobiological psychiatry, psychological testing, psychoanalysis and phenomenology. It has often been supposed that psychoanalysis and phenomenology are opposed to each other; it even seems that a few phenomenologists have at times expressed anti-analytic feelings and vice versa. This is the result of a complete misunderstanding. Psychoanalysis and phenomenology do not exclude each other any more than do, for instance, physiology and morphology. They are two distinct fields arising from two different starting points, using different methods and different terminologies. Far from excluding each other, they complement each other very well.

The impetus for *psychoanalysis* was Charcot's observation that there was a gap between the physiopathology of the brain and the clinical symptoms of neuroses and his demonstration that traumatic neuroses resulted from so-called "reminiscences"—*i.e.*, from the unconscious representation of the trauma. This led Janet and Breuer to cure hysterical patients by the unraveling of the forgotten "reminiscences" and brought Freud to explore systematically with new techniques the realm of repressed memories and man's unconscious life.

The impetus for *phenomenology* was quite different. It was the growing awareness of certain psychiatrists that the classical psychological frame of reference, inherited from the eighteenth century, was no longer adequate for the exploration of many psychopathological conditions. In 1914, for example, Blondel, a French philosopher, published a very interesting book *La Conscience morbide* [3] (Morbid Consciousness), in which, on the basis of his own studies of mental patients, he showed that we do not understand what the psychotic individual really experiences. When we say that "a hallucination is a perception without an object" or "a delusion is erroneous judgment which is maintained in spite of contrary evidence," we give verbal formulations that, without being technically untrue, are unable to convey to us anything of how a mental patient actually experiences a hallucination or a delusion. Even worse, these definitions give us the false impression that we understand the patient. Blondel emphasized the fact that the mental patient lives in another subjective world that we do not understand and cannot enter. This fact applies not only to the major psychoses but also to the subtle feelings of vague threat and depersonalization preceding the onset of acute schizophrenia. If we take into account Blondel's studies, we find ourselves in the following dilemma: either we give up hope of ever understanding the subjective experience of numerous mentally sick patients, or else we find more adequate methods for the accomplishment of this aim. Phenomenologists believe that they have found a new approach, which enables them to grasp the subjective experience of the patient more fully than could be done within the older, classical frame of reference.

The impetus for *existential analysis* was the same as for psychiatric phenomenology. It occurred to several psychiatrists, who had started to work with the phenomenological method, that existentialist philosophy (above all Heidegger's philosophy) was able to provide them with a frame of reference that was broader than that of phenomenology. Existential analysis does not supersede phenomenology; it integrates phenomenology as a part of its total system.

II *Psychiatric Phenomenology*

In both philosophy and psychiatry the word "phenomenology" has been used with a variety of meanings, and its philosophical and psychiatric aspects have not always been clearly distinguished. But here we are dealing only with psychiatric phenomenology and using the word "phenomenology" only in the sense of Husserl's concept.

Husserl's phenomenology is basically a *methodological principle,* intended

[3] Ch. Blondel, *La Conscience morbide* (Paris: Alcan, 1914).

to provide a firm basis for the foundation of a new psychology and of a universal philosophy. In the presence of a phenomenon (whether it be an external object or a state of mind), the phenomenologist uses an absolutely unbiased approach; he observes phenomena as they manifest themselves and only as they manifest themselves. This observation is accomplished by means of an operation of the mind which Husserl called the *epoche,* or "psychological-phenomenological reduction." The observer "puts the world between brackets," *i.e.,* he excludes from his mind not only any judgment of value about the phenomena but also any affirmation whatever concerning their cause and background; he even strives to exclude the distinction of subject and object and any affirmation about the existence of the object and of the observing subject. With this method, observation is greatly enhanced: the less apparent elements of phenomena manifest themselves with increasing richness and variety, with finer gradations of clarity and obscurity, and eventually previously unnoticed structures of phenomena may become apparent.

At this point, we can draw a comparison between Husserl's methodological principle and Freud's "basic rule." [4] The subject who follows Freud's basic rule must verbalize everything that occurs spontaneously to his mind, putting aside any consideration of shame, guilt feeling, anxiety, or any other emotion. Husserl's principle is the unbiased contemplation of phenomena, putting aside any intellectual consideration. The parallel could be drawn further: The analysand who strives to follow the "basic rule" is soon inhibited by "resistances," and it is the analyst's task to elucidate these resistances in terms of transference, defenses, etc. In regard to Husserl's principle, Merleau-Ponty [5] writes that "the greatest teaching of reduction is the impossibility of a complete reduction." [6]

We can pursue this comparison still further. For the psychoanalyst, the material furnished by the free associations constitutes the basis for such operations as focusing, emphasizing, restating, suggesting interpretations. In a similar way, the phenomenologist may submit the raw material furnished by the *epoche* to structural or categorical analysis, as we shall see.

Husserl exerted an immense influence on psychology and psychopathology.

[4] It is noteworthy that Husserl (1859–1938) and Freud (1856–1939) had almost the same dates of birth and death, and published their main works (Freud, the *Interpretation of Dreams,* and Husserl, the *Logische Untersuchungen*) in the same year, 1900. Husserl was the most prominent disciple of Franz Brentano, whose philosophical lectures Freud attended for two years.

[5] M. Merleau-Ponty, *Phénoménologie de la perception* (Paris: Gallimard, 1945), p. viii.

[6] After this first reduction, *i.e.* the *epoche,* or psychological-phenomenological reduction, Husserl instituted two further steps, the "eidetic reduction" and the "transcendental reduction." We do not need to enter into that properly philosophical part of his system. English-speaking readers will find an account of it in Marvin Farber's book, *The Foundation of Phenomenology* (Cambridge, Mass.: Harvard Univ. Press, 1943). See also the periodical, *Philosophy and Phenomenological Research,* published by the University of Buffalo, Buffalo, N.Y.

A wealth of psychological research was performed in all fields of psychology under the direct or indirect inspiration of his primarily philosophical school. There were, among many others, the studies of David Katz [7] on the phenomenology of colors, of Sartre [8] on emotions, of Merleau-Ponty [9] on perception. Because Husserl and his pupils were concerned with thorough descriptions of states of consciousness in their purest forms, as experienced by the subject, there is nothing surprising if these researches attracted the attention of psychopathologists in search of new methods. Psychiatric phenomenologists took over these methods from Husserl's school or devised new ones inspired by these researches.

The phenomenologist pays special attention to his own state of consciousness in the presence of a patient. Eugen Bleuler had already noted the importance of the observer's peculiar subjective feeling in the presence of a schizophrenic. Sometimes an alert examiner may be aware of the "feel" of schizophrenia before objective manifestations have appeared in the course of the illness. The psychoanalyst's analysis of countertransference is, in fact, an application of phenomenological methods. The main emphasis of psychiatric phenomenology lies, however, on the investigation of the patient's subjective states of consciousness. Three main methods have been applied to that effect:

1. *Descriptive phenomenology* relies entirely on descriptions given by the patients of their subjective experiences.

2. The *genetic-structural* method postulates a fundamental unity in an individual's state of consciousness and tries to find a common denominator, *i.e.*, a "genetic factor," with the help of which the rest can be made intelligible and reconstructed.

3. *Categorical analysis* takes a system of phenomenological coordinates, the most important of which are time (or rather "temporality"), space (or rather "spatiality"), causality, and materiality. The investigator analyzes how each of them is experienced by the patient, in order to achieve, on this basis, a thorough and detailed reconstruction of the patient's inner universe of experience.

These are the methods that we must now examine in some detail.

A *Descriptive Phenomenology*

Descriptive phenomenology was the first application of phenomenology to psychiatric researches. Karl Jaspers defined it as a careful and accurate description of the subjective experience of mentally sick patients, with an effort to empathize (*einfühlen*) as closely as possible with this experience.

---

[7] David Katz, *Der Aufbau der Farbwelt* (Leipzig: Barth, 1930).
[8] Jean-Paul Sartre, *Esquisse d'une théorie des émotions*. Actualités scientifiques et industrielles, No. 838 (Paris: Hermann, 1948).
[9] M. Merleau-Ponty, *op. cit.*

Jaspers and his associates devoted a great deal of time to interviewing patients about their inner world and compared the findings with accounts given by the same or other patients after their recovery, a great amount of which material was compiled by Jaspers in his textbook of psychopathology.[10]

Let us illustrate this by one clinical instance. Few states of consciousness are more mysterious than the subjective experience of catatonic schizophrenics. Jaspers found an excellent account of that condition given after her recovery by a patient of Kronfeld:

During the period of excitement, my mood was not fury, and not even a particular mood aside from a purely animal pleasure in moving myself. It was not the wicked excitement of someone who will commit a murder; far from it! It was completely innocent. However, the impulse was so strong that I could not help jumping. I can only compare myself, in such times, to a wild boar or a horse. . . . There was also a joyfulness, an exuberance, a pleasure in living which I had never felt so intensely. Concerning the memory of the attacks of excitement: it is generally good, but ordinarily does not retain the beginning of the attack. An external stimulation, such as a cold floor, may wake you up and bring back awareness. Then, you are oriented and you see everything, but you don't pay attention to it, you let the excitement continue its course. Above all, you don't pay attention to the people, although you see and hear them. On the other hand, you are careful not to fall down. . . . When you are stopped and put to bed, you are surprised by the suddenness of the change, you feel offended and you defend yourself. Then, the motor discharge, instead of jumping, takes the form of hitting around yourself; but it is not a sign of irritation. There is no concentration of mind. Sometimes, during a moment of lucidity, you notice it. Not always! But then, you notice that you are unable to build a sentence. . . . It seems to me as if this whole period was a total decomposition. . . . With all that, I had never the feeling of perplexity or insufficiency; I never felt that there was something disturbed in me, but that the chaos was outside of me. I was never anxious. In the bath, I still remember the many gymnastic exercises, the climbing up. . . . I remember how, some evenings, I often made long speeches, but I don't remember about what: all escaped from my memory, . . . confused thoughts, thoughts so pale and indistinct, nothing sharp. . . .

Such beautiful descriptions show how far we have come from Galen and the old psychiatrists who contented themselves with grossly behavioristic descriptions. But we are also very far from the analysis of psychopathological conditions in terms of symptoms, syndromes, and disease entities. The subjective experience of the patient is now the focus of interest and major concern of the psychiatrist, who strives to understand his patient's state of consciousness in order to establish contact with him, if possible. In other words, whereas Galen contented himself with a behavioristic approach, Zacchias with a two-dimensional behavioristic and psychological approach, nineteenth-century psychiatry with a three-dimensional approach including the

10 Karl Jaspers, *Allgemeine Psychopathologie* (Berlin: Springer, 1913).

study of symptoms, syndromes, and disease entities, now a fourth dimension is added, and a psychiatric investigation includes four steps: (1) the phenomenological study of states of consciousness, (2) the clinical study of objective symptoms, (3) syndromes, and (4) disease entities.

Even if the influence of phenomenology had been restricted to stimulating the psychiatrists' effort to gain an intimate comprehension of their patients, it would have meant remarkable progress. The psychiatrists' attention was belatedly attracted to a whole range of self-descriptions of mental conditions written by former mental patients, from *Aurélia,* by the French poet Gérard de Nerval (a description of the inmost subjective experience of an acute schizophrenic and a work of great psychological interest and literary beauty) to Clifford Beers's famous book, *A Mind That Found Itself.* Such accounts had not hitherto been taken very seriously by many psychiatrists; now they were sought for and systematically worked out by investigators.

One of the most remarkable works in the field of descriptive phenomenology was Mayer-Gross's study of mental confusion and oneirism [11]—a study of several modalities of alterations of consciousness based on self-descriptions by patients. We might also mention the studies by Jakob Wyrsch, in Switzerland, on how schizophrenic patients experience their disease and what their disease means for them in the various subtypes of acute and chronic schizophrenia. [12]

So much for descriptive phenomenology. However excellent was the work that Jaspers and his followers performed, it is doubtful whether descriptive phenomenology can provide us with full knowledge of the patient's subjective experiences. Only a few patients are able to remember what they were subjectively experiencing, and it is not certain whether they can find words to express what they are or were experiencing. For these reasons, a further development of phenomenological investigation was introduced by Minkowski: the investigation of the *structure* of states of consciousness using the methods of "structural analysis" and of "categorical analysis." Thus Jaspers's descriptive phenomenology became the first step toward a much more accurate investigation.

B *Genetic-structural Phenomenology*

Phenomenological observation does not merely provide the observer with a wealth of data. It may also lead to the recognition of connections and in-

11 W. Mayer-Gross, *Selbstschilderungen der Verwirrtheit. Die oneiroide Erlebnisform* (Berlin: Springer, 1924).

12 Jakob Wyrsch, *Ueber akute schizophrene Zustände, ihren psychopathologischen Aufbau und ihre praktische Bedeutung* (Basel and Leipzig: Karger, 1937); "Ueber die Psychopathologie einfacher Schizophrenien," *Monatsschrift für Psychiatrie und Neurologie,* Vol. 102, 1940, pp. 75–106; "Zur Theorie und Klinik der paranoiden Schizophrenie," *Monatsschrift für Psychiatrie und Neurologie,* Vol. 106, 1942, pp. 57–101.

terrelations between these data. It may even happen that in the total content of consciousness a general structure or gestalt shows itself spontaneously to the observer, who will subsequently try to describe and define it. Thus doing, he is performing what Minkowski [13] called "structural analysis" and Von Gebsattel [14] "constructive-genetic consideration" (*konstruktive-genetische Betrachtung*).

The aim of Minkowski's "structural analysis" is to define the basic disturbance (*trouble générateur*), from which one could deduce the whole content of consciousness and the symptoms of the patients. Von Gebsattel thinks that this method can also lead to recognition of the deep-seated relationship of the biological and psychological disturbances of the patient.

In their investigations of melancholic patients, both Minkowski and Von Gebsattel found the same basic symptom: time is no more experienced as a propulsive energy. The consequence is a flowing back of the stream of time, comparable to what happens to a river when a barrier is constructed. Therefore, the future is perceived as blocked and the patient's attention directed toward the past, while the present is experienced as stagnating. Many other symptoms may be deduced from this basic disturbance in the experiencing of time.

Minkowski's main field of research with this method was the psychopathology of schizophrenia, which he interprets as connected to a specific basic disturbance, the "loss of vital contact with reality." This use of the method he expounded in his book on schizophrenia.[15]

Another example of a genetic-structural analysis is Von Gebsattel's study of the world of the compulsive neurotic. Von Gebsattel starts with the classical distinction of "disturbing symptoms" and "warding off symptoms." Against what is the compulsive neurotic fighting? Against things which appear to him as ugly, dirty, repulsive, disgusting. On closer inspection, other particularities are manifested: the world of the compulsive is devoid of friendly forms, or even of inoffensive and indifferent forms. In this world, everything has "physiognomic" character; all objects are infected with decomposition and decay. In fact, the patient is fighting not so much against disgusting "things" as against a general background of disgust, a "counter-world" of decaying forms and destroying powers which Von Gebsattel calls *anti-eidos*. In the last analysis, this world shows itself as issuing from a specific type of hampering of self-realization. A condensation of Von Gebsattel's paper on the world of the compulsive neurotic is included in this volume. Another study on the same topic, and one which comes to fairly similar conclusions, is Straus's monograph on obsessions.[16]

[13] E. Minkowski, "La Notion de trouble générateur et l'analyse structurale des troubles mentaux," in *Le Temps vécu* (Paris: d'Artrey, 1933), pp. 207–254.
[14] V. E. von Gebsattel, "Zeitbezogenes Zwangsdenken in der Melancholie," in *Prolegomena einer medizinischen Anthropologie* (Berlin: Springer, 1954), pp. 1–18.
[15] E. Minkowski, *La Schizophrénie* (Paris: Payot, 1927).
[16] Erwin Straus, *On Obsessions*, Nervous and Mental Disease Monographs, 1948, No. 73.

C *Categorical Phenomenology*

Without discarding the classical psychological frame of reference, with its distinction of intellect, affectivity, will, etc., phenomenology can also use a "categorical" frame of reference. This means that the phenomenologist attempts to reconstruct the inner world of his patients through an analysis of their manner of experiencing time, space, causality, materiality, and other "categories" (in the philosophical sense of the word). The two basic categories of inner experiences are considered to be time ("temporality") and space ("spatiality"), which we must examine in some detail because of their great importance.

1. Temporality

In common psychiatric practice, the study of time is limited to checking whether the patient is or is not disoriented in time and whether his mental operations are accelerated or slowed down. The clinical psychologist will perhaps also measure the patient's speed of reactions and occasionally his appreciation of durations of time. In phenomenological investigation, however, temporality becomes a basic coordinate upon which the greatest emphasis is laid.

What is time? Time in terms of common-sense and everyday experience is but one form of a broader concept, *temporality*, easily demonstrable by a very short review of a few of the numerous concepts of time elaborated by philosophers, physicists, biologists, and psychologists.

Among philosophers,[17] Plato and the idealists assumed that time is a reflection of eternity, which is the true realm of reality. Bergson proclaimed that "duration" is the very stuff of reality, whereas the time of the physicists is a projection of spatial characteristics into the concept of time proper. For Kant, time is an "a priori form of sensibility" which we project into our vision of the world. There is also Dunne's [18] concept of "pluri-dimensional time," inspired by his parapsychological research.

Time to the physicists is an abstract, measurable continuum that is homogeneous, continuous, and infinitely divisible into identical and mutually exclusive units. In contrast to physical space, physical time has only one dimension, "duration," and this dimension has but one irreversible direction, the axis past–future. Another attribute is simultaneity, *i.e.*, each instant can contain several events; thus the instant can be considered as situated at the intersection of duration and simultaneity.

17 A good survey of the various philosophical theories of time was given by Werner Gent in his book, *Das Problem der Zeit. Eine historische und systematische Untersuchung* (Frankfurt a.M.: Schulte-Bulmke, 1934).

18 J. W. Dunne, *An Experiment with Time* (New York: Macmillan, 1927); The *Serial Universe* (London: Faber, 1934).

A concept of "biological time" was elaborated by Lecomte du Nouy,[19] a biologist who discovered that cicatrization of wounds is slower in proportion to the age of the patient and calculated the mathematical formula of this biological law. Lecomte du Nouy inferred that each individual possesses his own "inner physiological time," with a time unit of its own. If we measure cosmic time with this time unit, the days and years would be found to be shorter and shorter as we grow old (which corresponds only roughly to empirical experience). Ruyer [20] and the "neo-finalists" assert that certain biological phenomena cannot be accounted for without a special concept of "transtemporality."

To the psychologist, the problem of time is very different, because we dispose of the direct subjective experience of time and of the findings of experimental psychology. The main problem is that "psychological time" does not fit into the rigid patterns of physical time, although each is related to the other. Bergson's [21] contrast between experienced "duration" (which is "pure quality" and the very stuff of life) and "homogeneous time" of the physicists exerted an influence on psychiatric phenomenology, especially on Minkowski. Janet [22] distinguishes two forms of time, "consistent time" and "inconsistent time." "Consistent time" originates not from memory but from a specific form of action, i.e., "spoken report" and its derivatives, description, narration, history. From this phenomenon issue the concepts of temporal sequence and of chronological order. "Inconsistent time" originates when the narrative emancipates itself from its original conditions and purposes and becomes a play; this is what happens in poetry and legend and in confabulation.

To the phenomenologist, the category of time is of crucial importance and attracted the fullest attention of Husserl [23] and of Heidegger.[24] We may also mention the work of Volkelt.[25] The first study of the phenomenology of time in a clinical case was published by Minkowski in 1923; the reader will find it translated in this book. Other contributions of Minkowski were collected in his book Lived Time [26] in 1933. Minkowski's initial paper was followed by phenomenological studies by Straus, Von Gebsattel, Fischer, and others.

In order to investigate the phenomenology of time in clinical cases, let us first of all observe from outside the way in which various people deal

[19] Lecomte du Nouy, Le Temps et la vie (Paris: Gallimard, 1936).

[20] Raymond Ruyer, Eléments de psycho-biologie (Paris: PUF, 1946); Néo-Finalisme (Paris: PUF, 1952).

[21] Henri Bergson, Essai sur les données immédiates de la conscience (Paris: Alcan, 1889).

[22] Pierre Janet, L'Évolution de la mémoire et la notion de temps (Paris: Chahine, 1928).

[23] Edmund Husserl, Vorlesungen zur Phänomenologie des inneren Zeitbewusstseins (Ed. by M. Heidegger) (Halle: Niemeyer, 1928).

[24] Martin Heidegger, Sein und Zeit (Halle: Niemeyer, 1927).

[25] Johannes Volkelt, Phänomenologie und Metaphysik der Zeit (Munich: C. H. Beck, 1925).

[26] E. Minkowski, Le Temps vécu.

with time. Marked differences will strike us at once. Here is the activist, concerned with filling up every minute of every day with as much activity as possible; his slogans are: "Don't waste your time"; "Don't let people steal your time"; "Time is money." In contrast, there is the lackadaisical use of time, personified by the Italian *Lazzaroni* or, in Russian literature, by Oblomoff, the hero of Gontcharoff's famous novel. Between these extremes lies the contemplative, absorbed with his quiet vision of the universe and the silent growing up of his inmost self. The pseudo mystic, on the other hand, is striving to transcend common time by means of certain drug experiences in which he has the feeling of living whole years in a few hours. For certain neurotic or psychopathic personalities, time is boredom; one must "kill time" (which is perhaps a way of killing oneself). In a quite different style, the compulsive neurotic wastes his time by endless procrastination and suddenly becomes stingy with it (as shown by Von Gebsattel in his contribution to this book). It is obvious that such conspicuous differences in the time behavior of these individuals must be correlated with different ways of experiencing time subjectively.

Thus we come now to the phenomenological investigation of experienced time, of the subjective time of one's inner experience. What is the most immediate, subjective experience of time? It is of the *flowing of life*, experienced as a spontaneous, living energy. This is illustrated in such metaphors as "the stream of consciousness" (William James), "vital impetus" (Bergson), and *Werdezeit*, *i.e.*, "becoming time" (Von Gebsattel). This flowing is continuous; it exists in its own right, *i.e.*, independently from the sequence of events that may take place at the same time. Phenomenological investigation showed that the main and most disturbing experience in depressive conditions is an arrest—in other words, flowing back—of the stream of time.

Time is experienced as flowing with a certain *speed*. The speed of time, an intricate phenomenon, must not be confused with the "personal tempo" of movement and action proper to every individual [27] or with the conscious or unconscious appreciation of the duration of time.[28] The feeling of the

[27] William Stern was one of the first to give proper attention to this phenomenon. Later studies have shown that the "personal tempo" is a remarkably constant individual characteristic which is not modified with aging and is to a certain extent a hereditary characteristic. See Ida Frischeisen-Köhler, *Das persönliche Tempo* (Leipzig: Thieme, 1933).

[28] The unconscious appreciation of time is a very complex phenomenon. Experiments have shown that it depends to a large extent on the cellular metabolism: after absorption of thyroxine a certain duration of time seems to be longer than it really is; after absorption of quinine it seems to be shorter. On the other hand, there is a half-conscious appreciation of time gained by various means: becoming hungry, sensing daylight, hearing birds, etc. Finally, there are evidences of surprisingly accurate, totally unconscious appreciations of durations of time; such are the "inner alarm-clock" which enables certain individuals to wake up at any time at will, the accomplishment of post-hypnotic suggestions exactly at the required time even weeks or months after the suggestion under hypnosis, and the "secret calendar" (Stekel) according to which certain seemingly fortuitous events occur on the anniversary day of certain life-events.

speed of time (*Zeitgefühl*) is a specific factor which undergoes a fluctuating curve throughout human life. For the young child, time seems to be flowing much more slowly than for the adult, and the speed of time seems to increase with growing and aging. According to Martin Gschwind,[29] there are two periods in life when the speed of time seems to accelerate rapidly, the first one from the end of puberty up to twenty-two or twenty-four years and the other at a variable point of the second half of life. The feeling of the speed of time is modified in many conditions. One does not need to be a phenomenologist to know that time seems to flow more slowly when one experiences anxiety, boredom, grief, or sorrow but more rapidly in moments of joy, happiness, or elation. (However, the reverse is true for certain toxic conditions. Under the influence of opium, time seems to flow extremely slowly in spite of the euphoric condition.) One of the main symptoms of depression, from the phenomenological point of view, is the subjective experience of time flowing desperately slowly, stagnating, or even being arrested. Certain schizophrenics feel as if time were fixed at the present moment; hence the delusion that they are immortal, an assertion which is incomprehensible from the point of view of the normal mind, but which is quite logical when seen in the perspective of the distortions of the experience of time in these patients. The reverse experience, *i.e.*, the speed of time is increased, is a common experience in mania. According to Martin Gschwind, it is also what senile individuals experience; for them, years may seem to flow as quickly as days for the normal individual. In depressive conditions of old age, however, time seems to flow as slowly as in other depressive individuals.

Flowing time is *automatically structured* in the irreversible sequence of past, present, and future, each of them being experienced in a basically different way. Present is the "constantly now"; past is what "leaves us," although it remains more or less accessible to memory; future is that toward which we are going and is more or less open to previewing and planning. This subjective experience of the automatic structuring of time is to greater or less degree deeply distorted in many mental conditions.

The *present*, in our living experience, has nothing in common with the instant of physical time, an infinitely small point between the past and the future. Neither should it be confused with the psychophysiological "moment," *i.e.*, the minimum of time necessary to distinguish one sensorial stimulation from another.[30] William James [31] emphasized that we perceive the present as a certain quantum of duration, the "specious present," [32]

[29] Martin Gschwind, *Untersuchungen über Veränderungen der Chronognosie im Alter*, Basel, Diss. med. 1948.

[30] This characteristic has been found to be specific for each animal species. Cf. G. A. Brecher, *Zeitschrift für vergleichende Physiologie*, Vol. 18, 1932, p. 204.

[31] William James, *Principles of Psychology* (New York: Holt, 1890).

[32] William James had taken this expression from E. G. Clay, who, however, used it with a somewhat different meaning in his book *The Alternative* (1882).

which is "a saddle-back, not a knife-edge." Minkowski [33] insisted upon the difference between the "just-now" and the "present proper"; as he put it, the former is a peak and the latter a plateau. But above all, the present is experienced by the normal individual as awareness of his own activity and inmost drive to activity. "Real present," Janet said, "is for us an act, a somewhat complex state which we grasp in one act of consciousness in spite of its complexity and of its actual duration which may be more or less long." [34] Janet called this act the *présentification,* a concept not very different from what German authors termed *Eigenaktivität.* It is the act of grasping at once a certain field of phenomenal perception and a certain mental state, and bringing them into relationship with the continuity of one's past experience and expectation of the future. Some phenomenologists assume that the basic distortion in schizophrenia could be a weakening of the *présentification,* resulting in a disconnection between the past and the future.

For the normal individual, the *future* is "open" in that, although everything is uncertain except the certitude of our death whose date itself is uncertain, a large field is open to reasonable expectation and planning; in other words, a more or less precise tentative schedule is constantly projected into the future. [35] This may be deeply distorted in certain mental conditions. For the manic, as well as for many psychopaths, nothing is projected into the future, which is therefore "empty"; for the depressed, the future is inaccessible and "blocked," which is one of the worst sufferings of these patients.

The *past* is experienced as something that we "leave behind," as something that, although it no longer exists, is still for us a living reality with several special qualities: they could be described as "accessibility," "value," and "mutability." There are striking individual differences in the ways these qualities are experienced. As to *accessibility,* memory is always incomplete and imperfect; psychologists have long since demonstrated its distortions. But here there are important individual differences. Some people have a rather good and reliable knowledge of their own pasts, others not. Janet has pointed out how extraordinarily vague and inaccurate were the reports of their own lives given by the average patients of the Paris hospitals and clinics. (Freud considered this same feature as pathognomic for hysteria.) It seems that the more educated people are, the more accurate is their awareness of their own past, a fact which seems to confirm Halbwachs's theory of memory. [36] In regard to the *value* of the past, some people experience it

33 E. Minkowski, *Le Temps vécu,* pp. 30–34.

34 Pierre Janet, *Les Obsessions et la psychasthénie* (Paris: Alcan, 1903), Vol. I, p. 481.

35 Nathan Israeli undertook to study experimentally this particular point by asking a number of superior adolescents and of psychotics to write their "future autobiography." See his book, *Abnormal Personality and Time* (1936).

36 Halbwachs contended that our true, conscious memory retains almost nothing of the past; what we call "memory of the past" is always a reconstruction based on social indices and on other concrete relics from the past. See his book, *Les Cadres sociaux de la mémoire* (Paris: Alcan, 1924).

as a burden by which one is oppressed or perhaps ashamed, other people as a precious stepping-stone toward the future.[37] Regarding the *mutability* of the past, it is our common experience that the past is "closed" and cannot be changed. Of course, it may contain forgotten or repressed memories whose unearthing is as startling as might be any new, unexpected event. However, in certain paranoid patients the past is highly mutable, as observed in "hallucinations of memory": they feel as if the past had been artificially changed. This experience might be compared to the distress felt by the hero of George Orwell's *1984* when aware that the "social frame of memory" was continually changed by the state police; it would be made intelligible if we assumed that these patients experience Dunne's pluridimensional time.

In the normal individual, past, present, and future, although experienced, each of them, in different ways, constitute a *structured unit,* of which Minkowski[38] made a very fine analysis. He distinguished the following zones of experienced time, which have nothing in common with chronological time:

Remote past	Zone of the obsolete (*le dépassé*)
Mediate past	Zone of the regretted
Immediate past	Zone of the remorse
Present	
Immediate future	Zone of expectation and activity
Mediate future	Zone of wish and hope
Remote future ("the horizon")	Zone of prayer and ethical action

Each of these zones must be experienced in a specific fashion in order to fit into our normal experience of time. But here also numerous distortions are possible. To give only one example, in certain life situations such as banishment[39] or forced, prolonged unemployment,[40] individuals may become unable to experience the "immediate future," with the result of a gap between the present and the mediate and remote future, a stagnation in a hypertrophic and sterile present and an inability to organize their lives in a constructive way.

What we call the feeling of the "meaning of life" cannot be understood independently of the subjective feeling of experienced time. Distortions of the feeling of time necessarily result in distortions of the meaning of life. Normally, we look upon the future not only for itself but also for compensating and correcting the past and the present. We reckon on the future for paying our debts, achieving success, enjoying life, becoming good Christians. Wherever the future becomes empty, as with manics and certain psychopaths,

[37] Gerhard Pfahler, *Der Mensch und seine Vergangenheit* (Stuttgart: Klett, 1950).
[38] E. Minkowski, *Le Temps vécu*, pp. 72–120, 138–158.
[39] José Solanes, "Exil et temps vécu," *L'Hygiène mentale*, 1948, pp. 62–78.
[40] M. Lazarsfeld-Jahoda and H. Zeisl, *Die Arbeitslosen von Marienthal* (Leipzig: Hirzel, 1933), pp. 59–69.

life is a perpetual gamble and the advantage of the present minute is taken into consideration; wherever the future is inaccessible or blocked, as with the depressed, hope necessarily disappears and life loses all meaning.

The outlook on the future and the past involves the length of time that comes under our full awareness. De Greeff [41] summarizes it as follows: The one-year-old child lives in the present, the three-year-old child realizes that there are regular hours of the day; with four years comes the concept of the "today" and with five years the concept of the yesterday and tomorrow; at eight years, the child counts in weeks, each of which seems interminable; at fifteen, the time unit is the month, at about twenty the year; whereas the forty-year-old man counts in groups of years and the decades. De Greeff gives as one of the characteristics of the feeble-minded the inability to get an outlook on more than the preceding and following twenty days. A narrowing of the awareness of the past and future may also be found in many unstable and psychopathic individuals and in certain schizophrenics. The figures given by De Greeff may be somewhat schematic and subject to much individual variation, and, furthermore, people are interested to very different degrees in the past and the future.

This last point has led several authors to distinguish two types of individuals: the *"prospective"* and the *"retrospective."* The former are "looking forward" to the future, the latter "leaning on the past," as the French say. It would be wrong to equate the "prospective" with the young and healthy and the "retrospective" with the aged and sick. Some children manifest much interest for their own pasts, family tradition, and history; some aged people concentrate on the vision of the future and on working for their descendants and the centuries to come. These two types had been called by H. G. Wells the "legal type" and the "legislative, constructive type," by Porteus and Babcock the "retrovert" and "antevert." [42] Bouman and Grünbaum [43] demonstrated clinical implications of this type distinction, but rather than making the sharp distinction of two opposite types, they contend that in each individual there is a "temporal complexus" with prospective and retrospective aspects according to a formula which is specific for the individual. Minkowski believes that the distinction of the "prospective" and the "retrospective" is as important as the distinction of the "extravert" and the "introvert." However, one should not overlook the fact that there are different ways of looking toward the past and the future: as Israeli pointed out, an individual's concern with the future can be "constructive," "catastrophic," "confused," "delusional," etc.

41 Etienne de Greeff, "La personnalité du débile mental," *Journal de Psychologie*, Vol. 24, 1927, pp. 434–439.

42 Quoted by N. Israeli, *Abnormal Personality and Time*, p. 118.

43 Leendert Bouman and A. A. Grünbaum, "Eine Störung der Chronognosie und ihre Bedeutung im betreffenden Symptomenbild," *Monatsschrift für Psychiatrie und Neurologie*, Vol. 73, 1929, pp. 1–39.

Of the other phenomenological implications of time, we will mention only one more. We feel that time flows not only for us but also for the rest of the world. Our personal time must be *inserted into the social, historical, and cosmic time*. Minkowski states that schizoid individuals live more in their own, personal time than in the world time. This is still more the case in certain schizophrenics who seem to lose all awareness of the world time. The ordinary melancholic patient, on the other hand, is still aware of both forms of time, but his personal time flows much more slowly than the world time.

2. Spatiality

In common psychiatric practice, the concern with space is limited to determining whether the patient is disoriented in space or has some conspicuous symptoms such as micropsia. In phenomenological psychiatry, the investigation of spatiality is as basic and must be as thorough as that of temporality.

Space in common-sense and daily life is but one form of a more inclusive concept, spatiality, and many forms of spatiality have been described by philosophers, physicists, mathematicians, and psychologists.

Whereas certain philosophers identified space with matter (Descartes) or with one attribute of God (Spinoza), others consider it an abstraction, or an "a priori form of sensibility" (Kant) which we project into our vision of the world.

Physical concepts of space, to describe another of the forms, have changed greatly with the progress of astronomy and physics. The Babylonians and early Greeks (Anaximander) visualized space as having an absolute up and down. Parmenides visualized it as a finite sphere, outside of which there could be neither something (since all being was inside) nor nothing (since the "nothing" could not exist), and at the center of which was the earth. With Galileo and Newton, came the concept of a homogeneous and infinite space ("a sphere whose center is everywhere and its periphery nowhere," Pascal said). In our time, Einstein introduced the concept of space as heterogeneous and finite.

For the mathematician, on the other hand, space is an abstract measurable continuum in which each part is external to each of the other parts. Its attributes are homogeneity, continuity, infinity, and isotropism (the last term meaning that the three axes in which space can be measured have the same properties). Euclidian space, is said to be three-dimensional and homaloidal (meaning that one can construct in it similar figures on any scale). These two attributes disappear in the so-called non-Euclidian spaces, or *hyperspaces*. Mathematicians conceive and compute the properties of four-dimensional, five-dimensional, *n*-dimensional spaces, of space where the postulatum of Euclid is no longer valid. This means that in such spaces one can draw more than one parallel to a line through a certain point, or no parallel at all.

So numerous have been the studies by experimental psychologists on the perception of space, its genetic development, its individual particularities, its distortions, and the like that we must omit them altogether. But among the contributions of phenomenologists (over and above those of Husserl and Heidegger) there are publications by Straus,[44] Binswanger,[45] Minkowski,[46] and Merleau-Ponty's book on the phenomenology of perception is of great importance.[47]

In the clinical investigation of spatiality, we should start with the individual's most conspicuous attitude toward space. Individuals afflicted with agoraphobia or claustrophobia obviously must have a very disturbed subjective experience of space, but there are many other ways of dealing with space. One individual is striving to conquer or explore it, another to keep and defend it, a third to organize and utilize it, another to delineate and measure it. Some people "make themselves broad"; they need a large *Lebensraum*. Other people "constrict" themselves and content themselves with narrow life spaces. One can be "rooted" in a place or be "uprooted" and wandering. One can also escape from a place and take flight, either in real space through emigration, elopement, fugues, etc., or in the many modalities of sublimated or unsublimated phantasy. But this consideration is only a preliminary step to the properly phenomenological investigation of experienced spatiality. An individual can experience spatiality in very different ways, in normal and in abnormal conditions, and we want to sketch several of the most important of these modalities of spatial experience.

Oriented space is the form of spatiality of our most common experience. Even when we believe that "true space" is the abstract, homogeneous, infinite, and empty continuum of the mathematicians, our daily experience is of oriented space. In contrast to the isotropism of mathematical space, oriented space is "anisotropic," *i.e.*, each dimension has different, specific values. There is a vertical axis, with its up and down. There is a wide, horizontal plane, in which before and behind, right and left are differentiated. Two lines of the same length have a very different value if they are in our "near space" or "remote space," if they are between two objects or between us and an object. In oriented space, "great" and "small" are not relative measures but well-defined, qualitatively different sizes. We cannot

44 Erwin Straus, "Die Formen des Räumlichen. Ihre Bedeutung für die Motorik und die Wahrnehmung," *Der Nervenarzt*, Vol. 3, 1930, pp. 633–656.

45 L. Binswanger, "Das Raumproblem in der Psychopathologie (1932)," *Ausgewählte Vorträge und Aufsätze* (Bern: Francke, 1955), Vol. II, pp. 174–225. Binswanger gave the first detailed study of the phenomenology of spatiality in a clinical condition, mania, in his book *Über Ideenflucht* (Zurich: Orell-Füssli, 1933).

46 E. Minkowski, "Vers une psychopathologie de l'espace vécu," in *Le Temps vécu*, pp. 366–398.

47 M. Merleau-Ponty, *Phénoménologie de la perception*.

visualize oriented space as an empty continuum; it has limitations and contents; it is mapped by objects (which have an inside and an outside), distances, directions, roads, and boundaries. We know that the horizon and the celestial dome are not scientific concepts; but for our daily experience and for phenomenology, they are very important entities.[48]

One of the major features of oriented space is that it has a center of reference that is itself mobile: the body. It is the human body that conditions our experience of space. The vertical axis with its up and down is revealed to us by the effects of gravity on the changing positions of the body and the erect station. Because there is a variety of sensory organs, we are able to distinguish near space (through the touch) and remoter space (through audition and vision). Because the sensory organs are on different parts of the mobile body, we become aware of directions in space. The coordination of the various fields of perception and the fact that we are able to move in space result in the construction of our oriented space.

Much research has been devoted by experimental psychologists and by phenomenologists to the investigation of the various subtypes of space, as given separately by each of our sensory functions. Kinesthetic space, tactile space, visual space, auditory space have been described, as well as the special ways in which space is experienced by the blind, the deaf, the crippled. We cannot enlarge on these points and must point out the fact that phenomenology is also concerned with other forms of spatiality, of a very different nature.

Attuned space (*gestimmter Raum*) was described by Binswanger [49] as the spatial experience determined by one's feeling tone or emotional pitch. At the same moment that one is experiencing oriented space, the reference point of which is one's own body, one is also experiencing a special quality of space in accord with one's mood. The pitch or tone of one's inside oriented space may be one of fullness or emptiness; it may be felt as expanding or constricting. The outside oriented space may have a hollow tone or a rich, expressive, "physiognomic" tone.[50] Love, for instance, is "space-binding": the lover feels himself close to the beloved in spite of the distance, because in the spatial modality of love distance is transcended. Happiness expands the attuned space; things are felt as "aggrandized" (which is quite different from macropsia!). Sorrow constricts attuned space, and despair makes it

[48] One will find a phenomenological study on the horizon by J. Lindschoten and on the celestial space by Gusdorf in *Situation* (Utrecht: 1954), Vol. I.

[49] L. Binswanger, *Ausgewählte Vorträge und Aufsätze*, Vol. II, pp. 174–225.

[50] We regret that the frame of this chapter does not permit us to discuss the phenomenologically very important difference between "signal" and "indice" upon which Husserl has insisted. Expression and physiognomy should not be confused with signal and communication. As an illustration of the "physiognomic aspect of the world," see Von Gebsattel's paper showing how, for the compulsive neurotic, the physiognomic aspect of the world becomes overwhelming, taking on at the same time the specific physiognomy of decay. Straus contrasts this peculiar aspect to the "physiognomy of the wonderful," typical for the subjective experience in acute hashish intoxication.

empty. In schizophrenic experience, attuned space loses its consistency, either in a progressive way (as in the case of Ellen West, described in this book) or sometimes in a sudden, dramatic way (this is the *Weltuntergangsgefühl*, the feeling of the end of the world, of certain schizophrenics).

Binswanger pointed out the fact that, in organic diseases of the brain, the patient suffers deterioration of oriented space; in manic depressive disease and schizophrenia, more deterioration of attuned space. In experimental psychoses (hashish, mescaline, and others), there are distortions of both forms of spatiality.

Binswanger contended that his concept of attuned space includes, as subtypes, certain varieties of spatiality that have been described by other writers. A notable example is Straus's description of the "dance space." [51] Dance cannot exist in a "pure" state; it needs music which fills and homogenizes space. In the space of dance, as in all kinds of attuned space, there is no "historical movement"; the movement is of ebbing and flowing. The dance space is not determined by distance, direction, size, and limitation but is the elective medium of rhythm and of demonstrative movements; distance is not a quantity but a quality of that space. We refer to Straus's article on aesthesiology, included in this volume, in which such matters are discussed.

Minkowski's [52] descriptions of "clear" and "dark" space seem to constitute other subtypes of attuned space. *Clear space* is not only the space of horizon, perspective, and distinctness; its fundamental characteristic is what Minkowski calls the *distance vécue* (experienced distance): between individuals there is felt "free space" that enables the fortuitous, the unforeseen, the emotionally neutral and results in a certain "amplitude of life" (we would say a larger "playground of life"). *Dark space,* as we experience it in obscurity or in a fog, is more than the mere absence of light, of horizon and perspective. Phenomenologically, darkness is a black, thick, and gloomy substance. Since the "experienced distance" disappears, there is no more "life amplitude," vital space is narrowed, space is desocialized, it surrounds the individual and even penetrates his body. According to Minkowski, this kind of space experience is the substratum of delusions of persecution. "The normal opposite of delusions of persecution is not the awareness of benevolence . . . but the feeling of easiness in life, whether life be good or bad for us, a feeling intimately connected with the phenomena of experienced distance and life amplitude" (Minkowski). Thus, a certain type of paranoid hallucination becomes intelligible if one realizes its background of dark space superimposed on the patient's ordinary clear space.

To these dark and clear spaces, a third might be added—*luminous space,* where the subject is, as it were, blinded by an intensive light. This form of spatiality seems to underlie a number of mystical and ecstatic experiences,

51 Erwin Straus, *op. cit.,* pp. 633–656.
52 E. Minkowski, "Vers une psychopathologie de l'espace vécu," in *Le Temps vécu,* pp. 366–398.

and there is a considerable literature devoted to "mystic space." The apostle saint Paul speaks of "the breadth and length, and depth, and height" of the Love of God (Eph. iv:18). Jewish mystics of the Middle Ages devoted treatises to the measurement of the Glory of God, computed with mystic measurement units.[53] These strange speculations no doubt expressed profound and intimate experiences which these mystics were unable to convey in a clearer form. Experiences of a "mystic space" have been reported by an impressive number of seers in many countries and centuries. Guido Huber [54] collected a number of relevant texts and tried to define the common characteristics ascribed to mystic space: the fusion of the subject and the object in a "cosmic consciousness"; the experience of a radically different space in which distance and size are transcended, where immense spaces are contained in small ones, where the universe is at the same time empty and filled with blinding light, etc. The experience which Freud called "oceanic feeling" seems to be a subtype of this experience of mystic space.

Binswanger's study [55] defines other forms of spatiality ("historical," "mythical," "aesthetic," "technical," etc.), for which we cannot pause, although their existence should be kept in mind. We must now return to the topic of oriented space and mention that there are, at least theoretically, an infinite variety of oriented spaces, apart from the oriented space of our daily experience, which we described earlier.

Let us consider the structure of space in some of Chagall's paintings. We notice that space is less "anisotropic" than our common space, *i.e.*, the three dimensions of space are not so sharply differentiated. In the painting "Homage to the Eiffel Tower," trees cross the air horizontally from left to right and right to left; an angel floats through a window-pane, whereas the houses and people are in the vertical axis and the Eiffel Tower slightly curved. In others of Chagall's paintings there is no size and no proportions, things are superimposed while remaining distinct from each other. It is, in short, another type of "oriented space" different from our everyday experience, and in the same relation to the latter as is a non-Euclidian to Euclidian space.

Another example: People who attend certain kinds of three-dimensional moving pictures (the Cinerama) are often struck by the vague strangeness of the pictures; although perhaps more beautiful than nature, they have something unreal. Close observation will show that in that space there are fewer straight lines and more curves than usual, and that this space is also hypersymmetrical (not to speak of the predominance of certain colors). These slight modifications from our usual oriented space suffice to confer upon that world a queer aspect of unreality.

[53] Gershon G. Scholem, *Major Trends in Jewish Mysticism* (New York: Shocken Books, 1946), pp. 63–70.
[54] Guido Huber, *Akdçd—der mystische Raum* (Zurich: Origo-Verlag, 1955).
[55] L. Binswanger, "Das Raumproblem in der Psychopathologie."

We are now perhaps better prepared to come to the clinical use of spatiality. From the point of view of oriented space, Weckowicz [56] has shown experimentally that many schizophrenics have anomalies of visual perception, and Humphrey Osmond [57] has shown that these anomalies justify important implications for the architecture of mental hospitals. But the distortions of attuned space are no less important in schizophrenia (we recall Minkowski's considerations on the role of dark space as substratum of delusions of persecution). In another group of schizophrenics, the basic spatial disturbance seems to be rather an undue intrusion of mathematical space into oriented space. Minkowski [58] described the "morbid geometrism," the predilection for hypersymmetry, of certain schizophrenics. Another group of schizophrenics feel that they are watched from outside by invisible observers who are nowhere in our three-dimensional space; the patients hear voices whose reality they do not question, although they recognize that nobody could be there according to the known laws of reality. Such phenomena could be made intelligible if we assumed that these patients experience a four-dimensional type of spatiality and that the fourth dimension is open toward them: from it they are watched and spoken to.

In summary, one of the main findings of phenomenology has been that hallucination and delusion cannot be understood without the knowledge of the patient's spatial experience. As Merleau-Ponty [59] put it excellently: "What guarantees the healthy man against delusion or hallucination is not his reality testing but the structure of his space." [60]

This structure of spatiality is complex and differs greatly from one individual to the other. A phenomenological analysis of oriented space must examine its component elements, among which are its boundaries, right and left distance, direction, and the vertical axis.

The *vertical axis,* according to Binswanger [61] and to Bachelard,[62] is the basic axis of human existence to which our most vital experiences are related. Life is felt as a constant movement upward or downward. The movement upward is expressed metaphorically as becoming lighter, being "elevated, "uplifted" to a realm of light and peace; the movement downwards is expressed in being "abased," "falling," "becoming heavier," "dejected," "downcast."

56 T. E. Weckowicz, *Size Constancy in Schizophrenic Patients.* (Unpublished, communicated by the author.)

57 Humphrey Osmond, *Function as the Basis of Psychiatric Ward Design.* (Unpublished, communicated by the author.)

58 E. Minkowski, *La Schizophrénie.*

59 M. Merleau-Ponty, *Phénoménologie de la perception,* p. 337.

60 Distortions of experienced space occur also, of course, in other psychiatric conditions. An excellent study of such distortions in melancholia has been given by Hubert Tellenbach, "Die Räumlichkeit der Melancholie," *Nervenarzt,* Vol. 27, 1956, pp. 12–18, 289–298.

61 L. Binswanger, "Traum und Existenz," in *Ausgewählte Vorträge und Aufsätze.* Vol. I, pp. 74–97.

62 Gaston Bachelard, *L'Air et les songes* (Paris: Corti, 1943).

Distance also has many phenomenological implications. Alfred Adler [63] described the various ways in which a neurotic puts "distance" between himself and his life goal, the world, and his fellow men. Minkowski [64] analyzed another type of "experienced distance": the "free space" which we normally feel around us, which gives us "amplitude of life," and which is sorely missing in many neurotics and schizophrenics. Interesting clinical studies based on the phenomenological analysis of distance have been published by Roland Kuhn [65] and by D. Cargnello.[66]

Two specific types of distance are called by animal psychologists [67] the *flight distance* (the distance at which an animal takes flight from a man) and the *critical distance* (the distance—of course a shorter one—at which the animal turns from flight to counterattack). Both are specific characteristics of each animal species and can be accurately measured within an inch. It is by his perfect knowledge of these distances that the tamer is able to maneuver and, subsequently, to tame his animals. Recently, these concepts have been applied to the study of hospitalized chronic mental patients.[68] And it is possible to compare this use of spatial distance by the tamer with the use of psychological distance by the psychotherapist. Does not the psychotherapist, in his study of the defenses of his patient, constantly feel the emotional distance required to provoke withdrawal (flight distance) and aggressive responses (critical distance)?

It is not possible to do justice to the rich phenomenological implications of the concepts of symmetry and asymmetry (and the symbolic meaning of right and left) [69] and of the concepts of boundaries and limitations [70] within the scope of this paper.

3. Causality

In the experience of the normal, civilized man, the realm of causality is divided among three principles: *determinism, chance,* and *intentionality* (by which we mean either biological finality or free and conscious human

[63] Alfred Adler, "Das Problem der 'Distanz,'" in *Praxis und Theorie der Individual-Psychologie* (Munich: Bergmann, 1924), pp. 71–76.

[64] E. Minkowski, *Le Temps vécu*, pp. 366–398.

[65] R. Kuhn, "Zur Daseinsanalyse der anorexia mentalis," *Nervenarzt*, Vol. 22, 1951, pp. 11–13.

[66] Danilo Cargnello, "Sul Problema psicopatologico della 'Distanza' esistenziale," *Archivio di psicologia, Neurologia e Psichiatria*, Vol. 14, 1953, pp. 435–463.

[67] Heini Hediger, *Skizzen zu einer Tierpsychologie im Zoo und im Zirkus* (Zurich: Büchergilde Gutenberg, 1954), pp. 214–244.

[68] B. Staehelin, Gesetzmässigkeiten im Gemeinschaftsleben schwer Geisteskranker, *Schweizer Archiv für Neurologie und Psychiatrie*, Vol. 72, 1953, pp. 277–298.

[69] Stekel was probably the first to point out the meaning of right and left in the symbolism of dreams and neurotic symptoms. Cf. *Die Sprache des Traumes* (Munich: Bergmann, 1911).

[70] Cf. R. Kuhn, "Daseinsanalytische Studie über die Bedeutung von Grenzen im Wahn," *Monatsschrift für Psychiatrie und Neurologie*, Vol. 124, 1952, pp. 354–383.

intentions). We know that determinism predominates in the subjective experience of the melancholic and chance in the experience of the manic. The manic lives in a world of complete irresponsibility where he is bound neither by the past nor by the future, where everything happens through sheer chance; the melancholic, on the other hand, feeling himself crushed under the weight of his past, acts without feeling that he could change anything, because almost nothing is left to the realm of chance or free will. These two principles, determinism and chance, recede into the background in certain paranoiacs, who, in the most fortuitous incidents, see nothing but intentions analogous to human intentions.

4. Materiality (Substance)

After temporality, spatiality, and causality, a phenomenological analysis should take into consideration the substance of the world itself, as it manifests itself in its physical qualities: consistency (the fluid, the soft, the viscous); tension, shock, heaviness, and lightness; the hot and the cold; light, color (the depressed patient "sees in black" and the manic "in rose"), etc. For example, in his existential analytic study on flight of ideas in manic patients, Binswanger [71] found the following features, among others, in his patients' worlds: A consistency characterized by lightness, softness, plasticity, and multiformity; and optical qualities of brightness, colorfulness, rosiness, and luminosity.

Furthermore, a phenomenological analysis has to consider the distribution and relative predominance of the four elements—fire, air, water, earth—in the patients' subjective worlds. Bachelard's [72] research in this field is of basic importance. In the *Case of Ellen West*, which appears in this volume, the reader will see the role Binswanger ascribes to the elements of "air" and "earth" in the contrasting worlds of subjective experience of the patient.

The investigation of the category of materiality can be extended also to the vegetable and the animal kingdoms. An instance of such an analysis is Bachelard's study [73] of the French surrealist poet Lautréamont. Analyzing his metaphors, Bachelard found that a surprising number of them were borrowed from the animal kingdom, most involving ferocious animals and emphasizing claws and suckers. From this "animal index," Bachelard drew many inferences concerning the inner universe and deeper personality of Lautréamont. Such an approach reminds one of what a phenomenologically oriented psychologist may sometimes find in the "animal responses" of a Rorschach test.

[71] L. Binswanger, *Über Ideenflucht.*

[72] Gaston Bachelard, *La Psychanalyse du feu* (Paris: Gallimard, 1938); *L'Eau et les rêves* (Paris: Corti, 1942); *L'Air et les songes* (Paris: Corti, 1943); *La Terre et les rêveries du repos* (Paris: Corti, 1948); *La Terre et les rêveries de la volonté* (Paris: Corti, 1948).

[73] Gaston Bachelard, *Lautréamont* (Paris: Corti, 1939).

5. Reconstruction of Inner Worlds

Whatever the method used for a phenomenological analysis, the aim of the investigation is the reconstruction of the inner world of experience of the subject. Each individual has his own way of experiencing temporality, spatiality, causality, materiality, but each of these coordinates must be understood in relation to the others and to the total inner "world."

Take, for instance, the case of Minkowski's schizophrenic depressive patient included in this volume. Here Minkowski started his analysis with the patient's experience of time, which gave immediate clues for the investigation. But he also came to see that "the patient's mind had lost the ability to stop and fix itself at each object's boundaries" (thus, a distortion of spatiality) and that he did not believe that anything could happen by chance (causality). We find no mention of air, water, or fire in the patient's delusions but there are many references to metallic and earthly substances (materiality).

It is not less important to consider the relative importance of the phenomenological coordinates to each other. In certain schizophrenics, Minkowski [74] found that their time/space index was deviated, in the sense that they devalued time and overestimated space. This was expressed by the "spatialization of thought" and "morbid geometrism" of these patients. Reading the newspaper, one of them declared that the enlargement of a railway station—a spatial event—was much more important than the fluctuations of the financial situation—a temporal event. They lacked the ability to assimilate any kind of movement and duration. One of them wished he could keep an "intermediary" day between the "abyss" of the past and the "mountain" of the future. Their hatred of movement explained their predilection for rigid time schedules and their stiff and stubborn attitudes in life. "Spatial thought" was manifest in their love of symmetry, in the "architectural characteristics" of their reasoning, in their preference for big chests, massive building-stones, thick walls, and locked doors. This love of symmetry went so far that one of them deplored the fact that his body was not a sphere, *i.e.*, a perfect geometrical form.

Specific phenomenological worlds have also been described outside of psychopathology. Eduard Renner,[75] a proponent of "ethno-phenomenology," contended that there was no such thing as "primitive mind," but two fundamental, antagonistic outlines of the world: the *magic* and the *animistic* worlds, of which he gave excellent phenomenological analyses.[76] In the

---

[74] E. Minkowski, *La Schizophrénie*.

[75] Eduard Renner, *Goldener Ring über Uri* (Zurich: M. S. Metz, 1941).

[76] Example: In the tale *Peter Schlemihl* by Chamisso, the devil takes from his pocket a first aid kit, a telescope, and a horse. In a popular tale, the treasure of an enchanted castle was opened every year for a few minutes, at Christmas Eve. A woman entered there to

magic world, Renner said, space and time are properties of substances. In the animistic world, space and time not only contain the substances, but they are themselves substantified, endowed with the quality of a substance and therefore with wonderful properties. These concepts of Renner might seem to be far removed from psychiatry, but in fact it is striking to see how similar these "magic" and "animist" worlds are to some of the temporal-spatial structures that phenomenological investigations occasionally find in dreams and in certain schizophrenic conditions.

Remarks. Although phenomenology focuses upon subjective states of consciousness, there is often much overlap with the findings of behavioral and experimental psychology. On the other hand, psychoanalysis contributed to many phenomenological findings. But phenomenology essentially ignores psychic and physical causality, in contrast to psychoanalysis, whose orientation is historical and causal, even when considering the experiences of time and space.[77] Phenomenological and psychoanalytic studies may be mutually enriching because of the stereoscopic effect, as it were, of focusing from two different points of view.

III *Existential Analysis*

The reconstruction of the inner world of the patient may be an aim in itself for the phenomenologist, but if he is an existential analyst, it is a part of a broader task to which we are coming now. It is necessary at this point, however, to clarify the distinction between *existentialist philosophy*, *existentialist psychotherapy*, and Binswanger's *existential analysis*, since there is so much confusion concerning these three areas.

A *Existentialist Philosophy*

Existentialism is the philosophical trend of thought which takes as its focus of interest the consideration of man's most immediate experience, his own existence. Existentialist thinking has been implicit from time immemorial in many religions and philosophical systems. Kierkegaard was the

---

take some gold, but forgot her baby. Next year, she returned there at the same time, and found her baby alive, at the same spot: it had not changed, because time had not flown for it. In other tales, a traveler spends a few days on an enchanted island and, returning home, finds that fifty years have flown: whereas his companions were all dead or very old, he had kept the same age. All these instances are characteristic of the "magic" world where time and space are properties of things.

77 W. Clifford M. Scott, in his paper, "Some Psycho-dynamic Aspects of Disturbed Perception of Time," *British Journal of Medical Psychology*, Vol. 21, Part 2, 1948, pp. 111–120, gives good examples of distortions in the perception of time in connection with unconscious tendencies; these distortions disappeared through analytic insight into their psychogenesis.

first to make explicit its basic assumptions. In our time these concepts have been elaborated by Jaspers, Heidegger, Sartre, and the religious existentialists (Marcel, Berdyaev, Tillich). The main influence upon psychiatry came from Heidegger.

In Heidegger's thought we can distinguish three main sources:

1. Starting point was the old problem of being versus existence. Ancient philosophers contrasted "essence" and "existence." The abstract concept and knowledge of a triangle reveals to us the "essence" of the triangle; an actually drawn triangle demonstrates its "existence." Plato's essentialist philosophy contended that everything that exists is the reflection of an essence (or "idea"). Modern philosophers, notably Dilthey, focused the problem on the fact that the concept of existence must be very different for an inanimate object and for human beings. Heidegger's philosophy is based on the contrast between existence as *Vorhandensein* (characteristic of things) and as *Dasein* (for human beings). The untranslatable word *Dasein* designates the mode of existence peculiar to human beings. Thus Heidegger's philosophy is a *Daseinsanalytik* (analysis of the structure of *Dasein*).

2. Some of the main features of the structure of human existence had already been outlined by Kierkegaard. Man is not a ready-made being; man will become what he makes of himself and nothing more. Man constructs himself through his choices, because he has the freedom to make vital choices, above all the freedom to choose between an *inauthentic* and an *authentic* modality of existence. Inauthentic existence is the modality of the man who lives under the tyranny of the *plebs* (the crowd, *i.e.*, the anonymous collectivity). Authentic existence is the modality in which a man assumes the responsibility of his own existence. In order to pass from inauthentic to authentic existence, a man has to suffer the ordeal of despair and "existential anxiety," *i.e.*, the anxiety of a man facing the limits of his existence with its fullest implications: death, nothingness. This is what Kierkegaard calls the "sickness unto death."

3. Heidegger was a pupil of Husserl and took over from his master the principles of phenomenology. Heidegger's philosophy is, in the main, a phenomenology of human *Dasein*.[78] It is an analysis of unparalleled subtlety and profundity and one of the greatest philosophical achievements of all times.

This philosophical system influenced psychiatry in three ways: (1) It stimulated the development of an *existentialist psychotherapy*. (2) It exerted an influence on such psychiatrists as Alfred Storch [79] and Hans Kunz.[80]

[78] Martin Heidegger, *Sein und Zeit* (Halle: Niemeyer, 1926).
[79] Alfred Storch, "Die Welt der beginnenden Schizophrenie," *Zeitschrift für die gesammte Neurologie und Psychiatrie*, Vol. 127, 1930, pp. 799–810.
[80] Hans Kunz, "Die Grenze der psychopathologischen Wahninterpretationen," *Zeitschrift für die gesammte Neurologie und Psychiatrie*, Vol. 135, 1931, pp. 671–715.

(3) It inspired the elaboration of a new psychiatric system, Ludwig Binswanger's *Daseinsanalyse* (existential analysis).

B *Existentialist Psychotherapy*

Existentialist psychotherapy is simply the application of certain existentialist concepts to psychotherapy, without regard to phenomenology and psychoanalysis. It should not be confused with Binswanger's existential analysis. There is no standard system or method of existentialist psychotherapy, but three of its concepts are especially worthy of attention.

1. The concept of *existential neurosis, i.e.,* illnesses arising not so much from repressed traumata, a weak ego, or life-stress, but rather from the individual's inability to see meaning in life, so that he lives an inauthentic existential modality. The problem for him is to find meaning in life and to pass to an authentic modality of existence.[81]

2. Existentialist psychotherapy prefers, to the use of psychoanalytic transference, the use of another interpersonal experience, "encounter." Encounter [82] is, in general, not so much the fortuitous meeting and first acquaintance of two individuals, but rather the decisive inner experience resulting from it for one (sometimes for both) of the two individuals. Something totally new is revealed, new horizons open, one's *weltanschauung* is revised, and sometimes the whole personality is restructured. Such encounters are manifold, perhaps with a philosopher who reveals a new way of thinking or with a man of great life experience, of practical understanding of human nature, of heroic achievements, of independent personality. An encounter can bring a sudden liberation from ignorance or illusion, enlarge the spiritual horizon, and give a new meaning to life.

It is obvious that "encounter" has nothing in common with "transference" in the stricter meaning given to this word by Freud. Far from being a revival of an ancient interpersonal relationship, encounter works through the very fact of its novelty. On the other hand, it is not to be confounded with "identification." If the personality of the subject is changed, it means not that he copies a model but that the model serves as a catalyst in whose presence he comes to realize his latent and best abilities and to shape his own self (in Jung's terminology, to accomplish a progress in his "individuation").

81 Viktor Frankl, *Theorie und Therapie der Neurosen* (Wien: Urban und Schwarzenberg, 1956).

82 See, about the "encounter," F. J. Buytendijk, "Zur Phänomenologie der Begegnung," *Eranos-Jahrbuch*, Vol. 19, 1950, pp. 431–486—about the psychotherapeutic implications, Hans Trüb, *Heilung aus der Begegnung* (Healing Through Encounter) (Stuttgart: Klett, 1951).

3. Some psychotherapists make use of another existentialist concept, *kairos*. This Greek word meant, in Hippocratic medicine, the typical moment when an acute disease was expected to change its course for better or worse; "critical" symptoms would appear at this point for a short time, indicating the new direction; and the proficient physician would prove his capacity by his way of handling the situation. This long forgotten concept was revived in the theological field by Paul Tillich [83] and introduced in psychotherapy by Arthur Kielholz.[84]

Good psychotherapists have always known that there are specific times when a certain patient is inwardly ready for a certain kind of intervention and that the intervention is likely to be fully successful at such times, whereas it would be premature before and without prospects later. Agents of temperance societies have often demonstrated their ability to choose such a time for an interview with an alcoholic. They try to choose the moment when the drinker is close to despair, realizing that he is falling into the abyss and aware of his incapacity to help himself, yet has not completely given up any wish of salvation. According to Kielholz, similar instances of a critical, decisive point—of *kairos*—are not rare among neurotic, psychopathic, or even psychotic individuals. Unfortunately, the concept of a psychotherapeutic treatment is often associated with the idea of a standard course of development involving a slow elaboration and resolution of transference, without much concern for moments when time suddenly acquires a qualitatively different value. Such critical points, when adequately handled, enable a skillful psychotherapist to obtain a surprisingly rapid cure of cases which were considered severe, if not desperate.

C *Binswanger's Existential Analysis*

What Binswanger termed *Daseinsanalyse* (Existential Analysis) represents a synthesis of psychoanalysis, phenomenology, and existentialist concepts modified by original new insights. It is a reconstruction of the inner world of experience of psychiatric patients with the help of a conceptual framework inspired by Heidegger's studies on the structure of human existence.

Binswanger, a psychiatrist of the school of Eugen Bleuler, was one of the first Swiss followers of Freud. Then, in the early 1920's, he became, with Eugene Minkowski, one of the first proponents of psychiatric phenomenology. With his paper "Dream and Existence" (1930) and his studies on mania (1931–1932), he shifted toward existential analysis. His system was expounded in 1942 in his major work [85] and later illustrated in a number

83 Paul Tillich, *Kairos* (Darmstadt: Reichl, 1926).

84 A. Kielholz, "Vom Kairos," *Schweizerische Medizinische Wochenschrift*, Vol. 86, 1956, pp. 982–984.

85 L. Binswanger, *Grundformen und Erkenntnis menschlichen Daseins* (Zurich: Max Niehans, 1942).

of clinical cases, the first of which, "Ellen West," is given for the first time in English translation in this volume.

Binswanger was also influenced by Martin Buber's book *I and Thou*.[86] Buber described in poetic style how the pronoun "I" has two very different meanings, depending upon its relation to a "thou" or a "him." In the sphere of the I-Thou, "I" is expressed with one's whole being and expects reciprocity; it is the sphere of the "encounter," of the primary human relationships, and of the Spirit. In the sphere of I-Him, "I" is expressed with a part of one's being; it is the sphere of utilitarian relationships. Binswanger developed these ideas, with his descriptions of the "dual" and the "plural" modes of existence, to which he added a "singular" and an "anonymous" mode.

There are a few differences between phenomenology and existential analysis:

1. Existential analysis does not restrict itself to the investigation of states of *consciousness,* but takes into account the entire structure of *existence* of the individual.

2. Whereas phenomenology had emphasized the unity of the individual's inner world of experience, existential analysis emphasizes that one individual may live in two or more sometimes conflicting "worlds."

3. Phenomenology takes into account only immediate subjective worlds of experience. Existential analysis strives to reconstruct the development and transformations of the individual's "world" or conflicting "worlds." Binswanger stressed the fact that this study implies a biographic investigation conducted according to psychoanalytic methods.

Thus, existential analysis differs from phenomenology in that it operates within a larger frame of reference.

In his first existential analytic studies, Binswanger organized his descriptions around the distinction of the *Umwelt, Mitwelt,* and *Eigenwelt* of his subjects. Later he organized his analyses around a still larger frame of reference: the distinction of the "existential modes."

The "existential mode" is the dimension of *Dasein* in regard to the *Mitwelt* (fellow men). In contradistinction to classical psychology, which assumes continuity and sameness in the subject, existential analysis takes into account the fact that the "self" changes according to the various forms of "dual," "plural," "singular," and "anonymous" existential modes.

The *dual existential mode* corresponds very roughly to the current concept of "intimacy" and is an extension of Buber's views of the I-Thou relationship. There are several varieties of dual mode, such as the relationships of mother-child, brother-sister, lover-beloved, and even (according to Buber) of the faithful and God. Binswanger gave an extensive analysis of two of

---

86 Martin Buber, *Ich und Du* (Leipzig: Inselverlag, 1923).

these relationships, the dual modes of love and friendship.[87] In the dual mode of love, Binswanger says, space presents the paradox of being simultaneously infinite and all-near; distance and proximity are transcended by a particular spatial mode which bears the same relation to space that eternity does to time. The dual mode of love is also made manifest by an exigency of eternity, not only future but retrospective; the moment coincides with eternity by excluding transient duration. This *Heimat* (inner home of love), which transcends space and in which the moment and eternity fuse, forms the core of the normal existential experience, according to Binswanger.

Many problems have been considered by existential analysts in the light of the dual existential mode. Boss [88] analyzed the aspects of marriage: whereas normal marriage should imply the dual mode, there are "degraded forms of marriage," in which the partners live in the plural or in the singular existential modes.

The *plural mode* corresponds roughly to the area of formal relationships, competition, and struggle. Here, the intimacy of "Thou and I" yields to the co-existence of "one and the other," or of two beings who are "grappling" with each other. Binswanger describes at length the various ways of "seizing" and "yielding to" one's fellow man, through sensitivity, passions, morality, reputation, etc. Many psychopathological problems are thus viewed in a new light.

The *singular mode* includes the relationships of a man with himself (including his body). Psychoanalysis knows of narcissism, self-punitive and self-destructive behavior. Binswanger's concept is much broader and includes a wide range of intrapsychic relationships, which he analyzes in an extremely subtle way. These studies also cast a new light on certain problems; for instance, inner conflict is viewed as a variety of singular mode patterned on the model of the plural mode; autism is not only the lack of relations to one's fellow men but also a specific mode of relationship to oneself.

The *anonymous mode* was briefly sketched by Binswanger and its description developed after him by Kuhn [89] in his study of the interpretation of masks in the Rorschach test. It is the mode of the individual living and acting in an anonymous collectivity, such as the dancer in a masked ball or the soldier who kills and is killed by individuals whom he does not know. Certain individuals seek refuge in this mode as a means of escaping or fighting their fellow men; the latter is the case with the authors of anonymous letters, as Binder shows.[90]

[87] L. Binswanger, *Grundformen und Erkenntnis menschlichen Daseins*, pp. 23–265.
[88] Medard Boss, *Die Gestalt der Ehe und ihre Zerfallsformen* (Bern: Huber, 1944).
[89] R. Kuhn, *Ueber Maskendeutungen im Rorschachschen Versuch* (Basel: S. Karger, 1944).
[90] Hans Binder, "Das anonyme Briefschreiben," *Schweizer Archiv für Neurologie und Psychiatrie*, 1948, Vol. 61, pp. 41–134, Vol. 62, pp. 11–56.

IV *Therapeutic Implications*

In regard to the implications of existential analysis for psychotherapy, several points must be distinguished.

1. It should be understood that the activity of an existential analyst does not usually differ *seemingly* from what the ordinary psychiatrist or psychoanalyst does. He studies the patient's behavior, speech, writings, dreams, and free associations and reconstructs his biography. While doing this, however, he observes in a somewhat different way and classifies his observations within the framework of existential analytic concepts. This often makes possible a much deeper understanding and, consequently, may furnish new approaches for psychotherapy. In his interpersonal relationship to his patients, he will also be aware of the phenomenon of "encounter" and distinguish it from transference and countertransference reactions (in the stricter original sense of these words).

2. Phenomenology opens the path to a new type of psychotherapy which is still in its early stages of development. Every individual has his own subjective "world." Research in the field of perception, *e.g.*, by Gardner Murphy, demonstrates correlations between an individual's personality and his way of perceiving the sensory world; Murphy's research also shows that errors in perception can be corrected and the perceiver re-educated. This applies also to phenomenology in general. An individual's approach to temporality, spatiality, and the like can be reconsidered and readjusted—this, of course, independent of other methods, which keep their value. Take a case of agoraphobia. Psychoanalytic investigation will unravel the psychogenesis of the symptoms and treat them causally. Phenomenology will demonstrate subjective disturbances in the experience of spatiality, which could be treated in their own right concurrently to the analytic approach. Kuhn, in an above-mentioned article, relates how he treated a girl afflicted with anorexia nervosa, using the phenomenological concept of "distance" as a means of approach; his patient was cured. This is not to say that she could not have been cured with an analytically oriented psychotherapy or with both approaches simultaneously. In fact, it is surprising how accessible uneducated or very sick patients are to phenomenological considerations. Here lies a wide open field for research and discoveries.

3. Reconstruction of the subjective world of a patient is more than an academic exercise. Patients are not inert material; they react in one way or another to any kind of approach. Take a severe regressed schizophrenic who would be the object of an existential analytic investigation. If the psychiatrist is merely concerned with an intellectual, one-sided scientific study, the patient will feel that his personality is being disregarded; such an investigation could do considerable harm. On the other hand, if it is done with

genuine interest in the patient himself, the patient feels understood. He will be like the miner imprisoned under earth after an explosion, hearing the signals of the rescuers; he does not know when they will arrive or whether they will be able to save him, but he knows that they are at work, doing their best, and he feels reassured.

To conclude, I think that I cannot do better than to quote a few lines of what Professor Manfred Bleuler [91] wrote a few years ago about the meaning of existential analysis in the research on schizophrenia:

The existentialist point of view in research has gained independent and considerable significance in regard to schizophrenia. . . .

Existential analysis treats the patient's utterances quite seriously and with no more prejudice or bias than in ordinary conversation with normal people. . . . Existential analysis refuses absolutely to examine pathological expressions with a view to seeing whether they are bizarre, absurd, illogical or otherwise defective; rather it attempts to understand the particular world of experience to which these experiences point and how this world is formed and how it falls apart. . . . The existential analyst refrains from evaluations of any kind. . . . From the careful and tireless experience of what is expressed in a dialogue of this kind—in other words, in an entirely empirical way—the patient's transformed and different way of existence becomes clear. . . . From a description given by the patients themselves regarding the changes in their world of experience, their various expressions, hallucinations, gestures and movements can be logically understood in detail.

The remarkable result of existential analytical research in schizophrenia lies in the discovery that even in schizophrenia the human spirit is not split into fragments. . . . All of a schizophrenic's expressions (linguistic, kinetic, illusory, etc.) have an unmistakable relationship to one another, just as the various parts of a *Gestalt* are unmistakably interrelated. . . . In this way, existential analysis has opened new possibilities, comparable to the first attempts at Burghölzli to understand schizophrenic symptoms. . . .

If the mental life of a schizophrenic, as existential analysis shows, is not merely a field strewn with ruins but has retained a certain structure, then it becomes evident that it must be described not as an agglomeration of symptoms, but as a whole and as a *Gestalt*. . . .

Existential analysis . . . also helps—and this I find in my daily work—in the treatment of schizophrenics. An existential analytic attitude can sometimes quite unexpectedly help one to find the right word in talking with an "encapsulated" or withdrawn patient. If one introduces such a word into a conversation in the right manner and at the right time, a gap between patient and doctor is suddenly bridged. Thus, there is hope that a systematic psychotherapy can be built upon the basis of a thorough existential analytic examination of a patient. At the same time, as Ludwig Binswanger himself stressed again and again, such a psychotherapy will never suffice, for practical reasons of methodology alone, without illumination of the patient's entire life history, especially in the psychoanalytic sense.

[91] Manfred Bleuler, "Researches and Changes in Concepts in the Study of Schizophrenia," *Bulletin of the Isaac Ray Medical Library*, Vol. 3, Nos. 1–2, 1955, pp. 42–45.

PART II

Phenomenology

IV

Findings in a Case of
Schizophrenic Depression*

by Eugene Minkowski

IN THE YEAR 1922, a stroke of good luck—or, more exactly, life's vicissitudes—obliged me to spend two months as the personal physician of a patient. I was with him constantly, night and day. It is not difficult to imagine the unpleasant moments that such a symbiosis presents, but on the other hand it creates special conditions for the observer and gives him the possibility, by permitting him constantly to compare his own and the patient's psyche, of noting certain particularities that ordinarily escape attention.

Briefly, here is the clinical picture. The patient was a man of sixty-six who presented a depressive psychosis accompanied by delusions of persecution and extensive interpretations.

The patient expressed thoughts of guilt and ruin. A foreigner, he reproached himself for not having chosen French citizenship, seeing therein a heinous crime; he also stated that he had not paid his taxes and that he no longer had any money. An atrocious punishment awaited him as a result of his crimes. His family would have their arms and legs cut off and would then be exposed in some arid field. The same would happen to him; he would have a nail driven into his head and all sorts of garbage would be poured into his belly. Mutilated in the most horrible manner, he would be led, in the middle of a parade, to a fair and condemned to live, covered with vermin, in a cage with wild beasts or with the rats of the sewers until

* Translated by BARBARA BLISS. "Etude psychologique et analyse phénoménologique d'un cas de mélancolie schizophrenique," first published in *Journal de Psychologie normale et pathologique,* Vol. 20, 1923, pp. 543–558; re-edited in slightly condensed form in *Le Temps Vécu* (Paris: J. L. L. d'Artrey, 1933), pp. 169–181.

death overtook him. All the world was cognizant of his crimes and the punishment which awaited him; for that matter, everyone, with the exception of his family, would play some role therein. People looked oddly at him in the street, his servants were paid to spy on him and betray him, every newspaper article was directed at him, and books had been printed solely against him and his family. At the head of this vast movement against him was the medical corps.

These ideas of guilt, ruin, imminent punishment, and persecution were accompanied by interpretations of a really surprising scope. This was the "residue politics" (*politique des restes*), as he called it—a political system that had been instituted especially for him. Every leftover, all residue, would be put aside to be one day stuffed into his abdomen—and this, from all over the world. Everything would be included without exception. When one smoked, there would be the burnt match, the ashes, and the cigarette butt. At meals, he was preoccupied with the crumbs, the fruit pits, the chicken bones, the wine or water at the bottom of the glasses. The egg, he said, was his worst enemy because of the shell—it was also the expression of the great anger of his persecutors. When one sewed, there would be bits of thread and needles. All the matches, strings, bits of paper, and pieces of glass that he saw while walking in the street were meant for him. After that came nail parings and hair clippings, empty bottles, letters and envelopes, subway tickets, address-bands, the dust that one brought in on one's shoes, bath water, the garbage from the kitchen and from all the restaurants of France, etc. Then it was rotten fruit and vegetables, cadavers of animals and men, the urine and faeces of horses. "Whoever speaks of a clock," he would tell us, "speaks of the hands, cogs, springs, case, pendulum, etc." And all this he would have to swallow. In sum, these interpretations were boundless; they included everything, absolutely everything that he saw or imagined. In these conditions, it is not difficult to understand that the smallest thing, the most minute act of daily life, was immediately interpreted as being hostile to him.

Such was the clinical picture. Actually, it does not present anything particularly extraordinary unless it would be the scope, we would even say the universality, of his delusions of persecution and his interpretations. This universal character of the morbid manifestations is, however, an unquestionable advantage when we wish to penetrate the very nature of psychopathological phenomena. When these phenomena are limited to certain persons or objects, we first look for an explanation for this elective character. Why does the patient feel that this person persecutes him instead of another; why does he, in his delirium, attribute a particular importance to this thing instead of that one? Such are the questions that face us then. It is the *content* of the delusion or hallucination that attracts our attention, and it is there that the affective factors, the complexes and the symbolism that play such a great role in modern psychiatry, enter in. On the other hand, the cases where the content of the morbid phenomenon is in no way limited but has a universal character lend themselves better, I submit, to the study of a phenomenon as such; of the delusion, for example, as a phenomenon which is specific and unique.

Although my patient's case is relatively banal from a clinical point of view, this can hardly be said of the circumstances in which I was able to study him. I have already said that I lived with him for two months. Thus, I had the possibility of following him from day to day, not in a mental hospital or sanitarium, but in an ordinary environment. His way of reacting to the habitual external stimuli, his ability to adapt himself to the exigencies of daily life, the variability of his symptoms and their particular nuances come much more clearly to life under such conditions. To this must be added another point. We are unable to conserve a professional attitude twenty-four hours a day. We, too, react to the patient as do the other persons of his environment. Compassion, mildness, persuasion, impatience, and anger appear one by one. Thus it was that, in the above circumstances, I was not only able to observe the patient but also at almost each instant I had the possibility of comparing his psychic life and mine. It was like two melodies being played simultaneously; although these two melodies are as unharmonious as possible, nevertheless, a certain balance becomes established between the notes of the one and the other and permits us to penetrate a bit more deeply into our patient's psyche. The findings that were thus noted are on one hand psychological, on the other, phenomenological.

I *Psychological Findings—Alternating of Attitudes and Extension of the Delirium*

We have already outlined the clinical picture. The patient, however, did not invariably present the same tableau. We are not referring here to the fact that occasionally he behaved as a normal individual, taking part in the general conversation and in no way betraying his pathology. Our attention was much more drawn by the fact that in the area of his symptoms variations and changes occurred according to the circumstances. From the first, two different attitudes could be distinguished: now the depressive element was dominant, now it was the delusional and delirious patient that we saw before us. The alternating of these two main attitudes did not come about in an entirely disorganized fashion; on the contrary, it seemed to be determined at least partially by specific factors and to be subservient to precise motives. Here it is useful to confront the two melodies that I mentioned above. When, after a more or less violent scene, one felt the need to relax, and I, personally, wanted to tell my partner, "Okay, let's make peace," he would almost invariably react with an episode of simple depression. He would pity himself, list his misfortunes, and call on our compassion; the interpretations, on the other hand, scarcely entered the picture. It was as if, in so doing, he dug out of his arsenal of pathological attitudes the one which could be used to establish a certain contact with his fellow man. As he repeated his melancholic complaints and cries of suffering, they no longer moved us; nevertheless, they remained his "contact attitude" in our symbiosis. These were, in his pathological psyche, the last-ditch defenses of his syntonism. With reference to the contact with the environment, the attitude of the delusional, interpreting patient was obviously completely different. Then, often, he accused me personally. He could not stand my perfidy; on one hand, I was as friendly as could be with his family, but on the other, I was an active conspirator in the plot being woven against him. One day that my children came to visit me, I was supposed to have purposely had them bring a coin purse with some change in it; these coins, now, would also be put into his belly; it was shameful to make one's own children take part in such inhuman goings-on. Finally, he called me a murderer and gratified me with the name of *Deibler*. At that point, everything fell apart; nothing remained except two people who could no longer understand each other and, as a result, were hostile toward one another. I became angry. He translated his anger in his personal manner, adopting an antisocial attitude. He accused me of the most evil deeds, then, as if purposely, went to the garden and picked up every string and match stick that he could find.

The alternating of symptoms and their various forms establishes thusly a sort of current which runs between normal life and the pathological psyche. It is like the ebb and flow of the sea; now it is calm and the prevalent attitude is one of contact—one cannot keep from feeling an upsurge of hope; now it is a high sea, everything tearing loose, and once again all is submerged.

Besides this alternating of attitudes, a certain intellectual activity was evident concerning his delusions, and this activity brought a hint of life into the shadows of his ill personality. It had a special character, aiming at going over absolutely every object that might be put in his belly. I carelessly took a subway ticket from my pocket. "Hey," he said, "I hadn't yet thought about tickets." Then he would talk about train tickets, streetcar tickets, tickets for buses, the subway, etc. This question would preoccupy him for several days and, afterwards, would be brought up again from time to time in his conversation as a brief reminder. This, "My, I hadn't yet thought of that," was repeated at each item that he thought he had forgotten until then. Morever, with the same aim he named all the things that he saw around him or listed all the forms of the same general class of things. When germs happened to be mentioned, he listed all the microbes that he knew—those causing rabies, typhus, cholera, tuberculosis, and so forth. All of this would be stuffed down him. On another occasion it was acids that he ticked off—hydrochloric, sulfuric, oxalic, acetic, nitric, etc.—all with the same tone of voice. In this way, he pursued an intangible goal—to go through all the possible and imaginable objects in the universe. As he said, "That leads toward infinity." We will have occasion to bring this up again. For that matter, this activity was not limited to the above enumerations, and a certain retrospective work went on at the same time. Perhaps he might think of a hair-box in some barber shop that he once patronized; hair clippings were thrown into it, and now he was terrified to think of the mass of hair that must have been put aside for him. Another time, he might remember some dinner to which he had invited many friends; he would calculate how many eggs must have been used that day. At all costs, he wanted to know how long the "residue politics" had been in force.

There were still other problems that preoccupied him and that lent a more vivid note to the exasperating monotony of his stream of thought. Some of these problems were tinged with reality. For example, his "residue politics" would obviously necessitate enormous expenditures. All the bits of string and broken glass that had first to be put in his way and later collected again, the newspapers that had to be bought, and the books that had to be published—what a sum that must amount to! He supposed that donations were being requested all over France, as well as secret governmental funds being appropriated. He wondered, too, how they would manage to stuff all the canes and umbrellas into his stomach; "there my reasoning fails me," he would say. Then he found the solution: he would be made to absorb only a bit of each thing and the rest would be arranged around him when he was exposed to public derision in some side show.

II *Phenomenological Findings*

So it was that our patient's daily life was spent. *But where, exactly, is the discordance between his psyche and our own?* This question leads us to a study of the phenomenological findings.

From the first glance, it is obvious that his mental processes were quite different from our own; because of the delusions, this difference may even seem so great as to make us doubt whether there can be any correlation. However, we cannot be satisfied with such an attitude of psychiatric agnosticism. Modern psychiatry, aided by the psychology of complexes, has already demonstrated that many morbid symptoms can be traced back to normal drives and thus made intelligible. However, as we have already pointed out, most of these studies have been concerned with content. Here, our aim is quite different. We are trying to gain a fuller understanding of the nature of the pathological phenomenon itself by asking, for example, what is a delusion? Is it really nothing but a disorder of perception and of judgment? This brings us back to our present problem—namely, where is the discordance between the patient's psyche and our own?

From the first day of my life with the patient, my attention was drawn to the following point. When I arrived, he stated that his execution would certainly take place that night; in his terror, unable to sleep, he also kept me awake all that night. I comforted myself with the thought that, come the morning, he would see that all his fears had been in vain. However, the same scene was repeated the next day and the next, until after three or four days I had given up hope, whereas his attitude had not budged one iota. What had happened? It was simply that I, as a normal human being, had rapidly drawn from the observed facts my conclusions about the future. He, on the other hand, had let the same facts go by him, totally unable to draw any profit from them for relating himself to the same future. I now knew that he would continue to go on, day after day, swearing that he was to be tortured to death that night, and so he did, giving no thought to the present or the past. Our thinking is essentially empirical; we are interested in facts only insofar as we can use them as a basis for planning the future. This carry-over from past and present into the future was completely lacking in him; he did not show the slightest tendency to generalize or to arrive at any empirical rules. When I would tell him, "Look here, you can believe me when I assure you that nothing is threatening you—so far, my predictions have always been fulfilled," he would reply, "I admit that so far you've always been right, but that doesn't mean that you'll be right tomorrow." This reasoning, against which one feels so futile, indicated a profound disorder in his general attitude toward the future; that time which we normally integrate into a progressive whole was here split into isolated fragments.

One objection may well be raised at this point: isn't the disorder pertaining to the future a natural consequence of the delusional belief that execution is imminent? Here lies the crux of the problem. Could we not, on the contrary, suppose that the more basic disorder is the distorted attitude toward the future, whereas the delusion is only one of its manifestations? Let us consider it more closely.

What exactly was our patient's experience of time, and how did it differ from ours? His conception might be more precisely described in the following way: monotonously and uniformly, he experienced the days following one another; he knew that time was passing and, whimpering, complained that "one more day was gone." As day after day went by, a certain rhythm became evident to him: on Mondays, the silver was polished; on Tuesday, the barber came to cut his hair; on Wednesday, the gardener mowed the lawn, etc. All of which only added to the waste which was his due—the only link which still connected him to the world. There was no action or desire which, emanating from the present, reached out to the future, spanning the dull, similar days. As a result, each day kept an unusual independence, failing to be immersed in the perception of any life continuity; each day life began anew, like a solitary island in a gray sea of passing time. What had been done, lived, and spoken no longer played the same role as in our life because there seemed to be no wish to go further; every day was an exasperating monotony of the same words, the same complaints, until one felt that this being had lost all sense of necessary continuity. Such was the march of time for him.

However, our picture is still incomplete; an essential element is missing in it—the fact that *the future was blocked* by the certainty of a terrifying and destructive event. This certainty dominated the patient's entire outlook, and absolutely all of his energy was attached to this inevitable event. Although he might pity his wife and children for the atrocious fate that awaited them, he could do no more; he could no longer follow the events of daily life, he was no more up to date and was out of tune with the fortuitous events of daily living. If he had occasion to ask about some member of the family who was ill, his attention was short-lived and he seemed unable to go beyond the most banal questions. "It's always the same old thing," said his wife, and he, too, was aware of this. "It sounds phony. Nothing I say to my wife rings true." In other words, he presented the flattening of affect which we find so often in these patients.

Such was our patient's experience of time. How does it resemble ours and how does it differ? All of us may have similar feelings in moments of discouragement or dejection or when we believe that we are dying. Then the idea of death, this prototype of empirical certainty, takes over and, blocking off the future, dominates our outlook on life. Our synthetic view of time disintegrates and we live in a succession of similar days which follow one another with a boundless monotony and sadness. With most of us, however, these are only transient episodes. Life forces, our personal impetus, lift us and carry us over such a parade of miserable days toward a future which reopens its doors widely to us; we think and act and desire beyond that death which, even so, we could not escape. The very existence of such phenomena as the desire to "do something for future generations" clearly indicates our attitude in this regard. In our patient, it was this propulsion toward the future which seemed to be totally lacking, leading, as a result, to his general attitude. Nor would anything be changed for him if, quieted after a certain time, he would accept the fact that his punishment would not be for that very night but for a later date, such as Bastille Day or Armistice Day. The future would still be blocked as before; his life impetus could not spring from the present toward such a distorted future.

One might object here that, basically, this is the outlook of a person who has been condemned to death and point out that this patient reacted in this way to the delusion that he and his family were to be executed. I doubt this, although I have never seen anyone under a death sentence. Of course, I accept that this picture corresponds to that *idea* which we have of the feelings of someone in a death cell; but don't we draw this idea from ourselves? Don't we feel this way because all of us occasionally realize that we are sentenced to die, especially in those moments when our personal impetuses weaken and the future shuts its door in our face? Isn't it possible to admit that the patient's outlook is determined by a similar weakening of this same impetus, the complex feeling of time and of living disintegrating, with a subsequent regression to that lower rung which we all latently possess? Looked at in this light, a delusion is not something which is simply an outgrowth of phantasy but, rather, is a branch grafted onto a phenomenon which, as part of all of our lives, comes into play when our life synthesis begins to weaken. The particular form of the delusion, in this case the belief in execution, is only an effort made by the rational part of the mind (itself, remaining intact) to establish some logical connection between the various sections of a crumbling edifice.

Let us see whether or not we can look at the other delusions of this patient in the same light, beginning with his delusions of persecution.

The personal impetus is a determining factor in more than just our attitude with regard to the future; it also rules over our relationship with our environment and thus participates in that picture which we have of that environment. In this personal impetus, there is an element of expansion; we go beyond the limits of our own ego and leave a personal imprint on the world about us, creating works which sever themselves from us to live their own lives. This accompanies a specific, positive feeling which we call contentment—that pleasure which accompanies every finished action or firm decision. As a feeling, it is unique and has no exact negative counterpart where actions are concerned. In life, if we place contentment at the positive pole, that phenomenon which most closely approaches the negative pole is sensory pain. This latter, as we know, is one of the most essential factors in determining the structure of our relationship with the world about us; intrinsically bound up in pain is the feeling of some external force acting upon us to which we are compelled to submit. Seen in this light, pain evidently opposes the expansive tendency of our personal impetus; we can no longer turn ourselves outward, nor do we try to leave our personal stamp on the external world. Instead, we let the world, in all its impetuousness, come to us, making us suffer. Thus, pain is also an attitude toward the environment. Usually brief, even momentary, it becomes lasting when it no longer meets and is counteracted by its antagonist, the individual's life impetus.

When this latter fades, all of that world we live in seems to throw itself upon us, a hostile force which can only bring suffering. This is the reflection of a particular attitude toward the environment that, usually submerged by other attitudes, paints the entire universe in different colors when it emerges to rule the person. My patient would say, "Everything will be cut off of me except just what is necessary in order for me to suffer." He was aware only of pain and constructed every relationship with the external world exclusively on the model of this phenomenon of sensory pain.

It was against this hostile background that shadows came and went— silhouettes of other persons, of things, and of events. They were really only bas-reliefs growing out of the background. "Everything, everything turns against me," the patient whimpered. "Opposites all mean the same thing: the silence here makes me think of the deep and violent hatred of the people; the noise which those workers make outside reminds me of the nail that will be driven in my head; the most natural things are the most dangerous. How clever and infamous their scheme is. All one has to do is continue doing what one has always done—washing, combing one's hair, eating, going to the toilet—and all this will be turned against me." Everything spoke "the same clear and precise language"; black and white meant the same thing; everything was directed against him to make him suffer.

Here, again, he could not advance from a simple fact to a generalization. His attitude determined a precise picture of the universe which, then, was reflected on all the environment. Men were no longer perceived as individuals with their personal and individual values but became pale, distorted shadows moving against a backdrop of hostility. These were not living men who were persecuting him but men who had been transformed into persecutors and were no more than that. All the complex psychic life of human beings had disappeared; they were only schematic mannequins. All idea of chance, coincidence, of unintentional or unconscious acts was wiped out for the patient. The smallest bit of thread had been purposely laid in his way; horses were in on the plot and deliberately excreted beneath his window; the cigarette smoked by a passer-by was a signal; a failure of the electricity was caused so that people would light candles and that many more "remains" would be stuffed down him.

His thinking no longer was concerned with the usual value of an object, nor did he clearly delimit each one of them. An object was only a representative of the whole and his mind went beyond its particular meaning in ever-extending arcs. The address-band of his newspaper made him think of all the bands of all the copies of that paper which are distributed every day, which led him to all the address-bands of all the newspapers of France. A member of his family had a bronchitis and expectorated; the patient began to speak of all the sputum of all the tuberculosis sanitaria in the country and then went on to all the leavings of all the hospitals. When I shaved in front of him, he spoke of the soldiers in a nearby barracks who also shaved and then included all the soldiers of the army. "The minute that I do something," he confided while washing himself, "I must remember that forty million others do the same."

Let us remember here his way of searching to enumerate all the things which, one day, would be put into his belly. Perhaps one day we will be able to explain the genesis of delusions of enormity along these lines. What is particularly interesting to us at this point is the idea that the patient's mind had lost the ability to stop and fix itself at each object's boundaries but—as he said himself—had immediately to go further, gliding rapidly from the solitary object to infinity. This same sphere of immediate interest, which in the patient was spatially limitless, was temporally blocked in the future. Ours, on the other hand, is limited in space but extends endlessly into the future. The life impetus was missing in the patient and he was unable to project it onto either men or things; the individuality of external objects did not exist for him. In short, human beings and objects seemed to merge, everything speaking, to him, "the same clear and precise language."

Another observation may confirm this point of view. His mind not only fled toward infinity, it also decomposed every object that it met. The clock, as we have already mentioned, was not just a clock but an assemblage of instruments of torture—cogs, key, hands, pendulum, etc. Every object that he saw was like the clock.

One fact must be kept in mind—as soon as he performed some action his entire attitude changed, but once the act was finished he immediately fell back into his delusions. For example, when I wanted to weigh him, this interested him. He got on the scale, shifted the weights, and correctly found his weight. However, he was no sooner finished than he began, "What use is all that? This scale is only a lot of iron and wood and all that will be put into my belly."

In these circumstances, it is obvious that the essential values of an object or another being—such as the aesthetic value—could not be appreciated by him; he was unable to adopt the appropriate attitude. "You see these roses?" he asked me. "My wife would say that they are beautiful but, as far as I can see, they are just a bunch of leaves and petals, stems and thorns."

Thus, objects merged and seemed alike. Differences, always linked to the apperception of the individuality of each object, faded, and similarity was the only point of view under which they were envisaged. Thought, proceeding by analogy, discovered similarities which usually escape us as being practically unimportant; he, however, attributed great importance to them. The number of the house where we lived was the same as that of a sanitarium where he had spent a year; my pocket calendar was identical to that of one of the nurses at the sanitarium, and I paced the room just as she used to. Therefore, we must be applying the same methods here that they had used there. These similarities were discovered with amazing speed and he found them in places that it never would have occurred to us to look for them. For example, one 13th of July (the day before Bastille Day), he noticed that a pair of shorts that he put on was embroidered with the number 13 and immediately connected the two. His shirt, on the other hand, had the number 3, which also exists in 13. That year it happened that, as the National Holiday fell next to the week end, a three-day holiday had been declared. All of this proved that he and his family were to be executed on Bastille Day. Hundreds of similar examples could be given.

I think that the patient's attitude toward other men, events, and things concords with the view that we have taken of his delusions of persecution.

It must be pointed out that the patient's attitude toward others cannot be understood exclusively as that of a relationship of victim and persecutor. Through all this, he nevertheless attempted to safeguard a certain communion of thought with others. Although I was seen as a murderer and an executioner, he did not run from me; on the contrary, my presence helped him to a certain extent because I *knew* the same things that he knew and he could, thus, speak freely with me. If I were gone for a while, he needed to tell me all the new discoveries that he had made during my absence. Any attempt that I made to object was refused by, "Go on, you know all about this just as well as I do. You know even more about it than I do."

In summary, we arrived at the following conclusions. The individual life impetus weakening, the synthesis of the human personality disintegrates; those elements which go to make up the personality acquire more independence and act as entities; the feeling of time breaks up and is reduced to a feeling of a succession of similar days; the attitude toward the environment is determined by the phenomena of sensory pain; there remains only the person face to face with a hostile universe; the objects found in the environment insert themselves between the person and the hostile universe and are interpreted in consequence; the intellect translates this as all men being persecutors and all inanimate objects, instruments of torture. Thus, delusions should not be considered only as the products of a morbid imagination or distortions of judgment; on the contrary, they represent an attempt to translate the new and unusual situation of the disintegrating personality in terms of prior psychic mechanisms.

No matter how delusional the patient was, it seems difficult to admit that he would simply fancy such absurd and nonsensical thoughts as those that he constantly expressed. Wouldn't it help our thinking to assume that at the base of these ideas we will always find a natural phenomenon which has been more or less modified and, following a disintegration of the personality, has acquired an unusual independence? The patient attempts to express this situation by borrowing thoughts from his former life and, thus, ends by expressing delusional material. We then come along and augment this chasm by accepting the content of the verbalizations, seeing them only as aberrations of his imagination or his judgment.

So far, these are only suggestions. Perhaps it will be possible to continue along the same lines and, in so doing, to gain a better understanding of the nature of those phenomena which go to make up mental illness. Meanwhile, in the same general line, I should like to add a few more points relative to the same patient.

He expressed delusions of total ruin. Should we interpret these as ideas which just came to him? Does the depressive state alone explain the genesis of such thoughts? Sadness and emotional suffering, it would seem to us, could be attached to various other objects without giving rise to such bizarre and unrealistic feelings. Perhaps we would be closer to the truth if we conceived of such a feeling of ruin as translating what in everyday thinking is a distortion of the possession phenomenon, the phenomenon of that which is our own.[1] This sense of property is an integral part of our personality. As we have said, there is a close correlation between it and desire; we never wish for that which we already have and, on the other hand, the fulfillment of a desire in one way or another enlarges the sphere of our own possessions. Desire, in going beyond possession, always limits the boundaries of the latter. Wherever our life impetus and, conjointly, our desire dies, not only is the future shut off but also the boundaries of our possession-sphere disintegrate. The phenomenon of possession is disturbed and our ability to attribute something to ourselves is affected and altered. The person translates this both to himself and to others when he says that he is broke.[2] Ideas of negation, patients' complaints that they no longer have a stomach, intestines, or a brain, are perhaps only their way of expressing the same situation.

We may develop an analogous conception with reference to feelings of guilt. Here, too, the analysis of those phenomena which are the essentials of a human personality leads us to findings which seem to shed light on the genesis of such feelings. We must repeat our previous remarks concerning the asymmetry between good and evil. Once an error is made or a bad action committed, it remains engraved in the conscience, leaving palpable traces; from this point of view, it is static and a backward glance is enough to uncover it. On the other hand, the only remains of positive accomplishments or good acts is in the fact that we can do better in the future; such acts are really no more than bridges that we cross in our attempts to improve. Our entire individual evolution consists in trying to surpass that which has already been done. When our mental life dims, the future closes in front of us, while at the same time the feeling of positive actions of the past disappears. An intact memory remains, but everything is dominated by the static feeling of evil. Our patient would say that he was the world's greatest criminal, and he would see "concretized remorse" everywhere.

Perhaps, by more close study of those phenomena which make up the life of a human being, we may eventually gain a better understanding of the mysterious manifestations of mental illness. It is toward this goal that we have set our sights.

---

[1] E. Minkowski, *Le Temps vécu*, p. 117.

[2] It is useful to remember at this point that the word "poor" also means "unhappy," even when poverty is not the cause of the unhappiness. When we pity someone, we say, "poor man."

V

Aesthesiology and
Hallucinations*

by Erwin W. Straus

I *The Empiricist Held Captive*

THE UNDERSTANDING OF PATHOLOGICAL phenomena depends upon a preceding understanding of normal processes. When we discuss disturbances we refer by implication to the norm. Our knowledge of the norm may be fragmentary, open to many interpretations; nevertheless, the *actual* interpretation of the norm—even if not explicitly formulated—predetermines the *possible* interpretations of pathological manifestations. This is just as true for hallucinations as for all other phenomena. A better understanding of hallucinations therefore must wait for a deeper understanding of the norm of sensory experience. If this be the case—it will be objected—all waiting is in vain; for is there anything new to be said about sensory experience? Indeed, such an attempt would seem rash, in view of an age-old scientific tradition, and quixotic, considering our familiarity with these phenomena. Yet it is precisely tradition and familiarity that are most likely to prevent us from fully comprehending their meaning.

The world, as it unfolds in its sensory splendor, can never directly be made an object of mathematical science. Its qualities must in some way be effaced in order to allow quantification and measurement. The qualities must be debased, epistemologically, and metaphysically devaluated. In the course of this reduction the degraded phenomena cannot but suffer an as-

* An expanded version of a lecture which the author, as a member of a Medical Mission organized by the Unitarian Service Committee, delivered in the summer of 1948 at several German universities.

similation to the processes considered as real. Out of the wealth of sensory experience, we admit and finally notice and observe only that which yields to the process of reduction. The scientific transmutation of sensory experience terminates in a basic misconception of experiencing as such and of the mode of being of experiencing creatures.

Tradition is not uniform. One can compare it to the delta of a river mouth where waters from the same stream seek their course in many ways. These waters are not homogeneous; between source and mouth many tributaries have emptied into the main stream, yet they all flow for a long distance in the same bed in which they are largely, though not completely, mixed. The physiology and psychology of the senses, in spite of many variations, remain closely attached to that interpretation of sensuality which originated with Descartes and received its popular form from Locke and the later English empirical philosophers.

From the beginning of modern science, sensory experience, far from being studied for its own sake, has been forced, like the kulak in a controlled economy, into a rigid system with little respect for its own rights. Speculative dogmas of bygone days, handed down from generation to generation, are erroneously entered into our ledgers as matters of fact. Issuing from a small circle of philosophers and scientists, the development has come to influence the thinking of the man in the street. Paraphrasing the title of one of Molière's plays, one could say that all of us are "metaphysicians in spite of ourselves."

This tradition has its origin in the seventeenth century. It begins as a revolution, a rebellion formulated most succinctly by the French philosopher Descartes. The task was to emancipate man from revelation (the theological dogmas), from traditional philosophy (the "schools" was the term used then), and from the tyranny of nature. The moment man wanted to be completely independent, to rely on himself alone, he was forced to search for absolute knowledge. A science was to be created which once and forever would finish the perpetual arguments between the schools, a science that would conquer skepticism. How could it be obtained? Only as an insight which was beyond any doubt. The first matter which could not stand the supreme test of radical doubt was sensory experience. It was declared deceptive, confused, unreliable. Next came all traditional doctrines. Even mathematical evidence was rejected, because it could not be shown beyond doubt that the world was not created by a malevolent demon in such a way that we are always deceived just when we believe we have full insight.

Skeptical rejection of sensory experience was time-honored; the rejection of mathematical evidence was something new. Descartes felt that the best way to conquer skepticism was to outdo it and therefore to push doubt to its utmost possibilities. For this reason he introduced the argument of the evil demon as creator. Yet there was still another motive at work. With the assumption of the evil demon Descartes tried to establish the autonomy of human science. If it could resist that attack, then it was invulnerable; it need fear neither God nor the Devil. But the price paid was high; the demand was complete distrust of everyday life experience.

Descartes is credited with, or blamed for, the dichotomy of mind and body. This historic view is but half right and thereby doubly wrong. Descartes distinguished two finite "substances," and this distinction between a thinking and an extended substance goes far beyond that of mind and body. Indeed, in the day of Descartes, toward the middle of the seventeenth century, there was no need for anyone to invent such a dichotomy. It was the alpha and omega of Christian anthropology. There is, however, one decisive difference between Descartes's view and that of the Christian tradition. In the latter, the credo was that the body was mortal, the soul immortal; in death the soul departed from the body, but so long as a man was alive, body and soul formed a unit. They belonged together; they were mutually interdependent; the soul of living man was therefore intramundane. It was a part of our world. It was as an experiencing creature that man, with his sufferings and joys, his passions and sins, moved on earth. Descartes broke away from tradition at this point. As one of the two substances, the *res extensa* had been identified with physical nature; the other one, the thinking substance, the soul, had no place in nature. The exclusion of the soul from nature served a great purpose. It permitted the submission of all the rest, including the animals and the human body, to the principles of mathematical physics. The distinction of the two finite substances is, or was in Descartes's opinion at least, the prerequisite for the foundation of science as natural science.

The mathematical paradise lost in the universal doubt was soon regained. Mathematical evidence was readmitted after the characteristics of the two substances had been established. The stigma of incompetency, however, was not removed from sensory experience. Descartes continued to use the old terms, mind, soul, and intellect, but he gave them a new meaning, and he also added a new term—consciousness. The word *conscientia* with the connotation of "conscience" is a classical term; the use of the word *conscientia* with the connotation of "consciousness" begins with Descartes. The Cartesian consciousness is a worldless, bodyless, incorporeal, thinking substance. The Cartesian ego is extramundane.

When we today speak with little—in fact, too little—hesitation about an outside world, we are using Cartesian terminology and—whether we want to or not—are following the line of his thought. To what does the word "outside" in the phrase "outside world" ("external world") refer? It means that the world is outside of consciousness and that, reciprocally, consciousness—including sensory experience—is outside of the world, for it has been exiled to nowhere.

The Cartesian dichotomy therefore not only separates mind from body but severs the experiencing creature from nature, the ego from the world, sensation from motion. It also separates one person from another one, *me* from *you*. The Cartesian ego, looking at the outside world, is in no contact, has no direct communication, with any *alter ego*. According to Descartes, self-awareness precedes the awareness of the world. We are aware of ourselves before we are aware of things, we are aware of ourselves without necessarily being aware of anything else. In consciousness, each one is alone with himself. More correctly, one should say: Consciousness is alone with itself; for the Cartesian Ego is not identical with the man Descartes; it is "mind, soul, intellect." Sensory experience is transformed into sensory data; the sensations received into consciousness are worldless, incorporeal qualities. Although Descartes did not deny or seriously doubt the existence of the so-called outside world, he insisted, nevertheless, that it is never directly accessible to us. Its existence is not more than probable; it must be proved. In Descartes's philosophy, a demonstration of the existence of God and of his veracity guarantees the reality of the external world. However, this proof does not bridge the gap between consciousness and the world. The fact that a proof was needed emphasizes the distance. Even when our conviction of the existence of the outside world has been well established, we remain forever excluded from it, without any direct contact or communication.

This means that reality is reached only by inference, or by deduction or projection. Centuries after Descartes, Helmholtz related the experience of reality to unconscious inference, Freud to reality testing. In Cartesian philosophy, reality becomes a function of judgment. According to his interpretation, reality is posited as some kind of proposition; there is no direct experience of reality—*i.e.*, the one we have in mind when we say that we have seen something with our own eyes. Descartes's conception of reality could be expressed by the formula, "Something happens in the outside world in accordance with the laws of nature," whereas everyday-life experience of reality and its psychotic distortions adhere to the formula, "Something happens to me in the world." Descartes and his many followers could not accept the prescientific formulation of reality, because consciousness, substituted for the experiencing creature, had been turned into a neutral receiver of impressions, a remote observer of events. In other words, the prelogical sphere of the immediate experience of reality had been eliminated—a tremendous loss for psychiatry, because most psychotic experiences, such as hallucinations and delusions, belong in this very realm.

The popular formula of the subjectivity of sensations, indispensable for establishing the natural sciences, need not express anything but that the qualities of things found in everyday experience are relative to the constitution of Man. Descartes, however, and Galileo before him, went much further.

The doctrine of the subjectivity of the sensations is eventually formulated roughly thus: sensations, it is said, are not *modi* of things. They are not properties of matter, and they are not inherent in things. Where, then, are they? The answer is "in consciousness." And since they are in consciousness they cannot give any evidence of an "outer" world. They are purely subjective. Colors are not interpreted as attributes of visible things, relative to the constitution of man as an experiencing being. From visible things, colors migrated into consciousness. Seeing is no longer understood as the relation of an experiencing being to the world; it is rather an occurrence of sensory data in a worldless consciousness. In everyday life we see this wall as green, that table as brown. Descartes wants us to believe that originally such qualities of visible things are data in our mind. They will be related to an outside world by inference, or they are—as we say, using a meaningless phrase—projected outward. We are not affected by sensing; sensations merely occur in consciousness. The relation of consciousness to its sensory data, whether they are colors, sounds, scents, or what not, is always the same. They are interpreted as material handed over to reflection, memory, judgment; sensations are considered as an inferior type of knowledge, confused and confusing.

Descartes and Locke were aware that pure sensations could never be demonstrated in everyday experience. For we are convinced that we perceive things "outside" and that the qualities perceived are really theirs. Descartes explains this common tendency as the result of a habit acquired in early childhood. During those years of physical growth our interest was claimed particularly by what was beneficial or harmful to the body. Our sensations show us what benefits or harms the body. So it is not surprising that we finally come to look at our sensations as if we could experience immediately in them an external world and its nature. For Locke these relations are exactly reversed.[1] From childhood on, Locke claims, our mind is gradually filled with simple and complex ideas. But "the having the idea of anything in our mind no more proves the existence of that thing than the picture of a man evidences his being in the world, or the vision of a dream makes thereby a true history."[2] It is the manner of the reception of "ideas" which first makes known to us the existence of other things. From the effect we deduce its cause. "The notice we have by our senses of the existing of things without us, though it be not altogether so certain as our intuitive knowledge, or the deductions of our reason employed about the clear abstract ideas of our own minds; yet it is an assurance that deserves the name of knowledge."[3] But Locke holds fast to the primacy of self-certitude; "The knowledge of our own being we have by intuition. The existence of a God reason clearly makes known to us. . . . The knowledge of the existence of any other thing,

---

[1] John Locke, *An Essay Concerning Human Understanding* (New York: Oxford Univ. Press, 1924), Bk. II, Chap. VII.
[2] *Ibid.*, Bk. IV, Chap. XI.
[3] *Ibid.*

we can have only by sensation." [4] We have reasons for believing in the existence of a world outside, and they are very plausible. But they are no more than reasons and inferences; the world is not immediately accessible to us.

Physiology and the psychology of senses took over from philosophy the doctrine, by now raised to the rank of dogma, that the original, proper, and initial content of sensory experience is an aggregate of worldless sensory data. Receptors aroused by stimuli send impulses to the central organ, whose stimulation is "accompanied" by processes of consciousness. These data, supposedly without any extrinsic meaning, are then "projected outward" by a process X which is as incomprehensible as it is unproven. A sensation, Johannes Müller taught, "is not the transmission of a quality or state of external bodies to our consciousness but the transmission to consciousness of a quality or state of a sensory nerve as induced by an external cause, and these qualities differ in the various sensory nerves and are the energies of the senses." [5] Further on we read, "It is not in the nature of the nerves themselves to place the content of their sensations outside themselves; the cause of this transposition is the idea which accompanies our sensations, affirmed by experience." To Helmholtz, Müller's pupil, the sensations are signs for certain external objects.[6] Unconscious inferences lead to the assumption of the existence of an outside world. This theory of signs demands as a complementary postulate the constant co-ordination of stimulus and excitation, of excitation and conscious sign. For only when there is a constant co-ordination of a definite type of sign with a definite type of nervous process, and of that process with a definite stimulus, is there any guarantee of empirical knowledge. The starting point is always the same—the assumption that consciousness with all its numerous contents is alone with itself, cut off from the world. No longer does any road lead out of such a solipsistic dungeon.

The attempt to present sensory experience freed from traditional prejudices is designated here as *aesthesiology*. A new term was necessary, for the mention of sensations immediately recalls to mind those very dogmas whose dominance we should like to throw off. The word "aesthesiology"—the logos of *aisthesis*—hardly requires an explanation. Nor is it a new expression; it was used by Plessner,[7] yet it did not gain currency. The word "aesthetics" —in the sense still given it by Kant in the *Critique of Pure Reason,* where he speaks of "the transcendental aesthetics"—is no longer at our disposal. More than 150 years ago it was completely alienated from its original meaning. The circumstances of that alienation are characteristic of the dogmatism which has been forced upon sensory experience.

4 *Ibid.*

5 Johannes Müller, *Handbuch der Physiologie des Menschen* (Koblenz: 1837), Bd. II, Sect. 1, pp. 250 ff.

6 H. von Helmholtz, *Vorträge und Reden,* Vol. 1.

7 Helmuth Plessner, *Die Einheit der Sinne. Grundlinien einer Aesthesiologie des Geistes* (Bonn: 1923).

A. G. Baumgarten (1714–1762) made in his epistemology a distinction between a higher and a lower (sensory) form of knowledge. Sensory experience (he said, in agreement with Descartes) was a confused form of cognition; truth is the perfect conceived by the intellect, beauty the perfect perceived by the senses. Aesthetics is then a *gnoseologia inferior;* as a theory of sensory cognition it is a logic of the lower cognitive ability.[8] Baumgarten's work is a characteristic example of how sensory experience—with few exceptions—has been interpreted as a deficient mode of knowing. This means that it is misunderstood as a peculiar way of being and as a special form of "intentionality."

Knowledge lays claim to validity. It claims to be valid not only for me, not only for me at this hour—today perhaps and tomorrow no longer—but at any time, in any place, for every man. Whether or not we attain valid knowledge is psychologically unimportant. Insofar as we strive for knowledge, we detach ourselves from the vanishing moment of our existence, we cross over the boundaries of our Here and Now. We break through the horizon of our individual being. Knowledge begins with an abstraction from our own vital existence and its conditions. Truth is the same for all men; as knower I am everyman, not this one particular person. We say that observers are exchangeable. Whatever is related to my particular existence lessens and obscures knowledge. Even though the act of knowing be my own, in knowing I reach a ground which is accessible to everyone, which I myself can re-enter at any time. Knowledge is general, it can be shared. In knowing I seek to grasp things as they are intrinsically, not as they appear to me in relation to myself. In knowledge I seek to correct my perspectively-colored view and to project it on a neutral, general ground which can always be reconstructed. Any ground plan is such a neutral presentation. As soon as I open my eyes I find myself here, nearer to one place, farther from another. Much as I may take measurements for my ground plan, as a measurer I cannot escape from perspective views. But I enter what has been measured into a homogeneous space-grid, constructing a design which no longer tells anything about my shifting standpoints and performances.

Sensory experiencing, on the other hand, is mine; what I grasp there I grasp in relation to myself, to my existing, my becoming. In it is defined my present time, this moment in my unrepeatable existence, between birth and death. In knowing I seek to grasp things in their order and to grasp that order itself, which, as we all know, is indifferent to our existence. But in sensory experiencing all depends upon me, everything approaches me, I myself am affected, my existence is at stake. The formula for knowing is "something happens in the world" (in accordance with the laws of nature); the formula for sensory experiencing is "something happens *to me* in the

8 Kant, who in the *Critique of Pure Reason* was still opposed to this linguistic innovation, accepted it in his later work, the *Critique of Judgment.*

world." The reality of knowing is subjected to tests which decide whether an event obeys the general laws of nature; sensory reality knows no test and no proofs; it is enough that I feel myself affected.

A vast gulf has opened up between the certainties of everyday experience and their philosophical and scientific interpretation.

Philosophical criticism, which first dealt only with the cognitive value and the validity of the sensations, has construed the content of sensory experience to suit its own needs and in so doing has estranged itself completely from everyday experience. That is a paradoxical situation. For in all his performances—observing, testing, demonstrating, communicating—the scientist remains within the sphere of everyday experience. Science itself, to the degree that as human action it is rooted in everyday experience, presupposes the latter's validity. If we wish to understand sensory experience we must study everyday life, first as to its content and then as to its just claims, with respect to its validity, not its invalidity. There are axioms of daily life on which all intercourse of men with each other and with things is based. In them the essence of sensory experience is made known. If we wish to explore that, we shall do well not to start out from constructions in which the Who, the What, and the How of sensory experience have already suffered a fateful misinterpretation. The axioms of daily life are part of the "psychology of the human world." In this title we express a methodological principle: the human world has its basis, has one of its foundations in the experiencing of men. We accept as valid the human world, in the way it is familiar to us, and inquire into its psychological possibility.

II *Axioms of Daily Life*

1. First let us observe a witness in court. He swears that he will tell the truth, the whole truth, and nothing but the truth. All the participants, judge and accused, plaintiff and advocate, jurors and listeners, accept as a matter of course the claim contained in the oath. It may be that the witness is overburdened by the obligation which the oath imposes upon him. But that changes nothing in the situation. The testimony of a witness, which the whole world has regarded and still regards as indispensable to judicial processes, refers to the possibility of observing a happening, of detaching the content of the happening from its actual occurrence in time and space, of retaining it in memory, of recalling it when required, of putting what is recalled into words and communicating it to others.

So the witness reports: I saw this and that. He speaks of things and happenings, not of signs and pictures. He speaks of objects, not of stimuli, and it is good that he does. For what can be stated concerning objects and their relations does not, even in analogy, hold true of stimuli and reactions.

The witness does not speak only of objects, however; he also speaks of himself. He does not have his knowledge from hearsay; he reports what he saw "with his own eyes." Speaking about himself, he does not mean his brain. In the phrase "with his own eyes" the eyes are not understood as receptors. The witness speaks of himself as an experiencing being who, using his organs of sight, was personally affected by the happenings. He does not think of himself as "a consciousness," nor of things as its "intentional" objects. He speaks of objects which actually confronted him physically, and at the same time he speaks of himself in his physical existence. As one who sees he finds himself in one and the same world with the objects seen. He does not discover a world in his consciousness; he finds himself in the world. The subject that experiences is not a pure consciousness, nor is it an empirical consciousness; it is this unrepeatable, actual, living creature who experiences happenings within the context of his personal life history.[9]

The testimony follows the seemingly simple formula: I saw this and that. All this pertains to seeing, not just to what is seen. In seeing, the visible thing is *for me* an object, it is the *Other*. I see the *Other* as the *Other*. The word "as" calls for interpretation; it points to the true mystery of sensory experiencing. In seeing I grasp the object or I am affected by it; and yet it is precisely as the *Other* that I grasp the object, which shows itself to me in the act of being seen without being altered thereby. In my act of seeing, the object comes into my view, the object itself, not its picture. We are all too prone to visualize the relation between the thing seen and the sight of it as analogous to that of an object to its picture. Yet that which we rightly call a picture is itself a thing. Taken by itself, a picture—a photograph, for example—is a piece of paper covered with light and dark spots. It is not seen as a picture until we refer it to the "original," not regarding the texture peculiar to it, but interpreting it as the representation of an original. In seeing, however, I do not compare a picture with an original, nor do I interpret something as a sign which points to a designated but absent thing; I see the original, the object, itself. Although it is possible and necessary to distinguish the sight from what is seen,[10] in this polar relationship no spatial duplication of any sort is involved. This reaching-out beyond oneself, thus attaining to the *Other*—which reveals itself thereby as the *Other*—is the basic phenomenon of sensory experience, a relationship which cannot be reduced to anything in the physical world. If the visible object breaks, my sight of it does not break, but I do have the sight of broken pieces; if the object burns, my sight does not burn. Though one object affects another, one sight does not affect another.

The relationship to the *Other* in sensory experience is mutual and re-

9 Cf. L. Binswanger, "Über die daseinsanalytische Forschungsrichtung in der Psychiatrie," in *Ausgewählte Vorträge und Aufsätze* (Bern: 1947), Bd. I.

10 Husserl speaks of "thing-appearance" (*Dingerscheinung*) and "appearing thing" (*erscheinendem Ding*). However, as I differ in many respects from Husserl's standpoint, I considered it expedient not to adopt his terminology.

versible. In relation to the *Other* I experience myself in my own existence, determined in a peculiar way. Vis-à-vis a thing, whatever it may be, I feel myself as part and parcel of a relation in which the object is the *Other* for me, and vice versa. In sensory experience I always experience myself *and* the world at the same time, not myself directly and the *Other* by inference, not myself before the *Other*, not myself without the *Other*, nor the *Other* without myself. There is no primacy of awareness of oneself over awareness of an outside world. In sleep, I lose the experiencing of myself with my experience of the world. In dreams the two can still return together, though distorted.

In the wording of a witness's testimony there need be no mention at all of the reporter himself; all the same, he is always referred to. Every sentence includes the implied asseveration: so it was; I saw it with my own eyes, I can swear to that. Even in a wholly "objective" report the speaker talks of himself as one for whom the *Other* has become visible as the *Other*. The observed happenings are at once part of him, who has seen them, and no part of him, for they are the *Other*, the object of his observation. That something is at the same time mine and not mine, that I can establish a relationship with the *Other* and yet leave it as it is—that is the enigmatic and logically offensive aspect of sensory experiencing. In order to eliminate the paradox, theory either absorbs perception entirely into consciousness or locates sensations entirely in neutral processes. But since the theorist, trying to construe everyday experience in his own way, must at least accept it, he is at once forced into further hypotheses. He owes an explanation of how that which he claims was originally the content of a consciousness or the excitation in a nervous system can nevertheless be experienced as an object. That brings back the paradox. With such theories, therefore, nothing is won and much is lost. Lost is the possibility of grasping the phenomena, so essential in one's relation to the *Other*, of contact, distance, direction, freedom, and constraint. Yet theory does not simply discover this logical contradiction. Theory itself produces it by assimilating experiencing to what is experienced, by objectifying and spatializing it, so that the category "thing" is applied to the perception as well as to the visible object.

The relationship I-and-the-*Other* is replaced—after such misinterpretation—by the relation Outside-Inside or External-Internal. Although the former relationship is an inner-worldly one, although in experiencing I find myself in the world, although I and the *Other* belong together in one world, the "external-internal" hypothesis divides this unity of experience and calls two worlds into existence. The expression "outside world" speaks for itself. This seemingly meaningful word proves to be meaningless as soon as we try to fix its meaning precisely. The history of modern philosophy is a chronicle of the ever-renewed and always abortive attempts to define the relationship of these two worlds.

The translation of the two-world-hypothesis from metaphysics into physiological parlance has but increased the confusion. There is no reason that we cannot apply the word "external" to stimuli, "internal" to processes stimulated by them in the nervous system. Confusion begins the moment a place in the brain is assigned to experiencing, from which locality the so-called sensations are shifted "outward" by the mysterious process of projection. Thus, in a widely used textbook of physiology it is stated: "We may assume that all of our sensations are aroused directly in the brain, but in no case are we conscious of this. On the contrary, our sensations are projected either to the exterior of the body or to some peripheral organ in the body, i.e., to the place where experience has taught us that the acting stimulus arises. The exteroceptive sensations are therefore projected exterior to our body." [11]

Elsewhere in the same book we find: "We neither 'see' our retinae nor the images upon them; the stimulation of a particular point on the retina is the sign of an object in a particular position in the outside world agreeing with our other sense reports, particularly those of touch and muscle sense. Experience in the growing child builds up such an agreement." [12]

Such formulations propagate themselves from generation to generation like a heredodegenerative defect. Percepts in consciousness are supposed to correspond to things perceived, images to things remembered. A place, it seems, can be assigned to such mental things as sensations, perceptions, memories.

A consciousness projecting sensations outward behaves toward the "external world" like a sightseer who in his tour of a gallery views one picture after another. He looks at the world depicted, but he does not belong to it, nor does it belong to him. The frame separates the illusory space of a painting from real space. In sensory experiencing, however, no frame separates us from the object; it is one and the same world that embraces us and the *Other*.

Though we are often told that the mind is "part of what the brain does," no one dares to claim that projection is a physiological process. In breathing, air is "projected outward," but sensory projection is not an electronic breathing of the brain. Ganglion cells, fibers, circuits do not leave their places, they do not project themselves outward to the desk, to the wall in front of me, nor to the sky and clouds visible through the window. Hence, projection must be an activity of the mind itself; it is the mind or consciousness which does the trick of projecting. Although the hypothesis of sensory projection tacitly presupposes the mind-body dichotomy, it nevertheless is assumed that mind and brain share the same apartment—both are located

[11] *Howell's Textbook of Physiology*, ed., John F. Fulton (15th ed.; Phila.: Saunders, 1946), p. 328.
[12] *Ibid.*, p. 441.

within the skull. The mechanism of projection supposedly explains how we, in spite of this localization of our mind, experience events that are not within our brain and are aware of a world surrounding us. The doctrine of "projection" states in a most indistinct manner that the mind grasps as its initial content some events within the brain cortex, for instance the actual configuration of the calcarine field. This initial grip of the mind remains unknown to us. We are aware only of the results of the projection. Even so, we are sure that the original content undergoes through the process of projection surprising transformations. In some sensory modalities projection is connected with enlargement, in others not; in some the projected data have the taint of mine-ness, in others not; in some they have weight, in others not; in some the projected data form a continuum, in others they appear fragmentary. In vision the enlargement is enormous. The optical stimuli, which arouse an area measuring not more than a few square inches, when "projected" fill the whole horizon, encompassing the projecting cortex, brain, and body.

Assuming, nevertheless, that there were a process of outward projection, how could we understand its working? Outward projection is supposed to transplant my sensations to the external world. But I find outside not sensations but objects, and certainly not my sensations but precisely that which is different from me, the *Other*. Again, the sensation projected outward cannot have been shifted completely from inside to outside, for even after the projection is complete I continue to have sensations. I still see the object, I still have "in me" the view of the object. It follows that the sensation cannot be magically duplicated; it would be at once inside and outside. If there were an outward projection it would produce an absurd result. Outward projection is a meager hypothesis, neither physiologically nor psychologically verifiable; it belongs to the realm of scientific voodoo. Sensations and perceptions of things are not in themselves things that occupy space. There is no topography of sensations. In experiencing I comprehend the spatiality of the world, my Here is defined in contraposition to the There, the *Other*. If we free ourselves from the compulsion of conceiving experiencing as spatial, then it is not difficult to see the basic relationship peculiar to sensory experience—indeed, it is difficult to overlook it.

Descartes's *Metaphysics,* as pointed out, not only separates body and soul and evacuates consciousness from the world, it also bisects the unity of sensory experience and motion. According to Descartes, motion belongs to the *res extensa,* sensation to the *res cogitans.* Physiology and psychology adopted and adapted this Cartesian idea without much criticism.[13] In the schema of the reflex, sensation is located in the afferent, motion in the efferent, system. Action is understood as a coupling and integration of reflexes. The motor reaction necessarily follows the stimulus in a measurable

13 For a different view cf. V. v. Weizsaecker, *Der Gestaltkreis* (Leipzig: 1940).

time interval. In acting, however, we are directed in anticipation toward a goal. When a hand is stretched out toward something, the retina has always been struck previously by light rays. And yet I stretch out my hand toward something that stands before me as a future goal. This personal time system cannot be converted to the objective one. Future is always *my* future; future exists only for experiencing beings. In the conceptual system of physics, events are determined by the past; physics does not acknowledge any action into a distant future, there is no open horizon of possibilities. Only the relationship before-after is admitted in objective deliberation; both temporal moments, however, are observed and understood in retrospection. In grasping I experience the *Other* in relation to myself; in comprehending I arrange two events, both of which belong to the *Other,* in a scheme detached from myself. I experience in a state of becoming, conatively, what is happening; I understand, perfectively, what has happened.

The muscle, the *motorium,* cannot move by itself, for no world and no open space is at its disposal. Just as little is the *sensorium* capable of moving itself, for, taken by itself, it lacks a motion apparatus. Neither *motorium* nor *sensorium* can move itself, but I *can* move myself. Spontaneous motion can only be propounded of a living being as a whole, not of any single part of it.

The traditional conception of consciousness fails to recognize that experiencing beings find themselves in a unique relationship to the world, unparalleled by anything else; as experiencing beings they have a freedom and a power of action which reaches a peak in human technology. Only in wakeful experiencing do we have such power; in sleep we sink back into the constraint of vegetative, somatic existence. Even though our experiencing may be impelled by unconscious urgings and passions, these are enacted only in and by means of our conscious experience. "The *ego,*" says Freud, "controls the avenues of the motor center." The *ego* is thus compared to an engineer who works the levers of a machine. This interpretation is also in line with the traditional stimulus-reaction-pattern, in the last analysis with the Cartesian separation of body and mind, motion and sensation. The anatomical and functional separation of *sensorium* and *motorium,* however, is not equally valid for experiencing. In the basic relationship to the *Other,* sensuality and mobility interpenetrate each other in such a way that no neat division, according to the spatial *scheme* of afferent and efferent pathways, can be carried out. Man and beast are essentially mobile because as experiencing beings they are always directed to the *Other* beyond themselves. We could not experience the *Other* as such were it not delimited in relation to us, and it could not be so delimited if we could not behave actively toward it. Distance, direction, and besetment therefore belong to the original and persistent content of sensory experience in relationship to the *Other.*

It is not too difficult to realize that only a sensorily experiencing being can move itself; we have more difficulty with the reverse statement that only a being capable of spontaneous motion can have sensory experience. Nevertheless, these are two quite symmetrical statements, which together express the inner unity and the full content of experience.

Every attempt to present experience by means of categories of things should encounter the utmost suspicion. Actually, the opposite is true; it demands, so it would seem, coercion of oneself to turn away from tradition, to grant validity to experience as it presents itself, and therewith to recognize that experiencing beings, whether man or beast, have a relation to each other and to things such as does not occur in lifeless nature nor in the vegetable kingdom. In everyday life we are far from conceiving of existence as a mere addition to bodily processes. As theorists, however, we disavow our everyday behavior. Reversing an old adage, we could say: This is good in practice, but it is no good in theory.

2. Let us return, then, to everyday practice and to our witness. In court the witness formulates his observation in statements which lay claim to validity. Upon cross-questioning (but perhaps even without such pressure), the witness will consent to qualify his testimony. Now he will insist that he was able to observe the events in every detail; at another time he will admit that at first he was too far away, but that later he had moved closer in order to follow everything precisely.

For every observation there are more or less suitable vantage points, good or bad seats in a theatre. But whether we sit in the pit or the balcony, our eyes are directed to the same object. The nature of the object is always shown to us in some perspective, sometimes in a clear, sometimes in a distorting, perspective. In all shifts of perspective, the What remains the same. The perspective both shows and distorts the What, which draws us away from the perspective. The size-color-shape-constants are the constants of the What, which amid shifting perspectives persist as one and the same in a significant form. Never does the "What" show itself completely, never perfectly. Every view of it is only a partial view. Therefore each allows as well as needs completion. As we gaze at the same What from shifting perspectives, as we walk around the object, we experience at the same time each view of the *Other* as one phase of our own existence. Every individual moment has its place in the continuum of our becoming. Everything that is sensorily experienced is present—*i.e.*, present to me. The actual moment, the changing Now of my becoming, is determined with reference to the *Other*, by which I am affected. Each moment is in itself limited but not terminated; it is incomplete. The inner time-form of our sensory experiencing is that of becoming, in which every phase points to others, preceding and following it, for its completion.

3. The *Other*, the world, though a unit, shows itself composed of a

manyness of things and divided into a variety of aspects. The manyness is linked with unity, the diversity with complementariness. In everyday life we are not plagued by any doubt that the one world manifests itself in many aspects, as a visible, audible, tangible one. Again, we could speak of perspectives in which the *Other* shows itself as one and the same, but in no perspective as complete or perfect. To avoid confusion, however, it is expedient to follow established usage and limit the word "perspective" to the visual realm, applying a new term to the transition from one sensory sphere to another. We shall speak of aspects. This word cannot well disavow its derivation from the optical realm, either. But since it is as yet unburdened as a scientific term, and since it is familiar to us as designating our shifting relations to an identical object, let us employ it here as well to designate oneness in the multitude of modalities.

Distinguishing qualities from modalities, Helmholtz admitted the possibility of a transition from quality to quality, from color to color, from sound to sound. At the same time, however, he pointed to the chasm that separates modality from modality, colors from sounds, sound from scents. Their difference is easily noticed, their complementariness hard to understand.

In everyday life, to be sure, complementariness is no problem to us either. Without any hesitation we set foot on the ground, lift food to our mouth, seize a tool. We are sure of what we are doing, children and animals not excepted. Experience teaches us to make single distinctions. Experience operates within given predetermined possibilities and only helps us discover the single facts along courses already staked out. The principle of unification, to be sure, is different from the mere co-existence of two impressions, so that, for example, frequent co-occurrence arouses the expectation that when one appears the other will do so too. After all, co-occurrence is also an indispensable condition for making distinctions. What is more, we are not free to combine impressions of all modalities at will. We reach for the visible, but we do not finger sounds; we get the taste of the touchable, but we do not touch tastes.

Unification does not annul diversity. The various stimuli are not combined, nor are the sense organs and their excitations, nor the sensory nerves and their specific energies, nor the cortical areas, and not even the various impressions themselves. For they do not fuse into one; they are not superimposed; and in unification they remain separate. Color remains color and hardness remains hardness. The colored thing that I see and touch is the same one. It is the thing I touch, not the color. I seize my pencil, not the yellow. What unifies the aspects is the What, which can show itself at once in the one and in the other, but completely in none of them, and therefore permits and demands that it be complemented in a definite way. The unification of the divergent is made possible by the fact that I as one and the same in the diversity of my senses am oriented to the *Other* as one and the same.

What the senses have in common is not restricted to what has been designated by the ancients as object of the *sensus communis:* size and shape, rest and motion, oneness and number. Nor is it exhausted in the phenomena which have recently been designated as intermodal qualities. The intermodal qualities seem to close the gap between the modalities; a common factor, for example, brightness, is said to recur in different sensory spheres. Be that as it may, we still have no solution of this problem, one of principle: how to understand the unity of the senses without denying their difference. The Aristotelian doctrine of the *aisthesis koine* discovers a common Something, insofar as an object can be defined equally well by several senses.[14] As far as the determination may extend within one modality, each sphere as such is incomplete and needs to be complemented; it presents the *Other* in only one of its aspects, capable of further elaboration. The *Other* is common to all the senses; yet each sense perceives it specifically. In fact, the individual sense does not perceive, the experiencing person does so by means of one or several of his senses. Potentially we are directed toward the *Other* in a variety of ways. The actual is never more than a limited realization of the possible; it is experienced in its limitation—*i.e.,* always pointing to further actualization.

4. The spheres of sense are distinct not only with respect to their objective aspects, such as colors, sounds, and scents; they are also distinct in the manner of the contact which binds me to the *Other.* As I experience the *Other* in shifting aspects, so I also experience myself; in each sphere I am affected, seized, beset by it in a specific way.

In the streets of a city, many people meet us. We are not forbidden to look at them, but we should fare badly if we took a notion to go up to a girl we liked and embrace, kiss, and caress her. Convention does not make such rules arbitrarily. In formulating and formalizing the details of what is permissible or forbidden, it respects the differences established by nature between the sensory modalities. No one either receives or requires instruction to be certain as to the distinction of the contacts. Therefore we feel in many cases impelled, not to look on at a distance, but to attain to direct and close contact; in other cases we rebel against a contact with all our force. A burnt child learns that certain objects which can be observed with impunity from a distance when touched develop other most disagreeable energies. Again it is important to distinguish the teaching of experience from that which made it possible to learn from experience. This particular learning is made possible by the fact that to the experiencing child the same "What"

---

[14] Aristotle, *De anima,* 425a 14 ff. In a later passage, 426b 8 ff., he too raised the question: since we discriminate "white" from "sweet," what enables us to notice that they differ; in other words, what do they have in common?

appears in shifting aspects and that the child "knows" that the object it sees is also accessible to touch; more than that, in the shift of aspects the child experiences itself as the being that is affected by the same object in different ways. All this is part of the immanent content of sensory experience; it does not stem from empiric knowledge—it is its foundation. The unity of empiric knowledge is not the result of combining things originally separate. Only what belongs together can be united—*i.e.*, that which in the very peculiarity of its existence manifests itself as a part comprehended within a whole. Sensing unfolds into the multitude of the senses. And the manyness of the modalities is controlled by the oneness of sensory experiencing. While in the manyness of modalities the *Other* is shown in shifting aspects and perspectives I experience myself in the varying ways of my being-affected. For my own existence, too, is given only in the phases of my becoming, only in aspects, incomplete in each one and therefore in each case capable of and needful of complementation.

In sensory experience something happens to me. When I open my eyes the bright sunlight impinges upon me. I am forced to see, to hear, to smell this and that. I am beset, threatened, or protected in my existence between life and death, being and not-being. I do not act as a detached, impartial observer who merely takes cognizance of the occurrence of things, I feel their power. They are real to me, I am in the game myself, seized by the events in divers *modi*. In logic, real and unreal are opposites which belong to the same class. The term "real" used as predicate in a proposition has the attribute "not real" as a counterpart of equal footing. In sensory experience, reality has no counterpart; whatever enters into sensory experience appears as real—it is felt in its action and actuality. The "unreality" of phantasies, dreams, images has to be discovered. Only a later reflection may reveal something as unreal, a mirage, an illusion. The reality of sensory experience is immediate. It is not reached in an afterthought as a statement *about* some events, it is not a conceptual evaluation of initially indifferent data. Indeed, it means not the order and interconnectedness of things, but their relation to me.

5. In the different *modi* of contact each modality has a sociological function. We enter a shop to buy something. In everyday practice—apart from exceptional occasions—that is simple enough. A child can be sent to the baker for a loaf of bread. It will be admitted readily that the full understanding of the intricate methods of our economic organization requires intensive study. The elementary exchange process, however, on which ultimately that whole organization rests, seems easily comprehensible to everyone. All the same, the exchange action, simple as it is seen to be in practice, conceals an abundance of psychological problems.

In buying and selling, the attention of the participants, to be sure, is restricted to the concrete transaction and its objects. They are not surprised that an action can be undertaken in common. The "perception of the alter ego" is to them no problem. Buyer and seller will hardly hit upon the idea that their vis-à-vis belongs to another world, an outside world, into which they mutually hand each other outward-projected sensations. Buyer and seller act in the certainty that, each by himself and yet together, they can see, grasp, and hand each other the same object. In the simple, everyday business of exchanging, each of the participants is directed to something which, as a thing different from both of them, allows a unified action. In the difference of their roles as buyer and seller, in mutual giving and taking, they perform as partners a common action affecting the same object. In the shift of owners the object remains the same. We cannot have stimuli and sensations in common, they cannot pass from hand to hand; but that *can* be done by the object which I experience as the *Other,* different from me, separable and movable. Being-together and being-able-to-be-together are accepted as elementary facts in everyday life.

How indeed could it be otherwise if it is correct that sensory experiencing opens the world to us, that I experience myself *and* the world, find myself in the world—that the comprehensive *Other* organizes itself into many parts, and that among these I encounter such as behave meaningfully toward my intentions and such as do not? Meaningful reactions teach us to distinguish other experiencing beings from inert things that give neither a meaningful answer nor spontaneous cooperation. The orientation to partnership is an original one: being oriented to something together—*i.e.,* with-each-other or against-each-other. I am not aware of the "alter ego" as an object, nor can I be by making it the object of my study; I learn to know it in my action. I experience the "alter ego" as partner of my intentions; we meet on the same path in meaningful cooperation or in meaningful opposition. We find ourself in *one* world with the other, our fellow man, sharing the orientation toward some third entity. By means of a view peculiar to himself each grasps the same object, grasps the *Other* as the *Other.* In a medical demonstration many eyes are fixed on the same ·patient; all those assembled in the same auditorium hear the same words.

Lovers of cheap skepticism are inclined to object; there is no guarantee that we actually see the same object. This objection serves as its own refutation. For the skeptic appeals to the listener with the claim that his words can be heard in their acoustic shape and understood in their meaning just as he speaks them. The skeptic mistakes the view for what is viewed. The perspectives in which the "What" of an object appears differ. Each view has a particular limitation determined by present and past conditions. Despite the manifold limitations caused by differing views, what we see together is the same. Although an object appears desirable to two persons in different degree, still they see the same object, and although a definite sum has a value for the two which varies in relation to their wealth, they both understand it as the same number of monetary units.

Without differences in viewing the same object we should not have the relation of teacher to learner. The teacher conveys to his pupil a better view and ultimately a deeper insight into the What of the object. Difference of view is the practical prerequisite for a meaningful conversation about an object. In all these relationships, in exchanging as in teaching and in everyday converse, the same phenomenon is revealed: we as many can see the same thing together.

The organized exchange of things, no less than the rational exchange of ideas, demands a certain neutrality toward the object. There are things which we will not sell, matters about which we cannot talk. Even in the norm there are conditions under which we, too deeply concerned personally, can no longer arrive at an understanding with the other. In pathological cases, in psychosis, all possibility of con-versing breaks down. The world is no longer experienced in a neutral order which would permit one, distanced from the object, to change places with another person, to exchange standpoints, to perform an action in common. Synkinesis is abolished.

III *The Spectrum of the Senses*

Modalities can be studied separately and in isolation—*e.g.*, as visual and auditory sensations. As aspects, the realms of sensory experience want to be related to and compared with each other. A number of years ago I began to compare seeing and hearing as aspects of the world.[15] At that time too the inducement was an everyday observation: the ubiquity of the dance in all cultures and the universal coordination of the movement of the dance with rhythmic sounds. To the aspect of the world which is presented in rhythmical sound corresponds a characteristic *modus* of experienced space, of contact, and of motion. Let me refer here to the comparison of colors and sound begun in that study, and let me add some supplementary remarks.

1. For naïve experience, color is an attribute of things, sound is their utterance. Colors cling, sounds disengage themselves from the sounding body and can be heard as detached. We see the orchestra, we hear the symphony. The players and their instruments are and remain side by side, separated; the sounds press into the ensemble of the chords. The eye gives us the structure of the world, the skeleton of things; with the ear we listen to its heartbeat, its pulse. Hence language is fond of designating colors by adjectives, sounds by verbs.

2. We see the same things again, or can at least do so. We never hear the same sound again; it has died away. Color is constant; sound lasts, arising and dying away, only as long as it lasts. When I open my eyes in the morning my gaze falls upon the same things that I saw about me the evening before. There is the same room, the same house, the same street, the same town. But the words that were spoken have blown away with the moment

15 E. Straus, "Die Formen des Räumlichen," *Nervenarzt,* 1930.

which produced them. We salute each other again and again with the same greeting, but it is always a new salutation, valid for this day and this hour.

The eye is the agent for identification and stabilization, the ear an organ for perceiving the actuality of happenings. There exists in phenomena a temporal co-existence of sound and hearing, whereas the visible is peculiarly time-less with respect to the gaze which can rest on it, turn from it, and return to it. Cochlearis and vestibularis have their common origin in the inner ear. Yet it is not because of a housing emergency that they are tightly squeezed together in cochlea and semicircular canals. They are both parts of *one* organ, the actuality-organ.[16] The actuality of noises is more important than the reception of pure sounds. There are quite a few human beings to whom a musical ear and a musical memory are denied. In hearing we are directed to something going on. The cochlea informs us how our environment is at the moment directed toward us, the vestibularis directs us at the moment toward our environment.

3. The very forms of temporality—persistence in the visible, duration in the audible—differ. I see the clock before me, the sight of which persists, but I hear its unbroken ticking as a constantly renewed happening. Correspondingly, we experience motion in the optical field as a place-change of something identical, in the acoustic field as a time-sequence of changing data—*e.g.*, as a sequence of tones in a melody or in what the English language characteristically calls a "movement" in music.

4. In visible matters manyness is arranged in a side-by-side grouping, a disjoined array. Things show themselves in the continuum of a horizon which includes them and us. Noises and musical sounds appear singly or as single groups, arranging themselves in succession and juxtaposition. The boundary of visible things is spatial, that of audible ones is temporal. Contour separates thing from thing, the chord links tone to tone.

In the totality of the horizon, the eye must separate and detach thing from thing, arrange the whole in parts. The *eye's* procedure is predominantly analytical. The *ear* ties together the tones, which emerge singly, as parts of a sentence, a movement, or a melody. The ear is a predominantly synthesizing sense. In optical matters, beginning and end can be grasped simultaneously; hence in them finite magnitudes can be established and compared. We count size and number. In acoustics we perceive the accent and rhythm of the structure; we grasp a meter, a metrical pattern in verse. In optical matters there is multiplication, in acoustics repetition. Because beginning and end are not given simultaneously in a sound, the present moment points backward and forward; the single unit, present to us as a part, needs to be understood as a member of an entirety, developing in time.

5. The optical continuum continues on into darkness replete with quality.

16 In some species this has as third member the lateral organ, the lateral line system in the fish.

Darkness is visible in a mode different from that in which we perceive silence. Every sense has a form of emptiness peculiar to itself.

6. In the visible realm, the *Other* appears at a distance, yonder, opposite. The many "yonders" define my Here as peripatetic abode. Noise and tone, on the other hand, fill space, press in upon me. In the open horizon of the static optical continuum I can direct myself to the *Other,* move toward it. The *Other* lies as a goal before me; I see it in the present moment, as a point which I have not yet reached but which I can and shall reach. Optical space is open to the future, whereas sound lays hold on me in a particular moment; it is of the present and determines the actual uniqueness of my Now. When I am hearing, then I have already heard.

7. In seeing I direct myself actively to the visible; I "cast my eyes" upon something. But in hearing I am a receiver; the tones come at me and compel me. In hearing, obedience is foreshadowed. As German links *Hören* (hearing) and *Ge-horchen* (obeying), so the Greek *akouein* and *hypakouein,* the Latin *audire* and *ob-oedire* (the root of ob-edience), the Russian *slishim* and *poslocham.* Language knows of the fact that every modality has its special *modus* of contact, its specific form of being-affected (pathos); it knows about the activity of seeing and of the overwhelming power of sound. It also knows that our gaze, when directed to the *Other,* can encounter another gaze, meet it freely, or evade it—can indeed be unable to endure it. The psychopathologist has to tell still more about the reversal of direction in seeing, about the eyes that stare at the cocaine addict from every direction, threatening and persecuting, or about the eyes that look out from the Rorschach blots. All this reveals the peculiar freedom and besetment, the power-relationship that enters into every sensory experience, varying with each modality, and that emerges in the pathological sphere with increased violence.

The differences of the aspects remain in force, however physiology may regard the relation of stimulus and excitation and the conduction of excitations. The predominance of seeing and of the visible has made it the model of our world-interpretation and our self-understanding. It is true that in seeing I am normally with the *Other,* seeing objects in their relation to each other and in their independence. We easily forget the original meaning of the word "ob-ject." We speak of objective affirmations, meaning a cognitive view in which the basic relation to the *Other* has already been dissolved. Our conceptual system, our in-sight, is predominantly—if not exclusively—constructed with reference to the optical sphere. Subjected to this construction, the other aspects are not properly understood in their own special structure.

8. If the *Other* shows itself to the gazer as aloof, as tone it presses in upon the hearer, and to the toucher it is immediately present. Every touching is at the same time a being-touched; what I touch touches me, and it can

touch me throughout the entire scale of emotions, extending from horror and shudders to the quivers of lust. Our verbal expressions oscillate correspondingly between transitive and intransitive meanings. If I feel something, at the same time I feel (myself). Other languages act similarly. German *berühren* corresponds to English "touch," and in both languages "to touch" in the sense of physical contact can take on the sense of an emotional "touching" and "being touched." In no aspect is the reciprocity of one's relation to the *Other* as clear as in the tactual sphere.

This has a significant sociological result. Immediate reciprocity limits the possibility of participation. In the comprehensive horizon of the visible we can direct ourselves to something in common; the tone which, once detached from its source, fills space, embraces us all. But the immediate reciprocity of touch limits the sharing to two partners at a time. The tactile sense is exclusive. What you wish to seize I must first let loose. In drastic fashion language exploits the exclusiveness of the tactile sense in order to designate a claim to possession. It speaks of *pos-sedere* (German *be-sitzen*).[17] The tactile sense is the sense of the excluded third person.

Immediate reciprocity limits tactile impressions in still another way. Tactile impressions are fragmentary, they grasp Here without Yonder, a Here on the horizon of blankness. This blankness can, as touching goes on, be filled with new fragments of the *Other,* but the next groping move can also lead us into the bottomless pit. Surrounded by such blankness, which threatens us with annihilation, we cling to what is still presently tangible, seeking in suffocating fear for a handhold, of which we dare not let go. The immediacy of touching is burdened with a high premium.

The groping hand must repeatedly reach, seize, and release the *Other.* Sensuality and mobility are coordinated in the tactile sphere in an especially striking fashion. We pass our fingers over the table top and apprehend its smoothness as a quality of the object. The tactile impression results from the completion of the movement. When the tactile movement stops the tactile impression dies out.[18]

In the immediate, excluding, mutual grasping, the tactile sense is the medium of bodily connection to a greater degree than any other. Seizing and grasping refuse to come to a standstill. Affectionate touching is an endless process of approaching—really, of nearing and withdrawing. We must retreat to a distance in order to win nearness. The sexual embrace, too, is a crescendo of nearing and withdrawing which culminates in orgasm and breaks off. Communication is an event, not a state.

The reciprocity of touching and being touched is but rarely perfect. In such rare encounters we find ourselves stirred to the depths, experiencing

---

[17] American and Australian law have recognized so-called squatter's rights, the possibility of acquiring land by re-siding on it.

[18] Cf. D. Katz, *Der Aufbau der Tastwelt* (Leipzig: 1925).

with and through the partner the uniqueness and fullness of our existence.

Quite otherwise in handling things and utensils. There we are directed to the things. If we weary in our work, another can relieve us. So too in touching to test something, which ends in a tangible result, in a "statement." What is "found" can be repeated. In the reciprocity of affectionate contact no "finding" is arrived at. In this never-ending process of approach, we, you and I, are irreplaceable: no one else can take your place or mine. Yet the physician whose examination has led him to a conclusion can guide others to reach the same conclusion, and another can take his place. Physician and patient meet not as I and You but in definite social roles, in functions of a general character. The patient undresses before the other because he is a physician; the physician touches the other as a patient whose body, under his exploring hands, can yield stable findings. Reciprocity and immediacy are suspended; physiognomies are screened off. The Hippocratic oath demands the aloof behavior of the examiner despite the intimacy of touch. In the physiological relation of stimulus and excitation, in the reduction of excitation, in the tactile process as such, nothing has changed. What is altered is the attitude, and with it the direction to the *Other;* this transforms the object itself.

The reciprocity of touching can vary in two directions—on the one hand, toward the touching for testing purposes, in which, as remarked above, grasping is directed to the object, on the other hand, toward a being-touched, in which a ray of happening is aimed at me by the *Other.*

In active touching the hand functions as a tool whereby I secure information regarding the character of the object. On this point I exchange opinions with others. In the passivity of being touched, on the other hand, I am aware of my body in its sensitiveness, its vulnerability, its powerlessness, and its nakedness. The more powerfully the *Other* presses in upon me, the more I am overpowered by it—the more I sink back into the forsakenness and forlornness of my existence. Even pain is no mere passive state of being; in it too there is still an I-world relation. In the pain which robs us of our senses—in which, that is, things are no longer perceivable as they are—the world presses in upon us, imprisoning us in our body, which at the same time it alienates from us.

9. None of the modalities plays in only one key. Yet in each one the basic theme of I-and-the-*Other* is varied in a specific way, so that in the visible the persistent dominates, in the audible the actually present, in the tactile sphere the reciprocal, in the area of smell and taste the physiognomic, in pain the power-relation. In their totality the modalities are to be arranged in a broad scale, which extends from the visible to the area of pain. In this spectrum of the senses the aspects vary with respect to temporality, spatiality, direction, boundary, distance, movement, physiognomy, connection, freedom and constraint, contact, objectivity, enumerability, divisibility,

measurability, empty forms, and possibility of abstraction, of recollection, and of communicability. At one end of the scale insight predominates, at the other, the impression; *there* is found the communicable and actual communication in shaped wording and writing; *here* is the loneliness of pain, which can finally express itself only in unformed plaints and cries.

Every sense serves or denies itself to the intellectual existence of man in its own way. Arts have developed only in the fields of the visible and the audible. Scientific thinking takes its origin from there, too. Science and art are possible only when we can direct ourselves actively to the *Other*, delimit it from ourselves, separate the What from the This, and lay hold upon the What in its order and its connections. Such possibilities disappear when we ourselves are too strongly affected. At times this can happen even in the aspect of the visible, but as a rule it happens at the opposite end of the sensory spectrum. Fear, excitation, and pain are not conditions favorable to meditation. In an unfamiliar wood at night my reach shrinks, things close in upon me, direction is reversed and aims at me, the physiognomy of my environment is altered and with it the shape of all objects.

IV *Hallucinatory Modes of Being-in-the-World*

By way of a summarizing thesis we can say: Our everyday world is formed within the medium of sensory experience and in accordance with the characteristics of the modalities. *Hallucinations originate in the medium of distorted modalities.* They appear at points where the I-world relations are pathologically transformed. The causes of pathological alterations can be many and diverse, their attack peripheral or central. The severest disturbances can be expected where the I-world relations are most deeply altered, where a pathological disturbance of one's relation to the *Other* so alters direction, distance, and boundary that the *Other* appears, as it were, in new aspects.

Our being-affected determines the reality of experiences. For reality is not read off any dial of characteristics; it is not judged by a regulated order of occurrences, it is not a subsequent addition to data of sense; it is an original and inseparable factor of sensory experience itself. Sensory experiencing and experiencing the real are one and the same. In sensory experience there is no question of validity according to general rules. The reality of sensory experience needs no subsequent justification. It is before and above doubt. Its legitimation is sensory experience itself—*i.e.*, my being-beset, the appertaining of an event to my existence. The *Other* is real insofar as it affects and has affected me. In the pathological alterations of my being-seized, constructs are formed, with the character of reality and sensuality, which resemble the normal ones but which differ from them as "voices" do from utterances in speech. Let me make clear by some examples what aesthesiology can contribute to the understanding of hallucinations.

1. In alcoholic delirium the modality of seeing is distorted in a characteristic manner. The optical realm is that of stabilization and identification; alcoholic delirium is characterized by destabilization and loss of identification. Destabilization affects the spatial structure as a whole and visible things in detail. One may seek an explanation by pointing to the disturbances of the apparatus of equilibrium; these can indeed influence the relations to the *Other* in their optical aspect, but they cannot explain the totality of the hallucinatory symptoms in delirium. We find analogous disruptions of stability, a progressive unclarity of outlines, a paramorphosis and kaleidoscopic form-shifting even in cases of intoxication which have less, or no, effect on the apparatus of equilibrium. The motor unrest of visual delusions reveals—as do the mescalin experiments—no simple dependence upon motor excitation.[19]

Of seeing, it is normally true that we are directed to the things seen; even in delirium this attitude does not disappear entirely. The delirious subject often finds himself in a gruesome environment which threatens him with terrible tortures. But usually the scene is not constructed egocentrically. The patient becomes a witness of horrors which lay hold on him too but which are not aimed at him alone, are not meant for him to the exclusion of all others. This agrees well with the fact that the delirious drinker remains accessible to speech and is suggestible when contact is established, in contrast to the patient in alcoholic hallucinosis, who is completely under the spell of the voices conversing about and against him. We may recall at this point also that the acoustic experiences in mescalin and hashish intoxication generally do not appear to converge on the intoxicated subject. Noises fill and pierce space; they often have a voluptuous, "cosmic" character, they lay hold upon the hearer, penetrate his being, so that he feels the musical movement and himself as one (or feels himself one with the musical movements). This fusion contrasts sharply with the singling out and isolating of the person pursued by voices. Evidently, in the two groups, different varieties of involvement, of the relations I-and-the-*Other*, take effect.

Destabilization and the loss of identification can be recognized in the dreamlike state of delirium. The unstable, the metamorphic shifting, marks dream constructs in contrast with the solidity and constancy of things which we encounter in our waking existence. In spite of the certainty with which we distinguish, upon awaking, the wakefulness of daytime from the world of dreams, it is not easy to say what enables us to make that distinction— *i.e.*, how wakefulness apprehends itself. This at least is certain, that on each

19 Cf. Mayer-Gross, "Psychopathologie und Klinik der Trugwahrnehmungen," Bumke's *Handbuch der Psychiatrie* (Berlin: 1928), Bd. I, S. 449.

morning we again fasten the thread where we dropped it in the evening. One wakeful day joins the other as its continuation; but the dreams of one night are not in manifest connection with those of the preceding nights. Indeed, every moment of waking sensory experience has its place in a continuum from which it cannot be removed. In my recollection I can transport myself to past decades; in waking sensory experience I can only advance from present to present into the future. Conceptually, I can put minutes, hours, centuries into one total; in waking experience I remain bound to one point in time; it alone has the character of reality—*i.e.*, of reality in the development of my existence. In my imagination I can cross the ocean in one leap; in sensory experience there are no leaps. To reach the door of my room I must pass first this spot and then that. Waking existence has a heaviness [20] peculiar to itself, and no Pegasus can carry us away. By the same token, waking experience has its own peculiar order and precision. Every moment is directed to the following one in a meaningful anticipation. Temporal sequence and sequence as a meaningful order of the perspectives coincide. Sequence carries with it an inescapable consequence. In this continuum I can make the *Other* attain full concreteness and definiteness. It must show itself in a definite way, it must be definable. Only in physiological wakefulness do we have the power of anticipation, and in the continuum of anticipation we grasp our wakefulness. In falling asleep, in vertigo, in dreams, in disturbances of consciousness, the continuum falls apart, the present is no longer the fulfillment of an anticipation, nor does it reach out ahead of itself in new anticipations. Therewith the stability of things disintegrates, the order of experiential connections break down, and thus the possibility of abstraction and critical deliberation is abolished.[21] They require a breaching of the sensory horizon, a transcending of the moment. When awake we distinguish dreams from waking reality; in sleep, however we may age, we succumb again and again to the power of the dream. We cannot carry our critical awareness over into our dreams. We are completely held in bondage by the dream-experience. Not that ideas and recollections now attain the character of "real perceptions"—the type of reality is altered. The being-affected is decisive.

2. Direction and boundary change with involvement. Experiments with hashish and mescalin have contributed copious material to illustrate this connection. The saturation and intensive lustre of colors, the obtrusiveness

---

[20] We shall do well to conceive of this heaviness as physical, too. Sleeping and waking are biological phenomena, and like sensory experiencing, they belong to us, as embodied individuals. When awake we are aware of our constraint and gravity, and this precisely as mobile creatures which alone can experience gravity. The dreamer only dreams that he moves; he does not move, and he is not burdened by gravity. The one intoxicated by mescalin or hashish has the experience that "all heaviness falls away."

[21] The fantastic experiences of hysterics are as a rule characterized by the fact that they do not occur in a deformed, destabilized sphere, nor in a fragmented continuum.

of scents and noises, are but a prelude. As the intoxication develops, human features too become more expressive, insistent, significant. The physiognomies reveal to the intoxicated the very nature of their intentions. Yet, at a later stage, the alterations of the involvement and the variations of the power relationship are expressed in a manifest reversal of direction. The experimental subjects begin to feel influences: from the gaze of the *Other* issues a terrible, overpowering, irresistible effect. Such experiences may give rise to further paranoid elaborations and references, but they originate in the realm of immediate sensory awareness.

In every relation to the *Other,* in direction and counterdirection, in the often-mentioned power relationship, the experience of being influenced, overwhelmed, and persecuted is germinally present. With the shift of involvement the physiognomic characters stand out more clearly, first felt only as obtrusiveness and insistence, indicating that there is already a force emanating from the *Other* which lays hold on us with growing might.

The word physiognomy is to be used whenever the *Other* is not a neutral quality but reveals itself as luring or alarming, calming or threatening, as a friendly or hostile action-center. Hence, too, the calming or threatening physiognomies are not inferred but felt in the immediacy of sensory experience. Increasing passivity in mescalin intoxication brings with it heightened experiences of sensory dependence. Connected therewith are also the alterations of time and space: the stoppage of time, the boundlessness of spaces. Nearness and farness, including their visible forms, are not to be understood solely as optical phenomena. Depth of space, articulation into Near and Far, organize space with respect to a mobile being, organize an area of action. Near and Far are phenomena of reach, of reachableness. Passivity removes the reachable to a limitless remoteness. This conception is confirmed by the observation that in mescalin intoxication the blind undergo alterations of space like those of persons with normal vision.[22]

Vanishing of subject-object boundaries, fusing with the environment, has been observed with great regularity. Alterations of the body-schema, too, are probably variations in the experiencing of personal activity. The mescalin-intoxicated person may experience that his hand is raised and detached and remains floating in the air, even when he *knows* that it is resting on his knee. The body-schema is not an image of corporeal configuration but a "scheme" of possible action. The immediate involvement of freedom of action triumphs over contrary knowledge. Also, in a state of depersonalization the factual order of things is preserved. The visible distance is not altered, only the physiognomic aloofness. An impassable boundary separates the depersonalized person from the *Other,* which appears "unreal" to him. Patients who use this word refer spontaneously to the meaning of reality as it is established in sensory experiencing. The character of

22 Cf. K. Zucker, *Z. Neur.,* Vol. 127, 1930, p. 108.

reality is lost, because things can no longer be integrated into the temporal order of personal existence. The hashish-intoxicated may become a part of the *Other;* the depersonalized one faces it in helpless isolation.

3. We regard the voices that torment the schizophrenic as a symptom, in which a special mode of involvement is likewise manifested. The voices are heard, they are acoustic phenomena, but they are also different enough to contrast with all else that is audible. The mode of their reception is rather a being-affected, similar to hearing. The voices emerge in a deranged acoustic sphere and encounter the patient in a relation to the *Other* which most resembles hearing; they are quasi-acoustic.

Just as there are sounds that can detach themselves from the sounding body and, in permeating space, gain an independent existence, so there are the voices that speak to the patient—voices, not persons. Even when the patient can identify the voices—in a general way—as male or female, loud or soft, clear or scarcely distinguishable—or indeed when he assigns them to individuals—it is the voice that presses in upon him: the voice is present, not the speaker. The occasional reference to an apparatus that serves for transmission makes it clear that the voices alone are immediately present. Anyway, attempts at explanation play but a secondary part. The voices strike the sufferer with such violence that the question as to the How of their transmission, as to the possibility of their presence, remains irrelevant. In schizophrenic involvement a perturbing reality is manifested to which all critical opinion capitulates. Obstacles and distances are of no importance. The common order of things, in which each object has its place, with its own limited range and sphere of influence, is no longer valid. There are no boundaries, there is no measure and no standard of measurement, there is no organization of space into danger- and safety-zones. The *Other* is a realm of the hostile, in which the patient finds himself quite alone and quite defenseless, delivered up to a power that threatens him from all sides. The voices aim at him, they have singled him out, and they separate him from all others. He is certain that they mean him and no other; he is not surprised that his neighbor can hear nothing. Indeed, he is not surprised at all; he does not question, neither himself nor others nor things; he does not test his impressions, nor evaluate them according to general rules. "It happens to me in the world"; this characterization of sensory experience applies perfectly to the hearing of voices, which, as proved by that very fact, is a fundamental and primary disturbance of sensory experience. That is, it is a basic alteration of being-in-the-world, where the *Other* shows itself in an uncanny, incomprehensible way but, to the patient, with immediate certainty. In that world there is no co-partnership, no discursive elucidation. The patient cannot make himself understandable to us; indeed, he cannot understand himself and his world. He experiences it only in a sequence of moments of being overpowered. Understanding, shared or individual, demands some kind of indifference, the possibility of detaching one-self from the impact of impressions, of reflecting about oneself, of putting oneself into a general order in which places are interchangeable. The power of the voices resembles the power of all sound. Sound, although something, is not properly a thing, it is not one of the *pragmata* that we can handle. One cannot do anything to sound, and yet it is not nothing; it eludes our grasp, we are helplessly exposed to it. The power of sound goes on working in the articulated vocable, the Word, the creating command of God, the predestinating *fatum*—i.e., in the dictum, the judge's sentence, the voice of conscience. The voice of conscience warns and admonishes him who is free to act. The schizophrenic voice derides, persecutes, commands. It allows re-flection no freedom. The voices are everywhere; inescapably "they" press in upon the patient like a poison gas which our own breathing forces us to in-hale when it fills the atmosphere. The voice of conscience judges past things, weighs future ones. The schizophrenic voice is of the present, but always vanishing at the spur of the moment. If need be we can drown out one noise by a louder one, we can outshout a speech which we do not like; it is characteristic that this method of defense is hardly ever attempted by the schizophrenic. He is paralyzed in his actions, not only in his mobility—an impotent victim.

With the paralysis of action the boundary which separates the *Other* from the experiencing being is shifted. We who speak of hallucinations are con-vinced that the voices heard by the patient are his voices. He experiences something that belongs to him as belonging to the *Other*. I call "mine" what is at my disposal, what submits to me, pays attention to me, belongs to me, as also what I produce and have produced; conversely, finally, what I belong to and what makes definite claims upon me—narrowly defined, then, that over which I have the immediate power of production or dis-posal. The boundary-shift between Mine and His which takes place in the hearing of voices again points to the change in the sphere of freedom; it points to a central alteration of one's involvement.

A storm, an earthquake, heat and cold affect all of us. Voices are atmos-pheric, like gale and cold, but they aim at only one person, and they do not strike him only in his vital existence but also as this individual human being in his own Self. The voices behave like sounds in nature and yet they are speech, criticism, mockery; in seizing upon the individual, they attack him in his very humanness, in the realm of moral, aesthetic action. This circum-stance has occasioned doubts as to any sensory character of the "voices." So did the "composure" of the schizophrenic, the co-existence of hallucina-tory experiences and normal orientation. However, it is just this skepticism which points the way to the solution of the problem. For the illness attacks someone who up to its outbreak has lived and acted as a human being. The schizophrenic process corrodes that which has developed historically. In the elemental alteration of involvement, the *Other,* the world, shows a physiognomy corresponding to sensory experience. During the period of transition something uncanny announces itself, everyday things gain an enigmatic significance, till the familiar world collapses. Many of the delusional experiences and the so-called ideas of reference have a much more elemental sensory content than indicated by our customary terminology. Thus the hearing of voices stands midway between the so-called "kinesthetic" hallucinations and the realm of such phenomena as automatic thinking, ideas-snatched-away or thoughts-being-heard.

As the patient is a victim of the voices, so too with haptic hallucinations. He undergoes being touched but he touches nothing. The incubus that takes possession of a woman is not at the same time embraced by her in a hallucination. The reciprocity of tactile experience is annulled. A hostile power touches the patient, but eludes his grasp even when most insistently close to him. The touching is performed from a distance: the victim is blown at, sprayed, electrified, hypnotized. Optical hallucinations, rare in schizophrenia, may follow the same pattern: the direction of seeing is inverted, the patients are blinded, light beams are directed against them, pictures are thrown upon them. The hostile powers resemble the wind, the river, the fire. They are like the voices in their fluidity and volatility, in the impossibility of their being caught: they penetrate into the innermost existence of the patient, they clutch at his heart, they assault him sexually, and yet they remain at a distance. Attempts to explain the experienced effects technically, as transmitted by mysterious machines of which the persecutors make use, reveal once more that personal action is transformed into elemental happenings.

The automatisms of thinking indicate that the patient is denied any spontaneous and free survey of the world; his thoughts being heard, his mind being read, denote that the barriers of his intimate life have been leveled off, that the innermost sphere of his existence has been invaded. The structural proximity to many motor phenomena, such as induced movements, automatisms of command, echopraxia, or negativism, seems evident. The fundamental alteration of one's relation to the *Other* cannot be restricted to the sensory sphere. But we must be content for now with these suggestions.

Our purpose was to illustrate through some examples that, and how, hallucinations form in the realm of deformed modalities. They are variants, pathological variations, of the basic relation I-and-the-*Other.* They possess therefore that character of reality which pertains to all sensory experiencing, which is not one class of experience alongside many others. Sensory experiencing is the basic form of all experiencing, from which other modes of existing—such as thinking, remembering, imagining—separate off, but always return. Sensory experiencing is of the present. But the Now of the present is always *my* Now, a moment of my becoming. The essence of sensory experience itself, in its besetment at every moment, is to be sensitive to the efficacy—*i.e.*, the reality—of the *Other*. The schizophrenic does not withdraw from reality into a land of dreams; he is immersed in an alien reality with physiognomies which in the severest cases paralyze all action and cut off all communication.

VI

The World of
the Compulsive*

by V. E. von Gebsattel

I *The Problem*

WHAT ALWAYS FASCINATES US in encountering the compulsive person is
the unpenetrated, perhaps impenetrable, quality of his being different.
Seventy years of clinical work and scientific research have not altered this
reaction. Kept alive by the contradiction between the intimate closeness
of the presence of a fellow man and the strange remoteness of a mode of
being completely different from our own, the affect of psychiatric amaze-
ment never ceases. This excitement constantly thrusts upon us the question
about the world in which the compulsive lives; for our world, in which he
is found, does not seem to be his. Actually, the contradiction found in the
phenomenon of the compulsive does not distinguish him from others encountered by the psychiatrist; but the lucidity with which the compulsive
illuminates his own abnormality, without finding it out, and the consequently increasing paradox of his existence, only heightens, if possible, the
acuity of the psychiatric affect and keeps it going with particular emphasis.

The focus of our inquiry is the compulsive person *in toto* and primarily
the special way of existing by which he is set into a specific world of being
(*Daseinswelt*) different from our own. In this, we wish to go beyond the mere

* Translated by SYLVIA KOPPEL and ERNEST ANGEL. [This article has been considerably
abridged. The original paper contained three case histories. Only one is reproduced in this
translation, the one which best illustrates the paper's concepts.—EDITORS] The bibliographic
reference is Viktor E. Von Gebsattel, "Die Welt des Zwangskranken," *Monatsschrift für
Psychiatrie und Neurologie*, Vol. 99 (1938), pp. 10–74. Reedited in *Prolegomena einer medizinischen Anthropologie* (Berlin-Göttingen-Heidelberg: Springer-Verlag, 1954), pp. 74–128.

analysis of function, act, and experience, likewise beyond the depth-psychological drive theory of psychoanalysis, and beyond the simple character and constitution theories of compulsivity as stimulated through the compulsive phenomena in post-encephalitis. The results of these types of research form the premise of our method, which we should like to designate as a constructive-synthetic one. The following inquiry aims at a phenomenological-anthropological-structural theory, which will prepare the ground upon which the data obtained by clinical analysis can then take root and attain their proper meaning.

It is the psychiatric affect of astonishment, the experience of an encounter with an unexplainable other being, that should enter into the initial posing of our question. For what becomes effective in this encounter is just this unexplainable other being in his human totality. This "being-different" of a fellow human being—which stirs equally our sympathy and our intellectual curiosity—is not exhausted in the difference of his functions, his life history, his character, etc.—in other words, in what one usually calls the symptomatology of the sick person. The latter appeals to our curiosity, our intellect, our scientific understanding. But psychiatric wonder reaches deeper down than curiosity, interest, or scientific understanding. The wondering has an existential meaning. One wonders not only as a scientist or as a psychiatrist; one wonders much more as a fellow man—*i.e.*, on that level of being which precedes being a scientist or a doctor and which provides the foundation for both. In this fundamental wondering, indeed, is confirmed our engagement by the contradiction between a familiar human phenomenon and the strange form of being that is completely inaccessible to us. The fact is, indeed, that the greatest exertion of our will to knowledge never enables us to set foot on that place which the other person—*e.g.*, the compulsive—occupies. All psychiatric knowledge has, in relation to the object with which it is concerned, only the possibility of approximating it, never the possibility of completely penetrating it. This last separation, that keeps person from person and can be overcome only intellectually and not experientially, rings already in the sympathetic affect of wondering.

But in spite of this, or just because of it, existential-anthropological research is concerned with the whole of the compulsive person. That such efforts can be successful has been demonstrated unequivocally by the fine, meaningful work of Binswanger on the flight of ideas. Just in this realm of the contemplation of human beings, new insights often assert themselves through a reflection of the observer upon himself; thus, he includes in the formulation of his question factors which, although contained in his situation, were not considered in the hasty reaching out of the intellect to the cause of the event. Such a factor is, for instance, the sympathetic act of wondering which—because our own mode of existence in the form of "wondering" is always included in the question—is also capable of leading us beyond the bounds of the purely scientifically-oriented intellect and its inclination to functional-theoretical and functional-mechanistic trains of thought. As already mentioned, our aim is not a devaluation of the achievements of the intellect but their articulation within the new order of the existential-anthropological context, with a view to developing their true meaning.

II *A Case History*

Our considerations take as their starting point a clinical case. Each case of compulsivity offers the observer innumerable instructive features and can tempt him—through penetration into the individuality and uniqueness of the case—to plunge himself into the characterological specificity of the compulsive personality, its structure, and its logic. It must be explicitly emphasized that this is far from our purpose. Consequently the following case history will be presented only cursorily, for the sole purpose of gaining a clear background for the considerations to follow. We shall, furthermore, abstain from submitting to another revision the numerous classificatory principles for compulsive phenomena. Our example is representative for the type of "anankastic psychopath" (Eugen Kahn, Kurt Schneider, Binder). The anankastic [1] psychopath represents that kind of compulsive in whom the compulsion phenomena attain the most far-reaching systematic development. This type lives wholly in his very own special world and thus has a special meaning for the existential-anthropological way of thinking. (Something similar can perhaps be said also of the melancholic patient with anankastic symptoms, as established by Bonhoeffer.) We are firmly convinced that the cases which exhibit the symptoms in their purest form also represent model cases for demonstration.

Case H. H.

Patient is seventeen years old; gives an impression of being shy, embarrassed, dejected, introverted, inhibited. Intelligent—ambitious. Had earlier been the leader of his class, learned without an effort. Had to be removed from school ("Gymnasium") in August 1937 because of total failure—an eventuality which had been in the making for several years.

He complains about his compulsions, everything being compulsion with him; not for one second is he free of his compulsion. Wishes intensely for

1 [The word anankastic, derived from the Greek *ananke* (Fate) relates to "being tied by Fate"—*i.e.*, to the feeling of inevitability, of the impossibility of escape, which these patients subjectively experience. The term is spelled "anancastic" in Dorland's *Medical Dictionary*, and is loosely defined as "same as obsessive-compulsives." Actually, the "anankastic" is only one of several types of compulsives. The term "psychopath" has, in this context, a meaning which is quite different from the one assigned to it in our psychiatric language; it refers to constitutional psychopathological elements in such patients.—EDITORS.]

freedom from his suffering, but does not believe in a cure. Considers his case unique. He has been suffering from compulsions for eight years without knowing what was bothering him; considered himself abnormal. At the time of his first confession, his thought revolved exclusively around the confession, which he never considered valid because, in spite of hour-long efforts, he could never arouse a "perfect repentance" in himself. Anxiety about vows tortured him. In the prayer of angelic salutation, he felt he had to visualize each letter; should he fail to accomplish this, it would be a "mortal sin." He had then to vow to himself that he would accomplish it. Since, in spite of this, he did not accomplish it, he had broken a vow, an oath, and must confess he had perjured himself 150 times. In connection with the repetition of penitential prayer, there appeared a counting compulsion. With respect to the sixth commandment, he behaved as follows: One must confess when one has thought or done something unchaste. Actually, no such thing happened, but if a boy in school said something unchaste and he heard it, he did think it, because one cannot hear something without thinking, and he did do it because any thought is an act. Very severe scruples. Later he stopped confessing. At about twelve years, first nocturnal emission, which he took for "bed wetting." The next morning he noted an odor on himself and established that his penis was wet. Since then he observes that his urine drips. Hours on end he would sit on the toilet, waiting for the dripping to stop; he would dry his penis carefully and wrap it in toilet paper to prevent urine from getting on his shirt. Should he be disturbed in this, he would stand for one or two hours with pelvis pulled in, hands propped on the table in front of him, to prevent his shirt from becoming wet before his penis should have become dry. In spite of these measures, an "odor" developed that stuck to his clothes and his coat and controlled him all day long. This is still so today. He is constantly possessed with the thought of smelling bad and, thus, with being conspicuous, which prevents him from talking to and associating with people. He cannot even telephone because of his obtrusive body odor. Even when he is alone, this odor disturbs him in everything so that he cannot do anything. He is just about "nailed down" by it. Because of this odor which he considers to be something objective, he is shy and embarrassed.

In general, compulsions rule him in every performance. They begin at once with getting up in the morning. This must proceed according to a ritual that has been laid down exactly. He divides each action, each performance, into the very tiniest single movements. Each movement must be carried out exactly, and to each he must attend carefully. Everything is ordered and laid out this way—getting up, washing, drying, getting dressed: first this movement, then that one (dividing compulsion plus control compulsion). Often he must stand with arms upraised, clutching his sponge, before he can go further. Then again he must remain standing and think everything through once more, especially if he feels there is something he did not do right, or if he was "lost in thought" (*i.e.*, was not attending closely to his task). This recapitulation appears especially after some disturbance or omission in the completion of his ceremonial. He is often tortured by the impression that what he must do has not been done right, or not precisely enough or not consciously enough, and for this reason he is actually never "well washed" or "neatly clothed." He requires many hours for his toilet, never really gets through, and arrives late for everything. And for that reason he has a "guilty conscience." This compulsion for order rules everything, even the way he eats or goes through a door; in the latter act he must never come in contact with anything. If he touches something, he becomes dirty. If his father, in visiting the hospital, hangs his coat over his bathrobe, the coat is soiled with urine and he must take care not to hang his coat next to his father's in the closet at home, otherwise he cannot put it on again. By contact, dirt can be spread over innumerable objects.

A washing compulsion is also present. He can read only when he accidentally comes upon something readable. Should he *want* to read, he simply does not get to it because he must take each word apart into its single letters. He never has any peace; something always has to be analyzed or inspected, something always has to be recapitulated, or repeated, or washed—and in everything he is disturbed by his own repugnant body odor which is the most torturesome thing of all. He is depressed and without hope and thinks that people like himself, if left to themselves, could starve to death. No sexual life.

III *The Disturbance Aspect in the Compulsion-Syndrome: "The Anankastic Phobia"*

Our chronic anankastics confirm thoroughly the twofold nature of the compulsion-syndrome as recognized in psychiatric circles: first the "disturbance psychism" (*Stoerungspsychismus*) which generally takes on a phobic form and, in reaction to this, the "defense psychism" (*Abwehrpsychismus*) to which belong the conspicuous compulsive acts. The phobic aspect of the compulsion syndrome with its obtrusive, unshakable quality of possessedness is emphasized by French psychiatrists, who speak of "obsession" and of "obsessional neurosis," whereas German psychiatry underlines rather the factor of "compulsion." If, in what follows, we differentiate between the anankastic phobia and the compulsive defense psychism, we are dividing for the sake of orderliness what in the anankastic personality and in its world-relatedness forms a whole in which the succession of components is often interchangeable.

In contrast to many authors, we side with those investigators who consider the phobic touch of the compulsion syndrome almost indispensable. We recognize, however, that the anankastic phobia must be considered only a symptom of a more basal disturbance, pertaining to the fundamental disturbance in the patient's relation to the world—to the very thing that delivers him to the anxiety-world. But the nature of this disturbance—which precedes the phobic phenomena and is "basal" in relation to them (de Clérambault)—cannot be determined precisely, notwithstanding certain reports by patients, as we shall see.

Examples reveal these anxiety-worlds to us. They appear, for instance, in the form of a phobic odor of one's own body.

A Phobic Odor Illusion

In the center of the compulsive illness of H. H. stands, clearly recognizable as the "disturbance psychism," the being obsessed by an illusory body odor. We have learned that, biographically, this illusory odor originated from the first spontaneous ejaculation and, from there, quite consistently [2] implanted itself in the urinary and excretory system. This case stands out as a model for anankastic disturbance of volition. The cleaning process after elimination often takes hours—and in spite of this the penis remains moist, that is, unclean, and accordingly capable of transferring this uncleanness to clothing in the form of a repulsive odor. We see here a rather considerable impairment in getting things done and bringing them to an end; there is a complete failure to perform the *acte de terminaison* (Janet). If the process of cleaning the penis with the aid of special procedures does, at last, seemingly succeed, then the clothing odor which soon appears, and which is always the urine odor transformed by the specific properties of certain fabrics, immediately proves the contrary. The cleaning process itself and, indeed, elimination are defiling, and this defilement spreads on the one hand spatially (to clothing) and on the other temporally, in that from one point to the other it extends itself through the whole day. Indeed, completely in keeping with the anankastic illusory phobia, there is a complete absorption in the illusory urine odor. Every life situation now has the significance of serving as an occasion for realizing the latent obsession, regardless of whether it concerns meeting people, telephoning, working, reading, playing, eating, thinking, praying, etc. Becoming aware of the repulsive odor is always disturbing by nature. It is tied up with feelings of pain, aversion, shame, and disgust. The reflexive character of the phobic disgust-reaction is clear. It prevents, in general, every normal act, every normal occupation, every normal experience of rapport with people; it isolates the patient completely and confines him within the obsessive circle of nauseatedly having to smell himself.

Of all the symptoms in H. H.'s compulsion syndrome the odor is the most unpleasant, because it is always present and incombatable; and because of its localization in the center of the self-concept it is particularly painful. To himself and to others he is a "disgusting skunk." Changing

2 "Consistently" with reference to the regressive life-direction of the anankastic.

clothes from head to foot several times a day or frequent bathing does not bring relief; the impression of smelling bad or at least "funny" lingers on and forces the phobic, intense, cramping preoccupation with himself (*Reflexionskrampf*) which in anankastics, especially in puberty and adolescence, is often precipitated by a feeling of repulsion toward one's own body.

We see that the phobic odor-illusion is intimately bound up with a disturbance in the capacity to bring things to a close—especially with the incapacity to have done with the bodily act of cleaning. The persistence of the odor of the urine is the reverse side of the incapacity to turn to the tasks of the day—*e.g.*, school work—and to move further into daily activities and toward new goals. To the extent to which the incapacity for this decreases, the patient's preoccupation with the odor-illusion increases. Every problem the day brings in is left lying—and on this inhibition the reflexive occurrence of the odor illusion always rekindles itself, as it were, so that the preoccupation with the illusion forms a homogeneous continuum, filling up the time that is passing. Upon this odor H. H. is "nailed," thereby expressing fittingly that the persistence of his body odor is synonymous with being fastened to the past, at the cost of the future, which, in turn, is represented by the tasks that offer themselves. H. H.'s not getting rid of the past pollution is, at closer sight, the pollution itself in its genuine meaning. It appears as a personal emanation loaded with an offensive odor, but it only *appears* as this phenomenon. Behind this appearance, and making it possible, stands H. H.'s incapacity to let his energies stream into the implementation of a task-oriented self-development and thereby to purify himself from the stagnation of energy. This incapacity is the actual disturbance, perhaps related to the endogenic depressive inhibition; in any case, a choking or blocking of the life course is evidenced in it; therewith is impeded the temporalization of life—"Becoming" is blocked, and the past is fixated. This fixation can be experienced as a pollution which, in man, is expressed in the experience of the anxiety-producing body odor. For it is not at all a question of a real odor or of an actual soiling; rather, odor and soiling are symbols of a life deprived of one of the possibilities of purification—*i.e.*, of its orientation toward future. Thus, we recognize that the compulsive patient does what he does not mean to do; what he does mean, he cannot do. The lack of freedom which manifests itself in compulsive behavior belongs to the essence of his situation.

IV *The Defensive Side of the Compulsion-Syndrome and the Nature of Compulsion*

The case of H. H. is instructive still in another respect. Like many anankastics, he suffers from a disturbance in the capacity to act, which is revealed especially as an impediment to beginning something new and completing something. H. H. cannot finish anything because the inner life-historical articulation is missing from his outer action, and therewith the experience of completion. A splitting of action and occurrence is present; this takes on grotesque forms when H. H. stands in the room with his coat on and explains that he cannot go out, for he does not know whether he has really put his coat on. We see that an action can be completely executed, in the sense that it has served to implement a purpose, without being completed— or indeed, having occurred at all—in terms of its life-historical meaning. Although it is done, it is as if it had not been done. The person, as a living being moving ahead in time, does not enter into the objective performance of his action, and therefrom arises—after the completion of the action—doubt as to the reality of its occurrence. At least one more explicit action is needed —e.g., stamping one's foot, or swallowing, or clicking one's tongue, something—such as a command, a "fiat," in the sense James uses it—to give the impression that what was done was really done.

From the case history of H. H. we know that he met this disturbance in his capacity to act with a method that in France has been called *la manie de précision,* in other words, with a compulsion for exactness. His ceremonial consists in dividing every action into parts, into smaller and smaller movement particles, which are precisely determined according to their content, precisely marked off from one another, and precisely laid down in terms of sequence. One can speak of a *"dividual" (saccadierten)* [3] *form of action.* Thus, the morning toilet consists in a fixed number of single movements, precisely separated from, and following upon, one another. In order to keep to the schedule, it is necessary to put in a *control-compulsion* and to check, with alert attention, all the movements and their sequence. Mistakes that slip in undo the effect of the act, and hence immediately a *repetition compulsion* sets in—he must begin again from the beginning—or it suffices to carry out the repetition in mental form—by way of a *recapitulation compulsion.* Every imperfection that slips in is, in addition, experienced by the patient as guilt-laden and is punished, so to speak, by an intensification of the illusion of his body odor.

The intensification of the body odor illusion (which justifies H. H. in his feeling of being a "disgusting skunk"), running parallel with a failure in exactness, makes clear that the inexactness not only is considered as an impairment of the action but is experienced also as a soiling. One may recall that everyday language also draws a relation between "clean" and "exact": whoever shoots precisely, shoots "cleanly"; precise handiwork is described as "clean work." We call a piece of work "not clean" when it is not carried out with precision, and can thus not stand as completed. There is no doubt that H. H., with his "dividual" compulsion for exactness, is out to fight for perfection in his action, which constantly eludes him; for his

3 [*Saccadiert* connotes both fragmented and disrupted.—EDITORS.]

disturbance consists just in this—the outer completion of the task does not at the same time include the process of Becoming in the person, his unfolding in time, and an act of self-realization.

At the same time, H. H. defends himself with his dividual action—although unsuccessfully—against the possibility of pollution, which constantly lies in wait for him in the form of the repulsive and lasting body odor by which he is possessed, half as a hypochondriac, half as a depersonalized patient. It requires only a small outer disturbance or an insignificant failure in his apotropaic (warding off) ceremonial for the pollution to erupt from relative latency to actual fact.

We have already hinted that an intimate relation must exist between the anankastic "disturbance-psychism" on its non-ideational level, where it results in an inhibition in the capacity of Becoming, and the phobic feeling of pollution. Normally, life purifies itself through its devotion to the forces of the future and the tasks that challenge us from the direction of the future. If, through the inhibition in his course toward self-realization, the person is kept back from the deep wellspring of the capacity to "Become" and to repay the debt of existence, there awakens within him a vague sense of guilt, as we find it oftentimes in inhibited melancholics; this vague sense of guilt concretizes in the latter as self-reproach which may approach delusional thoughts—thoughts that are incorrigible because they are nourished by the generalized inhibition in the capacity of Becoming.

Now the feeling of being polluted might be only one particular form of the guilt feeling in which the inhibited life becomes indirectly aware of its stoppage. *Non elevarsi est labi* [4]—so does Franz von Bader paraphrase the popular insight that "whoever rests, rusts," that "standing water becomes stagnant," that "whoever does not go forward goes backward." It is a not-freeing-oneself-from-the-past that is revealed in the anankastic preoccupation with feelings of being polluted. The past must be dropped, like stool, and the healthy life, which is directed toward the future—be it explicitly or in the general condition of being-able—continually deposits the past, leaves it behind, thrusts it off, and cleanses itself from it. Not so in the compulsive; here the past does not take on the past perfect tense ("nailed to the past" says H. H. of himself); thus it cannot be eliminated and left behind, since this would call for the very condition of one's openness for the future. As something unfinished, it exerts pressure and makes demands on the anankastic as the future makes demands on the healthy person. Thus, the anankastic patient not only does not move from his position but also is flooded over by the past, through the symbols of the Unclean, the Soiled, and the Dead. As we already stated, it is an "un-form" (*Ungestalt*) hostile to life—which has the form of the ever-Becoming—an "un-form" in which the past, itself malformed, entrenches itself. It threatens with soiling, pollution, and

4 ["Not to rise means to drop."—EDITORS.]

putrefaction—all symbols of a tendency detrimental to the personality, its values, its beauty, and its perfection.

Anankastic behavior is to be understood as a defense against this tendency —a powerless defense, for the orientation toward non-Becoming (*Entwerden*) and de-essentialization (*Entwesen*), toward the anti-eidos, is fixated through a shutting out of the future, ultimately unknown to us in its nature, and asserts itself again and again in spite of all defense measures. The anankastic patient eventually succumbs to the pollution due to his stagnating, stopped-up life, in spite of the precision-aimed tension in his defenses, for this tension cannot be maintained; something is bound to interfere with it from within or without, and at once the negative in its "un-form" will triumph.

What is not sufficiently noted is the often possible proof that the compulsion phenomena take place against the background of a personality that is potentially intact but condemned to powerlessness in asserting itself. Already in everyday life it is characteristic for the experience of a compulsion that there is a simultaneous "yes" and "no"—a compliant act coupled with an inner refusal, or a refusal to act combined with inner compliance (if—*e.g.,* I feel compelled to sign a statement which I reject). In the case of psycho-pathological compulsion, both compulsion and being compelled originate in the ego-sphere: the ego is the *object* of the overwhelming force, but it is also the *principle* of the overwhelming force. The ego challenges the actions that spring from that very same ego. The challenging party and the challenged party are both of an ego nature, are both ego-spheres that do not coincide but stand in opposition to each other. This contradiction stems from the fact that in that portion of the personality which is altered in accordance with the compulsion syndrome, the free personality shines through in its disposition and in its idea. On the one hand, the nonsensicalness and strangeness of the anankastic disturbance is thereby increased; on the other hand, the reactive defense against this fundamental disturbance takes on the character of unfree acts, of an encroachment, of a compulsion. From case to case varying degrees of the shining through of the potentially healthy personality can be found, and it may be observed that with the weakening of this transparency phenomenon the painfully compulsive character of the acts also becomes weaker. Hoffman,[5] in an excellent paper, gathered statements from compulsive patients in love with their compulsions that bear eloquent testimony to this point. The more the compulsive lives in his phobic preoccupation and the nearer this approaches the overvalued idea (though criticism never is *completely* silenced), the more he is absorbed in his compulsion, and the less challenged—*i.e.,* the more unimpeded—remains the latter. But the more the compulsive distances himself from his phobic preoccupation, the stranger and the more nonsensical does

[5] "Der Gesundheitswille der Zwangsneurotiker," *Z. Neur.,* Vol. 110, 1927.

it seem to him, the more does he experience the necessity for defense as unavoidable, the more does its compulsive character stand out. Ultimately it is always the underlying personality which, potentially shut out, yet still healthy in its disposition, reflects like a mirror the experiencing and acting of the anankastic. This reflecting defines the experience side of the compulsive phenomena—a fact that up till now has not received sufficient attention.

Let us carry out a little further our analysis of a banal compulsive act— as, for instance, a compulsion for precision—by contrasting the compulsive precision with the healthy practice. In this setting it occurs to us that the healthy person reserves the special exertion of his will to perfection for certain activities where "it matters," whereas the greatest part of his activities takes place without being burdened by an explicit intention to be exact, but without lapsing thereby into inexactness. The healthy person trusts himself, along wide stretches of his way, to the automatically realizable "sure hit" in his conduct, without troubling himself about the difference between exact and inexact. Indeed, he allows himself errors and slips without being shocked where these are of no particular consequence. He knows that the human being is not a precision machine, and therefore he allows the irrelevant to come to expression without pinning himself down to any too-definite rule of conduct. For him, the approximate, too, has its right, and the preliminary its significance. Hence, he always lives in an atmosphere of freedom—where things can be so, but also otherwise, in a certain loose and capricious casualness of action. Harmless informality and variable irrelevance are, after all, important elements of our freedom. To take into account this side of existence does not prevent, but actually heightens, the readiness to precise action where precision is needed.

In contrast to the healthy person, the compulsive makes just this Unimportant and Irrelevant the object of his will to accuracy. A reversal of the normal relief map of what is important thus characterizes the practical world of the anankastic which simultaneously presents itself as a flattened one. Just where the healthy person bustles about freely in his business, cheered on by the irrelevance of the manner in which it is executed, we see the anankastic succumbing to the need for rigidly laid down, stereotyped executions, while the objectively important action drops out. An impoverishment in freedom now imposes itself in the fixating on irrelevant acts or part-acts and their sequence; there are no alterations; variations are forbidden and guilt-producing. Accuracy does not enter for the sake of attaining some purpose that matters, but has become an end in itself and has the characteristic features of the unmotivated, the reflexive, the formal, the sterile, and the rigid.

If the compulsive were a depersonalized individual and not merely his brother, he would complain that everything he does is incomprehensibly dead, empty, and meaningless, or even that it is not his own action but that of a stranger. The same void, which in the depersonalized patient is simply suffered, is found also in the anankastic: just as little as the other is he able to enter his task as a person who is "becoming" and to fill it with himself. But in his case, the incapacity to become stands in him as a non-Becoming (*Entwerden*), as an orientation toward formlessness which must be warded off but cannot be warded off. Precision is the counterpart of this orientation to formlessness to which his inhibition in Becoming inescapably delivers him. That the formless appears in the image of a possible contamination, we have shown repeatedly. Dirt is lack of order ("matter in the wrong place"); it is lack of form (excrement, for example, as matter) which un-forms itself (*entstaltend*) and causes "disformation" (*Entstaltung*). The necessity of defense by means of formal order and precise action would not exist if there were not constantly at work an orientation of the personality toward the formless, and it would not be *experienced* as compulsion if the possibility of something like a healthy performance of life did not form the background for the defense.

Just a few words about the repetition compulsion which is found in every compulsive illness. Here, too, we may remember that the life of the Healthy is unthinkable without repetition; his is, to be sure, not compa-rable with the anankastic repetition. For, in the strict sense of the term, the action of the healthy person, his daily toilet, breakfast, going out, etc., is already something other than repetition because it never appears detached from the orientation toward the future which controls the personality in its respective action. Through its temporal incorporation into the process of development of the personality, the regular morning and evening activities partake of the unrepeatable quality of a particular segment of development. It is just the absence of this relationship in the anankastic, however, and the resulting ineffectiveness and spiritlessness of his action that lead to the genuine anankastic repetition. This accomplishes what it does accomplish only through its purely volitional character—it brings the action to a kind of sham completion.

How should this performance of repetition be understood? Where do we find analogies for such unusual courses of events? We know this kind of repetition in the liturgic realm where formulas of prayer take on, through repetition, a meaning of conjuration. A kind of conjuring effectiveness also qualifies the anankastic repetition, even though it is not a spontaneous and fundamentally meaningful act: it conjures up a kind of completion which purely practically it cannot achieve at all. It achieves this in the way magical acts achieve effectiveness, the effectiveness of an undefined sorcery whose point of attack is the ego itself. The repetition does not bring about the real completion of the action, but a kind of sentimental belief that it has been completed, just as the magic of primitives has its main point of attack in the belief of the enchanting or the enchanted (cf. Levy-Bruhl, Jaide).

V *The Compulsive Patient and his World*

1. Our previous considerations converge in the insight that it must be possible to interpret the world of the compulsive patient (which according to Binswanger should always be understood as "his special way of being-in-the-world") from its inner logic.

Already the observation that the world of the compulsive patient appears even to himself to be set apart from the *koinos kosmos* [6] of average waking reality—without the latter undergoing any structural destruction as sometimes happens with schizophrenics—brings up a whole series of problems. These must be put aside in favor of the simplifying statement that the arrangement with the everyday world through action and self-realization is omitted by the compulsive and is replaced by another arrangement, proceeding according to other structural principles, with a differently structured existence-world.

In general it may be said that the world of the compulsive is constituted by forces inimical to form, whose quintessence we have called the "anti-eidos." A peculiar world opens up as soon as we use this kind of approach.

The actions and omissions of the compulsive are determined by encounters with an environment (*Umwelt*) that does not consist of the usual objects of our sympathetic experiencing and of our cognitive or practical conduct; rather, their coinage bears the stamp of a "physiognomic" character (Werner). If we accept the reports of certain compulsives that all objects around them take on "meaning," we must recognize that we are dealing here with a breaking through of archaic modes of experience to which there corresponds a "primal world," a world which, as Werner says, is "physiognomically given."

But it is not simply the unchanged resurgence of a primal reality that occurs here—as Jung and others assumed. When speaking of a physiognomic structure (which, incidentally, we see as a physiognomic-dynamic one) of the anankastic world, we do so with all reservations required by an analysis of the facts. Indeed, the broad sphere of physiognomic settings which constitute the world of children and primitives appears, in the specific anankastic world-structure, limited and restricted to a definite sector. Only that which is inimical to form, which moves toward "un-form" or is apt to bring it about, enters as a deciding factor into the anankastic world—which, because of its antithetical relationship to everyday reality, turns out to be a

[6] [Refers to the celebrated aphorism of Heraclitus: "When men dream, each has his own world (*idios kosmos*); when they are awake, they have a common world (*koinos kosmos*)." —Editors.]

physiognomic or, as we should say, a "pseudo-magic counterworld." Thus the physiognomic is here given as an energy—symbolizing "un-form"—that threatens and repels. Effective threat and repulsion are the physiognomic criteria of the anankastic counterworld—as when, for example, objects of daily use which had not been unpacked according to predetermined rituals and, therefore, are affected with the stigma of pollution, are also charged with the potency of the polluting magic force. Thus, the physiognomic construction of the anankastic counterworld also turns out to be a reduced structure.

To talk of the "revival of primal forms of reality" is actually a convenient way of covering up important facts, particularly the fact that physiognomic features are interspersed in our real world anyway. In our environment there is no object which, besides its categorical forming, does not have an expression, that is not somehow animated or tuned and can, therefore, speak to us in a fundamental way. It is only that these physiognomic structures become almost completely hidden from us through the categorical-rational ones. Only in the poetic atmosphere does the silent language of *things* come to life again, not because in such an atmosphere a person begins to phantasy, but because in the higher sympathetic receptivity of the poet the real language of things actually arrives at expression. Also in pathological states, in fever, intoxication, states of weakness, etc., the fundamental physiognomic structure of the environment (*Umwelt*) pushes back the categorical forms and determines the individual way of our being-in-the-world. Every reduction of the subject-object tension can give the physiognomic structure leeway whereby the so-called subjective factors (primarily the total affective state of the individual—*e.g.*, anxiety, grief, joy, etc.) can determine in a decisive way the physiognomic world structure; this is valid for the entire physiognomically-ordered world-design (*Welt-Entwurf*).

A series of questions demand answers in this context: first, the question of whether, in the reduced physiognomic structures of the anankastic counterworld, there is any worldness (*Welthaftigkeit*) at all. We saw in the course of our presentation that the dynamism symbolizing "un-form," implicit in the anankastic action upon things, results in an increasing derealization of those very things. It is never objectively demonstrable odors (cf. the case of H. H.) that cling to parts of the environmental and threaten the anankastic with their repulsive effect. These encounters do not seem to differentiate themselves from mere thoughts, which, as has been shown, display a stronger effect upon the patient than does, let us say, the dog or the garland that actually crops up.[7] In the sphere of the anankastic one must speak of a world that has been deprived of the quality of "worldness."

What about the transcendence-character of the anankastic world, if we

7 [This refers to case histories not contained in this excerpt.—EDITORS.]

understand "transcendence" in the Husserlian sense as the intentional potentiality of the "I" to reach out beyond itself before it has yet encountered
world—which forms the very basis for the constitution of world?

To this the following may be said: Fundamentally, the encounters of the
anankastic, his collisions with the powers of disformation (*Entstaltung*), do
not take place in a vacuum. Even if they do not invariably adhere to real
objects, the physiognomic features that determine his actions do impinge
upon him as though very much from the outside. In his own experience, it
is the world of things which in its taboo-like meanings takes its shape
toward him. . . . The intentional transcending of the anankastic takes place
within the immanence of his own possessedness and surroundedness by the
powers of the "anti-eidos." We speak of this particular situation and nothing else when we say that world-deprivation (*Entweltlichung*) is one of the
chief characteristics of the anankastic object-sphere. Just this reductive
character in the construction of the anankastic world differentiates it from
the equally physiognomic-dynamic world of the primitive. The world-design
(*Welt-Entwurf*) of the anankastic is concerned with a deforming of the magic
world of the primitive. A loss of world-content—of world containing density,
fullness, and form—and thereby of reality characterizes the environment of
which we are speaking. There is certainly some connection between the
physiognomic impoverishment of the anankastic world and the exclusive
receptivity of the patient to those contents that symbolize the loss of "eidos"
of existence, such as dirt, destructive fire, contaminating bestiality, images
of putrefaction, etc. Both belong essentially together, like the poles of
existence.

Let us return to our thesis that the physiognomic is here given as the
force symbolizing "un-form" which threatens and repels. Above all, our
thesis illustrates that the compulsive patient lives in a world different from
ours. This differentness of his world and the differentness of his existence
in it are two sides of one and the same fact which requires interpretation.
What entered our awareness from this other kind of world is a sum of ne-
gations. What struck us above all was that the friendly, inviting powers of
existence step back in favor of the hostile, repulsive ones. Everything that
normally draws the individual into the world and invites him to fuse with
it is condemned to a peculiar kind of ineffectiveness. Even taking nourishment is for H. H., according to his statement, a continuing torture because
the inviting appeal of food that effects its incorporation does not engage him
—rather is he threatened by the exclusive possibility of contamination
through it. So it is with all the features of the world which call for connection and union with it and thus make possible the extension of one's own
existence, the moving into the world and being active in it, penetrating
into it—conquest, joy, activity, spreading out. Indeed, it can also be plainly
shown that the world of the anankastic is characterized by the omission of

the harmless, the obvious, and the natural. What is called by Scheler the "ecstatic possession of world-contents" and by E. Straus "sympathetic communication" is here impeded. Threat and repulsion are all that remain. A world without mercy and without grace of Fate (*Schicksals-Huld*) opens up or, rather, shuts up before the anankastic. Its characteristics are narrowness, natureless monotony, and rigid, rule-ridden unchangeability—all of which are most essential alterations of the mode of moral, spatial, and temporal being-in-the-world. We must forego further interpretation of this.

2. The compulsive shies away from onlookers more than other patients do; the picturesque madness of his acts shuns the eyes of others, and hardly ever might a doctor succeed in watching when a patient like H. H. devotes himself for hours on end to the strange manipulations of drying his penis or to the bizarre exercising of his puppet-like compulsion for precision.

We have already expressed ourselves about the time-structure of this behavior, without exhausting its analysis. What may still be mentioned in a preliminary way is the peculiar mixture of dawdling and rushing that marks the temporal structure of anankastic behavior. In the execution of the ritual, time is always "lost" and therefore time must always be made up for. It is in the weaving of the ordered plan of passing time into the present-time of the patient that the slowing down of the anankastic time-events reveals itself as a feeling of "lost time," which is then followed by the necessity for having to make up time, with the feeling of torturing rush. Whoever is not master of time is its slave. In the attitudes of taking one's time and of hurrying, the person's patterns of mastery with regard to time take effect. Both possibilities of freedom are denied to the anankastic. What fails here, however, is the stream of inner happenings that can keep step with passing time; in the anankastic, for some unknown reason, this has fallen into a state of rigidity. At one point it binds the patient without rest to certain rituals, at another point it makes him race for lost time and delivers him to an even more ceaseless rushing.

Nowhere in the compulsive mode of temporal existing do we find the pleasing calm of healthy existence (*Dasein*). Still, reference to merely one change in the anankastic time experience brought about by inhibition does not suffice to explain the specificity of this change and, accordingly, the anankastic symptomatology. It is not merely the slowing down or hampering of inner time that differentiates the compulsive from other categories of patients, in whom the fundamental disturbance is likewise to be sought in the realm of Becoming (as in melancholics and depersonalized patients with syndromes of emptiness). What distinguishes the compulsive is his way of handling the disturbance of inner temporal events. He neither persists inactively in depressed inhibition nor develops a syndrome of emptiness, nor delusions (*Wahn*); seen quite naïvely, the fact is that the compulsive does act. True, anankastic activity is itself—as we could show—an expression of the disturbance in the capacity to act; nevertheless, the compulsive patient is forever in action. From early till late we see him in constant tension, ceaselessly at work to have it out with the enemy who, as H. H. says, is "forever at his heels," regardless of whether this encounter consists more in intellectual or in practical defenses.

Let us anticipate and name this "enemy" immediately; it is nothing else but the pseudo-magic counterworld of the anankastic, the quintessence of the forces that symbolize "un-form," which we have recognized as his world. From everywhere this world pursues him; from outside and from inside it breaks in upon him. Threat and repulsion (taboo) are its agents. In this double effect, however, the orientation of existence (*Dasein*) toward non-existence (*Nicht-dasein*) articulates itself; this orientation can appear only in images like excrement or dirt, poison or fire, ugliness, unchastity, "corpsiness" (*Leichenhaftigkeit*)—in short, in such images as are suitable to refer to the form-destroying powers of existence. The demon of this environment (*Umwelt*), or counterworld we have called the "anti-eidos," in order to define the quintessence of all form-destroying potencies of existence in one term. In the ubiquity of contaminating dirt, or of the urine-odor of H. H., the form-destroying potencies of existence in all the repulsive features of the anankastic world-image attain actual realization. Only this makes us understand the desperate and everlasting defense of the compulsive. His contest with the world has no other content than the battle with the form-destroying powers of existence, a battle that has the character of a powerless and fruitless undertaking since those powers have already seized possession of his own existence in the irrevocable manner of possessedness. They could, however, take possession of him only because the fundamental disturbance, the impediment to Becoming, has for the anankastic the meaning of a loss of form. This compelling orientation of his fundamental life process—not toward unfolding, growth, increasing self-realization, but toward diminution, going-down, dissolution of life-form—makes the compulsive susceptible to everything in which the form-destroying potencies express themselves, such as the reflection in objects of excrement, death, infectious bestiality, poison, fire, etc.

That the impediment of his own inner temporal happenings (unknown to the anankastic himself) is the premise for such a one-sided and monotonous orientation of anankastic experience appears probable in more than one respect. The decisive fact, as already stated, is not the impediment as such, but rather that particular disposition which is constitutive for the building up of the compulsive personality. Thus we must find and present the meaning of the "kinetic" impairment in its form-destroying effect. Of the various orientations which can issue from the elemental impairment in Becoming, the compulsive chooses—for reasons still unknown—that one which we have called the loss of form of the person. Of the various types of patients who are impaired in their Becoming, the anankastic represents that one for whom the inhibition in Becoming means a loss of form. That the impairment in Becoming can, on principle, be experienced in this way appears to us meaningful. For only in the process of Becoming does the form of life complete itself and the "eidos" of the person become realized. Incapacity to Become and nonactualization of one's own form are two sides of the same fundamental disturbance. This incapacity for realization of one's own form is not of itself a dissolution of this form, though much popular usage (*viz.*, pp. 177 and 178) has it so. In principle, however, the impairment in Becoming *can* be experienced as a dissolution of form. The compulsive, in any case, does experience it so. Every interval of passing time, then, is experienced as a threat of increasing the possible losses of form in the chained person and deepens the worry of those who have become deeply stuck—the worry about their ability to be. But threat and worry lie so very hidden in the depth of the anankastic being that they cannot come immediately to consciousness and become manifest and effective only in images and metaphors, namely, in the images of the form-destroying potencies of existence. These, then, draw the latent threat emerging from the ground of existence onto themselves and pursue the anankastic with it.

Now, indeed, begins the battle with his shadow which he himself is. Now the image of dirt or of death afflicts him with constant contamination. The whole world shrinks to this one repulsive physiognomy which can crop up in almost any content and which plagues him with its threat as it forces him into defense with its repulsion-producing energy. But only because the compulsive is threatened with the loss of his own form, of his own eidos, can the symbol of the form-destroying forces gain mastery over his imagination and determine his actions. The compulsive defends himself against the threatening effect of his own temporal impairment, but he does not know what the issue is and therefore defends himself against the threatening possibility of his own loss of form only by rejecting those objects and thoughts in which the form-destroying orientation of existence expresses itself. All individual compulsive acts can be explained on the basis of the fundamental disposition of the anankastic which we have here presented.

PART III

Existential Analysis

VII

The Existential Analysis School of Thought*

by Ludwig Binswanger

I *Existential Analysis—Its Nature and Goals*

By "EXISTENTIAL ANALYSIS" we understand an anthropological [1] type of scientific investigation—that is, one which is aimed at the essence of being human. Its name as well as its philosophical foundation are derived from Heidegger's Analysis of Being, "*Daseins* Analytics." It is his—not yet properly recognized—merit to have uncovered a fundamental structure of existence and to have described it in its essential parts, that is, the structure of being-in-the-world. By identifying the basic condition or structure of existence with being-in-the-world, Heidegger intends to say something about the condition of the possibility for existence. The formulation "being-in-the-world" as used by Heidegger is, therefore, in the nature of an ontological thesis, a statement about an essential condition that determines existence in general. From the discovery and presentation of this essential condition, existential analysis received its decisive stimulation, its philosophical foundation and justification, as well as its methodological directives. However, existential analysis itself is neither an ontology nor a philosophy and therefore must refuse to be termed a *philosophical anthropology;* as the reader will soon realize, only the designation of *phenomenological anthropology* meets the facts of the situation.

* Translated by ERNEST ANGEL from the original, "Über die daseinsanalytische Forschungs-richtung in der Psychiatrie," *Schweizer Archiv für Neurologie und Psychiatrie*, Vol. 57, 1946, pp. 209–225. Reprinted in *Ausgewählte Vorträge und Aufsätze*, Vol. I (Berne; Francke, 1947), pp. 190–217.

1 [Binswanger uses this word not in its usual American meaning, which is cultural anthropology, the comparative study of races, mores, etc., but rather in its more strictly etymological sense, that is, anthropology as the study of man ("anthropos") and specifically, as he goes on to say above, the study of the essential meaning and characteristics of being human.—TRANSLATOR.]

Existential analysis does not propose an ontological thesis about an essential condition determining existence, but makes *ontic statements*—that is, statements of factual findings about actually appearing forms and configurations of existence. In this sense, existential analysis is an empirical science, with its own method and particular ideal of exactness, namely with the method and the ideal of exactness of the *phenomenological* empirical sciences.

Today we can no longer evade recognition of the fact that there are two types of empirical scientific knowledge. One is the *discursive inductive* knowledge in the sense of describing, explaining, and controlling "natural events," whereas the second is the *phenomenological empirical* knowledge in the sense of a methodical, critical exploitation or interpretation of phenomenal contents. It is the old disagreement between Goethe and Newton which today—far from disturbing us—has changed by virtue of our deepened insight into the nature of experience from an "either/or" into an "as well as." The same phenomenological empirical knowledge is used regardless of whether we deal with the interpretation of the aesthetic content of an aristic style-period, with the literary content of a poem or a drama, or with the self-and-world content of a Rorschach response or of a psychotic form of existence. In phenomenological experience, the discursive taking apart of natural objects into characteristics or qualities and their inductive elaboration into types, concepts, judgments, conclusions, and theories is replaced by giving expression to the content of what is purely phenomenally given and therefore is not part of "nature as such" in any way. But the phenomenal content can find expression and, in being expressed, can unfold itself only if we approach and question it by the phenomenological method—or else we shall receive not a scientifically founded and verifiable answer but just an accidental *aperçu*. In this, as in every science, everything depends upon the method of approach and inquiry—*i.e.*, on the ways and means of the phenomenological method of experience.

Over the last few decades the concept of phenomenology has changed in some respects. Today, we must strictly differentiate between Husserl's pure or eidetic phenomenology as a transcendental discipline, and the phenomenological interpretation of human forms of existence as an empirical discipline. But understanding the latter is not possible without knowledge of the former.

In this we should be guided, to mention only one factor, by abstinence from what Flaubert calls *la rage de vouloir conclure,* that is, by overcoming our passionate need to draw conclusions, to form an opinion, or to pass judgment—a task which in the light of our one-sided natural-scientific intellectual training cannot be considered an easy one. In short, instead of reflecting on something we should let the something speak for itself or, to quote

Flaubert again, "express the thing as it is." However, the "as it is" contains one more fundamental ontological and phenomenological problem; for we finite human beings can acquire information on the "how" of a thing only according to the "world-design" which guides our understanding of things. Therefore, I have to return once more to Heidegger's thesis of existence as "being-in-the-world."

The ontological thesis that the basic constitution or structure of existence is being-in-the-world is not a philosophical *aperçu* but rather represents an extremely consistent development and extension of fundamental philosophical theories, namely of Kant's theory about the conditions of the possibility of experience (in the natural-scientific sense) on the one hand, and of Husserl's theory of transcendental phenomenology on the other. I shall not elaborate on these connections and developments. What I want to emphasize here is only the identification of being-in-the-world and transcendence; for it is through this that we can understand what "being-in-the-world" and "world" signify in their anthropological application. The German word for transcendence or transcending is *Ueberstieg* (climbing over or above, mounting). An *Ueberstieg* requires, first, that toward which the *Ueberstieg* is directed and, secondly, that which is *ueberstiegen* or transcended; the first, then, toward which the transcendence occurs, we call "world," whereas the second, which is transcended, is the being itself (*das Seiende selbst*) and especially that in the form of which a human existence itself "exists." In other words, not only "world" constitutes itself in the act of transcending—be it as a mere dawn of world or as objectifying knowledge—but the self also does so.

Why do I have to mention these seemingly complicated matters?

Only because through the concept of being-in-the-world as transcendence has the fatal defect of all psychology been overcome and the road cleared for anthropology, the fatal defect being the theory of a dichotomy of world into subject and object. On the basis of that theory, human existence has been reduced to a mere subject, to a worldless rump subject in which all sorts of happenings, events, functions occur, which has all sorts of traits and performs all sorts of acts, without anybody, however, being able to say (notwithstanding theoretical constructs) how the subject can ever meet an "object" and can communicate and arrive at an understanding with other subjects. In contrast, being-in-the-world implies always being in the world with beings such as I, with coexistents. Heidegger, in his concept of being-in-the-world as transcendence, has not only returned to a point prior to the subject-object dichotomy of knowledge and eliminated the gap between self and world, but has also elucidated the structure of subjectivity as transcendence. Thus he has opened a new horizon of understanding for, and given a new impulse to, the scientific exploration of human existence and its specific modes of being. The split of Being into subject (man, person) and object (thing, environment) is now replaced by the unity of existence and "world," secured by transcendence.[2]

Transcending, therefore, implies far more, and something much more original, than knowing, even more than "intentionality" in Husserl's sense, since "world" becomes accessible to us first and foremost already through our "key" (*Stimmung*). If for a moment we remember the definition of being-in-the-world as transcendence and view from this point our psychiatric analysis of existence, we realize that by investigating the structure of being-in-the-world we can also approach and explore psychoses; and realize furthermore that we have to understand them as specific modes of transcending. In this context we do not say: mental illnesses are diseases of the brain (which, of course, they remain from a medical-clinical viewpoint). But we say: in the mental diseases we face modifications of the fundamental or essential structure and of the structural links of being-in-the-world as transcendence. It is one of the tasks of psychiatry to investigate and establish these variations in a scientifically exact way.

As can be seen from all our analyses published so far, spatialization and temporalization of existence play an important part in existential analysis. I shall confine myself here to the still more central problem of time. What makes this problem so central is the fact that transcendence is rooted in the very nature of time, in its unfolding into future, "having been" (*Gewesenheit*), and present. This will help to explain why, in our anthropological analyses of psychotic forms of being-human, we are not satisfied with our investigation unless we gain at least some insight into the respective variations of the structure of our patients' time. . . .

In those forms of being-in-the-world which are generally called "psychotic" we have so far found two types of modifications of "world"-formation, one characterized by "leaping" (ordered flight of ideas) and by a "whirl" (disorderly flight of ideas), and the other characterized by a shrinking and simultaneous narrowing of existence along with its turning into swamp and earth (*Verweltlichung*).[3] We may describe the latter also in the following terms: the freedom of letting "world" occur is replaced by the unfreedom of

[2] Where we speak of "world" in terms of existential analysis, there world always means that toward which the existence has climbed and according to which it has designed itself: or, in other words, the manner and mode in which that which is (*Seiende*) becomes accessible to the existence. However, we use the expression "world" not only in its transcendental but also in its "objective" sense, as, *e.g.*, when we speak of the "dull resistance of the world," of the "temptations of the world," "retiring from the world," etc., whereby we have primarily the world of our fellow men in mind. Similarly, we speak of a person's environment and of his "own world" as of particular regions of that which exists in the objective world, and not as of transcendental world designs. This is terminologically troublesome, but not open to change any more. Hence, where the meaning is not self-evident, we have to place "world" always in quotation marks, or use the term "world design."

[3] *Viz.*, L. Binswanger, "The Case of Ellen West," Chap. IX.

being overwhelmed by a certain "world-design." In the case of Ellen West, for instance, the freedom of forming an "ethereal" world was replaced more and more by the unfreedom of sinking into the narrow world of the grave and the swamp. "World," however, signifies not only world-formation and predesign of world, but—on the basis of the predesign and model-image— also the *how* of being-*in*-the-world and the attitude *toward* world. Thus, the transformation of the ethereal into a grave-world could also be established in the change of the existence as expressed by an exultingly soaring bird to an existence in the form of a slowly crawling, blind earthworm.

All this takes us only to the outermost gate of Heidegger's fundamental ontology or "*Daseins* Analytics" and just to the gates of anthropological or existential analysis which has been inspired by and founded on the former. But I hasten to outline the method of existential analysis and the area of its scientific function. At this point, I have to mention that my positive criticism of Heidegger's theory has led me to its extension: being-in-the-world as being of the existence for the sake of *myself* (designated by Heidegger as "care") has been juxtaposed with "being-beyond-the-world" as being of the existence for the sake of *ourselves* (designated by me as "love"). This transformation of Heidegger's system has to be considered especially in the analysis of psychotic forms of existence where we frequently observe modifications of transcendence in the sense of the "overswing" [4] of love, rather than in the sense of the "overclimb" of care. Let us only remember the enormously complex shrinkage of the existential structure which we so summarily call "autism."

II *The Differentiation Between Human Existence and Animal Being*

"World" in Its Existential Analytical, and "World Around" (Umwelt) *in Its Biological Meaning*

HOWEVER SKETCHY and incomplete my statements have been so far, I hope they have indicated why in our analyses, the concept of "world"—in the sense of world-formation or of "world-design" (Husserl's "mundanization" [*Mundanisierung*])—represents one of the most important basic concepts and is even used as a methodological clue. For the *what* of the respective world-design always furnishes information about the *how* of the being-in-the-world and the *how* of being oneself. In order to clarify the nature of the world-design, I shall now confront it with some world-concepts of a biological nature. First comes to mind Von Uexküll's biological world-concept, par-

---

4 [This is a literal translation for the term *Überschwung*. Binswanger means the kind of transcendence which goes with love, an emphasis he introduced and which he contrasts to the transcendence arising out of "care" (one of Heidegger's concepts). His point is that the psychotic deviates particularly in regard to the former.—EDITORS.]

ticularly because it shows, in spite of its differences, a certain similarity in its methodological application. I shall start with the methodological agreement.

Von Uexküll distinguishes a perception world (*Merkwelt*), an inner world, and an action world of the animal and combines perception world and action world under the name environment (*Umwelt* or "world-around"). The "circular interaction" occurring between these worlds he designates as *function-circle*. And just as we would say that it is not possible to describe the psychosis of a person without having fully encompassed (*umschritten*) his "worlds," so Von Uexküll states: "It is not possible to describe the biology of an animal unless one has fully encompassed its function-circles." [5] And as we would continue by saying: "Therefore, we are fully justified in assuming the existence of as many worlds as there are psychotics," so Von Uexküll continues: "Therefore, one is fully justified in assuming the existence of as many environments (*Umwelten*) as there are animals." [6] He comes similarly close to our viewpoint when he says: "Also, to understand each person's actions, we have to visit his 'special stage.' " [7]

Von Uexküll's concept of environment however is much too narrow to be applied to man, because he understands by this term merely the "island of the senses"—*i.e.*, of sensory perceptions which "surround man like a garment." Hence it does not surprise us that in his brilliant descriptions of his friends' environments he continuously transgresses that narrow concept and demonstrates throughout how these friends are really "in-the-world" as *human beings*.

We further agree, for the present, with Von Uexküll's statement: "It is nothing but mental inertness to assume the existence of a single objective world [we psychiatrists naïvely call it reality] which one tailors as closely as possible to one's own environment, and which one has extended in all directions in space and time." [8]

However, Von Uexküll overlooks the fact that man, in contrast to animal, has his own world as well as an objective one which is common to all. This was known already to Heraclitus, who said that in the state of wakefulness we all have a common world, while in our sleep, as in passion, emo-

[5] *Theoretische Biologie*, II Aufl., 1928, S. 100.

[6] *Ibid.*, S. 144.

[7] *Nie geschaute Welten. Die Umwelten meiner Freunde*, S. 20.

[8] See *Umwelt und Innenwelt der Tiere*, 2, Aufl., 1921, S. 4: "Only to the superficial observer it seems as if all sea-animals were living in a homogeneous world, common to all of them. Closer study teaches us that each of those thousands of forms of life possesses an environment peculiar to itself which is conditioned by and, in turn, conditions the 'building plan' of the animal." Also, viz., *Theoretische Biologie*, S. 232: "We now know that there is not one space and one time only, but that there are as many spaces and times as there are subjects, as each subject is contained by its own environment which possesses its own space and time. Each of these thousandfold worlds offers to the sensory perceptions a new potentiality to unfold themselves."

tional states, sensuous lust, and drunkenness, each of us turns away from the common world toward his own. That common world—and Heraclitus recognized this, too—is one of phronesis, or rational deliberation and thinking. We psychiatrists have paid far too much attention to the deviations of our patients from life in the world which is common to all, instead of focusing primarily upon the patients' own or private world, as was first systematically done by Freud.

There is, however, one factor which not only differentiates our existential analytical concept of world from Von Uexküll's biological concept but places it even in diametrical opposition. It is true that, in Von Uexküll's theory, the animal and its environment form at times a genuine structure within the function-circle and that they appear there as "made to order for each other." However, Von Uexküll still considers the animal as subject and its environment as an object separated from it. Unity of animal and environment, of subject and object, is, according to Von Uexküll, guaranteed by the respective "blueprints" (action-plans, but also perception-plans) of the animal which, in turn, are part of an "overwhelmingly vast planful system." It now becomes clear that in order to proceed from Von Uexküll's theory to existential analysis, one must perform the Kantian-Copernican turn; instead of starting with nature and its planful system and dealing in natural science, one has to start at transcendental subjectivity and to proceed to existence as transcendence. Von Uexküll still throws both into one pot, as one deduces from the following ideas (which are quite impressive in themselves):

Let us take as an example a certain oak tree and then ask ourselves what kind of an environmental object will that oak tree be, in the environment of an owl that perches in its hollow trunk; in the environment of a singing bird that nests in its branches; of a fox which has its hole under its roots; of a woodpecker which goes after wood-fretters in its bark; in the environment of such a wood-fretter itself; of an ant which runs along its trunk, etc. And, eventually, we ask ourselves what the role of the oak tree is in the environment of a hunter, of a romantic young girl, and of a prosaic wood-merchant. The oak, being a closed planful system itself, is woven into ever new plans on numerous environment stages, the tracing of which is a genuine task for the science of nature.

Von Uexküll is a natural scientist and not a philosopher. So it should not be held against him that he, like most natural scientists, makes light of the essential difference between animal and man and does not "keep sacred" (Spemann) the division between them. And yet, just at this point, this division becomes almost tangible. In the first place, the animal is tied to its "blueprint." It cannot go beyond it, whereas human existence not only contains numerous possibilities of modes of being but is precisely rooted in this multifold potentiality of being. Human existence affords the possibility of being a hunter, of being romantic. of being in business, and thus is free to design itself toward the most different potentialities of being; in other words, existence can "transcend" the being—in this case the being which is called "oak"—or make it accessible to itself, through the most diverse world-designs.

Secondly, we remember—now departing completely from the biological point of view—that transcendence implies not only world-design but, at the same time, self-design, potential modes of being for the self. Human existence is a very different being for the self, according to whether it designs its world as a hunter and *is* a hunter or, as a young girl, is a romantic self, or as a wood trader is a prosaic-calculating self. All these are different ways of being in the world and of potential modes of the self which are joined by numerous others, particularly that of the genuine potentiality of being oneself, and of the potentiality of being *we* in the sense of love.[9]

The animal, not being able to be an *I-you-we*-self (since it is kept from even saying "*I-you-we*") does not have any world. For self and world are, indeed, reciprocal concepts. When we speak of the environment (*Umwelt*) the paramecium, the earthworm, the cephalopod, the horse, and even man *has*, this "*has*" possesses a very different meaning from the one we use when saying that man "*has*" a world. In the first case, the "*has*" signifies the establishment of a "blueprint," especially of the perception-and-action-organization, limited by nature to quite definite possibilities of stimulation and reaction. The animal has its environment by the grace of nature, not by the grace of freedom to transcend the situation.[10] That means, it can neither design world nor open up world nor decide independently in and for a situation. It is, and always has been, in a once and for all determined "situational circle." [11] On the other hand, the "having" of a "world" on the part of man implies that man, although he has not laid his own foundation himself but was thrown into being and, insofar as that, has an environment like the animal, still has the possibility of transcending this being of his, namely, of climbing above it in care and of swinging beyond it in love.

Somewhat closer to our viewpoint than Von Uexküll's theory is Von Weizsaecker's concept of the "gestalt-circle" as a self-contained biological act. "In so far as a living being through its movement and perception inte-

---

9 We therefore differentiate in the structure of the existence as being-in-the-world: (a) the ways in which it designs world and builds world—in short, the ways of world-design and world images; (b) the ways in which it, accordingly, exists as a self—*i.e.*, establishes itself or does not establish itself; (c) but also the ways of transcendence as such, that is, the ways in which the existence is in the world (*e.g.*, acting, thinking, creating, fancying). Thus, doing existential analysis in the area of psychiatry means to examine and describe how the various forms of the mentally ill, and each one for himself, design world, establish their self and—in the widest sense—act and love.

10 [See explanation of the term "transcend" in Chap. I.—EDITORS.]

11 This was already emphasized by Herder in his essay, "On the Origin of Language": Each animal has its circle within which it belongs from its birth, in which it remains for its life time, and in which it dies. (*Ausgew. Werke* [Reclam.] III, S. 621.)

grates itself into an environment, these movements and perceptions form a unit—a biological act." [12]

Like Von Uexküll, Von Weizsaecker also prides himself on "having consciously introduced the *subject* as a matter of biological research and on having obtained recognition for it as such." [13] That which produces the relation between subject and object is now no longer named "function-circle" but "gestalt-circle." According to Von Weizsaecker, the fundamental condition is "subjectivity" (which already shows a deeper view than the reference to the subject). But that fundamental condition cannot be recognized explicitly because it cannot in itself become the object; it is the "court of highest appeal," a power that "can be experienced either as unconscious dependency or as freedom." Von Weizsaecker, then, rejects the "external substantial dualism of Psyche and Physis"; he believes in replacing it by "the polar unity of subject and object." "But," he explains very rightly, "the subject is not a stable property; one has continuously to acquire it in order to possess it." Actually, it is only noticed when in a "crisis" one is threatened with losing it and later is able to rally again, thanks to its strength and resilience. "Simultaneously with each subject-jump, an object-jump, too, takes place and although the unity of the world is questionable, still each subject gathers at least his environmental world (*Umwelt*) whose objects he binds together into a little universe in a monadic unit."

All these theories are not only of the greatest interest to psychology and psychopathology but in addition bring clearly into focus the fact that only the concept of being-in-the-world as transcendence is genuinely consistent and penetrating; at the same time, they demonstrate that this concept can be applied consistently only to *human* existence.

Finally, I would like to remind the reader of Goldstein's world-concept, which proves so fruitful for the understanding of organic disturbances of the brain. Even where he uses the expression "milieu" in place of "world," we are still dealing with a genuine biological world-concept. As we know, it is one of his fundamental propositions that "a defective organism . . . can produce organized behavior only by such limitation of its milieu as corresponds to its defect." [14] At other times he speaks of a "loss of freedom" and of a "tightening of the tie to the environment" on account of a defect. We remember the fact that certain organic patients are no longer able to orient and conduct themselves in the world of "ideas," while being perfectly able to do so in the world of action or of practice where, as Goldstein put it more recently, "effects can come about through concrete acts in handling material presently at hand." In speaking, like Head, of a "disturbance of the symbolic expression" or, jointly with Gelb, of a "disturbance of categorical behavior."

---

12 "Der Gestaltkreis," *Theorie der Einheit vom Wahrnehmen und Bewegen*, 1940, S. 177.
13 [The quotations in this paragraph are from Von Weizsaecker.—EDITORS.]
14 *Der Aufbau des Organismus*, 1934, p. 32.

Goldstein in both instances formulates only a modification of "being-in-the-world" as transcending.

This chapter has tried to demonstrate the degree to which biological thinking today endeavors to view and investigate organism and world as a unity in a unitary gestalt, symbolized by the circle. What prevails is the insight that everything here is connected with everything, that no partial change within the circle can occur without a change of the whole and that, in general, no isolated facts exist any more. This, however, carries with it also a change in the concept of *fact,* of the fact itself, and of the methods in studying facts. For the goal is now no longer to arrive at conclusions by induction through mere accumulation of facts but to delve lovingly into the nature and content of the single phenomenon. Goldstein is well aware of this when he says: "In the formation of biological knowledge, the single links that are integrated into the whole cannot simply be evaluated quantitatively, as though the insight became the more certain the more links we establish. Rather, all the single facts are of a greater or lesser qualitative value." And he continues: "If in biology we see a science dealing with phenomena that can be established by analytical natural-scientific methods alone, we have to forego all insight which grasps the organism as a whole, and with it actually any insight into the life processes at all." [15]

This already carries us close to a phenomenological view of life in the widest sense, a view, that is, which aims at the grasping of the life-content of phenomena and not at their factual meaning within a precisely circumscribed object-area.[16]

III *The Existential-Analytical School of Thought in Psychiatry*

As compared with biological research, which exhausts or interprets the life-content of the phenomena, existential-analytical research has a double advantage. Firstly, it does not have to deal with so vague a "concept" as that of life, but with the widely and completely uncovered *structure of existence* as "being-in-the-world" and "beyond-the-world." Secondly, it can let existence actually speak up about itself—let it have its say. In other words, the phenomena to be interpreted are largely language phenomena. We know that the content of existence can nowhere be more clearly seen or more securely interpreted than through language; because it is in language that our world-designs actually ensconce and articulate themselves and where, therefore, they can be ascertained and communicated.

As to the first advantage, knowledge of the structure or basic constitution

---

[15] *Ibid.,* S. 255 f.

[16] *Viz.,* again Goldstein, *Der Aufbau des Organismus,* S. 242: "Biological insight is the continuous process through which we experience increasingly the idea of the organism, something of a 'ken' which is always based on the grounds of very empirical facts."

of existence provides us with a systematic clue for the practical existential-analytical investigation at hand. We know, now, what to focus on in the exploration of a psychosis, and how to proceed. We know that we have to ascertain the kind of spatialization and temporalization, of lighting and coloring; the texture, or materiality and motility, of the world-design toward which the given form of existence or its individual configuration casts itself. Such a methodical clue can be furnished only by the structure of being-in-the-world because that structure places a norm at our disposal and so enables us to determine deviations from this norm in the manner of the exact sciences. Much to our surprise it has turned out that, in the psychoses which were so far investigated, such deviations could not be understood merely negatively as abnormalities, but that they, in turn, represent a new norm, a new *form* of being-in-the-world. If, for example, we can speak of a manic form of life or, rather, of existence, it means that we could establish a norm which embraces and governs all modes of expression and behavior designated as "manic" by us. It is this *norm* which we call the "world" of the manic. The same holds true for the far more complicated, hitherto incalculably manifold world-designs of the schizophrenic. To explore and ascertain the world of these patients means, here as everywhere, to explore and ascertain in what way everything that is—men as well as things—is accessible to these forms of existence. For we know well enough that that-which-is as such never becomes accessible to man, except in and through a certain world-design.

As to the second advantage, the possibility of exploring language phenomena, it is the essence of speech and speaking that they express and communicate a *certain content of meaning*. This content of meaning is, as we know, an infinitely manifold one. Everything, therefore, depends upon the precise criteria by which we explore the language manifestations of our patients. We do not—as the psychoanalyst systematically does—focus merely upon the historical content, upon references to an experienced or conjectured pattern of the inner life-history. And we do not at all watch the content for all possible references to facts pertaining to life function, as does the psychopathologist in focusing on disturbances of speech or thinking functions. What attracts our attention in existential-analysis is rather the content of language expressions and manifestations insofar as they point to the world-design or designs in which the speaker lives or has lived or, in one word, their world-content. By world-content, then, we mean the content of facts pertaining to worlds; that is, of references to the way in which the given form or configuration of existence discovers world designs and opens up world—and is, or exists, in the respective world. There are, furthermore, indications of the way in which the existence is *beyond-the-world;* that is, how it *is,* or *is not,* at home in the eternity (*Ewigkeit*) and haven (*Heimat*) of love.

In "The Case of Ellen West," my first study planned as an example of existential analysis as applied to psychiatry, conditions were particularly favorable for existential analysis. In this case I had at my disposal an unusual abundance of spontaneous and immediately comprehensible verbal manifestations such as self-descriptions, dream accounts, diary entries, poems, letters, autobiographical drafts, whereas usually, and especially in cases of deteriorated schizophrenics, we have to obtain the material for existential analysis by persistent and systematic exploration of our patients over months and years. First and foremost it is our task to assure ourselves, over and over again, of what our patients really mean by their verbal expressions. Only then can we dare to approach the scientific task of discerning the "worlds" in which the patients are or, in other words, to understand how all partial links of the existential structure become comprehensible through the total structure, just as the total structure constitutes itself, without incongruity, from the partial links. In this, as in any other scientific investigation, there do occur errors, dead ends, premature interpretations; but, also as in any other, there are ways and means of correcting and rectifying these errors. It is one of the most impressive achievements of existential analysis to have shown that even in the realm of subjectivity "nothing is left to chance," but that a certain organized structure can be recognized from which each word, each idea, drawing, action, or gesture receives its peculiar imprint—an insight of which we make continuous use in existential-analytical interpretations of the Rorschach test and recently also in the Word Association Test. It is always the same world-design which confronts us in a patient's spontaneous verbal manifestations, in the systematic exploration of his Rorschach and Word Association responses, in his drawings, and also, frequently, in his dreams. And only after having encompassed (*umschritten*) these worlds—to speak in Von Uexküll's words—and brought them together can we understand the form of our patient's existence in the sense of what we call "neurosis" or "psychosis." Only then may we dare to attempt to understand single, partial links of those forms of world and existence (clinically evaluated as symptoms) from the modes and ways of the patient's total being-in-the-world.

Naturally, the connections of the life-history, too, here play an important part but, as we shall soon realize, by no means in the same way as in psychoanalysis. Whereas for the latter they are the goal of the investigation, for existential analysis they merely provide material for that investigation.

The following examples will illustrate the kind of world-designs with which we have to deal in psychopathology; but the number of such deviations is infinite. We are still at the beginning of describing and investigating them.

For my first clinical illustration I shall report the case of a young girl who at the age of five experienced a puzzling attack of anxiety and fainting when her heel got stuck in her skate and separated from her shoe.[17] Ever since, the girl—now twenty-one years of age—suffered spells of irresistible anxiety whenever a heel of one of her shoes appeard to loosen or when someone touched the heel or only spoke of heels. (Her own had to be nailed to her soles.) On such occasions, if she could not get away in time, she would faint.

Psychoanalysis proved clearly and convincingly that hidden behind the fear of loose or separating heels were birth phantasies, both about being born herself and therefore separated from mother and about giving birth to a child of her own. Of the various disruptions of continuity which psychoanalysis revealed as being frightening to the girl, the one between mother and child was fundamental and most feared. (I am omitting completely, in this context, the masculine component.) Before the period of Freud, one would have stated that the skating accident, harmless as it was per se, had "caused" the "heel phobia." Freud demonstrated subsequently that the pathogenic effect is produced by phantasies connected with and preceding such an accident. Yet in both periods still another explanation would be drawn upon to account for the fact that a specific event or phantasy had such a far-reaching effect precisely upon this person—namely, the explanation of "constitution" or "predisposition." For each of us has experienced the "birth trauma," but some lose their heels without developing a hysterical phobia.

We do not, of course, propose to unfold, let alone solve, the problem of "predisposition" in all its aspects; but I dare say that we can throw some more light on it when we view it from an "anthropological" [18] angle. In later studies we were able to demonstrate that we could reach even *behind* the phantasies insofar as we could trace and investigate the world-design which made possible those phantasies and phobias in the first place.

What serves as a clue to the world-design of our little patient is the category of *continuity*, of continuous connection and containment. This entails a tremendous constriction, simplification, and depletion of the "world content," of the extremely complex totality of the patient's contexts of reference. Everything that makes the world significant is submitted to the rule of that *one* category which alone supports her "world" and being. This is what causes the great anxiety about any disruption of continuity, any gap, tearing or separating, being separated or torn. This is why separation from the mother, experienced by everyone as the arch-separation in human life, had to become so prevalent that any event of separation served to symbolize the fear of separation from the mother and to invite and activate those phantasies and daydreams.

17 *Viz.*, "Analyse einer hysterischen Phobie," *Jahrbuch Bleuler und Freud*, III.
18 [*Viz.*, p. 191, Binswanger's explanation of this term as applied to phenomenological and existential analysis.—TRANSLATOR.]

We should, therefore, not explain the emergence of the phobia by an overly strong "pre-oedipal" tie to the mother, but rather realize that such overly strong filial tie is only possible on the premise of a world-design exclusively based on connectedness, cohesiveness, continuity. Such a way of experiencing "world"—which always implies such a "key" [19]—does not have to be "conscious"; but neither must we call it "unconscious" in the psychoanalytical sense, since it is outside the contrast of these opposites. Indeed, it does not refer to anything psychological but to something which only makes possible the psychic fact. At this point we face what is actually "abnormal" in this existence—but we must not forget that where the world-design is narrowed and constricted to such a degree, the self, too, is constricted and prevented from maturing. Everything is supposed to stay as it was before. If, however, something new does happen and continuity is disrupted, it can only result in catastrophe, panic, anxiety attack. For then the world actually collapses, and nothing is left to hold it up. The inner or existential maturation and the genuine time-orientation toward the future are replaced by a preponderance of the past, of "already having-been-in." The world must stop here, nothing must happen, nothing must change. The context must be preserved as it has always been. It is this type of temporal orientation that permits the element of *suddenness* to assume such enormous significance; because suddenness is the time quality that explodes continuity, hacks it and chops it to pieces, throws the earlier existence out of its course, and exposes it to the Dreadful,[20] to the naked horror. This is what in psychopathology we term, in a most simplifying and summarizing manner, anxiety attack.

Neither the loss of the heel nor the womb and birth phantasies are "explanations" of the emergence of the phobia. Rather, they became so significant because holding on to mother meant to this child's existence—as is natural for the small child—having a hold on the world. By the same token, the skating incident assumed its traumatic significance because, in it, the world suddenly changed its face, disclosed itself from the angle of suddenness, of something totally different, new, and unexpected. For that there was no place in this child's world; it could not enter into her world-design; it stayed, as it were, always outside; it could not be mastered. In other words, instead of being accepted by the inner life so that its meaning and content could be absorbed, it appeared and reappeared over and over again without having any meaning for the existence, in an ever-recurring invasion by the

[19] [Or attunement (*Gestimmheit*).—TRANSLATOR.]

[20] [This adjective used as a noun, "the Dreadful," signifies the abstract quintessence of all that is dreadful, the epitome of dreadfulness. This and similar expressions which follow on this page and subsequently in this essay—such as "the Sudden," "the Uncanny," "the Horrid"—have been capitalized to indicate that the adjective has the substantive quality of a noun.—EDITORS.]

Sudden into the motionlessness of the world-clock. This world-design did not manifest itself [21] before the traumatic event occurred; it did only on the *occasion* of that event. Just as the a priori or transcendental forms [21] of the human mind make experience only into what experience is, so the form of that world-design had first to produce the condition of the possibility for the ice-skating incident in order for it to be experienced as traumatic.

It should be mentioned that this case is not at all an isolated one. We know that anxiety can be tied to various types of disruption of continuity; *e.g.*, it may appear as horror at the sight of a loose button hanging on a thread or of a break in the thread of saliva. Whatever the life-historical events are to which these anxieties refer, we are always dealing here with the same depletion of being-in-the-world, narrowed down to include only the category of continuity. In this peculiar world-design with its peculiar being-in-the-world and its peculiar self, we see in existential terms the real key to the understanding of what is taking place. Like the biologist and neuropathologist, we do not stop at the single fact, the single disturbance, the single symptom, but we keep searching for an embracing whole within which the fact can be understood as a partial phenomenon. But this whole is neither a functional whole—a "Gestalt-circle"—nor a whole in the sense of a complex. Indeed, it is no objective whole at all but a whole in the sense of the unity of a world-design.

We have seen that we cannot progress far enough in our understanding of anxiety if we consider it only as a psychopathological symptom per se. In short, we must never separate "anxiety" from "world," and we should keep in mind that anxiety always emerges when the world becomes shaky or threatens to vanish. The emptier, more simplified, and more constricted the world-design to which an existence has committed itself, the sooner will anxiety appear and the more severe will it be. The "world" of the healthy with its tremendously varied contexture of references and compounds of circumstance can never become entirely shaky or sink. If it is threatened in one region, other regions will emerge and offer a foothold. But where the "world," as in the present case and in numerous others, is so greatly dominated by one or a few categories, naturally the threat to the preservation of that one or those few categories must result in a more intensified anxiety.

Phobia is always an attempt at safeguarding a restricted, impoverished "world," whereas anxiety expresses the loss of such a safeguard, the collapse of the "world," and thus the delivery of the existence to nothingness—the intolerable, dreadful, "naked horror." We then must strictly differentiate between the historically and situationally conditioned *point of breakthrough* of anxiety and the existential *source* of anxiety. Freud made a similar distinction when he differentiated between phobia as a symptom and the pa-

21 [Binswanger is here using Kantian expressions.—EDITORS.]

tient's own libido as the real object of anxiety.[22] However, in our concept the theoretical construct of libido is replaced by the phenomenological-ontological structure of existence as being-in-the-world. We do not hold that man is afraid of his own libido, but we state that existence as being-in-the-world is, as such, determined by uncanniness and nothingness. The source of anxiety is existence itself.[23]

Whereas in the preceding instance we had to deal with a static "world," as it were, a world in which nothing was supposed to "come to pass" or happen, in which everything had to remain unchanged and no separating agent was to interfere with its unity, we shall in the following example [24] meet a torturously heterogeneous, disharmonious "world," again dating from early childhood. The patient, displaying a pseudo-neurotic syndrome of polymorphous schizophrenia, suffered from all sorts of somato-, auto-, and allopsychic phobias.[25] The "world" in which that which is—everything-that-is (alles Seiende)—was accessible to him was a world of push and pressure, loaded with energy to the point of bursting. In that world no step could be made without running the danger of being knocked against or knocking against something, whether in real life or in phantasy. The temporality of this world was one of urgency (René Le Senne), its spatiality therefore one of horribly crowded narrowness and closeness, pressing upon "body and soul" of the existence. This came clearly to light in the Rorschach test. At one point the patient saw pieces of furniture "on which one might knock one's shin"; at another, "a drum that strikes one's leg"; at a third, "lobsters which squeeze you," "something you get scratched with"; and finally, "centrifugal balls of a flywheel which hit me in the face, me of all people, although for decades they had stayed fixed with the machine; only when I get there something happens."

As the world of things behaves, so does the world of one's fellow men; everywhere lurk danger and disrespect, mobs or jeering watchers. All this, of course, points to the borderline of delusions of "reference" or "encroachment."

It is very instructive to observe the patient's desperate attempts to control this disharmonious, energy-crammed, threatening world, to harmonize it artificially, and to belittle it in order to avoid the constantly imminent catastrophe. He does this by keeping himself at the greatest possible distance from the world, rationalizing this distance completely—a process which, here as everywhere, is accompanied by the devaluation and depletion of the

---

[22] "Neue Folge der Vorlesungen zur Einführung in die Psychoanalyse," S. 117 (Ges. Schr., XII, 238 f.)

[23] Viz., Sein und Zeit, 40, S. 184 ff.

[24] [This reference is to the case of "Juerg Zuend," Schweizer Archiv fuer Neurologie und Psychiatrie, Vols. LVI, LVII, LIX, Zurich, 1947.—EDITORS.]

[25] [A reference to concepts by Wernicke, meaning simply phobias relative to the patient's own body, to his own psyche, and to the external world.—TRANSLATOR.]

world's abundance of life, love, and beauty. This is particularly demonstrated in his Word Association Test. His Rorschach responses, too, bear witness to the artificial rationalization of his world, to its symmetrization and mechanization. Whereas in our first case everything-that-is (*alles Seiende*) was only accessible in a world reduced to the category of continuity, in this case it is a world reduced to the mechanical category of push and pressure. We are therefore not surprised to see that in this existence and its world there is no steadiness, that its stream of life does not flow quietly along, but that everything occurs by jerks and starts, from the simplest gestures and movements to the formulation of lingual expression and the performance of thinking and volitional decisions. Everything about the patient is jagged and occurs abruptly, while between the single jerks and pushes emptiness prevails. (The reader will notice that we are describing in existential-analytical terms what would clinically be called schizoid and autistic.) Again, very typical is the patient's behavior in the Rorschach test. He feels a desire to "fold up the cards and file them away with a final effort," just as he would like to fold up and file away the world as such with a final effort, or else he would not be able to control it any more.

But these final efforts exhaust him to such a degree that he becomes increasingly inactive and dull. If in the first case it was continuity of existence that had to be preserved at all costs, in the present case it is its dynamic *balance*. Here, too, a heavy phobic armor is employed in the interest of that preservation. Where it fails, even if only in phantasy, anxiety attacks and complete desperation take over. This case, whose existential and world-structure could be only very roughly suggested here, was published as the second study on schizophrenia under the title of "Juerg Zuend."

Whereas the above case permitted us a view of the kind of world in which "delusions of reference and encroachment" [26] become possible, a third case, that of Lola Voss,[27] gave us some insight into the world-structure which makes possible delusions of persecutions. It offered us the rare opportunity to watch the appearance of severe hallucinatory delusions of persecutions, preceded by a pronounced phobic phase. This expressed itself in a highly complicated superstitious system of consulting an oracle of words and syllables, whose positive or negative dicta guided the patient in the commission or omission of certain acts. She would feel compelled to break up the names of things into syllables, to recombine these syllables in accordance with her system and, depending on the results of these combinations, to make contact with the persons or things in question or to avoid them like the plague. Again, all this served as a safeguarding for the existence and its

26 The Swiss School differentiates between delusions characterized by ideas of reference and being encroached upon (*Beeintraechtigung*), on the one hand, and of persecutions on the other.

27 "Der Fall Lola Voss," *Schweizer Archiv fuer Neurologie und Psychiatrie*, Vol. LXIII, Zurich, 1949.

worlds against catastrophe. But in this case, catastrophe was not felt to be in the disruption of the world's continuity nor in the disturbance of its dynamic balance, but in the invasion by the unspeakably Uncanny and Horrid. This patient's "world" was not dynamically loaded with conflicting forces which had to be artificially harmonized; hers was not a world-design reduced to push and pressure but one reduced to the categories of familiarity and strangeness—or uncanniness (*Vertrautheit und Unvertrautheit—oder Unheimlichkeit*). The existence was constantly threatened by a prowling, as yet impersonal, hostile power. The incredibly thin and flimsy net of artificial syllable-combinations served as a safeguard against the danger of being overwhelmed by that power and against the unbearable threat of being delivered to it.

It was very informative to observe how, simultaneously with the disappearance of these safeguards, a new, quite different, because now quite unintended, safeguard made its appearance, namely the actual delusions of persecution.

The place of the impersonal power of the bottomless Uncanny (*Unheimlichen*) was now taken by the secret (*heimliche*) conspiracy of personalized enemies. Against these the patient could now consciously defend herself— with accusations, counterattacks, attempts at escape—all of which seemed like child's play compared with the constantly helpless state of being threatened by the horrible power of the incomprehensible Uncanny. But such gain in the security of existence was accompanied by the patient's complete loss of existential freedom, her complete yielding to the idea of hostility on the part of her fellow men, or, in psychopathological terms, by delusions of persecution.

I am reporting this case in order to demonstrate that we cannot understand these delusions if we begin our investigation with a study of the delusions themselves. Rather should we pay close attention to what *precedes* the delusions—be it for months, weeks, days, or only hours. We would then surely find that the delusions of persecution, similarly to the phobias, represent a protection of the existence against the invasion of something inconceivably Frightful, compared with which even the secret conspiracies of enemies are more tolerable; because the enemies, unlike the incomprehensible Frightful, can be "taken at something" [28]—by perceiving, anticipating, repelling, battling them.

In addition, the case of Lola Voss can show that we are no longer constrained by the bothersome contrast of psychic life with which we can empathize and that with which we cannot, but that we have at our disposal a method, a scientific tool, with which we can bring closer to a systematic

[28] [A Heideggerian concept which, in this context, serves to emphasize that these enemies can be "handled" by the patient.—TRANSLATOR.]

scientific understanding even the so-called incomprehensible life of the psyche.

Of course, it still depends upon the imagination of the single researcher and physician how truly he is able to reexperience and resuffer, by virtue of his own experiential abilities, all the potential experience which existential-analytical research methodically and planfully opens to his insight.

In many cases, however, it does not suffice to consider only *one* world-design, as we have done so far for the sake of simplicity of presentation. Whereas this serves our purpose in the morbid depressions, as in mania and melancholia, in our investigations of what is clinically known as schizophrenic processes we cannot neglect the bringing into focus and the describing of the various worlds in which our patients live in order to show the changes in their "being-in-the-world" and "beyond-the-world." In the case of Ellen West, for instance, we saw the existence in the shape of a jubilant bird soaring into the sky—a flight in a world of light and infinite space. We saw the existence as a standing and walking on the ground in the world of resolute action. And, finally, we saw it in the form of a blind worm crawling in muddy earth, in the moldering grave, the narrow hole. Above all, we saw that "mental illness" really means for the "mind," how the human mind really reacts under such conditions, how its forms actually change. In this case it was a change to a precisely traceable narrowing-down, to a depletion or excavation of existence, world, and beyond-world to the point where, finally, of all the spiritual riches of the patient's world, of its abundance in love, beauty, truth, kindness, in variety, growth, and blossoming, "nothing was left except the big unfilled hole." What did remain was the animalistic compulsion to cram down food, the irresistible instinctual urge to fill the belly to the brim. All this could be demonstrated not only in the modes and changes of spatiality, of the hue, materiality, and dynamics of the various worlds, but also in the modes and changes of temporality, up to the state of the "eternal emptiness" of so-called autism.

As to manic-depressive insanity, I refer to my studies on *The Flight of Ideas* [29] and to the investigations of the manifold forms of depressive states by E. Minkowski,[30] Erwin Straus, and Von Gebsattel, all of which, although not existential-analytical in the full sense of the word, were definitely conducted in an empirical-phenomenological fashion. In mentioning E. Minkowski we must gratefully acknowledge that he was the first to introduce phenomenology into psychiatry for practical purposes, particularly in the area of schizophrenia where he immediately put it to fruitful use.[31] I wish

29 L. Binswanger, *Über Ideenflucht* (Zurich: 1933).

30 [Appears in English translation Part I of this book.—EDITORS.]

31 Also, his books *Le Temps vécu* (1932) and, particularly, *Vers une cosmologie* (Ed. Montaigne, 1936) should be mentioned. The latter is an excellent introduction into "cosmological" thinking in phenomenological terms.

to mention further the work of Erwin Straus and Von Gebsattel on compulsion and phobias, and of the late Franz Fischer on *Space and Time Structure in the Existence of the Schizophrenic*. Applications of existential-analytical thinking can be found in Von Gebsattel's excellent study, *The World of the Compulsive*,[32] and in Roland Kuhn's study, *Interpretations of Masks in the Rorschach Test* (1945).

Apart from the deepening of our understanding of psychoses and neuroses, existential analysis is indispensable to psychology and characterology. As to characterology, I shall confine myself here to the analysis of miserliness. It has been said that miserliness consists in persisting in the state of potentiality, in "a fight againt realization," and that only from this angle can the bondage to money be understood (Erwin Straus). But this is still too rationalistic an interpretation. One has rather to analyze the miser's world-design and existence; in short, to explore what world-design and what world-interpretation lie at the root of miserliness, or in what way that-which-is (*Seiende*) is accessible to the stingy.

Viewing the behavior of the miser and his description in literature (as by Molière and Balzac) we find that he is primarily interested in *filling,* namely the filling of cases and boxes, stockings and bags with "gold," and only consequently in refusing to spend and in retaining. "Filling" is the a priori or transcendental tie that allows us to combine faeces and money through a common denominator. It is only this that provides psychoanalysis with the empirical possibility of considering money-addiction as "originating" from the retention of faeces. But by no means is the retaining of faeces the "cause" of stinginess.

The above-mentioned empty spaces, however, are designed not only to be filled but, in addition, to hide their content from the eyes and hands of fellow men. The miser "sits" or "squats" on his money "like the hen on her egg." (We can learn a great deal from such phrases of idiomatic language since language has always proceeded, to a high degree, phenomenologically rather than discursively.) The pleasure of spending money, of giving it out —possible only in sympathetic contact with one's fellow men—is replaced by the pleasure of secret viewing, rummaging, touching and mental touching, and counting the gold. Such are the secret orgies of the miser, to which may be added the lust for the glittering, sparkling gold as such as the only spark of life and love which is left to the miser. The prevalence of filling-up and its worldly correlate, the cavity, points to something "Moloch-like"[33] in such a world and existence. This, naturally, carries with it (according to the unitary structure of being-in-the-world) also a certain moloch-like form of the self-world, and in this case particularly of the body-world and of body-

[32] Published in this book in an abridged form (Chap. VI).

[33] The author here refers not to the cruel aspects of Moloch-worship but to the hollowness of the idol which had to be filled.—EDITORS.]

consciousness, as rightly emphasized by psychoanalysis. As to temporality, the very saying that one can be "stingy with one's time" proves that the miser's time is here spatialized in a moloch-like sense, insofar as small portions of time are eagerly and constantly being saved, accumulated, and jealously guarded. From this follows the inability to give "of one's time." Of course all this implies at the same time the loss of the possibility of true or existential temporalization, of maturation of personality. The miser's relation to death which here, as in all existential-analytical investigations, is of the greatest importance, can in this context not be discussed. It is closely linked to his relations to his fellow men and linked also to his profound lack of love.[34]

In the same way in which we investigate and understand a characterological trait, we investigate and understand what in psychiatry and psychopathology is so summarily termed feelings and moods. A feeling or a mood is not properly described as long as one does not describe how the human existence that has it, or is in it, is in-the-world, "has" world and exists. (See in my studies on *The Flight of Ideas* the description of the optimistic moods and the feelings of exhilarant gaiety.) What has to be considered here is, in addition to temporality and spatiality, the shade, the lighting, the materiality and, above all, the dynamics of the given world-design. All this can be examined again through the medium of individual verbal manifestations as well as through metaphors, proverbs, idiomatic phrases in general, and through the language of writers and poets. Indeed, idiomatic language and poetry are inexhaustible sources for existential analysis.

The peculiar dynamics of the world of feelings and moods, their ascending and descending motion, their Upward and Downward, I have pointed out in my essay on "Dream and Existence." [35] Evidence for this kind of motion can be found in waking states as well as in dreams, introspective descriptions, and Rorschach responses. Gaston Bachelard, in his *"L'Air et les Songes,"* gives a brilliant, comprehensive presentation of the verticality of existence, *de la vie ascensionnelle* on the one hand and *de la chute* on the other.[36]

He impressively and beautifully demonstrates the existential-analytical significance of the fundamental metaphors *de la hauteur, de l'elevation, de la profondeur, de l'abaissement, de la chute* (earlier referred to by E. Minkowski in his *Vers une Cosmologie*). Bachelard quite correctly speaks of a psychology—we would call it an anthropology—*ascensionelle*. Without this background, neither feelings nor "keys" (*Stimmung*) nor "keyed" (*gestimmte*)

34 *Viz.*, L. Binswanger, "Geschehnis und Erlebnis," *Monatsschrift f. Psychiatrie*, S. 267 ff.
35 *Neue Schweizerische Rundschau*, 1930, IX, S. 678.
36 But we also know of a horizontality of existence, particularly from Rorschach responses. This horizontality is characterized by the road, the river, the plain. It does not reveal the "key" of the existence, but the ways of its "life-itinerary," that is, the way in which it is able or unable to stay, or not stay, in life.

Rorschach responses can be scientifically understood and described.[37] Bachelard, too, has realized what impressed itself so urgently upon us in the case of Ellen West—that the imagination obeys the "law of the four elements" and that each element is imagined according to its special dynamism. We are particularly happy to find in Bachelard insight into the fact that those forms of being which are characterized by dropping and falling, those of a descending life in general, invariably lead to an *imagination terrestre*, a turning into earth, or a bogging down of the existence. This, in turn, is of the greatest importance for the understanding of Rorschach results.

This *materialité* of the world-design, originating from the "key" (*Gestimmtheit*) of the existence is by no means confined to the environment, to the world of things, or to the universe in general, but refers equally to the world of one's fellow men (*Mitwelt*) and to the self-world (*Eigenwelt*) (as demonstrated in the cases of Ellen West and Juerg Zuend). For them, self-world and environment were only accessible in the form of the hard, energy-loaded material, while the world of their fellow men was only accessible by way of an equally energy-loaded, hard, and impenetrable resistance. When the poet speaks of the "dull resistance of the world" he demonstrates that the world of one's fellow men can be experienced in the form not just of a metaphor but of an actually and bitterly felt hard and resistant matter. The same is expressed in sayings such as "a tough guy" and "a roughneck."

Finally, what part is existential analysis equipped to play in the total picture of psychiatric investigation and research?

Existential analysis is not a psychopathology, nor is it clinical research nor any kind of objectifying research. Its results have first to be recast by psychopathology into forms that are peculiar to it, such as that of a psychic organism, or even of a psychic apparatus, in order to be projected onto the physical organism.[38] This cannot be achieved without a greatly simplifying reduction whereby the observed existential-analytical phenomena are largely

[37] However, Bachelard's investigations are still based on imagination (*le forces imaginantes de notre esprit, viz., L'Eau et les rêves* [José Corti, 1942]; *La Psychanalyse du feu* [Gallimard, 1938]; *Lautréamont,* [Corti, 1939]). The latter book also provides an exemplary interpretation of a case interesting for the psychiatrist. What is still missing in them is an anthropological, and even more, an ontological, basis for B.'s studies. He realizes not yet that his "imagination," too, is nothing but a certain mode of being-in-the-world and being-beyond-it, especially of the latter. But he approximates this insight when he explains (*L'Air et les songes*, p. 13): *"l'imagination est une des forces de l'audace humaine,"* and when he sees in the *verticalité*—characterizing the ascending life—not a mere metaphor, but *"un principe d'ordre, une loi de filiation."* B.'s works today are indispensable for the literary critic and language scientist as well as for the psychiatrist.

[38] We are speaking here of the role of psychopathology within the total frame of psychiatric medical research. We do not neglect the fact that in the psychoanalytical investigation, as well as in every purely "understanding" psychopathology, germs of existential-analytical views can always be found. But they indicate neither a methodical scientific procedure nor a knowledge of why and in what way existential analysis differs from the investigation of life-historical connections and from an "empathic" or "intuitive" entering into the patient's psychic life.

divested of their phenomenal contents and reinterpreted into functions of the psychic organism, psychic "mechanisms," etc. However, psychopathology would be digging its own grave were it not always striving to test its concepts of functions against the phenomenal contents to which these concepts are applied and to enrich and deepen them through the latter. Additionally, existential analysis satisfies the demands for a deeper insight into the nature and origin of psychopathological symptoms. If in these symptoms we recognize "facts of communication"—namely, disturbances and difficulties in communication—we should do our utmost to retrace their causes—retrace them, that is, to the fact that the mentally ill live in "worlds" different from ours. Therefore, knowledge and scientific description of those "worlds" become the main goal of psychopathology, a task which it can perform only with the help of existential analysis. The much-discussed *gap* that separates our "world" from the "world" of the mentally ill and makes communication between the two so difficult is not only scientifically explained but also scientifically bridged by existential analysis. We are now no longer stopped at the so-called borderline between that psychic life with which we can, and that with which we cannot, empathize. Quite a number of case reports show that our method has succeeded beyond earlier hopes in communicating with patients, in penetrating their life-history, and in understanding and describing their world-designs even in cases where all this seemed impossible before. This applies, in my experience, particularly to cases of hypochondriacal paranoids who are otherwise hardly accessible. Thus we also comply here with a *therapeutic* demand.

This insight—that the world-designs as such distinguish the mentally ill from the healthy and hamper communication with the former—also throws new light on the problem of the projection [39] of psychopathological symptoms onto specific brain processes. Now it cannot be so important to localize single psychic symptoms in the brain but rather, primarily, to ask where and how to localize the fundamental psychic disturbance which is recognizable by the change of "being-in-the-world" as such. For indeed, the "symptom" (*e.g.*, of flight of ideas, of psychomotor inhibition, neologism, stereotypy, etc.) proves to be the expression of a spreading change of the soul, a change of the total form of existence and the total style of life.

39 [The German term "projection" used here in the sense of localizing or assigning.— TRANSLATOR.]

VIII

Insanity as Life-Historical Phenomenon and as Mental Disease: The Case of Ilse*

by Ludwig Binswanger

I *Insanity as Life-Historical Phenomenon*

Life-history

OUR PATIENT is a thirty-nine-year-old intelligent woman. She was happily married, but not fully satisfied in her marriage, Protestant, religious, mother of three children, daughter of an extremely egotistical, hard and tyrannical father and an "angelic," self-effacing, touchingly kind mother who allowed herself to be treated by her husband like a slave and only lived for him.

From the time she was a child Ilse suffered greatly under these conditions, feeling powerless to change them. For three years she had shown symptoms of overstrain and "nervousness." Following a performance of *Hamlet,* the idea came to her mind to persuade her father through some decisive act to treat her mother more considerately. During her boarding school period, the precocious girl had developed a somewhat ecstatic love for her father, and she believed she had great influence upon him. Ilse's resolution to carry out her plan was reinforced through that scene in which Hamlet plans to murder the king at his prayer but shrinks back from doing it. If at that particular time Hamlet had not missed his chance, he could have been saved, Ilse felt. She confessed to her husband that she planned something unusual and was only waiting for the right moment. Four months after the Hamlet performance, when asked for help against her father by her mother, she told her husband that she wanted to "demonstrate to her father what love can do." If he forbade her to do it, he would make her unhappy for the rest of her life; she had to "get rid of that."

* Translated by ERNEST ANGEL, from the original, "Wahnsinn als lebensgeschichtliches Phänomen und als Geisteskrankheit," *Monatsschrift für Psychiatrie und Neurologie,* Vol. 110, 1945, pp. 129–160.

One day, when her father had once again reproached her, she told him she knew of a way of saving him, and in front of her father she put her right hand up to her forearm into the burning stove, then held out her hands toward him with these words: "Look, this is to show you how much I love you!"

During the act she was oblivious to pain, although she suffered severe burns of the third degree with subsequent suppuration. During the four-week treatment she displayed tremendous energy and perseverance. Immediately after the act she appeared to be in an elated, heroic mood and directed the people around her, who had gotten panicky. Her father did change his behavior toward her mother for some weeks, but, to Ilse's great distress, soon new conflicts occurred. And yet, her husband found her, in the following months, more vigorous, agile, energetic, and busy than ever. Now, she announced, she had no other duties and could devote herself wholly to her husband and children. When her fourth child died in the same year, she bravely overcame her grief but firmly believed that the loss was the atonement for her love for the doctor who had treated the child.

Eight months after the act she was busier and moodier than before and took too much upon herself, intellectually and physically; she read Freud, participated in a Dalcroze gymnastic class, became secretary of a Society for the Improvement of Women's Dress, but felt that her strength was decreasing, particularly before and after periods. One day, thirteen or fourteen months after the burning, she asked the family doctor whether in his opinion she could develop a mental disease. After another three months she decided to take a vacation. She felt like "staking everything on one card." She reported that she was tortured by thoughts which, she felt, were almost thoughts of insanity.

During her stay in the health resort, she believed that she was to be "made the center of attention" and that at lectures the ladies chose their seats so as to be able to watch her. In reading Gottfried Keller's story "Der Landvogt von Greifensee" she found numerous references to herself and to her family. In "Figura Leu," described by her as a "cute and graceful, but overdressed girl," she saw allusions to herself and, in the character of the girl's uncle, allusions to her own father. She believed that certain lines which appeared in the original only once were read repeatedly. "Over and over again those greeting scenes with gentlemen! Everything so funny! Every time the subject of overdressing came up, the ladies would laugh so inappropriately, as they never did otherwise. How silly! Well, they wanted to test me—how I would react." (On the other hand, she was troubled by compulsive doubts about how she impressed others with what she said and did.) Suddenly she jumped to her feet and shouted, "You think I don't notice that you are sneering at me! I don't care a bit, do whatever you want!" Whereupon the reading had to be interrupted.

After the patient was placed in our institute, the delusions of reference spread further, along with delusions of love. These latter manifested themselves not only in Ilse's belief that she was loved and tested by the doctors but also in her compulsion to love the doctors. "I cannot eat and drink anymore until the hunger and thirst of my soul are quenched. Please let me have the nourishment I need, you know it as well as I do." Ilse imagined that the doctors increased all the drives in her so as to make her purge her self of them [1]—the drive toward love and the drive toward the truth. That, to her, represented her "treatment," one which she felt was very strenuous. Soon she considered it merely a torture.

It is *not* my fault that I got this way. You think it is delusions—religious delusions —that I think, speak, write like this. But this is not true; it is my nature, my innermost nature, which clamors for an outlet in order to relax again, or rather which you have dragged out of me with your torturous tools which torment me deeply. There is nothing other in me than what I have shown you, there is no breath of falsehood and no sensationalism in it, that I know of.

I cannot know what is in you. What is in me, I know, and am telling you everything without reservations. But I *cannot* tell you what is in you; because from the way you have behaved toward me I could draw different conclusions, and I cannot know which is the right one. [*From a letter to her physician.*]

The fact that a picture of a winter scene was on the wall of her room was interpreted by her as an intention to make her "as cold as ice." Another time she had a feeling as though her fingers, hands, and forearms were of wet clay—as though they were swollen and did not belong to her body at all.

When asked about the burning, she explained: "I wanted to demonstrate to my father that love is something that overcomes itself, not by words but by deeds. This should have had an effect on him like a lightning bolt, like a revelation, and should have made him stop living as an egotist. When the idea first came to me, it was for my mother's sake, but then I thought if I were to do it for his own sake it would be the right thing. I pitied him, and since then had felt even more love and understanding for him. I guess I must love all men so much because I loved my father so much."

Ilse passed through severe states of excitation with suicidal tendencies, mistaking of persons, and numerous ideas of reference, but without ever suffering from actual hallucinations. After thirteen months of institutional care Ilse could return to her home completely cured of her acute psychosis.

The *theme* around which this biography revolves is *father*. At the same time, it shows an attempt at mastering its theme. A sharp dissonance is noticeable, the contradiction between ecstatic love (an almost idolizing veneration of the father) and energetic rebellion against his tyranny, pri-

[1] When she watched the cleaning of windows, she felt the urge to join in the wiping so that everything would become clean and pure. What Ilse called the "treatment" is, of course, her delusion. No psychoanalytical experiments whatsoever were conducted.

marily his tyrannizing of the mother. The dissonance in this theme signifies an open, never-healing life sore; it could only be resolved by a change in the mind and behavior of the father, by a divorce of the parents, or by eliminating the father. All these roads were blocked by insurmountable external and internal obstacles. Thus, living turns into suffering from the dissonance of its main theme, into grievous floating in the pains of hopelessness. What from the angle of the world appears as hopelessness is, in terms of the "ego," irresolution, indetermination, shrinking away from decisions. This is the situation Hamlet is in. In his fate Ilse sees her own as in a mirror. The decision which she cannot make for herself she can, at least, make for Hamlet. She believes he should have killed the praying king without consideration of the situation and thus would have saved himself. Only such resolution to act would have saved him "from insanity!" Now the stone starts rolling. In her own situation, the possibility of eliminating the tyrant is excluded. The idea of parricide cannot develop, and, if it did, her love for the father would interfere with the act. Both parents are dead set against divorce. What is left to her is an attempt to persuade the father to a change in attitude and behavior toward the mother. The theme that now offers itself is named *sacrifice*. For a sacrifice will offer Ilse the opportunity to prove her love to her father as well as to make the desired "impression." The "sacrifice of love" is designed to overcome the father's brutal tyranny. Through the sacrifice of love Ilse takes the brutality upon herself. It is she who submits to suffering from some brutal pain so that mother does not have to suffer any more. The father himself is "spared" throughout.

The intended effect of the sacrifice fails in the long run, the sacrifice proves in vain. The life-sore opens again, deeper and more painful than ever. The sacrifice was still a self-chosen decision, still a decision of the "self" to bring about a reconciliation of the discordant forces; but now the self is relieved of any decision. The self succumbs under the heavy task of pursuing further the leitmotif of its history. But the life task posed by the theme as such remains nonetheless and presses for a "solution." This self-effacing solution, according to her own insight, runs as follows: You *must* love all men so much because you love your father so much (*viz.*, delusions of love). This may be complemented by: You *must* attract the attention and interest of *all* people to yourself, because you have attracted the attention and the interest of your father to yourself; you *must* know what impression you are making upon *all* people because you wanted to make an impression upon your father; you must react to everything the others do because you wanted to know how your father reacted to *you;* in short, you must be "in the center of attention" of *all* people (*viz.*, delusions of reference). The lack of insight into the *must* of this loving and attracting-of-attention we call insanity. The cure for such insanity consists in the shaking off of the *must* and in the restoration of the rule of the self.

In our case, the restoration was a lasting one. Ilse stayed perfectly healthy up to her death at the age of seventy-three.

She was able to direct the theme "salvation" and "purification" into healthy channels, that is, to confirm it through social work. Advised and counseled by experts over a period of time, she successfully practiced as a psychological counselor and at times was also the leader of a psychological workshop group.

The Sacrifice

Much as war is described as a continuation of politics by different means, so in our case we could interpret Ilse's delusions as a continuation of her sacrifice, but by different means. Even the sacrifice itself could be explained as a continuation of the earlier life history, but with the help of a different instrument. Already the sacrifice was the outcome and expression of a very complex life-historical network of motives. The rational motive was the intention to make a deep impression upon the father so as to change his attitude and behavior toward the mother. This intention was to be carried out by way of the fire ordeal, of suffering extreme physical pain as proof of what love—her love for her father—could do. If one wants to emphasize convincingly a belief or an intention in the German language, one would say, "For that I would put my hand in the fire." Ilse actually did it. Thus she tried to confirm how serious she was in her belief and intention not to "let it go on," that is, not to tolerate her mother's treatment at the hands of her father any longer.

But by the same token, Ilse wanted to save the father himself by her sacrifice of love. This act also represents the realization of a salvation phantasy as we know it from psychoanalysis in connection with "incest phantasies." As such the sacrifice expresses a purification wish, the wish to be purged of the incest wish. The salvation of the father is, at the same time, the salvation of her own exaggerated love for her father. The fire offers itself as a proper medium since, like the water, it is in the service of purification and, in our case, of purification by self-inflicted torture, mutilation, repentance, and asceticism. Hence the sacrifice itself is an act of atonement. It serves the expression and confirmation of Ilse's love for her father as well as her atonement for this love. The ambivalent nature of neurotic and psychotic forms of expression has been, since Freud and Bleuler, generally recognized. Ilse appears as a twofold heroine offering her love sacrifice for the father (and only indirectly for the mother) as well as offering her self-sacrifice, the sacrifice of her love for the father. Furthermore, the meaning and countermeaning of the sacrifice are expressed in Ilse's idea that out of the (partial) death through sacrifice new life was expected to grow: on one hand, the father was to be awakened to a new life, on the other, her love for her father was to score a new living triumph. (The equation *fire = life* is known from antiquity—*e.g.*, from Heraclitus, and more recently from Paracelsus.)

The hand (as well as the foot) is known to psychoanalysts as a male symbol, the stove as a female one. But more important than this knowledge is the knowledge of the phenomenology of fire in general, that is, of the phenomenal modes of fire as a material manifestation (*Gewand*) of physical and psychic modes of existence, primarily of the "die-and-be-reborn" mode of existence (*Stirb und werde*). In putting the hand—the life organ of gripping and interfering, of taking-at-something [2] and penetrating-into-something, and of the most sensitive touch and pain sensations—in putting this organ into the flames of the stove, Ilse sacrifices not only her "loaded aggressivity" but also her explosive "inner fire" altogether; her inner red-heat is to be overcome and purged by the "outer" one. "*Le besoin de pénétrer, d'aller à l'interieur des choses, à l'interieur des êtres, est une séduction de l'intuition de la chaleur intime,*" says Bachelard quite fittingly.[3] And although he adds, "*Ou l'oeil ne va pas, ou la main n'entre pas, la chaleur s'insinue,*" our case shows that entering of the hand and of inner warmth can find expression in one and the same act. In insanity, as we shall see later, it is no longer the stove which Ilse torturously struggles to enter with her "*chaleur intime*" but it is "*les êtres,*" the fellow men. However we have not yet reached that point.

We have seen that a verbal testimony of love to the father—perhaps expressed in the words: "I would risk my right hand to prove that my love does not shrink from any sacrifice, if only *you* make the sacrifice of your egotism and your tyranny toward mother"—that such *verbal* testimony was replaced by Ilse's *manual* testimony, her palpable affirmation, the sacrifice of her hand. As any sacrifice this, too, is an act of self-denial, of self-effacement and self-surrender. Hence it would be wrong to dispute the ethical meaning and content of this sacrifice. But that it was not a pure, let alone an "absolute," sacrifice was realized by Ilse herself. The motive of worry about the mother receded more and more behind the motive of the testimony of love to the father and of the test by fire of her influence upon him. The sacrifice is not pure but clouded by passion. The self-surrender is also a surrender of her inner heat to the ice-cold father, it expresses the "insane idea" of touching the father's cold heart by "something decisive," a "de-

2 ["Taking at something" is an expression referring to a mode of being in which "I" and "you" are opposite each other, so that one can be "at hand" for the other for all kinds of purposeful intercourse or action. Later in this same chapter Binswanger uses this phrase, "taking at," to designate Ilse's relating to her father and other men as objects. This is in contrast to the "dual mode" of being which obtains, in Binswanger's view, in a genuine meeting of two persons and in love; *viz.*, L. Binswanger, *Grundformen und Erkenntnis menschlichen Daseins* (II. Aufl.; Zurich: 1953), Kap. 2.—TRANSLATOR.]

3 *La Psychoanalyse du feu*, S. 48 f.

cisive event." For that something, Ilse, by no means accidentally, uses again a metaphor from the realm of fire; she wants to touch her father's heart with a "lightning bolt," not in order to sear it, but in order to melt it in the "fire" of her love. Following this, we may rightly say—if not with Ilse's own words—the sacrifice was to be a purifying storm in the close and oppressive atmosphere of her parents' home. Ilse's faith in the power of love was accompanied by a will to power in general, an arrogant drive to trespass stormlike, "like a lightning bolt," the boundaries of man. But Ilse trespasses these boundaries by no means only for the sake of her father, but just as much for the sake of herself. In her attempt to purify her passionate love for her father she tried to accomplish by a sudden violent act against herself, by an act of forced asceticism, what man is permitted to accomplish only in a steady process of slow maturation.

But the sacrifice was in every respect in vain. The lightning did not hit the father as deeply and as decisively as Ilse had hoped, nor did she herself emerge from the cataclysm genuinely purified. We shall understand this the better the more we can clarify for ourselves the meaning of a sacrifice. Such meaning does not exhaust itself in active testimony and substituting symbol; the deepest meaning of any sacrifice lies in *founding,* the founding of a union. The testimony of love must become a union of love to make the sacrifice "meaningful." By my testimony, by my confession of love, I am testifying to my love for you, I am confessing my love for you; but only in the union are you answering me, and only this answer is the foundation for the We. In Ilse's case, however, this answer is missing. The "lightning" did *not* strike, the storm did *not* purify the air, the union was *not* founded. Hence the sacrifice of self-purification loses its meaning too. The founding of a new union with the father, purified, made sacred, and conditioned by the sacrifice, would have made the self-sacrifice, the extinction of passion, meaningful; through the failure of the union, of unity with the father on the level of a pure We, the self-purification becomes meaningless. The entire existence is now not only thrown back to the *status quo ante,* but faces a completely new situation: What now?

Insanity

Ilse's "innermost nature" was not made to resign. The inner fire continued burning until one day it threatened to kindle the whole existence. Her failure to establish the union, her shaken confidence, became distrust of all and of herself. The pride of self-conceit turned into the feeling of being threatened in her honor. Since her father cared little for her sacrifice, even spurned it, she came to feel not only misunderstood but actually wounded in her honor. To her love for father was added her extreme disappointment, her distrust in him as well as in her own mission and strength.

These feelings were joined by doubts which can be formulated as follows: Didn't he notice how serious I was about it? Did he believe that I was out for sensationalism, that I wanted to become the center of his interest only to "make an impression" on him and to test the power of my influence upon him? Didn't he notice how much I love him, doesn't he know how greatly he has hurt and offended me?

No discussion of all this came about, and none could come about. What could have been accomplished by words since not even the "deed" had been convincing (that is, not able to create the union). Now Ilse is forced into a defensive position. Everything now seems to depend upon her giving evidence of her good intention and sincerity, upon her defense of her honor and her definite purification of her passion. But here, again, she believes that she meets with resistance; the others refuse to believe her, deride her, scoff at her, just as her father had "scoffed" at her.

In insanity, Ilse's hands are actually "sacrificed"; they are swollen, feel like "wet clay," are ice-cold, and they "seem not to belong to her body any more at all." Also, the inner fire as such, the "hunger and thirst of the soul," are actually sacrificed; that fire, in the "process of purification," turns into "icy coldness." The "need to penetrate, to go into the inside of things," into the inside of the stove—in order to penetrate from there into the inside of the father—is now replaced by a new *séduction de l'intuition de la chaleur intime*. This is, namely, *le besoin de pénétrer à l'interieur des êtres*, the painful desire to penetrate with her inner fire directly into the inside of her fellow men, to learn "what is in you." But again the inner fire and the others do not melt into new life and a new union. Due to the resistance and "coldness" of the others, the "burning torture" within herself persists, and so does the painful doubt, the staggering back and forth between presumed knowing and not knowing, between tormenting distrust and faithful trust. In this, the boundaries between inner and outer fire are constantly shifting; sometimes it is Ilse's "inner nature" that pushes outward, sometimes her inner nature is pulled out by the others with the help of their "torturous instruments."

During her insanity, she repeats time and again protestations in defense of her honor, in defense against the reproach of sensationalism, of dishonesty, and of "delusions." They all sound like belated justifications of her sacrifice: *not* out of sensationalism, *not* to place herself in the center of (her father's) interest, *not* out of self-conceit did she put her hand in the stove! Rather, it was her genuine aim to help her mother to an existence worthy of a human being. Nonetheless, the self-reproaches that her sacrifice was not made in full sincerity could not be silenced. Therefore, to her the treatment had to be a purification of her "drive for love and truth." Here again we face the ambivalence of psychotic manifestations: on one hand, Ilse must love *all* men so much because she loves father so much, and she must feel she is in the center of interest for *all* because she wanted to be in the center of interest for the father. On the other hand, she must make (purifying) amends *for* that love and *for* that wish to be in the center. As far and as long as she believes in the doctors' purifying intention and believes that she can interpret their intention in this sense, the doctors remain her friends and helpers; insofar and as long as she is certain that this is not the case, they change into tormentors and enemies. But halfway between the two interpretive possibilities lurks the doubt about "what is in you," the lacking ability really to penetrate the inside of the others. Again, in her certainty about the others being ill-inclined toward her, watching her, testing her with innuendos, scoffing at her and torturing her, we recognize her bad conscience and feelings of guilt (because of her "burning" love for her father). In this way the others become just as tyrannical, inflexible, and inaccessible to her love as is her father! Thus the entire dialectics of her relation to her father continue in the dialectics of her relations to her fellow men in general.

Hence, the actual meaning of her insanity rests in the pluralization [4] of the father—in the transformation of the singular *thou* and of the dual *we* into the plurality of *you* (plural) and *we*. In this sense the insanity is an expression of the lifting of the "incest taboo." The "inner flames," heretofore constrained by this taboo, now break all dams and seize *all* men who come on the scene. Hence the *thou*, though desecrated and devaluated, is brought closer to its "natural destiny." But still, for Ilse, the married woman, the *thou* remains taboo, a cause of fear and reproach, the reproach that she was "man-crazy." In the dress-loving Figura Leu she sees as though in a mirror her own coquetry and craving for men, just as, in Hamlet, she saw a reflection of her own indecision. With Figura Leu she can identify in yet another respect; this girl is the most enchanting figure among the former lady-loves of the Landvogt; she is described as "standing bathed in light—a heavenly angel who celebrates a mystery." And it was she who refused to marry the Landvogt "because she never knew when she would be called away to that unknown land where the spirits travel."

The real sense of Ilse's insanity (or, as seen from the angle of the healthy, the non-sense of it) we have located in the leveling down and pluralization of the *thou*. We now see that this process is not confined to the positive love motion of attraction but that it extends to its "countermeaning," to the negative motion of repulsion. Ilse's disappointment in the father develops —always by way of the pluralization of the *thou*—into the delusions of reference. The pluralization of the *thou* is the order principle by which the

[4] [By "pluralization," a term which is used frequently on this and the following pages, Binswanger means the spreading, extending of Ilse's relationship to her father to cover her relationship with all men. Pluralization is a dispersing, a "leveling down," as Binswanger puts it on the following page, and thus changes the central and real value of the "We" relationship.—TRANSLATOR.]

alleged disorder ("insanity") can be understood; it is the principle which permits us to see not just chaos but method in this insanity.

Thus, the scientific problem which presents itself to the psychiatrist in the form of Ilse's insanity has obtained its methodical foundation.

Review

Ilse's life-history impressed us as appropriate to our topic because it contains only one key theme and because its various phases can with increasing clarity be recognized and presented as specific variations of this theme. This key theme serves us as the *constant* which provides the key to our understanding of Ilse's life as a *history*. History is always thematic. The kind of themes which a person (or a people) is assigned by destiny or which he selects for "elaboration," and the manner in which he varies them, are not only decisive for his history but *are* his history. In Ilse's case the constant is, as we saw, the father theme. This historic theme, like all others, is not "absolute," not separated from the entire life situation, but it is a very real life problem and as such dominates the life history. It is this father, this adored cold tyrant, who enslaves the beloved mother and poisons the life of Ilse and her family with a close and oppressive atmosphere from which Ilse the child, and Ilse the woman and mother, never manages to emerge and in which she drags her life on in complete helplessness and hopelessness. This marks the first phase of her life-history.

In her fourth life-decade the pressure of this atmosphere condenses so as to produce an intolerable torture. More and more Ilse realizes that only a storm, a lightning bolt, can purify the atmosphere. Her key problem sharpens into a crisis. Her entire existence is in a turmoil and she stakes everything on one chance. It is true, Ilse has independently reached a decisive resolution, but now the self is ruled by this resolution to the point of being driven; thus, it desires nothing more than to free itself from being driven by means of the act. Already, the self is not any more in control of itself; the key problem is overpowering it. This is the second phase of this life history. It comes to its close in the pathetically violent solution of the crisis through action, through the fire sacrifice.

The third phase is initiated by self-mastery regained through the act; but this control is soon upset by another compulsion to be driven, another seemingly aimless restlessness which makes her fall for all sorts of side aims, and is, about fifteen months after the act, replaced by a new variation of the never-ceasing key theme—to be sure, by very different means. First, the passive helplessness, then the active, self-chosen but no longer self-empowered act, and then the extreme "self-disempowering," the yielding to the "theme" that now assumes unlimited power. The theme, of course, is not just a theme but an argument between "I and the world," sharpened by a definite existential situation. This theme now no longer worries about limitations but sweeps the whole existence along with it, perceiving only itself and living only for itself. It forces the person whom it rules to meet the "father" all over in the world of fellow men (*Mitwelt*) and to struggle with it in love and hatred, fight and surrender, and again and again in conflict. The father, to Ilse, was not merely a *thou* but was at the same time an object of *sorge* (combination of "care" and "worry"), something to be "taken at something" [5] (potentially and actually), something to be impressed and influenced. And Ilse, similarly, was accepted and rejected by him, disappointed, her honor wounded and tyrannized. Accordingly, things now develop between her and the world-around (*Umwelt*). Instead of father, the latter is now the power with which no union can be formed, no peaceful agreement or accord can be reached. But where thou and object, love and worry, are in constant conflict, the power becomes an insoluble riddle, a riddlesome power. Just as the father's harshness and coldness, inaccessibility to love and sacrifice, turned into a torturous riddle for Ilse, so the entire environment now becomes an enigmatic power; at one time it is a loving You, one to which she would like to surrender not just her hand but herself altogether; at another time it is a harsh, loveless, inaccessible world which scoffs at her love, derides and humiliates her, wounds her honor. Her entire existence is now limited to the motions and unrest of being attracted and being rejected. But with the pluralization of the You, with the theme extended all over her existence without limit, and with the loss of the original thematic goal, the father, no solution of the problem is possible any more. The theme spends itself on an inappropriate object, it rotates in eternal repetition around itself. The only remaining question is . . . whether the existence will find a way out of this form of self-discussion, return to itself, and so clear the road for new possibilities for a solution or whether it will be blunted in the process by endlessly repeating and stereotyping the discussion as such through acts, behavior, or phrases. But as long as the theme remains the theme (even the stereotypization is . . . still thematic variation) there is life-history. . . .

Finally, we have observed a fourth phase in her life-history reaching to the end of life, a phase in which the self regained command and led the life-historical problem toward a new but this time definite solution. The pressure of helplessness and indecision, the pathos of lightning swift action, the submission to the problem's superpower, and the state of being insanely driven back and forth by it, are eventually all replaced by what can be termed a "sound" solution: the switching of the problems of love, cleansing, and resistance onto the track of goal-directed and methodical, painstaking, and patient psychological work—in short, into the world of practice. The thou and the world-around (*Umwelt*) were finally reconciled in readiness

[5] See footnote 1

to help and work for the fellow man. The gap between the thou and the resistance of the apathetic world was bridged, and that resistance showed itself no longer in the "other fellow's" harshness, coldness, contempt, and scorn but in his suffering, which is accessible to work and can be overcome by work.

We understand that in the invention of a musical theme and in the formulation of its variations the total musical existence of the composer plays a decisive part. Similarly, in the acceptance of a life-historical theme and in the formulation of its variations the total existence of the person prevails. The father theme, therefore, is by no means the ultimate; we must not absolutize the "father-complex" into an independent "being." Much less should we, in the manner of psychoanalysis, see in this history merely a history of the libido, of its fixation onto father, its forced withdrawal from father, and its eventual transference to the world-around. For in that way we would misinterpret essential possibilities of human existence into genetic developmental processes, reduce history to natural history. But only human existence is genuinely historical. Although its history is determined by the themes it has been assigned and on which it works and even though its history consists in having and working out these themes, still its historicity rests upon its attitude toward its "ground." Although existence does not lay its own ground itself but takes it over as its being and heritage, it still is left with freedom in relation to the ground. Having a father and a mother is part of man's being, just as is having an organism and a history. (Therefore, where parents are "missing" existence can be exposed to the most serious crises.) But that Ilse got just that father and that mother was her destiny, received as a heritage and as a task; how to bear up under this destiny was the problem of her existence. Hence, in her "father complex" were destiny *and* freedom at work. Both are to be held "responsible" for the choice of the life-historical theme and the formulation of its variations.

Finally, we have to confess that in our case we do not even know the theme in its original form, the form it had in Ilse's childhood. This is not only a flaw in our life-historical discussion, but a real gap. If we knew the infantile arch-form of the father theme, we would probably recognize in it the seeds of all possibilities which we found developed and utilized in the later variations.

Insanity, Existential Analysis, and "Empathy"

Speaking of the life-historical phenomena of helplessness, readiness to sacrifice, insanity, and eventually of work, we also feel obliged to investigate and describe these phenomena in respect to their phenomenal structure. This would be the task of existential analysis or of anthropological phenomenology. All these phenomena are phenomena of being-in-the-world.

beyond-the-world; they are specific forms of it and produce, in turn, specific forms of being-oneself and not-being-oneself, being-together and not-being-together, of spatialization and temporalization, etc. In this way, the life-historical analysis presses beyond itself toward a phenomenological existential analysis. Since we deal with these questions elsewhere, we may stop at this point. But it should be emphasized that the kind and mode of the given being-in-the-world-beyond-the-world also determines the way in which we fellow men communicate with the person in the various phases of his or her life-history, which is to say, the way we sympathize and come to an understanding with him. The degree of potential and real agreement between my world and his world determines the degree of possible communication, of "understanding."

We are now approaching the problem which is usually characterized by the very vague term "empathy." But this label does not help us to get farther; wherever feeling and feelings are introduced, we have to grope as in a fog. We can only proceed into clearer air when we submit to the necessary effort to examine and describe that feeling or feelings in regard to their phenomenal mode of being and their phenomenological content. In the case of "empathy," *e.g.*, we would have to examine to what degree it is a phenomenon of *warmth*, a phenomenon of the possibility or impossibility of fusing the *chaleur intime* (as in our instance); or a vocal or *sound* phenomenon, as when the poet Hoelderlin writes to his mother that there could not be a sound alive in her soul with which his soul would not chime in; or a phenomenon of *touch*, as when we say, "your sorrow, your joy touches me"; or a phenomenon of *sharing*, as expressed by Diotima in Hoelderlin's *Hyperion*—"He who understands you must share your greatness and your desperation"; or a phenomenon of *participation*, as in the saying, "I partake in your grief"; or, lastly, a phenomenon of *"identification,"* as when we say, "I would have done the same in your place" (in contrast to, "I don't understand how you could act that way.") All these modes of expression refer to certain phenomenal, intentional, and preintentional modes of being-together (*Mitseinandersein*) and co-being (*Mitsein*) which would have first to be analyzed before the total phenomenon of empathy could be made comprehensive and clarifiable. For this reason alone, the differentiation of psychic life with which we can empathize from psychic life with which we cannot empathize (schizophrenics) loses a great deal of its scientific value, apart from the fact that the limits of empathic possibilities are purely subjective and vary according to the empathic ability and "imagination" of the investigator.

Fortunately, today we are in a position to overcome the dichotomy between empathizable and nonempathizable psychic life, because we now have at our disposal a method that enables us to analyze phenomenologically the given being-in-the-world independently from that dichotomy. This method is the anthropological or existential-analytical one which owes its existence to Husserl's phenomenology and which received its decisive stimulation from Heidegger's existential *"Daseins* analysis." Without yet entering this area we have had to carry the problem of communication to this point in order to find the actual starting point for our approach to the problem, *insanity as a mental disease.*

II *Insanity as a Mental Disease*

Wherever in a scientific or prescientific context mental illness is discussed, one speaks of psychic disease symptoms in a certain person. But *what* makes its appearance in these symptoms is, just as in the case of physical illness, by no means "the disease." Indeed, the latter does not at all show in the symptoms; the symptoms rather refer to something which is hidden "behind" them. The disease itself has yet to be brought to light or to be revealed, with the symptoms serving as guides. What are these symptoms like?

At this point, let us look at our case and specifically at Ilse's sacrifice, and let us see how a layman would react to such an act. He would probably ask himself: Would I have done this, or could I have done this in Ilse's place? And his answer would be: No, no normal person would do a thing like this in our day and time. And in view of the pluralization of the "Thou," he would have felt even more emphatically: "Now this woman has gone completely crazy!" So we see that the judgment on the sickness or health is subject to the norm of the social attitude. If an act, behavior, or verbalization deviates from that norm, it is judged even by the layman as morbid, as a symptom of an illness. However, there may be people who see in the sacrifice the expression of a genuinely religious or ethical self-effacement, of a genuinely ethical readiness for sacrifice and love for one's fellow man; such persons would strongly reject the idea that the sacrifice be considered a symptom of disease. We realize that the norm of behavior is by no means fixed once for all, but that it varies according to an individual's education and culture or to a cultural area. What appears abnormal—or a deviation from the norm— to one person may look to another quite normal, or even like the supreme expression of a norm; the judgment "sick" or "sound" is accordingly formed within a cultural frame of reference. Naturally, the same is true for insanity. What we of the twentieth century consider a symptom of disease was seen by the Greeks as a blow from Apollo or as the work of the Furies and by the people of the Christian Middle Ages as possession by the Devil. What at the peak of Pietism could pass for an expression of supreme piety would today be considered a phenomenon of morbid self-reflection and morbid guilt feelings, and so forth. But all this cannot alter the fact that a person is judged "sick" wherever his social behavior deviates from the respective norm of social behavior and thus appears conspicuous or strange.

But we must not be content with this. Although we register by our judgment the deviation from the norm of social behavior, this judgment rests on facts that are pre- and irrational, namely, facts from the area of *communicatio* (social intercourse) and of *communio* (love). For example, someone who considers Ilse's sacrifice morbid discloses thereby that such an act or, more correctly, that Ilse in carrying through such an act strikes him as "strange," which is to say that something has got between him and her which is experienced by him as a barrier to *communicatio* and, even more so, to *communio*. Now Ilse is no longer "someone else" like any other, let alone a Thou, but another strange person and a You which is excluded from the possibility of a purely loving encounter. The barrier to *communicatio* and *communio*, the obstacle, turns into an object [6] (of conspicuousness, avoidance, pity, judgment, etc.). Thereby I separate or remove myself from my fellow men, and the closeness of sympathy and intercourse changes into the distance of objective regard, observation, and judgment. Since the manifestation of love and the possibility of communication also greatly depend upon the membership in a cultural community, the cultural relatedness of the judgment "sick" must still be upheld. But we did wish to demonstrate that the symptoms of disease with which psychiatry deals refer to facts in the fellow-human area of sympathy and intercourse or, more precisely, that they are facts of sympathy and intercourse, in short, of understanding in the widest sense of the word.

Even the psychiatrist proceeds at first not unlike the layman. He, too, *judges* Ilse's sacrifice, and he often does so still in a moralizing fashion. He would, for instance, characterize the strangeness of this action as an act of "exaggerated" or "eccentric" love, or as bizarre or deranged, just as he describes the behavior of a hebephrenic or manic as insolent, reckless, frivolous. It appears obvious that he cannot be satisfied with such "subjective" criteria which vary from person to person and from culture to culture, but that he will have to search for comparatively definite criteria. This calls not only for a conscientious review and sifting of the total empirical material of abnormal social behavior but also for a new frame of reference out of which and by which the psychiatric judgment is formed. Such a frame of reference he can find not in the culture, as we know, but in nature. Therefore he can only reach his scientific goal if he succeeds in understanding culturally related behavior as naturally conditioned.

To get to this point the psychiatrist had first to collect and classify his observational material like a botanist or zoologist, from a natural-scientific viewpoint, in order to survey and organize it within a natural-scientific system. He sees the complex and dramatic life-historical *phenomenon* of the sacrifice as an individual *event* "in time" and "in" a human being, he places it in the category of bizarre, absurd, or "eccentric" acts, traces them perhaps to the class of "schizoid" or schizophrenic behavior, and lists the latter as a

[6] *Viz.*, René Le Senne, *Obstacle et valeur* (Paris: Editions Montaigne).

symptom of schizophrenia. It is true that in so doing he has completely neglected the life-historical structure and significance of the sacrifice; instead, he has used the natural-scientific method of subsumption and now knows in which disease category to include the action.[7] With this, he has reached his first goal, the formation of a diagnostic judgment.

But now we have to ask ourselves: what has happened here? We have, to be sure, far surpassed the concept of abnormality. Where we speak of disease symptoms and make a diagnostic judgment, quite a different frame of reference appears to be in force. It is neither a cultural nor a purely natural-scientific-biological one, but a medical one; it is the reference system of medical pathology. If we judge abnormal social behavior—a cultural fact—psychiatrically as a pathological phenomenon, we have left the area of purely biological judgment and entered the area of judgment of biological *purpose,* just as if we had to deal with physical abnormal behavior. Health and illness are value concepts, objects of judgments based on biological purpose, regardless of whether we measure them with Virchow by the purpose of safety of the organism (illness as threat or danger), with Krehl by the purpose of efficiency and vitality (illness as their limitation), or with Freud by the purpose of enjoyment of life (illness as suffering). The psychiatrist who judges the life-historical phenomenon of insanity or of the sacrifice as symptoms of schizophrenia or generally of a mental disease expresses much more than the fact that he considers them abnormal behavior—namely, that he sees in them a threat, a limitation, a suffering. But he does not stop there, he does not rest until he has, at least, tried to retrace this threat, this limitation, this suffering, to events in a natural object—the one which alone permits us to regard man wholly as a natural object (or to reduce him to it) even if with the greatest loss in observable reality (*anschaulicher Wirklichkeit*). This natural object is the *organism* in the sense of the total context of living and functioning of a human individual.[8]

Hence, that which in this context is indicated or registered by the disease

[7] We have omitted the question of whether the sacrifice already constitutes the beginning of a schizophrenic episode, a suspicion which is supported among other things by the patient's state of schizophrenia.

[8] But it has to be mentioned that the *complete* reduction of man to his organism is only possible "in abstracto," and that the seeming riddle of the psycho-physical connection stems only from that abstraction. In "reality" there is no organism and no brain that could not be claimed by someone as "my" organism or "my" brain. The possessive relation, however, is fundamentally removed from the categories of natural science. It does not partake in determining what is to be considered an object of nature. This problem had already been touched by Kant when he emphasizes the "trap" in the question of the location of the soul in the bodily world, stressing that the body whose changes are *my* changes is *my* body, and that its location is *my* location. This points already to the fact that "my body" must always, at the same time, mean "myself." Later, Hoenigswald (Psychology of Thinking) placed the problem of the *praesenzielle Possessivbestimmung* in the center of the discussion on the coordination of the psyche with the physis, pointing out why the coordination of the psyche to *the* brain has to be dropped, and that only *my* brain, as the condition for the objectivity of thinking, has an original (*urspruengliche*) relation to the world of norms.

symptom, that hidden something to which the symptom refers, is threats to or restrictions of the organism—in short, disturbances in the efficiency or functions of the organism. Of course, what is meant here is only the reference system in general within which the psychiatric-medical judgment occurs.

In the act of passing the psychiatric judgment the psychiatrist does not have to be conscious of this (teleological) system of reference. Indeed, between this system of reference and the given facts to be judged extends the entire empirical knowledge of psychiatry and knowledge of the aforementioned "system" of psychiatric-medical *pathology* developed in accordance with purely natural-scientific principles. It is that knowledge alone on which the psychiatric judgment rests. "Diagnosis" (*diagnosko*) means to discern precisely, to examine accurately, and to *decide* on the basis of such examination and discernment. Only through exact investigation and differentiation of the signs and symptoms of illness—which calls for familiarity and experience with psychiatric pathology—is the physician able to diagnose the hidden disorder to which these signs and symptoms refer and through which it registers. Thereby, however, the hidden is only named—*i.e.*, determined as here and now existent in the organism—but by no means is it revealed in its being (*Sein*) or essence. What psychiatry wants to do and is in a position to do is not at all a revelation of that essence but an increasingly precise and ever deeper penetration into the existing medical fact—as, for example, the fact of schizophrenia—into the causes of its existence and the possibilities of fighting and removing those causes and their effects. Actual revelation of being (essence) is here as everywhere only possible by philosophical ("ontological") revelation.

The reduction of human life-history to events in the organism occurs not simply under the pressure of the natural-scientific-medical method and its successes; it can be and has been philosophically argued that on all occasions where illness is discussed, one has eventually to resort to the organism. . . . But there still remains the great psychiatric problem of what in a behavior diagnosed as pathological can be reduced from a disturbance in communication to a disturbance in the organism, particularly in the brain. This will always be determined by the currents of contemporary scientific fashion, as so alarmingly demonstrated by positivism. But at this point philosophical demand and empirical research join hands. Whereas the former warns us not to give up a method prematurely and to avoid a *Metabasis eis allo genos,* our very case shows how necessary it is to pursue the life-history all the way into insanity. We can demonstrate thereby that it is not permissible to isolate from that insanity single links, such as Ilse's delusions of love or her ideas of reference or the muddy feeling in her hands and their apartness from the body, and to project them separated into the organism or the brain. All we can say is that the total form in which the life-historical theme is treated, the form of solution to the task which is posed by the theme, can be pathological and thus dependent on disturbances in the central organ. Anything beyond this is in the area of brain-pathological speculation; for it is not the "brain" that thinks and treats a life-historical theme, but the "man" (*der Mensch*).

Of course, the question could be raised, what would have become of Ilse if the father had accepted her sacrifice, if he had formed a new union with her and if thereby her love to him had been "purified"? It is very possible, if not sure, that the illness would have come to a standstill or would have assumed a different form. This possibility in itself—and even more so the possibility of "active" psychotherapy in psychoneuroses—suffices to prove that man does not "consist of psyche and soma" but that the "organism" as such is much more than and something different from a mere organism and that the psyche is altogether something different from a mere psyche.[9] Man is and remains a unit. He is not "divided into" body and psyche; rather, the body is also psyche and the psyche is also body. Although not "identical" in empirical observation, the two are borderline concepts mutually calling for each other; considered in separation, however, they are purely theoretical constructs. Only from such a viewpoint are we able to understand that a life-historical turn may bring about a change in physiological events, that a change in the latter can cause a turn in the manner in which a life-historical theme is formulated.

Since we have touched on the mind-body problem, we would like to put in a word about the concept which considers mental diseases as "illnesses of the soul." [10] We must take exception to this formulation. "Soul" is a religious, metaphysical, and ethical concept. Apart from these spheres, we can admit it only as a theoretical, auxiliary construct within a specific field—as, for example, in psychopathology. What of this auxiliary construct in psychiatry? If in this area we speak of functions, occurrences, or mechanisms of the psyche, we double the organism into two objects of nature, one psychical and one physical. Both objects are then assumed to influence each other or to run parallel to each other, or are recognized as *one*—which, however, can be ultimately regarded from the inside or outside. But as soon as the psyche has become an object of nature or is objectivated in some way—as in psychopathology—it immediately ceases to be psyche; we can realize this by just considering the phrase, "psychic events."

If we wish to speak of the psyche in its genuine sense, it has to be understood as that which is opposite to everything objective, including nature. We may call this possibility "subjectivity," but must not identify it with

---

9 The assumption that these possibilities prove "to what degree psychic and physical events interact" could only be made if one wishes to ingratiate oneself with the psychophysical theory.

10 [*Seele* and *Psyche* are almost interchangeable in German usage.—TRANSLATOR.]

the "I" which is but a "hypostatized relational concept" (of the relation of I and Thou, I and He or It)—as was already clearly understood by W. von Humboldt. Rather, we have to realize that subjectivity (in contrast to objectivity) is again but a certain mode of "transcending," of being-in-the-world as such, as being-directed-to, or as a psychic phenomenon (Brentano), or as an intentional act (Husserl).

III *Insanity as Life-Historical Phenomenon and as Mental Disease*

The distinction between insanity as a life-historical phenomenon and insanity as mental disease is, as we saw, rooted in the distinction between human existence (*Dasein*) or being-in-the-world, on the one hand, and nature on the other. For where we speak of a life-historical phenomenon, we speak of historicity in general; and where historicity is discussed, existence (*Dasein*) or being-in-the-world is discussed. On the other hand, where we speak of nature, we speak of "world," because by "nature" we understand the "categorical quintessence of structures of Being of something encountered in the inner world." [11] Accordingly, the methodology of knowledge is completely different in each case; [12] with the former, it is phenomenological-anthropological interpretation, with the latter, knowledge of nature or natural science.

At this point, the reader may feel confronted with the question of whether this separation of ours between the methodology of, let us say, "the humanities" (*Geisteswissenschaften*) and of natural science does not split the primary unity of being human. The belief in this unity is, indeed, a valid one, as we pointed out earlier. In antiquity, Heraclitus could still bring this unity into consciousness in such a way that its anthropological, psychological, cosmological, and theological aspects would form a complete circle.[13] But today we must realize that the European mind, from the time of the pre-Socratic thinkers, has lost its innocence and subscribed to the spirit of *separation,* that is, to the spirit of *science.* Science, however, which by its very essence must rely on certain philosophical principles and methodical assumptions, can never be in a position to grasp a "primary unity"—that is, to focus on it and comprehend it. This cannot be changed by the currently fashionable catchword of the mind-body unity. Either the latter does not stand for anything but the well-known empirical relations between these spheres (which, because of being relations, can never be that unity itself), or else it implies the admission that behind the separations

[11] [This phrase from Heidegger—almost impossible to translate—is, in the original, *"Inbegriff von Seinsstrukturen eines bestimmten innerweltlich begegnenden Seienden."* —TRANSLATOR.]

[12] This distinction formed the basis of my paper, "Lebensfunktion und Lebensgeschichte," *Monatsschrift für Psych. und Neur.,* Bd. 68, 1928.

[13] *Viz.,* L. Binswanger, "Heraklits Auffassung des Menschen," *Die Antike,* XI, 1935.

effected by science—or rather by the sciences—there is a unity not accessible to them. Such insight, indeed, is already a philosophical insight, and precisely the one on which anthropology as applied by existential analysis rests and the basis of which is provided by the life-historical phenomena. If, on the other hand, we speak of psychology, biology, physiology, etc., and if we act as psychologists, biologists, physiologists, we can get this unity neither into our concepts nor into our acts, for it is accessible to man only in two ways: by way of philosophy and of philosophical systems, and by way of Love—which includes both Eros and Agape.

It is the lack of insight into this distinction which can be blamed for all the embarrassing transgressions of the humanities into clinical psychiatry and of clinical psychiatry into the humanities. Both camps are so slow in accepting this insight because each is used to considering its methodological aspect as absolute, that is, to making its science into a *Weltanschauung*. But the *Weltanschauung* of the psychiatrist is that of Positivism, whereas students of the arts (*Geisteswissenschaftler*) still adhere to idealism. Both have thereby, as Jaspers put it, settled all problems for themselves in a way peculiar to them.

"For Positivism, mental disease is only a natural process to be explored, while for Idealism it is something to be dismissed as abnormal and not to be concerned with, or to be exploited edifyingly and cleverly in its a-realistic attitude. All things are settled for both in their peculiar way." [14] Since they have "settled" the problem of insanity each in its own way, neither of them shows any interest in the opposing viewpoint.

In his recent controversy with Jean Wahl, Gabriel Marcel took a similar position: *"Qu'est-ce qui m'empêchera, si je suis médecin, de traiter la destinée de Nietzsche comme un cas clinique, syphiligraphique? Rien objectivement, absolument rien."*

But he wisely added: *"On est toujours libre de ne rien comprendre à rien."* [15] In other words, if either party is free not to comprehend anything of what the other is doing, they still make themselves guilty of a transgression of their science wherever they make statements about facts which can only be judged and understood by the method of the other party. The subjects affected by those transgressions are particularly in the ethical-religious and artistic-aesthetic sphere. The same phenomenon diagnosed under certain conditions by the psychiatrist as a symptom of disease is seen by the student of the arts (*Geisteswissenschaftler*) under certain conditions as an expression of true religiosity, ethical conscience, or supreme art; and where without doubt mental disease has caused mental decay, the latter would hold responsible the philosophical system (as in the case of Nietzsche) or the poetic phantasy world (Hoelderlin) or purely psychological pressure (Tasso).

14 Philosophy I, p. 232.
15 *Existence humaine et transcendance*, p. 116.

We have left out the area of religion and limited ourselves to ethics and art.

To go back to our case, we discussed in an earlier chapter whether and in what way Ilse's sacrifice could be seen as an ethical act. We realized that that act, although affected by passion, could not be said to be lacking in ethical motives (consideration of her mother's well-being, salvation of the father from his selfishness, submission to serious bodily suffering for the sake of reaching these goals). Here the psychiatrist *qua* psychiatrist has to keep his mouth closed, since the ethical judgment draws on a reference system which is incommensurate with his own. Surely, the ethical frame of reference, too, represents something new as against the life-historical one, but the latter does pave the way for the ethical judgment by disclosing the interplay of motives and providing a basis for its consideration. Already the life-historical view shows that we can speak of contexts of meaning, of continuity of meaning, of a meaningful organization, where the psychiatrist sees only fragments of chaos of meaning. Granted that the psychiatrist had to see in Ilse's sacrifice the symptom of disease and that he had to recognize in it—in combination with other phenomena—the signs of a mental illness; granted further that, already at that point, he would have had to declare Ilse irresponsible in court; but all this is quite irrelevant to a purely ethical consideration. The student of the arts (*Geisteswissenschaftler*) may aptly say that Ilse's resolution to take upon herself the sacrifice of burning was a creative moral act, an act of ethical intuition or imagination designed to remove a life situation felt to be immoral—an act emerging from the depth of conscience and from the conviction that mutilation of the hand had to be preferred to mutilation of the soul. *After* making the decision, however, she no longer remained free and creative, for as long as we are free, we are in a position to repeal a decision on ethical grounds, to revise it, to weigh our own ethical counterarguments and those of others. Ilse, however, was overwhelmed and driven by her decision, she had to "get it over with." The execution, therefore, was no longer merely an act of creative moral intuition but, at the same time, the effect of a compulsive drive.

More frequent than in the ethical sphere are transgressions of both parties on occasions when philosophical and, particularly, artistic works are involved. Here, too, life-historical exploration has to advance as far as possible. But it is not enough for the explorer to pursue the variations of purely life-historical themes; he must venture to penetrate into the history of ideas and symbols in order to trace in this sphere, too, every single theme down to all its roots and ramifications. In this he will not permit the psychiatrist to interfere, just as the psychiatrist will not permit him to interfere with the diagnosis. The judgment may become careless and false only where the student of the arts feels justified in excluding a disease on the basis of superior philosophical or artistic achievement, thereby meddling with the psychiatrist's job, or where the psychiatrist feels justified in evaluating a philosophical doctrine or a work of art on the basis of his diagnosis, thereby meddling with the task of his counterpart. Both types of transgression were actually experienced in the "cases" of Tasso, Hoelderlin, Nietzsche, Strindberg, van Gogh, to list only these few. (Credit is due to Karl Jaspers, who was the first to interfere energetically with such misconceptions.)

Just as the student of the arts (*Geisteswissenschaftler*) is not trained in the recognition and clinical evaluation of disease symptoms and is particularly unfamiliar with the theories of the causes of mental disease, so the psychiatrist *qua* psychiatrist is not an authority in judging a change of philosophical, poetic, artistic, or musical style. Uninformed conflict and suspicion in this area should be replaced by understanding cooperation and confidence. Only then can both parties proceed to collaborate in a purely scientific atmosphere on the problem which is equally important for both: the possible relations—impeding and aiding—between mental disease and creative work.

But if it is difficult for psychiatry and the arts to come to an understanding, the same is true for psychiatry and philosophy, since there, too, we find a variety of ideas about insanity and disease as well as attempts to clarify and deepen them, and the psychiatrist had better be aware of it. Earlier Plato expressed the opinion (in *Sophistes*) that cowardice, unruliness, and injustice altogether have to be considered "sickness within us." Obviously, the frame of reference in which sickness and health are here referred to is purely an ethical one. We also know the statement by Plato that the greatest things in man are due to the "divine gift" of insanity (insanity as prophecy, catharsis, poetry, and above all as Eros). He uses the term insanity since he sees in these events a "suspension" (*Aufhebung*) (*epallage*) of the usual orderly state of the person (Phaidros). The various forms of this divine insanity, the "theia mania," imply a divine distinction (*viz.*, Diotima in *Symposium*). We are dealing here with a philosophical mythological concept of insanity which, in turn, is deeply rooted in Plato's theory of Logos-Psyche-Eros-Idea. In contrast to this, Plato also treats insanity as an illness in the medical sense (*nosos*)—a distinction which appears so much a matter of course to him that he fails to tell us how to distinguish insanity in the clinical sense from its nonpathological forms.

The problem of agreement between philosophy and psychiatry gains in complexity when we realize that many philosophers attempted to understand insanity on a purely philosophical basis. We are here reminded of Schelling's idea of the "continuous incitement to insanity which may only be overcome but can never be completely missing"—a concept that is connected with his fundamental view that "the true and principal matter of all Life and Existence is, indeed, the Dreadful," and even that "deity rules over a world of dread." [16] More closely related do we feel to a contemporary

16 *Die Weltalter.*

and kindred attempt at a philosophical understanding of sickness in general and mental sickness in particular: Paul Haeberlin [17] derives on a strictly logical-ontological basis that "the psyche" can never be sick and that no man can ever be "sick in his psyche."

Finally, we must remember a great mind who developed both a new philosophical concept of illness and an understanding of insanity as mental disease. We are thinking of Kierkegaard and of his concept of "Sickness unto Death," of the "desperate" wish to-be-oneself and to-be-not-oneself. This "illness" and its ingenious description and philosophical-theological interpretation appears to us as one of the most important contributions to the purely "anthropological" understanding of certain clinical forms of insanity, and particularly of schizophrenia. As to insanity in the clinical sense, we refer to Kierkegaard's notes on the lack of "inwardness of infinity" in insanity and on the contradiction that something is here focused upon objectively which, at the same time, is grasped with passion; or, in other words, that "the small infinity has been fixated." [18]

What matters here is to call attention to these ideas. To what degree they may aid in the life-historical and existential-analytical understanding of insanity as a mental disease can only be demonstrated through the interpretation of extensive life and case histories.

[17] *Der Mensch,* 1941, pp. 65, 94, 135 ff.

[18] *Philosophische Brocken,* I, 2. Trans. into English by Walter Lowrie and published by Princeton University Press (1941) under the title *Sickness Unto Death.*

IX

The Case of Ellen West*
An Anthropological-Clinical Study[1]

by Ludwig Binswanger

I Case History[2]

Heredity

ELLEN WEST, a non-Swiss, is the only daughter of a Jewish father for whom her love and veneration know no bounds. She has a dark-haired brother four years older than she, who resembles his father, and a younger brother who is blond. Whereas the older one "has no nerves" and is very well adjusted and cheerful, the younger is "a bundle of nerves" and is a soft[3] and womanish aesthete. At seventeen he was in a psychiatric clinic for some weeks on account of a mental ailment with suicidal ideas, and even after his recovery he remained easily excitable. He has married.

The sixty-six-year-old father is described as an externally very self-controlled, rather stiffly formal, very reserved, willful man of action; internally, however, as very soft[3] and sensitive and suffering from nocturnal depressions and states of fear accompanied by self-reproaches, "as if a wave of fear closed over his head." He sleeps poorly and is often under the pressure of fear when he gets up in the morning.

---

* Translated by WERNER M. MENDEL and JOSEPH LYONS from the original, "Der Fall Ellen West." *Schweizer Archiv für Neurologie und Psychiatrie*, 1944, Vol. 53, pp. 255–277; Vol. 54, pp. 69–117, 330–360; 1945, Vol. 55. pp. 16–40.

1 [The term "anthropological" is used here, as it frequently is in European psychiatry, to refer to a science of man.—TRANSLATORS.]

2 In this and the preceding chapters the procedures developed in my work, *Über Ideenflucht* (*On the Flight of Ideas*), are extended to the study of non-manic-depressive psychoses.

3 [The word *soft* implies in this context all the varied meanings of the German *weich*—a frequently used and important term in this paper—including physically soft as well as tender-hearted, delicate, effeminate, weak, or malleable.—TRANSLATORS.]

A sister of the father became mentally ill on her wedding day (?). Of the father's five brothers, one shot himself between the ages of twenty and thirty (details are lacking), a second likewise committed suicide during a period of melancholy, and a third is severely ascetic, gets up very early, and eats nothing at noon on the ground that this makes one lazy. Two brothers fell ill with dementia arteriosclerosis and later each died of a stroke. The father's father is said to have been a very strict autocrat, the father's mother, on the other hand, to have had a gentle, always conciliatory nature; she had "quiet weeks," during which she spoke not a word and sat motionless. All this is said to have increased as she aged. The mother of this woman—that is, the patient's great-grandmother on her father's side—is said to have been severely manic-depressive. She stems from a family which produced many outstandingly capable men but also many psychotics, one of whom I have treated (an eminent scholar).

The mother of Ellen West, likewise of Jewish descent, is said to be a very soft, kindly, suggestible, nervous woman, who underwent a depression for three years during the time of her engagement. The mother's father died young. The mother's mother was especially vigorous, healthy, and gay; she died at eighty-four of dementia senilis. There were five siblings of the mother, somewhat nervous, short, physically delicate,[4] but all lived long; one died of tuberculosis of the larynx.

Life-History and Course of Illness

Normal birth. At nine months Ellen refused milk and was therefore fed meat-broth; nor could she ever tolerate milk in later years. On the other hand she liked to eat meat, not so well certain vegetables, some sweet desserts not at all; if these were forced upon her, a tremendous resistance set in. (As she later confessed that even as a child she had passionately loved sweets, this was clearly not a case of an "aversion" but probably of an early act of renunciation.) Unfortunately, in spite of two periods of psychoanalytic treatment in later years, we are completely in the dark about her early childhood; she no longer knows much about the first ten years of her life.

According to her own statements and those of her parents, Ellen was a very lively but headstrong and violent child. It is said that she often defied an order of her parents for hours and did not carry it out even then. Once she was shown a bird's nest, but she insisted that it was not a bird's nest and nothing would make her change her opinion. Even as a child, she said, she had had days when everything seemed empty to her and she suffered under a pressure which she herself did not understand. After attending kinder-

4 [The word zart, translated as physically delicate, is a key term in the case history. It means tender, petite, fragile, subdued, and sensitive—in short, just the opposite of fleshy and heavy.—TRANSLATORS.]

garten she went to school in her first homeland from her eighth to her tenth year. At ten she moved with her family to Europe, where, except for some trips across the ocean, she remained till her death. In her second land she went to a school for girls. She was a good student, liked going to school, and was very ambitious; she could weep for hours if she did not rank first in her favorite subjects. She did not want to stay away from school even when the doctor ordered it, fearing to fall behind the class or to miss something. Her favorite subjects were German and history; she was not as good at arithmetic. At this time too she was of a lively temperament, but still self-willed. She had already chosen the motto: *aut Caesar aut nihil!* [5] Up to her sixteenth year her games were boyish. She preferred to wear trousers. From her babyhood Ellen West had been a thumbsucker; at sixteen she suddenly gave that up, along with her boyish games, at the onset of an infatuation which lasted two years. In a poem written in her seventeenth year, however, she still expressed the ardent desire to be a boy, for then she would be a soldier, fear no foe, and die joyously, sword in hand.

Other poems from this period already reveal a marked variability of mood: now her heart beats with exultant joy, now the sky is darkened, the winds blow weirdly, and the ship of her life sails on unguided, not knowing whither to direct its keel. In another poem from the following year, the wind is rushing about her ears, and she wants it to cool her burning brow; when she runs against it blindly, careless of custom or propriety, it is as if she were stepping out of a confining tomb, as if she were flying through the air in an uncontrollable urge to freedom, and as if she must achieve something great and mighty; then her gaze falls back into the world again and the saying comes to her mind: "Man, in small things make your world"; she cries to her soul, "Fight on." She considers herself called to achieve something special, she reads much, occupies herself intensively with social problems, feels deeply the contrast between her own social position and that of the "masses," and draws up plans for the improvement of the latter. At the same age (seventeen), following the reading of *Niels Lyhne*,[6] she changes from a deeply religious person (despite the intentionally nonreligious upbringing her father gave her) to a complete atheist. In no respect does she care about the judgment of the world.

Still other poems from her seventeenth year are available. In one, entitled "Kiss Me Dead," the sun sinks into the ocean like a ball of fire, a dripping mist drops over sea and beach, and a pain comes over her: "Is there no rescue any more?" She calls upon the cold, grim Sea-King to come to her, take her into his arms in ardent love-lust, and kiss her to death. In another

5 [Literally, "Either Caesar or nothing!"—Translators.]

6 [*Niels Lyhne* is both the title and the central character of a famous Scandinavian novel by J. P. Jacobsen (1847–1885), published in 1880. Its stark and melancholy realism, religious nihilism, and moving plot (concerning a disillusioned idealist) combined to give it a tremendous appeal to restless European youth at the turn of the century.—Translators.]

poem, entitled "I Hate You," she sings of a boy, supremely beautiful, whom she now hates because of his victorious smile just as intensely as she had formerly loved him. In a third one ("Tired"), gray, damp evening mists well up around her and stretch out their arms toward her cold, long-deceased heart, while the trees shake their heads in disconsolate gloom, singing an old, mournful song, and no bird lets its late song be heard, no light appears in the sky; her head is empty, her heart is afraid.

In diary entries from her eighteenth year she praises the blessing of work: "What would we be without work, what would become of us? I think they would soon have to enlarge the cemeteries for those who went to death of their own accord. Work is the opiate for suffering and grief."—"When all the joints of the world threaten to fall apart, when the light of our happiness is extinguished and our pleasure in life lies wilting, only one thing saves us from madness: work. Then we throw ourselves into a sea of duties as into Lethe, and the roar of its waves is to drown out the death-knell pealing in our heart."—"When the day is done with its haste and unrest, and we sit by the window in the growing twilight, the book will fall from our hand, we stare into the distance, into the setting sun, and old pictures rise up before us. The old plans and hopes, none of which have been realized, the boundless barrenness of the world and our infinite minuteness stand before our tired soul. Then the old question crowds to our lips, 'What for—why all this? Why do we strive and live, forgotten after a short span of time, only to molder in the cold earth?' "—"At such a time spring up quickly, and well for you if there is a call for you, and work with both hands, until the shapes of the night disappear. O work, you are indeed the blessing of our life!"

She would like to gain fame—great, undying fame; after hundreds of years her name should still ring out on the lips of mankind. Then she would not have lived in vain. She cries to herself, "Oh, smother the murmuring voices with work! Fill up your life with duties. I will not think so much—my last address shall not be the madhouse! And when you have worked and toiled, what have you accomplished? What prevails around us and below us is still so much of boundless distress! There they are dancing in a brightly lighted hall, and outside the door a poor woman is starving to death. Starving! Not a crust of bread comes to her from the table of plenty. Did you observe how the fine gentleman, while speaking, slowly crushed the dainty bread in his hand? And outside in the cold a woman cried out for a dry crust! And what's the use of brooding on it? Don't I do the same? . . ."

In the same year (her eighteenth) the diary praises with the greatest enthusiasm everything new and beautiful that she experiences in Paris on a trip with her parents. New little sentimental love affairs develop. At the same time the wish now arises in her to be delicate and ethereal, as are the girl friends whom she selects. Even now her poems continue to show the contradictoriness of her mood. One sings of sunshine and the smiling spring, of radiant blue skies over a free, wide land, of pleasure and blissfulness;

in another she wishes that the greening and blooming of the springtime world, the murmuring and rustling of the woods, might be her dirge; in a third the only longing left to her eyes is that for the darkness "where the glaring sun of life does not shine": "If thou still rulest behind clouds, Father, then I beseech thee, take me back to thee!"

But through clouds and darkness the light of life breaks through again and again. A journey with her parents across the ocean, occurring during her nineteenth year, lives in her recollection "as the happiest and most harmless time" of her life. In a poem of this year floods of light and "golden hands" rest upon grainfields, villages, and valleys, and only the mountains stand in darkness. And yet on this trip Ellen can never be alone—*i.e.*, away from her parents. Although she has a very good time while on a visit to friends, she begs her parents to call her back to them. Returning to Europe, she begins to ride horses and soon becomes very skilled at it, no horse being too dangerous for her; she vies with experienced riders in jumping competitions. Like everything she does, she cultivates riding "with excessive intensity," indeed, as if it were her exclusive task in life.

Her twentieth year is full of happiness, yearning, and hopes. From her poems stream radiant joy of life—indeed, wild ecstasy of life: the sun stands high, spring gales "roar through the world," then how can one lag behind, lock oneself "into the tomb of a house"? Through her veins the blood "races and roars," youthful zest bursts her breast asunder; she stretches her strong young body, for the fresh marrow of life shall not stale, the ardent yearning for a wild joy shall not dry up, "pining away bit by bit." "The earth is too stale and still, I long for a storm that is shrill." "Oh, if 'He' would come now," now when every fiber of her is quivering so that she can hardly sit still to write, now, when she is "so completely cured in body and soul," when no sacrifice would be too great for her: "He must be tall, and strong, and have a soul as pure and unblemished as the morning light! He must not play life nor dream it, but live it, in all its seriousness and all its pleasure. He must be able to be happy, to enjoy me and my children, and to take joy in sunshine and work. Then I would give him all my love and all my strength."

In the same year (her twentieth) she makes her second trip overseas, to nurse her older brother, who is very sick. She takes pleasure in eating and drinking. This is the last time she can eat unconcernedly. At this time she becomes engaged to a romantic foreigner, but at her father's wish breaks the engagement. On the return trip she stops in Sicily and does some writing on a paper, "On the Woman's Calling." Here, according to her diary, she loves life passionately, her pulse hammers out to her fingertips, and the world belongs to her, for she has sun, wind, and beauty all to herself. Her god is the god of life and of joy, of strength and hope; she is filled with a consuming thirst to learn, and she has already had a glimpse of the "secret of the universe."

The first weeks in Sicily are the last of her happiness in life. Already the diary is again reporting the shadows of doubt and of dread; Ellen feels herself small and wholly forsaken in a world which she cannot understand. To be sure, she is glad "to be far from the cramping influences of home," the pinions of her soul are growing, but this growth does not take place without pains and convulsions, indeed, in the midst of her loveliest, most exuberant moments, fear and trembling appear again. Pityingly, she looks down upon all her fine ideas and plans and closes her diary with the burning wish that they might one day transform themselves into deeds instead of merely useless words.

Along with this, however, something new emerges now, a definite dread —namely, a dread of getting fat. At the beginning of her stay in Sicily Ellen had still displayed an enormous appetite. As a result she got so fat that her girl friends began to tease her about it. At once she begins to mortify herself by fasting and immoderate hikes. This goes so far that when her companions stop at some pretty spot Ellen keeps circling about them. She no longer eats sweets or other fattening things and skips supper altogether. When she goes home in the spring, everyone is horrified at how bad she looks.

Ellen is now twenty-one years old. In the summer after her return to Italy her mood is markedly "depressive." She is constantly tormented by the idea that she is getting too fat, and therefore she is forever taking long walks. She takes up her diary again, complains that she has no home anywhere, not even with her family, that she does not find the activity she is seeking, that she has no peace, that she feels a veritable torment when she sits still, that every nerve in her quivers, and that in general her body shares in all the stirrings of her soul: "My inner self is so closely connected with my body that the two form a unity and together constitute my 'I,' my unlogical, nervous, individual 'I.'" She feels herself to be absolutely worthless and useless and is in dread of everything, of the dark and of the sun, of stillness and of noise. She feels herself on the lowest rung of the ladder which leads to the light, degraded to a cowardly, wretched creature: "I despise myself!" In a poem, grim distress sits at her grave, ashy pale—sits and stares, does not flinch nor budge; the birds grow mute and flee, the flowers wilt before its ice-cold breath. Now death no longer appears to her as terrible; death is not a man with the scythe but "a glorious woman, white asters in her dark hair, large eyes, dream-deep and gray." The only thing which still lures her is dying: "Such a delicious stretching out and dozing off. Then it's over. No more getting up and dreary working and planning. Back of every word I really hide a yawn." (This and the following from a letter to her male friend at this time.) "And every day I get a little fatter, older, and uglier."— "If he makes me wait much longer, the great friend, death, then I shall set out and seek him." She says she is not melancholy, merely apathetic: "Everything is so uniform to me, so utterly indifferent, I know no feeling of joy and none of fear."—"Death is the greatest happiness in life, if not the only one. Without hope of the end life would be unendurable. Only the certainty that sooner or later the end must come consoles me a little." She wishes never to have children: what awaits them in the world?

In the fall of the same year Ellen gradually comes out of her depression. She makes preparations for the installation of children's reading-rooms on the American model. But along with her newly awakening joy of life and the urge to action, her paralyzing dread and despair continue. From her diary: "I have not kept a diary for a long time, but today I must again take my notebook in hand; for in me there is such a turmoil and ferment that I must open a safety valve to avoid bursting out in wild excesses. It is really sad that I must translate all this force and urge to action into unheard words instead of powerful deeds. It is a pity of my young life, a sin to waste my sound mind. For what purpose did nature give me health and ambition? Surely not to stifle it and hold it down and let it languish in the chains of humdrum [7] living, but to serve wretched humanity. The iron chains of commonplace life: the chains of conventionality, the chains of property and comfort, the chains of gratitude and consideration, and, strongest of all, the chains of love. Yes, it is they that hold me down, hold me back from a tempestuous revival, from the complete absorption in the world of struggle and sacrifice for which my whole soul is longing. O God, dread is driving me mad! Dread which is almost certainty! The consciousness that ultimately I shall lose everything: all courage, all rebelliousness, all drive for doing; that it—my little world—will make me flabby, flabby and fainthearted and beggarly, as they are themselves."—"Live? No, vegetate! Do you actually preach making concessions? I will make no concessions! You realize that the existing social order is rotten, rotten down to the root, dirty and mean; but you do nothing to overthrow it. But we have no right to close our ears to the cry of misery, and to walk with closed eyes past the victims of our system! I am twenty-one years old and am supposed to be silent and grin like a puppet. I am no puppet. I am a human being with red blood and a woman with quivering heart. And I cannot breathe in this atmosphere of hypocrisy and cowardice, and I mean to do something great and must get a little closer to my ideal, my proud ideal. Will it cost tears? Oh, what shall I do, how shall I manage it? It boils and pounds in me, it wants to burst the outer shell! Freedom! Revolution!"—"No, no, I am not talking claptrap. I am not thinking of the liberation of the soul; I mean the real, tangible liberation of the people from the chains of their oppressors. Shall I express it still more clearly? I want a revolution, a great uprising to spread over the entire world and overthrow the whole social order. I should

---

[7] [The German word *Alltag* literally means any day which is not Sunday, and for this reason it is used to refer to the common and trite, the ordinary, or the humdrum and conventional workaday world.—TRANSLATORS.]

like to forsake home and parents like a Russian nihilist, to live among the poorest of the poor and make propaganda for the great cause. Not for the love of adventure! No, no! Call it unsatisfied urge to action if you like, indomitable ambition. What has the name to do with it? To me it is as if this boiling in my blood were something better. Oh, I am choking in this petty, commonplace life. Bloated self-satisfaction or egotistical greed, joyless submissiveness or crude indifference; those are the plants which thrive in the sunshine of the commonplace. They grow and proliferate, and like weeds they smother the flower of longing which germinates among them."—"Everything in me trembles with dread, dread of the adders of my everyday, which would coil about me with their cold bodies and press the will to fight out of me. But my exuberant force offers resistance. I shake them off, I *must* shake them off. The morning must come after this siege of nightmares."

During the winter Ellen pushes with energy and success the installation of the children's reading-rooms, with the help of a benevolent association. But as early as the ensuing spring this no longer satisfies her. She longs for love and for greater deeds. In a poem entitled "The Evil Thoughts," she sees the "evil spirits" standing behind every tree: mockingly they "close her in" on all sides, fiercely they seize her, clutch at her heart, and finally they themselves speak:

> One time we were your thinking,
> Your hoping pure and proud!
> Where now are all your projects,
> The dreams that used to crowd?
>
> Now all of them lie buried,
> Scattered in wind and storm,
> And you've become a nothing,
> A timid earthy worm.
>
> So then we had to leave you,
> To dark night we must flee;
> The curse which fell upon you
> Has made us black to see.
>
> If you seek peace and quiet,
> Then we'll come creeping nigh
> And we'll take vengeance on you
> With our derisive cry.
>
> If you seek joy and gladness,
> We'll hurry to your side;
> Accusing you and jeering
> We'll e'er with you abide!

In the diary she continues to air her hatred of the luxury and good living which surround her, she bemoans her cowardice and weakness in not being able "to rise above the conditions," in letting herself at so early an age be made flabby "by the uglinesses and the stuffy air of the everyday. I still feel the disgrace of my imprisonment. How musty is the smell of this cellar hole. The scent of the flowers cannot drown the stench of decay. No wonder you have got such ugly yellow souls, you who have grown up in this atmosphere. Already you have ceased to notice how hard it is to breathe here. Your souls have grown dwarf lungs. Everything about you is dwarflike: thoughts, feelings, and—dreams. You look at me askance because the conditions in which you feel happy disgust me. You want to get me down . . . I want to go away, away—away from here. I am afraid of you! I pound on the walls with my hands till I sink down exhausted. Then you come out of your corners like rats, and your little eyes pursue me, like a nightmare." A month later Ellen composes a passionate riding song: she gives her horse the spur, but "the evil thoughts, the spirits of the night" follow close behind it "on bony mares, hollow-eyed and pale"; at last, however, "the pale shadows" fall behind the rousing gallop of her horse, and "life has triumphed again." But a month later she is again bewailing her "loneliness of soul"; she stands "lonely as on icy peaks," and only the winds understand her longing and her fear.

In the fall of the same year Ellen begins preparing for the *Matura*,[8] with the intention of studying political economy. She gets up at five, rides for three hours, then has private lessons and works all afternoon and evening until late at night, with the help of black coffee and cold showers.

The next spring (Ellen is now twenty-two) makes her melancholy, she cannot enjoy the awakening of spring, feels merely "how low she has sunk," not only from her previous ideal image, but from that which formerly she really was. Formerly the world lay "open before her" and she wished to "conquer" it, her feelings and sensations were "strong and vigorous," she loved and hated "with her whole soul." Now she makes concessions; she would have ridiculed anyone who had prophesied this to her; with every year she has "lost a little of her old strength."

In the fall of the same year—Ellen became twenty-three at the end of July—she breaks down. At the same time she has an unpleasant love affair with a riding teacher. Besides, she watches her body weight and reduces her food intake as soon as she threatens to gain weight. But now dread of getting fat [9] is accompanied by an intensified longing for food, especially sweets, and this is strongest when she has been made tired and nervous by being with

8 [This refers to the final examination in secondary school, which in effect qualified one for entrance to any university.—Translators.]

9 [The German is *dick*, a word which connotes thickness, stoutness, denseness, coarseness, and fleshiness. The word *dick* should be contrasted with *weich*, in Note 3, and with *zart*, in Note 4. This contrast is central to the existential analysis in Section II.—Translators.]

others. In the presence of others eating affords her no satisfaction; only when alone may she enjoy it. As always since the beginning of her dread of getting fat, she has suffered from the conflict between the dread of getting fat and the wish to be able to eat unconcernedly. Even now her old governess observes that this conflict is "the cloud over her life." Especially during vacations is she in a "depressive unrest"; this does not disappear until she has regular work and a fixed daily schedule. Her plan to take the *Matura* is again given up. Instead, within a few weeks she passes the teachers' examination, in order to be able to audit courses at the university. During the summer semester of her twenty-third and the winter semester of the beginning of her twenty-fourth year she studies in the town of X. This period is one of the happiest of her life. In the summer a love relationship with a student develops. The diary breathes joy of life and sensuality. After the close of the winter semester, in a poem entitled "Spring Moods," she writes:

> I'd like to die just as the birdling does
> That splits his throat in highest jubilation;
> And not to live as the worm on earth lives on,
> Becoming old and ugly, dull and dumb!
> No, feel for once how forces in me kindle,
> And wildly be consumed in my own fire.

Ellen is enthusiastic about studying and student life. She goes with others on long excursions to the mountains, and now too she cannot be alone; her old governess is constantly with her. Nor can she free herself of her "fixed idea." She avoids fattening foods and, since she feels that she is nevertheless getting too fat, she undertakes a reducing diet, with her physician's consent, in the fall of that year.

At the same time the affair with the student turns into an engagement. Her parents demand a temporary separation. In the spring Ellen goes to a seaside resort, and here once again an especially severe "depression" sets in (she is twenty-four and one-half years old). She does everything to get just as thin as possible, takes long hikes, and daily swallows thirty-six to forty-eight thyroid tablets! Consumed by homesickness, she begs her parents to let her return. She arrives completely emaciated, with trembling limbs, and drags herself through the summer in physical torment, but feels spiritually satisfied because she is thin. She has the feeling that she has found the key to her well-being. The engagement remains in effect.

In the autumn, at the beginning of her twenty-fifth year, she takes her third trip overseas. There the physician diagnoses a "Basedow syndrome" [10] and prescribes complete rest in bed. She stays in bed six weeks and this makes her gain weight very rapidly, for which reason she weeps all the time. On her return home in the following spring she weighs 165 pounds. Shortly

[10] [This is known to the English-speaking reader as Graves' disease, a condition of exophthalmic hyperthyroid goiter.—TRANSLATORS.]

afterward the engagement is broken off. In May she is in a (public) sanatorium, in the summer she attends a school of gardening; she is in a depressive mood, but physically she makes a completely healthy impression. Since she soon loses interest in gardening, she leaves the school prematurely. Again she has attempted to reduce her weight by much physical activity and scanty eating. In the fall her cousin, with whom she has been friends for many years, takes a special interest in her. Until the following spring they take long hikes together, often twenty to twenty-five miles in a day. Besides this, she engages eagerly in gymnastics, is active in a children's home, though without enjoying it much, and longs for a real vocation. Although the broken engagement with the student remains an "open wound," a love relationship with the cousin develops. The "fixed idea" has not disappeared, but it does not dominate her as it formerly did.

At this time there is a poem, evidently aimed at her former fiancé, in which she asks herself if he ever loved her at all, if her body was "not beautiful enough" to bear him sons:

> Woe's me, woe's me!
> The earth bears grain,
> But I
> Am unfruitful,
> Am discarded shell,
> Cracked, unusable,
> Worthless husk.
> Creator, Creator,
> Take me back!
> Create me a second time
> And create me better!

In her twenty-sixth year a love for music awakens in Ellen. She and her cousin plan to marry. But for two years more she vacillates between her cousin and the student, with whom she has resumed relations. Not until her twenty-eighth year, after another meeting with the student (see below), does she break off with him for good and marry her cousin. Previous to that she has taken several Mensendieck[11] courses, traveled a great deal, consulted several famous neurologists at the wish of her parents and her cousin; she has again taken thyroid periodically and gone on tremendous hikes; she has been saddened when she looked at herself in the mirror, hating her body and often beating it with her fists. Girl friends who, like her, want to be slender influence her unfavorably. She always grows depressed when she is with thin people or those who eat little.

She hopes after marrying her cousin to get rid of her "fixed idea," but

11 [Mrs. Mensendieck was a Swedish physician who developed a system of physical culture based on gymnastics and on certain weight-reducing devices. She opened many salons throughout Europe and even in California during the early part of this century. The popularity of her treatment program was at least in part a result of the increasing freedom for women and the new trend of fashion toward a slim figure.—TRANSLATORS.]

this is not the case. At the wedding she weighs 160 pounds, but even on the honeymoon trip she diets, and as a result she steadily loses weight.

In the summer following the spring of her marriage her periods cease. The conflict between the "wish for harmless eating" and her dread of getting fat torments her constantly. In the fall, at the time of her twenty-ninth birthday, while on a hike with her husband in a lonely neighborhood she has a severe abdominal hemorrhage, despite which she must continue to hike for several more hours. The physician does a curettage and finds a miscarriage; he states that a good diet is a prerequisite for the possibility of a new pregnancy!

During her entire following year (her twenty-ninth) Ellen is now torn this way and that between the desire to have a child and the dread of getting fat (from adequate nourishment). "The dread retains control." Her previously regular menstruation ceases. On the whole Ellen is again in a better mood, but she is at times depressed by her repeatedly disappointed hope of a new pregnancy. She works energetically and with a great sense of duty in social welfare, goes to the theater frequently, and reads a lot. But when she happens to discover that she has gained over four pounds in one week, she bursts into tears and cannot quiet down for a long time. When another gynecologist tells her that good nourishment is not prerequisite to a pregnancy, she at once resumes the use of strong laxatives.

In her thirtieth year Ellen is even more intensely active in social welfare. She takes the warmest human interest in the people committed to her care, with whom personal relationships are kept up for years. At the same time she impoverishes her nourishment systematically and gradually becomes a vegetarian. Even after a short siege of grippe she does not spare herself. A treatment in Pyrmont,[12] prescribed by a third gynecologist, is unsuccessful, especially since she so increases the laxative dosage that she vomits every night. When she finds that she is steadily losing weight she is very pleased.

The winter of her thirty-first year brings with it a rapid decline in her strength. She continues to work just as much, but cannot get up energy for anything else. Also, for the first time she discontinues the two daily hikes with her husband. She sleeps up to twelve hours, contrary to her previous custom. The laxatives are further increased, her diet is further impoverished. In spite of an occasional high fever, which she keeps secret, she goes out in the street in the hope of catching pneumonia. Her facial expression changes. Ellen looks old and haggard. However, since she thinks she has found in the laxatives a preventive against getting fat, she is not depressed.

In the spring of this year, during a hike with her husband, suddenly, with elemental force, the confession bursts from her that she is living her life

12 [Pyrmont is a town in Germany which is well known for its health-giving waters. —TRANSLATORS.]

only with a view to being able to remain thin, that she is subordinating every one of her actions to this end, and that this idea has gained a terrible power over her. She thinks she can numb herself by work, exchanges her volunteer work in the welfare agency for a paid position, which obligates her to seven hours of office work a day, and, after some weeks, in June she breaks down. During this entire time she has further impoverished her diet; her weight goes down to 103 pounds. At the same time she becomes intensely preoccupied with calorie charts, recipes, etc. In every free minute she writes recipes of delectable dishes, puddings, desserts, etc., in her cookbook. She demands of those around her that they eat much and well, while she denies herself everything. She develops great skill in not letting them know that she is eating almost nothing by filling her plate like everyone else and then secretly emptying the greater part of the food into her handbag. Foods which she thinks are not fattening, such as shellfish and clams, she eats with great greed and haste. Often on the way home she eats up things she has bought for her household and then upbraids herself severely for it. At every meal she sweats profusely. Ellen now goes with her husband to a sanatorium for metabolic diseases and at first follows the orders of the doctor, so that her weight increases from 99 to 110 pounds, but after her husband leaves she deceives the physician by dropping her food into her handbag and secretly carrying weights when she is weighed.

At the beginning of her thirty-second year her physical condition deteriorates still further. Her use of laxatives increases beyond measure. Every evening she takes sixty to seventy tablets of a vegetable laxative, with the result that she suffers tortured vomiting at night and violent diarrhea by day, often accompanied by a weakness of the heart. Now she no longer eats fish, has thinned down to a skeleton, and weighs only 92 pounds. Ellen becomes more and more debilitated, goes back to bed in the afternoon, and is terribly tortured by the feeling that "her instincts are stronger than her reason," that "all inner development, all real life has stopped," and that she is completely dominated by her "overpowering idea, long since recognized as senseless." Yet her mood is rather cheerful, and it affords her satisfaction that her friends worry about her.

At the age of thirty-two and one-half she undergoes her first psychoanalysis, with a young and sensitive analyst who is not completely committed to Freud. She regains hope, again attends lectures, the theater, and concerts, and goes on excursions, but is extremely restless and again overdoes everything. During the times when her husband is absent her old nursemaid must stay with her. She soon regards the psychoanalysis as useless.

In her letters to her husband, now and again her "burning love for life crops out," but it remains "pure mood," and the dread of getting fatter remains unchanged in the center of her doing and thinking: "My thoughts are exclusively concerned with my body, my eating, my laxatives."—"And the fact that from time to time I see emerge on the horizon the fabulous, sweet land of life, the oasis in the desert which I have created for myself, only makes my road the harder. For what good is it? It remains a Fata Morgana and disappears again. It was easier before, when everything was gray-on-gray around me, when I wanted nothing but to be sick and lie in bed. Now I'd like to be healthy—and won't pay the price for it. Often I am completely broken by the conflict which never comes to an end, and in despair I leave my analyst and go home with the certainty: he can give me discernment, but not healing."

Ellen feels the opinion of the analyst, that her main goal is "the subjugation of all other people," to be "marvelously correct and frighteningly true." But she says she has a test, a kind of touchstone; she need only ask herself, "Ellen, can you eat a good serving of beans or a pancake and afterward take no medicine?"—then, she says, she is seized by a veritable panic, and at the mere idea dread makes her turn hot and cold. "All good resolutions, all joy of life, break down before this wall over which I cannot climb." —"I still do not want to get fatter, or, in psychoanalytic language—I still will not give up my 'ideal.'" But now she no longer wants to die, she says, she loves life again, and longs for health, work, and her husband, but actually she "will not pay the price for it." She thinks it a matter for despair that she knows no way to "help herself out of this swamp."

During the analysis Ellen cuts down more and more on eating. Feelings of dread become more frequent, and now there appears above all the bothersome obsession of constantly having to think about food. She describes her feelings of dread as "the specters which constantly jump at my throat." Good hours seem to her like a "flood tide," but then "low tide" swiftly sets in again.

In a letter to her husband Ellen now compares her ideal, exemplified by her former fiancé, the student, with the ideal of being thin: "At that time you [the husband] were the life which I was ready to accept and to give up my ideal [the student] for. But it was an artificially derived, forced resolve, not one ripened from within. For this reason it did not work. For this reason I again started to send him packages and to be full of opposition to you. And only much later, when I was ripe within, when I had looked my ideal in the face and realized, 'I have made a mistake, this ideal is a fiction,' then, and only then, could I say 'Yes' to you calmly and with assurance. Just so I must now be able to look at my ideal, this ideal of being thin, of being without a body, and to realize: 'It is a fiction.' Then I can say 'Yes' to life. Before I do that, everything is a fallacy, like that time in X [the University town]. But it is simpler to get into the train and ride to Y [where the rupture with the student took place] than to bring to the light of day what lies buried and hidden in me. As for the comparison of you with life, and of St. [the student] with my ideal, of course it is a lame one; there is only a superficial analogy. My saying 'Yes' [to the husband after her visit with the student in *Y*] was also not yet the right thing. I chose you—but then I still did not really become your wife. The thought of my secret ideal, by which I do not mean St. [the student]—for that was something external—I mean my life's ideal, to be thin, continued to occupy me more than all else. I shall really become a wife only when I have finally given up my life's ideal. And that is so difficult that today I am again just as desperate as weeks ago. Poor ——, always I have to keep disappointing you! As for externals, I have not yet taken medicine again. But that makes me constantly touch my abdomen and eat with dread [13] and uneasiness."

At another time Ellen writes her husband, "The only real improvement, which must come from within, is not yet here; Nirvana in a figurative sense, 'the extinction of greed, hate, and delusion' has not yet been reached. Do you know what I mean by this? The greed to realize my ideal; my hatred of the surrounding world which wants to make this impossible; the delusion which lies in my seeing this ideal as something worth while." To which is annexed the very characteristic outcry: "The thought of pancakes is still for me the most horrible thought there is." Moreover, meat and fat, she says, are so repugnant that the mere thought of them nauseates her. For the rest, she now has (during the analysis) the will to become fatter, but not the wish. She describes it as a fight between duty and desire in the Kantian sense. However, as long as it remains that, she is not "redeemed"; for this categorical imperative, this "thou shalt," comes from the outside, as it were, and therefore can do nothing against the tenacity of the morbid urge which rules her. At the same time she feels her present state, just because she is making an effort to take no laxatives, to be "more torturing than all that I have gone through hitherto. I feel myself getting fatter, I tremble with dread of this, I am living in a state of panic."—"As soon as I feel a pressure at my waist—I mean a pressure of my waistband—my spirit sinks, and I get a depression as severe as though it were a question of goodness knows what tragic affairs." On the other hand, if she has a "good bowel movement" there is "a kind of calm" in her and she feels at ease. In spite of this she feels "the entire time, every minute," how terribly her life is dominated by her "morbid idea."

Now that Ellen knows her husband has told her parents what is the matter with her, she feels a great longing for her parents, especially for her mother; she would like to lay her head on her breast and have a good cry. But this, she says, is a passing mood. Basically she feels no desire at all to be at home, indeed, she feels dread of "the grave and serious nature" of her father.

13 [The German word is *Angst*, which may mean either dread or anxiety. For a discussion of the concept of dread, and some suggestions in regard to terminology, see Chapter II, p. 51.—TRANSLATORS.]

In August, soon after Ellen's thirty-third birthday, the analysis begun in February comes to an end for external reasons. Upon his return, her husband finds her in a state of severe dread and agitation. Her food intake becomes quite irregular; Ellen leaves out entire meals, to throw herself indiscriminately with all the greater greed upon any foods which may happen to be at hand. Each day she consumes several pounds of tomatoes and twenty oranges.

A three-week visit with her parents at first goes better than expected. Ellen is happy to be out of the hotel atmosphere, to be able to spend the evenings with her family, and to talk things out with her mother. From the second week on, however, the picture changes again. For days Ellen cannot get over weeping, dread, and agitation, walks in tears through the streets of her home town, and suffers more than ever from her hunger, especially since at home she has to sit at the table with others who eat normally. She now despairs completely of her illness being curable and can hardly be calmed down any more. The physician does a blood count and finds "irregularities in the composition of the blood." He advises a consultation with the internist at the University Clinic in X, where she had audited lectures, and where she returns at the beginning of October with her husband and her old nursemaid. The internist advises a clinical treatment. Ellen cannot make up her mind to it. Instead, she undergoes psychoanalytic treatment for the second time. The second analyst with whom she enters treatment is more orthodox than the first.

Ellen is now at the beginning of her thirty-third year. On the 6th of October her husband leaves her, at the request of the analyst but against his own wishes. After having previously expressed suicidal ideas, on the 8th of October she makes an attempt at suicide by taking fifty-six tablets of Somnacetin, most of which, however, she vomits up during the night. The analyst ascribes no importance to this attempt and continues with the analysis. For the rest, Ellen is left to her own devices and walks aimlessly and tearfully through the streets. These and the following weeks until the middle of November are, according to her own account, "the most horrible of her life." In her dreams, too, she is incessantly concerned with eating. Her husband is with her from the 16th to the 24th of October and again continuously after the 6th of November.

On the 7th of November she makes her second suicidal attempt by taking twenty tablets of a barbiturate compound. On the following day she is in a condition which the analyst describes as a "hysterical twilight state." She cries and whimpers the entire day, refuses all food, and declares that in some unguarded moment she will take her life after all. On the 9th of November she again takes food greedily. On the 10th, she attempts several times on the street to throw herself in front of a car, on the 11th she tries to throw herself out of a window in her analyst's office; on the 12th she moves with her husband into the clinic of the above-mentioned internist.[14]

From her diary, resumed upon the advice of the analyst, the following October entries are of special interest.

October 19. "I don't think that the dread of becoming fat is the real obsessive neurosis, but *the constant desire for food* [E.W.'S EMPHASIS]. The pleasure of eating must have been the primary thing. Dread of becoming fat served as a brake. Now that I see the pleasure of eating as the real obsessive idea, it has pounced upon me like a wild beast. I am defenselessly at its mercy. It pursues me constantly and is driving me to despair."

October 21. "The day begins like all others. I see it lying before me filled with the uninterrupted desire for eating and the dread of eating. I get up and go away. My heart is full of despondency. Shall I ever in my life be able to rejoice again? The sun shines, but there is emptiness within me. The dreams of the night are confused. I have slept without joy.

"What is the meaning of this terrible feeling of emptiness—the horrible feeling of dissatisfaction which takes hold after each meal? My heart sinks, I feel it bodily, it is an indescribably miserable feeling.

"On the days when I am not tortured by hunger, the dread of becoming fat again moves to the center. Two things, then, torture me: First, hunger. Second, the dread of getting fatter. I find no way out of this noose. . . . Horrible feeling of emptiness. Horrible fear of this feeling. I have nothing that can dull this feeling.

"Anyway, the picture has shifted. Only a year ago I looked forward to hunger and then ate with appetite. The laxatives I took daily saw to it that I did not put on fat. Of course I also chose my foods accordingly, avoided everything fattening, but still ate with pleasure and enjoyment the allowable things. Now, in spite of my hunger, every meal is a torment, constantly accompanied by feelings of dread. The feelings of dread do not leave me at all any more. I feel them like something physical, an ache in my heart.

"When I awake in the morning I feel dread of the hunger that I know will soon appear. Hunger drives me out of bed. I eat breakfast—and after an hour get hungry again. Hunger, or the dread of hunger, pursues me all morning. The dread of hunger is something terrible. It drives all other thoughts out of my head. Even when I am full, I am afraid of the coming hour in which hunger will start again. When I am hungry I can no longer see anything clearly, cannot analyze.

"I will briefly describe a morning. I sit at my desk and work. I have a great deal to do; much that I have been looking forward to. But a tormenting restlessness keeps me from finding quiet. I jump up, walk to and fro, stop again and again in front of the cupboard where my bread is. I eat some of

14 [It was not at all uncommon in European institutions at this time for the family of a wealthy patient, and even a corps of servants, to live in the institution with the patient. —TRANSLATORS.]

it; ten minutes later I jump up again and eat some more. I firmly resolve not to eat any more now. Of course I can summon up such will power that I actually eat nothing. But I cannot suppress the desire for it. All day long I cannot get the thought of bread out of my mind! It so fills up my brain that I have no more room for other thoughts; I can concentrate neither on working nor on reading. Usually the end is that I run out into the street. *I run away from the bread in my cupboard* [E.W.'s EMPHASIS] and wander aimlessly about. Or I take a laxative. How can that be analyzed? From where does this unconquerable unrest come? Why do I think I can dull it only with food? And why then does eating make me so unhappy? One might say, 'Eat up the bread, then you will have peace.' But no, when I have eaten it, I am unhappier than ever. Then I sit and constantly see before me the bread I have eaten. I feel of my stomach and have to keep thinking and thinking, 'Now you will get that much fatter!' When I try to analyze all this, nothing comes of it except a theory. Something thought up. All I can feel is the disquiet and the dread. [Here follows an attempt at analysis.] But all this is only fantastic pictures; I must exert my brain to think them up. It would be easy to analyze someone else like this. I myself, however, continue to wander about in my deathly dread and must go through thousands of frightful hours. Every day seems to me to have a thousand hours, and often I am so tired from this spasmodic [15] thinking that I no longer wish for anything but death. After dinner my mood is always at its worst. I would rather not eat at all, so as not to have the horrible feeling after dinner. All day I am afraid of that feeling. How shall I describe it? It is a dull, empty feeling at the heart, a feeling of dread and helplessness. Sometimes then my heart pounds so strongly that it makes me quite dizzy. We've explained it in the analysis in this way: I attempt to satisfy two things while eating—hunger and love. Hunger gets satisfied—love does not! There remains the great, unfilled hole.

"In the morning when I awake I begin to be afraid of the 'dread after dinner,' and this dread goes with me all day long. I even dread to go into a grocery store. The sight of the groceries awakens longings in me which they [the groceries] can never still. As though a person tried to quench his thirst with ink.

"Perhaps I would find liberation if I could solve this puzzle: The connection between eating and longing. The anal-erotic connection is purely theoretical. It is completely incomprehensible to me. I don't understand myself at all. It is terrible not to understand yourself. *I confront myself as a strange person* [L.B.'s ITALICS]. I am afraid of myself, I am afraid of the feelings to which I am defenselessly delivered over every minute.

"This is the horrible part of my life: It is filled with dread. Dread of

[15] [This word is used to approximate the German *kramphaft*, which refers to cramp-like, convulsive effort.—TRANSLATORS.]

eating, dread of hunger, dread of the dread. Only death can save me from this dread. Every day is like walking on a dizzying ridge, an eternal balancing on cliffs. It is useless to have analysis tell me that I want precisely this dread, this tension. It sounds brilliant, but it does not help my aching heart. Who wants this tension, who, what? I see nothing any more, everything is blurred, all the threads are tangled.

"The only work I do is mental. In my innermost being nothing changes, the torment remains the same. It is easy to say: everything is transparent. I long to be violated—*and indeed I do violence to myself every hour* [L.B.'s ITAL-ICS]. Thus I have reached my goal.

"But where, where indeed is the miscalculation? For I am boundlessly wretched, and it sounds silly to me to say: 'That is just what I want: to be wretched.' Those are words, words, words, . . . and in the meantime I suffer as one would not let an animal suffer."

In the clinic to which, as already mentioned, Ellen went with her husband on the 12th of November, a spiritual relaxation sets in, and a complete revolution in her nourishment. From the first day on she eats everything which is put before her, including things she has not touched for years, such as soup, potatoes, meat, sweet dishes, chocolate. Her weight, which was 102 pounds on admission, nevertheless does not increase to more than 114 pounds in two months. From the clinic Ellen attends lectures at the University in the morning and afternoon: in between, from three to four o'clock, undergoes analysis; and in the evening often goes for a walk or to the theater. In class she takes notes with great concentration. It seems to her husband as if real improvement were now beginning. Her notes and poems show new hope and new courage. She wants once again "to be human among humans"; "softly on sun-billows comes a new time"; "and thus I was reborn and the world has me again"; "deep gratitude quivers through my heart that I have lived through this night." But still she does not quite trust this peace:

> I see the golden stars and how they dance;
> It's night as yet, and chaos utterly.
> Will with the early morn's clear countenance
> Peace come to me at last, and harmony?

All these poems (reproduced here merely in small extracts) were written in the night of November 18–19. She writes, "As soon as I close my eyes, there come poems, poems, poems. If I wanted to write them all down I should have to fill pages and pages—hospital poems . . . weak and full of inner restraint. They only beat their wings softly; but at least something is *stirring*. God grant that it may grow!"

From the same night we have the following entries: "I have been awake for two hours. But it is beautiful to be awake. Once before it happened, in the summer. But then everything fell apart again. This time, I believe, it will not fall apart. I feel something sweet in my breast, something which wants to grow and become. My heart throbs. Is love coming back into my life? More serious, more quiet than previously, but also more holy and more purified. Dear life, I will ripen toward you, I spread out my arms and breathe deeply, timid and glad.

"I am reading *Faust* again. Now for the first time I am beginning to understand it. I am beginning; much will have to come, and many more heavy things in my life, before I may say, 'I understand it. Yes, now I understand it.' But I am not afraid of what is coming. It is sweet to fear and to suffer, to grow and to become."

But on the very next morning (November 19) "the beautiful mood of the night is as if blown away. I am tired and sad." She does continue to go to lectures, to write, and to read, but the thought of eating never leaves her. For the attraction of this thought she finds a very characteristic comparison: "The murderer must feel somewhat as I do who constantly sees in his mind's eye the picture of the victim. He can work, even slave, from early until late, can go out, can talk, can attempt to divert himself: all in vain. Always and always again he will see the picture of the victim before him. He feels an overpowering pull toward the place of the murder. He knows that this makes him suspect. Even worse—he has a horror of that place, but still he must go there. Something that is stronger than his reason and his will controls him and makes of his life a frightful scene of devastation. The murderer can find redemption. He goes to the police and accuses himself. In the punishment he atones for his crime. I can find no redemption—except in death."

Ellen is painfully aware that "by this fearful illness I am withdrawing more and more from people." "I feel myself excluded from all real life. I am quite isolated. I sit in a glass ball. I see people through a glass wall, their voices come to me muffled. I have an unutterable longing to get to them. I scream, but they do not hear me. I stretch out my arms toward them; but my hands merely beat against the walls of my glass ball."

At this time she begins to write the "History of a Neurosis." We quote from it: "Since I acted only from the point of view of whether things made me thin or fat, all things soon lost their intrinsic meaning. My work too. I sought it for the purpose of diverting myself: away from my hunger or my fondness for sweets. (During the time that I was working from nine to one and from two to six, I was not tempted to eat things that would make me fat.) For a time work served its purpose. It also gave me joy. When everything collapsed in me, that too broke to bits: Work neither diverted me nor gave me joy. However, that did not come till later.

"In the fall of 19—— (at the beginning of my thirty-second year) I felt dread for the first time. Only a very indefinite and faint dread; really rather an inkling of the fact that I had become enslaved to an uncanny power which threatened to destroy my life. I felt that all inner development was ceasing, that all becoming and growing were being choked, because a single idea was filling my entire soul: and this idea something unspeakably ridiculous. My reason rebelled against it, and I attempted by will power to drive this idea out. In vain. Too late—I could no longer free myself and longed now for liberation, for redemption which was to come to me through some method of healing. Thus I came to psychoanalysis.

"I wanted to get to know the unknown urges which were stronger than my reason and which forced me to shape my entire life in accordance with a guiding point of view. And the goal of this guiding point of view was to be thin. The analysis was a disappointment. I analyzed with my mind, and everything remained theory. The wish to be thin remained unchanged in the center of my thinking.

"The months which followed were the most terrible I have ever experienced, and I have not yet gotten over them. Now it was no longer the fixed idea alone which embittered my life, but something far worse was added: the compulsion of always having to think about eating. This compulsion has become the curse of my life, it pursues me waking and sleeping, it stands beside everything I do like an evil spirit, and never and nowhere can I escape it. It pursues me as the Furies pursue a murderer, it makes the world a caricature and my life a hell. It seems to me that I could stand any other pain more easily; if my existence were darkened by a really heavy sorrow, I would have the strength to bear it. But the torture of having each day to tilt anew against the windmill with a mass of absurd, base, contemptible thoughts, this torment spoils my life.

"When I open my eyes in the morning, my great misery stands before me. Even before I am entirely awake I think of—eating. Every meal is associated with dread and agitation, every hour between meals filled with the thought, 'When shall I get hungry again? Would I perhaps even like to eat something now? And what?' . . . and so on and so on; a thousand different forms, but always the same content. No wonder I can no longer be glad. I know only dread and sorrow, lack of pleasure and lack of courage."

Since the curve again takes a serious drop after the end of November, at the beginning of December Kraepelin is consulted and diagnoses *melancholia*. The analyst considers this diagnosis incorrect and continues the analysis. In the first half of December her course is again uphill: Ellen again attends lectures, reads *Faust,* Part II, but is torn to and fro by the differing views of the doctors regarding her illness and her treatment. The internist, who judges the illness most correctly, considers continued hospital treatment necessary, the analyst advises leaving the clinic and "returning to life." This advice completely shakes her faith in the analyst. In her diary she noted on December 19, among other things, "I continue living only because of a sense of duty to my relatives. Life has no further lure for me. There is nothing, no matter where I look, which holds me. Everything is gray and without joy. Since I have buried myself in myself and can no longer love, existence is only torture. Every hour is torture. What formerly gave me joy is now a task, an intrinsically senseless something contrived to help me pass the hours. What formerly seemed to me a goal in life, all the learning, all the striving, all the accomplishment, is now a dark, heavy nightmare of which I am afraid." For her condition she again finds pertinent analogies:

Karl (her husband) says, she tells us, that she does have joy in some things; but he should "ask a prisoner of war sometime whether he would rather stay in the prison camp or return to his homeland. In the prison camp he studies foreign languages and concerns himself with this or that; of course, only to help himself get over the long, hard days. Does he really enjoy the work? Would he for its sake remain in the prison camp even a minute longer than necessary? Certainly not, and nobody will even dream up such a grotesque idea. But of me it is required. Life has become a prison camp for me, and I long as ardently for death as the poor soldier in Siberia longs for his homeland.

"The comparison with imprisonment is no play on words. I am in prison, caught in a net from which I cannot free myself. I am a prisoner within myself; I get more and more entangled, and every day is a new, useless struggle; the meshes tighten more and more. I am in Siberia; my heart is icebound, all around me is solitude and cold. My best days are a sadly comic attempt to deceive myself as to my true condition. It is undignified to live on like this. Karl, if you love me, grant me death."

Another analogy: "I am surrounded by enemies. Wherever I turn, a man stands there with drawn sword. As on the stage: The unhappy one rushes toward the exit; stop! an armed man confronts him. He rushes to a second, to a third exit. All in vain. He is surrounded, he can no longer get out. He collapses in despair.

"So it is with me: I am in prison and cannot get out. It does no good for the analyst to tell me that I myself place the armed men there, that they are theatrical figments and not real. *To me they are very real* [E.W.'S EMPHASIS].

Ellen complains that for months she has "had not one hour of complete freedom." At the same time, she says the daily picture keeps changing. In one week the morning hours are the worst, in another the evening hours, in a third the midday or the late afternoon hours, but in no week is she "completely free." What is constantly denied her is unconcern. She "knows" about herself unceasingly, does everything "with awareness," can never be simply here and live. If once in a while she "grasps at the faith" that her life does still make sense, that she can still be useful to others and help them, then fear comes and "stifles this weak spark of life again." It becomes clearer and clearer to her that she cannot live on if she does not succeed in "breaking the ban" and getting out of this preoccupation with self. Her "spiritual confusion" during and after meals is terrible. She swallows every bite with awareness and an inexplicable feeling of sadness. *"The entire world-picture is disarranged* [L.B.'s ITALICS]. As if I were bewitched. An evil spirit accompanies me and embitters my joy in everything. He distorts everything beautiful, everything natural, everything simple, and makes a caricature out of it. He makes a caricature out of all life."—"Something in me rebels against becoming fat. Rebels against becoming healthy, getting plump red cheeks, becoming a simple, robust woman, as corresponds to my true nature. . . . It drives me to despair that with all my big words I cannot get myself further. I am fighting against uncanny powers which are stronger than I. I cannot seize and grasp them. . . ."

At the beginning of the new year, on the 3rd of January, the internist intervenes decisively, prohibits the continuation of the analysis, to which the patient agrees, and advises her transfer to the Bellevue Sanatorium in Kreuzlingen. On January 7th she writes her younger brother to pardon her for writing him so frankly, but she will no longer lie to him; she wants to tell him that she is full of dread, even though she does not know of what: "Life burdens me like a cloud." During the preparations for the trip, increased depression and agitation sets in. The trip, which takes place on January 13th and 14th, is undergone amid states of fear, feelings of hunger, and depression.

The Stay at Kreuzlingen Sanatorium
from January 14 to March 30, 19——

The referral note of the internist states that menstruation has been absent for years and that the salivary glands are slightly enlarged. Certainly, therefore, there are endocrine disturbances too. The neurosis has expressed itself for many years in obsessive ideas, especially in the fear of becoming too heavy and then again in a compulsive urge to eat copiously and indiscriminately. Between these opposing feelings the exceptionally intelligent patient, many-sided in her interests, vacillates back and forth. To this was added in July of the previous year a very severe cyclothymic depression with exacerbations approximately once a month, strong feelings of dread, and periodic suicidal ideas. During periods of increased depression the obsessive thoughts have been more in the background. In the clinic her condition improved decidedly during the constant presence of her husband, who has a very favorable effect upon her. Her body weight increased markedly on an initial diet of 70 calories/kilo and at the present time is steady at about 52 kilos (114 lb.) on a diet of 50 calories/kilo. Because of her last depression, she was to undergo the prolonged rest urgently recommended by Kraepelin in our institution. Admission to the locked ward seems unnecessary.

The second analyst states in his detailed report that the patient is suffering from a severe obsessive neurosis combined with manic-depressive oscillations. He is convinced that the patient is on the way to a cure! Evidence of this is also a far-reaching physiognomic alteration; for whereas during the summer she was repulsively ugly, since then she has grown more and more feminine and almost pretty. The report confirms in general the above anamnesis, but also contains some important additions and opinions of the psychoanalyst. He considers the depression as "strongly and purposefully aggravated." The patient stated at one time, he says, that her father did not understand her obsessive ideas, but that he did have full understanding of the depression. She had feared that by becoming fat she would displease her previous fiancé (the student), and anyway, for her, being thin was equated with a higher intellectual type, and being fat with a bourgeois Jewish type. After the termination of her engagement her first action was, with a sigh of relief, to raid her own larder! "But when she learned from a statement of the gynecologist that she would have no success along the womanly—motherly—line, despite her renunciation of higher intellectuality (in her marriage she concerned herself ostentatiously with the household and the copying of recipes, especially when in the presence of her younger brother's wife, who is a slim blonde, artistically oriented, has children, etc.), she now resolved 'to live for her idea' without any inhibitions, and began to take large daily doses of laxatives." Since she saw the blond, higher type in the person of her analyst, he succeeded in quieting her during the first consultation (a fact which her husband also confirms). She has also shown pronounced hysterical traits, visibly calculated to impress her husband. Anal-eroticism was the focus of the treatment for a long time. She recognized the relationship between chocolate and anal-eroticism, as well as the equation: "Eating = being fertilized = pregnant = getting fat." The transference then became so clear that on one occasion she sat down quite suddenly on the analyst's lap and gave him a kiss, which, in spite of their previous friendly relations, was very unusual. On another occasion she came to him with the wish that she might lay her head on his shoulder and he should call her "Ellen-child." Since the beginning of December the analysis had flagged more and more, and this as a sequel to their discussion of the father-complex, which however could only be treated peripherally. She had made it clear to herself that "her obsessional idea" meant turning away from the paternal (Jewish) type. For the incest-wish, no material could be obtained, not even from her dreams. The infantile amnesia, unfortunately, was not illuminated by either analysis.

During the intake interview at the sanatorium on January 14th, after a few words the patient bursts out into loud wailing and cannot be calmed down for a long time, but reports abruptly and intermittently disconnected fragments of her case history. She readily follows her husband to her room and is glad that she will have an opportunity at once to report details of her illness. She then tells circumstantially the main features in the development of her suffering, from its inception thirteen years before to the latest events in the University town. Kraepelin had rejected the analyst's assumption of an obsessive neurosis, had assumed a genuine melancholia, and had declared to her that the obsessional thoughts would surely disappear with the melancholia; what would happen to her fixed idea after that would soon be seen. Even now she differentiates between the obsessional idea of always having to think about eating and the "fixed idea," the "one goal" of not becoming fat. She reports that during the last weeks she has felt a slight improvement, but has never really been happy and glad. She has come here with a thousand good resolutions, but even on the way over she has become terribly hopeless. Every trifle now seems to her like an insurmountable obstacle. She has the feeling that if one of her symptoms is better, another is so much the worse. "I need the carefree feeling again while eating; to me every meal is an inner conflict. Constantly I have the feeling that if somebody really loved me he would not let me live on." In the clinic, she says, she finally became afraid of everyone because she must always expect they would tell her she looked well. "Everything agitates me, and I experience every agitation as a sensation of hunger, even if I have just eaten." Now she has the feeling that all inner life has ceased, that everything is unreal, everything senseless. She also reports readily on her suicidal attempts. Even now she wishes for nothing so much as to be allowed to go to sleep and not wake up again, for she does not dream that she can ever become healthy again. After the second attempt she had constantly thought only this: if only her husband would come back soon, otherwise she would throw herself under some car, she had constantly longed for him when he was away. She turns against psychoanalysis with particular vigor. In contrast with this, her husband states that she let herself be analyzed quite willingly and that she was by no means detached from the second analyst.

Further extracts from the case record:

January 16. After a discussion of the daily schedule as to rest, walks, etc., and the question of eating, the first night went well, with the help of a mild sedative. The patient is allowed to eat in her room, but comes readily with her husband to afternoon coffee, whereas previously she had stoutly resisted this on the ground that she did not really eat but devoured like a wild animal—which she demonstrated with utmost realism.

Her physical examination showed nothing striking. She is a woman of medium height, adequately nourished, tending toward pyknic habitus, whose body build is characterized in the case record as boyish. However, signs of pronounced male stigmatization are missing. The skull is described in the case record as relatively large and massive, but otherwise no signs of acromegaly are present. Facial form oval and evenly modeled. Salivary glands are markedly enlarged on both sides. Thyroid gland not palpable. An earlier gynecological examination is said to have revealed "infantile genitalia." On clavicle, callus formation from an old fracture while riding. Internal organs, no comment. Pulse full, soft, but the rate is unstable. Periods absent for several years. The neurological examination shows, except for a very weak (Jendrassik enforced) patellar reflex (with a moderately active Achilles' reflex), absolutely nothing remarkable, nor any tremor of hands.

January 21. The facial expression is very changeable, corresponding to frequent fluctuations from one affective state to another; on the whole, however, somewhat stiff and empty, her look now empty, now strongly "saturated with feeling." Also, her posture is somewhat stiff. Her gait is erect and very quick. Her behavior is very amiable; she seeks contacts but without noticeable eroticism. Basic mood hopelessly despairing. Even at this time I noted: "One has less the impression that she suffers under a genuine depressive affect than that she feels herself physically empty and dead, completely hollow, and suffers precisely from the fact that she cannot achieve any affect. Strong feeling of illness in the sense of a flagging of her mental energy. Seriously longs for death. In the foreground, vexation and torment because of the obsession of always having to think of eating. Feels herself degraded by this. Striking is the objectivity with which she reports things from which properly the release of a strong affect must be expected. Train of thought shows neither flight of ideas nor dispersion; but she has difficulty concentrating since her thoughts keep revolving about her "complex." Hence will not yet let her husband read to her. Power of apprehension, attention, and memory intact, however. The Rorschach test was unfortunately not available at that time; the result would have been of the greatest interest in presenting experimentally a picture of the patient's entire worldview.

January 22. Nights tolerable with mild sedatives. Only during her second night so agitated that her husband had to call the head nurse. Mood fluctuates from day to day and often several times during the same day. On the whole, quieter; slight attacks of dread beginning with a "fluttering" in the cardiac region, "as if there were bats there." Eats nearly everything that is set before her, only makes occasional difficulties about desserts. Has lost one pound in the last week, since then has eaten better. During walks lets herself be diverted from her despair with relative ease. Though as a child she was wholly independent of the opinion of the others, she is now completely dependent on what others think about her appearance and her being fat.

Since everything now depended on our arriving at a definitive diagnosis,

I asked the patient and her husband to work out an exact anamnesis, a labor which visibly calms the patient.

February 8. She suffers greatly from obsessional impulses to throw herself upon food and gulp it down like an animal (confirmed by observation). One night devoured seven oranges in succession. By contrast, during the meals there appear ascetic impulses, forcing her to deny herself this and that, especially the dessert. She is least restrained during walks but is also quite orderly with the other patients; however, she can never get away from herself and constantly has the feeling "of being like a corpse among people."

February 15. The findings already noted in the report of the internist are again shown here clearly: feelings of hunger, ravenous desire, and "compulsive thoughts" about eating superseded by a severely depressive dejection, indeed, despair. Suicidal impulses, self-reproaches for beginning to lie once more—it had come to that today. Had recently taken six tablets of laxative daily but in response to a direct question had lied to the physician, saying she was taking nothing.

February 26. Agitation, quickly subsided again. Has attached herself to an elegant, very thin female patient. "Homo-erotic component strikingly evident." Dreams very vividly and always about food or death; sees the finest things before her, feels terrible hunger, but at the same time the compulsion not to be allowed to eat. The death dreams are:

Dream 1: "I dreamt something wonderful: War had broken out, I was to go into the field. I say good-by to everyone with the joyous expectation that I shall soon die. I am glad that before the end I can eat everything, have eaten a large piece of mocha cake."

Dream 2: In a semisomnolent state she dreams she is "the wife of a painter who cannot sell his paintings. She herself has to work at sewing or the like, cannot do it because she feels sick, both have to go hungry. She asks him to get a revolver and shoot them both. 'You're just too cowardly to shoot us; the other two painters shot themselves too.' "

Dream 3: Dreams that on her trip overseas she jumped into the water through a porthole. Her first lover (the student) and her husband both attempted artificial respiration. She ate many chocolate creams and packed her trunks.

Dream 4: She orders goulash, says she is very hungry, but only wants a small portion. Complains to her old nursemaid that people are tormenting her very much. Wants to set herself on fire in the forest.

For psychotherapeutic reasons, an analysis of her dreams was not made.

During a morning agitation in a semisomnolent state she speaks of the deceased, who have eternal rest while she is still tormented; speaks of her burial. Will eat no oranges because her husband will tell the doctor. Offers a farmer fifty thousand francs if he will shoot her quickly. Speaks of her younger brother, who has left the New World because he has been tormented day and night by the buzzing of a fly; she herself, though in the same tormented state, is not allowed "to leave from overseas," but must continue to live. If she knows no other way of dying, she will set fire to herself or ram her head through a pane of glass. She says we are all sadists and take pleasure in tormenting her, the doctor included.

It is very easy for her husband to achieve rapport [16] with her, not only when she is half asleep but when she is fully asleep.

March 9. After fourteen relatively good days, there are five days of agitation, which reached their climax yesterday. In the foreground a "colossal gluttony," to which, however, she did not yield. She says she cannot wait until her "melancholia" is cured. It is terrible that her husband has such a "bad" influence on her, since his presence makes it impossible for her to take her life. Wants to look at the locked wards, possibly to transfer there. "I feel myself, quite passively, the stage on which two hostile forces are mangling each other." She has the feeling that she can do nothing at all about it and must look on in complete helplessness.

March 11. Her visit to the locked wards has had a rather unfavorable effect. "I would want to smash in the solid panes immediately." Feels gluttony again "as when a wild animal throws itself on its food." Full of self-reproaches for having eaten too much. Wants permission from the doctor to take her life. Attempts obstinately to convince her husband and doctor of the correctness of this trend of thought, rejects every counterargument.

Even as a young girl she could not sit quietly at home, but always had to be on the go, which even then struck those around her. At the age of eighteen she wrote to a girl friend, "Melancholy lies over my life like a black bird, which hovers somewhere in the background until the time has come to pounce upon me and kill me." Now, too, she has the feeling that in everything she does a ghost stalks her in order to kill her, or she is only waiting until "insanity comes and, shaking its black locks, seizes me and hurls me into the yawning abyss." Periods absent for four and one-half years, sexual intercourse discontinued for three years; previously normal.

March 21. Suicidal threats become more serious. Wants only to wait for the consultation scheduled for March 24. "If there were a substance which contained nourishment in the most concentrated form and on which I would remain thin, then I would still be so glad to continue living."—"I want to get thinner and thinner, but I do not want to have to watch myself constantly, and I do not want to forego anything; it is this friction between wanting to be thin and yet not wanting to miss any food which is destroying me."—"On all points I am clear and sensible, but on this one point I am insane; I am perishing in the struggle against my nature. Fate wanted to

16 [This word is not used here in its customary sense of a close and harmonious relationship but in the special sense of communication between a hypnotist and his subject. In hypnotic rapport the subject responds without awakening to the questions and commands of the hypnotist. The use of the term at this point may be taken to indicate the extent of the husband's influence over Ellen.—TRANSLATORS.]

have me fat and strong, but I want to be thin and delicate." The capacity to enjoy spring increases more and more, but also the torment while eating.

Second postscript to the anamnesis: She says she already had depressive dejections even before the appearance of the fixed idea in her twenty-first year. In her diary, some months before the appearance of this idea, she expresses wonderment that a damper suddenly tones down her cheerful mood, so that she feels like crying. She wonders whether she is too sensitive for the great battle of life. "How often I begin a morning cheerily, my heart full of sunshine and hope, and before I am able to understand why I am so happy, something comes and strikes my mood down. Something quite insignificant, perhaps a cold tone in the voice of a person whom I love, or some other usually insignificant thing to disappoint me in someone. I see how the world darkens before my blurred vision."

In response to my request her husband gathers together the following material on the theme of suicide: The wish to die runs through her entire life. Even as a child she thinks it "interesting" to have a fatal accident—for example, to break through the ice while skating. During her riding period (at nineteen, twenty, and twenty-one) she performs foolhardy tricks, has a fall and breaks her clavicle, and thinks it too bad that she does not have a fatal accident; on the next day she mounts her horse again and continues to carry on in the same manner. When sick as a young girl, she is disappointed each time the fever subsides and the sickness leaves her. When she studies for the *Matura* (at twenty-two), she wants her tutor to repeat this sentence over and over again: Those whom the gods love die young. The teacher is annoyed by this and finally refuses to do this again and again. When she hears of the death of girl friends, she envies them and her eyes shine at the death announcement. While working in the Foundling Home, despite the warnings of the supervisor she visits children who have scarlet fever and kisses them in the hope that she, too, will catch it. Attempted also to get sick by standing naked on the balcony after a hot bath, putting her feet into ice cold water, or standing in the front of the streetcar when there is an east wind and she has a fever of 102°. The first analyst at the first consultation in late December 19— calls her behavior a "slow attempt at suicide."

March 22. Was very cheerful yesterday during her walk; sat down to her meal at noon quite calmly, but then, as always, was suddenly as if inwardly transformed. Wonders then immediately whether she can make herself leave something on her plate. Becomes more agitated, the more the meal progresses. "Everything in me trembles, the desire to eat up everything fights within me a furious battle against the resolve not to eat everything, until finally I jump up and have all that I have left taken away, in order not to get into the danger of eating it up after all." Then feels as if beaten up, completely exhausted, her whole body covered with perspiration; all her limbs ache as if she had been whipped; would like to shoot herself at once. Only after some time (one to two hours) does this condition fade away.

March 24. Consultation with Professor E. Bleuler and a foreign psychia-trist.

The preliminaries of this consultation are as follows: In view of the in-creasing risk of suicide, continued residence of the patient on the open ward could not be justified. I had to put before her husband the alternative of giving permission to transfer his wife to the closed ward or leaving the institution with her. The very sensible husband saw this perfectly, but said he could give his permission only if a cure or at least a far-reaching im-provement of his wife could be promised him. Since on the basis of the anamnesis and my own observations I had to diagnose a progressive schizo-phrenic psychosis (schizophrenia simplex), I could offer the husband very little hope. (If shock therapy had existed then, it would have offered a tem-porary way out of the dilemma and a certain postponement, but it would certainly have changed nothing in the final result.) Since it was clear that a release from the institution meant certain suicide, I had to advise the husband in the light of his responsibility not to rely upon my opinion alone —certain as I was of my case—but to arrange for a consultation with Professor Bleuler on the one hand, and on the other hand with a foreign psychiatrist whose views were not too close to the Kraepelin-Bleuler theory of schizo-phrenia. The complete anamnesis (excerpts from which are given in the following section), as well as our case record, was handed to the consultants in advance.

Result of the consultation: Both gentlemen agree completely with my prognosis and doubt any therapeutic usefulness of commitment even more emphatically than I. For Bleuler the presence of schizophrenia is indubi-table. The second psychiatrist declares that schizophrenia can be diagnosed only if an intellectual defect exists. In our case he would label it a psycho-pathic constitution progressively unfolding. The "idea" of wanting to get thin he correctly designates not as a delusional idea (since logical motiva-tion is absent), but with less justification as an overvalent idea (we shall come back to this). All three of us agree that it is not a case of obsessional neurosis and not one of manic-depressive psychosis, and that no definitely reliable therapy is possible. We therefore resolved to give in to the patient's demand for discharge.

March 30. The patient was visibly relieved by the result of the consulta-tion, declared that she would now take her life in her own hands, but was much shaken when she saw that despite her best intentions she could not master her dilemma with regard to eating. Externally she controls herself powerfully and is quiet and orderly, but inwardly she is very tense and agi-tated. She ponders this way and that what she is to do now, and finally re-solves to go home with her husband this very day. She continues precisely her whole way of life until the last, since every change "confuses her and throws her completely off the track." She is tormented in the extreme by her "idea" up to the last moment. Weight upon leaving approximately the same as upon arriving, namely, 104 pounds.

Her Death

On her trip Ellen is very courageous. The reason for taking it gives her strength. The glimpse into life which the trip gives her hurts her. Even more than in the institution she feels incapable of dealing with life. The following days are more harrowing than all the previous weeks. She feels no release of tension; on the contrary, all her symptoms appear more strongly. The irregularity of her way of life upsets her completely; the reunion with her relatives only brings her illness more clearly into view. On the third day of being home she is as if transformed. At breakfast she eats butter and sugar, at noon she eats so much that—for the first time in thirteen years!—she is satisfied by her food and gets really full. At afternoon coffee she eats chocolate creams and Easter eggs. She takes a walk with her husband, reads poems by Rilke, Storm, Goethe, and Tennyson, is amused by the first chapter of Mark Twain's "Christian Science," is in a positively festive mood, and all heaviness seems to have fallen away from her. She writes letters, the last one a letter to the fellow patient here to whom she had become so attached. In the evening she takes a lethal dose of poison, and on the following morning she is dead. "She looked as she had never looked in life—calm and happy and peaceful."

II *Existential Analysis* [17]

Introduction

The foregoing account summarizes what we know, on the basis of credible autobiographical and biographical documents and testimonies, about the human individuality to whom we have given the name Ellen West. This knowledge is of a purely historical sort, for which reason we designate the entirety of the underlying facts or data as the (inner and outer) life-history of that individuality. On the basis of the life-history, her specific name loses its function of a mere verbal label for a human individuality—as that of this unique time-space-determined individual—and takes on the meaning of an eponym (*fama*). The name Ellen West (in this connection, of course, it makes no difference whether this name is real or fictitious) thus designates the totality of a historical figure or personage. However certain and definite

---

[17] [The reader should be forewarned that some sections which follow may seem difficult to understand in English. Binswanger's style, in line with much German scientific and philosophical writing, uses built-up concepts, especially by hyphenating verb forms with other words, which mean something more than do the separate words in English. In translating, we had to decide whether to paraphrase or to render Binswanger more accurately. We chose to do the latter. We are of course aware that this does not make for writing that, as Kierkegaard put it, can be perused during the afternoon nap. But such was scarcely our intention.—TRANSLATORS.]

the data of a life-history may be, the judgments regarding it remain uncertain, fluctuating, and incomplete. True, we say in ordinary life that on the basis of a report or a narrative we form an approximate "conception" or construct a more or less vivid "picture" of a human individuality; however, this conception or picture, as is well known, depends upon the varying standpoint and viewpoint of the person or group making it. Love alone, and the imagination originating from it, can rise above this single point of regard; judgment, even scientific judgment, as a form of grasping-by-something,[18] remains of necessity bound to one perspective. It is the task of historical science to test and compare "personal" judgments, trace them back to their basic perspectives, and to place them in a scientific perspective. However, since even a scientific perspective takes its directives from the present moment, "history is constantly rewritten," as Ranke put it.

The analysis of an individual's existence also adheres to historical data. If its purpose is only to analyze the present mood of this existence, then in some circumstances it may depend on a single one or at least on very few of such data.

Thus we were able to give an existential interpretation of the manic "upset" of a female patient from two relatively orderly, unrelated, written documents, one a reproachful complaint, the other a solicitous inquiry.[19] If the "disturbance" went deeper, however, and if the speech became so disconnected that we had to speak of a disordered or incoherent flight of ideas, we soon found ourselves dependent on knowledge regarding a large part of the life-history of the patient in question. If we actually find ourselves, as in the case of Ellen West, forced to analyze a human individuality not only as to its mood-key (*Gestimmtheit*) but as to its total existence, then the entire life-history must be spread out before us in as many details as is at all possible. In contrast, however, to the historical delineation of the individual configuration, we now leave out as far as possible all judgments on this individual, be they moral, esthetic, social, medical, or in any other way derived from a prior point of view, and most of all our own judgment, in order not to be prejudiced by them, and in order to direct our gaze at the forms of existence in which this particular individuality is in-the-world. (After all, "individuality is what its world, in the sense of its own world, is.")[20] The place of the historical figure built up out of impressions and

18 [This is the literal rendering of the German *Bei-etwas-Nehmen*. This is one of the "basic forms" of the encounter between persons, as explicated in Binswanger's major work (see Note 21). Many of the passages in Section II undertake to compare this basic form with others, such as Love, in the existence called Ellen West.—TRANSLATORS.]

19 Refers to an earlier work by Binswanger, *Über Ideenflucht* (*On the Flight of Ideas*), 1st and 2nd Studies.

20 [This famous sentence is from Hegel's *The Phenomenology of Mind*, written in 1807. The passage in which it occurs is: "Herewith drops out of account that existence which was to be something all by itself, and was meant to constitute one aspect, and that the universal aspect, of a law. Individuality is what its world, in the sense of its own world, is. Individ-

judgments, is taken here by the phenomenologically described and analyzed existence—*Gestalt.* Since this *Gestalt,* however, does not remain the same throughout her life but undergoes transformations, the existential analysis cannot progress in purely systematic fashion, but must rather adhere strictly to the facts of the life-history. This will be illustrated as we proceed.

Whenever we speak of forms of existence, therefore, we are speaking of forms of being-in-the-world and being-beyond-the-world, such as we already viewed in our studies on the flight of ideas, and worked out systematically in our book, *Basic Forms and Cognition of Human Existence.*[21] Structurally these forms refer to the forms of the world. Their unity can be articulated only phenomenologically. Indeed, it is "in" the world that an actual existence "lives." Hence these forms are "being-in" any given world, and refer to the self which corresponds to this being-in, and the loving We-ness which is beyond the finite world, secure in homeland and eternity.[22] For didactic reasons we now develop the problem of the existential forms in the case of Ellen West in terms of the forms of the world in which she "lives." Since "world" always means not only the What within which an existence exists but at the same time the How and Who of its existing, the forms of the How and of the Who, of the being-in and being-oneself, become manifest quite "of their own accord" from the characterization of the momentary[23] world. Let it be further noted in advance that the term "world" means at one and the same time the *Umwelt,* the *Mitwelt,* and the *Eigenwelt.*[24] This by no means constitutes a fusion of these three worlds into a single one, but is rather an expression for the general way in which "world" forms itself in these three world-regions.

Existential analysis (*Daseinsanalyse,* as we speak of it) must not be confused with Heidegger's analytic of existence (*Daseinsanalytik*). The first is a hermeneutic exegesis on the ontic-anthropological level, a phenomenological analysis of actual human existence. The second is a phenomenological hermeneutic of Being understood as existence, and moves on an ontological

---

uality itself is the cycle of its own action, in which it has presented and established itself as reality, and is simply and solely a unity of what is given and what is constructed—a unity whose ideas do not fall apart, as in the idea of psychological law, into a world given *per se* and an individuality existing for itself. Or if these aspects are thus considered each by itself, there is no necessity to be found between them, and no law of their relation to one another." Hegel, G. W. F., *The Phenomenology of Mind* (transl. J. B. Baillie) (2nd ed., New York: Macmillan, 1931), pp. 335–336.—TRANSLATORS.]

21 [This is Binswanger's major work: *Grundformen und Erkenntnis Menschlichen Daseins* (Zurich: Max Niehaus, 1953). Subsequent footnotes will refer to it as *Basic Forms.*—TRANSLATORS.]

22 See p. 312 for meaning of the terms "homeland" and "eternity."

23 [The word *momentary* approximates the German *jeweilig,* which has in this context the sense of "for the particular time being" rather than "for the moment, not lasting." —TRANSLATORS.]

24 [See the discussion of these important terms in the essay by May in this volume, chapter II, p. 61.—TRANSLATORS.]

level. The similarity of the expressions is justified by the fact that the anthropological or existential analysis relies throughout on that structure of existence as being-in-the-world which was first worked out by the analytic of existence. Both with respect to its scientific structure and its method, it therefore makes use in all seriousness of the "new impulses" which arise on the ontological level.[25]

The World

The first datum which Ellen West's case history gives us is the fact that at nine months she refused milk, so that she had to be fed on broth. The peculiarity and stubbornness in regard to taking food, which runs through her entire life-history can therefore be traced back to her infancy. This is a peculiarity of "sensory communication," not in the sense of a "reflex" but of a "behavior toward the world." In sensory communication, too, we live either as uniting with or separating from the *Umwelt*.[26] In this early refusal of milk a "line of demarcation" is revealed between bodily *Eigenwelt* and *Umwelt,* a "breach" in the uniting with the *Umwelt* in the sense that the former is set in opposition to the latter. Concurrently with this opposition to the *Umwelt,* there may already have existed a resistance to the *Mitwelt,* a resistance to those persons who tried to oppose Ellen's idiosyncrasy. In any case, the first verbal statement by Ellen reported to us stands in crass opposition to the *Mitwelt,* "This bird's nest is no bird's nest." This negative judgment, in which she repudiates a state of things recognized by the *Mitwelt,* shows that her uniting with the *Mitwelt* also suffered a severe blow or, anthropologically expressed, that the upbuilding of the *Eigenwelt* here proceeds quite early in sharp opposition to the *Mitwelt.* This is further indicated by the judgments about her which the *Mitwelt* makes: defiant, stubborn, ambitious, violent.

When we speak of resistance to the *Um-* and the *Mitwelt,* these terms take on the meaning of the boundary, specifically the resisting or encroaching boundary. Here the *Eigenwelt* does not go trustingly over into the *Um-* and *Mitwelt,* to let itself be carried, nourished, and fulfilled by it, but separates itself sharply from it. It is therefore not surprising to hear that even as a child Ellen suffered from a pressure "which she herself did not understand." With this pressure, however, there is already associated the feeling that "everything is empty." The experiencing of the *Um-* and *Mitwelt* as purely oppositional to one, and the rigid assertion of the *Eigenwelt* in contrast to it, may masquerade as an expression of the fullness of exist-

25 Cf. Heidegger, *Sein und Zeit* (*Being and Time*).
26 Cf. E. W. Straus, "Ein Beitrag zur Pathologie der Zwangserscheinungen" ("A Contribution to the Pathology of Obsessive Phenomena"), *Monatsschr. f. Psych. u. Neur.*, Vol. 98, 1938.

ence, but on the contrary it really constricts the span of the existential possibilities and reduces this span to limited sectors of possible behavior. What we call defiance and obstinacy is always an expression of this: existence deals with the particular situation not as "open to the world," that is, in its changing, flexible sense,[27] but in a sense that is fixated ("own-willed") once and for all, locked against or in opposition to *Um-* and *Mitwelt.* Instead of "dominating" the situation, that is to say, instead of surveying it in all its meaningful relations and reaching a decision on this basis, the situation in this case becomes overpowering and the existence is robbed of its very autonomy. For in the insistence on always differing from the others and the always having-it-my-way of defiance, the "negative" supremacy of the *Mitwelt* asserts itself with respect to one's own decision. (The *Mitwelt* shows its "positive" supremacy in being anonymous.) The self of the being-in-the-world as defiance and willfulness is therefore no independent, authentic, or free self, but a self that is defined, though negatively, by the *Mitwelt,* a nonindependent, unauthentic, and unfree self—in a word, a defiant-violent self.

But not only from the direction of the *Mitwelt* is this existence constricted, oppressed, and "emptied out," but from that of its own self, too—namely, from that of its actual thrownness [28] into the role of woman. The place of open defiance and open rebellion, however, is taken by the willful attempt at exchanging this fated role for an assumed role: Ellen West plays only boys' games until her sixteenth year, likes best to wear trousers (at a time when this was not nearly as usual for young girls as it is today), and at the age of seventeen still wants to be a boy, in order to be able to die as a soldier, sword in hand. We learn of her outspoken rebellion against her fate as woman only from the hatred which a former friend's victorious smile aroused in her. Here it is no longer the case of a rift between *Mit-* and *Eigenwelt,* but a real though artificially bridged rift between the *Eigenwelt* and the "world-of-fate." [29] Here, the existence experiences a further, much more "incisive" limitation in the unfolding of its proper possibilities; for instead of taking on the role into which she has been cast, Ellen West tries to deceive both herself and the *Mitwelt* as to this role. Being is replaced by illusion. Existence here dodges its own burden; in the popular phrase, it "takes it easy." With her self-willed "separation" between the *Eigenwelt,* on the one hand, and the *Um-, Mit-,* and fate-world, on the other, there go a certain own-worldly self-sufficiency, expansiveness, and aggressiveness. There is evidence for the former in her thumbsucking, strikingly protracted up to

27 Cf. E. W. Straus, "Geschehnis und Erlebnis" ("Occurrence and Experience"), 1930; in addition, my own paper with the same title, *Monatsschr. f. Psych. u. Neur.,* Vol. 80, 1931.
28 [For discussion of meaning of "thrownness," see Chapter II.—TRANSLATORS.]
29 [For further r°   "world-of fate," see Note 67 of this section.—TRANSLATORS.]

her sixteenth year, for the latter too, in her "ambitious" all-or-nothing principle: *aut Caesar aut nihil!*

And yet this existence had not only a passionate reliance on itself alone. The deep religious faith of which we hear, in which she stood in marked contrast to her outspokenly a-religious father, may have given Ellen a certain feeling of security in her existence until her seventeenth year. To what extent this faith was transmitted to her by her nursemaid (whom I must assume to have been a Christian) we do not know. From her lifelong, touching attachment to this nursemaid and the constant feeling of shelter in her presence, we may assume that from the beginning the nursemaid had a great influence on Ellen.

In her sixteenth and seventeenth years, which cut so deeply into her existence and in which, in connection with her first love affair, she gives up boys' games and thumbsucking, her religious faith crumbles forever like a house of cards under the influence of reading *Niels Lyhne*. Niels Lyhne himself speaks of his "oppressive, imageless world-view." "He had no star. He did not know what to do with himself and his gifts." He hopes that mankind will achieve strength and independence "if it self-confidently tried to live its life in harmony with what the individual in his best moments held highest, in accordance with what dwelt within himself, instead of transferring it away from himself into a controlling deity outside himself." But in the end Niels can no longer endure "the indifference of existence, the being-set-adrift from all sides and constantly being thrown back on oneself. No home on earth, no God in heaven, no goal in the future." He too would like once to have a home of his own. He finds such a home, but his beloved young wife dies early, in fact while believing in God, and he must "experience the great sadness that a soul is always alone." "It was a lie, any belief in the melting of one soul into another. Not the mother who took us on her lap, not a friend, not the wife who rested on our heart. . . ." He goes to war and is mortally wounded.

This rigorous esthetic individualism and religious nihilism, so characteristic of the late nineteenth and the early twentieth century, runs throughout this book which captivated so many young souls. It should be expected to strengthen the faith of a truly believing person. In Ellen West, however, it makes kindred strings vibrate; she suddenly discards her faith, which she had cherished in opposition to her father, and feels confirmed, indeed strengthened, in her individualism. Feeling no longer any trust in, or obligation to a deity, "nowhere caring" again about the judgment of the *Mitwelt,* she is now completely reliant on herself, determining the guide-lines and goals of her actions, in the words of Niels Lyhne, entirely "as a solitary individual," "by what she in her best moments ranks highest according to what there is in her." With such concepts as "best moments" and "highest," existence and idea are raised to the realm of the superlative. This superlative, however, requires as correlative a superlative measure of "strength and independence." After reading *Niels Lyhne,* Ellen credits herself with that measure.

Existentially, that is, always from the viewpoint of being-in-the-world-beyond-the-world,[29a] this means that the world in which this existence predominantly *is* continues to be the *Eigenwelt,* the *idios kosmos* of Heraclitus. But that also means that the self remains limited to passionately wishing and dreaming, that one is oneself restricted to the passionate affects, to wishes, and to dreams.[30] The fact that Ellen now composes poems and keeps up a diary in which she mirrors predominantly her own condition and in which her own goals are determined in detail shows that the horizon of her *Eigenwelt* has widened, as is indeed characteristic of early puberty, and that this widening is concurrent with a serious attempt at a deepened self-interpretation. The guiding lines of this self-interpretation can be derived with all the clarity one could desire from the previously mentioned superlatives. The supreme moment is the one in which one's gaze is directed toward the highest; but this highest is, again in the words of Niels Lyhne, "the strength and independence of the human race in its belief in itself." Her relationship to the *Mitwelt,* previously defined quite negatively by defiance and willfulness, is now bridged over by a positive ("linking") trait, in which, however, defiance and willfulness by no means disappear, but rather into which they are amalgamated. Defiance and willfulness change into ambition, specifically into ambition for social betterment, even social revolution.

If it is only love, the dual mode of existence, which really transforms the defiance and stubbornness dominated by the particular situation and which can give to the existence homeland and eternity, then the ambition born of defiance and stubbornness, the ambitious knowing-better and willing-better, means precisely the nomadization [31] and infinite unrest of existence. Instead of the authentic I-Thou relationship of the being-with-one-another, instead of being sheltered in the eternal moment of love, we find the *Mitwelt* consisting of merely togetherness of one with the others—specifically, in the form of the restless seizing-by-the-weak-point [32] and of the unceasing urge to dominate and lead others. The discovery of the weak point of "the

29a [It needs always to be made clear that in the expression "beyond-the-world" Binswanger is of course referring not to "other-worldliness" but to the fact that the humanness of man inheres in his manifold possibilities with respect to his world, and to other aspects of his capacity for transcending the situation discussed in Chapter II.—EDITORS.]

30 Cf. "Heraklits Auffassung des Menschen" ("Heraclitus' concept of man"), *Die Antike,* Vol. 11, 1935.

31 [We have coined the word *nomadization* as the least clumsy translation of the German compound word *Aufenthaltslosigkeit. Aufenthalt* refers to where one is sojourning at the moment or at a certain time, and it implies that one has a place where one belongs, a homeland (*Heimat*) as this word is used a few lines above. Nomadization, for which we might perhaps substitute "sojournlessness," connotes an utter loss of homeland, a being thrown into the nowhere.—TRANSLATORS.]

32 ["Seizing-by-the-weak-point" is another of Binswanger's forms of encounter between persons, mentioned in Note 18.—TRANSLATORS.]

others," of the *Mitwelt,* is guided by the defiance against that *Mitwelt* in which this existence has thus far predominantly moved, namely, the family. The family's weak point is its prosperity in the midst of the deprivations and sufferings of the "masses." Certainly we also encounter here a feature of "general love for mankind." The forms which this feature assumes, however, betray the fact that here this love for mankind, as so often, is not born of pure love and does not culminate in pure charity, but is driven by ambition and is put into the ambitious service of an "undying name." But let us also not forget the lifelong attachment of so many "others" who were the recipients of Ellen's care and her own real suffering over "social injustice." Neither would be possible without the germ of true love. The fact that this germ is so darkly overshadowed, indeed repressed, is one of the main sources of the suffering and torment of this existence. Without this (unrealizable) [33] longing for a homeland and an eternity in the sense of love, without a secret knowledge of the possibility of being-beyond-the-world, this existence would not have suffered from its emptiness and poverty to the degree that it actually did: this existence would not have become a hell. To him who is completely empty of love, existence can become a burden but not a hell.

So much for Ellen West's "urge" toward social service, which lasts almost to the end of her life. It is primarily through this urge that the world of doing or practical action, the practical world, reveals itself to her. If we say of a person that he stands with both feet firmly on the ground, we mean his standing in this world. It is practical action which places the existence on the earth, teaches it to stand and walk on it; more correctly expressed—in practical action, in everyday pre- and nonprofessional conduct (family, friendship, games, sports), and in professional activity, the existence establishes itself on the earth, creates its own *Lebensraum,* its possibilities of orientation and, at one with that, its "practical self." "For it is only through the practical that we first become truly certain of our own existence." He who stands with both feet firmly on the ground knows where he stands, where he is going, how he is going, and who he himself ("in practical life") is. Such a standing, going, and knowing we call "striding," that is a "ranging from one place to another" which knows about itself, its standpoint, and its goal. We have designated and analyzed this striding, using an old philosophical term, as the *discursive* form among the basic forms of existence.[34]

---

33 [The use of the parentheses by Binswanger at this point may be taken as a way of emphasizing the crucial distinction between an existential lack and a psychic wish or need. Since terms referring to hope or realization are usually taken to imply such needs and would therefore suggest a theoretical orientation differing from what is being developed here, the word is set off by parentheses to demonstrate that the use of it does not involve subscribing to the customary presuppositions. This provides an excellent instance both of the difficulty of expressing existentialist conceptions in unambiguous language and of Binswanger's extreme care in this respect.—TRANSLATORS.]

34 Cf. *Basic Forms.*

In the existence of Ellen West this basic form undergoes significant modifications. Her existence does not stand "with both feet firmly on the ground"; that is, neither its independence nor its possibilities of orientation can take root in practical action. The existence moves only with an effort, indeed convulsively, on the earth; its standing-on-earth is constantly opposed by a swaying and flying in the air and a being-confined in and under the earth. Both these directions of existence, or their possibilities at least, and the worlds implied by them, are clearly seen in Ellen's poems, diary notes, letters, and oral utterances.

The worlds in which this *Dasein* has its "*Da*" are, then, the world on the earth, the world of the air, and the world in and under the earth. Existential movement on the earth is striding, that in the air is flying, that in and under the earth is crawling. To each of these movements corresponds a specific form of temporalization [35] and spatialization, to each a specific material consistency, special lighting and coloring, and each represents a particular contextual [36] totality. If the first world meant a contextual totality in the sense of practical action, the second means the world of "winged" wishes and "highest ideals," and the third is that of the "pulling to earth" (Wallenstein) [37] "pressing down," burdening, encumbering "desire,"—in short, it is the world structured by the demands of the "natural existence." Let us establish right now that the world which narrows existence down to fewer and fewer possibilities, arrests, even imprisons it to a point where existence is finally overpowered and nullified by it, is the world of appetite and greed, therefore, again a specific sector of the *Eigenwelt*.

But let us again proceed historically. Even in her earliest poems, frequently reminiscent of *Niels Lyhne*, we encounter the contrast between the "airy" world, through which Ellen thinks she flies in an uncontrollable urge for freedom, and the narrow world, the tomb, out of which she rises. The first world is well known to us from our studies on the flight of ideas. It is the world of the "airy" thought, of the "windy spirit," as Sophocles [38] expressed it, the volatile, lightened world of optimistic cognition,[39] of the "high" spirits in general. But from the very beginning this world encounters contradictions. It is of the greatest interest, and very important

35 [The German word is *Zeitigung*, which was coined by Heidegger, is central to his thinking, and cannot be translated except in a kind of explanatory phrase. The closest one might come, is to say "engendering time" or "temporalization" in the sense of an ongoing process, which at least suggests the conception of the existence producing time as a necessary expression of itself.—TRANSLATORS.]
36 [This word, *Bewandtnis*, is another Heideggerianism. It refers broadly to the relationship, the contextuality in which something belongs, to its relevance to all the potentialities of a situation.—TRANSLATORS.]
37 [A play by Friedrich Schiller.—TRANSLATORS.]
38 Cf. the famous first choral song of *Antigone* (*pollata deina*), which gives a superb picture of Greek man.
39 Cf. *Über Ideenflucht*.

for our investigation, to trace out precisely what material occasion provokes this contradiction, and how the occasion itself is slowly altered. First, it is the darkening of the sky, the sinking of the sun's fireball into the ocean, the eeriness of the whistling of the winds, the pilotless drifting of the ship of life on the water, the rising of gray, damp evening mists, the hopelessly dreary shivering of the treetops, the gradual waning of the birdsong. (The icy coldness is added to this later.)

In addition to this contradiction appearing at first in purely atmospheric and scenic garb, there also appears a systematic bounding and limiting of her "airy," optimistically ambitious plans, by means of which, however, Ellen attempts at the same time to escape from the gathering dusk; Ellen West realizes that man must create his world in little things. To this end she calls on work above all: "practical action" is to help her, but again not for its own sake but as a means of gaining undying fame, as an opiate for sorrow and grief, in order to make her forget, to rescue her from a world out of joint, in which the light has expired and the joy of life has withered, to rescue her from insanity and the madhouse. We see how convulsively Ellen West endeavors to counter with an existential contradiction the extremes of mood into which her existence is thrown by trying to stand again with both feet firmly on the ground, which can always and only mean: to work. But this effort is not crowned with lasting success. The laborious building up of a world in little things is constantly opposed by the temptation of effortlessly flying through the breadth and brightness, the splendor of color, and the loud jubilation of the "airy" world.

But her failure to realize "the old plans and hopes" does not act as a new incentive for further building up and expansion of the world of practical action, rather it transforms the world into boundless desolation, soundless stillness, and icy cold, in which the *Eigenwelt* shrivels to an infinitely tiny point. Her soul is weary, the bells of death in her heart cannot be silenced.[40] What for, why all this, if only to molder forgotten in the cold earth after a short span of time? This existence is not lived existentially as duration—in other words, not steadily extended in view of death—but is reified as something extant [41] during a definite time-span, as something which one day will no longer be extant but will molder and be buried in oblivion.[42] The ambi-

---

[40] At this point it is manifest that the "lowering" announces the "shadow" of death descending on the world of life.

[41] [We have used this word to translate Heidegger's term *vorhanden*, or "on hand," which refers to the world of objects present merely as such, that is, as items; *vorhanden* is to be contrasted with *zuhanden*, or "to hand," which refers to the world of human things, which are present as instrumentalities for existing beings. This distinction is essential to the further distinction between a world in which meaningful action can take place and a world giving rise to various pathological modes. As one example of a pathological mode, see Note 157.—TRANSLATORS.]

[42] Death, in the sense of love and friendship, stands in extreme contrast to the death of an extant living creature, in the sense of ending, perishing, and sinking into oblivion. See *Basic Forms*, "Love and Death."

tion for an undying name, which is still to be on the lips of men after hundreds of years, is only the existential consequence of this reification of existence—namely, the numbing of existential emptiness and weakness by the prospects of as extended as possible a continuation of her fame in world-time.

In her eighteenth year, however, something appears in this life-history which does belong altogether to the volatile airy world but can by no means be understood as coming from that world alone. Ellen West would herself like to be petite and ethereal as her chosen girl friends are. By virtue of this wish the ethereal world, as we shall call it from now on in keeping with Ellen's own terminology, casts its spell not only on the *Umwelt* and the *Mitwelt,* but also on the *Eigenwelt.* Yet it is precisely a sphere of the *Eigenwelt* which must offer the most powerful resistance to etherealization by its very gravity, solidity, and compact filling of space—by its massiveness and opaqueness, that is, the body sphere. (For, as we may now just as well establish, the body [43] represents the identity of worldly condition, *my* body, and of inner body-awareness, *"existence-in-the-body."*) [44] With this wish the existence overstrains itself by its own weight. Everyday speech quite correctly calls such an overstraining wish "off the beam"; [45] for here the existence gets "off the beam" into a situation from which actually no way back seems to be possible. [46]

Simultaneously with the appearance of this wish—calamitous because it means that the conflict of two worlds comes to a head in one conflict situation and thus becomes fixated—the ethereal world as such assumes more and more distinct forms, but at the same time, too, the resistance of the uncanny, gloomy, dull, damp world is "fortified." The contrast becomes increasingly sharp between a world full of sunshine, sprouting and flowering springtime, rustling groves, and radiant blue skies over a free, wild landscape—that is, the infinitely vast, mobile, radiantly lighted, warm, and colorful world (in a word, the ethereal world) and the confined, unmoved, dull and dark, cold colorless world beneath the earth, the world of the tomb, "where the glaring sun of life does not shine." To this something else is added, how-

43 [In this passage Binswanger distinguishes between two senses of the word "body" and discusses as well the "relation" between the two senses, using the unusual word "figure" to denote both aspects of corporeality. Unfortunately, English has only the single word "body" to stand for the two German words *Leib,* meaning "the body as living," in the sense of the living body of a human being, and *Körper,* which refers to the body in its physical sense, the animate object on which the surgeon works.—TRANSLATORS.]

44 Cf. *Basic Forms.* Seemingly the first meaning takes precedence for Ellen West: her *soma* is an externally perceived, judged, touched, beaten body; basically, however, the very *existing* of her *soma* is hateful to her.

45 [The German word is *verstiegen,* from the verb *sich versteigen,* which refers to losing one's way, as in the mountains, at a point where one cannot go either forward or back. *Verstiegen* is used to mean extravagant, high-flown, eccentric, odd, or queer; the expression "off the beam" retains some of the spatial connotations.—TRANSLATORS.]

46 The expression "off the beam" should therefore not be understood in the moralistic but in the existential sense.

ever; whereas Ellen previously, at sight of the dipping of the fireball into the ocean and the sinking of damp fogs on sea and shore, called upon the grim, cold Sea-King to rescue her, saying that he should come and kiss her dead in ardent lust, now she beseeches the Father (God) reigning behind the clouds to take her back unto himself. Eroticism and religiosity (not quite dead, though aesthetically colored) enter into an alliance here for the rescue of the existence from the wet, dark tomb- and grave-world. In the ethereal world as such the existence cannot get a firm footing and starts back in fear of the moldy world beneath the earth, the world of the grave. As in the case of the patient bewildered in his flight of ideas,[47] existence needs a stable anchor of salvation, and this anchor is—as in that case—the bond with the father and the erotic-mystical longing for return to him and union with him. This union, however, as she says in so many words, is possible only in death. Ellen does not long for a death that would simply put an end to things, nor is her longing for an undying name. Again, the reification of existence is broken through by the dual mode of existence, by a secret inkling of loving encounter and homeland, of the possibility, then, of being-beyond-the-world. Ellen's being-beyond does not begin and end in being-in-the-world, however, as it does in the full existential phenomenon of love but—as we shall show—in a return to Nothingness.

As these longed-for possibilities of salvation in the water and the sky move into the foreground more and more, the salvation on earth, the "standing with both feet firmly on the ground," or practical action, increasingly recedes. The more radiant and animated the ethereal world becomes, the more the world in and beneath the earth consolidates itself.

To start with, the ethereal world becomes still more glowing, colorful, and picturesque. Waves of light, like golden ribbons, lie upon fields of grain, villages, and valleys, while spring storms race through the world. Her body, and this is again of the greatest importance, at first participates more and more in this world. Her blood rushes and races through her arteries, every fibre trembles, her breast is not wide enough for the exuberant joy of youth, her young, strong body stretches itself, and sitting still (which had already grown into a torture back in Sicily) becomes impossible. Walking is replaced by horseback riding and jumping, and no horse is too dangerous. It is clear that such activities do not admit of a fat body, but rather require a body that is elastic and strong.

In this world-design, too, which at least reconciles the ethereal world with the practice of sport, love has its say. Now she is no longer concerned with the gloomy, cold Sea-King in the depths of the ocean or the Father who rules behind the clouds, but with the male partner, her peer, who walks on the earth. Tall, strong, pure, and unblemished he must be; he

47 [This refers to Binswanger's *On the Flight of Ideas*, 3rd Study.—TRANSLATORS.]

must live life, he must enjoy sunshine and work, enjoy her and her children. Here we see the attempt, at least in phantasy, to harmonize the ethereal world and the earthly, practical world, a harmony on the home ground of (male-female) love.

In contrast to this youthful exuberance and the longing for love which bursts her breast, immediately, as always, restrictions show themselves, at first, again, coming from the *Mitwelt*. "The house" becomes a tomb, the influences of the home are felt as constricting and are rejected. Next they come from the *Umwelt;* whereas the restrictions were previously of a purely atmospheric nature, namely, damp fog and dark clouds, they now take on a "vital" character. The "cosmological" contrast, which at first took place "in the atmosphere," takes place now in the world of vegetation, specifically as a contrast between ascending life (growing, shining, flowering, thriving) and degenerating life (withering).[48] It now becomes increasingly clear how frail and exposed her life is; it is dedicated to death. Still Ellen fights victoriously against rusting, languishing, drying up, and the staleness of the earth, but the (immovable) world of the tomb, of degenerating life—the world of moldering and withering—nevertheless surrounds the restlessly stirring world filled to overflowing with the joy of life and the roar of storms.

This is the period when she becomes engaged to the "romantic foreigner." We must view this engagement as an unsuccessful practical attempt to harmonize the ethereal with the earthly world. But Ellen breaks off the engagement with surprising compliance at her father's request. That she does not mourn her fiancé can be seen from the fact that even now (in Sicily) she loves life passionately, has sun, wind, and beauty all to herself— indeed, that the world is hers. Her god is now the god of life, her world is the entire universe, of whose secrets she has already caught a glimpse. She is filled with a thirst to learn and writes an article about woman's calling. Ellen considers this last serious attempt at a fusing and harmonizing the ethereal world with the world of work as the last weeks of her happiness. She ends them with the ardent wish that one day her fine plans and ideas, upon which she is already looking down with pity once more, might change into actions instead of mere useless words. Tossed back and forth from one world to the other, feeling wholly at home in neither, repeatedly failing in her attempts to bring the ethereal world into harmony with the earthly world, more and more "pulled down" into the subterranean world of the tomb, and no longer hoping for rescue by either an earthly-practical or a supermundane love, she is even in her most exuberant moments beset by

---

48 [The significance of the vertical as a kind of measure of human existence is stressed by Binswanger in *Basic Forms*. At this point there appear a number of key terms: *aufsteigen*, to ascend; *absteigen*, to descend; and *abfallen*, to fall off or plummet lifelessly.—TRANSLATORS.]

"pains and spasms." Nowhere does her existence find a loving shelter, nor can it anywhere lay hold of its ground.[49] This means that her existence is threatened by its own nothingness. This being-threatened we call, with Heidegger, dread (*Angst*) or, as the life-history has it, fear and trembling. What existence dreads is being-in-the-world as such. The world in general now has the character of the threatening and the Uncanny. When these feelings of threat and Uncanniness become a dread of something definite, we speak of fear. Ellen's dread of becoming fat would therefore be more correctly designated as a fear of becoming fat; but let us keep to her own expression which corresponds to general language usage, especially as this specific fear actually is an expression of existential dread.

With the dread of becoming fat and the wish to be thin, the cosmological contrast undergoes a further, in fact a final, alteration. From the macrocosm it spreads over to the microcosm, into psychophysical structure. The contrast between light and dark, between rising and descending life, is now enacted in the *Eigenwelt*, without in the least losing thereby its macrocosmological features. The material garb in which this contrast is now clothed is however no longer one of airy atmosphere or vegetation, but is of a psychophysical type. Light and rising life now appear in the garb of an ethereally spiritualized young soul and ethereal young body, whereas the restrictions, dark, and descending life appear in the garb of a spiritless and clumsy soul and a deteriorating, aging body. Of decisive importance at this point, too, is the falling apart of "the world" into two irreconcilable worlds —a bright, light, wide, nonresisting world, the world of the ether, and a dark, massive, heavy, narrow, and resisting world, the world of the earth or the tomb. "The body," in contrast to the "soul," has always been assigned to this latter world; one need only think of how the body is spoken of as the fetter and prison of the soul in Plato's *Phaedo* and in Christian doctrine. In our life-history, however, this "assigning" serves neither a logical system nor a religious dogma but is of an existential nature; corporeality, as the quintessence of the "material" mode of being-in-the-world, related to both matter and desire, is experienced here as heaviness and as prison (resistance), as will be shown even more clearly later on. Apart from the frustrated attempt at making a sport of existence, which we have discussed earlier, corporeality represents the sharpest contrast possible to lightness or ethereal existence. To this extent it represents a veritable challenge to the tendency toward "etherealization."

Added to this is the *Mitwelt* factor of Ellen's identification with her ethereal girl friends and her vexation at their teasing on account of her getting fat. In her girl friends the ethereal world finds its "personal" fulfill-

---

[49] [The German *Grund*, ground, may mean either a foundation or basis, as of a valley, or a logical basis, or the very bottom or heart of something, or the ground of all things in the metaphysical sense.—TRANSLATORS.]

ment, and, conversely, this personal factor contributes on its part to the building up of the ethereal world. To be sure, Ellen's identification with her girl friends is not authentic love, but only infatuation. For to be fat, seen from the angle of the ethereal world (!), always means to be an old or aging, ugly woman, to be thin always means to be a young, attractive, desirable one. It is the latter, however, with whom Ellen West identifies, and vis-à-vis whom she is the seeking, wooing male partner. But let us not further anticipate our analysis.

The dread of becoming fat, which appears in her twentieth year in Sicily, and with which the true illness in the psychiatric sense manifests itself, has thus to be seen anthropologically not as a beginning but as an end. It is the "end" of the encirclement process of the entire existence, so that it is no longer open for its existential possibilities. Now they are definitively fixated upon the rigid existential contrast between light and dark, flowering and withering, thin equaling intellectual [50] and fat equaling the opposite. As Ellen West's own expressions and descriptions so clearly show, existence now gets hemmed in more and more, confined to a steadily diminishing circle of narrowly defined possibilities, for which the wish to be thin and the dread of getting fat represent merely the definitive (psychophysical) garb. The "way" of this life-history is now unmistakably prescribed: it no longer runs into the expanse of the future but moves in a circle. The preponderance of the future is now replaced by the supremacy of the past. All that remains are the fruitless attempts at escaping from this circle, from the ever more clearly experienced and described existential incarceration or imprisonment for which getting-fat is only the definitive guise. That which the existence now flees from and fears has long since drawn it into its net. That the direction of Ellen West's life history no longer points to the future but circles in a present closed off from the future, ruled by the past, and therefore empty, is dramatically expressed in her truly symbolic act in which she keeps circling around her girl friends who have stopped at a scenic point. Ellen West does not walk ahead and then return, since she cannot enjoy the present; nor does she dance in a circle around her companions, which would represent a meaningful movement in the present (E. Straus), but she walks—that is, moves—"as if" she were striding forward and yet she keeps going in a circle all the same. (And all this in the psychological garb of the dread of getting fat!) She offers the picture of a lioness imprisoned in a cage, circling along the bars, vainly looking for an exit. If in place of this picture we want to set down its existential expression, it must read—hell.

To what extent body and soul form for Ellen West an unseparated unit we have already seen in her own expressions. The flowering, thriving, grow-

50 The "ideal of slimness" is, as Ellen West once stated, basically the ideal of "being bodiless."

ing, and the withering, decaying, and moldering, the lightness and the heaviness, the wideness and the narrowness (the tomb), freedom and imprisonment, the flying, walking, and crawling—all these expressions refer equally to her psychophysical and to her bodily existence.

But Ellen herself now emphasizes the intimate connection, indeed oneness, of her self with her body: "My inner self is so closely connected with my body that they form a unity and together constitute my I, my illogical, nervous, individual I." Since she has no inner calm, it becomes torture for her to sit still (for sitting still would be imprisonment, the tomb, death); every nerve in her trembles, her body takes part in all the stirrings of her soul. The experience of this inner unity, this oneness of self and body, must constantly be kept in view; for only from the viewpoint of the inseparability of self and body, which Ellen West so clearly experiences, does it become understandable why the body "participates" so much in the ethereal world, and why the self is so much "involved" in the bodily sphere. The anthropologist [i.e., the psychiatrist or psychologist who takes the science-of-man viewpoint—EDITORS] for whom this inseparability is self-evident, does not see a puzzle or a problem here. It becomes a problem only for those who believe in a separation of body and soul in the religious sense or for those who make this separation for special scientific or theoretical reasons. The fact that corporeality (the body as well as the bodily appetite) assumes such a preponderant role in this existence poses for the anthropologist no psychophysical problem but, as will become increasingly apparent, an existential problem. It is most closely connected with the "supremacy of the past."

That all of Ellen West's dread is a dread of being-in-the-world as such is shown in the fact that she is now in dread of everything, of the dark and the sun, of quiet and of noise. She has reached the lowest rung of the ladder. The "entire" world now has become threatening. The self becomes cowardly; hence her self-contempt. Already Ellen sees herself in the grave, with gray, ashen-pale Distress sitting alongside; the birds are silent and flee, the flowers wither under its ice-cold breath. The world itself becomes a grave. Practical action is no longer tempting, work is replaced by "yawning and apathy." Once again, the only savior from this existence is Death, but now no longer seen as gloomy Sea-King or God-father, but closer to earth, as "the great friend," or a glorious woman "with white asters in her dark hair, large eyes, dream-deep and gray." No matter whether it be man or woman, if only it means "the end." But Ellen cannot even wait for the end! The slow dying off (rusting, withering, languishing, becoming stale and earthy) is hateful to her. Every day she feels herself fatter, which according to her own statement means getting both older and uglier. Here too we find the all-or-nothing principle at work: "If I cannot remain young, beautiful, and thin," we hear in her words, "then rather—Nothingness."

Existence is now constricted and burdened, indeed fettered not only by corporeality but also by the *Mitwelt* and the daily intercourse with it. The resistance of the *Mitwelt* now takes the form of hostile compulsion, even of persecution, and her defiance of the *Mitwelt* becomes hate and contempt. Ellen West shuns nothing so much as compromise. But this is what the *Mitwelt* and the workaday life demand of her; hence both are no longer experienced as mere limitations but as fetters, against which she revolts and from which she tries to free herself in wild insurrection. Such fetters are convention, possession, comfort, gratitude, even love. But behind this Hamlet-like rebellion against the "rotten" society there lurks the dread, indeed the certainty, that her "little world" is softening her, making her into a puppet, and that it will condemn her to mere vegetating. Here the contrast is expressed neither cosmologically nor psychophysically, but purely existentially.[51] If the expressions "rusting" and "languishing" have an existential meaning, this is even more true of "softening," "making-into-a-puppet," and "mere vegetating"; indeed, we are here confronted with an existence characterized by the nonresistance and the passivity of a plaything and by just plain drifting on from day to day.

And yet Ellen West would again like to do something great, to come closer to her proud ideal. Once again everything boils and pounds in her and wants to rend its shell. World revolution, the nihilist's life among the poorest of the poor, is now the goal. Once again we see an attempt at harmonizing the ethereal world ideal with the world of practical action, but in view of the powers available to her this attempt is so high-flown as to make us dizzy. The limits narrowing the ethereal world now assume a definite life-threatening character. Again it is first the *Mitwelt,* the petty workaday life which, with its suffocating atmosphere, chokes off, as do weeds, the flowers of yearning; satiated (that is, "gorged"!) self-satisfaction, egotistical greed,[52] joyless submission, crude indifference (as "the plants which thrive in the sun of the everyday")—all these adders [53] of everyday life coil around her with their cold bodies to press the fighting spirit out of her, to stifle her boiling blood. In fact, she even sees the others as rats which pursue her from their corners with their little eyes. But even this is not enough of the cruel game! Physical threat to life from the air and the animal kingdom now joins, to close the circle from all sides, the moral threat to her conscience from the realm of the spirits. Her high-flown plans and thoughts take the shape of evil, jeering, accusing specters, which close in on all sides, grimly seize her, and snatch at her heart, or of pale hollow-eyed shadows which

51 How much these modes of experiencing and expressing in general alternate with each other and interpenetrate, is shown in "Über Psychotherapie" ("On Psychotherapy"), *Der Nervenarzt,* Vol. 8, 1935.

52 Please note once again the terms originating in similar fashion in the spheres of vegetation and corporeality.

53 Here for the first time the animal world makes its appearance.

follow close on her heels astride bony mares. This personifying of her own thoughts and feelings is accompanied by a further enfeebling of her self. She herself has now become a Nothing, a timid earthworm smitten by the curse surrounded by black night. Accusing, jeering, annihilating, her own thoughts turn against her now cowardly, pitiful self. These are figurative expressions of the restrictions of her existence quite different from those we had previously found! Everything now becomes not only more uncanny, more poisonously threatening, more nocturnal and overpowering, but actually evil. The self now does no more than vegetate like a crawling animal smitten by the curse, like a blind earthworm. The air has meanwhile become still more stifling, the tomb still narrower. "How moldy smells this cellar-hole," we read in a note written by Ellen at this time. "The scent of flowers cannot drown out the odor of rottenness." At the same time we hear of ugly, yellowed souls, of dwarf lungs and dwarf thoughts—which Ellen fights all the more passionately because she knows herself to be encumbered with them. The shapes of degenerating life, the worm-like, vegetative existing under the earth, the yellowing and the moldering decay, the world of nausea, now appear clearly in essential connection with the figures of the threatened conscience, the derision, the annihilating accusation, the curse, with the world of evil or guilt.

It is not surprising but in keeping with the existential encirclement-process of this existence that the material restrictions also become still more massive: they are now walls against which Ellen West beats with her hands (as later she does against her own fat body) until her hands drop powerless. We see here, too, that existential dread isolates the existence and discloses it, in Heidegger's words, as *solus ipse;* even in an exalted mood Ellen is alone, no longer flying in airy heights, but standing, with a frozen heart, on icy peaks.

But still Ellen continues to make attempts, impotent though they are, to stand with both feet firmly on the ground, that is, to work. Now the time comes for her to prepare for her final examination. But whereas previously the world lay before her open and ready to be conquered, now Ellen makes weak concessions; and yet she would have ridiculed anyone who might have predicted this to her. Now she has not only lost some of her former strength, as she herself says, but for the first time (at the age of twenty-three) she has a complete breakdown. At the same time there occurs again an erotic adventure, the unpleasant love affair with the riding instructor.

With the desire to be thin and the dread of becoming fat, however, her corporeality now takes on more and more the leading role in the dramatic "game of the existence with itself" which we are watching here. Again and again we must emphasize that corporeality is not to be confused with the mortal frame [54] or the body in the anatomical and anatomical-physiological

[54] [*Leib;* see Note 43.—TRANSLATORS.]

sense, but that this expression is always to be understood existentially, that is, as bodily existing or existing-in-the-body, as we have repeatedly described it.[55] Much as the self, in the case of Ellen West, is threatened (to be strangled, poisoned, cursed), encircled, and enfeebled by the *Umwelt*, the *Mitwelt*, and the *Eigenwelt* of thoughts, there do not arise "allopsychic" [56] hypochondriacal delusions, nor ideas of reference and delusions of persecution, nor the delusion of having sinned. Even in the sphere of corporeality the imprisonment and dispowerment of the self does not lead to a ("somatopsychic") [56] insanity. (Whether it might have led to this state if the life had lasted longer, we shall leave undecided for now.) Nevertheless, the imprisonment of the self takes on such great proportions that the restrictions coming from the other "worlds," much as they fortify, deepen, and "autonomize" themselves, subside by comparison.

We note from her twenty-fifth year that along with the dread of getting fat goes an increased urge for sweets, such as seems to have existed in early childhood, even at that time probably opposed by a tendency to ascetic self-denial. Here, too, the existential maturing in the sense of authentic self-realization (*Selbstigung*) determined by the future, is replaced by the supremacy of the past, the movement in a circle, and the existential standstill. It may also be interpreted as a "regressive" trait that Ellen derives no satisfaction from eating in the presence of others, but only from eating alone. Aside from this, she can no longer be alone at all and must always have her old nursemaid with her. For the rest, the desire for sweets is especially strong when being with others has made her tired and nervous. That this being with others makes her tired and nervous is easily understood from what we know of her rebellion against the restrictions and burdens, caused by her everyday intercourse with others, her "little world." But it is important that now she cannot recover from this burden and oppression by means of self-analysis, work or athletics, but only through—eating!

Along with the great conflict between the increased urge to eat and the dread of becoming fat, the contrast between life in the ethereal world and in the world of the earth (which is also the world of being-fat) continues. Ellen does not want to live as the worm lives in the earth, old, ugly, dumb, and dull—in a word fat. She would rather die as the bird dies who bursts his throat with supreme jubilation, or she would rather wildly consume herself in her own fire. What is new here is that the longing for death flashes up out of the ethereal world itself. The existential exultation itself, the festive existential joy, the "existential fire" are placed in the service of death,

55 Cf. "Über Psychotherapie" and *Basic Forms*.
56 [This term is from Wernicke, *Grundriss der Psychiatrie (Basic Outline of Psychiatry)* (1900) in which he classified all mental diseases as: allopsychic, with disorientation in regard to the outer world; autopsychic, with disorder in the representation of one's own individuality; somatopsychic, with disorder in the representation of one's own body.—TRANSLATORS.]

are indeed expressive of the longing for death. Already death is longed for here as the highest completion of festive existence. The poem which expresses this falls into a period which Ellen, again, calls one of the happiest of her life. She has, to be sure, given up working for the final examination and instead taken a teacher's examination and become engaged to the blond student. This engagement represents the last, most serious, and most prolonged attempt at harmonizing the ethereal world with the world on the earth by way of male-female sexual love.

During and after this engagement her cousin and she become closer: there follows a long vacillation on her part between the two suitors, the blond beloved who is part of the ethereal world and the other who stands with both feet firmly on the ground, the future husband engaged in the practice of a responsible profession, the hoped-for father of her children.

Life on the earth [57] wins out once again. Ellen longs for fertility in the manner of the fertile, grain-bearing earth and bitterly laments her unfruitfulness. In this lament she no longer degrades herself to the worm, which is after all a living thing, but to lifeless, worthless material: she is nothing more than discarded husk, cracked, useless, worthless. Just as she hates the small world of the everyday, the everyday intercourse with the *Mitwelt*, so she now hates her body too and beats it with her fist.

We see that what Ellen West hates is all the restrictions of her emotionally untamed, desperate, defiant self, everything that limits it, threatens it, opposes its dominance. And at the same time all these restrictions are what she dreads! The corporeal restriction, that is, the one built up out of the bodily sphere of the *Eigenwelt*, seems to have attained such surpassing importance in the total existential transformation of the existence into dread, hate, and despair, only because the existence was threatened from its ground by its "earth-heaviness," by its bodily-sensual, earthbound greed.

True, this existence builds for itself a sky-castle in the ethereal world, but we can trace precisely how this airy structure is more and more pulled down into the earth and, indeed, by greed—that is, transformed into a tomb or a grave. The spacious rooms of the sky-castle become a narrow dungeon, the thin, movable walls become impenetrable, thick masonry. The most impenetrable wall, however, is the fat body which has greedily gorged itself to the full, indeed, in the final analysis, corporeality in general. (Cf. her own equating of being thin with bodilessness.) Hence the most passionate hatred is directed at the body; only in relation to the body does dread turn into panic. The (fat) body is the first and last bulwark of desires, and on this bulwark not only the ethereal world but the existence itself founders in despair; for the mightier the existential restriction, the more impotent the attempts to disengage oneself from them. The early harsh severance of

[57] As we see, earth has two contrasting meanings for Ellen West: here the (less common) meaning of Mother Earth, whereas usually it is the meaning of stale, dead earthliness.

the *Eigenwelt* from *Um-* and *Mitwelt* now "exacts vengeance" throughout her whole existence. Naturally, one cannot here speak of guilt [58] in the moral sense. The existence as such—in the metaphysical sense—is guilty, and indeed in this case to a greater degree than in many others: it is more in arrears to itself than to others.

It is not necessary to recapitulate here all the tricks and stratagems Ellen West used in her struggle against getting fat. Let it only be pointed out that more and more these tactics replace practical action in the sense of work and become the real sphere of her practical action, as exhausting as it is fruitless. Everything goes into the dread of becoming fat, everything that Ellen West sees as merely greed-bound or purely vegetating life participates in this dread of becoming fat—the becoming old-ugly-stupid-dull as well as the becoming-different from her ethereal girl friends. (In the latter respect we can call this dread a dread of the decline from her virginal or Artemis ideal.)

We have already shown why everything here ends in dread and not in mere disappointment or fearing. For dread is the inevitable result only when the existence has "at bottom" become prey to or been seized by that of which it is afraid. In the case of this existence, the fact of being seized as well as that which does the seizing has been discernible from the very beginning. First it was evident in atmospheric darkening, then in the form of plant-vegetative withering or moldering, then in the form of poisonous animals and evil spirits, and in addition at times in the form of purely material restrictions such as net, fetters, and walls. In all this, the existence has merely shown more plainly and obtrusively by what it was enslaved from its ground: mere greed, which means existential emptiness and existential pressure, the existential being-hollow or being-a-hole, being delimited, or being constricted—in a word, being-a-tomb. It is the being of the worm in swampy earth. Against this threat to the existence from its ground—a threat which develops in scope from the atmospheric darkening to the swamping, from the shroud of fog to the wall, from the narrowing of the horizon to the tomb or the hole, from the exulting bird ascending into the ether to the worm crawling in moist earth, from the virginally flourishing Artemis to the hollow-eyed, pale specter—against this threat the existence defends itself by its flight into ever dizzier ethereal regions. The heaviness and the pressure of the descending life, of the greed which consumes all life, are stronger however than the "buoyancy" of the ascending life, of the flowering, growing ripening. The dread of becoming fat is actually only one especially prominent feature in this deformation of the entire existence, but in no way something isolated or independent. The urge to eat is only a special trait of that long-foreshadowed enslavement or movement-in-a-circle of the entire existence. Because of the dread of and the fight against

---

[58] [*Schuld* means both *guilt* and *debt*, and therefore the word as used here must be understood as including both senses.—TRANSLATORS.]

this metamorphosis of the entire existence, there emerges the dread of, and battle against, the particular metamorphosis of the flourishing, elastic, slim young body to a rotting morass and finally to a mere hole, and against the transformation of her bodily shell from a delicate covering to a thick fat-layer, indeed, a wall against which one can beat one's fists.

The more immediately the enslavement to the heavy swamp-world comes to light, the more imperatively this world announces itself, the greater is the dread of it. The increasing immediacy and independence of this world now show in the fact that the desire for food which pertains to it grows to a burdensome pressure, to a frantic greed, indeed greed just for fattening foods like sweets. Mere vegetating becomes animalization, "bestial" greed. The ethereal world loses more and more the leading role in this existence, it is forced out of the offensive into the defensive. The heavy world draws the existence more and more under its spell: greed is joined by the constant pressure to think of eating, the "compulsive thinking." Even though from a psychiatric point of view we are dealing here with something new, with the appearance of a new symptom, there is little reason to consider it something new anthropologically. The "fabulous, sweet land of life," the ethereal world, the oasis in the desert, which Ellen herself says she created for herself, emerges now only intermittently on the horizon, as a quickly disappearing Fata Morgana; the dullness of the world more and more narrows down to bodily dullness, the dread increases to panic. To her the thought of pancakes is the most terrible thought there is. Ellen longs for Nirvana, which is the extinction of the desire for her ideal, the extinction of her hatred for the *Umwelt* which wants to make this ideal unattainable for her, for the extinction of the delusion of finding in this ideal something worth striving for. Thus the ethereal world faces capitulation. Simultaneously there arise the wish (which quickly disappears again) to lay her head on her mother's breast and the dread of the grave and serious demeanor of her father. Both the return to her mother, as the ground of life, and to her father, as the spiritual ground "reigning behind the clouds," is cut off. Severe states of dread and agitation, and attempts at suicide ensue.

In the medical clinic Ellen gains the insight, probably furthered by her psychoanalysis, that it was not the dread of getting fat but the constant desire for food, the gluttony, which was the primary factor in her "obsessional neurosis." Of the gluttony she says, "it fell upon me like an animal"; Ellen is defenselessly exposed to it and is driven to despair by it. (Anthropologically there can never be a differentiation between primary and secondary, for this manner of speaking is possible only in the realm of objectification. What is here quite correctly designated as primary or as a primary symptom, is for us an expression of the metamorphosis of the entire existence, the unfolding of an entire world and an entire way of existence.)

The horrible feeling of emptiness, which we already know from Ellen's girlhood, is now more precisely described as a feeling of "being discontented," that is, as the nonagreement of ideal and reality. We are no longer surprised to hear that this feeling appears just after meals, for eating has long since ceased to be an uncomplicated matter to Ellen: it means the "compulsion" to fill the hole, the belly, and to become fat, the enforced renunciation, that is, of the ethereal ideal, and the most cowardly concession to the supremacy of the dull, oppressive, and restricted world of the swamp. This "indescribably wretched" feeling (of discontent and of dread) is also felt by Ellen in strong bodily sensations: her heart sinks, there is a pain in it, it pounds so hard that she becomes dizzy; she feels hot and cold with dread. Her whole body is covered with sweat, all her limbs ache as though she had been whipped; she feels beaten, and completely exhausted. At the same time it is only an apparent paradox that precisely a full stomach increases her feeling of emptiness. The physical being-full and being-round, which is a partial phenomenon, representing the dull world of the morass and the tomb, of withering away, of glutted vegetating and rotting, of evil and of guilt, is, when seen from the ethereal world, the (experienced) quintessence of (spiritual) emptiness. The hungry greed for eating, the bestial hunger during which she can no longer see anything clearly, and the dread of becoming fat form a noose from which the existence can no longer disentangle itself. Each meal becomes a torment. Ellen runs away from the bread in the cupboard and wanders aimlessly about. And yet, because of the enslavement of her existence to the dull world, she can numb her torturing unrest solely by eating, only to be doubly unhappy after the meal. The circle is closed.

For this "being encircled" Ellen finds extremely eloquent similes: that of the prison camp in Siberia, that of the stage "whose exits are all blocked by armed men from whom she must retreat back to the stage," and, the profoundest of all, the simile of the murderer who constantly sees the image of his victim before his mind's eye and is drawn back overpoweringly to the scene of the murder which makes him shudder. The picture of the murdered victim is the picture of Ellen's murdered existence; the scene of the murder which makes her shudder is the meal. Her being drawn to food, which is stronger than reason and will, and which rules her life and makes it a fearful scene of desolation, stands for her gluttony. Nowhere did she express her way of existence better and more profoundly than in this metaphor. As does the murderer, so Ellen feels herself excluded from all real life, removed from people, totally isolated.

The place of her previous expressions for being put into a hole is now taken by the glass ball and glass wall through which she sees the people for whom she "longs unspeakably," the glass wall against which she hits her hands when she holds them out to people and through which their voices come to her muffled. But then, again, she describes the encirclement of her existence in purely anthropological terms: "Since I did everything only from the viewpoint of whether things made me thin or fat, all things soon lost their intrinsic meaning. So did work." (Cf. "History of a Neurosis.") Ellen speaks here also of the dread (which at first appeared only as a faint intimation) of her having become the slave of an uncanny power which threatened to destroy her life, of the dread that all her inner development was ceasing, all becoming and growing was suffocating, because a single idea was filling her entire soul. The "obsession" of always having to think about food pursues her like an evil spirit from which she can nowhere find escape, pursues her as the Furies pursue the murderer (again a simile of murder). This obsession turns her world into a caricature, her life into a vain, tortured tilting against windmills, into a hell. Since the time when she buried herself in herself and could no longer love, everything is gray (senseless); all striving and achievement is a dark, heavy, fearful nightmare. She is caught in a net in which she gets more and more entangled and whose meshes pull together tighter and tighter about her. Her heart is frozen, all around her is solitude and cold: "If you love me, grant me death!"

And yet, shortly before this, Ellen had once again believed she could be saved from disintegrating. She felt in her breast something sweet which wanted to grow and develop. At the same time Ellen reveals that she not only divines but knows what love is; she describes her love as more serious and quieter, more sacred and more impregnable than earlier. For the first time she wants to ripen toward life; once again she opens her arms to life and not to death. The possibilities of the truly singular or authentically existential and of the truly dual and authentically loving mode of existence are still open even to this *Dasein,* if only for swiftly passing moments.

But a further surprise is in store for us. Even though the entire world picture (in Ellen's own words) is disarranged in her mind, and the evil spirit turns all that is simple and natural into a caricature, a distorted picture, Ellen now does realize that becoming fat is part of what is natural; she equates it with becoming healthy, with getting-round-red-cheeks, with becoming a simple, robust woman, as would correspond to her true nature. We see that her insight into her existence does not lessen toward the end, but increases. With her confinement increasing, Ellen is more and more able to rise above herself and to reach true insight into her loving and existential conditions of being, as well as into her "natural" ones. But "something in her rebels" against this insight; it is, of course, the ethereal or Artemis ideal which no more tolerates the round, red cheeks and the womanly robustness, than becoming fat. All the greater becomes the torture, the hellishness of her existence; for so much the stronger is the effect of the contradiction of her imprisonment, her being tossed back and forth between an "un-natural" ideal and an "over-natural" greed.

The second analyst used the expression that for Ellen slim "meant" the higher intellectual type, fat the bourgeois Jewish type. As to the word "mean," however, we cannot possibly accept a symbolic meaning, a representation by a symbol; but, as we have seen, only the fact that Ellen's dread of becoming fat, as well as her dread of the parental milieu and of the petty world of the everyday life are, equally, an expression of her dread of the narrowing and "swamping" of her existence. Therefore, one dread does not "mean" the other, but both are "on the same plane," that is, "next to each other" in the same existential metamorphosis. We shall come back to this in the next section. In contrast to the fat bourgeois Jewish type, the wife of the blond esthetic brother, with whom identification is naturally easy, is as mentioned above slim, blond, and artistically oriented.

In the institution Ellen already has the feeling of being like a corpse among people. That she, who previously believed herself so independent of the opinions of others, should now completely depend on what the others think about her looks and her being fat, is another expression of her imprisonment. Stubbornness and defiance are revealed here not as independence of the others, but, as pointed out above, as merely a special type of dependence on them, their integration into the *Eigenwelt*. For the rest, Ellen now feels herself quite passively to be the battlefield on which opposing forces are mangling each other. She can only be a helpless onlooker at this spectacle. Thus her existence has really become a stage. But whereas in the "healthy person" existence unfolds itself more or less evenly among stage actors ("roles"), director, and spectators, here it is dichotomized into stage and events on the stage, on the one hand, and "passive" viewing on the other. Accordingly, the verbal expressions for her mode of existence are all the more strongly reified, and at the same time "personified." "Melancholy" lies on her life like a black bird which stalks her in order to pounce upon and kill her. "Madness" shakes its black locks, seizes her, and hurls her into the yawning abyss. Death gains such a power over her that at the news of the death of a girl friend her eyes shine, while the world darkens before her.

In covertly watching Ellen while she eats one observes that she actually throws herself on the food "like an animal" and also gobbles it down "like an animal."

As far as the few available dreams are concerned, they all deal with eating or death, or death and eating. The first death dream repeats, though in less heroic form, the theme of death on the battlefield which we know from one of her earliest poems; at the same time it seems to anticipate an actual happening, her being able to eat a fattening dish quietly in the face of approaching death, and her joy over this. As regards this "anticipation," however, one need think neither of a "prospective tendency" in Mäder's sense, nor of a "clairvoyant" quality of the dream; rather, the dream and its later fulfillment in reality are only the expression of one and the same anthropological fact, namely, the intertwined, inner connectedness of the motif of gluttony and death. For in this existence, gluttony as such means descending life, dying. We saw that the dread of becoming fat could be more and more clearly understood as the dread of being "holed-up." But once the existence has resolved upon death, then it has overcome the dread and burden of earthly things; the urge for sweets has lost its fearfulness and can again become enjoyment.

The second (painter-) dream follows the first one in creating—this time more inventively—a social situation which can motivate the double suicide of the married couple. (Actually, of course, the reverse is true: the death wish calls forth the dream situation.) The thought of a joint departure from life was familiar to Ellen in her waking hours too. The dream also repeats the reproach of cowardice made to her husband when awake.

The fourth dream mirrors without falsification the reality of her torment and her wish for death. She wants to set fire to herself, a wish in which psychoanalysis, as is well known, sees a libido symbol, just as Ellen herself once wants to consume herself wildly in the fire of love's ardor.

Although these dreams reflect quite openly the leitmotifs of the waking existence, as is so frequently the case with schizophrenics, the third dream (leap through a porthole into the water, attempts at resuscitation, eating of chocolate candy, and packing of trunks) requires a special discussion. In order not to hold up too much the progress of the investigation, we shall save the discussion of this dream for the section entitled "Existential Analysis and Psychoanalysis."

The Death

In view of the fact that the existential *Gestalt* to which we have given the name Ellen West "makes an end" of its existence, the existential analysis must more than ever suspend any judgment derived from any standpoints or points of view, be they ethical or religious, psychiatric-medical or psychoanalytic explanations or psychological interpretations based on motives. But also the "dignity-of-life" viewpoint held by the "healthy common sense" which looks down with pity or horror upon anyone "to whom dying happens," and especially on one who brings about his own death, is no criterion here. We must neither tolerate nor disapprove of the suicide of Ellen West, nor trivialize it with medical or psychoanalytic explanations, nor dramatize it with ethical or religious judgments. Indeed, the statement by Jeremias Gotthelf applies well to an existential totality such as Ellen West: "Think how dark life becomes when a poor human wants to be his own sun"; or the dictum of Kierkegaard: "However low a man has sunk, he can sink even lower, and this 'can' is the object of his dread." But this growing dark and this sinking must not be understood by existential analysis by

way of religion or ethics, but must be viewed and described anthropologically. This is not possible from any *one* perspective, however close to our
heart, however familiar to our understanding, however in keeping with our
reason; for, as Paul Valéry says, "Every time that we accuse and judge, we
have not reached the ground." The ground—since it remains a secret to
every human eye—is, to be sure, not *attained,* but it is grasped in imagination
whenever the human being steps out of the perspective of judgment, con-
demnation, or even acquittal, that is, out of the plural mode of existence.
The ground must be grasped prior to any subject-object dichotomy. But
this is only possible in the freedom from presumptions [59] of the dual mode,
through the uniting of the I and the Thou in the dual We. And this means
in the uniting of the human existence with the common ground which I
and Thou share and the anthropological formation emerging therefrom.

In this unitedness we also stand prior to the dichotomy which determines
our intercourse with ourself, the intercourse of society with the individual
and of the individual with society, and last but not least also rules "the
judgment of history." This union is also prior to the dichotomy between
freedom and necessity, guilt and destiny (fate), or, in psychological reductive
terms, the dichotomy of activity and passivity, of acting and suffering; for
the existence in its common ground encompasses both. As in the eyes of
love "all is possible," so too in the eyes of love "all is necessary." In other
words, love knows no answer to the question of whether Ellen West's suicide had to take place "of fateful necessity" or whether she had the possibility of escaping it. Instead of raising the question of fate or guilt in the face
of suicide, and trying to decide this question, love attempts "to get to the
ground of existence" and from this ground to understand the existence
anthropologically.

If Ellen West judged every food from the standpoint of whether or not
it was fattening, she also viewed eating from the point of view of guilt.
"*The man who eats,*" says Socrates in a work by Valéry,[60] "*nourishes both
good and bad in his body. Every bite which he feels melting and spreading
in himself will bring new force to his own virtue, just as it does to his own
vices. It sustains his turmoils as it fattens his hopes, and it divides somewhere between passion and reason. Love needs it as well as hatred; and my
joy and my bitterness, my memory and my plans, share as brothers the same
substance of the bite. . . .*" Basically, Ellen West nourishes by her eating
only "*her bad points and her vices, her turmoil and hatred, her passions
and her bitterness.*" On only one occasion do we see her eat something
which, in contradistinction to all nourishment, only gives her joy, only gives
her new strength, only "nourishes" her hopes, only serves her love, and only

---

59 [*Voraussetzungslosigkeit*—literally, a complete lack of premise or prejudice.—TRANS-
LATORS.]
60 *L'Âme et la danse (The Soul and the Dance).*

brightens her mind. But this something is no longer a gift of life but the poison of death.[61] As she becomes ever clearer about her existence, the closer she knows she is to death (let me remind the reader of the painful awakening of her knowledge of true love and true naturalness, as well as her increasingly profound similes) and the greater the clarity she achieves in the face of death.

To live in the face of death, however, means "to die unto death," as Kierkegaard says; or to die one's own death, as Rilke and Scheler express it. That every passing away, every dying, whether self-chosen death or not, is still an "autonomous act" of life has already been expressed by Goethe.[62] As he said of Raphael or Kepler, "both of them suddenly put an end to their lives," but in saying so he meant their involuntary death, coming to them "from the outside" "as external fate," so we may conversely designate Ellen West's self-caused death as a passing away or dying. Who will say where in this case guilt begins and "fate" ends?

That life and death are not opposites, that death too must be lived, and that life is "encompassed" by death, so that both from a biological and a historical point of view the saying holds true that the human being dies in every moment of his existence—this insight was in a certain sense familiar even to Heraclitus. Indeed, for Heraclitus, Hades, the god of the Underworld, and Dionysos, the god of the wildest intoxication of Life, "for whom everyone rages and raves," are one and the same.[63] Ellen West too would like to die "as the bird dies which bursts its throat in supreme joy."

As indispensable as all these insights are, they are not yet sufficient for the existential-analytical understanding of the fact that on the one hand "the intuitive death-certainty" (Scheler),[64] "the idea of death," as Ellen West's old nursemaid had noticed, "overshadowed her entire life," but that on the other hand her knowledge of the immediate proximity of death brightens her life. For Ellen West, in the vital exuberance of her longing for death, could have said, with Shakespeare's Claudio, "Striving for life, I seek death; seeking death, I find life." [65]

Existential analysis cannot be content with the psychological judgment that the suicide of Ellen West is to be explained by the motive of her suffer-

---

[61] [The German word *Gift* has the common meaning of *poison* and the less common meaning of *gift.*—TRANSLATORS.]

[62] Cf. "The conversation with Falk of January 25, 1813." [Binswanger means to emphasize here that death is an active part of life whether one dies voluntarily (by suicide) *or* involuntarily.—EDITORS.]

[63] Cf. Diels, "Fragment 15"—As is well known, this contrast already exists in Dionysos himself and in the great Dionysian revels. Dionysos is on the one hand the nourishing, inebriating donor of wine, the soother of mourning and sorrows, the liberator and healer, the delight of mortals, the joyful, the dancer, the ecstatic lover, but on the other hand he also belongs to the sphere of annihilation, of cruelty, of eternal night: Walter F. Otto, "Dionysos."

[64] Cf. "Tod und Fortleben" ("Death and Life after Death"). *Posthumous Papers:* I.

[65] [*Measure for Measure*, Act III, Scene 1.—TRANSLATORS.]

ing of torture and the wish arising therefrom to end this torture; nor can we be satisfied with the judgment that her festive mood in the face of death is to be explained by the motive of her anticipating the certain end of this torture and the joy over this end. These judgments fall back on the motive as a final basis for explanation, whereas for existential analysis the motives too are still problems. For us it remains a problem how to understand that these motives become effective, in other words, how they could become motives at all.

From the standpoint of existential analysis the suicide of Ellen West was an "arbitrary act" as well as a "necessary event." Both statements are based on the fact that the existence in the case of Ellen West had become ripe for its death, in other words, that the death, this death, was the necessary fulfillment of the life-meaning of this existence. This can be demonstrated by existential analysis, but conclusive evidence calls for insight into the kind of temporality which this existence engendered. For the moment, we shall only summarize this matter of her temporality as follows.

When we said that in the case of Ellen West the existence was ruled more by the past, when we spoke of a "supremacy of the past," we meant to include the existence being encircled in a bare, empty present and its being cut off from the future. Such an existence however is robbed of its authentic life-meaning, of its existential ripening, which is always and only determined by the future. The past, "weighing down" the existence, deprives it of every view into the future. This is the existential meaning of Ellen's continued complaints that she is caught in a noose, that all exits are blocked to her, that she is moldering, locked in a dungeon, buried and walled into a tomb. But where the past, the lived life, has become overpowering, where the life which is yet to be lived is ruled by the past, we speak of old age. As a young woman Ellen West had already become old. The life-meaning of this *Dasein* had already been fulfilled "in early years," in accordance with the stormy life-tempo and the circular life-movement of this existence, in which the *Dasein* had soon "run idle." [66] Existential aging had hurried ahead of biological aging, just as the existential death, the "being-a-corpse among people," had hurried ahead of the biological end of life. The suicide is the necessary-voluntary consequence of this existential state of things. And just as we can only speak of the gladness of old age as the "most intimate and sweetest anticipatory relish of death" when the existence is ripening toward its death, so too in the face of self-induced death only gladness and a festive mood can reign when death falls like a ripe fruit into the lap of the existence. And just as old age, ripening toward death, separating itself more and more from the needs of life, becomes more and more perceptive of the pure essence of the world and of existence, so also in the case of Ellen West the existence freed itself in the face of death from the spell of greed,

66 [The German *leerlaufen* refers to an engine racing in neutral.—TRANSLATORS.]

from the compulsion of the hunger which again and again had "pounced on her like a wild animal." In the face of death, for the first time she can again eat harmlessly; indeed, all problems and all guilt fall away from her. She reads lyric poems and relishes the humor of Mark Twain. That this feast of existence is a farewell feast can in no way seriously dampen her festive mood. She takes leave of her husband in walking together and in reading together, she takes leave of her doctors with final greetings, and in her last letter she takes leave of her last ethereal woman friend.

The existential-analytic fact that the intuitive certainty of death, the life-immanent death (Von Gebsattel) appears as a shadow over life, whereas the nearness of the life-transcendent death shows itself as brightness, indeed as festive joy of existence, must also be understood in the light of what death as such means to this existence. Indeed, the fact of suicide itself must be understood in this light. To Ellen West, disciple of Niels Lyhne and complete nihilist, death meant the absolute Nothingness—that is, not only the negation but the absolute annihilation of existence. True, we saw that in this existence death repeatedly took on a subordinate meaning of erotism; as in the wanting-to-be-kissed-dead by the gloomy, cold Sea-King, in the wanting-to-be-raised-up by the God-father enthroned above the clouds, and in the death-images of "the great friend" and the beautiful woman with the dream-deep eyes. But nowhere do we find an indication, let alone a proof, of the fact that death-erotism constituted an impelling motive of her suicide or even of her feeling of happiness in the face of death. On the contrary, with the letter to her last ethereal woman friend Ellen West takes leave of erotism just as she takes leave of everything. We must not forget that the carrying-out of the suicide means the last practical act of this existence-*Gestalt* and that it stems from the world of action, deliberation, and planning, and not from the ethereal world of phantasies and wishes. And although we know that "behind" rational motives emotional wishes very frequently "hide," still her very leave-taking shows us that it meant for Ellen a "parting forever," as corresponds not only to her skeptical but to her nihilistic *Weltanschauung*. We have no evidence for, but only against, her faith in any kind of continuation of life after death; indeed, against even an "ethereal wish" for such a continuation. We must realize that for Ellen West everything stops with death, the practical as well as the ethereal and the tomb-world. And only because she stands face to face with the absolute Nothingness can all (always relative) problems, all contradictions between her worlds disappear and her existence once again become a pure celebration. But in contrast to the festive joy of existence as such, which originates in existential fullness and is kindled on the beauty of existence as the primal ground of all art, in Ellen West it originates in the face of Nothingness and is kindled on the Nothingness. Herein we recognize the tremendous positiveness which can inhere in Nothingness in a human existence. When this is the case, as with Ellen West, the life-history becomes a death-history to a special degree, and we rightly speak of an existence consecrated to death.

The positiveness of the Nothingness has a very specific existential meaning: when the existence bases itself on or rests upon Nothingness (here again we are beyond guilt and fate) it stands not only in existential dread but, also—which is the same thing—in absolute isolation. The positiveness of Nothingness, and an existence in the sense of being a complete isolate, represent existential-analytically one and the same thing. Ellen West died her death not only not as an individual "alone before God," as the religious individual dies it, that is, in religious We-ness, not only not in the We-ness of earthly loving encounter, and not even in communication with "the others," but, after parting from the others, alone before Nothingness. From here a metaphysical shadow also falls on her gladness in the face of Nothingness.

The truth of the assertion that the way in which a person dies shows how he has lived is demonstrated with special clarity in the case of Ellen West. In her death we perceive with especial impressiveness the existential meaning, or more accurately, contra-meaning, of her life. This meaning was not that of being herself, but rather that of being *not* herself. If we wish to speak of a foundering of this existence, then this is what it foundered on. What the psychoanalyst explains as the "rebirth-phantasy" (and this has implications for the understanding of the suicide) is for us something quite different. When Ellen West states that fate has wanted her to be fat and robust, but she herself wants to be thin and delicate, and when she asks the Creator: "Create me once again but create me differently," she reveals that throughout her entire life she has suffered from that sickness of the mind which Kierkegaard, with the keen insight of a genius, described and illuminated from all possible aspects under the name of "Sickness Unto Death." I know of no document which could more greatly advance the existential-analytic interpretation of schizophrenia. One might say that in this document Kierkegaard has recognized with intuitive genius the approach of schizophrenia; for at the root of so many "cases" of schizophrenia can be found the "desperate" wish—indeed, the unshakable command to one's *Eigenwelt, Mitwelt,* and "fate"—*not* to be oneself, as also can be found its counterpart, the desperate wish to *be* oneself.[67] Even the physician of the soul who does not concur in the purely religious conception and interpretation of this "illness," who does not regard "the self" as eternal in the religious sense, does not believe in the religious sense in the power which posited it, who does not see in the human being a synthesis of the

[67] Every psychiatrist will recall a very great number of cases in which the patients are dissatisfied with their "fate," for instance because it did not make them man or woman, because it gave them these parents and not others, and because it endowed them with this nose, this face, this forehead, this stature, this character, this temperament, etc., and not another, because it made them grow up in this country, in this class, in this milieu and not in another. Still more frequently are we confronted with the complementary attitude of someone desperately trying to be one-self, *viz.*, this one and no other.

temporal and the eternal in the religious sense, but rather conceives existentially of despair in the sense of the sickness unto death—even such a physician, too, is deeply indebted to this work of Kierkegaard. That the self can only found itself "with a view to the power which posited it" is a truth which ontological *Daseinsanalytic* recognizes as much as does anthropological existential analysis, quite apart from how they define this power, this existential ground. That Ellen West on the other hand wants from her earliest youth on, "defiantly and stubbornly," "just to be herself," is no evidence against her desperate "not-wanting-to-be-herself" but rather evidence for it. For the one type of desperation is inextricably tied to the other; indeed, as Kierkegaard showed, the two can be traced back to each other.

Desperately not wanting to be oneself but "different," which can only mean "someone different," and desperately wanting to be oneself—such desperation clearly has a special relationship to Death. When the torture of the despair consists precisely in this, that one cannot die, that even the last hope, death, does not come, that one cannot get rid of oneself, then suicide, as in our case, and with it the Nothingness, take on a "desperately" positive meaning. The despair that death does not come "of itself" into her existence is transformed by Ellen West's suicide into the celebration of its self-induced entrance into her existence. This entrance is festive not only because death comes as a friend, and because freedom and liberation from the fetters of life come in its train, but also for the much deeper reason that in the voluntary-necessary resolve for death the existence is no longer "desperately itself" but has authentically and totally become itself! *Authentically* I am myself, or I *exist authentically* when I decisively resolve the situation in acting, in other words, where present and having-been unite in an *authentic* present. In contrast to the "affect"-laden short circuit reactions of her earlier suicidal attempts, this suicide was "premeditated," resolved upon after mature consideration. In this resolve Ellen West did not "grow beyond herself," but rather, only in her decision for death did she find herself and choose herself. The festival of death was the festival of the birth of her existence. But where the existence can exist only by relinquishing life, there the existence is a tragic existence.[68]

Time

Ellen West's desperate defiance in wishing to be herself, but as a different being from the one into which she had actually been thrown from the ground of her existence, shows itself not only in revolt and battle against her fate (her being-a-woman, her home, her social class, her desire for sweets, her tendency to get fat, and finally her illness) but also in revolt and battle

[68] The fact that with all this the problem of the joy of existence in the face of death has not been exhausted may be seen by reference to later passages.

against time. Insofar as she refuses to become old, dull, and ugly, in a word, fat, she wants to stop time, or, as the saying goes, refuses to "pay her tribute" to time. In her stubborn adherence to her separate self (this becomes transparent to her only toward the end of her life) which is however not her real self but a "timeless" ethereal wish-self, she does not run away from the ground of her existence—no one can do that—but runs into it, as into an abyss.[69] Man can no more escape from his ground than he can escape from his fate. But when, as in the life of Ellen West, we observe such a plain circular movement of the existence away from its ground and back into it as into an abyss, then the existence exists in the mode of dread. The place of authentic maturing in the sense of becoming oneself, of the self-possessing of the ground, and, even more so, the place of the dual We, is taken "of necessity" by the Self- and We-destruction, or the reversal of becoming (*Entwerden*, Von Gebsattel), or "sinking" (Kirkegaard). However all is not said with this statement. For a better understanding of the patients entrusted to us it will have to be our task more and more to observe the material or elemental garb in which such a process of destruction or sinking takes place and what forms it shows as it takes its course.

There are very different kinds of such "elemental" processes of being and metamorphosis of human existence. They all take place in the elemental primal forms of the air (the light and the sky), of water, of fire, and of the earth,[70] manifold as their individual existential meaning and their existential relationships among each other may be. It is, however, of the greatest existential-analytical importance to realize that these arch forms and their metamorphic shapes are forms of temporalization.[71] The "momentarily rising" metamorphic form from the earth to the sky, for example, we know in the garb of the flame. *"But what is the flame, O my friends, if it is not the moment itself! What is foolish and happy and tremendous in the very instant! . . . Flame is the act of this moment which is between earth and sky. O my friends, everything that passes from heavy state to subtile state passes through the moment of fire and light. . . . And flame, is it not also the intangible and proud form of most noble destruction?—What will never happen again happens magnificently before our very eyes!"* [72] By contrast with this example, the elemental and the temporal structure of existence in the case of Ellen West becomes particularly clear. The "destructive" element here is not the "momentarily" flashing up and quickly disappearing

---

69 [*Abgrund*, a fathomless depth, as the absence of *Grund*; see Note 49.—TRANSLATORS.]

70 Cf. in this connection L. Binswanger, "Traum und Existenz" ("Dream and Existence") *Schweiz. Rdsch.*, 1930, and *Über Ideenflucht*; C. G. Jung, *Wandlungen und Symbole der Libido* (*Metamorphoses and Symbols of Libido*); Michelet, *La Mer* (*The Sea*); and in particular Bachelard's recent *La Psychoanalyse du feu* (*Psychoanalysis of Fire*) and *L'Eau et les rêves* (*Water and Dreams*).

71 Cf. Emil Staiger, "Die Zeit als Einbildungskraft des Dichters" ("Time as Imaginative Power of the Poet"). (The rushing time represented by flux, the resting time represented by permeating light.)

72 Paul Valéry, "L'Ame et la danse" ("The Soul and the Dance").

flame, which rises from the earth to the sky (*from heavy state to subtle state*), but the gradually darkening, slowly settling or consolidating rotting or being made into earth,—passing from *the subtle state* to *the heavy state*, sinking down from sky to earth. As we have seen, Ellen West's existence moves "between heaven and earth," but with a clearly descending tendency, not between earth and fire, earth and water. Only twice does fire appear in the case history, as wildly consuming flame of passion and as "suicidal phantasy" (Dream No. 4); thus, both instances in the time-garb of the "momentary." The innumerable shapes of water manifested themselves as the eternal sea, now as the abode of the gloomy, cold Sea-King who is to kiss her dead, now, as in the third dream, as the direct medium of self-annihilation. In rotting or being made into earth, however, we have before us neither the temporal mode of suddenness nor that of eternity, but rather that of the painfully slow sinking and submerging, the uncanny creeping of time, indeed, its congealing. Opposed to this mode is that of the high-flown wishes which fly above the heaviness of the earth but swiftly vanish and that of fleeting time, which is however devoured again and again by the time-form of the blindly crawling worm of the earth. This being-devoured also "has" its time: it is the time-form of hell.[73]

That temporality is the fundamental horizon of all existential explication can be demonstrated in our case too. If only at this point we focus more closely upon it, it is because, as mentioned previously, it seemed to us didactically more expedient and easier, first to present the other forms of how the existence is in its world (*Verweltlichung*), namely, of spatialization, material garbing, illumination, and coloring, and only then to show the horizon from which the total "world" of this existence can be properly understood. For the existential presupposition for the fact that Ellen West's world can undergo such an unequivocal change—change from the vivacity, breadth, brightness, and colorfulness of the ethereal via the darkening, beclouding, withering, moldering, and rotting, to the narrowness, darkness, grayness, shallowness, that is, to the state of dead earth—the presupposition for such a change is that an unequivocal, unified phenomenon underlies this change. This phenomenon is a phenomenon of temporalization.

Before we turn to the interpretation of this phenomenon, let it be said once more that having world [74] and having temporality cannot be separated ontologically and anthropologically, but merely form two special problems

[73] In reference to Hell—not as an objective but an existential "sphere of being" in the sense of an "endless structure," a "never-ending agony," a "drowning of the soul in its own darkness"—cf. Berdyaev, *Von der Bestimmung des Menschen* (*The Destiny of Man*) (1937): *Die Hölle* (*The Hell*).

[74] [*Weltlichkeit*, which might also be translated as "world-iness," in the sense of one's being inseparably related to the world, not as a matter of opposition to a given world but rather as a matter of completely being-in, being-with, or residing-in the world. Our Cartesian tradition makes this conception difficult to grasp; it is discussed at some length by May in this volume.—TRANSLATORS.]

within the one problem of being-in-the-world. This follows from the fact that, as mentioned earlier, world (cosmos) never designates only a What but also a How, a basic mode in which the human existence in fact exists.[75] The various worlds of which we spoke, therefore, always are at the same time indicators of certain basic modes, according to which the existence, as in the case of Ellen West, is in the world and takes a stand in regard to that which is (*Seiendes*). This existing, being, taking a stand and holding to it must be explicated from the horizon of temporality.

When we speak of temporality we do not mean the experiencing of time, the consciousness of time, or the heeding of time. The fact that Straus's expression, "time experience," [76] can lead to serious misunderstandings and has actually done so, has been stressed by Von Gebsattel.[77] He proposes that we speak of lived time, *temps vécu*,[78] instead of speaking of time experience, and he states that lived time and experienced time are related to each other as are happening and heeding, the pathic and the gnostic, namely, as the real inner time-happening and the objectified, thought time. Under the former time-concept fall the true time-disturbances which Minkowski and Straus have proved to be basic to the anthropological understanding of endogenous depressions and have connected with inhibition or retardation of vitality. Under the latter falls what Von Gebsattel has quite correctly called "derealization-experience related to time" as well as all the observations reported by depressive or schizophrenic patients about a discrepancy between experientially immanent and experientially transcendent time— that is, everything that Minkowski has designated as disturbance of the synchronism.[79] What we ourselves understand by "temporalization" is wholly on the side of the former concept. But we go beyond what is meant by time-happening, by *temps vécu*, by pathic or experientially immanent time, insofar as we understand by temporality not what is-in-being, neither a happening nor a becoming which only emerges out of itself but the self-

75 Cf. Heidegger, "Vom Wesen des Grundes" ("On the Essence of Ground"), *Papers in Honor of Husserl.*

76 [In using this term (*Zeiterleben*) Straus means to stress the very temporal horizon which is intrinsic to the experiencing of time. For example, if one is cut off from the future, both one's present and one's past undergo change. To be distinguished from this are, first, time-happening (*Zeitgeschehen*), which refers to the way time "happens to" a person, to the inner flowing of time, and second, clock-time, or conceptual, objectivated time. Binswanger is here suggesting that for *Zeiterleben* there be substituted the conception of *Zeitgeschehen*, of "lived time" (*gelebte Zeit*) or time-as-lived, the latter based on Minkowski's Bergsonian conception of *temps vécu.*—TRANSLATORS.]

77 Cf. "Die Störungen des Werdens und des Zeiterlebens im Rahmen psychiatrischer Erkrankungen" (Disturbances of Becoming and of Time-Experiencing within the Framework of Mental Illnesses"), *Gegenwartsprobleme der psychiatrisch-neurologischen Forschung* (*Contemporary Problems of Psychiatric-Neurological Research*) (Stuttgart: 1939).

78 Cf. the book by this name by E. Minkowski, 1932.

79 [The synchronism referred to here is between immanent, or inner, experiencing of time and "transient" time.—TRANSLATORS.]

temporalizing of the existence as such. Temporalization means the original "outside-of-self" (ecstasy) in the oneness of the phenomena of future, having-been and present, which Heidegger quite correctly designates as ex-stasies or transfigurations (*Entrückungen*) of temporality.[80] Future, having-been, and present are ex-stasies insofar as they show the phenomena of the *toward which, upon which, with which,* namely, of the toward-oneself, the back-to, and the letting-oneself-be-met-by. To express it in another way, the three ecstasies of time are being-ahead-of-oneself (future), having-been (past), and being-with (present). Temporality, therefore, has for us an ontological meaning. This must always be kept in mind, even when, in the analysis of a specific human existence, we must limit ourselves to showing what anthropological metamorphoses this ontological meaning goes through.

As is evident from the above remarks, it does not matter at all whether and how the patients express themselves about their experiencing of time. With Ellen West such expressions are strikingly infrequent. That her inner development is stopping, that is, standing still, is one of the few "temporal" statements on her own part.

If it is our task to understand the modifications of the temporalization of this existence from its modes of being-in-the-world (*Weltlichung*), it is again not enough to determine, in accordance with the common understanding of time, merely the various tempi which are meant by the expressions "flying," "striding," and "crawling," and perhaps to dispose of them by the designations quick, deliberate, slow (allegro, andante, largo). Rather, it is the purpose of our undertaking to investigate these various existential ways of being moved "in time" to find the mode of their temporalization.

The primary phenomenon of the original and authentic temporality is the future, and the future in turn is the primary meaning of existentiality, of the designing of one's self "for-one's-own-sake." In this fundamental ontological interpretation of temporality we find confirmed the view of the "primary" significance of the future which Scheler had already expressed and which we also find in Minkowski, Straus, and Von Gebsattel.

The existential sense of temporality in general forbids us to conceive of "future" only as the empty possibilities of the pre-established, the wished-for, and the hoped-for, as it also forbids us to see in the past only that which was present and is now over. Rather we must understand by the past in the existential sense the has-been, which decides that we not only have

---

[80] [Binswanger is here dealing, in this passage which is difficult to translate at best, with the concept of ecstasy, from the Greek *ex-stasis*, literally, "standing outside one's self." To show it is the original and not the popular meaning of *ecstasy*, the word is spelled "ex-stasy" above. The three "ecstasies of time," namely, future, past (or more accurately, "having-been"), and present are from Heidegger's *Sein und Zeit* (*Being and Time*). This capacity of the human being to transcend his immediate temporal situation is discussed in Chapter II, p. 71.—TRANSLATORS.]

been but actually *are* from the viewpoint of "has-been." In this "having-been" are founded the "capabilities" by virtue of which the existence exists. Indeed, existence does not mean being-on-hand,[81] but being-able-to-be, and to know about this being-able-to-be means understanding. To this extent the future by no means hangs in the air, and the possibilities of the future are not "empty" but are definite possibilities. To this extent existence is determined not only by the future, that is, by the comprehending of being-able-to-be, but always also by its pastness; existence has always been "thrown" into its being; it is, as we have previously noted, already in its being, or is in a word already tuned to a certain key. All futurity of the existence is therefore "has-been" and all having-been is of the future. "Future and pastness join here to form the life-circle of existence, and in their oneness swallow up the present."[82] The existential meaning of the present, however, is the creating of the present by the decisive resolving of the particular situation in action.

The Temporality of the Ethereal World

Even though everyone lives in an ethereal world, that is, "has" his ethereal world (of phantasies, wishes, longings, hopes), the ethereal world of Ellen West is distinguished not only by the fact that it takes the leading role in this existence but also by the fact that she makes no concessions to the world of practical action, to *Umwelt*, *Mitwelt*, and *Eigenwelt*, communication and intercourse. In a word, she makes no concession to the realms of "taking-and-being-taken-by" something. Here the ethereal world does not enter into the world of practical action; the two realms do not permeate each other. Art, for example, would mean such a mutual permeation. But Ellen West, much as "a God gave her ways to say what she suffers" (Goethe, *Tasso*), was not born to be a poetess. Now the ethereal world must not only be conceived as the world in which we let the future "come up to us," but it must in the full sense be understood existentially, that is, as the self-designing for the sake of one's self. This self-designing, however, is possible only insofar as "the self" becomes transparent upon the (divine) power which posited it (Kierkegaard) or as it understands how to seize the (metaphysical) ground in authentic making of one's self (Heidegger) or as it is blessed by our common existential ground with the gift of the dual mode of being of love (as we ourselves have previously presented it). But where the existence shuts itself off obstinately from the ground of its being and

81 [See Note 41.—TRANSLATORS.]
82 Cf. Oskar Becker, "Von der Hinfälligkeit des Schönen und der Abenteuerlichkeit des Künstlers" ("On the Fragility of the Beautiful and the Adventurousness of the Artist"), *Papers in Honor of Husserl*.

defiantly evades it, there the future too assumes a different meaning, namely the meaning of self-designing toward an unauthentic self, that is a phantasy self.[83] Such a future is no longer a "having-been future," that is not one determined by the pastness which makes up the possibilities and capabilities of the particular existence, but it is now really a future of "empty possibilities." In such a future "everything is possible"; it is the future in the sense of unbounded, unimpeded, unrestrained, ambitiously optimistic wishing and yearning. The spatial meaning of this future is the unlimited, bright, radiant, color-gleaming expanse; its cosmic aspect is landscape, sky, ocean; its material garb is the air, the ether.[84] By now it should have become clear that the darkening, burdening, limiting, confining, and restraining of this ethereal world, the bird-like flying in it, the flitting over the practical world, have a temporal meaning too. The self-designing toward the "for-one's-own-sake" is replaced by the mere—*i.e.*, no longer future—pastness, thrown-ness and anywhere-ness, which is what the common time concept designates as "being cut off from the future." Such a being-any-whereness is rightly termed *Schwermut* (heavy mood or melancholy) by the German language, *dépression* (being-pressed down) by the French. But let us stay with the ethereal world. Since it is a world of "unauthentic" future, a world of a phantasy "ahead-of-oneself" and of a phantasy self, a world in which there is no shadow and no boundary, this world as such is thus constantly threatened by the shadow and the boundary, which means by the having-been.[85] For the temporal-historical structure of existence can indeed be modified in defiance, self-willedness, and ambition, but it cannot be broken through, still less turned about. The existence, indeed *every* existence, remains committed to its ground. In unauthentic futurization, in self-designing for the sake of a wish-self, the meaningfulness of the world is falsified and "artificially" leveled (as we have shown in our study, "On the Flight of Ideas.") To be sure, everyone may "swing himself up" into such a world temporarily, but with the full knowledge of its phantasy-nature—*i.e.*, of the fact that there is no staying in it. But when this contour-less world replaces the present world of practical action, in which "things collide harshly in space" (Schiller), ground makes itself evident once more, but now no longer as a call back to the having-been, as a knowing about the "having-to-return to earth," but as an unknowing, blind, uncanny being-threatened by the shadow—that is, as dread! And the farther the existence climbs away into the ethereal world, the more threatening, more compact, more impenetrable the garb of this shadow becomes.

[83] That in the case of Ellen West this self was transformed, with the decision to die, in the direction of an authentic self indicates as well that in the face of death the ethereal world also collapsed.

[84] Cf. *Über Ideenflucht*, the topic of "Optimism."

[85] Indeed, Griesinger noted that each manic mood is transparent to the depressive mood.

The Temporality of the Tomb-World

It must already have become clear that just as the ethereal world is ruled by the (unauthentic) future, the tomb-world is ruled by the unauthentic (because it is without future), everpresent past. As Kierkegaard says of despair: "Every real moment of despair is to be traced back to its possibility; every moment in which he [the despairing one] is in despair, he draws it to himself; it is constantly the present time, nothing past originates which is left behind in contrast to reality; in every real moment of despair the despairer carries all the foregoing in its possibility as a present thing.[86] The condensing, consolidating, straightening of the shadow, (developing into the vegetative rotting and inescapable encirclement until it becomes the wall of the tomb) is an expression of the growing dominance of the past over this existence, of the supremacy of the already-been in the whereabouts of hell and the inescapable movement back-to-it. This dread of hell is the dread the existence feels of being engulfed by its ground, by which it is the more deeply engulfed the higher it tries to leap or to fly from it. The self's grasping of its ground and its becoming self-transparent upon it are replaced by the dreadful being-overpowered by this ground and by sinking back into Nothingness.

When the existence cannot design itself toward the for-one's-own-sake, when it "is cut off from the future," the world in which it exists sinks into insignificance, loses its character of relevance, and becomes nonreferential.[87] In other words, the existence no longer finds anything there from which and by which it could understand itself; and this means that it dreads and exists in the mode of dread, or, as we say, it is in naked horror. But at this point it is important to keep in mind that the Nothingness of the world, of which the dread is in dread, does not mean that in dread the inner worldly contents are experienced as absent. On the contrary, the person cannot escape encountering them in their empty mercilessness.[88] Add to this the fact that the insignificance of the world as opened up in the dread reveals the utter futility of what can be taken care of in the practical world, namely, the impossibility of self-designing for a being-able-to-be of existence founded in practical action. "Dread feels anxiety for the naked existence having been thrown into the Uncanny."

We must first note in this connection that in the confinement of the tomb-world the world has not yet completely lost its referential character, has not sunk down to complete insignificance, that this existence still has something out of which it can understand itself, namely, the tomb, the

---

[86] Cf. Kierkegaard, "The Sickness unto Death."
[87] [See Note 36.—TRANSLATORS.]
[88] Heidegger.

dungeon, the hole in the earth. That this existence is nevertheless in dread shows that the narrowing and leveling of the significance of the world which is concurrent with the supremacy of the pastness and its very loss of referential character does indeed mean dread. We have pursued this *Gestalt*-loss of the world step by step as the "sinking down" from an extremely mobile, extremely fleeting world into an extremely rigid, amorphous (*Gestalt*-less) world, where the existence can no longer understand itself out of anything "new," but only out of the perishing and decaying of the accustomed and familiar. The existence, therefore, already dreads its very own possibility of being even where it can still freely "design itself." [89] What is on hand in the inner world, then, need not show itself in its empty mercilessness. It can suffice if it shows itself in the aspect of emptying, in our case, in the aspect of the earth, the tomb, or the hole in the earth. All these expressions, however, show that emptying of the significance of the world, *Gestalt*-loss of its referential character, and "existential emptiness" mean one and the same thing, founded on a modification of the one existential sense of temporalization. When the world becomes insignificant, loses its referential character more and more, and the existence finds less and less toward which it can design itself and out of which it can understand itself; when the world, then, shows itself in the aspect of emptying (of the earth, the hole, the tomb in the earth); when the existence is no longer ahead-of-itself,[90] but thrown back into the mere has-been in which it can no longer understand itself out of "anything new," only out of the circle of the accustomed and familiar; then all this means that, as our everyday speech puts it so well, there is "nothing doing" and "everything stays the same." This nothing-doing and staying-the-same, which applies to the world as well as to the existence, is nothing but a standing-still or, at best, a crawling. When Ellen West understands herself as a worm of the earth, she expresses thereby the same thing as with the statement that her "development has ceased," that she is cut off from the future and no longer sees wideness and brightness before her, but now only moves slowly in a dark, tight circle. Again, this means nothing but what psychopathologists, and Ellen West too, designate as a sinking down from the height of the spirit (*Geist*) to a lower level of complete or almost complete vegetating, the level of mere greed.

Greed can be characterized existentially by the closeness, narrowness, and emptiness of the world, by its hole-like aspect, in which the existence con-

---

[89] Von Gebsattel once correctly referred to a systematization of "pathology of freedom." "Süchtiges Verhalten im Gebiet *sexueller* Verirrungen" ("Addictive Behavior in the Realm of Sexual Deviations"), *Monatsschr. f. Psychiatr. u. Neurol.*, Vol. 82. It is really sad that the psychiatrist must be told by the internist that we physicians cannot use a psychology "which does not accept mental freedom as fact and problem." L. von Krehl, "Über Standpunkte in der inneren Medizin" ("On Points of View in Internal Medicine"), reprint from *Münchener Med. Wochenschrift*.

[90] [This phrase, ahead-of-itself, refers to the future mode of temporalization.—EDITORS.]

tents itself with whatever happens to be at hand, and, as we must say in our case, "at mouth"—that is, where it does not select and consider but quickly grabs or bites, swiftly throwing herself "like an animal" on whatever happens to be there. The form of temporalization of this being-in-the-world is no longer the expecting of the future, but solely a turning into present (a "presenting") of the mere Now neither born of the future nor leaving a past behind it. The "animal seriousness" of this present shows itself in the fact that everything "revolves" only around eating or devouring, as the only reference from which the existence can still understand itself. From everything we have set forth it must be clear that, as previously stressed, such a greed for eating, as expression of the emptying of the world of existence and making it into mere earth, is dread. When Ellen West "throws herself like an animal" on her food, that means that she is driven by dread, by the dread which, to be sure, she attempts to numb in the greed of eating (for in the devouring of nourishment there is still "something doing"), only to become its slave again in the next Now. This is the inescapable "noose" in which this existence is entangled. Thus the dread of becoming fat is revealed as another expression of the dread of perpetuating the greed in the form of fattening, cramming, becoming a worm, rotting, growing shallow and ugly, and the aging and de-spiritualization of the existence. Being fat is the eternal reproach which the existence directs against itself, its real "guilt." The contrast between the ethereal world and the grave-world, between existential overlighting and existential shadow, proved itself to be a contradiction between overstraining oneself on the weight of the temporality of the existence and being pulled down by it. This finds astonishingly clear expression in the life-history of our patient. That a conflict exists between the two worlds does not mean, then, that the one is a solely festive joy of existence, the other solely existential sorrow or depression; no, both worlds, if one may say so, are dread-worlds. The ethereal one expresses the dread of the real future caused by wanting to be different, and therewith also the dread of death; the tomb-world is bound to the dread of the mere pastness. In the one the existence consumes itself in the mere wishing done by phantasy, in the other, in the mere greed for life. The contradiction between the two worlds is not that between non-dread, being-sustained by existence, or "composure" (*Gelassenheit*) (E. Straus), on the one hand, and dread on the other, but that between two different forms of dread, the dread of old age and death and the dread of life. In both forms the one dread of the nothingness of existence can find expression, and the two dreads thus are interchangeable: Hades can mean Dionysos, and Dionysos Hades. The contradiction between the two forms of dread is a dialectic one in the sense of the antinomy of existence, that is, the close interlacing of life with death and death with life. The suicide, however, is the willful breaking through this antinomy by a "resolute" deed of practical action, in which freedom finally and necessarily triumphs over unfreedom. So deeply founded is the essence of freedom as a necessity in existence that it can also dispose of existence itself.

The Temporality of the World of Practical Action

We have seen sufficiently well that Ellen West's practical activity is not really in the service of her existential self-realization but originates largely in her ambition for an undying name, her drive for the betterment of the world, and directly in her passion for self-forgetfulness and diversion. This activity is to a great extent a passion for self-numbing, and Ellen West herself does indeed compare it to an opiate. So this existence has a craze not only for sweets and fattening foods generally but also for self-forgetfulness and running away from itself. Hence the restless, untarrying practical activity, the "nomadization" and craving for something new.[91] Escaping from her most individual selfhood, hence neither letting her authentic future come up to her nor really being-able-to-have-been, she never experiences any "undissembled," objective letting-her-self-be-met-by-something, such as corresponds to the authentic present, which is the temporality of the attentive taking-care-of or acting. To this extent she is at bottom never involved in "the matter itself," which can only be genuinely "encountered" by the true self and the dual We. Everyday speech says rightly that we deal here not with "objective motives" but with "personal" ones. But since Ellen West also shows existential tendencies, she attempts desperately to bring order into this scattering. In place of the authentic temporalization of ripening we see only a "taking care of time," a pedantic division of "her time" and a desperate, restless filling out of it.[92] But all this is part of the temporality of her enslavement to the world, although neither of the temporality of attentive *taking-care-of* nor, still less, of that of theoretical discovering or artistic creating Here too existence cannot properly temporalize itself nor hold itself in the authentic present of the existential moment; in other words, it cannot "at the moment" resolutely be "here" with respect to the opened-up situation. Only authentic resoluteness opens up the "Here" of the existence as situation. "Hence the opened-up can never so encounter the resolute one that he can thereby irresolutely lose his time."[93] Also the striding on the earth, the practical action, is in the case of Ellen West not a considered and circumspect, but a jumpy, desperately tense motion, threatened both by her tend-

[91] Nothing is more remote from this impatience than the insight expressed in Valéry's line: *Tout ici bas peut naître d'une patience infinie* (Everything down here may originate from an infinite patience).

[92] The circling of her companions in Sicily "in order not to become grossly fat" is but one especially characteristic example of the "filling out" of time.

[93] Heidegger. To understand the very important ontological and anthropological fact of the *situation,* cf. also *Sein und Zeit.*

ency toward flying and flying away and, even more, by her tendency to crawling and to "apathy." Everywhere in the case of Ellen West we find temporality falling apart more or less into its single ex-stasies, that is, lacking in authentic ripening or existential temporalization. This is the basic trait of this existence, from which, as we saw, she can escape only in the resolve for suicide.

Again, it is temporality which sharply illumines her gluttony and her dread of becoming fat. The having to fill up her time, this "taking care of time," is only an especially revealing characteristic of her desperate need for filling up, her need to fill up her existential emptiness. But this emptiness is nothing more than a phenomenon of the temporality of her existence; hence she can be "filled up with time," although only scantily, artificially, and temporarily. This filling up, then, is a makeshift. Like the need for food, it becomes a greed, indeed a mania, the more the existence empties itself (and vice versa: Cf. her quiet waiting for death after completing her existential resolve!). The need for filling up the belly with food and its perpetuation in getting fat is only another mode (though a very inexpedient one) of having to fill up the existential emptiness. Its character of greed or mania has the same origin as the passion for the filling up of time, the need, namely, to escape from the phenomenon of emptiness. But the dread of eating and getting fat does not spring from the dread of filling up as such—otherwise Ellen West would also have a dread of filling up time—but of the horror of filling up in the sense of purely sensual avidity. Only when Ellen West has resolved upon an exogenous death, suicide, when therefore she is no longer existentially empty but "completely filled" with this goal, that is, when once more there is "something doing," does she again *have* time and no longer needs to fill up her time greedily and again has unimpaired enjoyment from sweets. "Time" as well as eating have once again become harmless. Let us remind ourselves, however, that enjoying is also a mode of temporalization, an unauthentically momentary one, one which temporalizes itself neither out of the future nor out of the past. For this reason alone it is, and even more so in its manic form, an unsuitable means for filling up the existential vacuum, for fetching the existence from enslavement back to its authentic self. What makes enjoyment become a mania and greed is precisely this, that as a purely momentary satisfier and tranquilizer it places the existence ever anew into the existential vacuum and thus again and again causes it to be enslaved by the world (of nourishment or poison). The place of the possibility of authentic temporalization or ripening is taken by enslavement to the objective world-time. In such cases the existence has to rely and is dependent only on the time-points of the appearance of hunger and of the opportunities for its possible satisfaction (meals, alcohol, drugs, sexual satisfaction). The vicious circle, the noose, is thus drawn, the imprisonment is complete.

Let us note in conclusion that the time-span left to Ellen West between her resolve for suicide and the swallowing of the poison is merely "filled up" again, not, to be sure, with hasty greed and hasty devouring, but with "intellectual" reading, a walk, and harmless eating. Though she experiences the boundary of life resolutely as an authentic boundary situation, and though to this extent she becomes an authentic self, even now she cannot grow beyond herself.

Retrospect and Prospect

In the case of Ellen West, we can speak of authentic existence, of temporalization in the sense of the authentic singular mode, only when she faces death. To be sure, we had previously noticed certain "existential tendencies" [94] but they were smothered by the unauthentic singular mode, by the (plural) willful relatedness to herself. When this mode rules the existence, it not only cannot extend itself steadily in the sense of authentic existence or self-actualization—it cannot even tarry in *one* world! The enslavement to the world which appears in this mode not only brings about quite diverse, dissociated forms of being-oneself, but also causes the world to split into several dissociated worlds. If we want to designate such a mode of existence with one word, none is more fitting than despair, even from the neutral existential-analytical standpoint. This despair again has many subforms which can be more precisely described according to the character of their temporalization and spatialization and their material garb. In our case the temporalization shows the character of a shortening or shrinking of existence, that is, of the sinking of its rich and flexibly articulated ontological structure to a less articulated level: the unity of this structure falls apart into its different ex-stasies; the ontological relation of the ex-stasies to each other dissolves; the ex-stasy "future" recedes more and more, the ex-stasy "past" predominates, and coinciding with this the present becomes the mere Now or, at best, a mere time-span. With respect to spatialization, this modification of the temporalization results in constriction and emptying of the world; with respect to its material consistency, in making into swamp or earth; with respect to its lighting and coloring, it results in gray glooming and black darkening; with respect to its mobility, in congealing and petrification. And all this is—in accord with the indissoluble unity of world and self—only an expression of the modified being-oneself, of the existential narrowness and emptiness, of the existential darkening, and congealing, and being made into swamp.

That this existence can once again break through its congealing, that once more it is able to burst the prison of pastness, to exchange it for the world of an authentic present, and so once more to become authentically and

[94] In this connection, cf. *Basic Forms.*

wholly itself—this testifies to the power of freedom in general which, to some degree, makes itself felt even in the insidious form of schizophrenia. But let us make clear to ourselves once more under what conditions, in our case, this power is again able to unfold itself! It is not an everyday or merely difficult situation, nor one of mere life-significance which is here used by the existence once more to find itself; but the completely unique situation in which the existence as such delivers itself to Nothingness. What was needed, therefore, to make the world flare up once more, to cause the self once more to exist genuinely, was not a random decision, but the most extreme one of all. What suicide provides here, in a not very advanced case—namely, the condition for the possibility of breaking through the congealing, means in more advanced cases and in more primitive individuals perhaps a murder, a violent action of some kind. This condition might be provided also by an act of arson, or by letting a hand burn slowly in the stove in order to make a sacrifice and with it to make a decisive impression upon a beloved person, as I myself was able to establish on one occasion.[95] Frequently particular external situations and events touch off the breakthrough, such as a physical illness, the sudden death of a relative, an attack, a fright, and the like. What we psychiatrists judge and label from the outside as a striking, bizarre, morbid "act of a schizophrenic" can be understood existential-analytically as an often last attempt of the existence to come to itself! As we have seen, however, this is a problem of temporalization. When even such an attempt is no longer possible, when finally "nothing anymore moves" (there is "nothing doing"), then the patients themselves frequently speak of a cessation of "time" in the sense of an invariable eternal time [96] in which no resolving is possible any more and every possibility of a mutual understanding ceases. Similarly the "genius" patients understand the tragedy of the desperate struggle "to come to oneself," the "crazily-wild search for a consciousness." So wrote the ailing Hoelderlin in his notes to "Oedipus Rex." But Hoelderlin also knew that the coming to oneself required special conditions of existence, a special bit of good fortune, or, if that is no longer possible, then at least *fright:* "O thou, daughter of the ether, appear to me from your father's gardens and if you may not promise me mortal happiness, then frighten, O frighten my heart with something else." This final stanza of the poem becomes more readily understandable in our context when related to the second stanza: "Where are you? I lived little, but already my evening's

---

95 [Binswanger is referring here to his paper on the case of Ilse, included in this volume. —EDITORS.]

96 Cf. the self-description in K. Beringer's and W. Mayer-Gross' case of Hahnenfuss, *Zeitschr. Neur.*, vol. 96, 1925: "The basic trait and essence of the tragedy of the insane is that, as already indicated, there is no temporal standard at all, and the entire psychic condition might just as well be considered as eternal, that therefore fundamentally meaningful communication is excluded in every way and every free decision is paralyzed *a priori.*"

breath is cold, and like the shades I am quiet here, and songless my shuddering heart slumbers in my bosom." [97]

Eternity

When we speak of eternity, we no longer speak of being-in-the-world, but of being-in-the-world-beyond-the-world, of the dual mode of being-human or of the We of the I and Thou in Love. No longer do we talk here of existence (being oneself), of time and space, but of being We. We speak of "eternity and home." [98] Here the present no longer means "letting-oneself-be-met," means no longer, then, a decisive resolution of the situation, but a meeting of I and Thou in the eternal moment of love. This is no longer a case of being-able-to-be, but of a being-allowed-to-be, no longer one of self-possessing of one's ground, but of the grace of being We arising from one's ground.

Though or just because it is the authentic mode of being-human, the dual mode is the one most hidden, indeed the one most severely suppressed. Just as in the history of mankind it took a long time until the dual mode achieved its breakthrough in the religion of love, in Christianity, and just as this breakthrough subsequently changed the psychic countenance of mankind, so is this breakthrough too, likewise faced with the greatest obstacles in the individual existence. When it has taken place basically, this breakthrough transforms the individual existence; for now the existence is no longer a finite being-in-the-world, hurled from crag to crag (Hoelderlin), but, regardless of this is secured in the infinite fullness of homeland and eternity.

If we ask ourselves whether and how far this dual mode broke through in the existence-*Gestalt* which lives on under the name of Ellen West, or whether and why it only glimmers through, then we face the subtlest question of our entire examination. For just where one truly deals with love one does not reach the ground if one asks for reasons. Here more than anywhere we must be content merely to circle around the secret which, "at bottom," every existence-*Gestalt* represents.

When an existence, as in the case of Ellen West, is ruled to such a high degree by the existential forms of death, dread, and guilt, this means that it is claimed to an especially high degree as an individual one. When the existence is claimed so exclusively as an individual one, and especially when it exists to such a high degree as a desperate individual one and can throw off this desperation only through the sacrifice of life, then love, which claims existence as a dual one (*i.e.*, in the existential possibilities of eternity, of secure homeness, of guiltlessness, and true culture), has evidently not achieved a breakthrough. This shows, among other things, in the fact that

[97] "Entreaty (to Hope)." It need not be emphasized how much Frozenness, Silence, Shadow, Shivering (Shuddering in the second version) resemble the world of our patient.
[98] See Note 22.

Ellen West cannot wait, not even for death, but rather is constantly in dread of "losing time," even in regard to the resolve for death, whereas love is *passion infinie* per se and by no means "time's fool," as Shakespeare expressed it in such impressive fashion. What makes it further evident that Ellen West did not achieve true culture is the fact that it was not given to her to devote herself wholly, in loving imagination, to any one of the great "Spiritual objectives" (religion, art or science, politics, or education).

And yet even in this existence-*Gestalt* the dual mode does shine through to some degree, as, indeed there is scarcely a human being in whom no germ of love can be discovered. In discussing Ellen's suffering over "social injustice" we have already observed that this germ was present even though overshadowed and suppressed by ambition. This existence would not have suffered so agonizingly from its emptiness and impoverishment, experiencing them not only as a burden but as a hell, had it not had a secret knowledge of the possibility of being-beyond-the-world. We also spoke of an inkling of such a possibility to be seen in the face of the various forms which death took on in her eyes. Death is for Ellen West not only Nothingness. Nothingness it is for her intellect and her practical acting, *i.e.*, suicide. Seen from the tomb-world, death is the end of the existential rotting process; seen from the ethereal world, death is an erotic-legendary Figure (Sea-King); an erotic-religious one (God-father); an erotic-esthetic one (glorious woman, white asters in dark hair); an erotic-poetic one (the great friend). Everywhere here we see love, albeit not in its genuine form but in ethereal-mystic or ethereal-passionate, "decay-form"; [99] at least shimmering through. Furthermore, the case history showed us more or less fully realized Thou-shapes: the nurse-maid, father and mother, the younger brother, the student and the husband, the ethereal girl friends. An indication of Ellen West's "readiness for Thou" was also given to us by the lifelong attachment and gratitude of many of those entrusted to her care, and above all in the deep love which the husband bestowed upon her and which, as we now may add, he retained for her during his entire life. Even the reader of her case history must have seen Ellen West not only as an object of interest but also as Thou. Ultimately, the closer she feels herself to death, the more a genuine knowledge about true love breaks through.

But the life of Ellen West in the face of death can also be understood from the vantage point of eternity. If it is only in the face of death that she can completely shed defiance and self-willedness, ambition and the phantastic, indeed, "the dread of the earthly" in general; if in the nearness of death, and still more in the face of death, she can come to herself and even free herself of herself and of the world to such an extent, then once again we perceive a positive meaning of Nothingness. Only in the face of nonbeing does Ellen West actually stand in being, does she triumph in quiet calm over the finite-

[99] Cf. *Basic Forms.*

ness of being, including her own. But this is possible only where the exist-ence knows or senses itself as *Gestalt* of this being, as a passing expression of the eternal *Gestalt*-metamorphosis. This knowing or sensing is the knowing or sensing of love.

The fact that this knowledge breaks through only in the face of death and could not work itself through in life shows how enormous was the pressure under which this existence stood from the very beginning. That in spite of this it was able to break through indicates the power of the dual mode in being-human.

III *Existential Analysis and Psychoanalysis*

Psychoanalysis likewise has the life history as its experiential basis, but a peculiar form of "history" reduced to natural history. This distinguishing characteristic of psychoanalysis extends to all three phases of historical inves-tigation: heuristics, criticism, and interpretation.[100] Even in regard to heuris-tics, its obtaining of historical experience material follows its own principle. Not only is psychoanalysis concerned with a painfully exact and detailed procurement of the material, but it has also given us a new heuristic method. As is well-known, in this method it places chief emphasis on the ethereal world, as we may say in reference to our case, namely, the world of phantasy and dream. At this point it immediately is in contrast with existential analysis, which undertakes to work out all possible world-de-signs of human existence, faithful to the fact established by Hegel that the individuality is what its world is, in the sense of its own world.[101] The reason for this preference of the ethereal realm is that wishing (the "pleasure principle") is the basic vector of meaning in which Freud harnesses man. This, again, is most closely connected with Freud's anthropology, that is, with his idea of man. Whereas existential analysis approaches human ex-istence with no other consideration than the uncontestable observation that man is in the world, has world, and at the same time longs to get be-yond the world, Freud approaches man with the (sensualistic-hedonistic) idea of the natural man, the *homo natura*.[102] According to this idea, which is possible only on the basis of a complete taking apart of being-human as such and a natural-scientific-biological reconstruction of it, psychoanalysis has developed its entire critique and interpretation of the historical experi-ential material. History becomes natural history, essential possibilities of human existing become genetic developmental processes. Man, being thus

[100] Cf. L. Binswanger, "Erfahren, Verstehen, Deuten in der Psychoanalyse" ("Experience, Understanding, Interpretation in Psychoanalysis"), *Imago*, Vol. 11, No. 1, 1926.

[101] [See Note 20.—TRANSLATORS.]

[102] Cf. S. Freud, "Auffassung vom Menschen im Lichte der Anthropologie" ("Conception of Man in the Light of Anthropology"). *Nederl. Tijdschr. v. Psychol.*, Vol. 4, Nos. 5 & 6, 1936.

reconstructed, is at bottom a driven or drive-dominated creature, his nature is driven instinctively. If the primary concern in this is libidinous instinctuality, it is so because sexuality is seen by Freud throughout as the true history-forming force within the individual life-history, in direct contrast to existential analysis. Since the psychic representation of instinctuality is seen in the wish, the ethereal or wish-world achieves unique importance in this picture of man, which, as we know, is reduced to the point where the picture is lost in the theoretical scheme of an "apparatus" of psychic mechanisms. In the working out of the function-modes of this apparatus, its phylogenetic and ontogenetic natural history with its dominant sexuality and its reacting to biographical *Umwelt* and especially *Mitwelt* factors, I see (as did Freud himself) the real achievement of psychoanalysis, its real genius—which, however, like most achievements of genius, is scientifically fruitful only as long as its one-sidedness is recognized and appreciated.

Since existential analysis undertakes to work out being-human in all its existential forms and their worlds, in its being-able-to-be (existence), being-allowed-to-be (love), and having-to-be (thrownness), whereas psychoanalysis does so only in respect to the last of these, it is clear that existential analysis is able to widen and deepen the basic concepts and understandings of psychoanalysis. Psychoanalysis, on the other hand, can only constrict and flatten [103] the existential-analytic forms, that is, reduce them to the plane of its (one-sidedly naturalistic-evolutionary) viewpoint. To this must be added, above all, that existential analysis stands on phenomenological grounds and works with phenomenological methods. Hence being-man is not considered objectively, that is, as a thing-in-being ("on hand") like other objects in the world, and least of all as a natural object, but rather the phenomenon of his being-in-the-world is investigated, which phenomenon alone permits understanding of what the world-design in the sense of the natural world in general means.

Following these introductory remarks, in regard to which I must refer for details to my paper "On Phenomenology," [104] the above-mentioned lecture, and to my *Basic Forms*,[105] let us now turn to the question of how in our special case existential analysis and psychoanalysis are related. The themes here to be considered are the "equations" given by the second analyst:

1. Slender = spiritual (*geistig*); fat = Jewish bourgeois.
2. Eating = getting fertilized and pregnant.

The latter equation will occupy us particularly in the psychoanalytic attempt at interpreting the third dream.

As to the two psychoanalytic equations, slender = higher spiritual (soft, blond, Aryan) type, fat = bourgeois Jewish type, they must not be understood in terms of a direct reference of the two sides to each other, but only of the community of the worlds to which both sides of each equation belong. This means specifically in terms of their belonging to the ethereal world in the first and to the tomb-world in the second equation. Hence we must not say that slender "means" the higher, fat, the Jewish, type. Existential analysis shows that in this case no one-sided meaning or symbolic relationship of one side of the equation to the other is before us, but that both sides, on the basis of belonging to the same significance in respect to the world, have a common meaning, the meaning of the light-ethereal in the first equation, that of the heavy-oppressive in the second. To return merely to the second significance, we have, indeed, shown that the familiar *Mitwelt*, the little everyday world, has likewise taken on the meaning of the tomb, of the oppressive being-walled-in, as has the bodily shell. Against both walls Ellen rebels, against both she beats physically or mentally "with her hands." Only if from the onset one presupposes in being-human a primacy of sensations or "feelings" can there be a "symbolic" relationship between the separate sides of the equation as such. But existential analysis knows nothing of such a primacy, hypothetically assumed in the interest of a purely philosophical and psychological theory; for existential analysis, sensations in general are neither first nor last. For existential analysis the rejection of the *Mitwelt* and the rejection of obesity stand on the same plane "side by side." Whereas Ellen West can remove herself from the pressure of the *Mitwelt* and actually does so more and more, her ability to escape from the pressure of being fat vanishes more and more as her gluttony counteracts that flight.

What is true of these two equations is also true of an equation not mentioned by the analyst: slender = ethereal girl friends = young and pretty (which must be supplemented by: fat = plump matron = old, ugly). In these two equations we also have to deal with two worlds, the ethereal world of ascending life in the first and the "massive" world of descending life in the second. Here too one cannot say that the wish for slenderness "means" the wish for (identification with) youth and beauty and that the dread of becoming fat "means" the dread of aging and becoming ugly; rather, both wishes and dreads belong together because they belong to the same wish-world or the same dread-world. Here too the prevailing world is decisive, not the specific prevailing wish and the specific prevailing dread! This is one of the most important insights of existential analysis and one of the chief contrasts between it and psychoanalysis.

All this becomes still clearer if we turn to the equation (incomparably more difficult to solve) eating = becoming fertilized, pregnant, to which the third dream furnishes an interesting contribution. True, we learn from the second analyst that Ellen West "recognized" this equation. But when the analyst links this equation, and particularly the eating of chocolate, with anal-eroticism, Ellen West herself declares that she is unable to make the slightest use of anal-eroticism. Thus, her "recognition" evidently remains quite superficial.

As to anal-eroticism, we certainly find in Ellen West some very definite traits of the "anal character"; her tremendous defiance and self-willedness and a great punctiliousness in the filling up of her time. Beyond this, however, we found no features of conspicuous punctiliousness and, above all, *no* indications of miserliness. Moreover, the available psychoanalytic material is much too sparse, the childhood phase much too obscured, to permit *any* binding psychoanalytical conclusions to be drawn. If the equation, chocolate = feces, could not be demonstrated and documented in this life-history, still less could this be done for the equations which, according to psychoanalytic experience, come next: feces = money, and feces = child. If, in spite of all these considerations, we now go into the psychoanalytic interpretation of our special case, it is because by means of it we can demonstrate the chief contrast between psychoanalysis and existential analysis. The subject of anal-eroticism is especially suitable for this.

The main feature of anal-eroticism is tenaciously keeping-to-oneself or not-giving-away. It is a very important insight of psychoanalysis, with which existential analysis completely agrees, that such a basic trait is not tied to the mind-body distinction, but transcends it. But here the agreement stops. Here too existential analysis asks first of all what world-design is basic to anality. In regard to the case of Ellen West the answer is particularly easy: in this world-design the multiplicity and multiformity of the world are reduced to the forms of the hole. The form of being in such a world is that of being confined or oppressed; the self which designs such a world is an "empty" self, concerned only with the filling of the emptiness. Consequently a decided anality is concurrent with a decided orality, with a greed for "incorporating." But since this expression (as psychoanalysis has quite correctly observed) is not restricted to the bodily sphere, we prefer to speak of appropriating, but in the sense of mere filling up.[106] The "category" which dominates equally this world-design, the being-in-it and the self which designs it, is only and solely that of emptiness and fullness, of being-empty and being-full, of the starving and satiated self. The basic trait of such an existence-form is greed, the throwing-oneself-upon (food). This existential movement has, as we have seen, the temporal character of sud-

---

[106] In the case of Ellen West, too, the greed for being filled manifests itself not only in the form of voracity for food and of hunger but also in the form of her greed for life and power; that is, her all-pervading hunger for life and her hunger for power ("ambition"). Ellen West bites greedily into all of life and, to use the very appropriate expression of the scholar mentioned in connection with our discussion of heredity, she has a "strong bite on life."

denness, the spatial one of nearness. The world in which such an existence "moves" is temporally oriented to the mere Now of the filling-up possibility and the mere Here of the stuffing; such a world is lightless and colorless (gloomy), monotonous and monomorphous, in a word, joyless or dreary. To this emptied world corresponds—and is indeed prerequisite to it—the existentially empty self, the existential emptiness and the corresponding existential pressure. Both these characterizations we find in the beginning of our report on Ellen West, and we meet them again at the end in the formulation, "There remains the great unfilled hole." Where the world is nothing more than a hole, the self too is (bodily as well as mentally) only a hole; after all, world and self are reciprocal determinants (in accordance with the principle which cannot be repeated often enough, that the individuality is what its world is, in the sense of its own world).

The world-design, then, which is at the bottom of anality (and orality) is the world as hole, tomb, or grave. The (pseudo-)existential [107] mode prevailing in a hole-world is greed, as the reverse of the being-unfilled and being-unsated, of existential emptiness in general. But as greed it does not lead to the authentic appropriation or fullness, but only to satiety and bloating. But this means that what "just a moment ago" had the character of the attractive, the alluring, the seductive, has "now" the character of the "uninteresting," indeed of the repelling, disgusting, nauseating; the ascending life capsizes to become the descending life, the growing, flowering, thriving turns into the wilting, moldering, rotting. The more impetuously and uninhibitedly life ascends "into the ether," the more quickly and deeply it falls down again and becomes the tomb, which clings to the existence like a lead weight and pulls it down into death; for the greed for satiety cannot fill the existential emptiness, but only dull it momentarily; it can only mean a short delay on this road, a momentary flight from death. The attracting power of death, the mention of which makes Ellen West's eyes shine, rests also on the fact that it, and only it—apart from being the dreaded end—is the longed-for sole possibility of escape from greed itself. The last glad day of life before the night of death constitutes the factual test of this existential-analytical example.

The entire life-history of Ellen West is nothing but the history of the metamorphosis of life into mold and death. It is, in the words of Paul Claudel, a most impressive example of the *"dismal alchemy of the tomb"* (*alchimie funeste de la tombe*). What psychoanalysis calls anality is only a special segment of the history of this alchemy. Expressed in another way, anality belongs in the realm of the dull, moldering, rotting swamp-world and its "end-product," the cold grave. This world-design asserts itself from the beginning in the life-history of our patient, even though again and again contradicted and broken through by practical action and, particularly, by

107 [This expression refers to a form of existence which is not a real one.—TRANSLATORS.]

the ethereal world. This contradiction shows itself in Ellen's ascetic tendency, from the voluntary renunciation of sweets to the running away from the bread in the cupboard, and from the involuntary renunciation of sociability to the voluntary-involuntary renunciation of life.

If then existential analysis has no hesitation whatever in recognizing the concepts of anality and orality (just as it recognizes in general the somatomorphology, indeed somatography, of experiencing given us by Freud as one of the most valuable preliminaries for its own undertaking),[108] still, it must explicitly oppose the attempted explanation with which psychoanalysis approaches not only anality but the entire structure of experiencing. As phenomenology it cannot only not recognize Freud's general principle: "Postulated strivings must take theoretical precedence over observed phenomena," [109] but it also opposes the special attempt at explanation as such. To continue with the existential form of anality: phenomenology cannot revert to an anal-erotic drive-component as the cause or genetic condition for the construction and consolidation of the world of the swamp and the hole. It cannot do so, not only because phenomenology is not an explanatory science—it leaves explanation to the objectifying sciences—but also because it must reject this way of explanation as such. Existential analysis cannot admit that pleasure sensations during defecation, that is, the fixation of the anal zone as erogenous zone, can build up the picture of a hole-, grave-, or swamp-world, just as in general no world can be constructed from sensations and urges. That view belongs entirely to a former time, the time of Positivism. Rather, existential analysis is of the opinion that, conversely, only when a design of the world as hole-world is present, at a certain stage of childhood or with certain forms of "spiritual (*geistig*) decomposition," the being-a-hole, the being-filled and being-emptied, or the retaining is experienced as "pleasurable." This "Copernican switch" is basic to all existential analysis. Hence, anality in the psychoanalytical sense is only a segment of the total hole-world, the segment which is restricted to the bodily share in the *Eigenwelt*. Consequently the expressions hole-world and swamp-world are to be preferred.

The fact that "experiencing" is to such a great extent "somatomorphic" [110]

---

108 "Über Psychotherapie."

109 [This quotation is from Freud's *General Introduction to Psychoanalysis,* first published by the International Psychoanalytic Society. The sentence in the German (p. 64) is, *"Die Wahrgenommenen Phänome müssen in unserer Auffassung gegen die nur angenommenen Strebungen zurücktreten."* A literal rendering of this would be: "In our view, perceived (observed) phenomena must yield their place to merely postulated (assumed) strivings (tendencies)." In the authorized English translation, by Riviere, published by Liveright, 1920, the sentence appears on page 60 and is rendered in a somewhat weakened form, "In this connection, the trends we merely infer are more prominent than the phenomena we perceive."—Translators.]

110 [The English term "anthropomorphic" may serve as an analogy to "somatomorphic" and "cosmomorphic."—Translators.]

shows only how great a role corporeality in general plays in the building up of our world and correspondingly in the verbal expressions for the experiencing. It would be completely incorrect, however, to ignore the other regions of the world. It is particularly instructive to examine the language since it serves to "affirm" our world-picture. In fact, we have seen in our own case to what an extent the verbal expressions for experiencing are derived cosmomorphically, *i.e.*, from the cosmos (*Universum*) in general, as also from its various "regions." When it is said that the deteriorated schizophrenic has such difficulty in finding words for his experience for the reason that his experiencing is entirely "novel," the explanation remains superficial. The truth is rather that the schizophrenic has so much difficulty finding words for his experiencing because his *world* is so novel, so altered or even disintegrated, that he no longer finds "holding-points" to which he can "affix" his language.

We are now prepared to consider in an existential-analytical manner the psychoanalytical equation, eating = becoming fertilized = becoming pregnant. Here more than ever we must guard against conceiving the equation in the sense of a symbolic equation, a symbolic relation of meanings. If the (second) analyst was of the opinion that the gluttony was only a symbolic expression of the greed for love, that the dread of becoming fat "meant" a dread of becoming fertilized and pregnant, he was led to this opinion by his diagnostic preconception that the case of Ellen West was one of a "compulsive neurosis," in which of course one action replaces or "substitutes" for another ("repressed") action-intention. But if things are even in a compulsive neurosis not as simple as is assumed by the theory of the mechanism of "substitution," they are still less so in the case of Ellen West. After all, the urge to fill up the existential emptiness—the being-a-hole—and its bodily component, the gluttony, are by no means repressed here; for if we speak of the opposition of the ethereal world to the hole-world, this does not mean that Ellen West represses her greed, but, on the contrary, that she condemns it and fights it.[111] This is indeed, as Freud himself explained, something quite different from repression. So the fact is not, in the case of Ellen West, that the one world rules the "consciousness," while the other is "repressed into the unconscious," but that the world is split into two equally "conscious" worlds.

Of course, we do not by any means deny that the wish for fertilization and pregnancy, can also be, with Ellen West, in the service of her filling-up tendency (but not conversely, that the filling-up tendency can serve the wish for fertilization!). If we knew something about her infantile sexual ideas, we could achieve greater certainty here. Nor do we deny that a dread of

---

[111] Indeed, the laxatives serve no purpose other than to make the greed ineffective. This is something quite different, much more "aggressive" yet "much less appropriate" than repression, for in the long run its goal is unattainable.

being pregnant can lead to a dread of becoming fat and fuse with it; but, again, we do deny that the dread of becoming fat symbolically expresses or means the dread of pregnancy. Only if one regards being-human in the light of the primacy of a sexual theory can one arrive at such an interpretation. Existential analysis does not approach being-human with a theory, but regards it without a "theoretical" prejudgment. However, that greed for devouring (hunger) can come to fuse with greed for love, and the dread of becoming fat with the dread of pregnancy, is again derived from the fact that both desires are special forms of one and the same desire and both dreads special forms of one and the same dread, the dread of this one world; for it is the one world of the tomb for which this existence "lusts" in every way, and which it dreads in all possible forms. It is the dread of the metamorphosis of the world of ascending life (of youth and slimness) into that of descending life (aging, deformity, deterioration), in short, the dread of the *alchimie funeste de la tombe.* This can also be seen in the figure of Mozart's Don Juan. Not by chance does it occur that this operatic figure stands not under the symbol of life but of death: greed for love, too, is hostile to life. This is nowhere more drastically expressed than in Balzac's *"Peau de Chagrin"* (The Wild Ass's Skin): [112] *la peau de chagrin,* symbol of life's duration, shrinks in the same proportion as the greed for life and love "lives itself out."

The relationship of existential analysis and psychoanalysis may now be more fully illuminated through examination of the third dream. Since for psychotherapeutic reasons we could not consider an analysis of the dreams of our patient and thus there are no "free associations" available, we are limited to the manifest dream content, to psychoanalytic experience with dreams in general, and to the knowledge brought to light by our existential analysis up to this point.

The third dream read:

1. "While on a trip overseas she jumped into the water through a porthole.

2. "The first lover (the student) and her present husband attempted resuscitation.

3. "She ate many cream-filled chocolates and packed her trunks."

What strikes us first in this dream is that in it the "element" of water plays a role (as the element of fire did in the second dream). Water *and* fire we found quite infrequently in the case history, except in the poem "Kiss Me Dead," in which the sun sinks like a fiery ball into the ocean and the gloomy, cold Sea-King is called upon to press her into his arms in ardent love-lust and kiss her dead. This meeting of fire and water—an expression of love-lust—is a quite isolated happening in our case report. As we have

112 [Literally "Skin of Sorrow," it is the story of a magic leather skin which shrinks with each successive wish by its owner. The skin symbolizes time passing away, as opposed to time growing.—TRANSLATORS.]

seen, Ellen's world is one in which not fire and water but air (light) and earth (dark) battle each other. If fire and water are (among other things) elements of purification and thus also of passing away and becoming, air and earth are the elements of airy becoming and of swamp-ing and petrify-ing,[113] of elevation and depression, of being-ahead-of-oneself and being-already-in,[114] of wideness and narrowness. The existence in the case of Ellen West moves primarily in these existential directions. Now water (to confine ourselves to this element) is, particularly in the form of the ocean or the sea, the element of depth.[115] It is of great interest, but cannot possibly be further explored here, that—and why—it is just in the dream that this element gains such importance. It is striking that Ellen's suicidal attempts are not attempted drownings, but attempts to throw herself out of the window [to the earth], to be run over [on the earth], or to poison herself. In this matter existential analysis is as yet only in its infancy. Let us merely note that depth, and specifically the depth of water, has intimate relation-ships with the past. "*Could one actually describe a past without images of depth?*" asks Bachelard in his book, *L'Eau et les rêves*,[116] which is so im-portant for existential analysis. In summary he states briefly and clearly "*The past of our soul is a deep water.*" [117] If we may interpret Ellen's plunge into the sea as a plunging into her own past, this throws a clear light on the "maternal" significance of water [118] and the fertility-meaning of the very ocean, of which Michelet [119] says, "*Such is the sea. It is, it seems, the great female of the globe, whose insatiable desire, permanent conception, and child-bearing never end.*" In this interpretation, past and future, becoming and passing away, being born and giving birth, unite. If we interpret her throwing herself into the ocean as submersion into the past, we could interpret the attempts at resuscitation as an expression of her being fetched back into the present "on the earth." Once the dreamer is on the earth, she also lets herself be "put on her feet." Her relationship to things is once more so clear and simple that she can even eat chocolate candy again and is able to pack her trunks, indicating that the future too asserts itself.

113 When we refer here to earth, we mean only "dead" earth!

114 [The expressions used here are *Sich-vorwegsein*, which refers to transcending oneself temporally, in Heidegger's sense of living toward death, and *Schon-in-sein*, which refers to being caught, almost in the sense of trapped, in a narrowed realm of existence.— TRANSLATORS.]

115 Jung has cited Seneca's observation that many a lake was regarded as holy because of its depth. "Wandlungen und Symbole der Libido. I" ("Metamorphoses and Symbols of Libido. I"). *Jahrb. f. psychoanal. u. psychol. Forsch.*, ed. Bleuler and Freud, Vol. 3.

116 (Paris: José Corti, 1942.)

117 For a clearer understanding, cf. all of Section III, Chapter 4, "Les Eaux profondes" ("Deep Waters"). The relation between depth and "sentiment" ("mood") has been recog-nized by E. Minkowski ("Vers une cosmologie. La Triade psychologique") ("Toward a Cosmology. The Psychological Triad.")

118 Also cf. Jung, *loc. cit.*, Vol. 2, and other references, Vol. 4.

119 Calman-Lévy, "Histoire naturelle. Le Mer" ("Natural History. The Sea").

This is about the way one could approach this dream existential-analytically, in contrast to an interpretation and analysis based on the individual life-history. Existential analysis cannot regard it as its task to interpret a dream in the fashion of a psychoanalytic life-historical interpretation, quite apart from the fact that existential analysis is always aware of having to deal, in a dream, not with the whole person but only with a certain existential mode, that of the self-forgetting existence.

That the existential-analytic interpretation, however, can stake out the circle for what may be interpreted psychoanalytically in the dream becomes apparent when we see how psychoanalysis would regard this dream. The psychoanalytic interpretations then reveal themselves to be special (Freudian) symbol-interpretations on the ground of fundamental existential-analytical understanding.

Let us, then, turn to an interpretation based on the life-history. The two preceding dreams and the one following this reveal the death wish throughout in undisguised fashion. So does this one. Whether we read it forward or backward, it always begins and ends with the death wish, for, on the basis of psychoanalytic experience, even the trunk-packing (departing) symbolizes a wish to die. However, no psychoanalyst will be satisfied with this. He will immediately state:

1. The first sentence, "While on a trip overseas she jumped through a porthole into the water," represents one of the best known birth-and-rebirth-symbolisms (ship equals mother's body), the latter insofar as in "the unconscious" the phantasy of the birth of one's own child is always connected with that of (re)birth from one's own mother.[120]

2. "The first lover (the student) and the present husband attempted resuscitation," involves the two men who have played the greatest part in Ellen West's life, the one (blond, soft) as representative of the "higher spiritual and Aryan type," the other as representative of the practical-sober world and of "naturalness." Ellen West confronted the first as a mistress, the second as wife. Resuscitation attempts, the waking-one-up-from-death, are again a well-known "symbol," namely, a symbol of fertilization. The dreamer would like to have a child by both men.

3. "She ate chocolate candy and packed her trunks," reveals the trunk-packing not only as a death symbol but also as a pregnancy symbol (trunk equals body). This belongs in the region of orality and anality, the filling-up of an empty container. And here we actually encounter the eating of cream-filled chocolates. Having the idea of getting children by eating is actually a part of oral-anal pregnancy- and birth-phantasies. It is altogether possible that in early childhood Ellen West might have had such sexual ideas. On the basis of this infantile concept, but only on this basis, one could actually

120 Cf. in this connection my "heel analysis," "Analyse einer hysterischen Phobie" ("Analysis of a Hysterical Phobia"), *Jahrb. f. psychoanal. u. psychol. Forsch.*, Vol. 3.

say that eating means becoming-fertilized. Accordingly, in this third sentence of the manifest dream content we have before us a derivative of the earliest infantile layer of the life-history, whereas the second sentence already presupposes knowledge of the man's participation in fertilization and therefore stemmed from a "more recent stratum." In addition, sweets or bonbons in a dream, according to Freud,[121] "regularly represent caresses, sexual needs." Consequently, as is so often the case, we have to read the entire dream backward. Its translation then reads as follows:

She eats chocolate candy in order to allay her sexual need and to have a child. She discards this method since she now knows that for this a man is needed. She vacillates between the student and her own husband. The child is born; at the same time she is reborn.

We do not think that in this interpretation we have departed from the Freudian method of dream interpretation. After all, it is one of the most important of the insights of Freud that the paratactically arranged sentences of the manifest dream content must be "translated back" into a logical context. In exactly the same way we deal with the logically leveling, paratactic style of thinking practiced in the flight of ideas, which in many respects resembles dream language. In regard to both language styles the question naturally remains by what right we use this method of back-translation or, in other words, to what extent we equate the "seeds of thought," emerging in sentences or words loosely strung together, with thoughts and wishes born of actual thinking. But more of this later.

So far we have analyzed the porthole dream solely in regard to the fertilization, pregnancy, and birth motifs. But we must also consider its death motif which reveals itself in the manifest dream content as well as in the symbol of trunk-packing (departure).

Here too the second sentence of the dream is the cardinal point, regardless of whether we read the dream forward or backward. First, there is no doubt that we must take seriously the manifest content of the first sentence, and, as in the other dreams, must recognize a death wish and its fulfillment. Let us here recall that method of presentation in the dream which Freud recognized and described under the heading of "reversal into the opposite": Since we see that both the first and the third sentences of the dream contain the death motif, it would be remarkable if the middle sentence spoke only of life and not, "on the contrary," also of death. If we are to make use of this means of interpretation, we must recognize in the resuscitation attempts the wish for help in dying which, indeed, Ellen repeatedly expressed to her husband in waking hours. Thus the dream, read forward, could also be interpreted as follows:

I have the wish to die, and the student or my husband should help me; if

121 "Aus der Geschichte einer infantilen Neurose" ("From the History of an Infantile Neurosis"), *Coll. Works*, Vol. 3.

they do this, I can once again harmlessly eat chocolate candy and pack my trunks ("for the Beyond").

If, on the other hand, we should follow the manifest content of the first two sentences, that is, understand them according to their actual content, we would have to be content with the following "superficial" interpretation: Now I am alive again and can safely eat chocolate candy and take trips.

Now what has existential analysis to say to all this?

Though it is not within its competence and the scope of its tasks to interpret a dream, existential analysis will still note with interest that the psychoanalytic interpretation has disclosed such a close interrelationship of the birth and pregnancy motifs with the death motif in one and the same dream. It will certainly be able to insert this intertwining of motifs into its own analysis, regarding it as a partial phenomenon of that contrast of ascending and descending life which traverses the entire life-history. As to the presence of a rebirth phantasy and the attempt at amalgamating it with the suicidal tendencies, existential analysis will, however, point out that it is, to be sure, acquainted with Ellen West's rebirth-wishes through her waking expressions ("Create me once more, Fate, but create me differently"), but that it considered the interpretation "from the unconscious" too one-sided and not doing justice to the total existence. Psychoanalysis—existential analysis continues—bases its interpretation one-sidedly on instinctuality, completely neglecting the existential factor, that is, the fact that Ellen West would desperately like to be herself and yet be other than she is and that this desperation drives her to her death. An existence which was not desperate in this way would have come to terms with gluttony in some fashion or other. In that case, the place of desperation would have been taken either by a heroic-philosophic submission to "fate" or by a religious submission to "the will of God," or else by a renunciation of any "spiritual" existence and the resignation to a dull, animal mode of existence. Neither for the one nor for the other alternative was Ellen West created.

Finally, as for the psychoanalytic equation of food = fertilized = pregnant, existential analysis again notes with interest that an intertwining of the motifs of eating and fertilization is supposed to be present here. But after having proved that the gluttony is easily reducible to the world of the hole and the need for filling the hole, that it is only one feature of this "empty" mode of being-in-the-world, existential analysis cannot admit that in order to understand the greed for food we need to assume a greed for love "hiding behind it." Surely, traits of immoderateness and a "need for caresses" in Ellen's love life are recalled, but *no* indications of particularly strong "repressions" are seen in her case. But even if we may speak of a greed for love, existential analysis must once again state that although the two desires can enter into a connection or fusion, on the basis of their common relations to the underground- or tomb-world, it can by no means be said that the one is only the symbolic substitute for the other. In other words, it cannot be said that the greed for food "means" greed for love! And hence it can also not be admitted that the dread of becoming fat means the dread of pregnancy. Nor can the infantile sexual conception—according to which fertilization is caused by eating—be permitted to take on such paramount importance for the entire existence of Ellen West. Both contentions, that of the symbolic meaning and that of the paramount importance of the infantile sexual conception are, of course, possible only where the libido is hypothesized as the basis and motor of existence. But existential analysis does not engage in such hypotheses. We do not by any means deny that there are existential forms in which the existence is so narrowed or finally "fixated" [122] ("neuroses") that their existence-mode can be understood only from the "fixation" of infantile wishes and strivings. But what is true of our understanding of these forms of existence is not true with respect to the understanding of being-human in general and of the case of Ellen West in particular.

All this has brought us close to the question of what position existential analysis takes in reference to the Freudian conception of the unconscious. Earlier we have already posed the question whether the method of "back-translation" of the manifest dream content into latent dream-thoughts is justified. If one follows this method, one construes "behind" the conscious personality an "unconscious" second person, which is certainly not permissible in existential-analytical terms; for if the individuality is what its world is (in the sense of its own world) and if its world is only affirmed in language, in other words, needs language to be world at all, then we cannot speak of individuality where the language is not yet language, that is, communication and meaningful expression. Hence Freud did not at first speak of an "ego" in regard to the unconscious, but of an "id"; later, however, he lent support to the popular conception of the unconscious as a second ego or a second person by the assertion that "parts of the ego and superego," too, must be recognized as unconscious.

In the light of all this, existential analysis must state that the unconscious in the strict psychoanalytic sense (*i.e.*, not in the sense of nonattention or forgetting) may point to a being but by no means to an existence. For the latter means a being which is Here and has its Here, that is, which knows about it and is in relation to it. This Here is its opened-ness, its world. The unconscious however has, as noted, no world; world is not opened to it not even—as in the manifest dream—"conjured up," and it does not understand itself in terms of its world. An unconscious id is not in the world in the sense of existence (*Dasein*), for being-in-the-world always means to be in the world as I-myself, He-himself, We-ourselves, or anonymous oneself; and least of all does the id know anything of "home," as is true of the dual We, of the I and

[122] In regard to this expression, cf. Kierkegaard, *Philosophical Fragments*, Vol. 1.

Thou. The id is a scientific construct which objectifies existence—a "reservoir of instinctual energy."

Of course this does not imply that existential analysis is not interested in wishing, phantasying, or dreaming. Indeed, the present study testifies to that interest. But what it cares about ultimately is the particular world-design, the being-in-it, and the being-self corresponding to it. As for the dream, we have repeatedly touched upon this question ourselves and answered it by saying that the dreaming mode of being-in-the-world is to be understood as being entangled in the *Eigenwelt*,[123] as bodily existing,[124] as existing in the sense of self-forgetfulness [125] and, above all, in the sense of the optimistic flight of ideas.[126]

We have shown how existential analysis and psychoanalysis can cooperate in the understanding of an existence-*Gestalt,* but we must again and again remind the reader of the gulf opening between these two so different scientific endeavors. The one is the phenomenological, which devotes itself to the phenomenal content of every verbal expression, every mode of action, every attitude, and attempts to understand it from basic modes of human existence prior to the separation of body, soul, and mind, and of consciousness and unconsciousness; and the other is the objectifying natural-scientific one, which according to Freud himself subordinates phenomena to the "hypothetically postulated strivings," investigates the verbal content not with respect to the world-design which emerges in it, but with respect to those strivings or "natural" instincts, and which thus projects the being of man upon the conceptual level of the being of "nature." In this way the extrapersonal, nameless id (alien to I and We) [127]—involving man's surrender without escape to a *vis major* which he confronts without the possibility of any real counteraction—achieves such paramount importance. To be sure, existential analysis too, as has been repeatedly emphasized, starts from the assumption that the existence did not lay its ground itself; but it knows of a freedom in relation to its ground—a freedom in the sense of self-responsibility (Plato to Nietzsche), in the sense of man's being free in his attitude toward his own "character" (Le Senne), and it knows of the grace of the free meeting of the I and the Thou in love. In whatever way one wishes to understand this freedom metaphysically or religiously, existential analysis holds to the fact that being-human is not only a having-to-be but also a being-able-to-be and a being-allowed-to-be, a being-secure in being as a whole. To this extent it considers not only the ethereal world of wishes and phantasies and

---

123 "Traum und Existenz."
124 "Über Psychotherapie."
125 *Ibid.*, also, *Basic Forms.*
126 *Über Ideenflucht.*
127 Cf. Hermann Ammann, "Zum deutschen Impersonale" ("Remarks on Impersonal Expressions in German"), *Papers in Honor of Husserl,* 1929.

its "substructure," the tomb-world of desires, but also the authentic I-myself and the eternal We, existence and love, the being-able and being-allowed, and thus the being in truth, beauty, and kindness. Since Freud developed his image of man from the neurosis, completely ignoring his own exemplary being, his view (in any case the view of the naturalist) necessarily focused on the inescapable having-to-be. But since even the neurotic is not only a neurotic, and man in general is not only one compelled, we deal here with a one-sided distortion of the human image in the frame of a scientific theory of man. Hence psychoanalysis can become "humanology" only in the light of the total study of existence or anthropology.

IV *Psychopathological Clinical Analysis*

Before we turn to the purely clinical problems which our case raises, let us once more briefly sum up the results of our existential-analytical interpretation. For in this study we are interested not only in furnishing a casuistic contribution to the theory of schizophrenia but also in showing by way of this case how varied, indeed divergent, are the viewpoints and methods from and with which the mentally ill person can and must be brought into view and scientifically studied.

The existential-analytic conception of our case culminated in the finding that we have to do with an existence-*Gestalt* whose world takes on more and more the form of emptiness or of the hole and whose total existence-form can be described only as being-empty or being-a-hole. Indeed, it is part of the nature of existence as being-a-hole that it can be experienced both as emptiness and as being-limited and being-oppressed or imprisoned and as longing for freedom; and finally also makes its appearance as a specific mode of the self. This is equally true for all world-regions which this existence opens to itself, for the *Umwelt* as well as for the *Mitwelt,* and for the *Eigenwelt*. In all these world-regions we find equally emptiness, restriction, pressure, and longing for liberation from all this; and only he who can see and appreciate them in all regions can also see and appreciate them rightly in the region of the body-world. If, then, we attempt to summarize once more the individual features and phenomenal forms of this mode of being-in-the-world within the various world-regions, but without at all trying to present them exhaustively, we shall again do best to start out from the landscape-world: the being-limited and being-oppressed showed itself here as darkening, darkness, night, cold, ebb-tide; the boundaries or limits as moist fog-walls or clouds, the emptiness as the Uncanny, the longing for freedom (from the hole) as ascending into the air, the self as a hushed bird. Within the world of *vegetation,* the being-restricted and being-oppressed showed itself as wilting, the barriers as suffocating air, the emptiness as weeds, the longing for freedom as urge to grow, the self as withered plant. Within the world of things we found the being-restricted in the hole, cellar, tomb; the barriers in walls, masonry, fetters, nets; the longing for freedom in the vessel of fertility, the self in the discarded husk. Within the *animal* world, the being-restricted is seen as being-holed-in, the barriers as earth or black night, the self as worm no longer capable of any longing for freedom, the emptiness as merely vegetating. Within the *Mitwelt* being-restricted is seen as being subjugated, oppressed, impaired, and pursued; the emptiness as lack of peace, indifference, joyless submission, seclusion, loneliness; the barriers as fetters, or adders of the everyday, or suffocating air; the hole itself as the little world (of the everyday); the longing for freedom as urge for independence, defiance, insurrection, revolt; the self as rebel, nihilist, later as cowardly compromiser. Within the *Eigenwelt* as thought-world, we recognized being-restricted in cowardice, indulgence, giving up of high-flown plans; the barriers in accusing, jeering ghosts or specters encircling and invading from all sides, the emptiness in being-ruled by one single idea, even as Nothingness; the self in the timid earthworm, the frozen heart, the longing for freedom as desperation. Finally, within the *Eigenwelt* as body-world, we found the being restricted or oppressed in being fat, the barriers or walls in the layer of fat against which the existence beats its fists as against walls, the emptiness in being dull, stupid, old, ugly, and even being dead, the longing for freedom in wanting-to-be-thin, the self as a mere tube for material filling-up and re-emptying.

From all this it becomes evident that everyday speech, in using the expression "benighted," does indeed pick out one very essential "cosmological" feature of the total phenomenon that occupies us here, but that we could speak by the same token of darkening, beclouding, chilling, swamp-ing, devastating; or of narrowing, encircling, ensnaring, entangling, enveloping, overpowering; of being grabbed, being-attacked; of being chained, walled in, oppressed, suffocated, interred, emptied; of being imprisoned, isolated, captured, and enslaved. All these expressions, and many more, also single out certain cosmological features as well as features of the *Um-*, *Mit-*, and *Eigenwelt* of the total phenomenon of that existential transformation which in literary language is often described as becoming "benighted" (*Umnachtung*), but is labeled as "psychosis" by psychiatry. Characteristically, in our case the "spatially" derived expression "de-ranged" (*verrückt*) is missing. In the space-time-sphere belongs the expression "standstill" (of development). Purely temporal terms are also lacking. From the sphere of things stem such expressions as disintegrate, from the sphere of vegetation expressions such as die-off, wither, wilt, molder; from the animal, human, and spirit world, all the expressions pertaining to ensnaring, entangling, isolating, and in addition to jeering, cursing, accusing, watching, poisoning, etc. From the body-sphere come the expressions getting-fat, getting-ugly, and freezing; from the psychic sphere, becoming-dull, -stupid, -cowardly, yielding, succumbing, shuddering, not developing further, being merely a stage, struggling in vain, suffering tortures of hell, being a walking corpse, etc. The "world-picture" as such is distorted to a grimace.

In reviewing these findings of existential analysis, we immediately realize how radical is the process of reduction which the natural-historically oriented clinical method must use in order to be able to speak of a disease-process and to project it upon the "organism" and the structure and modes of functioning of the brain, instead of considering the total phenomena of such an existential transformation. Since we have previously sketched this psychopathological-clinical reduction process, in our studies on the flight of ideas, we shall be brief here.

Like existential analysis and psychoanalysis, psychopathological-clinical analysis, too, is dependent on the life-history. By virtue of just this "narrative" feature, as Bieganski [128] clearly recognized, not only psychiatry but also medicine in general differs from all other natural sciences. But whereas existential analysis penetrates into the meaning and content of the verbal speech and other phenomena of expression and interprets from them the world and the being-in-the-world as historical, and hence understands being-human as it shows itself in those phenomena in its own terms, psychoanalysis changes the temporalization into chronology (a sequence of life events "in time"), the existence into an object, the existential transformation into a genetic developmental process, the life-historical phenomena into symptoms of certain vicissitudes of instinctual forces, and so on. By contrast, for clinical analysis the life-history becomes the illness history, verbal and other phenomena of expression become indications or symptoms of something which, indeed, does not show in them, but hides behind them, namely, the illness, and the place of the phenomenological interpretation, is taken by the diagnosis: the exact natural-scientific investigation and assembling of the illness symptoms and their classification under already familiar types and categories of symptoms. When we speak of diagnosis, however, we speak of the organism, in psychiatry just as in the other branches of medicine (this cannot be fully elaborated here). Diagnostic judgments are biological value-judgments. What for existential analysis is the emptying of existence down to the mere being-a-hole is for clinical analysis a symptom of an illness-process in the organism, of a "damage" to and "disturbance" of its functions. The system of psychiatric pathology is built upon this basic concept, just as is the system of the pathology of "internal illnesses." One who makes a psychiatric diagnosis, therefore, not only knows about this basic concept but also is familiar with the entire experiential system which has been built upon and around it. Just as the botanist and the zoologist must know the system of plants or animals if he wishes to classify a plant or an animal, so one must know the types, orders, and classes of the psychiatric system in order to be able to compare the individual case with other cases, using the symptoms observed in it, and to place it correctly, *i.e.*, "classify" it, on the basis of such comparing.

Before we turn to this task, one further word about psychopathology and its relationship to existential analysis. Like much of traditional psychology, psychopathology, too, is diametrically opposed to existential analysis insofar as both objectify the existence and make of it an impersonal something called "psyche." In doing this both completely miss from the very beginning the sense of "psyche" in the primal sense of the word. In place of the *experience of the sequence* (to mention only one factor) they place a *sequence*

128 Bieganski, *Medizin. Logik* (*Medical logic*) (German transl. by Von Fabian) (Würzburg: 1909).

of experiences (events, processes, functions, mechanisms) in the soul or in the consciousness. This makes "the soul" or "the consciousness" into a second psychical organism or even apparatus existing beside or with the bodily organism. As we see in particular from the presentation of the case of Ellen West, we are dealing here with a tremendous oversimplification, reinterpretation, and reduction of human existence down to the categories of natural science. All this, however, psychopathology accepts in order to find that "connection" with biology which, as noted, alone warrants the concept of illness in the medical sense and the possibility of a medical diagnosis and a causal therapy. Thus, we arrive in psychiatry at a doubling of the organism, from which results the futile and pointless controversy as to whether the one organism acts on the other, whether they parallel each other or are "at bottom" identical. All of these are pseudo problems, arising from purely scientific theory. Once we have seen through this philosophically, these problems vanish. In their place emerges the problem of intentionality (Husserl) and upon and behind it that of existence or being-in-the-world; the phenomenological problem of subjectivity deepens to the ontological problem of existence.

After these brief remarks about the state of affairs out of which being and not-being must be understood according to the concept of psychopathology, we finally turn to our psychopathological clinical task. The place of the historical and existential *Gestalt* of Ellen West will now be taken by the *case* of Ellen West.

Janet's Case of Nadia and the Case of Ellen West

Whereas an unspoken *aversion* to becoming fat and manifold devices for keeping thin are often found in young girls and women—be it out of vanity or after disappointments in love—an outspoken *dread* of becoming fat, such as in our case, is not frequent. Only one similar case in the literature is known to me, namely, Janet's case of Nadia.[129] Janet reports it under the purely descriptive classification of obsession with body-shame (*obsession de la honte du corps*).

Nadia, twenty-seven years old and unmarried, who five years previously had been referred to Janet with a diagnosis of anorexia hysteria, had devised for herself a more than bizarre mode of nourishment (two small portions of bouillon, one egg yolk, one teaspoon of vinegar, and one cup of very strong tea with lemon). Attempts by her family to change this diet caused terrible scenes. Her motive for the diet was the fear of becoming fat (*la crainte d'engraisser*). Janet saw quickly that this was not at all a case of anorexia (*perte du sentiment de la faim*), but that Nadia, on the contrary, usually felt hunger, indeed at times so great a hunger, that she greedily devoured everything she found (*dévorer gloutonnement tout ce qu'elle rencontre*). At times she also secretly ate biscuits. Afterwards she had terrible pangs of conscience, only to do it again at the next opportunity. She herself admitted

129 "Obsessions et Psychasthénie" ("Obsessions and Psychasthenia").

that it cost her a great effort to keep from eating, so that she felt like a heroine. At times she would think only of food for many hours, so great was her hunger; she would swallow her saliva, bite her handkerchief, and roll on the floor. She would search in books for descriptions of banquets, in order to participate mentally in them and to trick herself out of her own hunger. "The refusal of food," Janet concludes, "is nothing but the consequence of an idea, of a delusion." Viewed superficially, he says, this idea is the fear of becoming fat. Nadia was afraid, it seems, of becoming fat like her mother. She wanted to be thin and pale, as would correspond to her own character. She was constantly afraid of getting a bloated face, strong muscles, a healthier appearance. One could not tell her that she looked better; such a comment once caused a serious relapse. She constantly required people to confirm her emaciation. From this a "compulsive questioning" about her looks developed which was very annoying for those around her. So far the symptomatology of this case closely coincides with that of ours, apart from the main difference that in the one a "questioning compulsion" developed, in the other a "thinking compulsion." In addition, in the case of Nadia, the rejection of being fat referred to her mother, whereas in the case of Ellen West the wish to be thin referred to her ethereal girl friends. Psychoanalytically speaking, however, both cases probably reflect merely two different aspects of the repression of love for the mother and the "return" of the repressed love—with Nadia by way of narcissism, with Ellen by way of homoeroticism.

Nadia's obsessive idea (*pensée obsédante*) was, according to Janet, by no means an isolated, inexplicable, fixed idea, but rather part of a complex thought-system. Being fat (*l'embonpoint*) did not disturb her only for reasons of coquetry, for she had *no* wish to be pretty; in the eyes of the patient it was something immoral, something "that to me is abhorrent" (*cela me fait horreur*). If she were ever to get fat, she would be ashamed to be exposed to anyone's gaze, both at home and on the street. Yet being fat (*l'obésité*) seemed not to be "shameful" (*honteuse*) to her as such, and in fact (in contrast to our patient), she liked people who were very fat, and thought that it was becoming to them (this shows the ambivalence of the mother-complex!) Only in regard to herself was being fat "shameful and immoral" (*honteux et immoral*). And this judgment applied not only to being fat but to everything connected with eating.

As with our patient, the illness began with her insistence on eating alone, as if in hiding. She felt, in her own judgment, like someone who is asked to urinate in public; when she ate too much she reproached herself as for something indecent. She was terribly ashamed when surprised in the act of eating bonbons. Once when she had eaten chocolates on an impulse "*de gourmandise et de curiosité,*" she apologized for it to Janet in innumerable letters. Not only should one not *see* her eating, but not *hear* her either. Her chewing—only her own chewing—caused a particularly ugly and mortifying noise. She was willing to swallow the food, but people should not think they could force her to chew it.

As the last symptom goes beyond the observable symptomatology of Ellen West, so do the following of Nadia's symptoms: though quite pretty and slim, Nadia was convinced that her face was bloated, reddened, and full of pimples. Anyone who did not see these pimples did not understand; there were pimples between the skin and the flesh!

From her fourth year Nadia had been ashamed of her figure because she was told she was tall for her age. From her eighth year she had been ashamed of her hands, which she found long and ridiculous. About her eleventh year she rebelled against short skirts because she thought everyone was looking at her legs, which she could no longer endure. When she was allowed long skirts she was ashamed of her feet, her broad hips, her fat arms, etc.

The onset of menstruation, the growth of pubic hair, and the development of her breasts made her half-crazy. Until her twentieth year she attempted to pull out the pubic hair. From puberty on, her total condition showed an exacerbation: the rejection of her usual food and the refusal to eat in company originated during this period.

By every means, in clothing and head-dress, Nadia attempted to conceal her sex (as was the case with Ellen until her eighteenth year), in order to make a masculine impression. She did everything to look like a young male student. However, Janet thinks that in this case it is not proper to speak of inversion, for Nadia would have been equally ashamed to be a boy: she wanted to be quite *without* sex, indeed, apparently without body, for all parts of her body give rise to the same feeling (*sentiment*); the refusal of food is only a very special manifestation of this one feeling.

As to the question of which idea determined all these evaluations (*appréciations*), Janet thinks he must grant an important role to the feeling of shame. From childhood on Nadia could not undress in front of her parents, and until her twenty-seventh year she had not permitted any physician to listen to her chest. Added to this was a vague feeling of guilt, a self-reproach for her gluttony and all sorts of vices. (About early childhood masturbation we have as little information as in the case of Ellen West. In both cases we are inclined to answer in the affirmative from psychoanalytical experience.)

One further motif plays a similar part in both cases: "I didn't wish," Nadia said, "to become fat, or to grow tall, or to resemble a woman because I always wanted to remain a little girl." And why? "Because I was afraid of being loved less." This motif may also have played a part in the case of Ellen West, of whose psychic life as a child we unfortunately know so little. At any rate, Ellen West did not want to be a child but only to remain young, a Hebe, like her ethereal girl friends. But the real reason that Nadia was afraid of being ugly and ridiculous is, according to Janet, the fear that people would mock at her, not like her any more, or find her different from the others. "The wish to be loved" and the fear of not deserving the love so fervently longed for certainly accompanies her feelings of guilt and shame (*aux idees de fautes possibles et aux craintes de la pudeur*), and calls forth the obsession with body-shame. (We ourselves would say: The guilt and shame feelings are the motif of the fear of loss of love and probably also the motif of the body-shame.)

So much for Janet's report. As pure "history of an illness," it is a report on the illness symptoms and their sequence "in time." Hence we do not find an anthropological interpretation of the total phenomenon of this human existence and its uniqueness, but a mere "taking of the particular person by something," namely, by its weak points.[130] And the characteristics seen here

---

[130] Cf. *Basic Forms.*

as the weak points are those in which a deviation from normal behavior can be recognized. The latter is presupposed as generally known (though by no means recognized). Finally, an attempt is made to explain psychologically the diversity of the illness-characteristics from a single morbid basic feeling, the body-shame. But where psychology or psychopathology speak of feeling, that vaguest and most equivocal of all psychological expressions, there the scientific task for existential analysis only begins. For it, the word "feeling" means only the horizon of the statement of a problem.

Janet stops when he has determined that in the case of Nadia all parts of the body elicit the same feeling of shame, indeed, disgrace, so that according to him we have to do with a pervasive body-shame. But what, we must begin by asking, is the existential meaning of such a body-shame, how is it to be understood existentially? Nadia is even more high-flown [131] than Ellen: she would want not only to be slim but to be even without a body or, so to speak, to lead the existence of an angel.[132] She too does not stand firmly with both feet on the earth, she wants to escape from the corporeal part of man's destiny and wishes neither to have a sex nor to be nourished nor to be seen or heard at all. The latter means nothing other than that she would like to withdraw from the *Mitwelt* and lead a purely solipsistic existence. Her body-shame is not a being-ashamed *because* of the body but because of her *existing* as a body or, better, as lived body (*Leib*). If one speaks of corporeal shame, the body is not seen in its unity of identity as externally perceptible body (object) and body-consciousness, but, as is the case with Nadia herself, only as a hateful, loathsome object to be hidden from the eyes of the body-world. But my body is never only an object, only part of the external world; as Wernicke thought, my body is also always "I." If I wish to escape from my body, to get rid of, or to hide my body, then I always wish also to escape from myself, to get rid of "something of myself," and to hide "something of myself." I, as angel, wish to get rid of and hide from the others something devilish in me, or to get rid of and hide myself as a devil. Whatever way this consciousness of sin may have arisen—through early childish masturbation or masturbation-substitute, or through aggressive tendencies toward the mother—does not matter here. Indeed, it is precisely our task, in contrast to the one-sided overemphasis on genetic origins and the exclusive explanation drawn therefrom, to bring to light the essence (*eidos*), the *Gestalt* of the particular being-in-the-world, without which the genetic explanation remains hanging in mid-air. For even if we all suffer from the same "complexes," still it must be shown how the world-picture and the

131 [See Note 45.—TRANSLATORS.]

132 It is very instructive, as well as characteristic of the intrinsic relationship between the two cases, that Ellen, too, though on only one occasion, identifies being thin with being without a body: ". . . this ideal of being-thin, of being-bodiless."

being-in-the-world change when it comes to something like a neurosis or a psychosis.

To return to the case of Nadia, not only the feeling of shame but also the feeling of guilt is more clearly evident here than in the case of Ellen West. But this does not mean at all that the latter is missing in Ellen's case. Ellen's trait of asceticism, very probably appearing in early childhood, already points that way. Besides, her self-reproaches for eating sweets also show definitely the character of reproaches of conscience, much as such reproaches have in both patients "got on the wrong track." What both reproach themselves for and what both would like to hide from the *Mitwelt* is their greed, again as an expression of the bodily-"bestial," creaturely, "evil" side of their existence. Here too, early childhood ideas of a Christian nature (by way of the nursemaid in the case of Ellen) may play a part. In general, Nadia, with all her aggressiveness, is still the one more dependent on the *Mitwelt;* Ellen West is the more self-powered nature. This can also be seen from the fact that Nadia develops a *Mitwelt*-oriented "questioning compulsion," whereas Ellen West's "compulsive thinking" is a purely *Eigenwelt*-oriented "compulsion." Also, the fear that she will be less liked by *others* if she is fat is clearly expressed by Nadia, whereas at bottom Ellen cannot love herself any more if she is fat.

Moreover, Nadia, aside from the dread of being conspicuous and the suspicion that others are making fun of her, also shows traits of the hypochondriacal form of Kretschmer's *paranoia sensitiva*.[133] Consider in particular the incorrigible, in my opinion thoroughly delusionary hypochondriacal ideas with respect to chewing, pimples, and being bloated, in which the reference to the *Mitwelt* appears to play an even greater role than does that of the bodily *Eigenwelt*.

This brings us to the diagnosis of the case of Nadia. Both Eugen Bleuler and Jung are known to have believed that the majority of Janet's cases must be considered schizophrenic. Similarly, Manfred Bleuler[134] recently stated correctly that the various subforms of *paranoia sensitiva*—as a psycho-reactive ailment—cannot be clearly distinguished from advanced schizophrenic illnesses. Even if in the case of Nadia we cannot speak of an advanced schizophrenia, I think that here too the diagnosis of schizophrenia has to be made. And indeed it is very easy to think, on the basis of the anamnesis, of an attack occurring in early childhood which may have been followed by a second attack at puberty. Kraepelin has already pointed out that infantile schizophrenic traumas seem to occur much more frequently than we are inclined to assume. I myself can only confirm this assumption on the basis

133 [The reference is to the monograph by Kretschmer, *Der sensitive Beziehungswahn* (*The Sensitive Delusion of Reference*) (Berlin: Julius Springer, 1927).—TRANSLATORS.]

134 *Fortschritte d. Neur. u. Psych.*, No. 9, 1943.

of my own material, particularly in such cases as take a "neurosis-like" course. This cannot be entirely excluded in regard to the case of Ellen West either. Unfortunately Janet tells us nothing about Nadia's heredity.

Although in this section we have to do with the diagnostic reduction, we must, at its close, attempt to interpret more thoroughly the case of Nadia in existential-analytic terms—as far as this is possible on the basis of Nadia's symptoms—particularly with reference to Ellen West's case.

The main difference between the two cases in their mode of existence has already been emphasized. In the case of Ellen West—we refer here only to the "final state"—the existence is primarily absorbed in the being-to-itself, the intercourse with itself, or in the existence-realm of the *Eigenwelt,* whereas in the case of Nadia predominantly in the realm of the *Mitwelt,* in the intercourse of the one with the others.[135] To what degree the two modes of existence are basically dependent upon or intertwined with each other we shall see more and more clearly. True, Ellen West too feels herself in a "glass ball," "separated" from the *Mitwelt* by "glass walls," but she suffers from this separation. This suffering is nevertheless, not the main suffering for her; what she suffers most from is the suffering in or from herself, from her "violence-to-herself." Hence her inability to escape from herself, her being imprisoned, her being-in-the-noose of her self, from which noose she can free herself only through suicide. Hence also we find in her very little trace of shame in front of the others. True, she too must separate herself (hide) from the others while eating, but she is primarily ashamed before herself and correspondingly goes through her fight with fate alone and takes it into her own hands, disregarding the others. True, the others must confirm to her, too, that she is not fat, but in this respect not they but she is the highest court. Her "greed" she experiences primarily as detestable to herself, much less so to the others. The increasing emptying, earthifying, and entombing of her existence, her being-a-hole, concerns predominantly the *Eigenwelt;* the emptying of the realm of the *Mitwelt* appears only as the existential consequence of this.

Things are quite different with Nadia. She flees from the others, would like to conceal herself from them, and suffers because she cannot do this as she would like. She is afraid to be conspicuous to the others, to be different from them, to be less loved by them, and she protects herself from all this by innumerable "devices," whereas the devices which Ellen West uses serve as protection from herself. What appears to us in the case of Nadia as "feelings of shame and disgrace," morbidly aggravated both extensively and intensively, is just that wishing-to-conceal-herself from others. However, we must not view these very manifold symptoms of being ashamed as the authentic or essential thing, for they are merely the indications by which we recognize that this existence must conceal itself from the others. These indications are only the breakthrough-points of an existence stricken by the curse of

135 Cf. *Basic Forms,* Part I, chapters 2 and 3.

shame. Again, we can understand this form of existence only if we see that Nadia appears to herself as damnable, vile, repulsive, indeed, disgusting. Whereas Ellen retreats from herself into the body-world and for her protection seizes upon laxatives, Nadia retreats from herself into the *Mitwelt* and for her protection seizes upon measures of concealment from it. These measures of concealment are her protection against the insight into her existence as shame. The existential or, as Erwin Straus calls it, the protecting shame, becomes purely concealing shame.[136] In the latter, according to Straus, it is not a question of primal shame, originally intrinsic to being-human (and not acquired in the course of the life-history), but of the *Mitwelt*-connected or public shame stemming from one's own reflection thrown upon the others. This shame does not guard "the secret of the existence," facing which one can also be ashamed before oneself; rather, it is in the service of "social status" (Straus).

The Shame Phenomenon

Here we must pause a moment. Important and justified as Straus's distinction is, it must not lead us to lose sight of the shame phenomenon as a whole. At the bottom of the shame phenomenon, existential (protecting) and *Mitwelt* (concealing) shame belong together, just as existence (being-oneself) and *Mitwelt* (being-with) belong together. This comes to light perhaps more clearly in the shame phenomenon than anywhere else; for existential shame, too, shows itself in blushing, that is, in a partially *Mitwelt*-connected phenomenon! I can of course say that I blush before myself, but in reality I blush before another or the others. And here again lies a fact which is uncommonly important for the understanding of our cases, namely, that shame shows to the other precisely what it wants to hide from him, that is, the secret of the existence. I recall an epigram by Hebbel:

> Shame in a human marks the inner border of sinning;
> Where he will blush there begins surely his nobler self.

Whether I blush because I myself have touched the inner border of sin, or because another has touched it, I always show him by blushing something which at bottom I do not wish to show at all, namely, the "point" where the inner border of sin "in me" is touched. If we call "sin" a spiritual (*geistiges*) phenomenon and blushing a bodily one, it becomes clear that the very shame phenomenon as a whole contradicts this separation, much as it, on the other hand, rests upon it. No one has grasped this more profoundly than Scheler: "Only because having a body is part of being-human," he puts

---

136 For this distinction, cf. the (Zurich) lecture by E. Straus, "Die Scham als historiologisches Problem" ("Shame as a Historiological Problem"), *Schweiz. Arch. Neur. u. Psychiat.*, 1933. It seems to me important to mention at this point that in accordance with his theory of man, Freud saw and attempted to "explain" only the latter form of shame.

it, "can a person get into the position of *having to be ashamed;* and only because he experiences his spiritual (*geistiges*) being-a-person as essentially independent of such a 'body' and of all that can come out of the body, is it possible for him to get into the position of *being able* to be ashamed.

"In shame, therefore, in a peculiar and obscure way, mind and flesh, eternity and temporality, essence and existence touch each other." (Of course, existence is not meant here in Heidegger's sense, but, as the antitheses show, in the sense of being in general and in *contrast* to essence.) "All the various kinds and forms of the feeling of shame . . . have this one great, all-inclusive background: that the person feels and knows himself in the depths as a 'bridge,' as a 'viaduct' between two orders of being and essence, in both of which he is equally strongly rooted and of which he cannot give up one even for a second if he still wishes to be called a 'human.' " [137]

It requires no great sagacity to see that Ellen and to an even greater degree Nadia do not recognize this double destination of being-human, but want to overthrow it and desperately fight against it. But that is an illness of the "mind" (*Geist*).

Now, since shame leans so much toward the concealing, *Mitwelt*-oriented shame, the peculiar dialectic of shame—namely, that it reveals to the others just what it wants to hide—becomes all the more evident. But this brings us to the core of what we can call "mania to get attention." [138]

We see this with especial clarity in the case of Nadia. Her desperate revolt against corporeality as the ground of the having-to-be-ashamed results in her corporeality coming more than ever into the fore, as nothing but an attention-target. But this means: the communication or intercourse with the others (co-working, co-playing, co-struggling, co-enjoying, co-suffering, etc.) is restricted to the merely "being-taken" by the others in the sense of being-observed, that is, to a special form of objectification of existence and the distance peculiar thereto. Nadia is a reversed *voyeur*, namely, if one may put it thus, an *"homme-à-voir"* (one to be seen). Shame here is not the delicate psychic shell "that envelops the body" (Madame Guyon) and hence an expression of a "positive self-worth," [138] but the cloak of invisibility [139] behind which she tries to hide her body, the visible and audible part of her existence, completely from the eyes and ears of the others, the expression of an absolutely negative self-worth. In this case the anonymization goes even further than in the "mask" responses in the Rorschach test. [140] Here the self not only hides behind the anonymous mask but wishes not to be seen at all

---

[137] "Über Scham und Schamgefühl" ("On Shame and the Feeling of Shame"), *Posthumous Papers*, Vol. 1.

[138] Cf. Scheler.

[139] [*Tarnkappe*, literally a mask which makes one invisible and is itself invisible.—TRANSLATORS.]

[140] Cf. Roland Kuhn, *Über Maskendeutungen im Rorschach'schen Versuch* (*On the Mask Response in the Rorschach test*) (Basel: 1944).

any more, not even as mask-wearer; for what Janet designates here as body-shame is, as we have seen, nothing but the shame of being seen, of being observed, or, more correctly, of possibly being seen (*de pouvoir d'être vu*). Hence the dread of all that meets the eye as regards bodily figure, body functions, clothing, skin. Added to this, as we have seen, is the *honte d'être entendu* (while chewing). Nadia, too, wishes desperately to be herself, but as another, humanly impossible self, namely, as invisible and inaudible, hence nonbodily self. Since this wish is still more "off," more "alien to reality" than that of wishing-to-be-thin, we get from Nadia an even "sicker" impression than from Ellen, and we must designate her "case" clinically as even "more severe" than the case of Ellen West. Consequently, the dread of getting fat must have a different psychopathological evaluation in the two cases. In the case of Ellen West it is an expression of her dread of apostasy from her self-chosen, desperately maintained Hebe-ideal and of her dread of descending life in general; in the case of Nadia it is an expression of her dread of the creaturely, bodily existence insofar as that is the condition under which one can be seen and heard. This fear is therefore expressive of a much more "off the beam" existence, because it denies the creaturely basis of any being-human. In short: Nadia struggles desperately to lead in public an unpublic existence. A person who wants to lead such a humanly impossible existence we have every right to call deranged (*verrückt*).

The wishing-to-exist in a manner not observed by the *Mitwelt* (invisible and inaudible, altogether intangible) seems to me to contain one of the basic problems of schizophrenic modes of existence. Observing things superficially one might explain that Nadia withdrew from the *Mitwelt* (the public) to the point of complete impalpability because she was ashamed for reasons of her figure, her clothes, her pimples, etc. But a deeper consideration must lead to an opposite conclusion. As in so many insidiously progressive cases of schizophrenia (among them Ellen's) we find early in Nadia's case history a self-willed, stubborn revolt against the way in which she herself was "thrown" into existence, in short, against a special mode of the human fate. (In my own cases this revolt was often directed against the patient's sex and, with female patients especially, against being-taken-as-woman.) In this revolt (carried to the point of despair), in which the existence presumes to want to be a self other than it is and can be, it manifestly runs counter to the structure of existence in general, tries to break through it, indeed to shatter it, even though holding desperately to being-oneself as such. But this structure does not let itself be broken through, still less shattered, but reasserts itself again and again, only in another ("abnormal") way, as we have already shown in our studies, *On the Flight of Ideas*. With Nadia, as already mentioned, we see it in the fact that the more obstinately she wishes not to be conspicuous, the more striking targets she produces for the *Mitwelt*, ending with the pimples "under her skin." Thereby the structure of existence reasserts itself again. The more stubbornly (dictatorially) the human being opposes his being-thrown into his existence and therewith into existence in general, the more strongly this thrownness gains in influence. Applied to the case of Nadia: the more invisible, inconspicuous she wants to appear, the more conspicuous her existence becomes, that is, the more she thinks she is striking to the *Mitwelt,* the others, in some way "leaping into their eyes." From Nadia's conviction that she is conspicuous to the others it is only a short step to the conviction that the others are jeering at her; for that former conviction, in its very conception, carries in it the character of being disagreeably and ridiculously conspicuous. Nadia *must* be ashamed before the others, because the mode of her existence is a ridiculous one. If we could bring her to see this in the full existential sense—which is no longer possible with schizophrenics of this kind—she would indeed have to "enter into herself" (*in sich gehen*) but she would no longer need to feel shame before the others. If however she should gain a purely intellectual understanding of it—which at times is still possible in such cases—she would either take her own life or, as experience shows, the schizophrenic process would bring up still heavier artillery.

The Problem of Shame and the Schizophrenic Process

We will once more take a closer look at this process, particularly in connection with the shame phenomenon. The problem, as is evident from our foregoing discussion, revolves about the phenomenological "relationship" between existential and concealing shame within the one shame phenomenon. When we speak of existential shame, *i.e.,* where "the inner boundary of sin" is existentially experienced, hence, where the "nobler self" (Hebbel) is divined and guarded as secret, there the human being is his own lord and judge, the self is master of itself. The less, on the other hand, it is its own master, the more it drifts into dependence on the *Mitwelt,* the more the *Mitwelt* becomes lord and judge of the self. Hence the child, as a still dependent existence, is to a high degree dependent on the "judgment" of the *Mitwelt.* But the child—as Freud did not see—would not be able to depend upon the judgment of the *Mitwelt* if it were not capable of feeling, or at least divining, the inner border of sin as shame. In this sense, "morbidly exaggerated" shame is merely a relapse into childhood; but we must point out that it makes a great difference whether the human being must first acquire an existential position or falls back again from one already gained to an earlier one!

Now in regard to the understanding of the schizophrenic process by way of the problem of shame, the chief point is that here we have to do with a modification of being-human in the sense that "the inner border of sin" is no longer freely movable or fluid according to the standard of the self which "decides" in every case afresh and freely as to occasion, degree, and intensity of the having-to-be-ashamed, but that this border is fixed once and for all, *figé* (*i.e.*, "coagulated"), as Masselon has put it in his thesis (Paris, 1902).[141] However, Masselon applies this term still one-sidedly to the thinking (*la pensée*) of the schizophrenics. Here, as everywhere, we must not take thinking as our starting point but must fix our gaze on the total form of existence. The exploration of shame, as we have seen, is eminently suitable for this. The reason that the inner border of sin is no longer fluid—*i.e.*, variable according to the inner and outer situation—but is "coagulated," is just this—that the place of the self is taken by the *Mitwelt* (which always corresponds to an existential emptiness or emptying). For the *Mitwelt* is not one's own standard but an alien one, and as such it is no longer dependent on myself but faces me as something immovable and foreign. What we so casually call the "outward projection" of the shame feeling (and of other feelings) is nothing but the transfer of the center of gravity of our existence from our own self to the judgment of the others, experienced as fixed. Thereby the self, as we pointed out above, becomes a state of things, judged by the others and accordingly by me—in other words, it becomes objectified, made into a "fixed" object or thing, with fixed contours, fixed dimensions and weight. Consequently, just that sphere of being-human comes into the foreground which most readily corresponds to these conditions, namely, the body! "The body" signifies the sphere of our existence which is on hand here and now, spatially expanded, present *here, i.e.*, in evidence to eyes and ears, in contrast to that duration of the self which is independent of (world-)time and (world-)space. Because the objectified self can now no longer experience itself, in direct contrast to its desperate struggling, as essentially independent of its body, it can no longer be existentially ashamed but must conceal itself from the others. Body-shame (*honte du corps*) is pure concealing shame, that is, an unauthentic shame which one does better to designate as disgrace than as feeling of shame. So the schizophrenic process is primarily a process of existential emptying or impoverishment, in the sense of an increasing congelation ("coagulation") of the free self toward an ever-unfreer ("less independent") self-estranged object. Only from this viewpoint can it be understood. Schizophrenic thinking, speaking, acting, are only part-phenomena of this basic process. Existential emptying or impoverishment is, as we already know, nothing but a metamorphosis of freedom into compulsion, of eternity into temporality (Scheler), of infinity into finiteness. Hence Kierkegaard could rightly say that in insanity "the small finiteness has been fixated—which can never happen with [the inwardness of] infinity."[142]

This discussion was merely intended to show that we no longer satisfy the

---

141 Cf. Jung, *Über die Psychologie der Dementia praecox* (*On the Psychology of Dementia Praecox*), 1907.
142 *Philosophical Fragments*, I.

scientific demands made on us by the problems of schizophrenia if we speak of a loss of intellectual activity (*perte de l'activité intellectuelle*) (Masselon), a loosening of the associative structure (Bleuler), a primary insufficiency of the psychic activity (Berze), or an alteration of the consciousness of the activity (Kronfeld). All these are theoretical (psychopathological) interpretations of the schizophrenic process, attempts to explain it by way of formulae, which use an explanatory theoretical judgment to skip over what really goes on and what must serve as starting point. Here too our watchword is: back from theory to that minute description of the phenomena which today is possible with the scientific means at our disposal.

To avoid misunderstandings, let it be emphasized that by "process" we do not at all mean only the psychic process in general—in the sense of Jaspers—but the schizophrenic process, that is, the transformation of the existence or being-in-the-world concurrent with the still unknown schizophrenic *noxa*.

Further Observations on Gluttony

Under the heading of "*Les Phobies des fonctions corporelles*," Janet also mentions a girl of eighteen without hysterical anorexia, whose feelings at the sight of food show some similarities with those of Ellen: "When I see foods, when I try to bring them to my mouth, then something tightens in my chest; it makes me choke, it burns in my heart. It seems to me that I am dying and above all, that I lose my head."

He further mentions a female patient who, at the age of twenty-one, after suckling a child began to have a detestation and dread of eating and to refuse food. This syndrome disappeared, returned, only to disappear again, and finally manifested itself during the menopause in the following form: The patient ate normally but was now afraid that her illness would return and prevent her from eating so that she would have to die of hunger; thus she ate in dread, because she dreaded that she would get another dread of eating.

Janet correctly delimits these "phobias" from the *phobie de la digestion*, but he classifies them nevertheless among the *phobies des fonctions corporelles*.

Löwenfeld, in his book *On Psychic Compulsive Phenomena* (1904) mentions ravenousness among the symptoms which can be the equivalents of anxiety attacks. He adds that according to Magnan the desire for food can take on the character of a compulsion (sitiomania) accompanied by dread, which overwhelms the patient in spite of his resistance; for example, a patient, in despair over her compulsion to eat constantly, voluntarily submitted to institutional care.

Stähelin mentions an increased desire to eat in certain psychopaths, in connection with a suddenly increased sexual drive: "Thus I could prove that with certain psychopaths the breakthrough of a vital impulse, *e.g.*, the sudden onset of a violently increased sexual drive, was at times followed at brief intervals by complete insomnia, excessive restlessness, and a mania for smoking, eating, and drinking; that is, that one elemental urge dragged the other along with it, until eventually the 'depth-person' completely prevailed, whereas the higher parts of the personality were either paralyzed or completely in the service of the instincts." [143] I myself can only confirm these observations.

In schizophrenia, gluttony is such a well-known occurrence that there is no need to go into it. Here too it is often connected with sexual processes, wishes, and fears. A patient of Nelken, for whom ejaculation was "the most terrible thing there is," after each one felt thirst and "gluttony." [144] We may further mention Weber's instructive observation that especially in cases of nihilistic delusion, are attacks of ravenousness and refusal of food frequently found.[145] In the case of Ellen West we learn very little about the manifest relationship between gluttony and sexuality. Nor do we receive any information as to whether the gluttony was greater or less before, during, or after the menstrual period. We know only that after (or with?) the cessation of her periods Ellen's gluttony still increased.

An observation which is of interest in regard to our case was reported by Stähelin: [146]

A moderately athletic girl of eighteen, reserved, difficult, sensitive, vivacious, and intelligent, has suffered for three months from languor, headaches, and depressive thoughts. But she feels considerably better in body and soul after meals and also between meals as soon as she has eaten bread, fruit, and chocolate. At twenty, cessation of periods; depressed, suicidal impulses; "eats with pathological speed and abundance." Though otherwise not impulsive, she gobbles down repeatedly, without appetite, let alone hunger, whole loaves of bread and quantities of sweets, and afterwards she sometimes attempts to vomit. She offers this as the motive for the symptom: "It is like a mania. Others too have repulsive passions and thus lose their minds, and I have the gluttony mania just as the alcoholic has dipsomania, and now I am destroyed." She wants to numb herself with food, purposely to let herself sink into emptiness and irresponsibility. "By doing nothing but eat, I am decaying mentally." Then followed blocking, grimacing, and a rigidly depressive bearing.

We see that gluttony and its existential meaning is the same here as in the case of Ellen West. The latter, too, feels that gluttony represents her spiritual (*geistig*) death. In contrast to the other patient, however, Ellen fights against

---

143 "Psychopathologie der Zwischen- und Mittelhirnerkrankungen" ("Psychopathology of Diseases of the Diencephalon and Mesencephalon"), *Schweiz. Arch. Neurol. u. Psychiat.*, Vol. 53, No. 2.

144 "Analytische Beobachtungen über Phantasien eines Schizophrenen" ("Analytical Observations of the Fantasies of a Schizophrenic"), *Jahrb. f. Psychoanal. u. psychol. Forsch.*, Vol. 4.

145 *Über nihilistischen Wahn und Depersonalisation* (*On Nihilistic Delusions and Depersonalization*) (Basel: 1938).

146 "Über präschizophrene Somatose" ("On Pre-schizophrenic Somatization"), in "Papers in Honor of A. Gigon," *Schweiz. Med. Wochenschrift*, No. 39, 1943.

this, only gradually coming to the decision for suicide as the only possibility for release from the conflict between greed and spirit and for escape from the danger of complete mental decay. In contrast to this, the patient of Stähelin accepts spiritual decay and replaces suicide by greed. "Earlier I wanted to throw myself out of the window; now I won't commit suicide any more." This is followed directly by the statement quoted above: "By doing nothing but eat, I am decaying mentally."

In the case of Ellen West we had to throw the light of existential analysis on the inner relationships between gluttony and decay, but in this case they are plainly visible. The fact, however, that they are so plainly visible and that the patient so unemotionally prefers mental decay to suicide shows that here the process runs its course much more rapidly than with Ellen West.

The medical examination in this case showed a brachycardia as well as certain pathological findings concerning blood and metabolism, so that a complex endocrine disturbance, specifically a disturbance in liver metabolism, was suspected. After the patient was given a high carbohydrate, liver-protecting diet, with Karlsbad salt, ephetonin, thyroid and female hormones, she became more relaxed and able to work; after three weeks menses started again; after five weeks, patient was in a pronouncedly hypomanic condition (with normal eating). After four months of unremarkable and stable behavior occurred an onset of increasing agitation resulting in a severe catatonia. With insulin and cardiazol, substantial improvement. Course variable. Stähelin considers it an apparently diencephalic disturbance of the nutritive instinct with only secondary psychic motivation. A completely healthy sister of the patient likewise suffers from gluttony, especially when she feels listless; after eating, she feels fuller and stronger, but she too suffers pangs of conscience.

We shall come back to this case and to the problem of preschizophrenic somatosis in discussing the diagnosis of our case. We turn now to the psychopathological-clinical analysis of our case.

Anxiety Equivalent? Hysteria?

There is, in my opinion, no reason to regard Ellen West's gluttony or "ravenousness" as the equivalent of an anxiety attack. In our case, the constant existential dread is by no means "replaced" by gluttony; instead, it not only persists as such before, during, and after eating, but even continues to increase. At most one might speak of the momentary dulling of the dread during the greedy gulping down of food. Nor can there be any idea that the dread, as would be the case with an equivalent, is elicited by a repression of the gluttony. For the rest, we must clearly differentiate between (vegetative-neurotic) ravenousness (bulimia) and gluttony. Bulimia as such need not express itself in the form of bestial gluttony, the animal-like devouring of food. Where this is the case we leave the area of the so-called neuroses.

If in the case of Ellen West's gluttony we had real anxiety-equivalents, then one would have to think first of all of an anxiety hysteria. Aside from the fact that it is not at all a question of single attacks of dread but of a constant dread, for this diagnosis the releasing factor in the life-history is lacking. The anxiety here is neither attached to a definite "traumatic" event, nor does it develop from and during such an event, for which reason psychoanalysis in this case could not illuminate anything or be therapeutically effective. Nor is there any evidence of a conversion hysteria. When the second analyst designates her depression as being "strongly and purposefully aggravated," obviously it is a matter of an error stemming from therapeutic optimism. Also, when he speaks of "traits visibly calculated to impress her husband" and designates these as hysterical, still the outcome of the case must prove that the patient did not really "put on a show" for her husband. Even if her symptoms had actually appeared to be more obvious and severe in the presence of her husband—which I myself was never able to observe— this too would be easily understandable from the total configuration of the case. After all, we cannot even speak of a hysterical character here, assuming that one would want to call this case hysteria at all. Nowhere with Ellen West is there a question of the so-called hysterical urge for self-assertion, of "hysterical" lying, deceiving, or exaggeration. Her burning ambition is anything but a hysterical striving for importance. After all, she attempts with all her strength to fulfill her ambition and suffers because the attained lags behind what she willed, but without her disguising this or trying to bridge it by pseudo successes.

Addiction and Existential Craving (Süchtigkeit)?

A further psychopathological question is this—whether and to what extent we may call gluttony an addiction—which Stähelin's patient seems to suggest by her own words. But even here it is shown, as will appear again and again in the course of our psychopathological observations, that the symptomatology in the case of Ellen West can only with great difficulty be held to unequivocally defined concepts.

An authentic addiction to sweets, which he designates as saccharomania, was described by Von Stockert.[147] A twenty-one-year-old student, whenever he came from the battlefront to the rear, felt an unaccustomed desire for sweets, and would run from one candy shop to another to bolt down candies. This addiction persisted after the war was over. Not having entered a candy shop for weeks, he would suddenly visit four or five such shops in turn; then for several weeks he would feel no such need. The occasion for such an

---

147 "Zur Frage der Disposition zum Alkoholismus chronicus" ("On the question of the tendency toward chronic alcoholism"), *Z. Neur.*, Vol. 106, 1926.

excess was mostly a slight ill-humor in the morning, which prevented him from making up his mind to go to class. Out of vexation over the missed lecture he would run to the sweet shop and then, once the inhibition was overcome, from one candy shop to another, without much taste for what he ate, until he would run out of money or slowly give in to the demands of the day. Von Stockert correctly places this case close to the reaction of the alcoholic to feelings of displeasure. Even though eating sweets was pleasurable to the patient, this in itself in his opinion does not explain the "not-being-able-to-stop."

This case shows that there exists a genuine addiction to sweets which, in its prognosis, symptomatology, and course, resembles dipsomania. But the need for sweets in the case of Ellen West differs from it in its major points: it does not appear as something "unaccustomed" but is constantly present; it requires no special occasion and finds no termination; there is no simple "not-being-able-to-stop" in spite of complete satiation of the need but, on the contrary, the need as such is never satisfied but is constantly lying in wait.

Much rather could we compare Ellen West's "hunger" and the compulsion to think about it with the "morphine hunger" of the chronic morphine addict and the craving for alcohol of the chronic alcoholic. Just as many addicts must think of the syringe, alcoholics of the bottle or the glass—or must visualize them with almost "hallucinatory" clarity,—so Ellen West must think constantly of food or visualize it almost as in a hallucination. But there is no question of authentic compulsive thinking in either case; rather should one speak of a compulsive need, which, however, I reject with Bleuler, Binder, and others. In those chronic cases of intoxication it is not a matter of "compulsive ideation" but of a partly somatic—*i.e.,* metabolically conditioned—need, which can be more or less quickly and more or less permanently stilled by its temporary satisfaction. In cases where there is no cessation, as with Ellen West or those alcoholics who, in spite of being senselessly drunk, keep on drinking mechanically, no compulsion is present but a much profounder alteration—as a rule, in my experience, a schizophrenic one. (With the morphine addict the narcotic itself finally forces the cessation.) In the case of Ellen West, therefore, no lasting stilling of the hunger occurs, because the hunger is here, as with very many toxicomanics, not only a somatically conditioned need but at the same time the need for filling up the existential emptiness or vacuum. Such a need for filling out and filling up we designate as an existential craving (*Süchtigkeit*). Hence, if Ellen West does not suffer from an addiction in the clinical sense, still her "life-form" falls under the psychopathological category of existential craving. In this respect she is close to the life-form of toxicomanics and of many sexual perverts. At the same time, for lack of sufficient material we had to leave quite unresolved the question of the extent to which her own homoerotic component contributes to her unfulfilled and unfillable existence. (In the case of Nadia, too, this question remains open, despite Janet's assertion to the contrary.)

We completely agree in our conception of existential craving with Von Gebsattel, who in an earlier paper,[148] following ideas by Erwin Straus, set forth fundamental observations about craving and developed them still further in his latest paper.[149] In toxicomania he sees only an extreme, clinically particularly striking case of universal existential craving to which the "decision-inhibited" man falls prey. Under the term "decision-inhibited," however, he understands neither a "vital inhibition" nor an instinctual inhibition in Freud's sense, but a modification of the time-structure of the being-in-the-world in the sense of a definite "disturbance of becoming," or, as we say, of existential ripening. What for him is controlling for the time-structure of existential craving is the factor of repetition: "The addict, having lost the contextual continuity of his inner life-history, exists therefore only in punctate fragmentation, at the moment of illusory fulfillment, that is, discontinuously. He lives from moment to moment but is finally dissatisfied in everyone. Barely has he covered up the emptiness of the present by means of enjoyment, sensation, intoxication, gain, success, etc., when he is already gripped by the unreality of his experience in the form of dissatisfaction and hangover—compelling an immediate repetition of his doings. The manic always does the same, experiences the same, and in the medium of experientially immanent time moves nowhere." Anyone to whom our own discussion has not made it clear that the existence-form in the case of Ellen West bears all the earmarks of the "addictive" being-in-the-world must surely be convinced by this description.

In this connection it should be pointed out that Hans Kunz has adopted Von Gebsattel's viewpoint with respect to perversions.[150]

Compulsion, Phobia?

In our earlier statement that in Nadia a questioning-compulsion had developed, in Ellen a compulsion to think, we used the word compulsion in its popular sense. Purely clinically, we cannot speak here of a compulsion. The true questioning-compulsion of the anankastic concerns questioning as such, and the true compulsion to think concerns thinking as such—so that

148 "Süchtiges Verhalten im Gebiet sexueller Verirrungen" ("Addictive Behavior in the Realm of Sexual Deviations"), *Monatsschr. f. Psychiat. u. Neur.*, Vol. 82, 1932.
149 "Die Störungen des Werdens und des Zeiterlebens. Gegenwartsprobleme der psychiatrisch-neurologischen Forschung" ("Disturbances of Becoming and of Time-Experience" in *Contemporary Problems of Psychiatric-Neurological Research*) (ed. Roggenbau) (Stuttgart: 1939).
150 "Zur Theorie der Perversion" ("On a Theory of Perversions"), *Monatsschr. f. Psychiat. u. Neur.*, Vol. 105.

one can say that in one patient the compulsion consists in the necessity of questioning *qua* questioning, in the other in that of thinking *qua* thinking, while that which is questioned and that which is thought changes constantly, is irrational or wholly senseless.[151] In the cases of Nadia and Ellen, on the other hand, something specific must be asked and something specific thought, and always the same things. Here the "compulsion" does not extend to a certain form of being-with-others or of being-with-oneself, but is solely an expression of the "overvalent" interest of the patient in a particular state of things which in her view is not at all irrational but extremely meaningful and existential—that is, threatening to the entire existence,[152] indeed, calling the existence in question. (Nadia: "Do I really look bad? Am I really thin?"[153] Ellen: "If only I didn't have to eat any more, if only I didn't get fat from eating; I want to eat only enough so I can remain thin; if only I could once again eat harmlessly, if I only got something more to eat, if I could only eat chocolate creams again, for God's sake, no more pancakes, etc., etc.) Here, then, no substitution in the Freudian sense takes place, no diversion of asking and thinking from an authentic, "meaningful" content of question and answer to unauthentic contents which replace the former and, being "meaningless," cannot be settled, but "go into the infinite." Everything revolves, rather, about the one "overvalent" content, which "completely fills" the patient and upon which the bliss of her soul depends. Hence, it would also not be correct to speak here of a "psychic disturbance-mechanism" in Binder's sense.[154] Nadia does not at all experience that "about which everything revolves in her" as disturbance, Ellen at any rate not as "disturbing mechanism" but as threat, namely, as violation, indeed destruction of the core of her being. Nor can one speak in either case of a compulsive "defense mechanism." Nadia's illness is so far advanced that she identifies herself completely with her overvalent interest, whereas Ellen defends herself again and again with all her powers against her gluttony as well as against the dread of becoming fat, but without the occurrence of genuine compulsive defense-phenomena. Neither Nadia nor Ellen are anankastics in the clinical sense.

[151] Cf. the brooding-, question-, doubt-, scruple-obsession, and the counting-, computing-, recording-, precision-, contrasting-compulsion.

[152] Anankastic patients, too, frequently sense the compulsion as threatening to their existence, though not because of its factual "content"—that is, because of a certain kind of fact expressed in it—but because of this sort of experiencing: having-to, tied to otherwise nonsensical content.

[153] In advanced cases of schizophrenia we frequently find such questions in stereotyped form. For many years, during her states of excitation, one of my patients used to ask, with a suffering demeanor and in a tone of torment, "Am I beautiful? Am I ugly?"—of course, without expecting an answer.

[154] *Zur Psychologie der Zwangsvorgänge* (*On the Psychology of Obsessions*) (Berlin: 1936).

In both cases, however, we *can* speak of an obsession. Both patients are obsessed by their idea, their "ideal." But this obsession is by no means "ego-alien," much as Ellen regards it "intellectually" as foolish, contrasensical;[155] etc. On the contrary, "the ego" has a great share in it and, indeed, identifies itself with it time and again; what is rejected by Ellen with abhorrence on one occasion, is pounced upon by her at another time with wild greed. To be sure, she speaks of evil powers, demons, specters, which have violated her, but she knows only too well (and even expresses it) that she has violated herself! We see that nowhere in this case do rigidly circumscribed psychopathological categories suffice.

Can we, then, designate the "dread of becoming fat" as a phobia?

In our existential analysis the dread of becoming fat has revealed itself as a concretization of a severe existential dread, the dread of the "degenerating life," of withering, drying up, moldering, rotting, becoming a husk, eroding, being buried alive, whereby the world of the self becomes a tomb, a mere hole. Part of this is the fear of putting on fat and turning into material. It is the "earth-heaviness" which "pulls her down," and what she dreads is this being-pulled-down. It is, to quote Von Gebsattel,[156] the dread of the (existential) *Gestalt*-loss, dread of the "un-*Gestalt*," the "anti-*eidos*," in short, of the "un-becoming," (*Entwerden*) or, as I should like to say, of the "dis-being" (*ver-Wesen*). Hence, Ellen West's dread-filled battle is with the "*Gestalt*-dissolving powers of existence," with becoming-fat and becoming-ugly, becoming-old and becoming-dull, in brief, with dis-being. In contrast to the anankastic phobias, however, this defensive battle does not take place in a derived, phobic form (as for example the battle against the unclean in the form of the compulsive disgust at a dog [cf. Von Gebsattel's "A Case of Dog and Dirt Phobia"] or in the form of endless cleansing procedures [cf. his "Case of a Phobic Odor-Illusion"]), but in a direct, unmediated, and underived form, namely, in the form of a rational rejection and flight. When Ellen locks the cupboard in which the bread is kept, this is not a phobic but a purely rational, "sensible" measure of precaution; the same is true of her "exaggerated" dietary measures. The defense, therefore, takes place not in a phobic but in a rational form.

But we must ask once again, can the dread of becoming fat as such be termed a phobia? Yes and No! Yes, if we see in it the concretization or sharpening of the primordial dread of degenerating life, of the powers hostile to life and *Gestalt*, so that we could say that this dread concretizes itself in her dread of her own (psychosomatic) deformity (her "monstrousness," ugliness, and greediness). No, if we take into account the fact that

155 Contra-sensical (paradoxical) is not the same as *non*-sensical!
156 Cf., also, his excellent paper, "Die Welt der Zwangskranken," *Monatsschr. f. Psychiat. u. Neur.*, Vol. 99, 1938. [Chapter VI in this volume.—EDITORS.]

this state of things, namely, the connection between the concrete dread-content and the primordial dread is clearly and consciously known to her (which is precisely not the case in a true phobia and which explains why the analysis cannot achieve anything in this case). We could speak of a true phobia only in case the dread of becoming fat "meant" a masked dread of fertilization and pregnancy—which we have rejected.

Since the psychoanalysts from the start approached the case of Ellen West with the diagnosis of compulsive neurosis, they had to assume from the very beginning such a "substitution mechanism" and conduct their therapy accordingly. Though Ellen West supposedly accepted the equation, being fat = being pregnant, we must by no means take this acceptance too seriously, in view of her general skepticism toward psychoanalysis, her purely intellectual way of dealing with it, and the completely negative results. In consequence, our No has greater weight than our Yes! The dread of her own un-*Gestalt* is not a true phobia but an intensive dread of the threat to, indeed the collapse of, her existential ideal, immediately understandable from the peculiarity of the patient's world, namely, from the predominance of the ethereal world and its contradiction to the tomb-world.

But with the authentic phobias, too, we must of course not fail to investigate by ways of existential-analysis the patients' world, if we wish to understand the phobias thoroughly. This holds for the hysterical phobia, which corresponds to the anxiety-hysteria in Freud's sense (the genesis of which I myself have analyzed in my "heel analysis") [157] as well as for the anankastic [158] and the psychasthenic [159] phobia, which Von Gebsattel has already interpreted largely in existential-analytical terms. Certainly, the dread of becoming fat belongs in the area of the pathology of the sympathetic rela-

[157] "Analyse einer hysterischen Phobie" ("The analysis of a hysterical phobia"), *Jahrb. f. psychoanal. u. psychol. Forsch.*, III. In that case we are not dealing with either the world- or self-phenomenon of emptiness or the hole, but rather with a break in continuity or with a splitting asunder. The dread, here effusing to all tearing and separating, to being separated and being torn apart, is biographically focused in the phobia concerning the heel being torn off and herself being separated (being born) from the mother. But since every child is born of a mother, and some occasionally lose a heel without becoming hysterical, the biographical motivation and substituting do not become understandable unless we acknowledge that this is possible only on the basis of a primary disturbance of the "sympathetic relationships" or, more positively stated, on a personal peculiarity of the person's world-design. To the world-design, or project, of mere continuity or con-glomeration from which arises the anxiety of separation, there also belongs the symptom of fear, occasionally erupting into extreme horror, of a loose button (dangling by one thread) and of the spitting of saliva. No matter whether a loose heel, a loose button, or saliva is the biographically determined theme, we are concerned throughout with varia-tions of one and the same coarctated and emptied mode of being-in-the-world and the corresponding world-project.

[158] Cf. Von Gebsattel, Chapter VI.

[159] Cf. "Zur Pathologie der Phobien: I. Die psychasthenische Phobie" ("On the pathology of phobias: I. The psychasthenic phobias"), *Der Nervenarzt*, Vol. 8, Nos. 7 and 8, 1935.

tionships,[160] but not in that of the secondary, hysterical or compulsive elaboration of these disturbances of relationships; rather, it belongs in the area of those psychic forms of illness in which the alteration of the sympathetic relationships is either clearly evident or assumes delusional or hallucinatory forms. This area is that of the schizophrenic group. That the hysterical and obsessional forms of neurotic illness are so frequently observed along with the schizophrenic ones and not infrequently degenerate into them can be understood from the community of their pathological bases.

Overvalent Idea? Delusional Idea?

We recall that the foreign consultant had designated the dread of becoming fat as an overvalent idea. To what extent can we really regard Ellen West's desire to be thin and her rejection of being fat as an "overvalent idea," in the strict sense of Wernicke? We *can* do so insofar as this idea actually "determined all her doing and not-doing" [161] and insofar as it is not at all judged by the patient to be an alien intruder into her consciousness; we *can not* do so insofar as the patient does not see in this idea the "expression of her truest nature" and does not fight for it but against it. Not in a battle for the idea but *against* it does Ellen fight for her own personality; the "idea" is not looked upon (by the patient) as "normal and justified," as completely "explained by its mode of origin," but on the contrary as morbid and abnormal and by no means as explained by this mode. All this implies only that the "idea" in question must not be designated as delusional, that Ellen West does not (as yet?) suffer from a delusional idea. As is well known, Wernicke distinguishes between a "preponderant" or "heightened" interest, *e.g.*, a professional one, and the overvalent idea, but he also speaks of the latter, for example, in connection with "a definite, impulsive urge to suicide." What clearly distinguishes the overvalent idea from the "preponderant interest," however, and what in our case decisively tips the scales, is that Wernicke speaks of an "overvalent idea or conception" (this applies also to the above-mentioned case of suicidal urge), indeed defines it as such, only where the respective "ideas" appear as "recollections of some particularly affect-laden experience, or of a whole series of such interconnected experiences." But since "such experiences which because of their content are

---

160 Cf. Erwin Straus, "Ein Beitrag zur Pathologie der Zwangserscheinungen" ("A Contribution to the Pathology of Obsessive Phenomena"), *Monatsschr. f. Psychiat. u. Neur.*, Vol. 98, 1938. Here we find, didactically well expressed, the distinction between manifest and hidden properties. To prevent misunderstandings, it may be added that the expression "sympathetic" is not to be taken here in the specific sense of sympathetic communication, as this was used by E. Straus in his book *Vom Sinn der Sinne* (*On the meaning of the senses*).

161 Wernicke, *Grundriss der Psychiatrie* (*Basic Outline of Psychiatry*), 2nd ed.

difficult to assimilate cannot be avoided even by the healthiest mental life," a further special condition must prevail "if the overvalence is to be characterized as morbid." This condition is seen in the inaccessibility of any counterideas, hence, in the incorrigibility of the idea in question, and in the "simultaneously" appearing clinical earmark of paranoia. In the case of Ellen West the idea in question by no means originates from especially affect-laden experiences, as is the case, for example, with Michael Kohlhaas [162] upon the refusal of compensation for a mishap, a severe shock-experience connected with his own wrong-doing; but it is based on an *anidëic* (de Clérambault, Von Gebsattel) or pathological-sympathetic foundation (Erwin Straus).[163] Furthermore Ellen West is by no means inaccessible to counterideas, indeed she is constantly presenting such counterideas to herself, so that one cannot speak of an inaccessibility, but only of an ineffectiveness of counterideas. Consequently, in contrast to Nadia, Ellen does not develop a true observation-mania. Only in outbursts does she express the idea that those around her take a sadistic pleasure in tormenting her, and only in similes does she speak of evil powers, spirits, ghosts which torment her and violate her. Let us once again state that Ellen West's psychosis is in general oriented less toward the *Mitwelt* (as invariably is the case with Wernicke's overvalent idea) than toward *Umwelt* and *Eigenwelt,* that is, predominantly toward the bodily-*Eigenwelt.* But this does not mean that hers is somato-psychosis in Wernicke's sense; [164] whereas Nadia shows a clear inaccessibility to counterideas and obvious somatopsychotic traits.

The Vacillations of Mood:
Schizophrenic or Manic-Depressive Psychosis?

We have noted that Kraepelin designated as melancholia the condition which Ellen West showed at the time of his consultation. Thus he regarded this case as one belonging among the group of manic-depressive psychoses, and his prognosis (of the current episode) was quite favorable. However, the depressive as well as the manic dysphorias of Ellen West show certain peculi-

162 [The hero of a short novel by Kleist. The work is based on the life of an actual person of the seventeenth century, a paranoid querulent who suffered the loss of his horses at the hands of a nobleman. After failing in his attempts to obtain compensation, he became a vengeful criminal who waylaid innocent persons and destroyed property.— TRANSLATORS.]

163 Hans Kunz, in his excellent paper, "Die Grenze der psychopathologischen Wahnin-terpretation" ("The Limit of Interpretation of Delusions in Psychopathology"), Z. Neur., Vol. 135, 1931, has shown in regard to the primary schizophrenic delusion that, and why, the psychopathologist's explanation reaches a limit at this point; we can go beyond this limit only if we note, and consider, why in schizophrenia we deal with a "fundamentally different and unique way of existence." In this connection let me also refer to the same author's paper "Die anthropologische Betrachtungsweise in der Psychopathologie" ("The Anthropological Point of View in Psychopathology"), Z. Neur., Vol. 172, 1941.

164 [See Note 56.—TRANSLATORS.]

arities. True, despite the constant change of mood and the increasing gravity of her condition, everything remains predominantly within the sphere of dysphoria; yet we observe no inhibition on the one hand, no sign of flight of ideas on the other. As for the "urge to motion and occupation" it is less a question of a "vital" urge than of an "ideagenous" "motion-craze" (recall the encircling of her girl friends in Sicily) or a "true occupation mania" or an "occupation rage" for filling up her emptiness. The voluminous flood of poems during the night from November 18th to 19th is the clearest purely manic sign, yet even here there is no flight of ideas. Here as elsewhere we deal with an "ecstatic feeling of happiness experienced as a lift out of the flux of temporal events" rather than with a purely vital euphoric affect.[165] In Ellen's depressive dysphoria, again, we miss the symptom of depressive guilt-feelings, of the not-being-able-to-make-amends, and in general of the "ultimate determination (content-wise) by the past" (which points to a different phenomenon from the one we designate as the "supremacy of the having-been!"). Ellen's depressive dysphoria shows many traits which remind one more of a psychopathic [166] dysphoria than of an endogenous depression: When affected by it she is not cut off from the future but threatened by the future! So her depressive dysphoria belongs to the relationship of the I to fate. Time does not begin to halt; rather, the *Gestalt* in which what-is-to-come presents itself is "rejected, avoided, or combatted." Here the dysphoria does not originate only from a "pathological variation of psychophysical functions" but is also a "reaction to a variation," not of the *Umwelt* but of the *Eigenwelt*.[167] E. Minkowski was the first to undertake, long before E. Straus, the phenomenological analysis of depressive dysphoria, advancing it greatly.[168] But a comparison with the case described in his paper of 1923, as also with the one published in 1930,[169] shows how different our case is from his. This is the more noteworthy since the second case in particular shows a striking similarity in content to ours, in that Minkowski's patient speaks on the one hand of a "feeling of engorging materiality" (*sentiment de matérialité accrue*) and on the other hand "of being immaterial and airy" (*d'être immatériel et aérien*). But insofar as he complains "of being, in spite of himself, nothing but a devourer and defecator, nothing but walking

<hr>

165 Cf. Erwin Straus, "Das Zeiterlebnis in der endogenen Depression und in der psychopathologischen Verstimmung" ("Experiencing of Time in Endogenous Depressions and Depressive Reactions"), *Monatsschr. f. Psychiat. u. Neur.*, Vol. 68, 1938.

166 ["Psychopathic" in Swiss-German psychiatric terminology simply refers to psychic pathology and not to the American identification of "psychopath."—EDITORS.]

167 *Ibid.*

168 Cf. "Etude psychologique et analyse phénoménologique d'un cas de mélancolie schizophrénique" ("A Psychological Study and Phenomenological Analysis of a Case of Schizophrenic Depression"), *Journal de Psychologie*, Vol. 20, 1923.

169 "Etude sur la structure des états de dépression—Les Dépressions ambivalentes" ("A Study of the Structure of States of Depression—The Ambivalent Depressions"), *Schweiz. Arch. f. Neur. u. Psychiat.*, Vol. 26, 1930.

intestines, a species of vegetative functions that, furthermore, does himself ill" (1930), it appears that here we already have to do with a somatopsychosis, somewhat in the sense of Wernicke's hypochondriacal melancholia, even though our own case lies close to the border of, but still not within, the domain of somatopsychosis.

Add to all this the observation—most important for the total diagnosis—that in Ellen West we are by no means dealing only with phasic manic-depressive upsets after whose evanescence the previous *status quo* once again sets in, nor, by any means just with ever-deepening depressive dejections, but that the darkening of the world, which announces itself first as a temporary depressive upset, progresses also outside the authentic depressive phases, first assuming the form of withering and decaying, then that of being walled in and holed in, to end up finally as hell. What actually occurs is a progressive shrinking—becoming only the more clearly evident in each successive depression—of the total structure of the being-in-the-world, from its full *Gestalt* to an un-*Gestalt*. The gluttony and being-fat stand at the end of this shrinking process, in that the *Eigenwelt* (of both the soul and the body) is not only experienced as un-*Gestalt* but also lives itself out in this un-*Gestalt*, though still constantly opposed by the ethereal world of ideals, now condemned to impotence. The existence moves now in a vicious circle; it is the snake which bites its own tail. But existence, still being able to "reflect upon itself," can in its freely chosen death finally break through this circle and crush the head of the snake. This marks the victory of this existence over the power of "hell."

The Diagnosis:
Development of a Personality, or a Schizophrenic Process?

In the preceding section (III) as well as in the present one, we have shown in detail why in the case of Ellen West there can be no question either of a neurosis or of a mania or of an overvalent (delusional) idea. Having, furthermore, demonstrated why despite the decidedly endogenous vacillations of mood we must not be content with the diagnosis of manic-depressive psychosis, we have left only two further diagnostic possibilities: the development of a psychopathic constitution or a schizophrenic process. The first possibility had been carefully considered by the foreign consultant, the second seemed certain to Bleuler as well as to me.

The development of a psychopathic constitution can only point to what Jaspers in his "General Psychopathology" calls "development of a personality," by which he understands the totality of the growth of the original disposition (*Anlage*), its interactions with the milieu, and its corresponding reaction to experiences. He is thinking, for example, of the paranoid developments of the querulous and the jealous, but also of cases such as that of Reiss,[170] in which he presents a hypomanic personality, focused upon mere "importance" and form, in its change from a successful businessman to a frugal, psychopathic, itinerant preacher. This existence is understandable on the basis of a "mere" "remodeling of the façade" because of altered environmental conditions and an early decline in sexual potency, with the character remaining unchanged. It is immediately clear that the case of Ellen West cannot be subsumed under the concept of this personality-development; with her it is a question neither of a growth of the *Anlage* nor of a comprehensible interaction of *Anlage* and milieu (only the revolt against her family can be understood as such) nor of a consistent reaction to definite experiences corresponding to a characterological *Anlage* (as was pointed out before in connection with the controversy over the presence of an overvalent idea). But Jaspers himself quite correctly states that not infrequently we meet individuals "who in their entire life-course offer the picture of a specific personality development but in single features point to a slight process which lends an abnormal note to this development." This, he thinks, prevents the discussion from reaching a result.

If we ourselves feel that we *have* arrived at a result in our case, it is because it not only shows features pointing to a slight process, but also is itself a traceable process. Whereas, however, Jaspers does not consider every such psychic process schizophrenic, in our case we see no other possibility than this: an unknown something, which cannot be entirely explained from *Anlage,* milieu, and experience, appears to initiate and maintain this process. That the process is suspended, as it were, just before death cannot surprise us in view of the occurrence of such suspensions even in far advanced schizophrenias, and in particular cannot argue against the diagnosis of a mild, very insidious schizophrenia.[171] Whether Ellen West went through a first mild attack as a child, as is entirely possible from her known early traits of defiance, obstinacy, excessive ambition, emptiness, and pressure as well as from her delayed puberty, must be left undecided. It must, of course, also remain undecided how the process would have developed further if Ellen West by prolonged hospitalization had been prevented from carrying out her suicidal intention. None of the three physicians participating in the consultation believed in an improvement, much less a cure. On the other hand, there will probably be unanimous agreement that it could hardly be a question of a schizophrenia leading to complete mental deterioration. Yet it does

170 *Zeitschrift für Neurologie,* 70.

171 Kläsi's assumption seems justified that the occurrence of such "suspensions," as I call them, still does not give us the right to speak of remissions. Confining himself to the occurrence of ambivalence and insight, Kläsi states: "Ambivalence and insight into the illness may indeed occur in a remission, but they may just as well herald the process and accompany it throughout its entire course." *Praxis,* No. 42, 1943.

not seem impossible to me that, with Ellen West as with Nadia, a "somato-psychosis" marked by hypochondriacal delusions and an "allopsychosis" with paranoid ideas might have developed.

If we said above that in Ellen West we deal with a demonstrable schizophrenic process, we have already presented this proof by way of existential analysis. It culminates in the determination, if not of a definite break, at least of a decided "kink" in her lifeline. We shall come back to this below. But this proof can also be given by way of clinical symptomatology. In such "neurosis-like" cases the schizophrenic process is demonstrated by the vagueness and multiformity of the symptoms—which is still too little heeded. Thus we find in the case of Ellen West a general craving, to be sure, but no real mania in the clinical sense; we find a compulsive obtrusion of psychic contents, but neither anankastic-psychopathic traits nor, still less, compulsive neurotic mechanisms; [172] we find phobic elements but no authentic phobia, overvalent "interests" but no "overvalent idea," near-delusional somato-psychic phenomena but no delusion, decided endogenous dejections but no purely manic-depressive course; we do find traits of a pathological "development of the personality" but alongside it an irresistibly advancing illness process. It is the sum total of these symptomological observations which must lead to the diagnosis of schizophrenia and, in fact, as we shall bring out still more clearly in conclusion, the polymorphous form of schizophrenia simplex.

We need not repeat now the existential-analytically presented proof of the "kinking of the lifeline" from its beginning throughout its entire course to its final sinking down to the level of bestial greed, especially since we summarized the result of our existential analysis at the beginning of the present section. Besides, we have already brought this result not only in the case of Ellen West but also in the case of Nadia to its existential-analytic denominator. In the latter case we spoke of an increasing freezing or "coagulation" of the free self into an ever unfreer ("more dependent") thing-like object. In both cases existence was to a great extent deprived of its sovereignty and became extensively objectified; in both cases freedom was converted more and more into constraint and distress, existence into mechanical, constrained happening. We have shown in some detail what this means.

However, this is not yet the end. We find such an existential alteration in some "neuroses," especially in the compulsive neurosis, in psychopathic developments, and even in the development of individual passions. In the latter respect Gotthelf described this alteration so clearly and plainly, from the contrast between eternity and finitude, as did Kierkegaard, that we must let him have his say: "It is very remarkable in regard to the striving of man

---

[172] The difference between these two "psychogenic compulsive phenomena" is clearly stated by Binder in his paper, "Zur Psychologie der Zwangsvorgänge" ("On the Psychology of Compulsive Processes"), 1926.

that one mostly does not know how the striving will grow, what direction it will take, and whether in the end the goal will not become a magnet and man a will-less being. Many a striving is at the beginning worthy of honor and praise, and in its course becomes a millstone which pulls the person into the abyss. . . . If beyond these efforts there is not a most high striving which goes beyond all that is finite, whose goal lies in Heaven, all earthly striving degenerates and becomes vicious, grows into a passion to which one always sacrifices better things, until in the end one has nothing worth while left; it is like the blight in the clover which pullulates over the entire field until all the clover is consumed." [173]

In our case, too, the human being is yoked between finitude and infinity ("Heaven"), and it is shown that the "small finitude" is fixated as soon as it leaves the inwardness of infinity or, in our own terms, the duality of love.

It still remains for us to show by what criteria the fixation of finitude called schizophrenia is distinguished from such nonschizophrenic "fixations." This criterion is "time."

In the *Critique of Pure Reason* we read: "One gains a great deal if one can bring a multitude of investigations under the formula of one single task." The formula of our task, then, reads: investigate how matters stand in regard to temporalization when a "fixation of finitude" is to be called a schizophrenic fixation.

Here too we need only repeat what has already been worked out. For us, the temporality of the tomb-world became decisive for the fixation of existence in the case of Ellen West: "The development from the condensing, consolidating, narrowing of the shadow, through the vegetative rotting and inescapable encirclement, to, finally, the wall of the tomb," we noted, "is an expression of the increasing supremacy of the past over this existence, the supremacy of the already-being in the latitude (*Befindlichkeit*) of hell and the inescapable pull back-to-it. This dread of hell is the dread the existence feels of being engulfed by its ground, by which it is the more deeply engulfed, the higher it tries to leap, to fly from it. The place of the self-possessing of the ground and the being-self-transparent upon it is taken by the dread-full being overpowered by it as the sinking back into Nothingness."

But we are also familiar with a "supremacy of the past" in the endogenous depression, even though not concurrent with such a systematic, progressive transformation of the material garb of the world as in the case of Ellen West. But what is added in this case is the falling apart of the temporality into its ex-stasies and the extensive autonomizing of these, with the result that "time" actually "runs" no more. Where this is the case, we speak in psychopathological language of a "dissociation of the personality." In the case of

---

[173] "Erlebnisse eines Schuldenbauers" ("The Experiences of a Farmer in Debt"), *Complete Works*, Vol. 14. The fact that Gotthelf described these changes in terms moralistically colored in no way alters the truth of the meaning of his description.

depression we cannot speak of a falling apart of the individual ex-stasies of time, because "time" here, even though more or less slowed down, still "runs" ("extends"); which is precisely the reason that patients must feel as so torturing the tension, the contrast, between the "time" in which they "live" and the authentic "extended time." If the depressed patient could become entirely merged with the past without "knowing" anything further about future and present, then he would no longer be depressive! The depressive "experience of being determined by things past" and the "restriction of future freedom" conditioned thereby (Erwin Straus) is, as a statement of a psychopathological fact, something quite different from what we have, in our case, interpreted existential-analytically as the "predominance of the ex-stasy of the having-been." The predominance of the past (or more correctly of the having-been) in unison with the falling apart of the ex-stasies of time, so that, according to the patient Hahnenfuss, "The entire constitution of the soul can be taken [not as finite-timely but] equally well as eternal," seems to me fundamental for the understanding of what we call the psychic life of the schizophrenic. The proof of this conception, however, will have to wait for the existential-analytic investigation of advanced cases. The most important conclusion we must draw from this insight is that where an individual temporalizes (zeitigt) the world in a way so different from ours, as Hahnenfuss also says, "Mutual understanding is completely blocked off in every direction," or, at least, is made very difficult. However, this is not what E. Minkowski has called a disturbance of the synchronism, that is, a disturbance in world-temporal human communication and intercourse (and what psychopathology designates as "defective adjustment to reality"), but represents a different mode of temporalization of the existence as such, which, in turn, only conditions the disturbance of the synchronism. But since in these cases of disturbance we speak of autism, those different modes of temporalization must underlie autism too. The falling apart of the ex-stasies, the abolishing of the possibility of temporalization as a steadily extending one, has the effect of mutual understanding (in the sense of communication in general) being excluded or made difficult. Autism shows itself first, like all psychotic "symptoms," in a certain type of disturbance of communication. Since autism however does not by any means signify a mere mood-upset, such as depression or mania, but a much deeper modification of the temporalization of the existence, here communication is also made much more difficult. And yet even here, as we have seen, the existence can still be investigated and understood existential-analytically; in this respect, Jaspers' differentiation between empathic and unempathic mental life, as a purely "subjective," psychological one, should not disconcert us. Existential analysis has no reason whatever to refrain from investigating schizophrenic psychic life, even though, as was done here, it must first try its methods out on insidious processes.

Autism, like every existence-form, has its forms of expression and its "grammar" of expression (Scheler). Even in Ellen West we found a somewhat stiff and empty facial expression, a gaze which was now empty, now "drenched with feeling"—*i.e.*, not "filled with feeling" in the normal sense— and a rather stiff bearing. All these are expression-forms of existential emptiness in the sense of the schizophrenic process. Added to this is the "feeling" that all inner life has stopped, that everything is unreal, everything senseless. Also, in regard to the "contact" with the patient—the sympathetic communication (Erwin Straus) as well as the existential one—we must speak of autism: Ellen West was no longer able to be absorbed in the being-with-each-other of love or friendship [174] or to open herself up to existential care. Correspondingly, the *Mitwelt*-intercourse with the patient was also made difficult. Her irritability, sensitiveness, turning into herself, and her suspicion that people did not want to help her and were only letting her suffer, indeed, only wanted to torment her, repeatedly set up insurmountable barriers to mutual understanding. Since Ellen West on her deepest ground existed only as a having-been, all attempts to transfer her to the present (that is, to call her into the momentary situation) and to open the future to her had to fail.

As far as heredity is concerned, Ellen West evidently tends predominantly toward the manic-depressive side. But we cannot judge at all how far the heavy, serious characters among her forebears, or the adventuresome and nervous ones, suggest schizoid types. It is, at any rate, not too far fetched to conceive as schizoid characters the following: her externally very self-controlled, somewhat stiffly formal, very reserved and serious-mannered father; the father of her father, depicted as a very stern autocrat; and the markedly ascetic brother of her father (to whom we shall return at once). Also the short, physically delicate, nervous siblings of Ellen's mother and the soft, "aesthetic" younger brother of the patient could be placed in the category of schizoid types. Thus we would have to deal here with a mixture of manic-depressive and schizoid heredity. On the basis of recent studies in biological

174 That schizophrenic autism is a form of lovelessness and incapacity to love is implied in both word and concept. Thus, for example, Binder, in "Zum Problem des schizophrenen Autismus" ("On the Problem of Schizophrenic Autism"), *Z. Neur.*, Vol. 125, speaks of a "decrease in the ability for an experience of intimate directness in its manifold forms." This absence, with all its consequences, was demonstrated in a remarkable paper from Beringer's department: Hans Kuhn, "Über Störungen des Sympathiefühlens bei Schizophrenen. Ein Beitrag zur Psychologie des schizophrenen Autismus und der Defektsymptome" ("On Disturbances of Sympathy Feelings in Schizophrenics. A Contribution to the Psychology of Schizophrenic Autism and Symptoms of Defectiveness"), *Z. Neur.*, Vol. 174, No. 3. However, "moral defect" and egotism exhibit the lack of this ability in a way similar to autism (cf. Binder and Kühn). Therefore it remains our task to show, by means of further existential analyses, in what this similarity consists and how the various forms of the incapacity for intimate directness (coming-from-the-heart and going-to-the-heart) can be distinguished (cf. *Basic Forms*). However, this problem cannot be solved exclusively by means of an analysis of the absence of intimate experience; rather, it demands an analysis of the total design of an individual form of existence.

heredity we know how frequently schizophrenias develop on just such genetic soil.

We have still to discuss in particular the ascetic uncle, since his behavior shows in its content a striking agreement with that of his niece, Ellen West. He too displays ascetic tendencies in regard to the intake of food and leaves out entire meals because he believes that regular eating made people fat. We see from this little trait how right Manfred Bleuler [175] is in considering it indispensable to investigate the psychological behavior patterns of the relatives of our patients. One of his students, Hans Jörg Sulzer,[176] found for each of the various abnormal idea-worlds of the three members of a family investigated by him a corresponding content in the idea-world of the healthy members of the family, though not carried to delusional extremes. "Hence the abnormal thought-contents of the schizophrenic family member do not depend on his schizophrenia but obviously on his prepsychotic personality." This conclusion is important for us because it serves as a warning against prematurely attributing the symptom of gluttony in our patient and the abhorrence of it solely and directly to a pathological occurrence in the brain.

Our patient shows a body build which gives the definite, if not pronounced, impression of being pyknic. As to the endocrines, presumptive variations to be mentioned are the slightly acromegalic skull, the thickening of the salivary glands, which was traced by the internist back to an endocrine disturbance, the infantile genitalia reported by a gynecologist, and the absence of menstruation for years. In regard to the intensified sensations of hunger, we must, of course, guard against immediately inferring an endocrine basis.[177] The findings of our investigation are not sufficient to decide whether Ellen West starves only because she allows herself too little nourishment on psychic grounds, is at the same time wild about sweets, and, in general, has a healthy appetite, or whether we are confronted here with a physiologically abnormal feeling of hunger. Nor can we decide whether her case is one of an endocrine-conditioned increase in fat production, in view of which her dread of getting fat, though by no means caused by it, would obtain a semblance of justification. If in view of the pathoplasty of our case endocrine ço-determinants are to be assumed—which at least cannot be ruled out—then primarily pituitary and ovarian influences would come into consideration; in which case we must remember, however, that just these disturbances may, in turn, be "psychogenically conditioned" in psychoses. In

[175] "Schizophrenie und endokrines Krankheitsgeschehen" ("Schizophrenia and Endocrine Pathology"), *Arch. d. Julius Klaus-Stiftung*, Vol. 18, 1943.

[176] "Zur Frage der Beziehungen zwischen dyskrinem und schizophrenem Krankheitsgeschehen" ("On the Question of the Relationship between Endocrine and Schizophrenic Processes"), *Arch. d. Julius Klaus-Stiftung*, Vol. 18, 1943.

[177] In regard to the well-known relationship between "vital feeling" and midbrain and cerebellum, cf. Stähelin, "Psychopathologie der Zwischen- und Mittelhirnenkrankungen" ("Psychopathology of Diseases of the Diencephalon and Mesencephalon"), *Schweiz. Archiv. f. Neur. u. Psychiat.*, Vol. 53, No. 2.

no case, however, does it seem admissible to us to think of a form of pituitary cachexia, since Ellen West's loss of weight could be traced back to intentional undernourishment and, as Janet has also properly stressed in the case of Nadia, there was no anorexia at all but, on the contrary, an increase in appetite. Since we share M. Bleuler's opinion—based on his own and his students' investigations—"that in schizophrenia the shaping of the illness (in regard to its course and its symptomatology) is to a great extent dependent on certain endocrine relationships," this question, for the sake of completeness, was brought up for discussion. Unfortunately, data on endocrinological findings concerning Ellen West's relatives are also completely lacking.

In conclusion, the question arises whether we should designate the case of Ellen West as "preschizophrenic somatosis" (Stähelin) or as schizophrenia. I decide unconditionally for the latter diagnosis. In Stähelin's case too (*viz.*, p. 343) I would from the very beginning (that is, dating from the abnormal phenomena in her eighteenth year) speak of a schizophrenia. Stähelin rightly calls attention to the "alterations of the vital drives" accompanying the "gluttony" (sudden, apparently unmotivated alcoholic excesses, inhibition and disinhibition of sexual and motor drives, of sleep-waking regulation, such as I could frequently observe in my own patients), but he regards them as symptoms "which one finds not rarely in the years before the outbreak of schizophrenia." Here, of course, everything depends on what one understands by "outbreak of schizophrenia." If this means, as is customary, the emergence of severe secondary symptoms, especially in the sense of "acute attack," then, naturally, Stähelin's designation is quite correct. If, however, one understands by outbreak of schizophrenia the earliest signs of a schizophrenic process, however slight, then it no longer makes sense to speak of preschizophrenia—as little sense as it would make to speak of pretuberculosis on the first appearance of clinical indications of the presence of an apical tuberculosis or on the X-ray finding of a mere pinpoint-sized focus in an apex of the lung or on enlargement of the hilar glands. If we do not speak of the outbreak of a schizophrenia until we see massive secondary psychotic symptoms appear, then the internist too might only speak of tuberculosis when severe destructive processes in the lung can be pointed to. Since for purely clinical and especially for forensic reasons we must continue to differentiate between preschizophrenia (not to be confused with latent schizophrenia) and "overt" schizophrenia, we must, if we wish to continue purely medically, have at hand a single name for the entire schizophrenic process from its faintest beginnings to its end. Even though, in agreement with Stähelin, we see in those disturbances of the vital urges, and especially in overintense gluttony, diencephalic disturbances (gluttony, as is known, is regarded also as a hypothalamic symptom), still, even today we are not as yet justified in designating schizophrenia as a diencephalosis. I would, therefore, propose that we group preschizophrenia as well as latent and manifest under the name of Morbus Bleuler, just as one might designate all forms of tuberculosis as Morbus Koch. It should go without saying that what I am dealing with here is not verbal games but, considering the present status of schizophrenic research, a purely medical requirement. Of course, schizoidism, as a character disposition (*Anlage*), would not come under the heading of Morbus Bleuler. Schizoidism is no more a sickness than is syntony. On the other hand, upon the appearance of "neurotic" or neurotic-like phenomena in a severely schizoid personality we should think more often than hitherto of a Morbus Bleuler, as we must think of the beginning of a depression upon the appearance of such phenomena in a markedly syntonic personality. I know from experience that much too often neuroses are diagnosed when we should already speak of a psychosis, and I still side with E. Bleuler [178] when he declares that he "regards the concepts of the neuroses as artifacts, if they are not to count merely as symptom-complexes."

Finally, as far as therapy is concerned, today certainly a hormonal therapy would have been initiated, the direction of which is prescribed by the afore-mentioned endocrine disturbances. But even in the present state of our knowledge and skills we are far from sure of the possibility of a cure. The same is true in regard to shock therapy, the first precursors of which were not yet known at that time. In the very responsible situation in which the physician was placed by the total state of the case, shock therapy would surely have offered a very welcome temporary expedient. In view of the special symptomatology of the case (dread of becoming fat, strong feelings of hunger), one would probably for the time being not have attempted insulin therapy but electro- or cardiazol shock. It is possible that thereby a temporary improvement might have been achieved, but upon a critical scrutiny of modern "curative results" it must be assumed that, especially in view of so insidious a process and a personality so much focused on the "either/or," it could have been merely a question of postponing the final catastrophe.

A Final Word

It may to some colleagues seem striking, even devious, that we begin our attempt to elucidate from the anthropological side the problem of schizophrenia with a case which shows "no intellectual defect," no secondary schizophrenic symptoms such as delusion and hallucinations, blocking or stereotypy, and which exhibits a multitude of apparently nonschizophrenic features, in addition to showing a predominantly manic-depressive heredity. I would like to counter these objections with the statement that precisely in this case we were able to trace and display step by step, through the tangle and vagueness of the symptomatology, the progressive narrowing, loss of power, and "mundanizing," (*Verweltlichung*) or, psychopathologically ex-

[178] Forel's attitude on psychoanalysis, published in *Jahrb. Bleuler u. Freud,* IV.

pressed, the emptying of the personality as observed in the schizophrenic process. Our task was made easier by the good gift of self-observation and self-description on the part of the intelligent patient, the slow advance of the process, and the availability of sufficient observations extending over a period of seventeen years. In cases leading quickly to mental deterioration, and with unintelligent patients, the transitions from the healthy to the abnormal, which are for us just as important as for the physiopathologist, if not more so, cannot be observed as clearly, if at all. Where we observe the appearance of a "massive" schizophrenic symptom, as for example in a so-called primary insanity,[179] there we do not see the "genesis" of the schizophrenia but have before us the completed result, whatever else may follow. In this point of view I agree entirely with Wyrsch, whose merit it is to have pointed again to the particular scientific importance of schizophrenia simplex.[180] Our case joins ranks completely with his case of Anna K. (Case 13) who so consciously "has the experience of inner instability and the standstill of development" and who makes such "fruitless and exhausting attempts" to "shape existence and herself." But what was for Wyrsch a "special case" is found rather frequently in my case material.

In his basic work, "On the Simple Demented Form of Dementia Praecox," [181] Diem has already pointed out that the prognosis is obvious, "but that only the most precise observation of the initial phase can lead to a clarification, which can probably only be obtained with educated patients." To be sure, he doubts very much whether any number of such cases can be found among the more cultured classes, and as proof of this he cites Kahlbaum's work, "On Heboidophrenia." [182] On the basis of my own material, however, I must take issue with Diem's doubts; from the very beginning of my psychiatric work in this institution it was impossible for me to get along diagnostically with the three main forms of schizophrenia; even the introduction of the fourth form, dementia praecox simplex, seemed to me in the beginning not to suffice for the distinguishing and classification of my cases. It seemed to me indispensable to group a number of not infrequently observed cases, on the basis of their peculiar symptomatology and course, under a special heading: the polymorphous type of schizophrenia. However, I soon realized that a purely clinical analysis must nevertheless assign these cases to the category of schizophrenia simplex, however much they stand

179 In this connection, cf. especially Schultz-Henke, "Die Struktur der Psychose" ("The Structure of Psychosis"), *Z. Neur.*, Vol. 175.

180 Jakob Wyrsch, "Über die Psychopathologie einfacher Schizophrenien" ("On the Psychopathology of Simple Schizophrenias"), *Monatsschr. f. Psychiat. u. Neur.*, Vol. 102, No. 2, 1940. Less convincing to me, on the other hand, is his essay of the following year (1941): "Krankheitsprozess oder Psychopath. Zustand?" ("Disease Process or Psychopathic Condition?"), *ibid.*, Vol. 103, Nos. 4/5.

181 *Archiv. f. Psychiatrie*, Vol. 37, 1903.

182 *Allg. Zschr. f. Psych.*, Vol. 46.

apart, through their wealth of apparently nonschizophrenic symptoms, from the "unproductive" cases that simply deteriorate.

Under the heading of "polymorphous" form I listed all those schizophrenias without marked hebephrenic, catatonic, and paranoid symptoms, which showed clear manic-depressive vacillations, seeming psychopathic-anankastic, compulsive-neurotic, "hysterical," or "neurasthenic" symptoms, a tendency to addiction (alcohol, morphine, cocaine), moral defects, and sexual aberrations (especially homosexuality). (Criminal acts were rarely involved.) [183] Apart from these foregoing conditions, the following characteristics also are involved in the syndrome of polymorphous form: long duration of the symptoms or their slow course or years of standstill, the patients' loss of intellectual capability (though with preservation of formal intelligence and speech), the patients' frequent change and final relinquishing of their social tasks (study, profession, founding a family) or the sinking down from their social level, their unsusceptibility to psychoanalysis, and the relative ineffectiveness in their cases of shock treatment. Naturally, not all cases showed those "complications," but as a rule several could be observed. In a considerable number of cases, however, paranoid or catatonic phenomena could years later, in follow-up studies, be observed; yet nevertheless there scarcely ever occurred a true schizophrenic dementia. In the strict application of the concept of this polymorphous form—that is, excluding all those cases where from the beginning and even after years there was no evidence of hebephrenic, catatonic, or paranoid symptoms—these cases constitute about 5 per cent of my schizophrenics; in a wider sense—that is, including those cases which sooner or later have shown one or the other of those symptoms—about 10 per cent. In contrast to the frequency of this polymorphous form of schizophrenia simplex, the unproductive, merely deteriorating cases constitute in my case histories a rare exception.

[183] For a case of this kind see Hans Binder, "Zwang und Kriminalität" ("Compulsion and Criminality"), *Schweiz. Arch. f. Neur. u. Psychiat.*, Vol. 54 ("The case of Joseph B").

X

The Attempted Murder of a Prostitute*

by Roland Kuhn

IT IS ALWAYS MEANINGFUL to present the story of a criminal if we "care infinitely more about his thoughts than his deeds, and again far more about the sources of his thoughts than about the effects of those deeds" (Friedrich Schiller). But there are men who cannot, themselves, realize either their thoughts or the sources of their thoughts. When such a person commits a crime without any apparent external cause, even our best intentions to understand him cannot solve the riddle. In such cases, psychology often enables us, if not to solve the psychic riddles, at least to throw some light upon them by teaching us to reconstruct the person's external and inner life history, to gain insight into his dream and phantasy life, and to see him within the frame of his predisposition and in interrelation with his family environment. Also, psychology makes use of an understanding description of all the attitudes of a person toward his fellow men, including his doctors. Furthermore, psychology examines him under experimentally simplified conditions and understands him in the terms of diagnostic-clinical psychiatry on the basis of classifying criteria which were found by comparing numerous cases with one another.

However, it is possible to describe a person independently of any normative concept and, therefore, apart from the distinction between healthy and sick and, as far as this is possible, without passing any judgment. We are here referring to the phenomenological method of E. Husserl [1] which,

* Translated by ERNEST ANGEL from the original, "Mordversuch eines depressiven Feti-schisten und Sodomisten an einer Dirne," *Monatsschrift für Psychiatrie und Neurologie*, Vol. 116, 1948, pp. 66–151.

[1] E. Husserl, *Logische Untersuchungen* (II. Aufl.; Halle: 1913). Bd. 2.

extended into existential analytics by M. Heidegger [2] and L. Binswanger,[3] has made possible this particular way of understanding.

We shall not, here and now, present a description of the method of existential-analytical investigation nor an argument on behalf of it. Instead, a practical case (which, in any event, is original enough to deserve interest) will serve as a test to determine whether existential analysis can contribute more to our understanding of a person than the usual clinical and psychological approach and, if so, in what fashion. It was natural to select for such an investigation a particularly enigmatic and difficult case. However, other cases are no less suited.

I Evidence and Psychiatric Testimony

On March 23, 1939, Rudolf R., a twenty-one-year-old, hard-working, inconspicuous butcher boy, having no police record, shot a prostitute with the intent to kill.

He had left his job in the morning, donned his Sunday clothes, purchased a pistol and ammunition, and gone to Zurich on a one-way ticket. There he roamed the streets all day, stopping at several taverns but without drinking much. At 5 P.M. he met a prostitute in a bar, accompanied her to her room, had intercourse with her, and, after they had both dressed again, fired the shot. She was hit by the bullet but only slightly injured. Shortly after the criminal act, Rudolf surrendered to the police.

Nothing in Rudolf's behavior, before or after the act, made him conspicuous except, perhaps, his superior calm. Questioned about his motive, he said he had noticed that the prostitutes in Zurich made their money too easily. He had spent much of his time at the movies and in the reading of trashy literature. It was his ambition to become famous as a hero.

After a thorough psychiatric examination, the preceding events and Rudolf's personality were presented as follows: at the age of twelve Rudolf was involved in the theft of church offerings; later he was sexually seduced by women. Subsequent guilt feelings resulted in psychological isolation and made him somewhat reticent toward the outside world. Before committing the criminal act, he had worked himself more and more into a phantasy world in which he played all sorts of heroic roles. During the preceding night he had slept for only two hours and had roamed the streets in a state of sexual excitement, trying, without success, to find an opportunity for sexual intercourse. There and then the idea of shooting a prostitute in

---

[2] M. Heidegger, Sein und Zeit (Halle: 1935); "Vom Wessen des Grundes," Jahrbuch f. Phil. und phaenomenologische Forschung, Husserl-Festschrift, 1929; Platons Lehre von der Wahrheit (Bern: 1947).

[3] L. Binswanger, Grundformen und Erkenntnis menschlichen Daseins (Zurich: 1942); Ausgewaehlte Vortraege und Aufsaetze (Bern: 1947), Bd. I; case histories of "Ellen West und Juerg Zuend" in Schw. Archiv fuer Neur. und Psych., Bd. 53–59.

Zurich formed in his mind. Rudolf struggled against it, and by the time he left for work the idea was forgotten. But while at work, the idea suddenly re-emerged, and, from then on, everything he did seemed to happen automatically. He was no longer able to muster any counterimpulses against the criminal drive.

The testimony came to the conclusion that Rudolf was a schizoid, hysterical psychopath who had acted in an exceptional, neurotically-conditioned state. He was pronounced irresponsible, placed under guardianship, and on September 1, 1939, brought to Muensterlingen, his home-canton institution, for extended psychotherapeutic treatment. No symptoms were found at that time to support a diagnosis of schizophrenia or any other psychosis.

II *Information about Rudolf's Immediate Family* [4]

After the mother's early death, Rudolf's father had gone through a rather serious depression for about a year. He was unable to work, lamented a lot, and reproached himself. From that time on he suffered increasingly from a trigeminal neuralgia which he traced back to colds he had caught when poaching as a youth. He was operated on at a time when occasional states of arteriosclerotic confusion had already occurred and died from apoplexy at the age of sixty-four. He had always had a strong urge to collect and hide things away. Hidden money was found after his death.

Rudolf's mother was rather intelligent and of a very sentimental nature. Within fourteen years she bore ten children. She did not recover from the birth of the last child and, after five-and-a-half months of illness, died in 1922.

Rudolf's maternal grandfather owned a fairly large farm and did some business on the side. He was known to have been very inconsiderate to his wife and to have had intercourse with prostitutes well into old age. He gladly let his family work for him, liked to travel a lot, and would bring dubious girl friends home to his wife, even in the midst of harvesting.

III *Rudolf's Memories*

We shall now report those facts from Rudolf's life history which have proved essential to the understanding of his personality. At the time of the testimony, Rudolf was aware of only a few of these experiences. We shall present the events without discussing the method and particular conditions under which they were recalled.

Rudolf's first childhood memory reaches back to his fourth year of life. His mother had recently died. Rudolf would sleep in his dead mother's bed,

4 [That part of this chapter which deals with Rudolf's relatives beyond the immediate family unit has been omitted. It should, however, be mentioned that one of his uncles and one of his cousins had been committed to mental hospitals.—EDITORS.]

next to his father, who frequently at night would pick him up and place him on the chamber pot (the child was a bed-wetter). His father would then use the pot himself—a procedure which greatly impressed the boy. For a time, his father would put a compress on a sore on Rudolf's leg, during which time the boy had the opportunity to observe deep scars on his father's leg (childhood osteomyelitis). In connection with these procedures the father often hugged Rudolf in an access of impetuous affection, which left a weird impression on the boy. It is probable that Rudolf slept next to his father for two-and-a-half years.

During this period, the boy was given his first pair of pants. He wet them on the same day and smeared them all over with feces.

Most of the time he stayed in the house and tried to communicate with his father's housekeepers, but was unkindly rebuffed. All day long he would search the house from cellar to attic, rummaging through every corner and every piece of furniture.

When Rudolf was six years old, his father married one of his housekeepers. Rudolf still remembers how she asked him to call her "mother" and how he at first refused. Around that time, he once urinated into the vegetable water in the kitchen. Soon his stepmother would send him out to the village on all kinds of errands, such as to buy wine for her. She would get drunk on it, become very angry, and lock herself for days in her room, leaving the household to the older children. Rudolf did not like his stepmother, yet he suffered from her strange behavior during her periods of depression. The woman was committed for some time as an alcoholic; she was probably schizophrenic.

When Rudolf was not yet of school age, he was taken to see the body of a deceased neighbor, an old man with a large beard. He was thoroughly frightened and later, at the age of thirteen, refused to look at the body of his dead grandmother. After having seen the dead old man, he began to be afraid at night. He imagined meeting the devil; and in the sounds of the wind in attic or cellar, in corridors or toilets, he imagined he heard the moaning and sighing of people doomed soon to die. At night he would wander about the house with closed eyes.

In his first years at school he was greatly impressed by the illustrations in the children's Bible—particularly by that of the beheading of John the Baptist, and of Christ and the Tempter standing on the parapet of the Temple at Jerusalem. At that time, he jumped from the hayloft to the threshing floor and, overestimating the thickness of the haystack on the ground, suffered a fracture across his right foot. The distal fragment moved over the proximal one and healed in this position because his father refused for economic reasons to place the boy in a hospital, as advised by the physician. When, after many weeks, Rudolf returned to school, he was laughed at because of his report that he had broken "a little bone" in his foot. For a long time, Rudolf believed that he had been born with two club feet; that he had once broken the left one, which had become normal in the process; and, therefore, had now only one club foot—the right one.

As a result of the accident, his anxiety increased. He hardly ventured to cross a bridge for fear of falling off. Towers and roofs, too, aroused in him the idea of falling. He also visualized falling into the canal of some industrial plant and being drawn into a machine where he would be ripped to pieces—like Max and Moritz [5] (we are not certain that he knew of the book at this time). After hearing about a body, nibbled by rats, which was said to have been found nearby, he developed a fear of being eaten alive by rats in the woods. He then also became afraid that "something could happen" in games with his friends, and he withdrew more and more. Soon he got the impression that his schoolmates bore him some grudge and did not care for him any longer, and he had a peculiar feeling about it.

From one of his older brothers, Rudolf had taken over the job of collecting church offerings during Mass. One of the boys showed him how to open the box. From early childhood Rudolf had loved coins and glittering things. He yielded to temptation and took some of the money. Some of it he used to buy cigarettes for his schoolmates in an effort to make himself popular again. He also became industrious, purchased and sold rabbits, and entered barter deals. He acquired a construction game. He bought fireworks and made himself conspicuous by setting off too many. He was watched in church and caught at a new theft. Rudolf was then probably about twelve years old. As soon as he came home after having been found out, he masturbated in the toilet and furiously threw the rest of the fireworks into the manure pit. Next day in school he was beaten by his teacher and later, again, by his father. The priest is said to have cursed him with the punishment of Hell. He was thoroughly questioned by the churchwarden, but was so choked by tears that he could hardly speak. He was inwardly angry, and his helplessness made him angrier still. While he was making a forced apology, in the presence of the authorities and before a candle-lit crucifix, he was inwardly vowing vengeance by way of murder and arson. Whenever roasted rabbit was served at home, he suffered further humiliation from family innuendoes that the meal was sponsored by the church. Most significantly, Rudolf began to stutter in school, inviting ridicule from teacher and students. Only several years later, during his apprenticeship, did the stuttering disappear.

Rudolf's father would slaughter the rabbits in the cellar while the boy looked on. On these occasions Rudolf often asked why his mother had died.

[5] [Characters of a popular German children's book by Wilhelm Busch whose text and illustrations vividly portrayed the punishments visited upon two bad boys for their incessant practical jokes.—TRANSLATOR.]

The father seems either to have dodged the question or to have mentioned jaundice. Rudolf remembers having hated anything yellow when he was a child. He would call one of his sister's friends, who wore a yellow skirt, "the yellow danger" or "yellow fever."

Physically, Rudolf was robust and well-developed. Puberty began at an early age. Shortly before the church stealing incident, Rudolf's older brother, who shared his bed, seduced him into mutual masturbation under the pretense of sexual education. During the following years he masturbated a lot, most of the time in the toilet and alone. During this he felt a strong fear of being seized by a skeleton hand through the window or of falling through the toilet pan into the sewage. He then imagined he might get stuck in the pipe, get a view of female genitals, and get his face smeared with feces and menstrual blood. He would go through terrible anxiety, tinged with sexual excitement, and imagined feeling the touch of ghosts in various bodily sensations, particularly that of chill on his skin.

In the period after the theft he was drawn to a woman of about his mother's age. But subsequently, the woman observed him making mischief in church again and informed his father. After he was punished, Rudolf's love for the woman turned into hatred, and he decided to kill her. In the meantime he had to go on seeing her in spite of his disappointment. When he was told to take her shoes to the shoemaker, he followed an immediate instinctual impulse and went to the toilet where he masturbated with one hand while holding her shoes with the other.

Before the stealing episode, Rudolf had always been very impressed by church procedures. Especially on Ascension Day (probably confused by Rudolf with Resurrection), which was celebrated by picturesque presentations and accompanied by flourishes of trumpets, the boy was shaken by experiences of a gruesome beauty. After his misdemeanor he began to hate and resist the priest, the church, the school, and, particularly, religious teaching. Among other matters, he objected to the commandment "Thou shalt not kill!" because again and again, when anything adverse happened to him, he entertained thoughts of murder and revenge. He had always been very sensitive to disappointments and, as a small child, would cry for hours if a promise or an expectation was not fulfilled.

When he finished school Rudolf started working for a maternal uncle who was a butcher and lived about fifteen miles from his parents' house. He had to deliver meat and, on his errands, met all kinds of adventures. Once he watched workers pulling a horribly disfigured corpse out of the river. He talked a lot with the apprentices and butcher boys. Crude sexual themes were regular topics. Mutual masturbation and homosexual acts were frequently indulged in. One Sunday night the older boys arranged for the fifteen-year-old Rudolf to have normal sexual intercourse in his room with a servant girl who was still a minor.

At the age of sixteen, Rudolf began serving his apprentice-time with a butcher in Appenzellerland. He had said once as a boy that he would like to be a butcher because butchers had the most beautiful wives. Later, he became anxious, was less ready for this kind of work, and would have preferred to become a mechanic, but his father insisted on the earlier plan. At first the job of killing animals gave Rudolf trouble and, several times, nauseated him, but he quickly adjusted to the work and soon liked it very much.

During the early phase of his apprenticeship Rudolf was again charged with delivering meat. On these occasions he would get into elaborate conversations with the housewives. He would attempt to learn about their intimate affairs, such as menstrual periods, births, marital relations. One of the women told him the terrible story of her son, who had shot to death a neighboring couple in the belief that they practiced witchcraft and were responsible for mishaps in his stable, for the death of his younger brother, and the difficult birth of his sister.[6] The killing took place when young T. (who was later committed because of schizophrenia) passed his neighbor's house and was asked by the woman about the birth of his sister. Believing that she already knew and did not have to ask him, he became furious and fired the shot.

During this time and, probably, partially in connection with this story, Rudolf experienced sexual excitement mixed with murderous impulses toward the women as they were telling him things. Usually he was able to ward off these feelings simply by leaving, yet he felt these impulses to be strange, and grew anxious. He liked to be called "Sebastian" by a Mrs. R. and thought of the saint, his deeds and martyrdom. But when his employer accidentally accompanied him to this woman's house, his real name was disclosed and Rudolf was very ashamed.

At the time of these visits to Mrs. R., Rudolf was having an affair with his employer's wife, who had told him how unhappy her married life was in its sexual aspects and who had seduced the apprentice into serving as a substitute. Subsequently she confessed her misconduct to her husband, and Rudolf had to leave his job. When Rudolf's father learned of the incident, he couldn't help admiring his son for having been able, at his age, to have intercourse with a fully clad woman—to him a sign of particular potency.

A new attempt by Rudolf to become a mechanic was foiled by his father's stubbornness, and he was placed with another butcher for continuation of his apprenticeship. It was there that Rudolf one day found the maid lying unconscious on the couch. He first inspected her, then touched her body to find out whether she was alive, tried to open her eyes, and eventually attempted, unsuccessfully, to have intercourse with her. Gradually she came to. Soon an intimate relationship with the girl ensued, with frequent inter-

6 The case was published by Hermann Rorschach; *viz.*, "Ein Mordfall aus Aberglauben" ("A Case of Murder from Superstition"), *Schweizer Volkskunde*, Bd. 10, 1920, S. 39.

course in his or her bed. When Rudolf's master got wind of this, he flew into a fit of rage, entered the boy's room, and beat him out of his sleep.

From the time of his first apprentice-job on, Rudolf would on Sundays be almost manically driven to cheap movies on crime, often three in one day. He also read a great deal of trashy literature and, always and everywhere, waited for opportunities to have sexual intercourse. Since with his brutal ways he hardly ever succeeded, he once tried to seduce one of his older sisters but was rejected. All that day he spent in criminal and sexual phantasies.

After being beaten by his master, Rudolf fell into a serious depression. When he came home, one of his sisters asked him what was wrong with him. Not answering, he telephoned for a taxi and left the same evening, planning to slit the driver's throat with a butcher knife he had with him. He did not carry out this plan but, after leaving the taxi in a nearby town, stole an automobile. He drove aimlessly about, cheated a garageman out of gasoline, and ended up against a garden fence in the early morning. He abandoned the car and managed to reach the house of one of his brothers, who supplied him with money and sent him back to his job.

Soon after these events, his apprenticeship completed, Rudolf started on a paid job. This produced new conflicts with his father, who expected him to send money home; whereas Rudolf could hardly get along on his wages. He frequently went to town, roamed half the nights through dubious places, and sought the company of prostitutes. Once he slept with one, a rather middle-aged and intoxicated barmaid who had wrapped her body in a blue veil. Another time he bought champagne for a night club performer, whereupon she left him in the lurch. Frequently he found himself in a state of indefinable urge and sexual excitement. As his way of life and financial situation did not permit him to obtain satisfaction and relaxation for himself, he resorted to earlier practices. He masturbated a great deal, partly applying perverse procedures such as the use of coins, ladies' silk stockings, silk handkerchiefs, and parts of animal intestines. Occasionally he would practice sodomy with pigs before he slaughtered them. He also accepted money from a homosexual physician for being used as a male prostitute.

A friend persuaded him to participate in a burglary. Rudolf hoped to get money this way, but, thanks to external circumstances, his friend went ahead on his own, was caught and sent to prison. Later he told Rudolf that it wasn't so bad in prison, that he had been allowed to work all the time and had liked it there.

During this period, Rudolf maintained a friendship with a farmer's daughter. They met occasionally on Sundays and he would go with her to her father's "Alp" where sometimes some "necking," but never actual intercourse, occurred. He got along well with his employer and was a diligent worker. He was described as rather inconspicuous. When his employer's landlady antagonized the employer, Rudolf had phantasies of killing her.

Rudolf had been home for the last time on Christmas Day of 1938. His father had again reproached him for not sending any money. When, subsequently, his sister wrote that his father had suffered a stroke and might soon die, he was glad. On January 18 word of his father's death reached him. His master's wife told him that he didn't look like someone whose father had died. Except for a slight temperature and some coughing, he was in a gay mood when he went home. He found his father's body in his bed. He was rather timid at first, but when his stepmother permitted him to touch the body, he did, and behaved quite crazily. Again and again he opened and closed his father's eyes, wanted to examine the body more and more thoroughly, offered to shave the face and carry the body out and prop it against the wall of the corridor where his brother was waiting—afraid to enter the room. After the body was placed in the coffin Rudolf asked to examine the bed, but was refused.

The funeral took place on the following day. Rudolf had had little sleep and did not feel well. Before the mourners convened he wanted to listen to very loud popular music on the radio. But at the moment when the coffin was carried out of the house, he began to cry without control or inhibition and was scolded by the family. En route to the cemetery he became very sad at the thought that his father was now passing these houses for the last time. When they passed the school he was somewhat cheered by remembering how, as a pupil, he had always envied the people who passed in funeral processions because they were allowed to take a walk while he was forced to sit still and study. The actual ceremony was terrible to him, and he cried again as the casket was lowered into the grave. At the funeral repast at which meat and red wine were served, he was offended by the merrymaking of the others and refused to eat anything himself.

On the following morning, a Sunday, he saw the woman neighbor to whom, as a child, he had taken such a great liking and who had so bitterly disappointed him. In the course of conversation with her, he became more and more aware that his father, unhappy with his second wife, must have had an intimate relationship with this woman who lived in discord with an alcoholic husband.

Contrary to the wishes of his brothers and sisters, he left at noon of the same day, with the intention of stopping off at Zurich for a visit to a prostitute. As he rode a trolley down *Bahnhofstrasse,* his father's funeral procession came to his mind. He felt as if he *were* his father in the hearse, riding through the streets of his town for the last time. Simultaneously he was seized by an irresistible desire to strangle the prostitute he planned to visit. He entered a bar and soon found what he was looking for. He followed the prostitute to her room, still possessed by the idea of choking her to death.

While he drew the blinds at her request, she told him she would not undress. At this very moment the murderous impulse suddenly disappeared. He had normal intercourse with the girl and subsequently returned to his job.

Nothing special happened during the following weeks, except that he could not see his girl friend. On Wednesday, March 22, 1939, he went to a nearby town and looked, fruitlessly, for a whore in a cheap bar. A waitress whom he knew from earlier visits helped him to his satisfaction manually. He missed the last train and, as at previous times, roamed the streets for most of the night and returned home in the early morning.

At 8 A.M. he was carrying a tray with cuts of meat on it and suddenly put it down. Thereafter everything took its course automatically, as it were. To what degree, at this stage, memories of the previous night's murderous impulses had emerged, we were never able to clarify. Those connections which were obtained for the testimony had emerged during hypnotic states and were not again mentioned later.

As described before, he arrived at Zurich early in the morning. He could not yet expect to find a prostitute in a bar so he visited various taverns, without drinking much. A waitress told him a long story about a murder case in Basel which had just been written up in the newspapers. She remarked that the murderer would now have to go to the penitentiary for many years . . . so what did he get out of it?

In the early afternoon Rudolf returned to the bar he had visited some weeks before. Soon three prostitutes entered. He chose a blond one and went with her to her room. When she suddenly stood, stark naked, before him, he became very frightened. He undressed, but could not achieve ejaculation during intercourse. Subsequently the girl had to satisfy him manually. Then they both dressed.

He paid her twenty francs, then slipped out his revolver, holding the weapon somehow hidden in front of him. The woman took it for a lighter, and he asked her to try it. Whereupon, he pulled the trigger without actually taking aim. She was hit in the neck and collapsed. He ran away without looking back . . . feeling as if he had wakened from a dream.

At first he roamed the street aimlessly. Then it occurred to him to phone the police to say that something had happened, that they should go there and look. . . . Following this, he telephoned his master to say that he had done something wrong and would not return.

In the meantime the ambulance had arrived and, among the spectators, he watched the removal of the injured girl. Later he called the hospital in an unsuccessful effort to learn about his victim's condition. Eventually, feeling very hungry, he went to a restaurant and ordered meat and red wine. From the restaurant, he called the police and told them where to find the man who had attempted the murder. They arrived before he had a chance to eat.

He had concealed the revolver in the bread basket. In the police car, he said he felt so hungry that he could eat a horse, shoes and all.

When questioned, Rudolf showed a strangely cool and relaxed attitude. He did not know why he had done what he had. He kept very calm, too, during the early part of his stay in prison, and worked steadily. Nevertheless, he was disappointed, since he had had a very different picture of everything from his friend's report. At Easter when he heard the bells ring and saw the flawless blue sky, he began to cry convulsively. The warden then reminded him:

> "The illusion is short,
> the remorse is long."

Shortly after, he was transferred to Burghoelzli for examination and evaluation.

IV *From Rudolf's Early Childhood*

We have now to refer to those events which Rudolf can not longer remember. He has phantasied a great deal about them and, on the basis of these phantasies, we have made thorough inquiries. The following material is the result of these inquiries which, incidentally, agree in great measure with the phantasies. Rudolf had numerous dreams which formulated his earlier experiences.

Rudolf was born, the eighth of ten children, on October 9, 1918. Another boy was born after him who died in infancy from pneumonia. Subsequently, a girl was born. The mother never recovered from the last birth. Bedridden, she suffered repeatedly from genital bleeding, jaundice, and fever and died on February 23, 1922.

During the five-and-a-half months of her illness, Rudolf slept in his mother's bedroom and spent his days in her bed. He climbed about her body while she was talking to him. He wore a skirt. Since the older children had the care of the house, they were glad that the mother took the three-year-old upon herself. The youngest sister, still an infant, made no trouble. The mother died at night, after a long and bitter struggle which was attended by the entire family and the priest, who administered holy water. As her bed was dirty and bloodstained and her body light, the father carried it to another room. Rudolf slept the night in the room in which all this took place.

Next morning he looked, as always, for his mother, rummaging through her still unclean bed. He was then dressed and told that Mother had died.

The nocturnal transfer of the body had left bloodstains on the floor. Rudolf, in all probability following these traces, had entered the room where his mother's body lay. He pulled a chair over to the bed, climbed up on it, and knelt on his mother's body. He touched the face with his hands and spoke to his mother: "You aren't dead, Mother, are you? Mary says you are. . . . You are asleep, aren't you?" One of the older sisters, looking for the boy, took him up and carried him away. He is said not to have cried or shown any symptoms of fear. (It is possible, but cannot be proved, that a similar scene was enacted on the following day.)

The mother died on Thursday. The funeral took place the following Sunday. It was Carnival time. It is likely that Rudolf spent a lot of time at the window, watching the riotous fun and the masquerades. Possibly Rudolf's first real memories stem from that period. He remembers something about horses pulling a carriage but seems, somehow, to mix up his mother's hearse and his stepmother's moving van.

The brothers and sisters emphasize that, from the day of the funeral, Rudolf turned into a different person. The scene at his mother's body was always considered very touching by the family, and the poor child was pitied for having to suffer so much from the subsequent housekeeper misery.

V Observations of Rudolf's Attitudes in the Institution

From the very beginning Rudolf set himself apart from the average patients by his good external control and reasonable behavior, and therefore he was granted many privileges.

While employed in housework at Burghoelzi, Rudolf met a housemaid and started a friendship which he tried to keep up after his transfer to Muensterlingen. At Burghoelzi he began to suffer temporary serious depressions, during which he wept convulsively and appeared quite desperate. At other times he told of stage-like phantasies.

In Muensterlingen Rudolf again was thoroughly controlled, friendly, pleasing, and very eager to work. Soon he was made substitute for the houseboy who was absent on military duty. Only after a year did it become apparent that Rudolf had early abused this job and started an affair with a kitchen girl, against almost insurmountable odds and with great skill at camouflage. With an intricate tissue of lies and fictitious dreams and in every way conceivable, he misled the doctors and attendants. His supervision was also made difficult by the fact that his regular meetings with the doctor were frequently canceled because of the latter's military duties.

During the sessions Rudolf was at first quite reticent and shut-in. He did anything rather than associate freely. He did not even want to be treated—partly because he was afraid, and rightly so, that things would emerge which would prolong his internment, partly because he had a bad conscience on account of the kitchen maid, and, finally, because he wanted to remain the way he was and did not conceive of changing his mode of existence. His friendly and engaging attitude and his diligence secured him a favorable reception everywhere. His robust build and well-cut features won him a great deal of sympathy, particularly with nurses and female patients. So he could very well be pleased with his life.

On March 11, 1940, while Rudolf was still carrying on his secret love affair, something unexpected happened. Suddenly Rudolf changed completely. He thought a lot of his father, he said, and he had had almost no sleep for several nights. He had lost his appetite; food seemed "silly" to him and he had a feeling of fullness in his stomach. The sex urge was extinguished, as it were. Rudolf complained about headaches and stopped smoking. He felt as though smoking stupefied him. He felt he was sick but could not tell what was wrong with him. He felt tired, battered, spent, and weak, and he no longer liked working. He was sick and tired of everything. Rudolf said that he didn't know what had happened, only that he saw no future and was therefore desperate. He believed he would deteriorate more and more and never get out of the hospital . . . that no one could help him . . . that he couldn't even die any more . . . that he ought to be beaten and transferred to the violent ward . . . that he deserved nothing else. He told us that he was confused . . . had no feeling left, but was different from before in that he was not at all afraid, but quite calm, and could again kill at any time . . . that it would make no difference to him, and leave him quite cold. However, he insisted he had a clear mind and knew exactly what he was doing and saying.

In the days that followed Rudolf's state alternated between improvement and deterioration. The patient said that he could only "think so far and no further" and that not only he himself but all people around him seemed strange and cold. Again and again the thought struck him that all people knew why he was here and, therefore, did not respect him.

He remained in this state for many weeks, with some variations. At first, complaints about experiences of change in his psyche prevailed. He explained that his thinking was as though under a spell. Several times he had suicidal impulses or called upon the physician for help with theatrical, hysterical-looking gestures. Later he became calmer and, at worst, complained about his general weakness and a variety of physical ills. Only afterwards did he admit how tortured he had felt. He had tested himself with difficult arithmetic problems to determine whether his power of thinking was still intact—hoping the disturbance would in this way vanish. Once he had cut into his left forearm in the belief that he might be relieved by the sight of the flowing blood.

About three months later a complete reversal of his mood took place within a few days. Rudolf leapt into high spirits, talked loudly and much, and hopped from one topic to another. In this period he would, quite uninhibitedly, invent complex stories in order to cover up his relations with the kitchen help. He entertained grandiose plans for the future . . . wanted to learn English and see the world. He grew impatient of his commitment and urged his release within the shortest time.

For the first time in many years he went to Confession and Communion. He was very enthusiastic about them and told everyone who was willing to listen about the miracle that had happened to him—as if a weight had been lifted from his spirit. Subsequently he busied himself as a ladies' man and spent long hours on the beach. He dressed with great care, acquired loud neckties, used skin creams and hair pomade, and managed to consume fifteen bottles of perfume within a few weeks. His sleep and appetite were "excellent," and "no trace" was left of any physical symptoms. Occasionally he became irritated and insolent and began to grumble about the institution, saying that even in prison he had had a better time. He also clashed with co-workers and frequently threatened them, whereupon we finally felt compelled to transfer the patient to a closed ward. This put an end to his operations.

Already these first periods of strong moodiness were distinguished by their lack of consistency and continuity. In the midst of his almost manic activities Rudolf could become quite desperate and weep for one or two hours. During the next few years, moodswings were still conspicuous to the superficial observer, although they were less extreme than in the beginning. At seemingly irregular intervals Rudolf would develop low spirits with depressive dejection, desperation, disgust, and a feeling of being under a spell. Then, suddenly, he would become irritable and quarrelsome, with a feeling of being discriminated against, or he would become gay and unrestrained. Often these moods extended only over hours or days. Sometimes they seemed to appear without any external cause. At other times they were closely connected with everyday events of Rudolf's life. Everything that was unexpected would touch off low moods, as, for example, the escape of a patient. The depressive moods were generally stronger in the Spring.

Underneath that strong depressibility there occurred other emotional processes which were not easy to trace. The serious depressions of 1940 were followed by a distinctly depressive disposition, particularly in the somatic area—and extending over a period of two years. Rudolf felt chronically and indefinably ill and, again and again, tended toward hypochondriac reactions. His mind was a great deal occupied with his mother. He never felt quite free, and his handwriting was very small.

From the end of 1941 to the end of 1943 Rudolf's basic disposition was rather reverse. He spoke almost always with a very loud thunder-voice, developed a giant's appetite, wrote in large letters, fluently, and with a left slant. Anxiety and suicidal impulses receded, and, at the same time, he was discontented with the institution, the doctor, and himself. He thought himself misunderstood and became the confidant of a married woman who frequently visited the hospital. At a hospital party he danced exclusively with this woman and was again gossiped about to such a degree that again we had to intervene. For the following two years, well into 1945, Rudolf remained basically in a depressive state with corresponding fluctuations in his somatic feelings—his writing was small and straight, his voice lower. Also his giant appetite gradually decreased, and he adjusted more readily to the hospital rules. In the Spring of 1944—and rather reluctantly, at first, since he stubbornly clung to the idea of remaining a butcher—he was able to start working as a gardener's apprentice in the institution. At that time Rudolf had to fight the strong impulse to throw himself in front of an approaching train.

However, while he eagerly carried on his gardening work and was, in secret, lovingly devoted to a nurse, his condition improved more and more. His personality grew more balanced, and he began to read good books. In the Spring of 1947 he passed the final apprenticeship examination as the second highest among the three hundred apprentices in the Thurgau Kanton. He was then permitted to take a leave from the hospital. He has since held a job as a gardener for a year, to the satisfaction of his employer, and without being conspicuous in any of his reactions. In the spring of 1948, nine years after committing his crime, he was definitely released from the institution and went to a trade school for further training. The guardianship was continued for the time being.

VI *Rudolf's Daydreams and Dreams*

It can be assumed with certainty that Rudolf, before his crime, was a great daydreamer for years and that his acts can be understood only on the basis of those phantasies. But, because of their nature, the content of these experiences never became clearly conscious, and Rudolf could not inform us about them. In the course of the psychiatric treatment various fragments of such phantasies from earlier times came to light which, however, could never be composed into a whole; that is to say, in a way from which Rudolf's behavior could have been altogether explained. Forgotten phantasy-contents which are subsequently reproduced are almost always falsified and can, therefore, only with reservations be used to explain puzzling behavior.

Later, however, during Rudolf's stay in the hospital, we observed a vast amount of phantasy and, particularly, of dream contents which we shall present in the following pages.

At first Rudolf dreamed hardly at all and took great care not to reveal any of his daydreams. Due to his general lack of interest it was difficult to find any topics for talk. Being a nonbeliever, he did not go to church either—all the while feeding his imagination ever new material through his secret reading of trash just as he had drawn earlier upon the movies and cheap literature to provide material for his phantasies.

In the second half of September 1939 we had a talk with Rudolf and explained to him how we planned his treatment. Whereupon, on September 25, he made a beginning with a dream in which the physician was shot to death.

During the next half-year Rudolf related only six dreams. In one of these the physician was shot again. Twice he dreamed about the stealing, wrapping, and transportation of female bodies. Two dreams could not be interpreted at that time. Later they turned out to refer to Rudolf's secret relations with the kitchen maid and to his cheating the physician.

The dreams of female bodies could be traced to memories of films about the wax figures of Mme. Tussaud and about a sadistic murderer who turned his victims into wax figures. Also, shilling shockers that had been read by Rudolf at an earlier time played their part. He often spoke of phantasies which would come to mind again and again, as, for example, that people whom he met outside would drop dead all around him. Also, he phantasied about himself as the victor in athletic contests—although he had never been active in sports—and he imagined himself, the Champion Shot, being kissed by pretty girls. He seemed to have some vague feeling that something was wrong in his psyche, and he believed he could be helped only by having as much sexual intercourse as possible. This is why, from the very beginning, he was in such a hurry to be released and vigorously protested against his castration, although nobody had ever suggested such an operation to him.

During his depressive state, which was observed in March 1940, Rudolf was predominantly concerned with himself and his health. He reported one dream only—namely, that his face was covered with ugly scabs.

In the period during which everything seemed to him cold and strange, he remembered having felt something similar on earlier occasions, particularly toward his girl friend shortly before his crime, which was one of the reasons he had not seen her during that time. In his talks with the physician Biblical history was often a subject—particularly its bloody events. It was in this period that he reported his night-ride in the taxi and his murderous impulses toward the driver.

In his maniform phase Rudolf struck us by talking a great deal about death. Death enters as an invisible force or disguised as a human and bends over the person who, thereupon, dies. The small child is visited by a white-robed woman with a kindly smile, the soldier by an officer. Only the aged are approached by a skeleton, who takes their hands and is welcomed as a friend. Rudolf had always been terribly afraid of death and whenever someone talked about dying he had hardly dared to go to bed by himself. Wax figures were supposed to help conquer death.

Subsequently Rudolf had some extended stage-like dreams which made use of childhood memories of local holidays,[7] films, books, circus shows, and

7 [Such as the *Sechseläutenfeier*, a popular festival celebrated at Zurich, at which a strawman is carried through the streets, burned, and thrown into the river.—EDITORS.]

Biblical history. In several, women were threatened, tortured, and killed. He also told of grandiose daydreams in which he saw himself as a general in the midst of bloody battles and celebrated as a conquering hero; or he was a great statesman or politician, or had discovered a drug for a perilous disease, or, as an explorer, went through daring adventures. All these and numerous other phantasies, some about murder and dismemberment—particularly in connection with women with whom he was alone and who excited him—he had had for years. He related his experiences in Zurich on the day after his father's funeral. He also told us that all day in the hospital his mind forced him to think that next time he wouldn't miss the woman, that he would shoot more calmly and aim better, and that he would kill not only one but several of them, etc.

He would also describe horrifying states of anxiety which befell him when he was alone with a woman and the murderous impulse emerged—an impulse he could fight off only with the greatest of effort. More and more frequently he became afraid of cold corpses at night. He would believe that one had been put in his path to the toilet and expected, at every step, to touch the ice-cold body with his bare foot. Soon he even believed he had a female body next to him in bed and no longer dared to bring his hand from under the blanket, taking the sensation of cold air for the cold touch of the corpse. For hours, his body covered with cold sweat, he dared not move in his bed.

In such a mood Rudolf had a dream in which he saw two arms and two feet sticking out of a sandhill. In the dream someone explained something about it, and he assured me that under the sand was lying the body of a man whom he had seen under a train earlier in the dream. In the sessions Rudolf continued to be occupied with dead people, coffins, blood, and similar topics. The heap of sand led to the image of a heap of wood in a small room of his parents' house—the same room in which his mother was said to have lain on the bier. Then, on the third day after the dream, in a wild emotional outburst, he phantasied the crucial scene at his mother's body—until then forgotten by him and unknown to us.

In a parallel development Rudolf produced occasional dreams which seemed to resist any attempts at interpretation; but, actually, they alluded to his secret affair and caused him to devise a complex tissue of lies so as to allay the suspicion of his doctor. This was one of his typical reactions in his maniform states.

Subsequently Rudolf dreamed much more frequently and even daily at certain times. In his dream-contents two new images could be discerned which showed many variations in the course of the following years. At first Rudolf saw himself as a small child, later as a little prince to whom all kinds of accidents happen. On the days following his dreams of the prince Rudolf phantasied that he had not been his parents' child. In those dreams Rudolf— through an old, unused, rusty door—enters underground passages which lead to palatial rooms or a labyrinth of caves or a church or cellars and vaults. There solemn rituals are performed in the dim light of colored torches; and often a chest or coffin or cash box or the like containing some secret treasure is unearthed. Again and again that content was connected with human corpses and dead creatures in general, but the box is also, and at the same time, a device to resurrect the dead. Killing and being killed was a frequent theme in these dreams. For instance, in one of the dreams Rudolf, at the bottom of the sea, was entwined by the hair of a girl who had stepped out of a shipwreck and who threatened him with a dagger.

After he had admitted his relations with the kitchen maid—relations terminated quite some time before—he was more at ease and, as was frequently confirmed later on, more reliable in his communications. His girl friend had meanwhile married and become pregnant. He dreamed he attended the birth. What was born was "a brown little heap that looked like a child."

In this period Rudolf phantasied a great deal about his mother's death and tried in various ways to recall the image of her body. Dream interpretations brought back the horses of the funeral procession, the cabinetmaker who had made the coffin, and the gravestone sculptor. Corpses appeared time and again and the most diversified ways of killing were perpetrated in Rudolf's dreams—either by Rudolf or on Rudolf or sometimes just witnessed by him. The entire circle of friends from earlier years emerged. Boys with whom he used to roam about—particularly those who later went astray or insane—played their parts in the most manifold, adventurous, and bloody enterprises. Only rarely did he meet former girl friends in his dreams.

In the spring of 1941 Rudolf went through an extended depressive state, but with far less extreme symptoms. Murder was still frequently featured in his phantasies. Especially after masturbation he imagined how it would feel to kill women. In such phases he became always more hostile to his doctor. Although he preserved his composure on the surface, he phantasied a great deal about killing him and about ways and means of killing him. Treatment became unproductive and dangerous.

In March and April of the preceding year Rudolf had confessed his taxi ride and his plan to murder the driver. Also, he told of his homosexual adventures from the years preceding his crime. They must have, in part, taken place at the same time of the year. Now he began to dream with conspicuous frequency about fellow patients on the ward. At that time he got into repeated tussles with them, saw them masturbate in his dreams, and was supposedly examined by them "in the genitals"; in discussing his dreams he would, spontaneously and over and over again, mention operations and castration.

During the following summer the motif of chopping, which had occasionally come up in dreams of dissection, came more and more to the fore, accompanied by light maniform states—recognizable by the patient's talk tiveness and irritability. Increasingly, daytime phantasies of dismemberment and mutilation, with reference to the patient's own body, made their appearance. Rudolf began to tell about the strange hunger sensations after his crime and felt a growing disgust at eating meat. Sometimes he had the feeling it smelt of corpses. He also reported feeling extreme thirst while suffering from depressed moods.

Whereas in October 1940 Rudolf occupied himself with his mother's body, in the same period of the following year he paid more attention to his own. He boasted of his strength and ran about with rolled-up sleeves, coming to the doctor's office dressed this way. As in an earlier maniform phase, he nursed his skin and hair, used various cosmetic medications, and tried to look his best. He prided himself upon his "favorable appearance," but felt, at the same time, very conscious of his crippled right foot, which gave him a feeling of pain and which he blamed for his lack of success with women. The functioning of his genitals was watched hypochondriacally. He felt tension and pain in them and talked about them endlessly.

About the end of 1941, when Rudolf's depressive mood slowly changed, he had a dream which differed from all earlier ones. He looked through a window at a wonderful snow scene. At the same time real experiences of shame began to occur in Rudolf—in his dreams as well as in his talks with the doctor—while his hostile attitude toward the latter gradually disappeared. He phantasied that the doctor, too, had committed murder as he had; that he, too, suffered from the same daydreams, and similar things.

Something new came to light during a depressive state in March, namely, the confession of sodomy. It introduced a quality of animal and butcher expertness into Rudolf's dreams and phantasies, which now showed horrifying and repelling sadistic motifs. Again, a maniform phase replaced the spring depression in 1942. The autumn again found him turning his attention to his body. The dreams often produced fire, and phantasies centered around hell-fire and purgatory.

In March 1943 Rudolf reproduced his early fears on the toilet. Subsequently the chopping motif receded and the sewage-mud-and-mire motif became ever more important. For more than a year Rudolf's phantasies and dream contents were focused upon birth. As a small child Rudolf had imagined that the stork bites the mother's leg and the child arrives through the wound; later he believed in birth through the bowels and imagined that the child is delivered like feces amidst bad smells. Again Rudolf's dreams produced boxes and cases, this time containing human parts and a stinking broth. Priests handled them in a mysterious way. Rudolf told about his childhood belief that children were made in church during Mass, even that the priests killed people in order to make children, since dead people and babies were always carried to church.

Mixed with these contents there appeared in dreams, and even on Sundays in church, sacrilegious ideas in connection with carnivalistic disguises, transformation of the sexes, and hermaphroditism. Choir boys who had soiled their garments with urine exhibited themselves in church, and children brought animals which were married by the priest. In one of his dreams Rudolf saw an idiot or a nude woman crucified. Another time he dreamed of his "twelve fellows," whereupon it came to light that for years he had phantasied being Christ and doing miracles. Moreover, he had thought out a complex device for crucifying himself in the woods, quite on his own and without anybody's noticing it, so as to make those who would find him believe in a new miracle.

Time and again, a gloomy mood prevailed in Rudolf's dreams. Corpses and skeletons appeared almost daily, and Rudolf's productivity in this respect seemed inexhaustible. Once in a dream Rudolf saw stone statues of women holding clocks in their hands.

Late in March 1944—about the time of the fifth anniversary of his deed—Rudolf again dreamed of a chest in the cellar which was locked with a clock. It was easy for Rudolf to take apart the clock and open the chest. He could not remember what was inside, but he did report subsequently that for years he kept hidden a box filled with buttons, splinters of glass, and pieces of cloth. He said that from early childhood he had searched for such objects and, whenever he found one, would seize upon it, enjoy it hugely, and cherish it like a treasure. He also derived great pleasure from glittering coins. In earlier years he had masturbated with the help of buttons and coins and had carried small change in his mouth. This fancy could be traced to the time after his mother's death when he searched the entire house and occasionally from the window saw something glitter out in the fields. He would then go out and comb the fields for the object.

Various dreams suggested that there was a close connection between those glittering things and the sparkle of eyes, particularly the eyes of his deceased mother. Then, during puberty, the sparkling objects—now including the gloss of silk—became at least partial goals of the sexual drive and led to a fetishism which, among other things, prevented Rudolf from having sexual intercourse with women who were not dressed. The significance of the clothes was determined on the one hand by the buttons, on the other by the fact that Rudolf as a child ran around at carnival in his dead mother's clothes. To this, various frightening experiences with masks have to be added.

On September 22, 1944, Rudolf had the following dream: He was in a ward of the institution, but from the outside the building looked like his parents' house. A brook ran past the house, and from its stinking, muddy waters Rudolf pulled fish. The brook was teeming with fish. Inside the house Rudolf fastened two music notes high up on a curtain. Then he sat on a washing stand in a room and looked into the mirror where he saw a door in the opposite wall. Through this door a woman entered and stopped behind him. "I tore myself around, embraced her, and kissed her passionately on the mouth . . . horrible . . . her eyes popping out, white, extinguished, face pale, mouth voluptuous—as if bloated—and in it, a stinking broth . . . the whole figure, a rigid, unyielding mass. Then people came and looked into the room. . . . I tore away and, because of the woman, had to make believe by rolling on the floor and emitting high sounds. Then I lay on the bed in the other room. A white shine followed me to the right side of the bed, but slowly lost its strength. My inner turmoil calmed down, and I could fall asleep. . . . Later I saw the same woman, in black, standing before my door." [From Rudolf's dream-book.]

It was obvious that this dream could only be interpreted as a reexperiencing of Rudolf's meeting with his mother's body; and to Rudolf, himself, this interpretation was a matter of course. He concluded from the dream that he must have kissed his mother's body and, by moving on it, must have caused putrid, evil-smelling air, or even liquid, to pour out of the mouth.

During the following months Rudolf suffered from strong suicidal impulses and, simultaneously, from great disturbances at contact with his fellow men. He felt misunderstood and was unable to comprehend why we had to bar his relations with a married woman. The woman in question appeared to him as a ghost in his dreams. He still occasionally phantasied about dismembering, but the putrefaction contents receded noticeably.

Naturally we had always tried, for many reasons including therapeutic ones, to feed Rudolf's need for phantasy material with the help of good books. In this we had never succeeded in practice, as he would read a great deal without paying attention to the contents of the books unless they complied with his interest in blood and mire. However, in the summer of 1942, our patients, at a garden party, produced the Clown Comedy from *A Midsummer-Night's Dream*. Rudolf played the part of Pyramus. He then became interested in the entire play and was enthusiastic about its fairy-tale and magic mood. Of his own accord he continued to read Shakespeare's plays and, in *Richard III* and *Timon of Athens*, discovered plays which satisfied his taste for goriness. During subsequent years, especially from the summer of 1943 on, he repeatedly read through the entire dramatic work of Shakespeare and, later, used his first self-earned money to acquire a ten-volume edition.

In the winter of 1944–45 Rudolf went to trade school for the first time and, therefore, stayed more often outside the institution. While working very well in school, he visualized how, on the last day, he would drown himself in the lake under the pretense of an accident. He believed he was insane and could not resist dreadful ideas and impulses of suicide (he felt drawn to his mother). He wanted to leave life with honors and have people say of him, "What a pity! . . . now that he is cured, that such a thing should happen to him!"

Once, before he could carry out the suicidal plan, he had to wait for the train for about an hour. He had entered a Catholic church, said the Lord's Prayer in front of the main altar and continued before the altar of Mary with Gretchens' prayer from *Faust*. Whereupon the image of the Virgin and Child had shown a strange shimmer and looked as though it were alive. Rudolf was shaken and cured of the impulse to take his life—an impulse he had experienced as a compulsion. He said afterwards that he didn't know whether he had imagined things, or what had happened. This took place on February 23, 1945, the twenty-third anniversary of his mother's death, but Rudolf had not noticed the date.

In the weeks that followed the incident, Rudolf fell in love with the nurse. For several months he was dissatisfied, again felt discriminated against, thought that the more he ate the better he'd be, wrote dreams down in a language of confused grammar, and occasionally made the impression that his affective rapport was really very poor. This was the phase, if any, in which schizophrenia could be suspected for some good reasons, although no definite symptoms could be found.

Gradually Rudolf's state improved. He could again make contact, and threw himself more and more into his trade training. He read various literary works with growing understanding and stuck to his beloved one, the nurse.

He was very afraid of taking his final trade school examination and, in fact, failed the first time. But, after a few psychotherapeutic sessions, he made out very well. The suicidal impulses, the anxiety states, the phantasies and excessive dreams have vanished more and more during the last two years. The depressive states still occur but are scarcely different from those experienced by the "normal." Disturbances of rapport are not noticeable, either subjectively or objectively. Rudolf never dared to approach his beloved one. Occasionally he saw her and felt inhibited. Increasingly he regretted his deed and his former life. He felt newborn and declared he was discovering the beauties of the world, one by one, and was gradually getting to know people.

VII *Clinical-Psychiatric and Forensic Evaluation*

Emotional Life

Rudolf's personality is greatly dominated by his emotional life and equally as much by his psychopathological condition.

At first we meet numerous features characteristic of a *cycloid* temperament. Rudolf has without doubt a particularly sensitive nature. He can be deeply touched by poetry and classical music. Although he became accessible to emotional experiences of this type only after several years of treatment, the disposition must have been always present. Indeed, it had revealed itself in impressive experiences of religious emotions and in his participation in singing societies. He also pays a great deal of attention to feminine beauty, and tries to celebrate it in poetic-romantic emotional outpourings.

In his everyday communication with others there is reflected Rudolf's capacity for affective experience. Wherever Rudolf goes he is popular and well liked. He is able to adjust to situations, is friendly and obliging, knows what to say, is interested in other people, and knows very well how to win his way into another's favor. Rudolf is also capable of expressing his emotions. He is not inhibited except in his relationship to his girl friend who, to be sure, does not respond to his love. Rudolf enjoys working to an unusual degree and is highly proficient in and gifted for practical work, and very handy. He knows how to organize his time and how to help himself. His movements are fluent—not angular by any means—and he is a good dancer.

Finally, Rudolf is extremely inclined to fluctuations of disposition which range from light manic states to serious depressions and symptoms of depersonalization. These states show great variations as to the vital layer of the emotional experience. One has to distinguish phases which extend over years from those whose mood is based on reactive and endogenous conditions and which may change from week to week, often from day to day, and occasionally even from hour to hour. The vital phase determines the affective expressions such as the volume of voice, size of handwriting, appetite, and the relation to his own body as, for example, expressed in hypochondria; while external behavior, the acute mood and feeling of contentment, and the way of dressing vary more readily.

Apart from all this, Rudolf shows unmistakable features of a *schizoid* [8] temperament. Rudolf's emotional experience, as described above, does not completely fill him . . . it does not completely fuse with him. There is something artificial and affected in it, a certain lack of transparency. It contains more reflection than is usual with the cycloid temperament and thus Rudolf's personality gets a touch of the complex and the problematic, not found in the pure cyclothymic person. In his childhood Rudolf was decidedly timid. In order to overcome his shyness he took dancing lessons. He had to observe other people so as to learn how to get along with them. He often reacts in a touchy way, and he actually made an impression of sensitivity in the court-psychiatric examination.

Rudolf tends toward a complex-like (*complexhaft*) elaboration of many experiences, to phobic and compulsive reactions, and shows a perverted sexuality. Among his schizoid features, one should not forget to mention Rudolf's crime and his cool, calm behavior during and after it. Deep down,

8 [This term has here to be understood as originally defined by Bleuler and Kretschmer. The latter differentiated between the "syntonic," who responds to stimulation with his total personality, and the "schizoid," who responds with only part of it, as does Kuhn's patient, Rudolf.—EDITORS.]

Rudolf still feels lonely, particularly since he has left the institutional environment and faces life again. For two years he idolized a nurse in the institution without getting a sign of response to his affection. Nor did he ever find a friend. But only rarely or passingly did we observe a real disturbance in his affective rapport. It was the exception for Rudolf to be nervous or irritable—if ever, this was most likely to happen during psychotherapeutic sessions. By no means is he unsociable or humorless. His emotional life gained a great deal of freedom through treatment in the institution. Thus Rudolf offers the picture of a motley mixture of cycloid and schizoid temperamental features wherein the former prevail in the external appearance whereas the latter, perhaps, share to a greater extent in the structure of the inner personality. In his body structure, too, the pyknic-athletic features prevail. We may assume a very mixed temperament based on heredity—which is confirmed to some degree by the family picture. The particular form of Rudolf's depression and, with it, his crime become somewhat more comprehensible when seen in the light of the schizoid components of his temperament. His act, however, cannot be explained through Rudolf's emotional life alone, as we do not find a disposition for affective acts proper, and the crime, itself, cannot be considered such an act.

Instinctual Life

Rudolf's instincts, as far as their force is concerned, fluctuate widely according to his mood. Also, his instinctual life is perverted.

The act iself—an attempt at murder—most easily reveals the perversion. It shows a sadistic trend. To be sure, it was not Rudolf's intention to inflict pain on his victim—he simply wanted to kill her. Nor do we find any features of sadism, in the narrow sense, in Rudolf's earlier life. It is true that he was a butcher; but we do not find any proof of his inflicting torture on animals or of experiencing any pleasurable excitement from killing them. He would not generally treat women brutally. At most he hatched plans to take revenge on them because, as he saw it, their attitude barred him from finding sexual satisfaction (*e.g.,* he indulged in the idea of making as many girls pregnant as possible and of then taking his own life). Certainly, this crime does not at all belong in the category of murder for lust. The idea of murder did not increase his sexual excitement but rather inhibited the course of sexual function. The act was not performed to attain the highest possible sexual, or any other, excitement, but was carried out coldbloodedly in the depressive state following the sexual discharge. On the other hand, one has to consider the fact that sexual discharge could not be obtained in a natural way and certainly did not result in real satisfaction. It is true that in the following years Rudolf's dream-life and his daydreams showed extremely sadistic (and also masochistic) features, including the dismemberment motif, and that.

before the crime, such images were over and again sought and cultivated by way of cheap movies and detective stories. Nevertheless, sadism alone does not appear to be a sufficient basis for understanding the act.

More evident than the sadistic features are the fetishistic ones in Rudolf's instinctual life. As we have seen, objects of this fetishism are glittering things—particularly buttons, coins, ladies' silk underwear and stockings. If we want to investigate the possible relationship between Rudolf's perversions and his murderous assault, we have to begin with an exploration of his somatic experience.

Although in the literature about fetishism, the relationship of the fetishist to his fetish has been often described, the person of the fetishist has so far been neglected. No attention has been paid to the question of how and whether a disturbed relation to the body of one's mate may be connected with a disturbed relation to one's own body. Among the many possible forms of this relationship, it seems that incapability of one's own body, the peculiar emphasis on it, and the rejection of it may play a part in the genesis and preservation of fetishist tendencies. This we shall demonstrate in an example where it shows more clearly than in Rudolf's case:

A shoe-and-stocking fetishist, afflicted with hereditary imbecility, psychotic and suicidal tendencies, and lability, has crippled feet which oblige him to walk with the help of a stick. He still remembers exactly how, as a small child, he stood in water in his shoes and stockings, and how he experienced excitement at the chilly smoothness which he felt on his feet. Later he felt sexual sensations at this—feelings which recurred when he looked upon his glossy shoes and touched them fondly. Gradually his interest in girls' shoes and stockings became more obvious, and he became excited when he saw females step into water in their shoes. On such occasions he would masturbate; and he felt especial satisfaction when he was able to imagine, particularly vividly, women with their feet dipped in water. Actually they had to behave as if they, themselves, had crippled feet and so enjoyed this activity as much as he did.

Returning to Rudolf, we find that he did not take a merely negative attitude to his crippled right foot. His teacher once presented it to the entire class, saying that female dancers had feet like that. Hence Rudolf became proud of it and felt on various occasions like being a girl. He also insisted for a long time that originally both his feet had been misshapen and that, through an accident, one of them became normal again. At the same time that he nurtured phantasies of dissecting women, he imagined how he himself would fall victim to a traffic accident, lose his limbs, and have to be nursed and cared for. He ostensibly enjoyed this role. One time he saw himself as a murderer in his phantasies. Another time he phantasied his own violent death, as on the cross. In other words, to the murderous impulses were added suicidal ones. All this expresses, among other things, his attitude to his own body and to that of woman. In his esteem for his own deformation (the deformation of his own bodily figure) one could possibly find one of the roots of his tendency to deform the body of his sex partner—an explanation for the dismemberment and murder motif in his phantasies, dreams, and impulses.

We have thus been led, in a rather direct way, to the concept of "deformation" which, in the more recent theories of perversions, particularly those of Straus and von Gebsattel, has assumed a general and central significance. According to von Gebsattel's ideas about fetishism,[9] one could assume that the idea of killing the human carrier of the fetish is not very foreign to the fetishist! For the fetishist, because of the deformation of his instinctual life, is incapable of grasping the total love reality. The total human partner, then, is in the way of his concentration on the part with which he is fetishistically in love. The suggestion to simply eliminate the disturbing factor (the human partner) is obvious. Certainly, there are cases in which the external facts largely correspond with this theory:

A man who suffered from a typical fetishistic attraction to women's stockings—he constantly carried some of them with him, even wore them—continuously clashed with his wife until once, during a quarrel, he abruptly shot her to death. He mentioned no other cause but his hatred against the woman.

Rudolf's murderous impulses could be doubly understood if one assumes that Rudolf actually expressed love to his mother through the fetish and felt hampered in his realization of her image by the fetish-carriers. Killing then, would mean not only removing the annoying object from this world but also, by turning it into a corpse, making it similar to the original beloved image which is also dead. True, a great many fetishists are neither deformed nor aggressive in their attitudes. In any case, such observations and considerations may aid our understanding.

However, it appears that in this case the factual basis for such an interpretation of the patient's experience is too weak. As tempting as the deformation-hypothesis may be and however valuable the references it supplies, it cannot clarify our case without steering us toward a theory of unconscious motivation, which means that we would have to take a methodological step which we try to avoid.[10]

The next step should be to clarify whether and, possibly, in what manner Rudolf's sexuality is at all related by inner context with the crime.

Such context can hardly be challenged, considering the fact that it was a sexual partner whom Rudolf tried to kill. However, the attempt was cer-

[9] *Nervenarzt*, Bd. 2, 1929, S. 8–20.

[10] Of course, from the psychoanalytic view many points could be made. However, since they would hardly contribute much that is new, we refrain from bringing them up, assuming that each reader will add whatever seems conducive to his understanding.

tainly not a perverted act in the narrower sense of the word since the goal of such an act is the satisfaction of the sex drive—a satisfaction that can only be achieved in an abnormal fashion. What makes for the abnormality is that sexual satisfaction is possible only through impediments which are determined through the "World-Design" of the perverted, in that this World-Design does not permit of any other way (as Boss has convincingly shown). However, Rudolf's murderous assault occurred *after* the sex act, and its goal was to prevent any such act in the future. The fact that the deed did not actually accomplish its objective may have contributed to its evaluation as a sexual crime. Thus the crime becomes, at least partially, a consequence of the perversion, without itself being a perverted act. Perversion, the inability to love and, consequently, to achieve a satisfactory sex and love experience are among the preconditions for the crime, but not its only cause.

One such further precondition can be found in the sodomistic acts. When Rudolf found sexual satisfaction with pigs and afterwards killed them (as happened several times), he set a pattern for his deed. But it cannot be definitely proved that the killing was in any way more deeply tied up with the sex act.

In the sodomist's mind the distinction between man and animal is, as a rule, not sufficiently developed. There is the type who attributes to the animal personal human values. If, for instance, Rudolf dreams of children taking animals to church for a marriage ceremony, it is not merely a sacrilegious dream but also shows the assigning of personal values to animals. Another patient, a young farm laborer, chose for his sexual satisfaction only one particular cow. Because of her name, her beauty, and her ability to ring her bell melodiously, he took such a liking to her that he actually fell in love.[11] On the other hand, there is a type of sodomy that knows of no personal values in either man or animal. In such cases the killing of a person is not too far removed from the killing of an animal. This was probably the type of sodomistic impulses present in Rudolf at the time of his crime.

11 Acts of sodomy, we believe, should always be understood on the basis of the general relations between man and animal. In rural areas sodomy is by no means as rare as may be assumed. We have had in our institution at least eight definite cases within the last eight years. To these should be added a number of cases in which relations to animals were conspicuous although no evidence of actual acts of perversion was available. For the understanding of sodomy such cases should not be neglected either. The relationship between man and animal should be investigated in all its various forms. Already the totemism of the primitives offers plenty of material and tasks to psychology. We have to remember that animals in myths and fables have the gift of language—which points to personal values assigned to them. The relation of the individual person to the animals develops from an early age toward more and more differentiation. Only gradually does the image of man separate from the realm of the animalistic, and often the two spheres remain mixed in many respects. Today, the Rorschach test offers the most perfect method for the investigation of this problem; in many cases it reveals to us, as it were, the animal pages in the book of a person because the phantasy of most people has at its disposal an "animal realm" that serves them for the formation of their world. (*Viz.*, in regard to this entire problem, G. Bachelard, *Lautréamont* [Paris: Corti, 1939]).

(The above-mentioned dream occurred at a later period.) Finally, we have to consider the homosexual component in Rudolf which should particularly facilitate the murder of a woman. Actually, homosexuality was never very obvious in Rudolf and was of a predominantly passive nature. But, nevertheless, it was present and decisively took part in the development of Rudolf's sex drive through his mutual masturbation with his brother. It was also amply confirmed by recurring dreams during the period following the crime. Of course, the relations of the homosexual male to woman vary a great deal. But the specific form which leads to misogyny, to the torture of women in various ways, and, eventually, to murdering them is well enough known and frequently so transparent psychologically that we refrain from any further discussion of it.

In summary we may say that Rudolf is, indeed, a sexually perverted personality—that perversion has facilitated and paved the way for his crime. However, the execution of the act at its specific time cannot be understood merely in terms of the instinctual situation. The attempt at murder was, indeed, much more an *automatic* act than an *instinctual* one, since the fact that Rudolf chose an object is completely outweighed by the fact that his crime left Rudolf actually quite indifferent—that it remained alien to him (he ran away immediately after committing it)—that, in terms of experience, it took place outside of him—and that he did not, in any way, feel responsible for it.

It could be argued that Rudolf's mood fluctuations also caused fluctuations in the intensity and mode of expression of the perverted instincts, and that this could serve as an explanation of the crime. This objection, although not altogether incorrect, does not change the basic phenomenological fact that the attempt at murder cannot be understood simply as an act of perversion.

The Compulsion Symptoms

Rudolf's is, without doubt, one of those rare cases in which a crime originated out of a genuine compulsive experience.[12] We find the first compulsoid (*zwangsartigen*) ideas in Rudolf's childhood fears of falling from a bridge, from the roof, into a brook—of being cut up in the factory or eaten by rats. Rudolf had to struggle against these ideas and, in the process, anxiety states were produced. Of a more definite compulsive character were the impulses to murder housewives when delivering meat to them. From these he suffered greatly and developed serious spells of anxiety when he repressed them. Already these compulsive impulses occurred in connection with sexual excitation.

The compulsive experiences were peculiarly fixated to locations. As far as

12 [But, as Kuhn goes on to say, the immediate act itself cannot be explained as a compulsive act proper.—EDITORS.]

we know, they made their appearance only when he stood in a doorway and found himself facing a woman. Very probably this can be traced to the story of the superstitious murderer from Appenzell whose drama, too, began in a doorway. Only after Rudolf had learned that story did his compulsive impulses start. He, too, shot at the woman who stood in front of him. Originally he had planned to commit the crime in the corridor and had returned to the room only to keep the shot from being heard in the hall. As clearly as these circumstances show a close psychological tie between the compulsive impulses and the crime, just as certainly is it true that the crime did not come about under the *immediate* influence of such an impulse. Thus we are here not dealing with a compulsive act *proper,* since no inner conflict took place and, generally, no "defense mechanism" of any sort can be shown.

Furthermore, the sadistic sex phantasies never occurred in a compulsive fashion. Hardly ever did Rudolf struggle against them, nor did they appear alien to him, whereas the murderous impulses toward the housewives were something completely different, something alien to him, something he, himself, could not understand.

During treatment, drives of a compulsive nature were occasionally felt by Rudolf. When attending services in the Muensterlingen church among the Catholic patients, Rudolf, for many months, had to fight the compulsion to plunge from the gallery down into the midst of the congregation. Time and again he had to picture to himself how he would lie smashed on the stone floor, what the churchgoers would say, what panic would ensue, and the like. That drive, too, was alien to Rudolf and was felt by him as something very different from the phantasies of suicide, self-mutilation, and accidents. These compulsive drives produced serious anxiety states, so that Rudolf hardly dared continue going to church. Here, too, the compulsive impulses were bound to definite locations.

Once Rudolf had admitted his compulsive impulses, he could be helped to overcome them through a discussion of that plunge which had caused the crippling of his right foot and of various related dreams and phantasies about Christ's temptation on the parapet of the Temple at Jerusalem.

Surely Rudolf's case does not represent an "anankastic psychopathia," as the essential features of such a character are missing in him, and compulsive experience occurs only occasionally. His compulsive experiences are typical *psychogenic symptoms* originating from a definite constellation of complex-forming experience (*Komplexhaften Erlebens*) and probably therefore fixed to certain locations.

Thinking and Consciousness

Rudolf's intelligence is normal. His thinking shows no abnormal peculiarities—apart from periods of exceptional states. In times of depression it appeared occasionally somewhat loose in its connections, although not typically inhibited. During manic states it tended slightly toward flight of ideas. In our many talks with Rudolf we never observed any signs of scattered schizophrenic thinking or of delusions.

Rudolf's states of consciousness are difficult to judge. We do know that Rudolf, up to the time of his crime, generally lived in a state of reduced clarity of consciousness and remained in a world of reveries. Although working hard at that time, he nevertheless never quite completed the transition from the child phantasy world to the world of the grownups with its objects and its reality. Stimulated by detective novels and movies, he liked to drift farther and farther away from wide-awake daytime consciousness.

Real twilight states—with amnesia—can hardly be established, except for a short time before the crime when Rudolf tore up the photograph of his girl friend. There is no amnesia in regard to the "quasi-poriomanic" nocturnal automobile ride at the end of his butcher apprenticeship. Nor is there any gap in Rudolf's memory as to the crime itself, whereas the phantasy contents, and thus the motives for the act itself, are poorly or not at all remembered. His crime was as unintelligible to Rudolf as it was to those who had to sit in judgment on it.

At any rate, certain periods during the nocturnal ride on the day of the father's funeral and during the day of the crime turn out to be clearly delineated episodes within a special state of consciousness. There the action is completely automatic. Although consciousness of these acts is not eliminated and not even impaired, active thinking does not in the least interfere with the psychic and action process.

We refrain in this context from bringing up all the problems which could be discussed in connection with the concepts of disturbance of consciousness and automatism. We are under the impression that, in this area, research has not advanced far enough to provide us with more understanding than we can gain from the clearest possible phenomenological formulation of the facts. As to this, we consider it essential that, despite his perception of the proceedings, no counterimpulses were produced in Rudolf. This argues against a completely ego-alien impulse, originating in some organic illness—such as, for example, the murderous impulse of the epileptic. It is true that in the epileptic automatic acts sometimes occur without counterimpulses and without loss of consciousness, but no proof of the epileptic basis of the disturbance can be seen in such acts.

Physiological Problems

There is not much to report about this aspect of the case as no laboratory studies could be made. However, we want to mention that the heavy depressive states that occurred in the beginning of Rudolf's stay at the institution were partly related to external influences. For instance, exposure of the body to intensive sunlight produced a markedly depressive state within a few hours. At first we tried to treat it with Thyroxine and then proceeded, over the years, to prescribe very small doses of Iodine Potassium (*Jodkali*). From that time on the patient definitely improved. Shock therapy or prolonged sleep therapy were never indicated and, therefore, never performed.

Psychiatric Diagnosis

If we want to fit the picture of Rudolf's case into the accepted pattern of clinical diagnosis in our terms, then the seriousness of the depressive states, their symptomatology, and the accompanying syndrome all point definitely to a psychosis. Primarily, we must consider a manic-depressive psychosis, but have to add immediately that the picture is colored by features which are alien to that disease, such as schizoid, definitely hysterical, reactive, and perverse tinges. The depressive states, marked by experiences of depersonalization, remind us of cases such as described by Von Gebsattel [13] and A. Weber; [14] the sadistic phantasies, of Schilder's reports on manics.[15]

There are no findings whatever which would permit us to diagnose schizophrenia. And yet, the crime and the schizoid features in Rudolf warrant a certain suspicion. Perhaps schizophrenia, possibly of a paranoid nature, will develop later, after many years.

Finally, one could think of an epileptic influence in the light of heredity, Rudolf's tendency to disturbances of consciousness, the violence of the act, and the phantasy contents, but, as we have shown, there is little probability that these disturbances were epileptic manifestations. There is nothing more we can say, today, about this question. Epileptic seizures were never observed.

Forensic-Psychiatric Opinion

Surely, the earlier judgment of irresponsibility, derived from the psychopathological syndrome of Rudolf, was an accurate opinion even if, at that time, a complete diagnosis could not be made. This case demonstrates again how extremely difficult it can be to give a correct forensic-psychiatric opinion and that, occasionally, many years have to go by before a conclusive insight can be gained.

Today we must assume that Rudolf committed his crime in a depression which has to be considered an actual mental illness. Generally not much forensic significance is assigned to endogenic depression, whereas in psychoanalytic literature [16] the criminal tendencies of depressives are assigned a

13 Von Gebsattel, *Nervenarzt*, Bd. 10, 1937, S. 169, u. 248.

14 A. Weber, *Ueber nihilistischen Wahn und Depersonalisation* (Basel: 1938).

15 P. Schilder, *Entwurf einer Psychiatrie auf psychoanalytischer Grundlage* (Zuerich: 1925), S. 139.

16 H. Nunberg, *Allgemeine Neurosenlehre* (Bern: 1932), S. 121, 149.

degree of importance far beyond that of a merely extended suicide. But we are dealing, here, with only a seeming contradiction; for everything depends on our definition of "depression." The wider the concept becomes, the greater the number of criminal cases that will be covered. Pertinent in this same context is the interesting study, *Melancholische Kriminialitaet,* by the Hollander, Hutter,[17] which unfortunately, in our opinion, is insufficiently supported either by case histories or by bibliography. This study, too, uses psychoanalytic theories. But perhaps it is still correct, in cases of incomprehensible crimes and strikingly unconcerned behavior on the part of the criminal, to consider the possibility of a depression. Thus one may, not too rarely, find cases in which a somewhat atypical psychotic depression is closely tied up with the crime.

VIII *Attempt to Understand Rudolf's Crime through Existential Analysis*

So far, the case of Rudolf has been considered predominantly in terms of the life-historical content. However, in the light of diagnostic considerations other aspects of his personality come into focus.

The puzzle of Rudolf's crime has been somewhat elucidated by clarification of his life history, by some insight into his dream and phantasy life, and by way of clinical-diagnostic considerations. However, we have avoided drawing solid connections by way of theories (which by their very nature always tend to stretch experience) where actually only loose relations can be seen— or even only sensed. Of course, if one wished to operate in the realm of "possibilities" here, as in every case, infinitely more points could be made. Those connections, however, which were pointed out by us are anchored in Rudolf's spontaneous experiences and could be recognized by *him*. A selection had to be made from the vast material at our disposal (the records of our sessions comprise more than three hundred single-spaced typewritten pages, the dream-notes many more). We have concentrated upon the most important facts and particularly upon whatever seems to contribute to the understanding of the enigmatic criminal act. We shall now try to proceed further in making that act understood by means of the existential analytical method already referred to in our introduction. In this context we shall present the "world" in which Rudolf existed. "World" is not here used in its idiomatic meaning (either in the sense of "ways of the world" or in the very different biblical sense of "worldly desires"). The word "world" is rather used in the sense of a "world-design" which is laid, as it were, by every human upon everything that exists, through which he interprets everything that exists, and from which he gets a context of reference (*Bewandtnis-*

17 Schweiz. *Zeitschrift fuer Strafrecht,* Bd. 62, 1947, S. 280.

Zusammenhang) wherein each person's existence (*Dasein*) is determined.[18]

Our primary task will be to seek out that "world" of Rudolf's in which his crime was not just possible, but unavoidable. This of course will confront us with all sorts of difficulties. Existential analysis is not a finished, beautifully rounded theory which allows us to "explain" some, or all, events that occur in a psyche. Furthermore, we are at present still at the beginning of work in this direction. Often it can be recognized only belatedly that this or that point should have been clarified more accurately. Even the first exploratory steps must be steered in a direction unfamiliar to us in many respects. All this results in various imperfections which today still affect our existential-analytical work but which should not prevent us from applying the method, since only by application can we improve it.

Although our investigation is aimed at understanding Rudolf's crime, it is still necessary first to shed more light on his everyday existence—the manner of his everyday acting, his practical life.

Everyday Life

A small boy is searching the house looking for his dead mother. After having found the body he speaks to it and touches it. Later, after the body is lost to him through the funeral, he rummages through the entire house—around all its furniture and into all its corners. In all these instances Rudolf is *acting*, behaving in a peculiarly active fashion which already reveals a certain industry. There is nothing contemplative to be found in his early memories. For example, he has other children pull him around in a little cart through the village, or he entertains his comrades for money by walking naked through the River Thur. He watches all incidents of street life, sees fierce dogs bite people, horses go wild, ugly corpses being fished out of the river. Money becomes important to him at an early age.[19] With the coins he took in church he immediately starts a real business, buying and selling rabbits. He also engages in barter and quickly trades his Christmas toys for new ones. Later his industry shifts to his jobs and he becomes an efficient and ambitious worker. He does more than his share, works diligently even without supervision, and is praised and appreciated for this. It is true that in his work making money was his primary goal, but he worked just as assiduously at his unpaid jobs in the institution, even though he couldn't there be employed as a butcher, the one line with which he was particularly familiar. Also after his release from the institution he at once went zealously to work.

18 On the concept of "world," *viz.*, M. Heidegger, "Vom Wesen des Grundes."

19 The various ways in which money and an eminently assertively acting life style are interrelated, emerge from the numerous facts investigated by G. Simmel in his *Philosophy of Money* (3 Aufl., Muenchen: 1920). It should only be mentioned that money is called "the purest form of tool" (S. 205). Goethe, too, calls money a "tool" (in a letter to Schiller, Dec. 25, 1794).

He rummaged the village attics for antiques, accepted them as gifts, and later sold them.

Not only his working life but his entire existence was charged with bustling activity on a broad scale. Often on one Sunday he would attend three different movies; and, in earlier periods, he would read quantities of trashy literature. Even in his sexual relations he only sought action. He would hurry from bar to bar to find a prostitute and would content himself with sexual satisfaction that was manually attained with the help of a waitress. It was natural to him to handle his relations with prostitutes in a manner in which one closes a business deal.

On the other hand, he did not know what to do with his girl whom he saw frequently over a period of time before his crime. She did not permit herself simply to be used by him; consequently this relationship faded out before it could be interrupted by external events.

To a large extent Rudolf is consumed by work and activity. The street— with its continuous promise of new encounters, with its infinite abundance of ever-changing people and things, with its unlimited forward extension— this is what he likes. The street is actually that space in which Rudolf's existence primarily takes place; that is to say, he moves horizontally. The street, with its busy restlessness, with its hurriedly advancing movement, represents also a symbol of the "time" in which Rudolf lives. The panting hurry, the impatient craze for experiencing the ever-new, the actual curiosity as expressed by the need to elicit intimate information from women, the enjoyment of the unexpected, the thrilling, the dangerous—all of this charges this existence with the element of suspense. Living in expectant suspense is the basis of Rudolf's world-design. "World" for Rudolf is only that which appears to him in the form of suspense and puts him in a state of suspense. Where there is no suspense, there is no "world" for him—there is nothing, emptiness, coldness, senselessness, boredom. This existence is without continuity, without history. It is "leaping" in L. Binswanger's sense; [20] it is Time chopped up.

Doubtless the work of a butcher contains a great deal of suspense; while gardening, a skill acquired by Rudolf in the institution, has much less of it and was, therefore, for a long time rejected by Rudolf as too boring.

Another aspect of an existence in suspense is its fascination with criminals. We find this feature in Rudolf to a marked degree; and he cultivated it by attending cheap movies, reading detective stories, and mixing with criminal persons from the street. In being fascinated by the criminal, Rudolf becomes a man of the crowd, since we here face, at least in the big cities, a mass psychological phenomenon. [21]

[20] L. Binswanger, Über Ideenflucht (Zurich: 1933).

[21] J. E. Stähelin in a recent paper (Schw. Arch. f. Neur, u. Psych., Bd. 60, v. 1947, S. 269–278) investigated the relations of mass psychology to clinical psychiatry. Primitivation and loss of integration of Man in the crowd, as described impressively by Staehelin, can also be found in Rudolf when he acts as a member of a larger social unit.

By its very nature, an existence in suspense is always referring to other people and therefore has a social aspect.

The existence in suspense has its own laws which, as far as we know, have not been sufficiently investigated by psychology and psychiatry; whereas the history of literature has, for a long time, dealt with the expectant style of life by occupying itself with the subject of *the dramatic* in art and living. From the history of literature we know that an existence in suspense is slanted toward an ending—perhaps self-destruction by a tragic act, perhaps some other solution such as *the comic*. Could it be that we have to understand Rudolf's crime as an attempt to step out of the suspense in order to dissolve its tension? Are there any clues to this? It cannot, of course, be the task of a scientific study to "dramatize" Rudolf's act; but we have to keep clear of the prejudices which are implicit in the "clinical" approach—prejudices which represent a tremendous simplification of Man. They could easily cause us to state that Rudolf's crime was not sufficiently "motivated." Rather we should try to point out what meaning the crime could have had for Rudolf in the world of everyday life. Maybe we shall then be in a position to find out whether he was involved in something that could be termed tragic.

In the beginning of the legal and psychiatric investigation Rudolf listed three groups of motives for his crime. He withdrew them later, after becoming aware of the effect of his statements. These were the three groups:

1. Rudolf wished to take his revenge on prostitutes because he had spent too much money on them. In his opinion, they made their money too easily.

2. He wished to appear as a hero who dares to fight prostitution, who eliminates and publicly exposes this evil. (It was important to him that the name of his victim would appear in the papers; that this would put her to shame; he believed that, as a result, all other prostitutes would be frightened and would change their calling.) He also believed that it did not matter if a prostitute were killed.

3. Finally, Rudolf wanted to avoid the temptations of the world and continue his life in the seclusion of a prison cell.

If we take these motives seriously—and for the time being we have no reason whatever, from an objective point of view, not to take them seriously —then we must attribute to Rudolf's crime a "pathetic" [22] meaning which makes it reach into the realm of the dramatic style; for Rudolf is "moved by what ought to be, and his movement is directed against what now exists." [23] He wants to fight prostitution and employs himself to act toward that ideal goal. By that he lifts himself out of the crowd; he differentiates himself from others. He also suffers; and his suffering is to be recognized by everybody; but at the same time he is destroyed. "Pathos consumes the individuality" and is "ruthless in every sense." [24]

---

[22] ["Pathetic"—here used in the sense of deeply affecting and moving.—TRANSLATOR.]
[23] Emil Staiger, *Grundbegriffe der Poetik* (Zurich: 1946), p. 164.
[24] *Ibid.*, p. 168.

The "pathetic" act which lifts Rudolf out of the crowd is related to all those phantasies in which he plays a hero's role; as when, for example, he imagines himself a prize athlete carried on his comrade's shoulders in a festive procession; or when he sees himself, riding high above the others, triumphantly leading his troops through the conquered city. Quite generally Rudolf gains height in this way, moves up the vertical axis of existence and thereby steps out of its horizontal plane. Of course it is a very laborious and by no means nimble way of rising. Apparently in his vertical movement he is being pulled down by some strong force. We shall return to these problems later when discussing the world of dreams and daydreams which also includes the phantasies about heroic roles.

In the tragic existence, the pathetic act is tied up with the "problem," the "fore-cast" with which one must catch up—*i.e.*, the goal cast in advance toward which all strivings are directed. In Rudolf's case the veil is to be torn from the eyes of mankind where the vicious nature of prostitution is concerned. There is a starting point of this problem—a point from which one starts to catch up with the "fore-cast." For Rudolf this starting point is the moral corruption of man in the form of prostitution or, more exactly, his own evaluation of that fact.

Just like the tragic hero, Rudolf is most closely intertwined with what is, and what ought not to be. He is himself a victim of prostitution and, by daring to rise against this fatal evil, he wants also to extricate himself from its meshes. But what is actually his goal? That there shall no longer be prostitution is a merely negative goal. Rudolf is not in a position, either in general or for himself, to set a positive goal; by merely striving for external separation from the worldly temptation he has essentially nothing to gain for himself. This is what distinguishes Rudolf from the genuinely tragic hero.

In still another way are the motives for Rudolf's crime internally related with his active life. By saying that prostitutes make their money too easily, he relates the nature of prostitution to work. Thus he rebels against the fact that there are people who make money more easily than others. We see here the flash of a motive which is connected with a general social resentment, and we can conjecture that Rudolf may not be always equally enthusiastic about his work. However that may be, his shot was aimed not only at a prostitute but also, beyond her, at his own entire active life, with its diligence and work, its moneymaking, and everything connected with it. All of that should stop; and so it turns out that Rudolf through his act tried, in fact, to bring about a solution to the suspense of his life.

Since we could, in this manner, get a glimpse of some connections in the functioning of Rudolf's personality, it seems appropriate to go one step further and examine still other peculiarities of his being from the point of view of suspense. As to his murderous intention toward the taxi driver, we know no more than that it originated in a state of severe depression. Here again we find the tendency to step out of everyday life—if, in this case, primarily into the adventurous. There was no pathetic impulse present on this occasion.

Of special importance in Rudolf's world are the courts. As so frequently occurs in such cases, Rudolf's imagination was very preoccupied with the idea of appearing in court. By being judged irresponsible, he was deprived of the experience. He found a substitute experience to some degree in being presented at lectures. Years later he would still dream of these presentations and be impressed by his own importance. He also produced various dreams in which the court was directly represented. Lastly, we found a peculiarly moralizing content in the records of one of his Rorschach tests. This affinity to the idea of judgment is again a characteristic of the *drama* in which life, decision, and action are *judged*. "This is why the inner forces also press toward the external form of judgment." [25]

Finally, we must consider the tremendous influence of Shakespeare's plays upon Rudolf during the period of treatment. Although he was actually enthusiastic about the plays, he could not warm up to Shakespeare's sonnets. The latter seemed to him to reveal that their author was "nothing but a human being." In the dramatic plays, Rudolf sees something which goes beyond the mere person—namely, the *action* of persons—the decisive *deed* by which they take their destiny into their own hands—man's gaining a more general, quasi-exemplary significance by the conquering of himself and his limitations through his *deed*. Because Rudolf could not find that deed in the sonnets—only resignation—he was disappointed by them.

The presentation of the tragic in Rudolf's existence has shown us, among other things, the possibility of a view different from one which sees only the "moral abyss" in those "few murderers who commit their crime in order to become famous." [26] But we do not yet know why Rudolf committed his crime at just that moment—that is, what occasioned it. We can only conjecture that there happened to him something that had a tragic effect. Such is the case when the event "deprives man of his hold, of the last remaining goal that matters; so that from now on he staggers and is quite out of his mind; when not only some desire or some hope is destroyed, but also the very joints of the world's meaningful context." [27] The date of the crime— Thursday, March 23—may offer a clue, considering that Rudolf's mother died on Thursday, February 23, seventeen years earlier. (The disparity of four weeks seems to have something to do with the holidays of the Catholic Church—Day of Ascension and Corpus Christi Day, also celebrated on Thursday. We cannot further discuss this here.) We could assume that there are

[25] *Ibid.,* p. 192.
[26] Goering, "Kriminal Psychologie." in Kafka's *Handbuch der vergl. Psychologie,* Bd. III, S. 182.
[27] Staiger, *op. cit.,* p. 201.

connections between his mother's death and his crime; but it came to light that Rudolf was not conscious of such connections during the act itself. Therefore, we refrain from spinning this theoretical yarn any further. However, there is another connecting link which we shall more closely pursue in the following section.

Rudolf's Crime and his Father's Death

Rudolf's crime—his murderous assault on a prostitute—has, above all, an obvious temporal connection with the death of his father, since he had felt the first impulse of this kind on the day after the funeral. Here we find a decisive starting point for an existential-analytical investigation of Rudolf's crime. Existential analysis will first try to elucidate the structure of Rudolf's experience at his father's death and, for the time being, rely on three established facts which have been confirmed by observations of witnesses:

1. When Rudolf learned of his father's severe illness and, later, of his death, he remained apparently quite unmoved.

2. His behavior in the presence of his father's body was peculiar; he performed all sorts of bizarre acts which on the surface were incomprehensible.

3. At his father's funeral, Rudolf expressed great grief by impetuous and loud crying.

These observations were added to by Rudolf himself in an apparently convincing way; he professed that at first he felt outright joy at his father's death and that this feeling emerged as a completely spontaneous affect, just as did his subsequent grief. He could give as little information about either of these emotions as about his impulse to handle his father's body, which was equally incomprehensible and puzzling to him.

It will now be our task to describe as adequately as possible Rudolf's experiences and attitudes without judging their causes and effects from without; otherwise we would have to accept Rudolf's judgment which found them "incomprehensible" or resort to a hypothetical "unconscious" without experiential basis. But we prefer to demonstrate how that which is commonly described as "unconscious" can be comprehended by way of existential analysis.

A joyful reaction to the news of his father's death on Rudolf's part could hardly be understood by what we know of him, since there was neither money nor any other assets for him to inherit; nor did the idea that death could have been a salvation for the miserable man who suffered from a painful ailment ever enter his mind. His quarrels with his father were not of the kind that would cause a man to wish for his father's death. On the other hand, Rudolf had always been aware that as a child he had already envisaged his father's death as an approaching joyful event about which he phantasied whenever external occurrences offered an occasion. As a schoolboy, he envied the people in the funeral processions which passed the schoolhouse, partly because they did not have to study, partly because they obviously participated in some way in the joyful event. Wherein the pleasure would actually lie, Rudolf knew neither during his father's lifetime nor after he got word about his father's death. Since the fate of the deceased left him unmoved and he was merely concerned with his own pleasure, his relationship to his late father must have been somewhat remote; also, Rudolf must have had at that time a particular idea about death, one that was lacking in horror. All these are conditions of his experience at his father's death, but they do not in themselves suffice to explain his behavior.

The further course of events, however, does suggest in what way Rudolf could expect pleasure from his father's death. Even if he himself was not aware of it, we are bound to assume that he must have found with his father's body what he so joyfully expected. We have to consider that generally impulses strive for their satisfaction in a certain direction without our thinking necessarily being aware of the goal; indeed, the formulation of an affective goal as an idea is often not only a facultative, but also a widely derivative, process.[28]

Our assumption that Rudolf found in his preoccupation with his father's body what he had joyously expected can only be correct if the activity was actually pleasurable. And we did learn from his relatives that once he had started with it, he could hardly be induced to leave the body, and that in the process he had worked himself into a visible excitation. That situation was later reproduced in various dreams in which he occupied himself, mostly with the help of complicated machines, with the body of his father or of people unknown to him, predominantly of the female sex. In most of these dreams he succeeded in bringing the dead back to life, a result that gave him the feeling of indescribable happiness. Later, he was inclined to remember that when facing his father's body, his foremost feeling was doubt whether he was really dead, and that this gave him perhaps the first impulse to open the body's eyes. In any case, it is certain that in that night during his bizarre activities he did not feel like mourning.

When on the following day Rudolf saw how the coffin with his father's body was placed in front of the house, only then did he become aware of the real significance of death; now the idea crossed his mind that his father was about to pass by these houses for "the last time." Now he could not doubt any more that death had actually occurred, that he was in no position to change anything about it, and that he was being deprived of the object which had given him a brief joyous expectation. Thus, joyous expectation of pleasure, pleasurable activity for the satisfaction of a need, and mourning about the loss of the object which produced the pleasure followed each other in Rudolf's mind in a perfectly comprehensible succession, whereby only the

28 *Viz.,* M. Scheler, *Der Formalismus in der Ethik und die materiale Wertethik,* S. 263.

means by which pleasure was attained, namely, the body, seems abnormal and strange. In clinical diagnostic terms we would describe this as a tendency toward necrophilia, although, in the present case, a particular sexual tinge in the necrophilic pleasure could not be noticed.

What Rudolf did with his father's body, we know very well. Among other things, he touched especially his face, opened and closed his eyes, and moved his jaw. These manipulations remind us of those performed by Rudolf on his mother's body at the age of three years, four months. But these earlier scenes he could not at all remember for many years, and he again forgot them soon after they were described to him by members of his family. The events upon his mother's death were brought to light only with the greatest of effort during Rudolf's psychotherapeutic treatment and were never actually remembered. On the other hand, Rudolf was well aware of the fact that he had once before manipulated the maid's body whom he had found unconscious in a very similar manner and that he had managed to bring back to life the seemingly dead girl. Furthermore, from detective films and similar literature, Rudolf had learned something about "associating with corpses," and he always became extraordinarily excited and fascinated by such reports.

We further know how hopeful Rudolf was in the presence of his dead mother whose death he expressly denied. As long as he occupied himself with her body he felt apparently quite comfortable, whereas his entire nature changed "from the day of the funeral," as his oldest sister told us. That was the time when he began to search the house restlessly. Not only were the manipulations on the body repeated after a lapse of seventeen years but also, after these acts and subsequent to the funeral, another fundamental change in Rudolf's state of mind took place. This does not necessarily imply that Rudolf's experiences in connection with his mother's death brought about a repetition after seventeen years, on the occasion of his father's death, as a necessary consequence. One should rather be able to assume that the opposite is true, namely that the behavior of the three-year-old was largely due to the infantile state of his emotional and mental development and that in the course of seventeen years his personality underwent a change. Certainly, a great deal had happened in the meantime, but it is equally certain that the fundamental experiential structure was essentially the same in the case of both the mother's and the father's death.

In trying to define more closely this fundamental experiential structure we must consider that we are dealing here with an experience which is divided into two distinct aspects: the first is the joyous expectation which reaches its climax in the enjoyment of the expected; but this pleasure precipitously stops and is followed by another experience whose time structure shows no definite limit. This is not the place to point out the general significance of such an experiential structure; rather must we try to exhaust to the best of our ability the particular content of these experiences of Rudolf. It now serves our purpose to turn, for the time being, to the second point the disappointment over the loss of a beloved person by death, and the ensuing mourning.

On Mourning

"Mourning for the loss of something we have loved or admired seems so natural to the layman that he declares it a matter of course. But to the psychologist mourning is a great enigma, one of those phenomena which one does not clarify oneself, but to which one retraces other obscure matters."

These statements by Freud are still valid today. A phenomenological investigation of mourning would certainly permit us to grasp its essence but would carry us too far off our topic; hence we confine ourselves to reporting the results of such an investigation as far as they are useful for the understanding of Rudolf's crime.[29]

In the extensive literature on the problem of death the phenomenon of mourning is mostly skipped, as it were, which, in our opinion, causes us to lose sight of the fact that the image of death which each one has in his mind is essentially coined by one's personal suffering in mourning.[30]

We are here only concerned with mourning for the loss by death of a beloved person.[31] We must, hereby, differentiate between the mourning affect which consists in the emotional experience in the bereaved touched off by that loss, and mourning in the sense of a profound and lasting transformation of existence which replaces the mournful affect, if the deceased

---

29 [The sources which the author consulted for his outlining of a phenomenology and psychology of mourning include a number of philosophical and literary works from Martin Luther to Jeremias Gotthelf, Karl Jaspers, Max Scheler, and Ludwig Binswanger. We are listing only his references to the psychiatric treatment of the subject.—EDITORS.]

S. Freud, "Zeitgemaesses ueber Krieg und Tod," in *Werke* (London: 1946), Bd. X, S. 325-355; "Vergaegenglichkeit," in *Werke* (London: 1946), Bd. X, S. 359-360; "Trauer und Melancholie," in *Werke* (London: 1946), Bd. X, S. 425-466; "Aus der Geschichte einer infantilen Neurose," in *Werke* (London: 1947), Bd. XII, S. 46-47. K. Abraham, "Ansaetze zur psychoanalytischen Erforschung und Behandlung des manisch-depressiven Irreseins und verwandter Zustaende," *Klinische Beitraege zur Psychoanalyse*, Wien, 1921, S. 95. K. Landauer, "Aequivalente der Trauer," *Int. Z. Psychoan.*, Bd. XI, 1925, S. 194-205. H. Deutsch, "Ueber versaeumte Trauerarbeit," in *Festschrift Josef Reinhold* (Bruenn: 1936), S. 44-52. O. Kanders, "Der Todesgedanke in der Neurose und in der Psychose," *Nervenarzt*, Bd. 7, 1934, S. 288-297.

30 An extensive bibliography on the problem of death has been recently compiled by H. Kunz and utilized in his book, *Die anthropologische Bedeutung der Phantasie* (Basel: 1946), Bd. II, S. 71, and particularly in the footnote on p. 75.

31 Mourning in its wider sense includes homesickness and reactions to losses which are not caused by death (abandoned lovers, financial losses, *et al.*). Rudolf's case could lead us to believe that a comparison with crimes out of homesickness or love pain could be fruitful; but our insight into such cases is still rather limited and we cannot expect to illuminate darkness through something equally obscure.

From the pertinent literature the following references may be mentioned: K. Jaspers, "Heimweh und Verbrechen," *Archiv fuer Kriminalanthropologie und Kriminalistik*, Bd. 34, 1909, S. 1-116. Siefert, "Der Fall Fischer," *Arch. f. Kriminalanthropologie*, Bd. 9, 1902, S. 160-178. Voss, "Beitrag zur Psychologie des Brautmordes," *Mschr. fuer Kriminalpsychologie*, Bd. 8, 1912, S. 622-630, und Bd. 9, 1913, S. 244-246.

has been loved in the full meaning of the word. Thereby, "mourning work" in the Freudian sense—namely a withdrawal of libidinal energy from the lost object and a turning to other objects—does not occur; but rather (as particularly shown by Binswanger) the mourner himself, by bidding farewell to the departed, gets into bidding farewell to his own earlier way of existence, and the bereaved takes over somehow the being of the deceased.

The outward forms of expression of the mourning affect vary a great deal; they range from noisy crying, wailing, lamenting, and acting out of destructive impulses, particularly by children and primitives, to quiet, solemn, and often rigid restraint. Noisy and quiet manifestations of grief turn easily into each other, or the mourning affect may suddenly disappear, being generally an extremely dynamic phenomenon.

Custom has largely regulated the manifestations of mourning. This facilitates false expressions of mourning not based on adequate emotional experience. The two contrasting forms of mourning, noisy and quiet affective utterances, are reflected in the customs, too. Downright aggressive acts are often committed against the self as well as against anything that constitutes "world," particularly, and not accidentally, against what the fashion calls for. But then, again, the mourner is expected to display a dignified attitude.

Subjectively, the mourner experiences pain, a pain which calls for a vehement outbreak. He feels burdened, heavy of head and limbs; his strength, his courage, and his gusto for anything have vanished. He hates to eat, food chokes his throat, digestion is poor, and sexual desire is extinguished. To the mourner, everything seems deserted and empty, as though seen through a veil; the eye stares into space, the voice is muffled, feet move with caution. All thoughts are always with the dead; the eye seeks him and wants to retain him as long as possible; time and again, the steps would turn toward the body. Whenever the outside world obtrudes itself, grief breaks out again loudly, as at the burial. When this is over, mourners often feel obvious relief.

What actually takes place in the mourning affect was described by M. Heidegger with unexcelled clarity: "The 'deceased,' who in contrast to the 'dead' has been torn away from the 'bereaved,' becomes an object of 'care'—by way of the funeral rite, the burial, the grave-cult. And this occurs because the deceased, in his way of being, is 'still more' than just some 'stuff at hand' in the environment [*Umwelt*]. In their mournful-commemorative remaining with him, the survivors *are with him* in a mode of honoring care. The relation to the being of the dead must, therefore, not be understood as a mere dealing with something at hand. In such being-together with the dead, the deceased himself is in fact no longer 'there.' But being-together always means being together in the same world. The deceased has left and relinquished our world: Only out of it can the remaining ones still be with him." [32]

With the statement that "such being-with-the-dead does not at all make one experience the actual having-come-to-an-end of the deceased," Heideg-

[32] M. Heidegger, *Sein und Zeit*, S. 238.

ger leaves this analysis. What, then, do these sentences imply for the understanding of mourning? If "being-with" always means "being-together-with in the same world," with the deceased "having left and relinquished ours," then in dwelling with the deceased we are no longer in the same world in which we were with him as long as he still lived. Through our "being-together-with-the-dead" who "himself is factually no longer there," our world of the factually existing, of the real—or, more simply put, the world in which we had lived before—takes on a touch of the unreal; it is changed. We may say it has become more phantastic, dreamy, or mystical, and we thereby indicate that the mourner has turned away from the real world of everyday life, toward the past. The world which tempts us and attempts to fascinate us loses in power and significance; we step out of it to turn to the deceased. If Heidegger says "Only out of it [their world] can the remaining ones still be with him," then this has to be understood also in the sense of a movement *out* of the world, that is, out of that world in which they had been together with the deceased before. And if we learn that in the quiet phase of mourning one always thinks of the deceased, what is meant is identical with what Heidegger terms "being-with-the-dead."

The desolation and emptiness, the lack of interest in any interference with the ways of the world are all expressions of the feeling that the mourner has been ejected from the world heretofore familiar to him. The muffled behavior corresponds to an empty world, just as we behave less noisily at night.[33] The destructive impulses can be understood partly as a rebellion against the temptations of the outside world; partly, they may be related to the inhibition. To understand the inhibition is, of course, much more difficult, although it is possibly the original phenomenon which is responsible for the transformation of the perceived world. The feelings of inhibition and heaviness are probably related to the experience of motionlessness of the dead body and refer to an original meaning in which motion and life are identified. In trying to overcome the inhibition, the mourner has the best chance to succeed if he assumes forms of movement which he "knew" in the deceased. On the other hand, we know from the Rorschach test that respondents with inhibited movements tend to vivify the *Umwelt* and *Mitwelt*. But here we have reached a point where the mourning affect has been overcome and mourning in the existential sense commences.

Rudolf's Mourning

The results of a phenomenological description of the mourning affect can very well be applied to a single case, even to the case of a mentally-ill per-

---

[33] In reference to this question and particularly to the phenomenological distinction between stillness and darkness which becomes significant in the continuation of the investigation into the mourning affect, *viz.*, E. Minkowski, *Vers une cosmologie* (Paris: 1936), S. 173-178, "Le Silence et l'obscurité."

son, since the validity of phenomenological descriptions is not limited by judgments on normality or abnormality. Although many aspects of the mourning affect are very similar with different persons, particular individual differences are encountered. Such particular forms of the mourning affect as occurred in Rudolf we shall approach by tracing the individual history and development of mourning affects throughout his life.

Mourning for Mother. As far as we know, Rudolf met the phenomenon of death for the first time at the age of three years and four months, when his mother died. But we should be careful not simply to transfer what we know about the mourning affect in adults to a three-year-old child, . . .[34]

In observing the child's encounter with death we have clearly to separate insight into the nature of death—which in itself can touch off affective reactions similar to mourning—from the real experience of loss by death of a beloved person. What we do not know, however, is what happens if a child experiences the death of a beloved *before* it has actually understood the significance of death. This seems to have happened in the case of Rudolf. It is quite possible that the words which Rudolf is said to have spoken at his mother's body were correctly conveyed. If this is so, we would have to conclude that Rudolf did know about dying but did not recognize the fact that death had befallen his mother. He believed the body to be his mother in a state of sleep. The observation that Rudolf in the presence of the body showed no signs of fear or horror also supports the assumption that he did not comprehend what he was dealing with; children usually react to the sight of a dead body with fear and horror (Weber, Zulliger). Nevertheless, Rudolf probably did perceive the opacity in the eyes of his mother's body even if he could not interpret it correctly at that time. Generally, children do not recognize the lusterless eye as a symptom of death, partly because they usually see dead bodies with their eyes closed.

Since Rudolf later assigned such special significance to the luster of eyes and the lack of it, we must look for the cause in the individual nature of either his personality or his life-history.

From his misunderstanding of the situation at his mother's body stems the peculiar form which Rudolf's mourning assumed. Since he did not believe that his mother had died, it was natural and made sense to him to search for the lost mother. Had he understood the true significance of death, he would have never acted the way he did. The fact that Rudolf changed so much from the day his mother was buried, certainly indicates sadness; but that affect was not essentially different from the sadness he would have felt if his mother had gone on a trip; he could still hope that in any event the missing beloved mother would return. Since nothing of the kind could be

---

[34] [Omitted is a reference by the author to a paper of A. Weber on the experiencing of death in small children: "Zum Erlebnis des Todes bei Kindern," *Mschr. f. Neur. u. Psych.*, Bd. 107, 1943, S. 192–225.—EDITORS.]

promised to him, he proceeded on his own, and he felt the more justified in so doing since his search had once before resulted in at least finding the body. Of course, his could not be a planful search, as the context of events which had resulted in the loss remained hidden for him. This is what made it so hasty and nervous a search, the kind in which one is apt to make the most absurd provisions, to rummage places that have not been touched for a long time, and to inspect locations where success is out of the question for mere reason of space proportions. One reaches the point where the search is performed for its own sake, as it were, and where true anxiety is produced as the existence finds itself again and again confronted with something it has not. The more meaningful the lost object, the greater the anxiety as long as the object is missing. Such restless hurry and flurry certainly does not reflect the attitude of a person who feels the impact of a mourning affect and who is, as we have seen, rather inhibited. But without that inhibition, the paths that could lead to overcoming the mourning affect are blocked.

We can be reasonably sure that originally Rudolf was looking for the mother who was alive, who spoke to him and loved him. And one must assume that even after having found the body he was yet looking for the living mother, as he believed her to be asleep and expected her to awake. Later, he may have realized the meaning of the opacity which he had observed in his mother's eyes; but in the meantime he had found the glittering objects. In describing to us how he discovered them, he showed true emotions, and the happiness he must have felt about it as a child was still vividly present in the adult. That must have been an event of extraordinary importance to him.

Man generally reacts to shiny things. We know how early the infant responds to the luster of eyes and how he later grabs glittering objects. But even in the adult's life shiny things have significance (*viz.*, the role of eyes in ogling [35] or of glitter in the psychology of adorning oneself, and of jewelry).[36] Just as a personality is, so to speak, extended and its sphere intensified by glittering jewelry so that it turns into something "more" than the unadorned personality, so is man "lesser" without the luster of his eyes. But this is only true in respect to a second person who observes the luster in the first. And that luster does have its effect although it is strictly external and conveys no suggestive power or significance of personality whatsoever (all this according to G. Simmel). Indeed, the phenomenology of the glittering phenomena tells us that the lustrous light is never placed in the plane of the object on which it occurs, but always *in front* or *above* that plane.[37] This externalization of the luster and its loose relation to personal values

[35] G. Simmel, *Grundfragen der Soziologie* (Goeschen: 1917), S. 62.

[36] G. Simmel, *Soziologie* (Leipzig: 1908), "Exkurs ueber den Schmuck," S. 365-372. Stephane Mallarmé, "La Mode" (article on jewelry).

[37] D. Katz, *Der Aufbau der Farbenwelt*, II. Aufl., Leipzig 1930, S. 30.

permits its significance to become autonomous; the glittering, then, is desired for its own sake (or, as we know, feared in a phobic fashion; *viz.*, dizziness at the sight of glittering objects).[38]

Something of that sort happened in Rudolf. In glittering objects he found again the luster from the eyes of his late mother. These connections were uncovered by dreams and their interpretation by Rudolf himself. This makes it more understandable that the finding of glittering objects made Rudolf so happy and that in stealing the church money he yielded to the tempting splendor of the coins. Also, in this context it does not seem so strange any more that later, in puberty, his sex drive should have turned toward glittering things.

Surely, the glittering objects could never offer Rudolf all he was seeking in them. Hence, he could never be satisfied with what he found, and he had to continue seeking. What, then, was it that would have to be added to the glittering objects to make them into a whole? It could only be a human being *without* the luster of eyes—that is to say, a corpse. Now we understand why Rudolf, in the daytime, always felt the desire to see bodies and why, at night, he was afraid of an imagined icy body in his bed; why in his dreams bodies appeared time after time; and why he formed, from sheets and pillows, a body on his bed and alternately covered and uncovered it.

Once he had admitted his fetishism and relinquished his craze for glittering things, his dreams and phantasies about bodies practically ceased.

Features of Sadness Remaining in Rudolf's Life. From the time of his mother's death sadness never completely left Rudolf; "He never became like others," as his brothers and sisters put it. In viewing his active life, we must not overlook the fact that joy is completely missing in it. Rudolf did not tell us of any time when he might have been joyful. He was, for a long period of his childhood, inclined to easy crying. When he met with disappointment he would cry disconsolately for hours. His particular sensitivity to the solemn and ceremonial, as for example in experiencing religious feelings, must be understood as a readiness to emphasize the seriousness of life, all of which should be taken as a manifestation of a sad disposition.[39] We are further reminded of Rudolf's calm composure when committing the criminal act and after the crime, particularly during the inquiry, during which he definitely displayed a somehow ceremonial behavior.

But we know even more about the development of Rudolf's sadness after his mother's death. We know that later, probably at the age of about six, he saw the body of a deceased neighbor, the "looks" of which frightened him terribly; very likely he saw his extinguished eyes. Subsequently he could not eat anything for days, which suggests a strong mourning affect although he had been in no way especially close to the man before his death. At the same time he began to feel afraid; the dark of night assumed life, apparitions

---

[38] Von Gebsattel, "Die psychasthenische Phobie," *Nervenarzt*, Bd. 8, 1935, S. 337–398.
[39] *Viz.*, O. F. Bollnow, *Das Wesen der Stimmungen* (Frankfurt/M: 1943).

produced by anxiety emerged. Subsequently the boy refused to look at the body of his grandmother. Apparently for the first time Rudolf realized what belonged with the glittering things; he learned the meaning of a dead body, experienced a mourning affect, and we may assume that along with this experience the inhibition entered his life. Hereafter he not only saw phantoms but also grew generally anxious and fearful of dangers.

Rudolf's job as a butcher must have decisively influenced his affective life and, thus, his sadness. We know that he conducted studies of animals to find out how eyes "die"; he began to feel like a master over death and life, apparently with something of that magic power which, in bygone times, turned the hangman into a healer.[40] Thus Rudolf was extremely excited when in an emergency slaughter of a pregnant animal he succeeded in saving the calf. In that period he often had phantasies about being Christ and performing miracles; and he even experienced a confirmation of these phantasies when the seemingly dead maid revived under his hands. In these reveries of power over life and death we find the infantile features which, according to A. Weber,[41] serve the small child in overcoming the experience of death. To be sure, Rudolf enormously expanded this psychological device and clung to it for years, whereas in the normal child it supplies the material for questions and games for a period of perhaps several weeks or months.

Rudolf's Mourning for his Father. As shown above, Rudolf felt grief only at his father's funeral and not when he received the news of his death. That he cried with wild unrestraint and that the feeling of grief remained in his memory both point to a genuine mourning affect. Immediately after the funeral the bereaved gathered for the funeral repast. The general mood was, as is usual on such occasions, depressed at first, but soon became so elated that a parsimonious uncle decided to remit a major debt to the children of the deceased (a generous impulse which he later regretted and tried to cancel). Rudolf alone remained sad, was unable to eat anything (as he had been ten years earlier after having seen the neighbor's body), and resented the pleasure of the others. Since his mourning affect had emerged only an hour before, it is not difficult to understand that he was unable to conform with the general mood of the funeral meal. Whereas for the normal mourning affect the disappearance of the body helps dissolve the inhibitions, which, in turn, makes possible the first overcoming of this affect, in Rudolf's case the affect emerged precisely because of the loss of the body. Lastly one has to consider that he probably had hoped, with his manipulations, to awaken his father from death, too. Thus he found himself in a situation similar to the one at his mother's body, in that he really did not recognize death or at least did not believe it to be true.

On the day after the funeral Rudolf was still given over to his grief. When

---

40 [In Germany, *e.g.*, the hangman was thought able to treat fractures of the bone—perhaps because in those days criminals were broken on the wheel.—Editors.]

41 A. Weber, "Zum Erlebnis des Todes bei Kindern," S. 192–225.

he relates how, in the trolley car in Zurich, he was reminded of the funeral procession of the day before, and how he felt as though he were his father moving along in the hearse and passing all the houses "for the last time," he describes the same phenomenon which Heidegger calls "remaining with the dead." More precisely expressed, in that moment the mourning affect became again acute. It is certainly of the greatest importance that at the same moment the murderous impulse, too, made itself felt. How closely the murderous impulse was connected with the mourning affect is also demonstrated by the former's sudden disappearance. This instability is precisely typical of the mourning affect.

Rudolf's mourning affect at his father's death was touched off not by the loss of a beloved living person but by the loss of a body—that is, of a "stuff at hand" (Heidegger). In this case, one cannot expect that the mourning affect be followed by an inner transformation of personality in the existential sense of mourning, for this is possible only if the survivor has loved the deceased. However, loving another person and considering him as "stuff at hand" are mutually exclusive. A mourning affect which is not followed by an existential transformation may suddenly disappear. It may reappear with equal suddenness and in precisely the same way as it did at first, since nothing, indeed nothing, has happened in the meantime.

The question of the way in which mourning affects were operating in Rudolf before and during his crime can for the time being be answered only indirectly, because it is certainly no mere accident that Rudolf, after his crime, had a sort of funeral meal on his own by ordering in a tavern just those dishes which he had left untouched at his father's funeral feast. We also know for sure that he felt intensely hungry after his arrest, apparently being in a state similar to that of the bereaved after the burial. We shall now have to describe and understand what happened in and about Rudolf between his departure from the house of mourning and the time of his crime. We have learned that the mourning affect causes all a person's experience to shift toward "remaining with the dead," into the reality-alien sphere of the past, which brings about his alienation from the present and from the reality surrounding him. The question is then: what kind of world was it into which Rudolf was carried by his father's death? In a quite general way we may say that it was the world of phantasies and dreams, which now shall be presented in more detail.

The World of Reveries and Dreams and its Relation to Everyday Life

Since Rudolf's "remaining with the dead" leads him on the one hand to a dead body and on the other into his phantasies and dreams, we have first to ask what role he assigns to the bodies in these phantasies and dreams. To begin with, we know that Rudolf could produce no memory image of his mother's body, nor of his mother alive. Furthermore, we have to assume that in his childhood, at some indeterminable time, Rudolf had some theories about a causal connection between the church and the death of a person; he believed that the priests at mass made little children out of corpses in the ceremony of transubstantiation, a process which was accompanied by foul odors. The veneration of miraculous relics seems to have played some part in this connection. And lastly, we know that Rudolf's attitude toward bodies was never an indifferent one but that there must always have been necrophobic and necrophilic features in it, at times even simultaneously.

Nothing can be gained by pointing out the ambiguity in such attitudes nor by recognizing the diversity of man's reactions to bodies in general.[42] Real understanding becomes possible only when we realize in what way necrophobia and necrophilia belong to two different world-designs; we have seen before that the necrophilic features are related to the world of active life in which obviously there is no place for necrophobia.

Necrophobia, however, should be linked to a nocturnal existence, as we know from Rudolf that he was afraid of bodies only at night. We also remember the horror dream in which he kissed the body: this again took place in a dark environment (and, at the same time, brought the entire period to an end, since afterwards no more symptoms of a body phobia could be noticed). But the night is also the world of dreams and reveries. Out of the almost unfathomable abundance of dream and phantasy contents, the constituent characteristics of that world of body phobia can be gathered.

The dream contents refer time and again to the *earth* as to the material-elemental basis of imagination.[43] The prominent role of dirt, of mud, and of feces was pointed out earlier; we called attention to the stone statues, to the "brown little heap" of a newborn child, and also to the money in the

42 The terms necrophobia and necrophilia are here applied in a wider sense. How closely related the two contrasting tendencies are is illustrated by the statement of a patient who suffered from a serious phobia and compulsion neurosis; he considered a human corpse the cleanest thing on earth since it did not sweat any more nor eliminate anything; on the other hand, we know that many phobic persons are particularly afraid of corpses. The psychasthenics who do not dare pass a cemetery are juxtaposed to people who, as did one of our patients, play the flute at midnight over the grave of a deceased friend.

Hans-Joachim Rauch recently distinguished between "genuine necrophilia" (corpses being the primary aim of the sexual instinct) and "pseudo-necrophilia" (transference of the sexual instinct from the original aim—the life sexual partner—to corpses) (Z. Neur., Bd. 179, S. 54–93). In addition, he discusses the necrophilic-sadistic acts and symbolic necrophilia. To the literary references with descriptions of necrophilic tendencies we may add the novel by Anton Francesco Doni, *Eine Liebesgeschichte Karls des Grossen* (Manesse Bibliothek). Also, Zarathustra's wanderings with the body of the tightrope walker (Nietzsche) and Joanna the Insane, come to mind.

43 In reference to dreams and reveries, *viz.*, the following books by G. Bachelard—*La Psychanalyse du feu, L'Eau et les rêves, L'Air et les songes*. (A study about the earth was published too late to be here considered.)

form of coins. In all of these we are dealing with *matter*. We may add that concrete matter is also the basic material from which machines are made, those machines which so predominantly and recurrently pervaded Rudolf's life, daydreams, and dreams, either in the form of a wish to become a mechanic, of more or less complicated instruments which permit their master to awaken the dead, of mechanical devices that in Rudolf's phantasy would help him to crucify himself, or of the clock which frequently emerged in his dreams and which, in the shape of a lock on the mysterious trunk, indicated that "time is up." Only material substances have those qualities which are so important for Rudolf, namely, luster and warmth. And only a material substance can be cut up, can be eaten, digested, and make its appearance again; only something that consists of matter can be killed.

For Rudolf, the body, too, is a piece of matter; hence it can be worked upon manually like any other such piece. Since to him the matter of the body represents its essence, man and animal seem so close to each other that they are treated alike by him, in dismembering as well as in the sodomistic act. Similarly, living man and dead body are not so very different, in certain conditions; indeed, the materiality of man is more fully represented by the dead body, since in man, alive, other factors disturbingly interfere.

It is in the nature of earth that one cannot easily penetrate it. However, in certain places it is open and accessible by way of abysses and caves. But such entrances have to be long and laboriously searched for. It is also possible to enter the earth by force, by digging holes and trenches, building tunnels, and the like. Only concrete, material objects have a real outside and inside. Rudolf, then, connects his interest in earthy-material substances with the wish to penetrate into the inside of such substances in their most diverse forms: into the inside of the earth, of buildings, boxes and chests, even of bodies—human as well as animal—and even into the inside of his own body by way of phantasies of self-inflicted damage. To pierce earth and matter from the outside calls, of course, for strength and force. The sexual act, too, is included in this concept of piercing the inside, although it does not necessarily represent the original image of these strivings. However, from here we may gain access to the understanding of the close link between aggression and sexuality in Rudolf.

The other elements played only an incidental role in Rudolf's dreams, as for instance the fire, since Rudolf saw all sorts of magic lights, or the water, mixed with earth in the form of mud. When, as an exception, in one of his dreams he found himself on a ship, it would sail along a jungle, or he would see a garden on top of a rock which protruded high above the sea. Generally, he needs earth in order to gain height—*e.g.*, he uses a house so that children can leap down from it, or a perilous fall occurs in the depth of a chasm. To the *air*, Rudolf has virtually no relation.

What clearly emerges from his dreams is also present in his everyday world, if in a more concealed way. There, too, matter is predominant, as in his work as a butcher and gardener, in his peculiar relation to money, or in his fetishism in the realm of sex.

As we recall the existential space of his phantasies and dreams, we find that almost exclusively they take place within closed spaces, such as the interior of a butchery, a moviehouse, or a bar; in rooms—although also in church or in the woods—whereas wide open spaces, free sight, altitude and depth, as primarily encountered in nature, are hardly mentioned. The lighting is usually gloomy to dark. There are few objects in these spaces, except for occasional tools, money, corpses; human relationships are out of place. If human beings are present, they act brutally or obscenely or in measured rituals; no words are heard, only screams of men and animals.

In dreams, those space-building forces of personality which are obstructed by reality come into their own. In Rudolf's dreams particularly the underground is being opened; we learn about subterranean vaults, catacombs, labyrinthine caves, passages, and cellars. They are more or less dimly lit by torches. Thus, the ritually measured, mysteriously violent actions—including the performance of murder—can unfold without impediment. We should point out that certain illustrations from Rudolf's child's Bible became determining factors in the set-up of this world, particularly one which shows the decapitation of John the Baptist in a dusky vault. In this underworld one meets corpses, coffins, chests, boxes, and the like which contain decaying, smelly stuff, manure, and feces.

The opening of the underworld refers to the vertical axis of existence which we encountered when we discussed the extension of the *horizontal existential plane* of the active everyday world by means of phantasies and the pathetic act. Ascension and descension in the particular form of being "lifted into height" and of "penetrating into depth" [44]—*i.e.*, the existence in the *vertical axis*—proves to be the actual spatial existential form of Rudolf's dreams and reveries. There is quite some evidence for this; we refer, for example, to the music notes fastened high up in the room in which Rudolf kissed the body, in one of his dreams. With the notes high above, and Rudolf, at the end of the dream, rolling on the floor, the dream tends toward a spatial organization which is clearly vertical. Attention should also be given to how great an effort is required to lift Rudolf high up, and how heavily he is held back by the depth.

Remembering that we described once before one category of existential space of Rudolf, that of practical life and of busy action, we now realize how

44 In reference to the problems of the vertical plane of existence, *viz.*, L. Binswanger, "Traum und Existenz," *Ausgewaehlte Vortraege*, (Bern: 1947), S. 74–98; *Über Ideenflucht* (Zuerich: 1933). E. Straus, "Die Formen des Raeumlichen," *Nervenarzt*, 3, S. 633–656.

different it was from the one we are encountering now. A juxtaposition of the two types of time structure in the experience of these two world-designs will help to differentiate them still more clearly and distinctly.

In the existential space of Rudolf's dreams and reveries, everything is ancient. We find there old chests, rusty doors, relations to old biblical stories, to mummies and corpses; even the vaults themselves in which all this takes place are ancient and have not been entered for a long time. The objects in them are rotting and decaying, and quite generally we are dealing here with a world of the has-been. Quite to the contrary, in the space of practical life, the New plays the main role; there is an actual greed for the New (*Gier nach Neuem*), a definite curiosity (*Neugierde*), and the forward-rushing movement seeks ever-new impressions and encounters. The new, in general, is also likely to shine. Whereas the space of dreams and daydreams is oriented toward the ancient and gloomy, and thus to the *having been*, the space of active life is directed toward the new and shiny, and thus toward the *expected*. With certain reservations, we may well designate the two worlds as Rudolf's past and future.

So far, we have viewed Rudolf's two worlds—*i.e.*, the bright world of the street and the decaying world of the cellar—only outside his body. But it appears that the same analysis can be made in regard to his body experience, too. The external appearance of man, which generally includes clothing, corresponds to the bright existence, whereas the world of the cellar is repeated in the inside of the body. There, too, darkness prevails and accessibility is limited; mysterious processes (called digestion) take place which seem to have an unmistakable relation to what occurs in the underground vaults. We should also have in mind procreation and, connected with it, the infantile theories about the origin of children. Again, verticality with its above and below can be found in body consciousness. To Rudolf, the line of separation between above and below cuts through the mouth. Hence, the vertical is divided into two quite unequal halves, a smaller upper and a tall lower one.

Relations and Transitions between the Worlds of Reality and Phantasies; Their Relation to Mourning and to the Crime

The world of phantasies and the world of active life do have points of contact with each other. In the outside world, the door permits communication between the street and the inside of a house. In the sphere of the body, outside and inside are connected through the body openings. Rudolf sees in the female genitals the point of transition of the two worlds. Undressing represents an approach to the inside world and is feared to the degree to which an approach to the world of phantasies is avoided in reality. We have already pointed out that dying and being killed also effect a transition from one world to the other, since the living person belongs to the active world, the dead one to the phantasy world. In a certain sense, the transition from one world to the other also represents the step from phantasy to reality, and vice versa. Within the phantasy world, great care is taken lest the psychic contents turn into reality. This explains the phobic feature inherent in this world. As long as one succeeds in keeping the two world-designs strictly separated from each other, no danger exists that the criminal phantasies and dreams could be transformed into action or that the actions could be determined by influences from the world of dreams.

However, Rudolf does not always succeed in maintaining the separation completely, as demonstrated by his sexual relations with women. He seeks and finds his sex partner outside, in the street. As long as she stays dressed, she remains in the realm of the active world. She *must* remain there, or else he would have to kill her, since no living human being fits into the world of phantasies. Therefore, he has to trick himself into the sex act, as it were, by keeping up the pretense of remaining in the active world while in reality he is penetrating into the inside and thus into the realm of the other world. He can more easily maintain this pretense as long as the sex partner remains dressed and as long as he can perform the act *en passant,* in a casual and haphazard way. But even if Rudolf is able to maintain that pretense in the act, he nevertheless gets into so intimate a contact with the "inside" that the phantasies with their macabre contents gain in power; this helps us to understand why sexual intercourse produces in Rudolf a severe depression in which, as we know, the temporal orientation toward the future always suffers, too.[45]

What, then, is going on in the butcher's shop, when observed from this angle? We see Rudolf standing there at a crucial point of his existence where the two different worlds in the form of life and death touch each other most closely. Rudolf is *acting* in this situation, he is part of the active life. But by killing the animals, he is turning them over to the other world. In being killed, the animals become components of the world of dreams and day-dreams—they are, as it were, incorporated into that world—and, through their transformation into foodstuff, gain also access to the somatic inside world. In fact, the killing of animals—as turning live animals into dead ones—represents actually a realization of phantasies, if only in the animal realm. It is well to realize that killing is, in its design, closely related to the sex act and that sexual misuse of animals is an act that comes pretty close to slaughtering animals.

We must now go back to Rudolf's compulsive impulses to murder the

45 Von Gebsattel, "Zur Frage der Depersonalisation" (Beitrag zur Theorie d. Melancholie), *Nervenarzt*, 1937, 10. Jahrg. S. 169. E. Straus, "Das Zeiterlebnis in der endogenen Depression und in der psychopathischen Verstimmung," *Monatsschrift fuer Psychiatrie und Neurologie,* 1928. 68, S. 640–656.

women he met when delivering meat. Facing him as acting, living, and clothed persons, they are able and liable to excite him sexually. But by emerging from the inside of a house, they stand in a place where they do not belong unless they are actually corpses. In this way, Rudolf's murderous impulses can be understood.

Eventually, we have to examine how Rudolf's mourning for his late father structured the relations between his two world-designs. From our general discussion of the mourning affect we have gathered that "remaining with the deceased," as effected by the mourning affect, brings about a retreat from active, everyday life and a proclivity to the world which in Rudolf has disclosed itself as that of phantasies and dreams. That world gained in power on account of the loss. But it must be added that in Rudolf's case this increase in power on the part of the phantasy world occurred in a very specific form; the mourning affect broke through when Rudolf observed how the coffin with his father's body was carried through the door. And with this, the contents of the dream existence, until then confined to the inside of the house, poured out, too; the borderline between the two worlds was broken and the phantasy world superimposed itself, as it were, upon the everyday world or, in other words, the everyday world was at that moment "tuned" (*gestimmt*) by the world-design of phantasies and dreams. For Rudolf, this brought about a fundamental change in his entire existence. We now understand that for him the mourning affect is linked with sexual desire, for it is precisely the piercing of the inside which is sought in the sexual act. Since the day of his father's funeral Rudolf is, so to speak, much closer to that inside. But the impulse that earlier occurred only in the door of a house—where the sexually exciting women stood in the wrong place and were therefore liable to be killed—has spread, under the influence of the mourning affect, so that every sexually exciting woman now stimulates this murderous impulse, as the world of phantasies covers the whole existence. Nor are we surprised any more that it is just the prostitute, the woman who is out to seduce men, who becomes Rudolf's primary target and the object of his murderous assault. For the prostitute is a creature of the street and as such has been one of the constituents of Rudolf's world of real, everyday life. But the image of the street, its "tune," has changed under the influence of the mourning affect which, in turn, has changed the nature of Rudolf's meetings with prostitutes. A counterdrive against the murderous impulse could not come about because Rudolf no longer stood on the border of his two world-designs and so could no longer view one from the angle of the other, as he had done earlier, whenever the murder impulse emerged. He now was totally in the world of phantasies and dreams, which had fused with the world of everyday life—or one may say that phantasy and reality agreed. Viewed more from the outside, one could say that phantasies broke into the realm of reality or that the active world took possession of the phantasies.

The close link between the mourning for the late father and the murderous impulse toward a prostitute against which no resistance could develop so that it ruthlessly prevailed to the point of violent realization—all this, it seems to us, has become amply comprehensible.

We have yet briefly to consider the postponement of the criminal act. It can only be understood if one realizes that the presence of the mourning affect is a definite prerequisite for the occurrence of the act. When Rudolf, on the day after the funeral, stayed with a prostitute, the world of reality gained ground in two ways; first, the girl refused to undress, as if she wished to retain the physiognomy of the active, phantasy-alien world; secondly, at the same moment in which Rudolf learned of the girl's refusal to undress, he took a look through the open window from the inside of the house while shutting the blinds. This, too, oriented him toward that world which had always been outside. (Which reminds us of a similar process that occurred later, in prison, when Rudolf looked through the window of his cell at the blue sky and heard the Easter bells ring. Again, at that moment the world of reality grew in power, and Rudolf became aware of the significance of his crime and of the meaning of his situation, and began to cry.)

The sudden disappearance of the murderous impulse on the day after the funeral can be retraced to the sudden disappearance of the mourning affect which yielded to the temptations of the real world; it is the same process which time and again can be observed at funeral meals, the only difference being that there the temptation of reality rather assumes the form of food and drink. It could be asked why the murderous impulse did not appear at the moment when mourning broke through in front of the father's house. The answer is that at that time no object for that impulse was yet at hand. Rudolf had first to meet the prostitute outside, on the street, or at least be intensively occupied with her.

It is true that he planned to see a prostitute *before* he became aware of the murderous impulse, in the Zurich trolley car. But this, too, becomes transparent as soon as we consider how labile the mourning affect is and how greatly it fluctuates with regard to intensity. The murderous impulse emerged when, in the trolley, Rudolf was strongly reminded of his late father and so must have experienced an elemental recurrence of the mourning affect from the preceding day; but now that affect, instead of erupting in crying and lamenting, emerged in the form of the murder impulse. The displacement of the affective discharge from crying to the impulse of killing —as we would have to describe the psychological process from an outside viewpoint—is peculiar but not incomprehensible if one considers that in both cases vehement affects are experienced which can no longer be controlled and overcome by rational thinking and everyday action. Strange as it may look at first sight, we must say that Rudolf's crime comes closer to an "affective act" than could be expected on the basis of a clinical approach. This, of course, only applies if one recognizes both the murderous impulse and the crying as manifestations of the mourning affect. (This is quite legitimate, since we know of numerous examples of aggressions as expressions of the mourning affect, particularly in children but also in primitives. Readers of Goethe's *Faust* may remember that Dr. Faust first cries and later curses the world—*i.e.*, destroys it.)

Now we have once more to ask why the murderous impulse about seven weeks later made another appearance and why this time no brake was applied. The answer can only be that the mourning affect re-emerged and that the world of reality remained powerless in the face of it. It is in the nature of the mourning affect that it can suddenly re-emerge after a long lapse of time, once its path has been cleared. This may occur where a further development of the mourner in the sense of "incorporating" the being of the deceased is *not* achieved. This certainly was the case with Rudolf on the occasion of his father's death. What did touch off the mourning affect on the day of Rudolf's criminal act we could not definitely determine, since these processes, interfered with by earlier explorations under hypnosis (for the purpose of the psychiatric testimony), were no longer accessible in their original form. But we are in a position to state that on the day of the crime Rudolf had no chance to enforce the world of reality. The chatter of the waitress about the murder case certainly did not help Rudolf out of his fusion of phantasy and reality any more than the fact that the prostitute suddenly stood in front of him stark naked (which altogether frightened him).

But after the crime had been committed, Rudolf awoke "as from a dream," as he put it himself. We would assume that at that time the mourning affect had receded again. Rudolf's further actions (his telephone call to the police, the call to his boss, his surrender) are, then, those of a man who has returned into the world of everyday life. This provides us with a fitting demonstration of how this everyday world is also a world of community with other men, whereas in his phantasy world Rudolf, as everybody else, stands quite alone. The sudden extinction of the affect after the act can be explained through the phenomenology of normal mourning. We know that mourners feel a similar relief after the body has been buried. For days, the body had been in some sense the object of their mourning; with the disappearance of this object, a certain relief occurs. Of course, the mourner would like to retain the demised; but since the beloved person turned into a thing—namely, into a body—the same estrangement develops in relation to the dead as in relation to things. As these turn into a burden of which one rids oneself under the influence of the mourning affect, so, generally, the body turns into a burden. In regard to Rudolf's mourning affect, it is the living, seductive woman, the woman with sexual demands, who becomes a burden to Rudolf and of whom he rids himself by his criminal act. Subsequently, he is relieved and feels hungry, as does the normal mourner after the funeral, when he can get hold of reality again.

The mutual effect of the two world-designs upon each other and their mutual overlapping, one can hardly envisage in dynamic enough terms. Just as they will never actually coincide, so they will hardly ever be totally separated; through their prevailing relationship at any given time they determine Rudolf's present.

This present of Rudolf, in its changing structure, makes us speak clinically of a depression, of a manic state, or of a perversion of the sexual instinct, of compulsive experience, automatic acts, twilight states, and the like. But it was our intention to understand Rudolf's act in terms of existential analysis, and not to analyze the states in question; naturally, we would have been no less justified in doing the latter.

Thus, our investigation has come to some kind of conclusion by disclosing why Rudolf arrived at his criminal act and how the latter is linked with the mourning for his late father. But so far we have learned nothing about the way in which Rudolf came upon the two described world-designs nor about the effect of psychotherapy on him. We have to refrain from continuing the investigation in this direction, but wish to outline in a brief final section how the analysis would have to be carried on.

Some Comments on the Relations between the Death of Rudolf's Mother and his World-Designs

We took up Rudolf's behavior at his mother's death because it could help us understand why the boy subsequently began his search, and why what he found (the glittering objects) assumed special significance. Our further analysis dealt primarily with the mourning affect. But we have also learned that Rudolf's being changed after his mother's death; that he could no longer really enjoy himself and that he remained disposed to feelings of sadness. This might indicate that some sort of mourning had stayed with him from the time of his mother's death. If we compare other features of Rudolf's personality with descriptions of his mother given by relatives, we are struck by conspicuous agreements: both displayed the same obliging, peaceful, and courteous behavior. These character traits need not necessarily be inherited, since we know that frequently after the death of a beloved person his traits are taken over by the survivor, that an incorporation of the dead person's being (*Wesenseinbildung*) takes place in which the survivor's own earlier existence undergoes a fundamental change. Surely, a precondition of any such existential transformation is genuine *love* for the deceased. To be sure, not even to the small child should we deny the ability to love, and as for Rudolf, all the prerequisites of loving his mother were present for him. But then, it is questionable whether we can expect from a child of this age the faculty of "incorporation of being" in the sense of an existential transformation. To our knowledge, nothing definite is known about it. The possibility of such a transformation should certainly not be excluded. Indeed, certain peculiarities in the psyche of small children lead us to believe that the child undergoes such changes in a still more pronounced degree than the adult (notwithstanding some distinct differences between the two types of phenomena). Certainly, compared to the adult the child is with all of his being much more related to his environment and to the world of his fellows and particularly to the firmly fixed web of circumstances (*Bewandtniszu-sammenhang*) in which he meets another person. The deceased remains in the context in which the child had experienced him, as would a fellow man who has gone on a trip. (This is why a child after a short time of separation does not readily recognize his nurse when meeting her on the street.) Since the dead does not reappear in another context, nothing is changed in the totality of circumstances in which he has left the surviving child. Hence the relation to the deceased cannot further develop in any way. But we know that children playfully repeat situations which they experienced earlier, when special circumstances offer them a chance. It might well be that in such ways something at least related to the "incorporation of being" occurs in small children, too.

In Rudolf's case, one would have to add that he suffered, well into the period of psychiatric treatment, from a rather severe and disturbing pruritus, which vanished immediately after his mother's jaundice was discussed, without Rudolf's ever having learned that in jaundice such pruritus also appears. This may be a rather external symptom, and yet it shows how closely oriented toward his mother Rudolf remained even at a much later stage. Of course, we would need far better proof of the assumption that Rudolf was mourning for his mother in the existential sense of the word, but by no means can this simply be discarded. By contrast, no change of being and no existential mourning occurred subsequent to his father's death. And yet, his readiness for sadness must have been related to existential mourning, which would explain why the death of a neighbor to whom Rudolf was not very close could touch off such a severe mourning affect. On the other hand, it should not be concluded that any kind of existential mourning makes the mourner disposed to mourning affects; rather, what we find in Rudolf is a very special form of existential mourning.

We get closer to that particular form of mourning for the mother when we realize that Rudolf, though retaining his mother in regard to her "being," forgot her as an "object"; or we could also say that he forgot her as a "body." Phenomenological research has shown that "forgetting" and "corporeality" are closely connected with each other; we look for the lost word in our mouth; we say, "it is on the tip of my tongue"; we seek it there where it got lost, and that seems to be somehow in the periphery of the body.[46] Rudolf, too, searches for the lost and the forgotten in the periphery of the body, namely, in the luster of eyes and garments. On the other hand,

[46] *Viz.*, L. Binswanger, *Grundformen und Erkenntnis menschlichen Daseins*, S. 472–474.

in his world of phantasies, he skips the periphery, avoids the surface and penetrates directly into the inside where nothing lost or forgotten can ever be found. Probably, his wishes to trace the forgotten are opposed by other wishes which try to prevent the finding—a contraposition we have encountered before in Rudolf's relation to the corpses, with its necrophilic and necrophobic features. In this context, we should not be surprised by the fact that just that which is phobically feared is the central theme in phantasies and dreams. It is the *realization* of those dream-and-phantasy contents which is feared, and of this the phobia is an expression; it is not the contents in themselves which are repressed through the phobia.

The problem becomes especially acute when in puberty the sex drive is aimed at the body of another person. A world-design which is phobically forgetful of the body could very well cause the sexual interest to shift to objects. Once the "forgotten body" is recovered in form of a glittering object from the realm of things, serious consequences for the further fate of the person will ensue. Experience has shown that he who has incorporated in himself the being of a beloved person is able to find again and love again that being in another person. But if the "memory" of a beloved dead is split into two "parts" which can no longer be fused because the object can never be one with the being it ought to be (a glittering button can never be a "being"), then the path to love is completely blocked, both the existential mourning and the fetishist tendency remain, and along with them the special disposition to mourning affects.

This process—here only sketchily suggested—has been neatly confirmed by the way in which a psychotherapeutic effect upon Rudolf could be achieved. At a certain point in his treatment a church picture of the Virgin Mary came to life for him as her eyes assumed an extraordinary luster. The kind of smile which the picture showed must have been related to the smile so strikingly characteristic of Rudolf himself—which, we may assume, is likewise linked with his mother's facial expression. At that moment, he was somehow reminded of the forgotten object or body *gestalt;* and at that moment being and body fused into a unit again, and the path toward love was open for him. (Incidentally, "being," which has been mentioned here so frequently, seems to be related to "movement" in a still quite mysterious way.)

Finally, we are confronted with the problem of why, after all, "object" and "body" were forgotten. Of course, one cannot account for the "process of forgetting" in oneself. But it is an obvious assumption that recognition of the fact that the body was dead, and of its repulsive sight, caused Rudolf to forget it. Furthermore, he could only manage to see a substitute for the lost object in the glittering things if the object itself were forgotten; because this alone made it possible to ignore the monstrous discrepancy. We believe that at this point one could advance considerably further if L. Binswanger's notes about retaining and forgetting being primarily erotic and not intellectual phenomena [47] and E. Husserl's "Investigations on the Phenomenology of the Inner Time Consciousness" [48] were applied to our case. This would bring to light deep connections in completely new areas between forgetting and phantasies on the one side and these two phenomena and the crime on the other. We have to refrain from continuing the analysis in this direction as it would carry us into the most difficult fields of pure phenomenology. We may, however, suggest in this context that beyond the present investigation a phenomenological inspection of *forgetting* and *killing* would show up their close inner relations. This would lead to obscure areas where the "extinguishing" is joined by the "being unable to forget" (*viz.*, Shakespeare's *Macbeth*). The motive of killing, omnipresent in Rudolf's phantasy world (from his vows of vengeance after the disclosure of the church theft to the dream in the beginning of his psychotherapeutic treatment in which the therapist was shot to death, and numerous times in between and after), could in this way be understood in its widest context and seen in its tie-up with compulsive experiences. We cannot elaborate on all this any further.

But we do have to discuss briefly some cases from the research literature in which an analysis of the patients' "worlds" yielded results similar to those in Rudolf's case. We are thinking of the patients described by Von Gebsattel [49] and of L. Binswanger's case of Ellen West.[50] Notably in this latter case a "hole-" and "grave-world" was found to prevail which greatly resembles Rudolf's phantasy world. If one considers only the clinical presentation, one could hardly conceive of comparing the two cases; in Ellen West we find a psychosis developing underneath an obesity-phobia and taking a catastrophic course, a process in which the ability for emotional experience is increasingly impoverished to the point where suicide is the only way out. Rudolf, on the other hand, remains capable of emotional experience throughout his psychosis, and psychotherapy succeeds even in liberating the affects to a point where the initially perverted instinctual life admits of genuine love. Whereas Ellen grows unproductive and bogs down (*versandet*), Rudolf stays productive and alive. The difference in terms of world-designs throws some more light on the difference in outcome of the two cases; Ellen West's grave-world more and more dominated her entire existence and turned her whole condition into something static, whereas Rudolf's world of phantasies with its macabre mood gradually retreated from his existence as we succeeded in giving his past a new and different significance. This is the place to refer to Rudolf's aforementioned suspense-experience and to his "dramatic style of life." As long as neither of his two

[47] *Ibid.*, S. 472–474.

[48] E. Husserl, *Vorlesungen zur Phaenomenologie des innern Zeitbewusstseins* (Halle a.d. Saale: 1928).

[49] Von Gebsattel, "Die Welt des Zwangskranken," *Monatsschrift fuer Psychiatrie und Neurologie*, Bd. 99, 1938, S. 10–74.

[50] L. Binswanger, "Der Fall Ellen West" (Chap. IX).

world-designs prevails in his existence, he is still free to judge the one from the angle of the other.

As pointed out before, judging is inherent in the nature of a dramatic existence. But where in this context of circumstances is the break which caused Rudolf to carry out a pathetic act? Here the path to understanding may take a turn back to the joy which Rudolf felt upon the news of his father's death. An expectation built up over years and linked with hope and consolation (even if we do not know exactly what was expected) seemed about to be fulfilled—and ended in bitter disappointment—be it because he did not manage to awaken the dead or because he was deprived of the object of his joy or whatever else may have been involved.

Even if occasionally under the dominance of one of his world-designs a particular destiny runs its course, Rudolf can yet achieve—subsequently—a viewpoint outside that destiny and so can judge again. Thus the dramatic is made possible although it remains aimless. Ellen West, too, has a possibility to step out of the grave-world, but only in the face of imminent death. So we see on the side of Rudolf the labile dynamics of world-designs mutually shifting and overlapping each other, but, on the side of Ellen West, fatal stagnation and immutability. In one case action, in the other freezing.

Are we here, perhaps, at the point where the problems of manic-depressive psychoses, with their antinomic structure, and those of schizophrenia, with its progressive destruction, are opposing, touching, and intersecting each other so that the existential-analytical investigation finds itself rechanneled into clinical fields?

The time for answering such all-embracing questions has not yet come. For the present, we have to remain in the realm of the single case which often opens wide enough views in various directions. The death of a mother is one of those events whose influence upon a small child's psychic development can hardly be completely understood.

E. A. Poe was another such child—Poe, whose stories and poems are so similar to Rudolf's dreams and daydreams that they could almost be mistaken for one another (without Rudolf's ever having read E. A. Poe). It is known that Poe in his third year of life spent entire days in the immediate neighborhood of his mother's dead body.

Quite a different development of a child who went through a similar experience is disclosed in the *Histoire d'une ame* of the Sainte Thérèse de l'Enfant Jésus who, too, saw a picture of the Virgin Mary smile to her.

Finally, I wish to quote a verse from the *Sonnets to Orpheus* by Rainer Maria Rilke which at first may sound mysterious but bears witness to his deep insight into the human soul:

> Killing is one of the forms
> of our wandering mourning . . .

Biographical Notes
of Translated Contributors

Biographical Notes
of Translated Contributors

EUGENE MINKOWSKI, M.D.—Born in Poland in 1885, Minkowski finished his secondary studies in Warsaw and then entered the medical school of the university in that city. When the school was closed because of revolutionary activity among the students, he went to Germany to continue his studies and received his medical degree at the University of Munich in 1909. Minkowski's life story reads like a reflection—which in truth it is—of the intense political and intellectual crosscurrents in the Europe of his times. In 1910 he received a medical diploma in Kazan, Russia, and then he went to study philosophy in Germany. At the outbreak of the first World War he escaped to Switzerland and became a resident at the Burghölzli, the psychiatric university hospital, under Eugen Bleuler, from 1914 through 1915. He then became a volunteer in the French army, and received the *croix de guerre* and *legion d'honneur*. Taking French citizenship, he was awarded a French medical diploma and practiced in Paris for many years as a psychiatrist. He also served as consultant at the *Hôpital Henri-Rouselle,* the *Fondation Rotschild,* and was Medical Director of the *Foyer de Soulins,* an institution for children with character disorders.

During these central years, Minkowski experienced the decisive influence of Bergson and Husserl and their schools. His medical thesis had been on the subject of medical biology, but by the end of his medical studies he had shown marked interest in problems of human psychology and philosophy. His first publications, appearing before World War I, were on the theory of color perception and psychophysical parallelism, thus foreshadowing the broad studies he later was to make in phenomenological psychiatry.

He is past president of the *Société Médico-psychologique* (1947) and of the *Société Française de Psychologie* (1950) and is now a member of the Commission and Medical Superior Committee for mental patients at the French Ministry of Public Health. A founder and past president of the *Evolution Psychiatrique,* he also served as chief editor of the journal of the same title. His honors include being *Officier de la Légion d'Honneur,* honorary membership in the Swiss Society of Psychiatry, and an honorary medical degree from the University of Zurich.

Minkowski's numerous publications in French and foreign journals on clinical psychiatry and psychopathology are all informed with the viewpoint of phenomenological psychiatry. His most important books are *La Schizophrénie,* 1926, revised in 1954; *Le Temps vécu,* 1933; *Vers une Cosmologie,* 1936.

FREIHERR VIKTOR E. VON GEBSATTEL, PH.D., M.D.—Von Gebsattel was born in Munich in 1883. As a young man he studied philosophy and history of art in Berlin, Paris, and Munich, receiving his first doctorate in the last-named city. Beginning his career as an author, he wrote, among other publications, *Moral in Gegensätzen.* At the beginning of World War I, he decided to study medicine and received his medical degree in 1920. His education as a psychiatrist and neurologist was under Professor Kraepelin and Professor Malaise. In 1924 he assumed the directorship of the *Kuranstalt Westend,* the largest private sanatorium in Berlin, and in 1926 he founded the *Schloss Furstenberg,* a sanatorium for nervous diseases near Berlin. During this period Von Gebsattel produced a number of scientific publications. In 1939 he accepted an invitation to teach at the *Zentral-Institut für Psychologie und Psychotherapie* at Berlin and in 1944 took the directorship of a psychotherapeutic clinic in Vienna.

In late years Von Gebsattel's career has been increasingly identified with universities. He was called to teach medical psychology and psychotherapy in Freiburg in 1946, then assigned to the directorship of the *Nervenklinik* at the University of Würzburg in 1951, and later called to the chair of Anthropology and Human Genetics at the same university, a position he still occupies.

From his writings we mention only the books *Christentum und Humanismus,* and *Prolegomena einer medizinischen Anthropologie.* The *Handbook der Neurosenlehre und Psychotherapie,* in which he is now collaborating, is in preparation.

ERWIN W. STRAUS, M.D.—Like other pioneers in phenomenological and existential psychiatry, Dr. Straus's education and experience bridge several disciplines, and the breadth of his background includes association with leaders of diverse schools of psychiatry and psychology. Born in Frankfort, Germany, Dr. Straus studied at the University of Berlin Medical School from 1909–11, then at the University of Munich from 1911–14 (where he attended Kraepelin's lectures), and during this period also attended the summer school at Zurich where he heard Bleuler and Jung. After the first World War he received his medical diploma in Berlin. He then served on the staff of the University Hospital for Nervous and Mental Diseases in ascending capacities until his appointment as Professor of Psychiatry at the University of Berlin in 1931.

These years in the late '20's and '30's found Dr. Straus also continuing his private practice as a psychiatrist in Berlin, lecturing at several universities in Europe, serving as co-editor of the periodical, *Der Nervenarzt,* and producing numerous scientific papers as well as several books. In 1938 he became one of the gifts to America which the European upheavals unwittingly contributed, and served from that year until 1944 as Professor of Psychology at Black Mountain College, North Carolina. Though he continued to write and publish (chiefly in German and other European presses), the significance of his contribution was not appreciated in this country for a number of years. After a fellowship in psychiatry at Henry Phipps Psychiatric Clinic, Johns Hopkins University, he took his psychiatric and neurological boards in America. Though several attempts have been made to lure him back to Germany (the Chair for Psychotherapy at the University of Berlin was offered him in 1948), he has elected to remain in America as Director of Professional Education and Research at the Veterans Administration Hospital in Lexington, Kentucky and Assistant Professor in Psychiatry at the University of Louisville Medical School.

LUDWIG BINSWANGER, M.D., HON. PH.D.—Since the background of Dr. Binswanger is better known in this country than our other contributors, particularly after the publication of his personal memoirs of his friendship with Freud (*Sigmund Freud: Reminiscences of a Friendship,* published by Grune & Stratton in 1958), we shall give only a few notes here. He was born in Kreuzlingen, Thurgau, Switzerland, in 1881, into a family which had been distinguished for several generations for its famous physicians and psychiatrists. His medical studies were in Lausanne, Heidelberg, and Zurich, and he received his medical degree at the University of Zurich in 1907 in connection with studies under C. G. Jung. He served as Psychiatric Interne under Eugen Bleuler in Zurich, then, later, as Resident at the Psychiatric Clinic for Nervous Diseases of Jena University under his uncle, Professor Otto Binswanger. At this time his father, Robert Binswanger, was director of Sanatorium Bellevue at Kreuzlingen, and Ludwig Binswanger served as his associate from 1908–10. In 1911, Dr. Ludwig Binswanger succeeded his father (and followed his grandfather) as chief Medical Director of this sanatorium, and, although he relinquished the directorship in 1956, he is still active there.

Visitors to this sanatorium on the shore of Lake Constance tell of Dr. Binswanger's never-failing interest in leisurely and penetrating discussions of almost any topic related to his broad intellectual and scientific concerns. His humanistic breadth as well is shown in this partial listing of some of his writings: *Introduction Into the Problems of General Psychology,* 1922; *Changes in Understanding and Interpretation of the Dream from the Greeks to the Present,* 1928; *On the Flight of Ideas,* 1933; *Basic Forms and Cognition of Human Existence,* 1943, revised in 1953; *Selected Essays, On Phenomenological Anthropology,* 1947; *The Problems of Psychiatric Research,* 1955; *Henrik Ibsen and the Problem of Self-Realization in Art,* 1949; *Three Forms of Unsuccessful Dasein—Eccentricity (Vertiegenheit), Queerness (Verschrobenheit), Affectedness (Manieriertheit),* 1956, *Man in Psychiatry,* 1957; *Schizophrenia,* 1957. A complete bibliography of Binswanger's writings in German would be too long to include here. Though the above-mentioned works are not translated into English, they are cited here in translated titles.

Binswanger's professional honors include the following: Corresponding Member (former) of the Academia Nazional de Medicina, Madrid; Honorary Member of the Swiss Society for Psychiatry; Honorary Member of the Society of German Neurologists and Psychiatrists; Honorary Member of the Austrian General Medical Society for Psychotherapy and the Viennese Association for Medical Psychology; Membre associé étranger, Société médico-psychologique (France), Neuilly s/Marne. In 1956 he was awarded the International Kraepelin Medal in Munich, Germany.

ROLAND KUHN, M.D.—The youngest of our contributors, Roland Kuhn was born in 1912, in Biel, Switzerland. He studied in Biel, Berne, and Paris and received his Medical Diploma in the spring of 1937. He took two years of residency at the University Psychiatric Hospital of Waldau, near Berne, and since that time has been Associate Director of the Cantonal Mental Hospital of Munsterlingen, Thurgau, Switzerland.

Kuhn is particularly noted for work on the phenomenological approach to the Rorschach test. His other fields of psychiatric interest, in addition to Existential Analysis, are aeronautical psychiatry and the psychiatric applications of electro-encephalography. Among his scientific publications are: *Über Maskendeutungen im Rorschach'schen Formdeutversuch,* 1943; "Daseinsanalyse eines Falles von Schizophrenie," *Monatsschrift für Psychiatrie und Neurologie,* Vol. 112, 1946; "Daseinsanalyse im psychotherapeutischen Gespräch," *Schweizer Archiv für Neurologie und Psychiatrie,* Vol. 67, 1951; "Zur Daseinsstruktur einer Neurose," *Jahrbuch für Psychologie und Psychotherapie,* Vol. 1, 1954; "Daseinsanalytische Studie ueber die Bedeutung von Grenzen im Wahn," *Monatsschrift für Psychiatrie und Neurologie,* Vol. 124, 1952; "Der Mensch in der Zwiesprache des Kranken mit seinem Artz und das Problem der Uebertragung," *Monatsschrift für Psychiatrie und Neurologie,* Vol. 129, 1955; "Über die Ausbildung zum Spezialartz für Psychiatrie," *Schweizer Archiv für Neurologie und Psychiatrie,* Vol. 77, 1956.

Index

Index

About the Editors